MW00638325

Ancient Jewish and Christian
Perceptions of Crucifixion

Discard

JUN 22 '23

David W. Chapman

Ancient Jewish and Christian Perceptions of Crucifixion

Library St. Vincent de Paul
10701 S. Military Trail
Boynton Beach, Fl 33436

Baker Academic

a division of Baker Publishing Group
Grand Rapids, Michigan

© 2008 by Mohr Siebeck, Tübingen, Germany

Paperback edition published in North America in 2010 by Baker Academic
a division of Baker Publishing Group
P.O. Box 6287, Grand Rapids, MI 49516-6287
www.bakeracademic.com

ISBN 978-0-8010-3905-8

Originally published in 2008 in Tübingen, Germany, by Mohr Siebeck GmbH & C. KG Tübingen
as *Ancient Jewish and Christian Perceptions of Crucifixion*, Wissenschaftliche Untersuchungen
zum Neuen Testament, 2. Reihe 244.

Printed in the United States of America

All rights reserved. No part of this publication may be reproduced, stored in a retrieval system,
or transmitted in any form or by any means—for example, electronic, photocopy, recording—
without the prior written permission of the publisher. The only exception is brief quotations
in printed reviews.

Library of Congress Cataloging-in-Publication Data is on file at the Library of Congress, Washington, DC

In keeping with biblical principles of
creation stewardship, Baker Publishing Group advocates the responsible
use of our natural resources. As a
member of the Green Press Initiative,
our company uses recycled paper
when possible. The text paper of
this book is comprised of 30% post-
consumer waste.

green
press
INITIATIVE

Tasha, Leela and Karis:
In love and thanksgiving

Preface

This book sets out to accomplish two goals. The first part aims to provide a full accounting of ancient Jewish perceptions of crucifixion through the talmudic era based on currently-extant Jewish literary and material remains. The second part (consisting of the final chapter) seeks to suggest some ways that those perceptions affected both Jewish and Christian understandings of Jesus' crucifixion. Both sections are inductive, working from sources to syntheses. However, the first section aims to be comprehensive, the second merely seeks to be suggestive. My hope is that the final chapter spurs scholarly interest in further pursuing ways that Jewish perceptions of crucifixion affected views of Jesus' death in both Judaism and Christianity.

At least three audiences should benefit from this work. First, scholars of Judaism in antiquity could make substantial use of the sources on crucifixion gathered and analysed in chapters two through six. While there has been some intense interest in crucifixion in early Judaism, researchers have not previously interacted comprehensively with all pertinent sources. Second, students of early Jewish and Christian interactions may find the final chapter helpful in illumining ways that Jewish perceptions of crucifixion impacted Jewish and Christian polemic and dialogue. Third, scholars of the New Testament and early Christianity may consider the whole thesis as a charge to further consider how Jewish perceptions of the cross influenced Christian thought.

Translations below are generally my own unless otherwise noted. The major exception involves the regular use of the Josephus volumes in the Loeb Classical Library, upon which I consistently found it difficult to improve. My translations here tend toward a high degree of formal equivalence. Though at times sounding stilted, hopefully such renderings should benefit the reader's interaction with comments on the literary, grammatical and idiomatic features of the original texts.

This study constitutes a substantial revision of my doctoral thesis written at the University of Cambridge. Without the space constraints of the university protocols, it was possible to expand substantially all chapters, to update some secondary literature, and to add a chapter on crucifixion in symbology and magic.

I would like to express profound gratitude to Prof. William Horbury, my doctoral supervisor, whose depth of knowledge is only equaled by his charity and good will toward his students. Also I wish to thank Drs. Markus Bockmuehl and Andrew Chester, each of whom supervised me for a term. Part of this book was written while for several months I was a guest of the

Institut für antikes Judentum und hellenistische Religionsgeschichte at the Universität Tübingen. For that time I have primarily to thank Prof. Hermann Lichtenberger, who kindly arranged all aspects of our stay. While we were there, Profs. Hermann Lichtenberger, Martin Hengel and Otto Betz, as well as Drs. Anna Maria Schwemer and Gil Hüttenmeister, all thoughtfully read portions of my work. The thesis was examined by both Prof. Graham Stanton and Dr. Catrin Williams, who each made helpful suggestions for revision.

For funding, my appreciation goes to the directors of the Overseas Research Student Award scheme. Also, St. Edmund's College provided me assistance to attend the British New Testament Conference in Glasgow and the Evangelical Theological Society conference in Orlando – in both venues I read a paper related to material in this thesis.

Subsequent papers have been read at the annual meeting of the Society of Biblical Literature, and at Wheaton College. The interaction with colleagues at these conferences has been most appreciated. Tyndale House, wisely governed at the time by Bruce Winter and well staffed by David Instone Brewer and Fiona Craig, provided us with needed accommodation and assistance during doctoral studies, as well as with a wonderful working environment with many good comrades. Among these, Larry Lahey and John Lierman especially should be named for their friendship and for their willingness to interact frequently with me about this material.

I wish to convey my gratitude to Prof. Jörg Frey for accepting this book into the WUNT series. I am also thankful for the diligence and patience of the good people at Mohr-Siebeck, especially for the assistance of Dr. Henning Ziebritzki, Tanja Mix and Lisa Laux. They have been most long-suffering with me as several other projects, archaeological excavations, and life issues have delayed the publication of this volume until long after it was due. My hope here is that the time spent in revision and typesetting will be worthwhile for the reader. In this regard some students at Covenant Theological Seminary willingly assisted in copyediting – especially Rick Matt, David Rapp, and Cheryl Eaton. Richard Hiers assisted in recovery of data from various computer malfunctions. Other colleagues at Covenant have encouraged me along the way, among whom I should mention Drs. Hans Bayer, Donald Guthrie, Sean Lucas, Jay Sklar, Greg Perry and Jimmy Agan. In expressing my great appreciation to these many people in this preface, I am quite aware that the contents (especially any errors) are indeed my own responsibility.

Most of all, my wife, Tasha, and our daughters, Leela and Karis, have been a constant source of joy and encouragement. Our parents, Cecil and Mabelann Chapman and Donald and Carolyn Neeper, have also always provided their characteristic unceasing support and care for us.

Saint Louis, Missouri David W. Chapman
May 2008 *SDG*

Table of Contents

Part Two: Ancient Jewish Perceptions of Crucifixion and the Cross of Christ

Abbreviations

For most Jewish and Christian works the abbreviations follow *The SBL Handbook of Style*. Citations of Classical authors follow Liddell & Scott or the *Oxford Latin Dictionary*. Exceptions and additions are:

Alcalay   Reuben Alcalay, *The Complete Hebrew-English Dictionary* (Tel-Aviv—Jerusalem: Massadah, 1965).

EVV   English Versions

Jastrow   Marcus Jastrow, *A Dictionary of the Targumim, the Talmud Babli and Yerushalmi, and the Midrashic Literature*, 2 vols. (New York: Pardes, 1950; reprint, New York: Judaica Press, 1971).

Lewis & Short   Charlton T. Lewis and Charles Short, *A Latin Dictionary* (Oxford: Clarendon Press, 1896).

Liddell & Scott   Henry George Liddell and Robert Scott, *A Greek-English Lexicon*, Revised by Henry Stuart Jones and Roderick McKenzie. 9th ed. (Oxford: Clarendon Press, 1996).

OLD   P. G. W. Glare, ed., *Oxford Latin Dictionary* (Oxford: Oxford University Press, 1968–82).

Midr. Tannaim   D. Hoffmann, *Midrasch Tannaïm zum Deuteronomium*, 2 vols. (Berlin: M. Poppelauer, 1908–1909).

Sifre Num.   Sifre Numbers

Sifre Deut.   Sifre Deuteronomy

Sokoloff   Michael Sokoloff, *A Dictionary of Jewish Palestinian Aramaic of the Byzantine Period* (Ramat-Gan, Israel: Bar Ilan University Press, 1990).

Rabbinic authorities are occasionally designated according to their generation; e.g., T2 = second generation Tannaite. These designations follow those in Stemberger's, *Introduction* (see bibliography).

Chapter One

Introduction

Given the mode of death of its central figure, crucifixion has been a topic of profound interest to Christians throughout the centuries. Christianity, of course, did not spread in a vacuum; rather, it was constantly in contact with the cultural pre-conceptions of the day. Hence, early Christians, proclaiming a crucified Messiah, necessarily interacted with the various perceptions of crucifixion in the ancient world.

For the contemporary scholar of early Christianity, the study of the views concerning crucifixion in antiquity can thus potentially illumine the ways in which Christianity itself developed in its understanding of the death of its central figure. Moreover, given the importance of ancient Jewish thought in the formation of early Christianity, the study of Jewish perceptions of the cross forms a necessary, if perhaps sometimes neglected, context in which to view early Christian references to the cross of Christ.

Jewish people in antiquity were frequently in contact with acts of crucifixion. For example, Josephus, in some nineteen separate accounts,[1] numbers several thousand victims as suspended on the σταυρός (Gr. "cross") – most of these in Judaea.[2] Frequent references to crucifixion in rabbinic texts demonstrate this gruesome penalty to be a matter the rabbis considered a common part of life.[3] And the rabbis sometimes defined their own teachings

---

[1] The figure "nineteen" treats as single events parallel narratives in the *Antiquities* and in the *War*. This includes the *Testimonium Flavianum*, despite the intense debates over its authenticity. "Nineteen" also includes those events, described with σταυρός terminology, which speak of the suspension of a dead body (e.g., *Ant.* vi.374). For more on the semantic range of σταυρός see §2.2 below.

[2] For example, in *Ant.* xvii.295 Josephus states that two thousand were executed by crucifixion; and he speaks of "incalculable numbers" being executed in this fashion in *Bell.* ii.253. Even given the famous tendency of Josephus to exaggerate numbers, one can nonetheless infer from his accounts of the Second Temple period that this form of execution was quite evident in Palestine in the first century.

[3] E.g., note the way crucifixion terminology creeps into aphoristic sayings such as לקיש לסטים בכיר לצלובים ("the last of the robbers is the first of the hanged," in *Eccl. Rab.* vii.37). Similarly, H. Cohn notes, "The extent of such crucifixions [in Judaea] is demonstrated by the legal rules which had to be elaborated to meet contingencies." Cohn cites passages such as *m. Yebam.* xvi.3; *m. Ohol.* iii.5; and *m. Šabb.* vi.10; also note *t. Giṭ.* vii.1; see Haim Hermann Cohn, "Crucifixion," in *Encyclopaedia Judaica*, vol. 5 (Jerusalem: Keter, 1972), 1134; and chapter 2, §3.7 below.

over against the frequent crucifixions that were so much a part of the Roman world.[4] In this light, the study of crucifixion in the numerous references from ancient Jewish sources can help amplify themes that are important for the student of Judaism itself. Thus such an analysis of Jewish perceptions of crucifixion can also rightly be justified as helpful for the scholar of Jewish, as well as Christian, antiquity.

The first part of this book seeks inductively to draw out ancient Jewish views concerning the penalty of crucifixion through the period of the completion of the Talmuds. This work indicates that the numerous references to crucifixion in ancient Jewish literature manifest a variety of perceptions of the cross. These perceptions are often overtly negative both toward the punishment and toward the person so executed. Yet, more positive views can also be found. The second part of the book then briefly suggests how such understandings may have influenced early Christianity.

While other scholarly works have provided helpful insight into the history of crucifixion in the ancient world (and even in Palestine), the emphasis throughout this book is on *perceptions* of crucifixion. In what ways did Jewish people in this period perceive of crucifixion and of a crucified person? Such perceptions can include both well-developed concepts as well as the less tangible "gut-reactions". In short, what would immediately have sprung to mind if someone learned of a person being crucified? And how did those understandings affect Christianity?

This first chapter discusses introductory matters, beginning with a brief summary of the previous scholarship on the subject. Then follows a short study of ancient crucifixion terminology. Next an overview of Jewish law and practice concerning death penalties provides necessary background for future discussion. Finally, a working methodology for this study is suggested.

1. Crucifixion and Judaism in Contemporary Research

Most extended works on crucifixion written by contemporary scholars focus on the Graeco-Roman world at large. Hence, previously there has not been a comprehensive analysis of the many crucifixion and suspension passages found within ancient Jewish literature – especially an analysis that has focused on the variety of ancient Jewish perceptions concerning this penalty.

For example, when one examines Martin Hengel's treatise *Crucifixion*, perhaps the best-known book on the subject available in the English language, one notes that Professor Hengel devotes only two powerful, but all too brief,

---

[4] Thus תולים אותו חי ("hanging him alive") is specifically ruled out as a form of Jewish death penalty *vis-à-vis* its connection with the Roman government in *Sifre Deut.* 221; cf. *b. Sanh.* 46b; *Midr. Tannaim* (Hoffman p. 132, line 7).

pages to "Crucifixion among the Jews."[5] Hengel, explaining his emphasis on Gentile sources throughout this book, states: "The history of crucifixion in Judaea and in the Jewish tradition really needs a separate investigation..." (p. 84). In this regard, Hengel continues the focus on Graeco-Roman analysis that is evident previously in the classic studies of crucifixion by Lipsius and Fulda.[6] Even the important later survey by H. W. Kuhn only provides a few pages more of discussion on Jewish materials.[7]

Many previous studies on the cross in ancient Jewish literature do not focus on the perceptions of Jews toward the penalty; rather, they tend to ask whether ancient Jewish leaders practiced crucifixion. Thus, the modern study of crucifixion in Judaism significantly advanced with the work of Ethelbert Stauffer, but Stauffer was clearly concerned about when crucifixion was first practiced by Jews in Palestine (Stauffer believed the priest Alcimus was the first to crucify fellow Jews).[8] Later, in a carefully argued study, Stauffer's student Ernst Bammel contended that some Jewish people would have regarded crucifixion as a legitimate method of execution.[9] There were, however, also important voices that insisted crucifixion was never a sanctioned practice within Judaism.[10]

In the last few decades, a significant portion of the work on crucifixion within Judaism has focused on two short passages from Qumran (4QpNah 3–

---

[5] Martin Hengel, *Crucifixion in the Ancient World and the Folly of the Message of the Cross*, trans. John Bowden (London & Philadelphia: SCM Press & Fortress Press, 1977), 84–85; reprinted in Martin Hengel, *The Cross of the Son of God*, trans. John Bowden (London: SCM Press, 1986), 176–77. It should be noted that Hengel does make multiple references to Philo and Josephus throughout this work. This book forms an expansion of Martin Hengel, "Mors turpissima crucis: Die Kreuzigung in der antiken Welt und die 'Torheit' des 'Wortes vom Kreuz'," in *Rechtfertigung*, ed. Johannes Friedrich et al. (Tübingen: J. C. B. Mohr [Paul Siebeck]/Göttingen: Vandenhoeck & Ruprecht, 1976), 125–84. The French version has material not found in the English; see Martin Hengel, *La crucifixion dans l'antiquité et la folie du message de la croix*, trans. Albert Chazelle, Lectio divina 105 (Paris: Cerf, 1981), 1–113.

[6] Hermann Fulda, *Das Kreuz und die Kreuzigung: Eine antiquarische Untersuchung* (Breslau: Wilhelm Koebner, 1878). J. Lipsius, *De Cruce libri tres* (Amsterdam, 1670).

[7] Heinz Wolfgang Kuhn, "Die Kreuzesstrafe während der frühen Kaiserzeit: Ihre Wirklichkeit und Wertung in der Umwelt des Urchristentums," in *Aufstieg und Niedergang der Römischen Welt*, ed. Wolfgang Haase, vol. II.25.1 (Berlin/New York: Walter de Gruyter, 1982), 665–69, 706–18, 724–27.

[8] Ethelbert Stauffer, *Jerusalem und Rom im Zeitalter Jesu Christi* (Bern: Francke, 1957), 123–27.

[9] Ernst Bammel, "Crucifixion as a Punishment in Palestine," in *Judaica: Kleine Schriften I*, WUNT I.37 (Tübingen: J. C. B. Mohr [Paul Siebeck], 1986), 76–8; originally published in *The Trial of Jesus*, ed. Ernst Bammel (London: SCM Press, 1970), 162–165.

[10] This claim is made as early as Emil G. Hirsch, "Crucifixion," in *The Jewish Encyclopedia*, vol. 4 (New York/London: Funk and Wagnalls, 1903), 373–74; also see Paul Winter, *On the Trial of Jesus*, ed. T. A. Burkill and Geza Vermes, 2nd rev. ed., SJ 1 (Berlin: Walter de Gruyter, 1974), 90–96 (posthumous revision of the 1961 edition, in which see pp. 62–66).

4 i 6–8; 11QTemple 64:6–13). The Nahum Pesher was released first.[11] Its intriguing line about the Lion of Wrath who "hangs men alive" led to an initial appraisal of this phrase as a reference to crucifixion. Though some discussion ensued, an appeal to *Sifre Deut* 221, which contains a similar phrase, appears to confirm this as a reference to crucifixion.[12] Later, Yigael Yadin caused a sensation by suggesting that the Temple Scroll indicates that Qumran halakhah (based on Deut 21:22–23) mandated suspension as a form of execution. Based on this evidence, he asserted that the Qumranites in the Nahum Pesher actually commended the Lion of Wrath (= Alexander Jannaeus) for his use of crucifixion in opposition to the Seekers-after-Smooth-Things.[13]

The Temple Scroll passage has naturally fascinated NT scholars, especially given Paul's application of Deuteronomy 21:22–23 to the crucified Christ in Galatians 3:13.[14] And Yadin's striking interpretation of the Nahum Pesher has helped provoke even more interest in how various Jewish sects viewed crucifixion.

Many have since penned articles either agreeing or disagreeing with Yadin's proposal.[15] They frequently appeal to the inclusion in *Targum Ruth* 1:17 of צליבת קיסא (often translated as "hanging on a tree") among the four accepted Jewish death penalties, taking the place of strangulation (חנק) in the standard rabbinic list (cf. *m. Sanh.* 7:1).

Many studies also note the 1968 discovery at Givʿat ha-Mivtar in the vicinity of Jerusalem of a crucified man from the first century. This discovery has been cited as evidence of crucifixion in first-century Judea, and it has also

---

[11] Prior to its inclusion in *DJD* 5 (pp. 37–42), the text was first released in J. M. Allegro, "Further Light on the History of the Qumran Sect," *Journal of Biblical Literature* 75 (1956): 89–95.

[12] N. Wieder, "Notes on the New Documents from the Fourth Cave of Qumran," *Journal of Jewish Studies* 7 (1956): 71–72; see the next section in this chapter for further discussion.

[13] Y. Yadin, "Pesher Nahum (4Q pNahum) Reconsidered," *Israel Exploration Journal* 21 (1971): 1–12 (on 11QTemple lxiv.6–13). Though clearly indebted to Josephus' account of Alexander's crucifixion of 800 Jews (*Bell.* i.97; *Ant.* xiii.380) in his historical reconstruction of 4QpNah (see p. 2), Yadin himself uses the terminology "hanging alive" and not explicitly "crucifixion." But he does in a later comment state that he doubts Baumgarten's contention that the sectarians would have differentiated between "hanging alive" and "crucifixion"; see Yigael Yadin, *The Temple Scroll*, 3 + suppl. vols. (Jerusalem: Israel Exploration Society, 1977–1983), 1:378n.

[14] On Paul's usage cf. Max Wilcox, "'Upon the Tree' – Deut 21:22–23 in the New Testament," *Journal of Biblical Literature* 96 (1977): 85–90; Ardel Caneday, "Redeemed from the Curse of the Law: The Use of Deut 21:22–23 in Gal 3:13," *Trinity Journal* 10 (1989): 196–99.

[15] E.g., Daniel R. Schwartz, "'The Contemners of Judges and Men' (11Q Temple 64:12)," in *Studies in the Jewish Background of Christianity*, WUNT 60 (Tübingen: J. C. B. Mohr [Paul Siebeck], 1992), 81–88. See further chapter three §4.3 below.

led to multiple studies on the exact methods employed during crucifixion (i.e., how would a person be positioned on the cross).[16]

Drawing on this material, the one work that has presented the most methodical and comprehensive study of crucifixion in Jewish literature, an article by Luis Díez Merino,[17] seeks to prove that there is pre-Mishnaic evidence that crucifixion *ante-mortem* was an acceptable penalty for some Jewish groups (Sadducees and Essenes), but not for others (Pharisees). Díez Merino contends that the Qumran sectarian literature (Essene documents) contains two texts applauding crucifixion in certain cases (11QTemple 64:6–13 and 4QpNah 3–4 i 6–8). And, after an extensive analysis of targumic evidence, he holds (based on the principle that "what is anti-Mishnaic must be pre-Mishnaic") that the targumim contain pre-Mishnaic strands of legislation that favour crucifixion (especially Targum Neofiti on Num 25:4; all the targumim on Deut 21:22–23; *Tg. Ruth* 1:17; and *Tg. Esth II* 9:24). Hence the tensions between Luke 24:20 and John 18:31 can be resolved when one realizes that they deal with different Jewish sects (Sadducees and Pharisees respectively). However, Díez Merino's analysis has not gone unquestioned, with attention being paid to whether the targumic material is truly anti-Mishnaic and to whether the Qumran texts bear out his Yadin-influenced interpretation.[18]

In contrast, Hengel has proposes that there was a time when even Pharisees crucified. He argues that the famous account of Simeon ben Shetaḥ hanging eighty witches in Ashkelon (*m. Sanh.* 6:4; as developed in *y. Ḥag* 2:2 [77d–78a]; *y. Sanh.* 6:9 [23c]) is actually an encoded narrative describing the Pharisaic backlash against the leadership who supported Alexander Jannaeus, who had crucified eight hundred of the Pharisees' countrymen.[19]

Roughly speaking, among modern scholars addressing these issues there are three sets of opinions concerning the legality of crucifixion within ancient

---

[16] Cf. Joseph A. Fitzmyer, "Crucifixion in Ancient Palestine, Qumran Literature, and the New Testament," *Catholic Biblical Quarterly* 40 (1978): 493–513. For bibliography, see chapter two (§3.6) below.

[17] Luis Díez Merino, "El suplicio de la cruz en la literatura Judia intertestamental," *Studii Biblici Franciscani Liber Annuus* 26 (1976): 31–120. He has also provided two succinct versions of the same argument in Luis Díez Merino, "La crucifixión en la antigua literatura judía (Periodo intertestamental)," *Estudios Eclesiásticos* 51 (1976): 5–27; and Luis Díez Merino, "La crocifissione nella letteratura ebrea antica (Periodo intertestamentale)," in *La Sapienza Della Croce Oggi: Atti del Congresso internazionale Roma, 13–18 ottobre 1975*, vol. 1: La Sapienza Della Croce Nella Rivelazione e Nell'Ecumenismo (Torino: Leumann, 1976), 61–68.

[18] See especially Joseph M. Baumgarten, "Hanging and Treason in Qumran and Roman Law," *Eretz Israel* 16 (1982): 7*–16*.

[19] Martin Hengel, *Rabbinische Legende und frühpharisäische Geschichte: Schimeon b. Schetach und die achtzig Hexen von Askalon*, AHAW.PH 1984,2 (Heidelberg: Carl Winter, 1984). See discussion below in chapter 2.

Jewish law: (1) crucifixion was upheld as a viable means of execution by
certain Jewish sects (i.e., Essenes, possibly Sadducees) and rejected by others
(esp. Pharisees)[20]; (2) crucifixion was universally rejected by all major Jewish
sects – the Qumran and targumic passages either speaking to a different
time,[21] or to a different mode of punishment[22]; (3) crucifixion was accepted
within ancient Jewish law at some early stage only later to be rejected by the
formative rabbinic movement.[23]

At times the ensuing debate was entangled with emotional issues sensitive
to both Christians and Jewish people. Some articles strongly questioned the
veracity of the Gospel accounts of Jewish participation in the crucifixion of
Jesus.[24] Other authors feared the looming spectre of anti-Semitism, so often
rationalized throughout Western history by claims of Jewish participation in
Jesus' death.[25] However, while the present-day social consequences of historical analysis cannot be blithely ignored, and the pure objectivity of any
interpreter is philosophically dubious, one must appreciate the historiographic
contribution of those who, like J. Baumgarten of Baltimore Hebrew College,

---

[20] Yadin apparently held this position; see esp. *Temple Scroll*, 1:375. Among others, also
note: J. Massyngberde Ford, "'Crucify him, crucify him' and the Temple Scroll," *Expository
Times* 87 (1975–1976): 275–78; Fitzmyer, "Crucifixion," 498–507; Torleif Elgvin, "The
Messiah who was Cursed on the Tree," *Themelios* 22 (1997): 14–16. And recall the work of
Díez Merino mentioned above.

[21] Zeitlin repeatedly argued a later date for the Qumran finds, and especially for 4QpNah;
e.g., Solomon Zeitlin, "The Dead Sea Scrolls: A Travesty on Scholarship," *Jewish Quarterly
Review* 47 (1956–1957): 31–36 (though not directly addressing the issue of crucifixion).

[22] Especially Joseph M. Baumgarten, "Does *TLH* in the Temple Scroll Refer to Crucifixion?" *Journal of Biblical Literature* 91 (1972): 472–81; also *idem*, "Hanging," 7*–16*.
Baumgarten argues that תלה at Qumran and צלב in the Targumim refer to execution by
hanging on a noose.

[23] See esp. David J. Halperin, "Crucifixion, the Nahum Pesher, and the Rabbinic Penalty
of Strangulation," *Journal of Jewish Studies* 32 (1981): 32–46.

[24] In a well known article published in the same year as the Nahum Pesher, Samuel
Rosenblatt argued that it was impossible that Pharisees could have been involved in the call
for Jesus' crucifixion. One of Rosenblatt's primary arguments was that death by hanging was
not an authorized form of capital punishment in Pharisaic legal practice. See Samuel
Rosenblatt, "The Crucifixion of Jesus from the Standpoint of Pharisaic Law," *Journal of
Biblical Literature* 75 (1956): 315–321, esp. 318–20.

[25] Note, for example, the opening paragraph of Solomon Zeitlin, "The Crucifixion of
Jesus Re-examined," *Jewish Quarterly Review* n.s., 31 (1941): 327. The danger of anti-
Semitism in historical scholarship on crucifixion can also be seen against the backdrop of the
Medieval and modern history of Christian accounts of Jewish ritual murder of Christians by
crucifixion; e.g., see Haim Hillel Ben-Sasson, "Blood Libel," in *Encyclopaedia Judaica*, vol.
4 (Jerusalem: Keter Publishing House, 1972), 1121–22; Gavin I. Langmuir, "Historiographic
Crucifixion," in *Les Juifs au Regard de L'Histoire*, ed. Gilbert Dahan (Paris: Picard, 1985),
109–27; Samuel Krauss, *The Jewish-Christian Controversy from the Earliest Times to 1789*,
ed. William Horbury, vol. 1, TSAJ 56 (Tübingen: J. C. B. Mohr, 1995), 74, 76, etc.

seek primarily to argue positions based on the indications inherent within the primary sources.[26]

In any case, noticeably lacking among all the works surveyed above is a thoroughgoing attempt to provide a broad-based study of the many perceptions of crucifixion in the various ancient Jewish corpora. These studies have almost invariably focused on the historical issue of whether Jewish people in the time of Christ practiced crucifixion.[27] Certainly any study of the perceptions within ancient Judaism with regard to crucifixion necessarily includes whether or not it was viewed as an acceptable Jewish penalty. Thus, this issue will occasionally be in the background of the present work (see esp. §3 below). However, this study concentrates on what Jewish people in the Second Temple and early rabbinic periods would have thought when they saw, or heard about, a crucified person. A sustained treatment of all facets of the evidence directed toward this particular issue has yet to appear.

2. Crucifixion Terminology

This section offers some preliminary comments concerning the terminology most often used to designate crucifixion events. Probably in large part due to the impact of centuries of Christian art and symbols, the English term "crucifixion" typically designates the execution of a living person on a cross (particularly one shaped like †).[28] "Crucifixion" has become a technical term for a very specific and gruesome form of capital punishment. Similar connotations are seen in the German *Kreuzigung*, the French *crucifixion* and *crucifiement*, and the Spanish *crucifixión*. This is significant to recognize here because these are the languages in which, along with English, appear the most important recent writings on ancient Jewish views of crucifixion. However, ancient Hebrew, Greek, and Latin terminology is, to varying degrees, more flexible. This section elaborates this point, along with noting some pertinent lexical debates for the study of Jewish sources on crucifixion.

---

[26] So Baumgarten carefully states, "… I do not take *tlh* to mean 'to hang' [as opposed to 'to crucify'] because I find crucifixion repugnant to Jewish law, but rather because crucifixion, in my view, does not harmonize with the indications of the Qumran texts and the other pertinent sources." See Baumgarten, "Hanging," 15*n10.

[27] A rare exception is Thornton's brief essay treating the impact of Jewish conceptions of crucifixion associated with the book of Esther on later Christian writers; T. C. G. Thornton, "The Crucifixion of Haman and the Scandal of the Cross," *Journal of Theological Studies* n.s., 37 (1986): 419–26.

[28] E.g., cf. *Oxford English Dictionary*, vol. 2, (1933), s.v.; by extension the term can also refer metaphorically to torture or anguish, and to the mortification of sin, desires, etc.

2.1 Latin Terminology

The English terminology has roots in the Latin verb *crucifigo* (the dative of *crux* with the verb *figo*, often written separately; cf. also *cruci affigo*) – "to fasten to a *crux*." A *crux* was a wooden instrument of execution upon which a person was suspended.[29] Other terms may be used to refer to the victim (e.g., *cruciarius*)[30] or to indicate verbally the action of crucifixion (e.g., *crucio* in ecclesiastical Latin).[31] It is common for modern authors to distinguish four shapes of crosses: *crux immissa* (shaped like †), *crux commissa* (T), the Greek cross (+), and the *crux decussata* or St. Andrew's cross (X).[32] The crossbar of the *crux*, a kind of yoke, is sometimes designated a *patibulum*.[33] Criminals can also be spoken of as being fixed to a pole/stake (*palus, sudis*) or to a piece of wood (*lignum*[34]).

However, even the so-called technical terminology could give the misleading impression that execution via the *crux* had only a limited range of shapes and practices. A well-known quote from Seneca indicates otherwise: "*Video istic cruces non unius quidem generis sed aliter ab aliis fabricatas: capite quidam conversos in terram suspendere, alii per obscena stipitem egerunt, alii brachia patibulo explicuerunt.*" ("I see there crosses, not merely of one kind, but fashioned differently by others: a certain one suspends [a

---

[29] For the following Latin terminological discussion, see Charlton T. Lewis and Charles Short, *A Latin Dictionary* (Oxford: Clarendon Press, 1896), s.v.; and P. G. W. Glare, ed., *Oxford Latin Dictionary* (Oxford: Oxford University Press, 1968–1982), s.v. Idiomatic extensions of *crux* can designate "torture, trouble, misery, destruction"; the term can also be used in reproaches such as "gallows bird," "go and be hanged" (cf. *dierectus*). Of course, verbs other than *figo* can be used with *crux*: e.g., *sustollo* "to raise on high"; cf. Plautus, *Mil.* Act II, scene 3; see Paul Nixon, *Plautus*, 5 vols., LCL (Cambridge: Harvard University Press, 1916–1938), 3:154.

[30] *Cruciarius* can also be used adjectivally in reference to "tortured." Ecclesiastical Latin could employ *crucifer* for the victim and *crucifixor* for the executioner.

[31] "Only in eccl. Latin" according to Lewis & Short, *Latin Dictionary*, s.v. The semantic range of *crucio* also encompasses "to torment, torture."

[32] So Hirsch, "Crucifixion," 373; D. G. Burke and H. E. Dosker, "Cross; Crucify," in *The International Standard Bible Encyclopedia*, ed. Geoffrey W. Bromiley, Fully rev. ed., vol. 1 (Grand Rapids: Eerdmans, 1979), 826. Others have fewer categories; for example, Gerald G. O'Collins, "Crucifixion," in *The Anchor Bible Dictionary*, ed. David Noel Freedman, vol. 1 (New York: Doubleday, 1992), 1208. The four-fold distinction also appears in E. A. Wallis Budge, *Amulets and Talismans* (New York: University Books, 1961), 342. However, Budge examines these in the context of a much fuller discussion of various cross symbols, rightly implying that these four shapes used in Christian art may not correspond to actual Roman executionary forms.

[33] However, note that *patibulum*, at least by the seventh century CE, can designate a "gallows" for hanging as opposed to a "cross-bar" (Isidore, *Etymologia* v.27.34). The term can also indicate a forked prop for vines, or a bar for fastening a door. Related adjectives are *patibulatus*, and *patibulus*.

[34] Cf. Seneca, *Ep.* 101.14.

person] with his head upside down towards the ground, others impale a stake through the sexual organs, others extend the arms by a yoke [*patibulum*].")[35] Understanding the three clauses beginning with *capite* as explications of "*video istic cruces...*", then even impaling of the genitals on a *stipes* ("tree, branch") can be considered affixing to a *crux*. That Seneca distinguished what he "saw" from any possible expectations to a unity of appearances of the cross ("*non unius quidem generis*") may show both (1) that under the Romans in this time execution on the cross tended to follow a fairly common routine, and (2) that there could be significant exceptions that are designated by the same terminology.[36] Indeed the affixing of a dead body to a *crux* could also be described as crucifixion in Latin (cf. Pliny, *Nat. Hist.* xxxvi.107).[37]

Thus a variety of words could be used to speak of crucifixion, and even the most technical Latin terms could refer to the suspension of humans in ways only vaguely resembling execution on a *crux immissa* (†). This relative flexibility in terminology is all the more obvious in the extant Greek sources.

2.2 Greek Terminology

The familiar New Testament terms for the crucifixion of Jesus include the verbs σταυρόω (46 times, though not all of Jesus), συσταυρόω (5 times),[38] and ἀνασταυρόω (in Heb 6:6), as well as the noun σταυρός. Also NT authors speak of the event with προσπήγνυμι ("to affix"; in Acts 2:23)[39] or with the passive of κρεμάννυμι and ἐπὶ ξύλου ("to hang upon a tree"; cf. Acts 5:30; 10:39; Gal 3:13).[40] Combining this terminology with that in

---

[35] Seneca, *De Consolatione ad Marciam* xx.3. Text from John W. Basore, *Seneca Moral Essays*, 3 vols., LCL (Cambridge, Mass.: Harvard, 1965), 2:68. The translation here is mine. Basore translates *cruces* as "instruments of torture" (*Moral Essays*, 2:69); however, although this is a possible translation of *crux* in some circumstances, note that here the three postures Seneca lists all indicate a death by suspension, and note that Seneca distinguishes these three from the expectation that the *cruces* he sees are not of a single kind (implying that a *crux* was normally in his reader's mind associated with a particular form of execution, rather than a more generic term for an "instrument of torture"). Cf. Hengel, *Crucifixion*, 25.

[36] Note also in this regard: Tacitus, *Annals* xv.44.4 (the Christians are pinned to crosses and set on fire – though the textual issues here are significant); see Erich Koestermann et al., eds., *Cornellii Taciti libri qui supersunt*, 2 vols., Bibliotheca scriptorum Graecorum et Romanorum Teubneriana (Leipzig: Teubner, 1965–1986).

[37] Pliny describes this situation as unique, but that may well refer to post-mortem suspension in cases of suicide.

[38] This term may be a NT neologism, since a search of *TLG* and *PHI 7* only surfaced 136 uses – all NT or post-NT Christian authors.

[39] Also προσηλώσας αὐτὸ τῷ σταυρῷ ("nailing it [the χειρόγραφον] to the cross") in Col 2:14.

[40] Depending on the context, κρεμάννυμι alone can refer to a crucified person (see Luke 23:39). Also note the use of ξύλον by itself in Acts 13:29 and in 1 Pet 2:24 to designate the cross; this usage may be relevant to Luke 23:31 as well. Wilcox has suggested a Christian

Lucian's *Prometheus*[41] and in other works of Greek antiquity, several more words surface that, in context, can designate a crucifixion event: particularly ἀνασκολοπίζω (verb) and σκόλοψ (noun),[42] and including verbs such as ἀνακρεμάννυμι, κατακλείω, καταπήγνυμι, πήγνυμι, προσηλόω, and προσπατταλεύω (= προσπασσαλεύω).

Nevertheless, in Greek it is rare for the semantic range of any single term to be confined to "crucifixion." For example, a σταυρός appears originally to have referred to an upright pole. Thus a σταυρός can be a stake in a σταύρωμα ("palisade"; e.g., Thucydides, *Hist.* vi.100)[43] as well as a pole on which a person is impaled or crucified. Hence it naturally follows that both ἀνασταυρόω and σταυρόω can refer to the building of stockades as well as to the setting up of poles (especially for the purpose of suspending people on σταυροί).[44] Elsewhere a σταυρός can be used as a place of scourging, with the death following from some other method.[45]

A σκόλοψ likewise generally refers to "anything pointed" (Liddell & Scott, s.v.), including pales, stakes, thorns, a point of a fishhook, and (in the plural) a palisade. And similarly, the cognate verb ἀνασκολοπίζω need not exclusively refer to "fix on a pole or a stake, impale."[46]

---

dependence on Deut 21:22–23 in the application of ξύλον to the cross of Jesus (see below chapter 7, §6); cf. Wilcox, "Upon the Tree," 85–99.

[41] See Hengel, *Crucifixion*, 11 (repr., 103). Add to Lucian's vocabulary the use of σκόλοψ as a term for "stake" on which one is impaled (cf. Euripides, *IT* 1430) and the verbs such as ἀνακρεμάννυμι, ἀναπήγνυμι, and πήγνυμι, which are often used for affixing a person to a σκόλοψ or σταυρός.

[42] Possibly also ἀνασχινδυλευθήσεται in Plato, *Rep.* 362a; see Henry George Liddell and Robert Scott, *A Greek-English Lexicon*, Revised by Henry Stuart Jones and Roderick McKenzie. 9th ed. (Oxford: Clarendon Press, 1996), 120, 122. Also cf. ἀνασκινδυλεύεσθαι (specifically related to ἀνασκολοπίζω) in Hesychius 4583.

[43] Other palisade terminology is likewise related to the σταυρ- root (e.g., ἀποσταυρόω, διασταυρόω, περισταυρόω, προσσταυρόω, προσταυρόω, σταύρωσις) – most terms can be conveniently witnessed in Thucydides, some also occurring in later historians such as Polybius and Dionysius of Halicarnasus.

[44] Nairne has briefly contended that "ἀνασταυροῦν is good Greek for 'crucify,' 'impale,' whereas σταυροῦν, which is always used elsewhere in the N.T. [i.e., outside Hebrews], meant in the classical period 'make a palisade'"; see A. Nairne, *The Epistle to the Hebrews*, CGTC (Cambridge: Cambridge University Press, 1922), 67. In fact, σταυρόω in the Hellenistic period was widely used for "crucify"; see, for example, Polybius (*Hist.* i.86.4), Strabo (*Geog.* xiv.1.39), Lucian (*Prom.* 1, 10 – parallel w/ ἀνασταυρόω and ἀνασκολοπίζω) and Josephus (*Ant.* xvii.295; xix.94; cf. ii.77, which is parallel with ἀνασταυρόω in ii.73).

[45] See Dio Cassius (*Roman History* xlix.22.6), where the Jewish king Antigonus is flogged by the Romans while tied to a σταυρός, and is later slain.

[46] This is the only definition given in Liddell and Scott, s.v. In fact, it does cover the majority of instances in Greek literature. However, compare ἀνασκολοπίζω in Aquila's translation of Isa 36:2 and 40:3; see Joseph Ziegler, *Isaias*, Septuaginta (Göttingen: Vanden-

However, the "fundamental" references to an upright pole in σταυρός and its cognates, and to pointy objects in σκόλοψ and its cognates, does *not* rightly imply such that terminology in antiquity, when applied to crucifixion, invariably referred to a single upright beam. This is a common word study fallacy in some populist literature.[47] In fact, such terminology often referred in antiquity to cross-shaped crucifixion devices. For example, Lucian, in a brief dialogue that employs most Greek crucifixion vocabulary, refers to the "crucifixion" of Prometheus, whose arms are pinned while stretched from one rock to another.[48] Such a cross-shaped crucifixion position in the Roman era may actually have been the norm; nevertheless, the point to be sustained at this stage is that this position was not the only one to be designated with these Greek terms.

In addition to recognizing the broader semantic ranges of these terms, it is helpful to note that different authors prefer certain terminology. Thus, while Philo knows σταυρός as a "cross" (see *Flacc.* 72, 84; contrast σταυροί as fortifications in *Agr.* 11; *Spec. Leg.* iv.229), he does not use the cognate verb ἀνασταυρόω, preferring instead ἀνασκολοπίζω.[49] Josephus, on the other hand, employs only ἀνασταυρόω and σταυρόω but never ἀνασκολοπίζω.[50] Hengel contends that in the Classical period Herodotus utilized ἀνασταυρόω and ἀνασκολοπίζω with different nuances from one another (ἀνασκολοπίζω of the suspension of living men and ἀνασταυρόω of dead men), but that after Herodotus these two verbs become synonymous. Such a picture may require some more nuance,[51] but it is certainly the case that after Herodotus some

---

hoeck & Ruprecht, 1939), 249, 266. Also note that Field (*Origenis Hexaplorum*, 2:500) indicates a use of ἀνεσκολοπισμένη in Symmachus (as well as Aquila) on Isa 36:2.

[47] Thus, falling prey to the etymological fallacy, some assume that σταυρός can *only* designate a single upright pole, as does W. E. Vine, *An Expository Dictionary of New Testament Words*, 4 vols. (London: Oliphants, 1939), s.v. This error is often found in Jehovah's Witnesses literature. The diachronic study of these terms likely might sustain the possibility that the earliest means of penal bodily suspension involved single pointed poles, and hence was associated with the σταυρ- and the σκολοπ- stems. However, later (at least by the time of early Roman military incursions into Anatolia) suspension devices developed other shapes, while the terminology remained attached to all such bodily suspensions.

[48] Lucian, *Prom.* 1: ἀνεσταυρώσθω ἐκπετασθεὶς τὼ χεῖρε ἀπὸ τουτουὶ τοῦ κρημνοῦ πρὸς τὸν ἐναντίον. Text in A. M. Harmon et al., *Lucian*, 8 vols., LCL (London: William Heinemann/Cambridge, Mass.: Harvard University Press, 1913–1967), 2:242. See also (Pseudo-) Lucian, *Jud. Voc.* 12 (where the σταυρός is shaped like a Tau).

[49] Most often Philo employs ἀνασκολοπίζω to clearly refer to a means of death: e.g., *Post.* 61 (οἱ ἀνασκολοπισθέντες ἄχρι θανάτου); and also *Flacc.* 84 (ζῶντας δ᾽ ἀνασκολοπίζεσθαι προσέταττεν). See also Dio Chrysostom, *Orationes* xvii.15; and multiple references in Lucian (esp. *Prom.* 2, 7, 10; *Pisc.* 2; *Philops.* 29). Also likely Polybius *Hist.* x.33.8; Dionysius of Halicarnasus, *Antiq. Rom.* v.51.3.

[50] This phenomena was already noticed by Hengel, *Crucifixion*, 24 [repr. 116].

[51] Concerning Herodotus, the instance in *Hist.* vi.30 (τὸ μὲν αὐτοῦ σῶμα αὐτοῦ ταύτῃ ἀνεσταύρωσαν) is at least ambiguous (similarly with many of Herodotus' uses of

authors use the terms interchangeably and that both verbs can designate acts of crucifixion (even in the narrow English sense of the word).[52]

The sources testify at times to a variety of means of suspending a person from a σταυρός. For example, Josephus reports the monstrous incident of the Roman soldiers who "out of rage and hatred amused themselves by nailing their prisoners in different postures," affixing them to σταυροί.[53] Roughly contemporary to Josephus is the use of σταυρός in the account by Plutarch concerning Parysatis (mother of Artaxerxes): "ἐγχειρίσασα τοῖς ἐπὶ τῶν τιμωριῶν προσέταξεν ἐκδεῖραι ζῶντα, καὶ τὸ μὲν σῶμα πλάγιον διὰ τριῶν σταυρῶν ἀναπῆξαι, τὸ δὲ δέρμα χωρὶς διαπατταλεῦσαι." (*Art.* xvii.5).[54]

Perhaps most importantly, there is often ambiguity in crucifixion and suspension accounts as to whether the person is being suspended before or after death. So Josephus, while most often utilizing ἀνασταυρόω to indicate a means of execution,[55] can also say that the Philistines "crucified" the *dead* bodies of Saul and his sons "to the walls of the city of Bethsan" (*Ant.* vi.374; τὰ δὲ σώματα ἀνεσταύρωσαν πρὸς τὰ τείχη τῆς Βηθσὰν πόλεως). Thus

---

ἀνασκολοπίζω), if not actually implying that the means of death was through ἀνασταυρόω, since the use of the term is not preceded by the death of Histiaeus. In the later period it is possible that Plutarch distinguished crucifixion on a σταυρός from impalement on a σκόλοψ (cf. "ἀλλ᾽ εἰς σταυρὸν καθηλώσεις ἢ σκόλοπι πήξεις;" – "but will you nail him to a cross or impale him on a stake?" in *An vitiositas ad infelicitatem sufficiat* 499D; see text and translation in Frank C. Babbitt, et al., *Plutarch's Moralia*, 16 vols., LCL (Cambridge, Mass.: Harvard University Press, 1927–1969), 6:498–99). Schneider calls ἀνασταυρόω and ἀνασκολοπίζω "identical," which may be too strong; see J. Schneider, "σταυρός, σταυρόω, ἀνασταυρόω," in *Theological Dictionary of the New Testament*, ed. Gerhard Kittel and Gerhard Friedrich, trans. Geoffrey Bromiley, vol. 7 (Grand Rapids: Eerdmans, 1971), 7:583.

[52] E.g., Lucian (second century CE) uses ἀνασκολοπίζω, ἀνασταυρόω and σταυρόω interchangeably to refer to the crucifixion of Prometheus (*Prom.* 1, 2, 4, 7, 10, 15, 17).

[53] προσήλουν δὲ οἱ στρατιῶται δι᾽ ὀργὴν καὶ μῖσος τοὺς ἁλόντας ἄλλον ἄλλῳ σχήματι πρὸς χλεύην... (*Bell.* v.451). See analysis below in chapter 2, §3.5. Throughout this book texts from Josephus are cited from Benedictus Niese, *Flavii Iosephi Opera*, 7 vols. (Berlin: Weidmann, 1887–1895) (here vol. 6, p. 496). Translations of Josephus are from H. St. J. Thackeray et al., *Josephus*, 10 vols., LCL (Cambridge, Mass.: Harvard University Press/ London: William Heinemann, 1926–1965).

[54] "...she put the eunuch in the hands of the executioners, who were ordered to flay him alive, to set up his body slantwise on three stakes [τριῶν σταυρῶν], and to nail up his skin to a fourth." Text and translation from Bernadotte Perrin, *Plutarch's Lives*, 11 vols., LCL (Cambridge, Mass.: Harvard University Press, 1914–1926), 11:167.

[55] Note especially *Vita* 420–21, where the three crucified individuals are removed from the cross at Josephus' request (one of them survives). Also see *Ant.* xi.267 (καὶ κελεύει παραχρῆμα αὐτὸν ἐξ ἐκείνου τοῦ σταυροῦ κρεμασθέντα ἀποθανεῖν); xii.256 (ζῶντες ἔτι καὶ ἐμπνέοντες ἀνεσταυροῦντο); and xiii.380 (= *Bell.* i.97); most likely also *Ant.* xix.94; *Bell.* iii.321. In other situations in Josephus the context is not necessarily determinative as to whether the σταυρός was the means of death, though often it is possible to assume so.

hanging a dead body on a pole (or, in the case above, in a similar fashion to a wall) may be associated terminologically for Josephus with the hanging of a live person for the purpose of execution. This fluidity of σταυρός terminology also appears in other Greek authors (especially in Polybius and Plutarch).[56] In fact, most often our sources do not present us with clear contextual indicators that would allow us to decide in any one text which manner of penalty is projected. For example, are the criminals' dead bodies being impaled, or are they being nailed alive to a cross in Philo *Spec. Leg.* iii.151–52?

In part, this calls for the interpreter to be sensitive to matters of personal and regional lexical style. But it is quite conceivable, especially when considering the ἀνασταυρόω word group, that the fundamental distinction within the terms is not "crucifixion vs. other post-mortem suspensions," but rather "suspension of persons vs. suspension of other objects." Crucifixion represents a subset of the larger conceptuality of human bodily suspension. In fact, many (if not most) of the concepts in a Greek-speaking audience concerning human suspension (both as a means to and as a subsequent penalty after death) may come into play when that same audience hears of an act of crucifixion.

2.3 Hebrew, Aramaic, and Syriac Terminology

While Hebrew and Aramaic are distinct languages, it is still reasonable to treat them together in our discussion of terminology. Naturally, both are part of the larger family of Semitic languages. More importantly, there appear significant similarities in usage between Hebrew and Aramaic in words from roots such as *tlh* (cf. Aramaic *tly* and *tl'*) and *ṣlb*. Further, Syriac terminology originated from Aramaic. Thus the following section analyzes crucifixion terminology from these three languages – noting both continuities and discontinuities between them.

---

[56] In his Polycrates account, Herodotus certainly represents ἀνασταυρόω as a penalty *post mortem* (*Hist.* iii.125), though later authors understood this same event as death by crucifixion; see Hengel, *Crucifixion*, 24n. (repr. 116n.). Note the mention in Philo, *Prov.* ii.24–25 = Eusebius, *Praep.* viii.14.24–25; see Karl Mras, *Eusebius Werke Achter Band: Die Praeparatio Evangelica*, 2 vols., GCS 43,1 (Berlin: Akademie-Verlag, 1954), 1:468–69. However, the Armenian version varies here; cf. F. H. Colson et al., *Philo*, 10 (+ 2 suppl.) vols., LCL (Cambridge, Mass.: Harvard University Press, 1929–1962), 9:543–44. Polybius clearly reports the crucifixion of both the living (*Hist.* i.86.6, employing σταυρὸν with ἀνέθεσαν ζῶντα; cf. σταυρόω in *Hist.* i.86.4) and the dead (*Hist.* v.54.6–7; viii.21.3 – both ἀνασταυρόω). Most notable is how Plutarch can use ἀνασταυρόω both for the suspension of a dead body (*Tim.* xxii.8; *Cleom.* xxxix.1 [cf. xxxviii.2]) and for a means of execution (*Caes.* ii.7; cf. σταυρός in *De sera numinis vindicta* 554B; also note, since listing no other mode of death, the uses of ἀνασταυρόω in *Fab.* vi.3; *Alex.* lxxii.3; *Ant.* lxxxi.1; *De Garrulitate* 508F–509A).

2.3.1 TLH and ṢLB

Ancient Hebrew and Aramaic literature often denotes bodily suspension of a person after (and sometimes before) death with the Hebrew phrase תלה [אתו] על עץ (in Aramaic with the corresponding תלי or תלא)[57] and with the Hebrew and Aramaic verbal root צלב.[58] Jastrow notes that the device on which a person is suspended is designated by the nominal cognates of צלב in Hebrew (צְלוּב) and Aramaic (צְלִיבָא), and that the suspension itself may be signified by Hebrew צְלִיבָה and Aramaic צְלִיבְתָא.[59] However scholars debate whether these terms and phrases by themselves can typically designate, beyond mere bodily suspension, an act of "crucifixion" in the limited sense of the English word.

For example, when the Qumran Nahum Pesher was published, there was some discussion as to whether אשר יתלה אנשים חיים ("who hangs men alive") in 4QpNah 3–4 i 7 was a reference to crucifixion.[60] However, most

---

[57] E.g., the phrase תלה [אתו] על עץ appears for bodily suspension of humans in the MT in Gen 40:19; Deut 21:22; Josh 8:29; 10:26; Esth 2:23; 6:4; 7:10; 8:7; 9:13, 25 (cf. Esth 5:14; 7:9) – the Esther accounts likely indicating a means of execution. The word תלה by itself functions in a similar way in Gen 40:22; 41:13; Deut 21:23; 2 Sam 4:12; 21:12; Lam 5:12; Esth 9:14. For Aramaic תלי: Sokoloff lists as one of the definitions "to execute by hanging" (citing *Lam. Rab.* 5:12 [Buber 157:8]); see Michael Sokoloff, *A Dictionary of Jewish Palestinian Aramaic of the Byzantine Period*, Dictionaries of Talmud, Midrash and Targum 2 (Ramat-Gan, Israel: Bar Ilan University Press, 1990), s.v. The penal suspensionary use of the Aramaic term תלי appears as early as text no. 71 in A. Cowley, *Aramaic Papyri of the Fifth Century B.C.* (Oxford: Clarendon Press, 1923), pp. 180–81 (line 19).

[58] Jastrow defines the verb צלב in both Hebrew and Aramaic as "to hang, impale"; see Marcus Jastrow, *A Dictionary of the Targumim, the Talmud Babli and Yerushalmi, and the Midrashic Literature*, 2 vols. (New York: Pardes, 1950), s.v. However, Sokoloff more specifically understands the Aramaic term as signifying "to impale, crucify"; see Sokoloff, *Dictionary*, s.v. Cf. Modern Hebrew, which signifies "to crucify" with צלב and indicates the cross or a crucifix by צְלָב; see Reuben Alcalay, *The Complete Hebrew-English Dictionary* (Tel-Aviv/Jerusalem: Massadah, 1965), s.v.

[59] Jastrow (*Dictionary*, s.v.), indicates "stake, gallows" as definitions for צְלוּב (also, in a separate entry, "impaled, hanging"). Jastrow provides similar definitions for צְלִיב, and for the Aramaic צְלִיבָא (variant צְלִיבָה). For צְלִיבָה and צְלִיבְתָא Jastrow lists "impaling, hanging." However, here again Sokoloff is more specific in defining צְלִיב as the "pole for crucifixion" (*Dictionary*, p. 465).

[60] Doubts against a crucifixion understanding of the phrase אשר יתלה אנשים חיים have been unfairly associated with the name of H. H. Rowley; see the remarks by Wieder, ("Notes," 71); and Baumgarten ("TLH in the Temple Scroll," 478n.). Actually, Rowley states that, based on the versional renderings of OT passages that use תלה, this phrase may possibly be a reference to crucifixion but the lexical data alone cannot limit the term תלה to this meaning. Rowley himself, however, also contends that the "...horror caused by such action suggests that it was some non-Jewish form of death, and this elevates the possibility that crucifixion is meant into a probability"; see H. H. Rowley, "4QpNahum and the Teacher of Righteousness," *Journal of Biblical Literature* 75 (1956): 190–91.

rightly favour a crucifixion understanding of the Nahum Pesher phrase, due to the comparison of this phrase with a similar idiom also found in *Sifre Deut* 221 (יכול יהו תולים אותו חי, "is it possible they hung him alive?"), which itself is explicated in important manuscripts by כדרך שהמלכות עושה ("in the manner which the [Roman] government does").[61]

On another matter, H. Cohn argues that, while צלב in Hebrew designates "to crucify," in Aramaic צלב means "to hang." He bases this on the etymologies of the two words, which he claims are different – the Hebrew is derived from the Hebrew root "*shelov*" (שלב), which he defines as "fixing or bracing wooden planks or beams together," while the Aramaic comes from the Assyrian *dalabu* (glossed as "causing pain or distress").[62]

It is surprising that Cohn can argue a strong distinction between two identical consonantal terms used in such similar contexts in two languages with such a long history of intermingling. The spectre of the etymological fallacy suggests itself. Also, the etymologies he provides are striking for the improbable consonantal shifts required (שׁ to צ in Hebrew; and Assyrian *d* to Aramaic *ṣ*).[63] Rather, Baumgarten's proposal that צלב is related to the

---

[61] So Wieder, "Notes," 71–72. Zeitlin, having erroneously stated on the basis of a "minor midrash" concerning Judith that the phrase "to hang alive" in 4QpNah was an expression "coined in the Middle Ages," uses this as evidence for a very late date to the Nahum Pesher; see Zeitlin, "DSS: Travesty," 33–34. Upon Wieder's publication of the *Sifre Deut* 221 evidence to the contrary (see Wieder, "Notes," 71–72), both Zeitlin and Wieder crossed swords concerning whether the omission of the phrase כדרך שהמלכות עושה in the Vienna edition of the *Sifre* changes matters; see S. Zeitlin, "The Phrase יתלה אנשים חיים," *Journal of Jewish Studies* 8 (1957): 117–18; N. Wieder, "Rejoinder," *Journal of Jewish Studies* 8 (1957): 119–21. The textual issue in the *Sifre* is discussed below in chapter 3, §4.7; but for now observe that יכול יהו תולים אותו חי occurs in all manuscripts of the *Sifre Deut* (thus undermining Zeitlin's Medieval thesis in any event) and note that the manuscript evidence for the phrase "as the [Roman] government does" is significant.

[62] Haim Cohn, *The Trial and Death of Jesus* (New York: Ktav, 1977), 209. The same claim is found in the earlier Hebrew version of this book; thus see Haim Cohn, משפטו ומותו של ישו הנוצרי (Tel Aviv: Dvir, 1968), 132–33. For the etymology from שלב Cohn relies on Elieser Ben-Yehuda and Naphtali H. Tur-Sinai, *Thesaurus Totius Hebraitatis et Veteris et Recentioris [= מלון הלשון העברית]*, 16 vols. (Jerusalem: Hemda, 1908–1959), 11:5482. Actually Ben-Yehuda is more cautious than Cohn (stating "שלב: קרוב ואולי"); and, more significantly, Ben-Yehuda draws an explicit connection between the Hebrew צלב and its Aramaic counterpart ("מן הארמ' צלב"; see p. 5482n.).

[63] Descriptions of typical consonantal shifts with these consonants (and their relationships to "proto-Semitic") can be found in: Carl Brockelmann, *Grundriss der vergleichenden Grammatik der semitischen Sprachen*, 2 vols. (Berlin: Von Reuther & Reichard, 1908/1913), 1:128–36, 170–173, 234–38; or more cursorily in Sabatino Moscati et al., *An Introduction to the Comparative Grammar of the Semitic Languages: Phonology and Morphology*, ed. Sabatino Moscati, PLO, n.s. 6 (Wiesbaden: Otto Harrassowitz, 1964), 31–37. These standard works fail to support the consonantal shifts that Cohn proposes. Brockelmann notes the shift of Aramaic *ṣᵉlībā* to Persian *čalīpā* (meaning "Kreuz") in *Grundriss*, 1:208 (also in his *Lexicon Syriacum*, 303).

Assyrian *ṣilbu* ("a crosswise arrangement [of bandages or wood]") seems more worthy of consideration.[64] Even more detrimental to Cohn's belief is the evidence of the Aramaic sections in the midrashim where Aramaic צלב clearly designates crucifixion.[65] Further, Cohn's subsequent discussion about צלב in the Nahum Pesher is misplaced, since the term in the Pesher is תלה and not צלב.[66] Thus, Cohn's strong separation between Aramaic and Hebrew צלב must be rejected.

However, in a meticulously argued article, J. Baumgarten contends that the phrase ותליתמה אותו על העץ וימת ("and you shall hang him on the tree and he shall die") in the Qumran Temple Scroll does *not* refer to death by crucifixion, but to execution by hanging on a noose.[67] Baumgarten's essay essentially combines (1) an assertion that hanging on a noose was an accepted means of execution in Second Temple Judaism (and signified by both תלה and צלב) with (2) an argument that תלה by itself could not designate crucifixion for the Qumran community (and hence must refer to hanging from a noose). Because Baumgarten's thesis involves several issues of lexical semantics, his arguments are worth reviewing:

(1) Targum Ruth 1:17, which lists צליבת קיסא as a form of capital punishment, does so in the place of execution by strangulation (חנק) in the standard rabbinic list, thus indicating that hanging from a noose is intended in this use of צלב (pp. 473–74).[68]

---

[64] Baumgarten, "*TLH* in the Temple Scroll," 474. The definition is from *CAD* 16, p. 187 (which Baumgarten also cites). However, other lexicons are less certain of the meaning of the term *ṣilbu* (cf. *AHW* 3, p. 1100). Further, etymological relationships with its more frequent relatives (cf. *ṣalāpu* in *CAD* 16, p. 71) would probably also need to be explored before affirming Baumgarten's proposal. Díez Merino remarks that the known occurrence of *ṣlb* in the Punic dialect (see *RES*, vol. 1, no. 125) is not certain enough to contribute significantly to the etymological debate ("Suplicio," p. 32). Z. Harris suggests the Punic term might designate "impale on a razor" – see Zellig S. Harris, *A Grammar of the Phoenician Language*, AOS 8 (New Haven: American Oriental Society, 1936), 141. Concerning the Punic word, Hoftijzer and Jongeling are even more cautious when they suggest "to impale? (highly uncert. interpret.)" on the strength of the usage of *ṣlb* in Hebrew and Aramaic; see J. Hoftijzer and K. Jongeling, *Dictionary of the North-West Semitic Inscriptions*, 2 vols., HdO I.21 (Leiden: E. J. Brill, 1995), 2:967.

[65] Some Midrash Rabbah examples of overt application of Aramaic צלב and its cognates to designate crucifixion: *Eccl. Rab.* 7:37 [21c] (on *Eccl* 7:26; of brigands); *Esth. Rab.* 10:5 (on Esth 6:11 = Vilna 14d [28]; note use of nails).

[66] Cohn, "Trial," 210–11. Cohn's lack of awareness of the Hebrew manuscript of 4QpNah is all the more obvious in the earlier Hebrew edition of Cohn's book (משפטו, p. 133) where his reference to the Pesher Nahum citation varies wildly from the actual text.

[67] Baumgarten, "*TLH* in the Temple Scroll," 472–81.

[68] Also supported by an appeal to one MS of Targum Ruth, which reads חניקת סודרא ("the strangulation of the scarf") in the place of צליבת קיסא (MS De Rossi 31). Baumgarten seems to imply that, since צלב is the normal rendering of תלה in the Targumim (p. 474), this Aramaic evidence may be relevant to the Hebrew expression as well.

2. Crucifixion Terminology

(2) That hanging from a noose was seen as a legitimate variant of strangulation is borne out by the use of תלה in the suicide account of Jakum (=Jaḳim) of Zeroroth, who hangs himself from a pole to produce strangulation (*Gen. Rab.* 65:22; *Midr. Psa.* 11:7).[69] Baumgarten also claims similar support from Simeon b. Shetaḥ's hanging of eighty witches in Ashkelon (תלה in *m. Sanh.* 6:4; וצלבונן in *y. Ḥag* 2:2 [78a]; אייתי לצליבא in *y. Sanh.* 6:9 [23c]).[70]

(3) The essence of crucifixion, as practiced by the Romans, was "the deliberate protraction of torture" combined with the disgrace of leaving the body unburied. But, since this contravenes the command to bury the executed person within the day (Deut 21:22–23) – a command explicitly known and kept by the Qumran community (11QTemple lxiv.11–12) – the Qumranites could not have envisioned their law to execute someone by "hanging him on the tree" as involving crucifixion. Rather this Qumran legislation must have involved a more instant means of death, such as by strangulation on a noose.[71]

(4) Most significantly, both the Qumran community and the rabbis addressed crucifixion as the act of "hanging men alive" (יתלה אנשים חיים in 4QpNah 3–4 i 7; also line 8 לתלוי חי על העץ; cf. *Sifre Deut* 221 תולים אותו חי). The need for the explication "alive" demonstrates that "...*tlh* by itself did not signify impalement on a cross, but a form of execution resulting in immediate death" (p. 478).

(5) Contrary to Yadin's contention, it is unlikely that 4QpNah 3–4 i 6–8 reflects a positive affirmation of the Lion of Wrath's crucifixion of the Seekers-after-Smooth-Things.[72]

Although Baumgarten's article focuses on the use of תלה at Qumran, his work leaves the clear impression that תלה nowhere means "to crucify" apart from the technical phraseology produced when it is combined with "alive" (חי or חיים). He does allow that תלה in the biblical Esther narratives may be a reference to impalement on a pole, but these instances do not amount to evidence that this was a legal punishment in Jewish law (pp. 476–77).

---

[69] Baumgarten (p. 474) notes a similar account to that of Jaḳim in the execution of Balaam as recorded in *b. Sanh.* 106b. As indirectly acknowledged in Baumgarten's footnote 12, the major contribution to Baumgarten's argument in the Balaam traditions actually comes in Rashi's medieval commentary on the Bavli here (esp. note שתלאוהו). The evidence from Ginzberg that Baumgarten cites in his footnote 12 does not help his case.

[70] Baumgarten (p. 476) also cites Büchler's references to execution by hanging in the Ben Stada accounts (*b. Sanh.* 67a – in uncensored manuscripts), and to the renderings of הוקיע (in Num 25:4; 2 Sam 21:6, 9, 13) in *Sifre Num.* 131 and *b. Sanh.* 35a.

[71] Note that Baumgarten, without evidence, inferentially rules out any means of hastening the death of the victim by a *coup de grâce* such as the breaking of the legs of the victims (pp. 477–78). But, since John 19:31–33 portrays such a procedure without explaining its efficacy to the readers, such a *coup de grâce* likely was known in the Mediterranean world. Some have also pointed to such a procedure in the early reports of the archaeological evidence from Givʿat ha-Mivtar, but later assessments have not confirmed that this crucified man's legs were intentionally broken; see Joseph Zias and Eliezer Sekeles, "The Crucified Man from Givʿat ha-Mivtar: A Reappraisal," *Israel Exploration Journal* 35 (1985): 24–25 (see chapter 2, §3.6 below).

[72] Section 2.4 below on 4QpNah in chapter 2 examines Baumgarten's arguments for point five.

In a later article Baumgarten clarifies his understanding of the semantic range of צלב: he allows a few instances where צלב does refer to crucifixion,[73] but maintains that the targumic usage of צלב signifies hanging and not crucifixion (pp. 8*–9*). Those uses of *ṣlb* in Syriac, Mandaic, and Christian Palestinian Aramaic (which use the term to signify "crucifixion") are dominated by Christian theological assertions, and are thus not relevant when examining צלב in targumic Aramaic (p. 8*). Furthermore, the targumic passages that use צלב reflect standard rabbinic interpretations of those biblical passages – thus showing that the targumim did not contravene the standard rabbinic understanding of bodily suspension (i.e., that crucifixion is not a viable means of execution; p. 9*).

An article by D. J. Halperin portrays an almost entirely opposite view from that of Baumgarten, since Halperin holds that צלב generally designates crucifixion.[74] Halperin emphasizes the evidence of Syriac, Mandaic, and Christian Palestinian Aramaic with regard to *ṣlb* (pp. 37–38). He also contends that צלב in the targumim is only used in reference to the penal bodily suspension of humans either living or dead (p. 38).[75] And Halperin, noting certain rabbinic Hebrew uses of צלב and its cognates that clearly denote crucifixion in the rabbinic writings (38n.), argues that the Esther Targumim "plainly intend" crucifixion in their use of צלב (p. 39). Finally, he contends that there are places in rabbinic Hebrew where תלה actually replaces צלב as a term for crucifixion, thus showing that the meturgeman could very well have thought that תלה in the biblical texts referred to a form of punishment implying "crucifixion or something resembling it" (on this basis צלב, a term normally designating crucifixion, was extended to include post-mortem suspension).[76] With this argumentation Halperin states:

One gathers that the primary meaning of Targumic *selab* – meaning that surfaces when the writers are composing freely and without the restrictions imposed by the Hebrew text – is crucifixion.... There is no evidence that the verb is ever used for hanging by the neck. In *Targ. Ruth* 1:17, where a form of execution is obviously designated, the burden of proof rests heavily upon the scholar who would see in *selibat qesa* anything other than crucifixion (pp. 39–40).

---

[73] See Baumgarten, "Hanging," pp. 8* (on *t. Sanh.* 9.7) and 9* (esp. note 15, citing *m. Yebam.* 16:3).

[74] Halperin, "Crucifixion," esp. 37–40.

[75] Halperin does allow that the Samaritan Targum, unlike the other targumic traditions, uses צלב to render the biblical תלה uniformly ("Crucifixion," 38n.), even where not speaking of human bodily suspension (he notes Deut 28:66). Baumgarten seizes on Halperin's admitted exception in the Samaritan Targum, noting that thus צלב is used "...even where the verb does not pertain to execution" (Baumgarten, "Hanging," 8*).

[76] Halperin, "Crucifixion," 39–40. He cites *t. Sanh.* 9.7 (צלב) and "its parallel" in *b. Sanh.* 46b (תלה) as his example of תלה replacing צלב in denoting crucifixion.

How ought one arbitrate between the lexical studies of Baumgarten and Halperin? Of all modern authors Baumgarten has certainly presented the best lexical arguments so far for limiting the range of תלה and for guarding the targumim from bearing a crucifixion meaning in their usage of צלב. Yet, there are reasons to remain unconvinced of his analysis.

First, an appeal to the later Aramaic dialects remains fruitful. What is interesting about the other Aramaic traditions is not simply that they use *ṣlb* for "crucify" (and its nominal cognates for "crucifixion"), but that, in the semantic field of terms for crucifixion, *ṣlb* is distinctive in several Middle Aramaic dialects for having the exclusive meaning of "crucifixion" while other crucifixion terms have broader semantic ranges.

For example, in Syriac both ܙܩܦ and ܨܠܒ can designate "to crucify," with their corresponding nominal forms (ܙܩܝܦܐ and ܨܠܝܒܐ) designating the cross itself. However, while the semantic range of ܨܠܒ appears focused on "crucify,"[77] ܙܩܦ can signify *"erexit, suspendit, crucifixit; erexit se, horruit."*[78] Thus ܙܩܦ appears to be a term that includes crucifixion within its semantic range (especially in the NT Peshitta),[79] but that more broadly has to do with "lifting up" or "erecting." In a similar way the verb ܬܠܐ, while having a basic concept of *suspendit*, can in certain contexts signify *crucifixit*.[80] In contrast, the nouns ܙܩܝܦܐ and ܨܠܝܒܐ are much closer to *termini technici* for the cross and for crucifixion, as is ܨܠܒ for "to crucify."[81]

---

[77] For ܨܠܒ see R. Payne Smith, ed., *Thesaurus Syriacus*, 2 vols. (Oxford: Clarendon Press, 1879/1901), 2:3403–3405. The elder Payne Smith is naturally followed in J. (Mrs. Margoliouth) Payne Smith, ed., *A Compendious Syriac Dictionary* (Oxford: Clarendon Press, 1903), 478. Also Carl Brockelmann, *Lexicon Syriacum* (Edinburgh: T. & T. Clark/Berlin: Reuther & Reichard, 1895), 303. Other lexica have similar entries: Carolo Schaaf, *Lexicon Syriacum Concordantiale*, 2nd ed. (Leiden: Typis Joh. Mulleri, Joh. fil; Apud Cornelium Boutesteyn & Samuelem Luchtmans, 1717), 483; Louis Costaz, *Dictionnaire Syriaque-Français/Syriac-English Dictionary/Qamus Siryani `Arabi*, 2nd ed. (Beirut: Dar El-Machreq, [1986?]), 302.

[78] So R. Payne Smith, ed., *Thesaurus*, 1:1148–49 on ܙܩܦ (also endorsing the further meanings *"vocali Zekopho insignivit"* and *"ingruit* mare, tempestas"). To this the supplement adds "to hold oneself erect, stand erect"; see J. P. Margoliouth, *Supplement to the Thesaurus Syriacus of R. Payne Smith, S.T.P.* (Oxford: Clarendon Press, 1927), 115. Brockelmann also has *"erexit; crucifixit*; and (intransitive) *surrexit, horruit"* (*Lexicon Syriacum*, 98).

[79] So J. Payne Smith (*Dictionary*, 119) notes concerning ܙܩܦ "in the N. T. *crucified* but in other books ܨܠܒ is usual."

[80] R. Payne Smith, ed., *Thesaurus*, 2:4440–44. NT influence here is quite possible, especially given the usage (and potential subsequent influence) of the Ethpeʿel in Gal 3:13 (ܕܡܬܬܠܐ ܐܠܗܐ). However, remember that תלי in Palestinian Jewish Aramaic can also be used in contexts of execution.

[81] This concerns the noun ܙܩܝܦܐ, not the passive participle of the same form. It may be due to connecting the participle and the noun in the same entry that Brockelmann remarks that, in addition to *"cruci fixus"* and *"crux,"* ܙܩܝܦܐ can also function (apparently adjectivally) to mean *"erectus, altus"* (*Lexicon Syriacum*, 98; citing the Benedictus edition of

Similarly, Christian Palestinian Aramaic evidences a limited application of *ṣlb* and its nominal cognates to crucifixion, while *zqp* is a more general term that can designate crucifixion in certain contexts.[82] Also, in Mandaic the central definition given for *ṣlb* is "to crucify," though *tla* can likewise be legitimately used for human bodily suspension.[83]

As these Aramaic dialects progressed, *ṣlb* was the Aramaic term already in use that presented itself as the most likely candidate for a technical term for crucifixion in Christian and Nasoraean literature. Other terms were also available that could mean crucifixion, but only *ṣlb* was the clear choice to bear such a focused meaning. Thus it is wholly possible that *ṣlb* may have had some proclivity to bearing crucifixion signification in other Aramaic dialects with which Syriac, Christian Palestinian Aramaic, and Mandaic were in contact, and from which they developed – including both Babylonian and Jewish Palestinian Aramaic, as well as their predecessors. It is this possibility that Baumgarten too quickly dismisses. Though the focus of this lexical analysis will be on synchronic evidence, such diachronic development might provide subsidiary support.[84]

Second, it is worth re-emphasizing Halperin's point that צלב is always only used in the targumim for human bodily suspension (rendering each time the Hebrew תלה). In fact, צלב in rabbinic literature also only designates human bodily suspension (while its cognate nouns only speak either of the device on which such suspension occurs, or of the event itself). The only example that Baumgarten adduces to the contrary is from Halperin's own admission that the Samaritan Targum uses צלב uniformly to translate תלא, even in Deut 28:66. However, in Deut 28:66 a person's "life" is in suspension before him, a metaphor that the Samaritan meturgeman could easily have sought to vividly render with bodily suspension terminology.[85] In any case,

---

Ephraem's works, vol. 2, 89a) – note that R. Payne Smith (*Thesaurus*, 1149) includes this same reference under the passive participle. Naturally, other cognates of ܣܡܝ and ܙܩܦ can be used to indicate related crucifixion concepts: e.g., ܣܡܩܐ and ܙܩܘܠܐ ("crucifier"); ܙܩܝܦܘܬܐ and ܣܡܝܩܘܬܐ ("crucifixion").

[82] Fridericus Schulthess, ed., *Lexicon Syropalaestinum* (Berlin: George Reimer, 1903), pp. 170–71 for *ṣlb*; p. 57 for *zqp* (noting ܣܡܝܩܘܬܐ in Acts 2:23 refers to "*crucifixistis*").

[83] See E. S. Drower and R. Macuch, *A Mandaic Dictionary* (Oxford: Clarendon, 1963), p. 395 for *ṣlb*, p. 387 for *ṣaliba*, and *tla* on p. 487. Also in Mandaic, as in Syriac, *zqp* can be used of setting up or erecting something, though Drower and Macuch do not note any uses of this term for human bodily suspension (169–70).

[84] Such diachronic evidence against Baumgarten's position is strengthened if the original derivation of צלב is from Assyrian *ṣilbu* ("a crosswise arrangement [of bandages or wood]") as Baumgarten himself suggests (this was mentioned above); see Baumgarten, "TLH in the Temple Scroll," 474.

[85] Lack of good indices hampers an exhaustive search of Samaritan Aramaic and Hebrew. Some qualification may be in order to Halperin's point, since the medieval Samaritan Aramaic-Arabic-Hebrew dictionary המליץ lists צלב as equivalent in meaning to the Hebrew

the point remains that for rabbinic and Jewish targumic Aramaic, as well as for Rabbinic Hebrew, צלב always speaks of human bodily suspension. This point is not at odds with Baumgarten, but it is crucial to understanding how צלב functions.

Third, as Baumgarten himself admits (though without proper emphasis), there are many instances where צלב and its cognates are clearly used to designate an act of crucifixion. Baumgarten lists two examples: *t. Sanh.* 9.7 and *m. Yebam.* 16:3. Halperin also notes the parallels to *m. Yebam.* 16:3 in *t. Yebam.* 14:4, *b. Yebam.* 120b, and especially in *y. Yebam.* 16:3 [15c], where a matron can ransom the crucified man. Furthermore, Halperin additionally lists the following instances of Hebrew צלב: *t. Git.* 7(5):1[86]; *y. Git.* 7:1 [48c]; *b. Git.* 70b (a crucified man signals for a writ of divorce); *m. Šabb.* 6:10; *y. Šabb.* 6:9 [8c]; *b. Šabb.* 67a (a nail used in crucifixion); *m. Ohol.* 3:5; *t. Ohol.* 4:11; *b. Nid.* 71b (the dripping blood of a crucified person). To these add some of the Aramaic passages cited earlier in our discussion of Cohn's work; and further passages will arise in later chapters of this book.[87]

Fourth, Baumgarten unduly limits his study of the way in which ancient Jewish translations and interpreters rendered the use of תלה in the Hebrew Bible. Having confined צלב to "hanging" (by the neck), Baumgarten goes on to say that it is the normal targumic way of rendering תלה.[88] Indirectly he thus implies that the versional evidence would suggest only a "hanging" interpretation of תלה in OT texts by Jewish translators. However, the full evidence indicates that at times Jewish translators understood תלה more broadly. For example, the Septuagint of Esther uses σταυρόω to encapsulate the Hebrew תְּלֻהוּ עָלָיו ("hang him [Haman] on it," i.e., on the tree; Esther 7:9).[89] Indeed, later Jewish renderings of the Esther narratives are replete with crucifixion terminology associated with the Hebrew phraseology

---

תלא and חלא, צלוביה as representing תחלאיה, צלובה representing תחליה, as well as שאלף צליבה representing שלה; see Z. Ben-Ḥayyim, *The Literary and Oral Tradition of Hebrew and Aramaic Amongst the Samaritans*, 5 vols. (Jerusalem: Bialik Institute, 1957–1977), 2:474, 597, 609. Also Macuch's Aramaic grammar indicates an instance where the Ethpaʿal participle (מצטלבה) signifies "wird verbrannt."

[86] Note that the victim must still be breathing (כל זמן שיש בו נשמה); also cited with Tannaitic authority in *y. Git.* 7:1 [48c].

[87] Especially note the rabbinic works analysed in chapter five, §§2 and 3 (including *Šem.* ii.11, which assumes that the body decays until it is unrecognizable while being crucified – using צלב). Perhaps here it also should be noted that *ṣade* is connected with Jesus' crucifixion in the early medieval *Midrash ha-ʾOtiot* version B – a fact that Figueras attributes in part to the crucifixion term צלב and in part due to the shape of the letter צ; Pau Figueras, "A Midrashic Interpretation of the Cross as a Symbol," *Studii Biblici Franciscani Liber Annuus* 30 (1980): 159–63 (dating the passage to the fourth–seventh centuries).

[88] Baumgarten, "*TLH* in the Temple Scroll," 474.

[89] The B-text (=LXX) reads Σταυρωθήτω ἐπ᾽ αὐτοῦ. Cf. both the A and B texts of the "addition" E18 (= 16:18 = Rahlfs 8:12[r] = L 7:28). See below in chapter three.

of תלה אתו על העץ.[90] When the Targumim on Esther then apply צלב, a term that certainly can bear crucifixion associations, to render the Hebrew תלה, they are in good company. And a similar picture arises in reference to the suspension of the baker in Genesis 40:19 (וְתָלָה אוֹתְךָ עַל־עֵץ; cf. 40:22; 41:13). Both Josephus and Philo employ clear crucifixion terminology in interpreting this incident,[91] while the targumim use צלב.[92] Thus, some ancient Jewish authors were fully comfortable designating "hanging on a tree" (and hence תלה) at certain junctures with crucifixion terminology.

Fifth, Baumgarten's distinction between halakhic and haggadic exegesis misses the point in his discussion of *t. Sanh.* 9.7. In that passage, Rabbi Meir compares Deut 21:23 to a story of two twin brothers, one of whom is cruci-fied.[93] Baumgarten, noting that this refers to a Roman crucifixion, contends that such a haggadic passage can "...hardly suffice to prove that in the legal exegesis of the time Deut. 21:22–23 was understood to refer to crucifixion."[94] This is true. The story of R. Meir, though occurring in a legal context, does not make a legal point. However, it does associate crucifixion with the hanged person (תלוי) of Deut 21. And thus it provides evidence that the Hebrew word תלה (and especially תלה in Deut 21:22–23) can be understood to designate crucifixion.

Sixth, some of Baumgarten's notations of execution by hanging on a noose are ambiguous at best. The accounts of Simeon b. Shetah's hanging eighty witches in Ashkelon have also been adduced as instances of crucifixion.[95] In fact there are no textual markers that would signal strangulation on a noose in

---

[90] E.g., Josephus, *Ant.* xi. 208, 246, 261, 266–67, 280. Two uses of צלב in *Esther Rabbah* are best explained as acts of crucifixion: Prologue 1 (note the likely Roman context); 10:5 (note the use of "ropes and *nails*" חבלים ומסמרים; for nails cf. *m. Šabb.* 6:10). Other occur-rences of צלב and its cognates in the Midrash Rabbah refer to the Esther narratives: *Gen. Rab.* 30:8; *Exod. Rab.* 20:10; *Lev. Rab.* 28:6; *Esth. Rab.* 2:14; 3:15; 7:3, 10, 11; 9:2; 10:15.

[91] So Josephus *Ant.* ii.73 (ἀνασταυρόω) and ii.77 (σταυρόω); Philo, *Jos.* 96–98 (ἀνασκολοπίζω); *Som.* ii.213 (analogous to the baker the person is described as προσηλωμένος ὥσπερ οἱ ἀνασκολοπισθέντες τῷ ξύλῳ). Naturally, Josephus and Philo could have based their understanding on a Greek version, but the point would still stand that "to hang someone on a tree" (be the phrase in Greek or Hebrew) could be rendered with cru-cifixion terminology by representatives of Second Temple Judaism.

[92] So Targums Onkelos, Neofiti, and Pseudo-Jonathan on Gen 40:19, 22; 41:13; and a Cairo Geniza targumic text on Gen 41:13. Also note the Samaritan Targum on these verses (except for ms A in 40:19).

[93] The narrative is treated in detail below in chapter three.

[94] Baumgarten, "Hanging," 8*. If Baumgarten's point were conceded here (which seems unwarranted), then a similar distinction between halakhic and haggadic evidence may tell against Baumgarten's own strategic use of the narrative of Jakim of Zeroroth, since the Jakim narrative represents a clear haggadic passage.

[95] Defended most fervently by Hengel in *Rabbinische Legende*, 27–36.

the texts referring to this event. Thus these texts, without more detailed argumentation than Baumgarten provides, do not positively contribute to his thesis that hanging on a noose, rather than crucifixion, was practiced in pre-Mishnaic Judaism.[96]

Seventh, when Baumgarten follows Büchler in noting *b. Sanh.* 67a and 35a as instances of hanging on a noose, he involuntarily weakens his thesis. In the first passage, some have considered the Ben Stada narrative in *b. Sanh.* 67a to be a covert reference to the crucifixion of Jesus of Nazareth (which may explain its omission in the censored editions of the Talmud) – though this is debated.[97] In any case, the narrative sequence in the Talmudic manuscripts that contain the passage implies that stoning preceded the hanging; thus it is irrelevant to Baumgarten's case for hanging on the noose as an early form of strangulation.

In addition, the second Talmudic passage (*b. Sanh.* 34b–35a) defines וְהוֹקַע in Num 25:4 as תלייה ("hanging"), arguing this definition in part based on the lexical connection with וְהוֹקַענוּם in 2 Sam 21:6 and the way Rizpah four verses later in 2 Sam 21:10 defends the bodies of the slain from birds. Thus the Talmud implies an extended time of "hanging" in the 2 Samuel passage (as well as presumably in Num 25:4).[98] But one of Baumgarten's key arguments is that תלה in rabbinic (and Qumranic) thinking must refer to the relatively quick hanging by a noose (in keeping with Deut 21:22–23), rather than a long-term suspension (such as on a pole or cross) as we find suggested in this Talmudic passage.

Eighth, the debate over the four means of execution acknowledged in Targum Ruth 1:17 permits an alternate interpretation to that of Baumgarten. So Halperin in fact contended that the phrase צליבת קיסא in this Targum is a reference to crucifixion.[99] As noted above, Baumgarten makes reference to a single manuscript (MS De Rossi 31) that reads וחניקת סודרא ("and the strangulation of the scarf") in agreement with the Mishnaic halakhah, thus suggesting to him that צליבת קיסא was just an alternative means of strangulation. However, apart from the scant support, internal criteria would suggest that this one manuscript is actually seeking to bring the Targum back into agreement with the Mishnah (or at least back into agreement with *Ruth Rabbah* 2:24 [on Ruth 1:17] which reads וחנק). Perhaps this manuscript even

---

[96] A similar point could be made regarding the *Sifre Num.* 131 citation in Baumgarten, "*TLH* in the Temple Scroll," 476n.

[97] Travers Herford defends the identification with Jesus in R. Travers Herford, *Christianity in Talmud and Midrash* (London: Williams & Norgate, 1903), 79–83 (cf. 37–41; 344–47).

[98] So the footnote in the Soncino *Hebrew-English Edition of the Babylonian Talmud* on *b. Sanh.* 35a infers that, since Rizpah protected the bodies from birds of prey, "They must have been hanged on trees."

[99] Halperin, "Crucifixion," 37.

testifies to the discomfort felt by its scribal circle in acknowledging צלב as a viable means of execution.

Baumgarten also appears to argue that the very fact that in Targum Ruth צליבת קיסא is in the place of strangulation in the standard rabbinic list implies that צליבת קיסא was a mere variant form of strangulation (via suspension from a noose), dating back to a time before the sanctioned rabbinic method (via a padded rope pulled by the two witnesses, as described in *m. Sanh.* 7:3) was universally applied. However, if the tradition in the Targum Ruth passage is earlier than the Mishnaic legislation (as Heinemann maintained),[100] then it is possible that it doesn't represent a mere variation on the idea of strangulation, but a completely different penalty altogether. This is not to imply that the whole of Targum Ruth is pre-Mishnaic, only certain traditions contained in it. To state this another way: If Baumgarten finds in Targum Ruth an exception to the standard *means* of rabbinic strangulation (possibly predating the later codification), then similar arguments also favour it being viewed as an exception to the standard *list* itself – the difference is a matter of degree in how great an exception *Tg. Ruth* 1:17 appears to the scholar. All this is to say that there are alternatives to Baumgarten's suggestion that he has not adequately countered, and thus *Tg. Ruth* cannot provide indisputable evidence that hanging on a noose, and *not* crucifixion, was practiced in the pre-Mishnaic period.

Ninth, the phrase "hanging *alive*" in the Nahum Pesher and in the Sifre on Deuteronomy may not be the only means of expressing crucifixion with תלה in ancient Judaism. While חי in these two texts may have been added for emphasis (the suspended victim is *alive*), it may not be required in talking about crucifixion with תלה. So in *Sifre Deut.* 221 the emphasis on suspension of the "living" person helps set off the point that the sequence in the biblical text speaks of death first and then hanging. Its use in 4QpNah likewise seems emphatic on the living status of the suspended victims. On the other hand, the author/redactor of 11QTemple may not have felt the need to emphasize that the person suspended was "alive," since the word order alone was sufficient for this. Certainly, one cannot infer (as Baumgarten apparently does)[101] from the adjectival use of חי an extensive time of suspension unto death as opposed to an immediate one – חי in this context does not speak of the *extent* of time one spends alive hung on a tree, but emphasizes the *fact* that one is alive when suspended.

---

[100] So Joseph Heinemann, "The Targum of Ex. XXII,4 and the Ancient Halakha," *Tarbiz* 38 (1969): 295–96.

[101] Thus Baumgarten says of the word "alive" in 4QpNah and *Sifre Deut* that it "demonstrates that *tlh* by itself did not signify impalement on a cross, but a form of execution resulting in *immediate death*." Baumgarten, "*TLH* in the Temple Scroll," 478 (italics mine).

When combined, all nine objections to Baumgarten's thesis indicate that תלה could be understood in the Second Temple period as a designation for crucifixion – even "by itself" without the emphasis added by "alive." Also צלב bears strong crucifixion associations in both Hebrew and Aramaic.

However, listing objections to Baumgarten's argumentation does not necessitate wholehearted agreement with Halperin, who contends that the "primary meaning" of צלב is "to crucify" and that it was never used of hanging by the neck. Several cautions are worth noting.

Some targumic passages utilize צלב (and its cognates) in a word order implying that the person is already dead prior to suspension.[102] And this fact is enough to call into question whether "crucifixion" (in the English sense of the word as a means of producing death) is the "primary" meaning of צלב. If צלב had inevitably referred to "crucfixion", then why not use another Aramaic term (e.g., תלא or זקף) in passages where the person is dead before suspension?[103] Rather, it appears that the semantic range of צלב was broad enough to include both the bodily suspension of the dead and the living.

Also, the one text Halperin cites for תלה occasionally replacing צלב with the meaning "crucify" (*t. Sanh.* 9:7 to *b. Sanh.* 46b) may not be a linear passing of tradition from the Tosefta to the Bavli (with a conscious supplanting of צלב with תלה), for the traditions may have come from common stock (see chapter 3, §4.7 below). Halperin's argument is possible, but not lock tight.

Furthermore, as Baumgarten notes, the story of Jaḳim of Zeroroth, who (while employing all official means of execution upon himself) hangs himself from a pole to produce strangulation (*Gen. Rab.* 65:22; *Midr. Psa.* 11:7), does seem to allow that תלה in this passage (and hanging by the neck) could be seen as the equivalent of strangulation – at least in this remarkable suicide. Also, though we have opposed Baumgarten's lexical arguments, his understanding of the Ruth Targum is well worth considering in more detail, as are his two suggested reconstructions of 4QpNah and some of the broader points he makes on 11QTemple.

In summary, although צלב does not only signify "to crucify," it does frequently bear strong crucifixion implications. Certainly צלב is a term devoted to describing the penal suspension of the human body (either living or dead) in the context of execution. Beyond that, the actual means of suspension (and the timing of it in relation to death) may be signaled by the literary context of any one occurrence. Where not signaled, likely the ancient audience would come to its own conclusions – undoubtedly influenced by a

---

[102] See *Tg. Onq.*, *Tg. Neof.*, and especially *Tg. Ps.-J.* on Deut 21:22; *Tg. Josh.* 10:26; possibly also *Tg. Ps.-J.* Lev. 24:23. Halperin also admits this much.

[103] That is to say, Halperin's concept ("Crucifixion," 39) of the Hebrew Bible "restricting" the meturgeman, who is unable to "compose freely," makes scant linguistic sense. A competent meturgeman had other Aramaic options, and thus had the power of lexical choice.

social world in which they witnessed frequent governmental employment of crucifixion.

In this regard, צלב and its cognates function semantically in some ways similar to the Greek semantic field of (ἀνα)σταυρόω and its cognates. Both terms convey a technical sense of "bodily suspension" in contexts of execution (though ἀνασταυρόω, unlike צלב, can at times be employed in other broader contexts). Both terms can convey the bodily suspension of the living (including what is usually meant by "crucifixion" in English) and of the dead. Certainly, such words can designate crucifixion in the right context. Yet, more importantly, such Greek, Hebrew and Aramaic vocabulary appear to indicate that "crucifixion" was terminologically associated in antiquity with a broader field of penalties that involved penal bodily suspension.

Concerning תלה, the basic meaning of the term is clearly "to hang," but in certain contexts it can speak of the suspension of humans (both before and after death). It is unwarranted to claim that תלה cannot be used of crucifixion unless it is joined with עץ. Rather, some of the examples cited above show that, at least by the Second Temple period, biblical passages using תלה could be understood to refer to crucifixion. Thus תלה by itself may be understood in certain contexts (and possibly in certain communities) to bear crucifixion associations.

2.3.2 Aramaic ZQP

An important passage in the Babylonian Talmud records that Rabbi Eleazar ben Simeon, in collusion with the Roman authorities, sent a man to the cross as a thief (b. B. Meṣ. 83b). This text uses both the verb זקף and its cognate noun: זקפוהו קם תותי זקיפא וקא בבכי – "They hung him [the suspected thief] up. He [R. Eleazar] stood under the pole and wept." That this represents an act of crucifixion is made highly probable by both the fact that the arrested man was thought to be a thief, and that a Roman execution penalty is involved.[104]

Halperin argues that "the Aramaic of the Babylonian Talmud uses *zeqaf* for crucifixion instead of *ṣelab*."[105] As he notes, though צלב *is* present in Hebrew sections of the Bavli, זקף can designate the bodily suspension of a person, and its cognate זקיפא (also זקופה) can indicate the pole upon which one is suspended, the hanged person, or the suspension itself.[106] These terms also occur in contexts of execution outside the Bavli.[107]

---

[104] On the crucifixion of thieves and brigands see chapter five, §2; also note the discussion of this episode in chapter two, §3.7.2.

[105] D. J. Halperin, "Crucifixion," 38n.

[106] See Jastrow, *Dictionary*, s.v. Uses of both זקף and זקיפא in reference to execution include: b. Meg. 16b (sons of Haman); b. B. Meṣ 59b ("if there is a case of hanging in a family record" – this contains a possible double entendre with crucifixion and suspension of a

However, it is necessary to qualify the above by noting that the vast majority of instances of זקף in the Bavli are more mundane – referring to the elevation, erection, or suspension of some other object. And likewise זְקִיפָא can also speak generally of something erect or upright. Thus it is better to conceive of צלב in a relation of hyponymy with זקף rather than in one of synonymy. While זקף can be used in contexts of execution, and may even clearly refer in those contexts to an act of crucifixion, its semantic range is actually fairly broad. On the other hand, צלב in extant Jewish literature invariably refers to the penal suspension of a human body.[108] Interestingly, as noted above, a similar hyponymous relationship exists between *ṣlb* and *zqp* both in Syriac and in Christian Palestinian Aramaic.

Finally, the one biblical use of the Aramaic זקף should be mentioned (Ezra 6:11; RSV: "a beam shall be pulled out of his house, and he shall be impaled upon it").[109] The complexities involved in interpreting this verse, especially in the relationship between זְקִיף and מחא in וּזְקִיף יִתְמְחֵא עֲלֹהִי, are analyzed below in chapter three.

2.3.3 Notes on the Hebrew YQ⁽

One final term worthy of study is the Hebrew יקע. According to the Masoretic pointing of the Hebrew Bible it occurs four times in the Qal,[110] thrice in the Hiphil, and once in the Hophal. Only those occurrences in the so-called "causative" *binyanim* (Hiphil & Hophal) seem to refer to execution. However, the manner of execution employed in these instances is a matter of some debate among contemporary lexicographers.

Among the major lexicons, Koehler-Baumgartner glosses the meaning as "to display with broken legs and arms,"[111] while Alonso Schoekel implies that the execution was by some form of impalement or suspension ("Empalar,

---

fish). Also see זקיפא in *b. ʿAbod. Zar.* 18b (the government is about to crucify a warder). Both BDB (new ed., p. 279) and KB (זקף, s.v.) suggest that זקף is related to Assyrian *zaqāpu*, which includes the impaling of a person among its more basic meanings of erecting, planting or lifting up something (see *CAD* 21, pp. 51–55; also note *zaqīpu* on p. 58).

[107] E.g., *Tg. 1 Chron.* 10:10 (of Saul's head; זקפו על זיקפא); *Tg. Esth II* 2:7 (Haman affixed to the זקיפא). And see זקף in *Tg. Esth I* 7:9; 9:13 (also note 3:2 in MS Paris 110; and cf. *Tg. Esth I* 5:14, though here the wooden post is being erected).

[108] As mentioned earlier, it is possible that *Samaritan* Aramaic may present an occasional exception, but even these are debatable.

[109] Hebrew זקף is testified with the idea of "raising up" in Psa 145:14; 146:8.

[110] Gen 32:26; Jer 6:8; Ezek 23:17,18. There is likely a close relationship between the Qal form of יקע and the Qal of נקע (Ezek 23:18, 22, 28); see Ezek 23:18 and cf. Robert Polzin, "HWQYʿ and Covenantal Institutions in Early Israel," *Harvard Theological Review* 62 (1969): 231n.

[111] *KB*, Engl. transl., s.v. A similar definition is given in David J. A. Clines, ed., *The Dictionary of Classical Hebrew*, 4+ vols. (Sheffield: Sheffield Academic Press, 1993–present), 4:274–75.

colgar, ajusticiar").[112] On the other hand, Brown-Driver-Briggs is content to admit that the meaning of this "solemn form of execution" is uncertain.[113]

In favour of the Koehler-Baumgartner translation is the relationship of the Hiphil of יקע as the causative form of the Qal, especially as the Qal is represented in Genesis 32:36 (Jacob's thigh is "dislocated"). Thus, one could argue that such an execution (employing Hiphil of יקע) likely involved *causing* the person's limbs to be dislocated.[114] However, this does not fully explain the Koehler-Baumgartner idea of "displaying" such a dismembered person. Other etymological explanations draw on Arabic parallels to either *waqaʿa* or *naqaʿa*;[115] but the range of meanings of the Arabic words, especially when examining *waqaʿa*, calls for some caution.

----

[112] Luis Alonso Schoekel, *Diccionario Bíblico hebreo-español* (Valencia: Institución San Jerónimo, 1990–1993), 305–6. Modern Hebrew can also apply הוקע to mean "expose, stigmatize, condemn, arraign; hang, impale, crucify" (see Alcalay, *Hebrew-English Dictionary*, s.v).

[113] *BDB*, 429. With only slightly more confidence the new Gesenius states, "Bedeutung unsicher: (?) hinrichten, (?) jemandes die Glieder verrenken oder brechen ([?] und ihn in diesem Zustand aussetzen), als Strafe für Verbrecher"; see Wilhelm Gesenius and Udo Rütersworden, *Hebräisches und Aramäisches Handwörterbuch über das Alte Testament*, ed. Rudolf Meyer and Herbert Donner, 18th ed., 2+ vols. (Berlin: Springer, 1987+), 2:488 (abbreviations expanded).

[114] See Arvid S. Kapelrud, "King and Fertility: A Discussion of II Sam 21:1–14," in *Interpretationes ad Vetus Testamentum Pertinentes Sigmundo Mowinckel Septuagenario Missae* (Oslo: Land og Kirke, 1955), 119–20; Martin Noth, *Numbers: A Commentary*, trans. James D. Martin, OTL (London: SCM Press, 1968), 197. Barrois rejects this argument, but his appeal to תָּקְעוּ in 1 Sam 31:10 is less convincing since this verb in the MT stems from תקע not יקע; see A.-G. Barrois, *Manuel d'Archéologie Biblique*, 2 vols. (Paris: A. et J. Picard, 1939/1953), 2:85. However, various scholars favour emending the text of 1 Sam 31:10 (and 1 Chron 10:10) to read הקיעו or some similar form from יקע, which would again make appeal to 1 Sam 31:10 possible; see esp. Julius Wellhausen, *Der Text der Bücher Samuelis* (Göttingen: Vandenhoeck & Ruprecht, 1871), 148–49; Henry Preserved Smith, *A Critical and Exegetical Commentary on the Books of Samuel*, ICC (Edinburgh: T. & T. Clark, 1899), 253; Karl Budde, *Die Bücher Samuel*, KHC 8 (Tübingen: J. C. B. Mohr, 1902), 192; Paul Dhorme, *Les Livres de Samuel*, Ebib (Paris: J. Gabalda, 1910), 260. While the possibilities of such an emendation may be suggestive, any lexical arguments based on it could well be circular – see also the concerns in Arnold B. Ehrlich, *Randglossen zur hebräischen Bibel*, 7 vols. (Leipzig, 1908–1914), 3:270; S. R. Driver, *Notes on the Hebrew Text and the Topography of the Books of Samuel*, 2nd rev. and enlarged ed. (Oxford: Clarendon, 1913), 230–31; and P. Kyle McCarter, *I Samuel*, AB 8 (Garden City: Doubleday, 1980), 442.

[115] For *waqaʿa* see *KB*, s.v. יקע, For *naqaʿa* (with the meaning "to split, rend" and specifically "to cut the throat of") note Polzin, "*HWQYʿ*," 232. Polzin makes too much of an Arabic sacrificial custom. Similarly, one might doubt W. R. Smith's suggestion that an Arabic etymology proves the method employed was casting from a cliff; see William Robertson Smith, *Lectures on the Religions of the Semites*, 3rd ed. (London: A. & C. Black, 1927), 419; and see Gray's comments to the contrary in George Buchanan Gray, *A Critical and Exegetical Commentary on Numbers*, ICC (Edinburgh: T. & T. Clark, 1903), 383.

The contexts of the four executionary uses of יקע in the Hebrew Bible provide crucial data for understanding the verb. In Numbers 25:4, Moses,
confronting a time when Israelite religious loyalty was being swayed by
Moabite women, is instructed to summon the leaders of Israel and then
"execute them" (וְהוֹקַע אוֹתָם) "before the Lord, opposite the sun"
(לַיהוָה נֶגֶד הַשָּׁמֶשׁ).[116] Clearly the executions involve a public dimension
(possibly involving prolonged exposure). Some have argued for an additional
cultic dimension based on לַיהוָה ("before the Lord").[117] Others see a more
covenantal context.[118] In Numbers 25:5, the narrative continues with Moses
instructing people to slay (הִרְגוּ) those who are thus joined to Baal Peor. Thus
there is fairly strong evidence of a paradigmatic relationship between הרג and
יקע, confirming the executionary aspect of יקע.[119] The narrative continues
when Phinehas immediately follows Moses' command by spearing Zimri and
his Midianite wife Cozbi in their tent – the terms being used are: נכה
("smite") and דקר ("pierce"; with his spear [רֹמַח] and through the belly
[אֶל־קֳבָתָהּ]). That Phinehas' used a spear in executing Zimri may reflect
assumptions that impalement satisfies the command of הוֹקַע in Num 25:4.
However, there is already at least one significant discontinuity in the Phinehas
narrative *vis-à-vis* 25:4 – Phinehas slays Zimri inside a tent and 25:4 implies a
public venue.

The other biblical narrative that uses the Hiphil and Hophal of יקע is in
2 Samuel 21:1–14. In 2 Samuel 21:9 it is said that the seven sons of Saul are
executed "on the mountain, before the Lord" (וַיֹּקִיעֵם בָּהָר לִפְנֵי יְהוָה). Again
public connotations are strong in the executionary form, and the cultic or
covenantal overtones may be present here as well. Also in 21:9 the enumera-
tion of the dead follows with standard wording (וַיִּפְּלוּ שְׁבַעְתָּם),[120] and the
seven are described as "put to death" (הֻמָתוּ). Most interesting is how they are

---

[116] The Samaritan Pentateuch has apparently harmonized 25:4 with 25:5 and removed the
difficult term יקע; see Alison Salvesen, *Symmachus in the Pentateuch*, JSS Monograph 15
(Manchester: University of Manchester, 1991), 138.

[117] Mentioned in Theodor Nöldeke, *Neue Beiträge zur semitischen Sprachwissenschaft*
(Strassburg: Karl J. Trübner, 1910), 198n. The cultic idea forms the central thesis of A. S.
Kapelrud, "King and Fertility," 113–22. That these people were given over to the Lord (as in
the ban) has been affirmed by Timothy R. Ashley, *The Book of Numbers*, NICOT (Grand
Rapids: Eerdmans, 1993), 518. Milgrom contends that, while לִפְנֵי יהוה implies a ritual at the
sanctuary, לִיהוה indicates a "nonritualistic dedication to the Lord outside the sanctuary"; see
Jacob Milgrom, *Numbers*, JPS Torah Commentary (Philadelphia: Jewish Publication Society,
1990), 213.

[118] R. Polzin, "*HWQY*ʿ," 227–40.

[119] Some hold Numbers 25:4 & 25:5 to come from different sources. Nonetheless, Second
Temple readers of the narrative as it now stands would naturally draw a connection between
the executionary terms in the two verses; and, if they are from separate sources, the editor
likely also made such a connection. Similar points could be made throughout this paragraph.

[120] Qere שְׁבַעְתָּם. For this use of נפל see 1 Sam 4:10 and note BDB, p. 657 (§2a).

left unburied from the beginning of harvest (21:9) until David provides for
their burial, presumably at the beginning of the rainy season (21:10). Meanwhile, Rizpah, Saul's granddaughter, defends their slain bodies from birds
and beasts. It is the Rizpah narrative that beckoned the rabbis to consider
הוקע as meaning "hung" (תלה; *b. Sanh.* 34b–35a). In any case, the aftermath
of this death, and perhaps the means of execution, involved prolonged exposure to the elements.

The obvious context of prolonged exposure, and the unclear meaning of
the verb itself, are enough to explain the many ways יקע is rendered in the
versions: παραδειγμάτισον ("make an example of"; LXX Num 25:4),
ἀνάπηξον ("transfix"; Aquila Num 25:4; 2 Sam 21:6, 9), κρέμασον ("hang";
Symmachus Num 25:4; 2 Sam 21:6),[121] ἐξηλίασαν ("set out in the sun";
LXX 2 Kgdms 21:9; see 21:6, 13 and cf. 21:14 [in many mss.]); ܒܘܪ
("spread out, exposed"; Peshitta Num 25:4),[122] ܕܒܚ ("slayed, sacrificed";
Peshitta 2 Sam 21:9; cf. 21:6), ܘܩܛܠ ("killed"; Peshitta 2 Sam 21:13); קטול
("killed"; *Tg. Onq.* Num 25:4); and various forms of צלב ("suspended, crucified"; Palestinian targumim on Num 25:4 and Targum Jonathan on
2 Sam 21:6, 9, 13).

In sum, there appears to have been early confusion as to the meaning of the
Hiphil and Hophal of יקע, and the etymological data provides no absolute
guidance. But the contexts of both Numbers 25 and 2 Samuel 21 imply some
means of official public execution with strong religious overtones that could
involve prolonged exposure to the elements. While יקע remains somewhat
mysterious, and cannot be shown with any degree of definiteness to be a suspension term (let alone a technical word for crucifixion), chapter three will
indicate that some ancient Jewish traditions found a plausible reference to
crucifixion in its few biblical usages.

2.4 Summary: Crucifixion Terminology and Suspension

The preceding discussion should be sufficient to sustain the following general
statements:

(1) While one might be able to speak of a general method of crucifixion in
Roman practice, in fact there were many variations on execution by suspension, though the same Latin and Greek terms designate both the variations and
the (hypothetical?) norm.

---

[121] Additionally, Codex Ambrosianus margin at Numbers 25:4 has φούρκισον; see
Fridericus Field, *Origenis Hexaplorum quae supersunt*, 2 vols. (Oxford: Clarendon Press,
1875), 1:257n. Presumably this is an imperative from φούρκιζω ("to attach to a fork"), from
which the related noun φούρκη (= Latin *furca*) is known (Liddell-Scott, s.v.).

[122] R. Payne Smith, ed., *Thesaurus*, 2:3276–77, lists ܒܘܪ as a Pali stem from ܒܘܪ
(glossing this occurence as "*expone*"); C. Brockelmann, *Lexicon*, 290, lists as from the quad-
riliteral verb ܒܘܪ ("*denudavit, revelavit*").

(2) In examining Greek, Hebrew, and Jewish Aramaic, we have seen that there was no single term that only designated "crucifixion" (in the limited sense of the English word) on a cross-shaped object. In this regard there is significant similarity in the various languages in the application of their most specific suspension terminology. These words generally permit a variety of means of suspending a human body. So, for example, צלב in Hebrew and Aramaic and (ἀνα)σταυρόω in Greek all have clear instances where they speak of the suspension of both living and dead bodies. Further, the shape of the device employed in many of these instances is unknown. Even in Latin, where there is a higher degree of rigidity in the means of punishment indicated by a certain word (e.g., *crux*), the standard terminology sometimes has broader reference to various means of suspension (even of the dead).

(3) This is not to say that the semantic ranges of these terms in the different languages completely overlap (i.e., that they had precisely the same application). For example, צלב in both Hebrew and Aramaic appears only to be used of human bodily suspension, but there is no such word in Greek (contrast the broader ranges of ἀνασκολοπίζω and ἀνασταυρόω).

(4) Each language evidences a semantic field of several terms for crucifixion (and bodily suspension), with some terms acting as hyponyms for others. Thus Hebrew uses צלב with more limited reference than תלה, Aramaic does the same with צלב and זקף, and Greek employs a variety of more general verbs with wider ranges than (ἀνα)σταυρόω and ἀνασκολοπίζω in contexts of suspension (e.g., [ἀνα]κρεμάννυμι, πήγνυμι, and προσηλόω). One consequence of this is the affirmation of the sound linguistic principle that the exegete discussing crucifixion must be duly wary of context.

(5) However, in acknowledging differences among the languages here surveyed, it is quite likely that the similarity in application (mentioned above) of suspension terms in the various languages displays significant "cultural overlap" (to use a term from contemporary linguistics). In other words, the fact that Greek, Hebrew, and Aramaic (and at times Latin) terminology for crucifixion does not inherently distinguish between ante-mortem and post-mortem suspension, and does not inevitably dictate the form of the object employed, might very well testify to a common cultural perception. Admittedly lexical semantics is not always a sufficient basis for determining cultural perceptions. Just because a single term does not exist for a certain concept, does not mean that a collection of terms cannot convey that concept. Certainly a cross-shaped ante-mortem crucifixion could be designated in antiquity by a series of words. But most often the ancients did not seem to care to be so specific. Instead they appear content to associate multiple suspension forms as a single penalty. The fact that this occurs in several languages leads us to conclude that generally in antiquity the form of penal bodily suspension was less significant than the fact that body was being suspended.

(6) Although words and concepts must not be confused, this word study evidence suggests a cautionary reminder about how to study crucifixion. It seems that crucifixion was often widely regarded in the ancient world as being within the general conceptual field of human bodily suspension. This point appears to me neglected in Baumgarten's studies considered above, and disregarded by those who would attempt to rigidly define crucifixion *vis-à-vis* other forms of suspension such that the associations of the one cannot partake of the associations of the other.

Certainly it was possible for the ancient authors to use a combination of terminology and context to designate "crucifixion" (English sense) as opposed to other forms of human bodily suspension; and likewise one could (again with appropriate contextual indicators) clearly delineate executionary suspension from a post-mortem penalty. The scholar must always be sensitive to individual lexical usage and other matters of style among the many sources. However, so often in the sources the context is not so determinative, the author's usage varies, and the reader is left to his or her own imagination as to the precise penal method employed.

This suggests that in studying the ancient world the scholar is wise not to differentiate too rigidly the categories of "crucifixion," "impalement," and "suspension" (as if these were clearly to be distinguished in every instance). Hence, any study of crucifixion conceptions in antiquity must grapple with the broader context of the wide variety of penal suspension of human beings.

One solution to the terminological complexities this produces in English would be to follow the Spanish approach of Díez Merino in labeling all acts of human bodily suspension as instances of "crucifixión" (only then distinguishing between forms of crucifixion: empalamiento, crucifixión *ante mortem*, exposición del cadáver *post mortem*).[123] However, following traditional English usage, we will continue to use "crucifixion" to mean the executionary suspension of a person on a cross-shaped object (allowing for a certain flexibility in shapes). Meanwhile "suspension" will serve as the broader term for the lifting up of a human body (living or dead) on some device for exposure.

Nevertheless, such an English divide between "crucifixion" and "suspension" should not be taken to indicate that these were perceived by people in antiquity (including Jewish people) as wholly different spheres of punishment. On the contrary, this discussion of terminology has sought to point out the likelihood that crucifixion on a cross was simply one specific form within the broader category of human bodily suspension. This dynamic goes a long way to explain how general references in the Hebrew Bible to suspended bodies could later be associated more specifically with crucifixion terminology (see chapter three). It also reminds us that perceptions associated in

---

[123] See L. Díez Merino, "Suplicio," 44–47; ibid., "La crucifixión," 5–6.

3. Suspension and the Death Penalty in Jewish Law and Practice

Jewish antiquity with any penal suspension of a human body could still very well inform ancient Jewish thoughts of crucifixion itself.

3. Suspension and the Death Penalty in Jewish Law and Practice

Perceptions of crucifixion in ancient Judaism were inevitably related to what Jewish people in this era viewed to be correct penal practice. As has emerged from the above summary of the history of scholarship on crucifixion, a significant modern debate has raged concerning whether or not some Jewish groups believed crucifixion was a viable means of execution – in fact, this has been the principal concern of many scholars. The aims of this thesis are much broader than this one question, encompassing the whole of ancient Jewish perceptions of crucifixion; but it is nonetheless necessary to understand the legal aspects of these perceptions, and to do so (albeit in a preliminary fashion) before setting out to chart the broader picture. Thus a few brief remarks are necessary about Jewish executionary law and practice as it concerns bodily suspension.

As was remarked earlier, the starting point of many scholars is to note that Mishnaic law, probably most immediately reflecting opinion of the late second century CE, prescribes four means of execution: stoning, burning, beheading, and strangling (*m. Sanh.* vii.1).[124] Further, rabbinic tradition explicitly rejects crucifixion as the correct legal understanding of the commandments concerning hanging and burial in Deuteronomy 21:22–23.[125] For some, these statements are sufficient to show that in the first century crucifixion was rejected as a viable death penalty (at least by the Pharisees). However, the date of the Mishnah leaves some room for question, and there are other materials to take into account.

The chief basis for the rabbinic legislation is, naturally, the Hebrew Bible. The Hebrew Bible lists a number of offenses punishable by the death penalty; and, while in many cases the means of execution is not specified, the MT legislates only two forms of death for individual crimes – stoning and burning.[126] Post-mortem suspension is endorsed, but limited to a single day (Deut 21:22–23). The context here does not specify which kinds of crime can merit such suspension, labeling it only a חֵטְא מִשְׁפַּט־מָוֶת ("sin bearing a

---

[124] Cf. also the tale about Jose b. Joezer (see chapter 2, §2.2)

[125] See above on: *Sifre Deut.* 221; *Midr. Tannaim* (Hoffman p. 132, line 7); *b. Sanh.* 46b.

[126] A helpful summary is provided in Roland de Vaux, *Ancient Israel: Its Life and Institutions*, trans. John McHugh (London: Darton, Longman & Todd, 1961), 158–59. Goldin less convincingly argues that decapitation is also a biblical form of capital punishment, since whole towns that are led astray (he labels this "communal apostasy") should be put to the sword (Deut 13:12–16); see Hyman E. Goldin, *Hebrew Criminal Law and Procedure: Mishnah: Sanhedrin – Makkot* (New York: Twayne, 1952), 28, 36.

judgment of death").[127] How such suspensions were to have occurred (e.g., tying or impaling) is not specified, though the extant ANE parallels would possibly argue for impaling (see chapter 3 §1).

In comparison, the standard rabbinic injunctions add two additional sanctioned forms of execution (beheading and strangling). Further, following *m. Sanh.* vi.4 one observes: (1) The rabbis also delineate which crimes result in post-mortem suspension (only blasphemy and idolatry, but with reported disagreement from R. Eliezer who wishes all those stoned to be hung). (2) The rabbis, focusing on the use of the word בְּאִישׁ ("in a *man*") in Deuteronomy 21:22, limit the penalty to males (again with reported disagreement from R. Eliezer). (3) Also the method of suspension was specified: two hands brought together and affixed (presumably tethered) to a crossbar of an upright post (with reported disagreement from R. Jose). Admittedly, reported disagreement is a frequent feature of Mishnaic writing; nevertheless, it is possible that these minority opinions indicate that the halakhic interpretation of Deuteronomy 21:22–23 was still in development.

In actual practice as reported in the Hebrew Bible, there were instances of sanctioned death penalties that involved long-term exposure (Num 25:4; and esp. 2 Sam 21:1–13) – as discussed in chapter 3 the rabbis viewed these as (exceptional) instances of prolonged hanging (contravening Deut 21:22–23).[128] Further, in the Hebrew Bible the recorded incidents of human penal suspension either diverge from the methodology implied in Deut 21:22–23 (see 2 Sam 4:12), or are not for crimes as such but are part of the conquest of enemies in war (Josh 8:29; 10:26). These divergences, to my knowledge, are not represented in extant records of early halakhic discussions.

When it comes to the actual Mishnaic methods of execution, these often seem unusual: so the strangulation procedure involves burying a person in dung to his knees, wrapping a rope (itself covered over with soft material) around his neck and then pulling (*m. Sanh.* vii.3); the sanctioned burning procedure involves burying the person in dung and then putting a burning object down his throat (*m. Sanh.* vii.2); and stoning involves the first witness pushing the person off an embankment (*m. Sanh.* vi.4)[129] – if that fails, a stone is thrown on him by the second witness and subsequently by the rest of the people.

---

[127] See the extended discussion of Deut 21:22–23 in chapter three.

[128] Also cf. the rabbinic discussion of Haman's hanging (see below in chapter three).

[129] Note how this procedure is projected onto the biblical account in *Tg. Ps.-J.* Lev 24:23 (and followed by hanging). For a likely example from the NT period compare Luke 4:29. Mendelsohn contends there are parallels to a Greek executionary form; see S. Mendelsohn, *The Criminal Jurisprudence of the Ancient Hebrews: Compiled from the Talmud and other Rabbinical Writings, and Compared with Roman and English Penal Jurisprudence,* 2nd ed. (New York: Hermon Press, 1968), 45, 158.

As Bammel has well observed, the rabbis themselves preserve indications that these death penalties had at one point varying forms.[130] Burning was at least on one occasion done at the stake (*m. Sanh.* vii.2, according to R. Eliezer b. Zadok). The Mishnah provides a live debate over whether beheading should be done by sword (as the Romans do) or by axe (*m. Sanh.* vii.3). Though one must exercise caution here, external sources imply that some stonings (at least in actions by the populace) involved throwing stones rather than hurling people off cliffs.[131] All these debates and variant practices indicate that the mode of execution was still being standardized in the late Second Temple and early rabbinic periods.

In a related way, when R. Eliezer appeals in *m. Sanh.* vi.4 to the tradition that Simeon b. Shetaḥ hung women in Ashkelon, this may be viewed as a different practice than that accepted in the Mishnah. Certainly this tradition varies from the Mishnah's majority decision to refuse to suspend women; and it also differs from the number of death penalty cases that can be tried in one day (both differences are admitted and excused in the Mishnah and in *Sifre Deut* 221). Further, later expansions in the Yerushalmi on the Simeon b. Shetaḥ incident clearly portray the suspension of these "witches" as their means of death.[132] Whether or not in the actual historical event the victims were truly executed in such a fashion or not, rabbinic tradition (despite its own insistence that only post-mortem hanging is permitted) retained a story that displays variance with its own approved methods.

It is in this context that talk of suspension as a means of execution (such as one finds in 11QTemple lxiv.6–13) may be part of a broader discussion within ancient Jewish communities as to what constituted viable death penalties outside those prescribed in the Torah itself. Indeed, the Temple Scroll, the Peshiṭta to Deut 21:22, and Philo's *Spec. Leg.* iii.151–52 all provide independent testimony to an ongoing executionary reading of the legal text of Deuteronomy 21:22–23.[133]

In this light, the variant four-fold listing of death penalties in *Tg. Ruth* i.17 is perhaps less surprising:

---

[130] Bammel, "Crucifixion," 162–63. Similarly, though perhaps overstated, see Ze'ev W. Falk, *Introduction to Jewish Law of the Second Commonwealth*, 2 vols., AGJU 11 (Leiden: E. J. Brill, 1972–1978), 2:157–60.

[131] So in the NT: John 10:31; cf. 8:7 (not in earliest MSS); Acts 5:26; 7:59; 14:19; 2 Cor 11:25. See Josef Blinzler, "The Jewish Punishment of Stoning in the New Testament Period," in *The Trial of Jesus*, ed. Ernst Bammel, SBT II.13 (London: SCM Press, 1970), 147–61. A similar point, though in a different discussion, is made in Torrey Seland, *Establishment Violence in Philo and Luke: A Study of Non-Conformity to the Torah and Jewish Vigilante Reactions*, Biblical Interpretation Series 15 (Leiden: E. J. Brill, 1995), 121–22 (Seland also has an intriguing discussion of the stoning of Stephen, esp. pp. 238–44).

[132] See the discussion in chapter 2.

[133] These texts are discussed in chapter 3.

אֲמֶר׳ נָעֳמִי אִית לָנָא אַרְבַּע מִינֵי מוֹתָא לְחַיָיבַיָּא רְגִימַת אַבְנִין וִיקֵדַת נוּרָא וּקְטִילַת
סְיָיפָא וּצְלִיבַת קֵיסָא

Naomi said, "We have four kinds of deaths for guilty people: being stoned of stones, and
burned of fire, and slain of the sword, and suspended of the tree."

The antiquity of this passage, which is deliberately given a closely literal
translation, has been asserted by some on the principle that what is anti-
Mishnaic must be pre-Mishnaic.[134] Such a principle may need some refining
since a period might be postulated in which the Mishnaic law grew into its
pre-eminence (conflicting viewpoints being also possible at this time), but the
point remains that the above text reflects a halakhic viewpoint at odds with
that in the Mishnah.

The discussion in the preceding section touched on the lexical issues in *Tg.
Ruth* i.17. While Baumgarten has appealed to it as a clear instance of execution by hanging with a noose, in fact the lexical range of צלב, as a technical
word for human bodily suspension, often encompasses crucifixion in writings
of the period. However, Baumgarten's case might be strengthened by appeal
to a fascinating list in Philo's *De Aeternitate Mundi* 20.[135] Here Philo illustrates his point that when substances perish they do so either through internal
or external causes:

ὁμοιοτρόπως δὲ καὶ ζῴοις ἐπιγίνεται τελευτὴ νοσήσασι μὲν ἐξ ἑαυτῶν, ὑπὸ δὲ τῶν ἐκτὸς
σφαττομένοις ἢ καταλευομένοις ἢ ἐμπιπραμένοις ἢ θάνατον οὐ καθαρὸν τὸν δι᾽ ἀγχόνης
ὑπομένουσιν.

---

[134] So Joseph Heinemann, "Early Halakhah in the Palestinian Targumim," *Journal of
Jewish Studies* 25 (1974): 119–22; also Heinemann, "Targum of Ex. XXII,4," 294–96 (and
English summary, page v). Cf. Étan Levine, *The Aramaic Version of Ruth*, AnBib 58 (Rome:
Biblical Institute Press, 1973), 60–62; Díez Merino, "Suplicio," 86–98.

[135] While the Philonic authorship of this treatise has been challenged, current consensus
appears to regard the work as authentic. See an overview in Schürer (revised), vol. 3.2, 858–
59; opinion in James R. Royse, *The Spurious Texts of Philo of Alexandria: A Study of Textual
Transmission and Corruption with Indexes to the Major Collections of Greek Fragments*,
ALGHJ 22 (Leiden: Brill, 1991), 145; and discussions in Colson et al., *Philo, LCL*, 9:171–77;
R. Arnaldez and J. Pouilloux, *De Aeternitate Mundi*, Les oeuvres de Philon d'Alexandrie 30
(Paris: Cerf, 1969), 12–37; and David T. Runia, "Philo's *De aeternitate mundi*: The Problem
of its Interpretation," *Vigiliae Christianae* 35 (1981): 105–51. Colson holds §20 to be the last
section that expresses Philo's own views. But Runia appears more correct in viewing §20 as
the start of a long section that represents a view Philo himself rejects in the missing conclusion of the treatise. Thus Runia claims: "the content of *Aet.* 20–149 should not
unreservedly be quoted as Philo's own opinions, even though the manner of expression is
indubitably Philonic" (ibid., 139). However, though in a section that likely represents a view
Philo ultimately rejected, the passage cited below could very well be a case where Philo is
putting another side's arguments in his own "manner of expression" (to use Runia's terminology). Alternatively, the passage could be from another philosopher, in which case Philo's
citation is still interesting in that it conveys some Jewish contact with a schema very much
like the one the rabbis ultimately adopt.

And in like fashion, death also comes at the end for living things either from themselves by being sick, or by things from without – by being slain (with the sword), or by being stoned, or by being burnt, or by suffering the unclean death that comes through [hanging on] a halter.

It is remarkable to find here in the first three members a list that corresponds to the classic rabbinic death penalties, while the fourth member deviates. Colson in his *LCL* translation rightly points to *Mut.* 62 to clarify the fourth external cause of death (δι' ἀγχόνης). In both contexts death occurs by *hanging* from a halter/noose, and in both contexts the death is considered unclean.[136] However, it should be admitted that the context of *Aet.* 20 does not claim that these four means of death are penal executionary measures. Moreover, the parallel in *Mut.* 62 appears to indicate that the halter is a means of death by suicide,[137] a connection also made in *Spec. Leg.* iii.161. Nonetheless, the fourfold parallel to the rabbinic list remains striking.

Thus, the Jewish practice of human bodily suspension, alongside the standard mode and listing of death penalties, appears to have been in flux during the late Second Temple and early rabbinic periods. Some have attributed these variations to recognizable groups (e.g., Sadducees and Essenes), but even the rabbinic documents themselves betray remnants of halakhic discussion and practical variation. On the other hand, as will be shown below, whereas Philo willingly associates Deuteronomy 21:22–23 with executionary suspension and even crucifixion, it appears that Josephus was much more reluctant to do so.[138] These two renowned Jewish authors may then further illustrate conflicting tendencies within the first century concerning executionary suspension.

In conclusion, a few points are worth emphasizing: (1) It appears that opinion on executionary measures (including penal suspension) was subject to flux and development in Second Temple and early rabbinic Judaism. (2) One can thus not assume that all texts from the period must conform to the Mish-

---

[136] *Mut.* 62: ἀπὸ γὰρ μικρᾶς καὶ τῆς τυχούσης προφάσεως ἐπ' ἀγχόνην ἦξεν, ἵν' ὁ μιαρὸς καὶ δυσκάθαρτος μηδὲ καθαρῷ θανάτῳ τελευτήσῃ. "...from a small and ordinary motive he turned eagerly upon a halter, in order that this defiled and difficult to purify man might not die a clean death." Text in Colson et al., *Philo* , 5:174; translation is mine. Liddell-Scott give the possible glosses of ἀγχόνη as "strangling, hanging." However, Lampe notes that it later takes on the meaning of "means of strangling, halter"; see G. W. H. Lampe, ed., *Patristic Greek Lexicon* (Oxford: Clarendon Press, 1961–1968), s.v. Souls are metaphorically hung from a halter/noose in *Post.* 27; *Quis Her.* 269; *Praem.* 151; and a necklace is compared to the ἀγχόνη (which is clearly a "halter") in Philo, *Som.* ii.44; *Jos.* 150. Whereas the meaning "strangling" could fit in the context of *Aet.* 20, the use of prepositions here and in *Mut.* 62, as well as the uses where "halter" is clear, makes it likely that the physical object (the noose or halter) is intended in *Aet.* 20.

[137] This seems the most likely intention of ἐπ' ἀγχόνην ἦξεν. So also Colson/Whitaker in *Philo*, LCL, 5:175; and R. Arnaldez, *De Mutatione Nominum*, Les oeuvres de Philon d'Alexandrie 18 (Paris: Cerf, 1964), 61.

[138] Note the individual summaries of Josephus and Philo in chapter six.

naic halakhah, though many texts certainly will. (3) As the central issue of this thesis concerns perceptions of crucifixion, it should be emphasized that different conceptions of death by crucifixion will be tied up with how that author's community understood the legality of the penalty.

4. Methodology in this Study

This study is largely inductive in orientation, drawing out the independent threads of the variety of testimony in the extant sources and synthesizing these materials only to the degree that they properly cohere.[139] Chapters two through five examine ancient Jewish texts and archaeological remains, sifting each for its orientation toward crucifixion as a penalty and toward the crucified person. The summary in chapter six then generates a list of perceptions of crucifixion evidenced among Jewish people in classical antiquity. The final chapter, starting from that list, seeks to find conceptual parallels as they are rejected or incorporated in those early Christian works that can reasonably be indebted to a Jewish milieu.

It is the author's conviction that, just as the views in Jewish literature should not be treated merely as subject material for the study of Christianity but as meriting study within their own cultural context, so too should the varieties of opinions and practices within ancient Jewish groups (including the identified "sects") be allowed their own expression. However, to the extent that trends can be testified in a variety of source groupings and over widespread geographical or temporal locales, then synthesis may rightly be permitted.

Also, though early Christian sources often evidence a marked self-identity and opposition to Judaism, they may still provide useful evidence of trends within Judaism itself. Some important early Christian figures (especially in the New Testament period) still saw themselves in significant continuity with Jewish tradition and thus may provide testimony from within.[140] And even *adversus Iudaeos* literature used with care may provide indications of contact with Jewish thought.

The above comments about crucifixion and suspension terminology influence the source selection for this study. The study thus encompasses those many texts that speak of the bodily suspension of a human being. And, while those texts that speak overtly about acts of crucifixion are most directly rele-

---

[139] Thus I have not sought to classify these texts within categories drawn from social-scientific study (such as shame and honour).

[140] A similar point, more broadly stated, can be seen in Geza Vermes, "Jewish Literature and New Testament Exegesis: Reflections on Methodology," *Journal of Jewish Studies* 33 (1982): 361–76.

vant to this study, texts that do not clearly denote crucifixion (*vis-à-vis* other forms of bodily suspension) may still be important to comprehending Jewish and Christian conceptualities of the more specific practice of crucifixion itself.

Part One

Ancient Jewish Perceptions of Crucifixion

Chapter Two

Crucifixion and Suspension in Extra-Biblical Jewish Historical Narratives

This chapter presents a survey of extra-biblical Jewish narratives of deaths by suspension, especially those involving crucifixion. In all cases they purport to describe historical events. To provide a context for these narratives, some brief comments are also made concerning the common practice of these penalties in the Graeco-Roman world (with which Jewish people were in contact). However, while all these texts speak of historical events, the more important contribution of this chapter to this study concerns the *perceptions* of suspension and crucifixion evidenced in the Jewish historical texts themselves.

Since the focus remains on general Jewish perceptions of crucifixion, the emphasis falls on the views of the authors and their communities, rather than on the historical reconstruction of the events. Thus this chapter does not, in principle, seek to present an actual history of crucifixion in Judaea,[1] although the question of the historical value of the sources is the subject of occasional comment. For convenience, however, these narratives are listed here in the approximate chronological order of the events they purport to represent. One benefit of this approach is that it allows for a comparison of perceptions in parallel accounts from more than one source regarding similar events and periods. This chapter also serves as the most natural place to discuss the archaeological evidence for crucifixion in Roman-era Judaea. The various Jewish perceptions of crucifixion found in these sources are summarized at the end of the chapter.

1. Suspension in the Graeco-Roman World

Classical Greek and Latin authors often record deaths associated with suspension. As noted in chapter one, several important modern surveys previously

---

[1] For brief histories of crucifixion in Palestine see Ethelbert Stauffer, *Jerusalem und Rom im Zeitalter Jesu Christi* (Bern: Francke, 1957), 123–27; Heinz Wolfgang Kuhn, "Die Kreuzesstrafe während der frühen Kaiserzeit: Ihre Wirklichkeit und Wertung in der Umwelt des Urchristentums," in *Aufstieg und Niedergang der Römischen Welt*, ed. Wolfgang Haase, vol. II.25.1 (Berlin/New York: Walter de Gruyter, 1982), 706–18, 724–27.

have discussed the use of crucifixion in the Hellenistic and Roman eras. Here we shall merely summarize the standard conclusions represented in these works. Only a very brief overview will be required in order to survey some general perceptions of crucifixion in antiquity, and in order to establish that crucifixion and related penalties frequently occurred in the various cultural environments in which Jewish people lived in classical antiquity.[2] These concepts of crucifixion found among their Gentile neighbours might well have influenced Jewish people in antiquity.

During this period, crucifixion was repeatedly employed as a punishment against robbers.[3] These were usually not mere thieves, but often they were violent criminals working in gangs. "Brigands" is perhaps the best term. In some contexts, such brigands were difficult to distinguish from rebels, and both brigands and rebels often faced the cross. Perhaps it was the (particularly Roman) concern with peaceful commerce that led to the regular implementation of such a gruesome penalty against those who would disrupt the peace of the empire through banditry and rebellion. Nonetheless, crucifixion could also be employed in general times of war.[4]

Slaves especially, if they participated in rebellion or sought to significantly harm their masters, could meet the cross as their final lot in life. Thus Dionysius of Halicarnassus records that the slave rebellion under the tribuneship of Agrippa Menenius concluded with the execution of its slave leadership.[5] This further highlights the social stratification within Roman society, in which Roman citizens (especially those of superior rank) were not commonly crucified. Indeed, when a prominent citizen was crucified, it could become a legal point against the governor responsible for the edict (see Cicero, *Against Verres* ii.5.165).

The penalty of crucifixion often was preceded by scourging.[6] Both cords and nails could be employed in crucifixion.[7] The crucifixion itself was typi-

---

[2] Consequently, the primary source texts cited in this section should be understood as exemplary, and not as by any means exhaustive.

[3] E.g., Petronius, *Satyricon* 111.5; Apuleius, *Metamorphoses* i.14.2; Plutarch, *Caesar* 2.4, 7; etc. See many more examples in Hengel, *Crucifixion*, 46–50 (repr. 138–142); Kuhn, "Die Kreuzesstrafe," 724–32. Kuhn tends to view these robbers as most akin to political revolutionaries.

[4] E.g., Polybius, *Hist.* i.24.6; i.79.2–4; and esp. i.86.4–7 (where Hannibal was said to have been crucified alive).

[5] Dionysius of Halicarnassus, *Antiq. Rom.* xii.6.7: τῆς δὲ πράξεως περιφανοῦς γενομένης συλληφθέντες οἱ πρῶτοι συνθέντες τὴν ἐπιβουλὴν καὶ μαστιγωθέντες ἐπὶ τοὺς σταυροὺς ἀπήχθησαν· ("And the revolt having been fully discovered, the leaders who had contrived the plot were seized and, after being scourged, were led away to their crosses."). See also his *Antiq. Rom.* v.51.3. Also cf. Plutarch, *Ant.* 81.1 (here a παιδαγωγός).

[6] See e.g., Dionysius of Halicarnassus, *Antiq. Rom.* v.51.3; xii.6.7 (noted above). Also cf. Lucian, *Pisc.* 2.

cally a public act, involving a march to the place of execution.[8] However, as noted in the previous chapter, the shape of the cross could vary, even while there is some evidence of a standard form.[9] In that chapter it was suggested that crucifixion should really be seen as part of the larger category of executionary suspensions – with the terminology often indicating that the ancients felt little need always to be specific about exactly how a person died relative to such an act of suspension.[10]

While regularly practicing crucifixion (or similarly horrible penalties), it is ironic that the Greeks and Romans themselves believed the origin of the cross to stem from barbarian practices.[11] Especially in recounting distant episodes in the historical or mythological past, classical authors might embellish the death of someone by inserting references to crucifixion.[12] One overt act of subsequent authors applying crucifixion terminology to a previous event can be found in the later accounts of the death of Polycrates, despot of Samos. Whereas Herodotus indicates that Polycrates was executed and then pinned to the stake (*Hist.* iii.125),[13] both Lucian and Dio Chrysostom summarize his death as an act of barbarous suspension (each of these authors employ the

---

[7] For both cords and nails see Pliny, *N.H.* xxviii.11.46. For nails see also Lucan, *Bell.* vi.543–49; Lucian, *Philops.* 17. All these report uses of crucifixion objects in magic, concerning which see further below in chapter 4, §2. Some of these and other sources are discussed in Joseph William Hewitt, "The Use of Nails in the Crucifixion," *HTR* 25 (1932): 42–44. Hewitt's ingenious attempt at limiting nail usage to nails in the hands (relying as he does on how easy it would have been to extract a nail from the foot) appears to be an exaggerated analysis of the sources, especially in light of the nail stuck in the calcaneum of the crucified victim from an ossuary at Giv'at ha-Mivtar (see later in this chapter in §3.6).

[8] For example, see Lucian, *Pereg.* 34. Also Plutarch, *De sera numinis vindicta* 554A–B: καὶ τῷ μὲν σώματι τῶν κολαζομένων ἕκαστος κακούργων ἐκφέρει τὸν αὑτοῦ σταυρόν ("and on the body of those who are punished each of the criminals bears his own cross"); text in Frank C. Babbitt, et al., *Plutarch's Moralia*, 16 vols., LCL (Cambridge, Mass.: Harvard University Press, 1927–1969), 7:214–16.

[9] Note sources referenced in the discussion of crucifixion terminology in chapter one, §2. Especially compare Seneca, *Dial.* 6.20.3 ("I see there crosses, not merely of one kind, but fashioned differently from others..."), which implies both a variation from any normative form and a possible expectation that "one kind" would be mostly anticipated. Also see Josephus, *Bell.* v.451.

[10] Again, see above in chapter one, §2.

[11] Hengel, *Crucifixion*, 22–24 (repr. 114–16).

[12] Note especially the repeated depiction of the legendary Prometheus as crucified in Lucian's *Prometheus*, as well as in his *On Sacrifices* (6) and *Zeus Catechized* (8).

[13] Herodotus, *Hist.* iii.125: Ἀποκτείνας δέ μιν οὐκ ἀξίως ἀπηγήσιος Ὀροίτης ἀνεσταύρωσε ("and, having killed him in a way unworthy of narration, Oroetes suspended him"). The tendency in later authors to view Polycrates death as an act of crucifixion may have been encouraged by Herodotus' use of ἀνασταυρόω, combined with the way that just a few clauses later he summarizes Polycrates demise with ἀνακρεμάμενος (i.e., Polycrates was "hung up").

term ἀνασκολιπίζω),[14] and Philo considers Polycrates to have been executed through his being nailed up.[15] This embellishing activity will be important to remember as we discuss the "actualization" of the biblical text in early Judaism (see chapter 3).

In at least one instance, later Roman authors could conceive of one of their own as facing the cross in apparent echoes of martyrdom.[16] Nevertheless, on the whole the penalty of crucifixion was viewed with great dismay. Certainly the pain was understood to be intense, and the public nature of the penalty would heighten the shame involved. Still, there were some strong personalities, who spat in the face of death, and who, even while pinned to the cross, refused to give the crucifier the satisfaction of seeing them admit defeat (Strabo, *Geog.* iii.4.18). However, in a culture well aware of the pain of crucifixion, and fully cognizant of despicable associations with the cross, the mention of Jesus' death provided an opportunity for Roman authors to deride the early Christian faith in a crucified messiah.[17]

2. Crucifixion and Suspension in the Hellenistic Age

Hengel has rightly argued that the Greek penalty of ἀποτυμπανισμός bears similarities to crucifixion; and the additional element of suspension was at times also reportedly brought to bear (e.g., Herodotus, *Hist.* ix.120).[18] Significantly, narratives about Alexander the Great (including his conquest of Tyre),

---

[14] Dio Chrysostom, *Orationes* 17.15 (in his "On Covetousness"): μηδὲ ῥᾳδίου γε θανάτου τυχεῖν, ἀλλὰ ἀνασκολοπισθέντα ὑπὸ τοῦ βαρβάρου διαφθαρῆναι ("he indeed obtained no easy death, but, having been impaled by the barbarian, he was murdered"). Also note the use of ἀνασκολοπισθήσεται in Lucian, *Cont.* 14. See further examples in Hengel, *Crucifixion*, 24n. (repr. 116n.).

[15] Philo, *Prov.* ii.24: πρόσθες δ᾿ ὡς ὑπὸ μεγάλου βασιλέως ἐκολάζετο, καὶ προσηλοῦτο, χρησμὸν ἐκπιπλάς ("and adding how he was punished by a great king [or 'by the Great King'], and was impaled, fulfilling an oracle"). Later, Philo (*Prov.* ii.25) summarizes Polycrates death with κρεμάμενος.

[16] The traditions concerning the Carthaginian torturing of the staunch Roman warrior M. Atilius Regulus are discussed in detail by Hengel (*Crucifixion*, 64–66; repr. 156–158), who notes that crucifixion was only added in later Regulus accounts, and who remarks that thus the crucifixion dimensions of his death were not likely to have been historical. However, regardless of the historicity of the Regulus traditions, these still demonstrate that in some circumstances crucifixion imagery could be attached to the death of a national hero.

[17] Consider the famous Alexamenos inscription, or Lucian's reference to Jesus as the "crucified sophist" (*Pereg.* 13; cf. 11).

[18] So Hengel, *Crucifixion*, 69–83 (repr. 161–75). On the lexicography of the term ἀποτυμπανισμός see esp. Hengel's note 11 on pp. 71–72; also add the opinion of Arthur Darby Nock, "Thackeray's Lexicon to Josephus," *HTR* 25 (1932): 361–62. The term is employed by Berossus as cited by Josephus (*C. Ap.* i.148).

as well as historical accounts of the Diadochoi, portray these arch-representatives of Hellenism as suspending – even crucifying – their conquered opponents.[19]

2.1 Persecution under Antiochus Epiphanes

It is not entirely surprising then that the Seleucids, as the Eastern heirs of Hellenism in lands once ruled by Persia, might be thought to have enacted such penalties.[20] And so, admittedly some 250 years after the purported events, crucifixion is listed by Josephus (in book twelve of the *Antiquities*) among the penalties inflicted by Antiochus IV Epiphanes upon the faithful Jewish nation:

(255) καὶ πολλοὶ μὲν τῶν Ἰουδαίων οἱ μὲν ἑκοντὶ οἱ δὲ καὶ δι᾽ εὐλάβειαν τῆς ἐπηγγελμένης τιμωρίας κατηκολούθουν οἷς ὁ βασιλεὺς διετέτακτο, οἱ δὲ δοκιμώτατοι καὶ τὰς ψυχὰς εὐγενεῖς οὐκ ἐφρόντισαν αὐτοῦ, τῶν δὲ πατρίων ἐθῶν πλείονα λόγον ἔσχον ἢ τῆς τιμωρίας ἣν οὐ πειθομένοις ἠπείλησεν αὐτοῖς, καὶ διὰ τοῦτο κατὰ πᾶσαν ἡμέραν αἰκιζόμενοι καὶ πικρὰς βασάνους ὑπομένοντες ἀπέθνησκον. (256) καὶ γὰρ μαστιγούμενοι[21] καὶ τὰ σώματα λυμαινόμενοι ζῶντες ἔτι καὶ ἐμπνέοντες ἀνεσταυροῦντο, τὰς δὲ γυναῖκας καὶ τοὺς παῖδας αὐτῶν, οὓς περιέτεμνον παρὰ τὴν τοῦ βασιλέως προαίρεσιν, ἀπῆγχον, ἐκ τῶν τραχήλων αὐτοὺς τῶν ἀνεσταυρωμένων γονέων ἀπαρτῶντες. ἠφανίζετο δ᾽ εἴ που βίβλος εὑρεθείη ἱερὰ καὶ νόμος, καὶ παρ᾽ οἷς εὑρέθη καὶ οὗτοι[22] κακοὶ κακῶς ἀπώλλυντο. (*Ant.* xii.255–56)

[255] And so, many of the Jews, some willingly, others through fear of the punishment which had been prescribed, followed the practices ordained by the king [Antiochus IV], but the worthiest people and those of noble soul disregarded him, and held their country's customs of greater account than the punishment with which he threatened them if they disobeyed; and being on that account maltreated daily, and enduring bitter torments, they met their death. [256] Indeed, they were whipped, their bodies were mutilated, and while still alive and breathing, *they were crucified*, while their wives and the sons whom they had circumcised in despite of the king's wishes were strangled, the children being made to hang from the necks of their *crucified* parents. And wherever a sacred book or copy of the Law was found, it was destroyed; as for those in whose possession it was found, they too, poor wretches, wretchedly perished.[23]

---

[19] Texts in Hengel, *Crucifixion*, 73–76 (repr. 165–68).

[20] Cf. Polybius, *Hist.* v.54.6–7; viii.21.2–3 (though both instances are post-mortem); see F. W. Walbank, *A Historical Commentary on Polybius*, 2 vols. (Oxford: Clarendon Press, 1957/1967), 2:97.

[21] Some manuscripts read μαστιζόμενοι, another word for "whip."

[22] The οὗτοι is in the Loeb edition, though Niese (despite the substantial manuscript support of οὗτοι) reads αὐτοί; see Benedictus Niese, *Flavii Iosephi Opera*, 7 vols. (Berlin: Weidmann, 1887–1895), 3:116. Texts from Josephus in this chapter will follow Niese's edition.

[23] Unless noted otherwise, translations of Josephus throughout this chapter will follow H. St. J. Thackeray, et al., *Josephus*, 10 vols., LCL (Cambridge, Mass.: Harvard University Press/ London: William Heinemann, 1926–1965).

That Josephus envisioned this to involve actual crucifixion is evident not merely from his employment of his standard term for crucifixion (ἀνασταυρόω), but also from his insistence that the victims were "still living and breathing" (ζῶντες ἔτι καὶ ἐμπνέοντες) when they were crucified. Scourging and mutilation would also appear as standard precursors to crucifixion in Josephus' day.

Probably this section of the *Antiquities*, despite some noticeable variations, is partially indebted to the text of 1 Maccabees 1:20–64.[24] Both in the *Antiquities* and in 1 Maccabees, Antiochus orders the cessation of Temple rites, the initiation of idolatrous sacrifices, the cessation of circumcision, and the destruction of the scrolls of the Torah. However, the closest corresponding passage in 1 Maccabees 1:60–61 (cf. 1:50, 57) does not mention crucifixion as part of the persecutions:

καὶ τὰς γυναῖκας τὰς περιτετμηκυίας τὰ τέκνα αὐτῶν ἐθανάτωσαν κατὰ τὸ πρόσταγμα καὶ ἐκρέμασαν τὰ βρέφη ἐκ τῶν τραχήλων αυτῶν, καὶ τοὺς οἴκους αὐτῶν καὶ τοὺς περιτετμηκότας αὐτούς.

And they put to death, according to the ordinance, the women who had circumcised their children; and they hung the infants from their necks, also their households and those (males) who had circumcised them.

Since the final two καί clauses in 1:61 have no verb,[25] and thus appear to be dependent on ἐκρέμασαν, Goldstein believes this verse forms the textual basis for Josephus' conclusion that the husbands were crucified. That is to say, in Josephus' understanding the males were "hung" (i.e., "crucified") just

---

[24] It is generally accepted today that Josephus used 1 Maccabees as a source; see the helpful review in Louis H. Feldman, *Josephus and Modern Scholarship (1937–1980)* (Berlin: Walter de Gruyter, 1984), 219–25. For a possible reconstruction of events see Emil Schürer, *The History of the Jewish People in the Age of Jesus Christ (175 B.C.–A.D. 135)*, ed. Geza Vermes et al., Revised English ed., 3 vols. (Edinburgh: T. & T. Clark, 1973–1987), 1:150–56 [Schürer will be cited below as *HJPAJC*]. A view more favourable to Antiochus is found in Otto Mørkholm, *Antiochus IV of Syria*, Classica et mediaevalia – Dissertationes 8 (Copenhagen: Gyldendalske Boghandel, 1966), 143–48. For possible motives of Antiochus, see Jonathan A. Goldstein, *I Maccabees: A New Translation with Introduction and Commentary*, AB 41 (Garden City, NY: Doubleday, 1976), 104–60. On Josephus' loose use of 1 Maccabees 1:20–64, see ibid., 56–61, 558–68. However, note the concerns in Louis H. Feldman, "A Selective Critical Bibliography of Josephus," in *Josephus, the Bible, and History*, ed. Louis H. Feldman and Gohei Hata (Leiden: E. J. Brill, 1989), 370–71.

[25] The manuscripts attempt solutions to the lack of a verb – so the so-called Lucianic texts, the Sinaiticus corrector, et al., read καὶ τοὺς οἴκους αὐτῶν *προενόμευσαν* καὶ τοὺς περιτετμηκότας αὐτοὺς *ἐθανάτωσαν* ("also their households *they plundered* and *they killed* those males who had circumcised them"). But Codex Alexandrinus and other manuscripts have the above text, which is preferred by Kappler and is clearly the more difficult reading; see Werner Kappler (ed.), *Maccabaeorum liber I* (Göttingen: Vandenhoeck & Ruprecht, 1990).

like the infants.[26] Alternatively, the detailed description of the persecution found in Josephus may be due to his reliance on an earlier source, thus possibly increasing the historical value of Josephus' account.[27]

In any case, regardless of the actual historicity of Josephus' narrative, clearly in his account of the pre-Maccabean persecution of Antiochus IV we have testimony to a first-century view that those persecuted Jews, who were often identified as martyrs (cf. 2 Macc 6:1–7:42), endured crucifixion.[28] A similar view is to be found in the *Assumption of Moses*, a text that shall be examined below.[29]

2.2 Jose ben Jo'ezer and his Nephew

A fairly late, but intriguing, story about the great Jose ben Jo'ezer and his nephew Jakim of Zeroroth appears both in *Bereshit Rabbah* lxv.22 (on Gen 27:23) and in *Midrash Tehillim* on Psalm 11:7. In the story Jose was apparently being led to his crucifixion, and his nephew Jakim (in contrition for his blasphemous disparagement of Jose and his God) enacts upon himself

---

[26] See Goldstein, *I Maccabees*, 227. Of course, this requires Josephus to have understood the masculine gender of the participle περιτετμηκότας as designating males who are performing the crucifixion (as in our translation above) rather than as a generic use of the masculine. Goldstein's thesis might be aided by noting that Codex Alexandrinus follows in 1 Macc 1:62 with πολλοὶ ἐν Ισραηλ ἐκρεμάσθησαν (where other MSS read ἐκραταιώθησαν), thus testifying to an early reading of 1 Maccabees that viewed the suspensions as including "many" individuals – again the Greek male gender is used (πολλοί), which would have naturally included men, as opposed to the neuter, which would have been more natural if the intent was to refer back to the suspended infants (τὰ βρέφη). An alternative depiction of the events appears in 4 Macc 4:25 (the women who circumcise their children are thrown from the city walls with their infants; cf. 2 Macc 6:10).

[27] Hengel suggests this might constitute basis for some trust in Josephus' account; see *Crucifixion*, 74–75 (repr. 166–67). Other sources that have been proposed for this section of the *Antiquities* include Nicolaus of Damascus, Jason of Cyrene, a (hypothetical) work by Onias IV, and the *Testament of Moses*. Contemporary Graeco-Roman authors, though not mentioning crucifixion, also know Antiochus' attempt to wipe out Jewish "superstition": e.g., Diodorus Siculus, fragments in Loeb collection xxxi.18a.1 (from Jerome, also speaking of Polybius), xxxiv/xxxv.1.1–5 (Antiochus is here presented more ambiguously); Tacitus, *Hist.* v.8.2; see also Josephus, *Contra Apionem* ii.84. Cf. Fergus Millar, "The Background to the Maccabean Revolution: Reflections on Martin Hengel's 'Judaism and Hellenism'," *JJS* 29 (1978): 12–17.

[28] Josephus himself speaks of the persecuted as οἱ δοκιμώτατοι καὶ τὰς ψυχὰς εὐγενεῖς ("the most esteemed and noble souls"; *Ant.* xii.255). Cf. 4 Macc 1:7–12; 5:1–18:19. For a key recent study and bibliography see Jan Willem Van Henten, *The Maccabean Martyrs as Saviours of the Jewish People: A Study of 2 and 4 Maccabees*, Supplements to the Journal for the Study of Judaism 57 (Leiden: Brill, 1997); unfortunately, J. W. van Henten does not provide significant discussion of the Josephus account.

[29] *As. Mos.* 8:1 (*qui confitentes circumcisionem in cruce suspendit*) is often taken as reference to the persecution of Antiochus Epiphanes; see §3.2 below in this chapter.

the four forms of death approved by the rabbinic masters. The Genesis Rabbah account reads:

יקים איש צרורות היה בן אחותו של ר' יוסי בן יועזר איש צרידה והוה רכיב סוסיה,
אזל קמי שריתא אזל למצטבלה, אמר ליה חמי סוסי דארכבני מרי וחמי סוסך דארכבך
מרך, אמר ליה אם כך למכעיסיו קל וחומר לעושי רצונו, אמר לו ועשה אדם רצונו
יותר ממך, אמר לו ואם כך לעושי רצונו קל וחומר למכעיסיו, נכנס בו הדבר כארס
שלחכנה, הלך וקיים בו ארבע מיתות בית דין סקילה שריפה הרג וחנק, מה עשה הביא
קורה ונעצה בארץ ועשה סביבה נדר וקשר בה ניניא [ועשה מדורה לפניה ונעץ את
החרב באמצע נתלה בקורה נפסקה נינייא] ונחנק, קידמתו החרב ונהפך עליו גדר
ונשרף, נתנמנם יוסי בן יועזר וראה את מיטתו פורחה באויר, אמר בשעה קלה קידמני
זה לגן עדן:[30]

Jaḳim of Ẓeroroth was the nephew of R. Jose b. Joʿezer of Ẓeredah. Riding on a horse he [Jaḳim] went before the beam on which he [R. Jose] was to be hanged [i.e., crucified], and taunted him: 'See the horse on which my master has let me ride, and the horse upon which your Master has made you ride.' 'If it is so with those who anger Him, how much more with those who do His will,' he [R. Jose] replied. 'Has then any man done His will more than thou?' he [Jaḳim] jeered. 'If it is thus with those who do His will, how much more with those who anger Him,' he [R. Jose] retorted.

This pierced him [Jaḳim] like the poison of a snake, and he went and subjected himself to the four modes of execution inflicted by the Beth Din: stoning, burning, decapitation, and strangulation. What did he do? He took a post and planted it in the earth, raised a wall of stones around it and tied a cord to it. He made a fire in front of it and fixed a sword in the middle [of the post]. He hanged himself on the post, the cord was burnt through and he was strangled. The sword caught him, while the wall [of stones] fell upon him and he was burnt.

Jose b. Joʿezer of Ẓeredah fell into a doze and saw his [Jaḳim's] bier flying in the air. 'By a little while he has preceded me into the Garden of Eden,' said he.

Jaḳim, also known as Jaḳum,[31] is in many respects the focus of the narrative. His death combines the four rabbinic means of execution in a most imaginative way. The current debate over acceptable rabbinic suspension practices has frequently referenced Jaḳim's manner of suicide, contrasting Jaḳim's hanging himself from a noose with crucifixion. The implication some draw is that suspension on a noose was acceptable rabbinic suspension practice, while crucifixion was not (see above in chapter one, §§2.3.1 and 3). However, it appears that this narrative was not concerned with precisely imitating correct rabbinic executionary forms (e.g., note that the death by sword involves impalement not beheading; the burning and stoning are also not in keeping with typical rabbinic descriptions of such procedures). Also, the hanging from a noose does not in the text invoke a fulfillment of Deuteronomy 21 (and the command to suspend), instead the text indicates that it is a way of producing

---

[30] Text from J. Theodor and Ch. Albeck, *Bereschit Rabba*, 3 (+ 2 Register) vols. (Berlin: M. Poppelauer, 1912–1936), 742–44. Translation by H. Freedman, *Midrash Rabbah: Genesis*, 2 vols. (London: Soncino Press, 1939).

[31] Jaḳim is spelled Jaḳum in one major manuscript (D) according to Theodor/Albeck, and appears under that spelling in other rabbinic texts and in modern translations.

"strangulation" (חנק) – long recognised as one of the four modes of rabbinic execution (see *m. Sanh.* vii.1). Rather than serving as a summary of correct rabbinic executionary practice, this story of Jakim's death merely developed, in a complex and imaginative way, the idea that a person could commit suicide while simultaneously invoking the penalties of the Beth Din.

However, while still investigating the suicide of Jakim, one should not overlook that Jose's death here is most likely represented in this narrative as a case of crucifixion. This conclusion is based not merely on the use of the verb צלב (למצטבלה)[32] and the concept of traveling with one's wood to the place of execution, but also on the narrative's implication that Jose underwent a protracted death. Note that while Jose was dying he fell into a doze (as overtly highlighted in his vision of Jakim and in his concluding utterance) – the very kind of doze expected of someone pinned to a cross.

Bereshit Rabbah is usually dated to the early fifth century; it collects Palestinian traditions that come to their final shaping in the Amoraic period.[33] The *Midrash Tehillim*, though often dated later, cites mainly Palestinian Amoraim of the fourth or fifth centuries. Jose b. Jo'ezer appears in *m. Abot.* 1:4 paired with Jose b. Johanan as the first of the *zugot*,[34] which would place him early in the second century BCE. The temporal distance from Jose's day to the time of writing, as well as some of the legendary features of this account, makes it difficult to assert definitively how much of this narrative corresponds to actual history, though many scholars have acknowledged some historical core to the crucifixion of R. Jose.

The figure of Jakim/Jakum has been identified by several modern scholars as the Alcimus in 1 Maccabees 7–9.[35] In 1 Maccabees Alcimus appears as the arch-Hellenist who calls upon the Seleucids (including Demetrius I Soter) to assist him in putting down the Hasmonean opposition. The identification is based on Josephus's *Antiquities* xii.385 – Ἄλκιμος ὁ καὶ Ἰάκειμος κληθείς; ("Alcimus who was also called Jakeimos"; also cf. xx.235). Aside from his

---

[32] Here we are following Jastrow's very sensible suggestion that this word should actually read למצטלבא; see Jastrow, *Dictionary*, 825 (= מצטבלה s.v.). The manuscript tradition is quite confused on this word, with several reading למצטלבא, and others reading למיצלבה, למצטבבלא, or למסתבלא; see Theodore and Albeck, *Bereschit Rabba*, 742.

[33] See the conclusions in Günter Stemberger, *Introduction to the Talmud and Midrash*, trans. Markus Bockmuehl, 2nd ed. (Edinburgh: T & T Clark, 1996), 279–80.

[34] On the Jose traditions see Jacob Neusner, *The Rabbinic Traditions about the Pharisees before 70*, 3 vols. (Leiden: E. J. Brill, 1971), 1:61–81. Neusner holds the *zugot* pairing to be a later rabbinic development.

[35] Cf. Schürer, *HJPAJC*, 1:168n. The identification also appears without argumentation in such articles as: Adolf Büchler, "Alcimus," in *The Jewish Encyclopedia*, ed. Isidore Singer, vol. 1 (New York: Funk and Wagnalls, 1901), 333; Abraham Schalit, "Alcimus," in *Encyclopedia Judaica*, vol. 2 (Jerusalem: Keter, 1971), 549. The identification is rejected (again without argumentation) in Neusner, *Rabbinic Traditions*, 1:77.

vicious power politics, Alcimus is also infamous in the sources for his executing some sixty of his fellow Jews all in a single day (even killing those Hasidaeans who were "first" among the sons of Israel; 1 Macc 7:13–17).

Having made the connection of Jaķim to Alcimus, Stauffer has gone on to identify the crucifixion of Jose b. Joʿezer with Alcimus' execution of the sixty *Ḥasidim*.[36] Thus, in Stauffer's estimation, Alcimus was the first Jewish person to crucify fellow Jews (including his own uncle). Stauffer also supports his assertion with his reading of the Nahum Pesher (see further below).

Stauffer's thesis is not impossible. However, it should be stressed that our better earlier sources (1 Macc 7:16 and Josephus, *Ant.* xii.399–400), which show no fondness for Alcimus and thus have no reason to hide his atrocities, do not report him conducting such an awful manner of execution. On the other hand, the Jaķim death story in these midrashim to Genesis and Psalms is full of legendary description (contrast with 1 Macc 9:54–56 and Josephus, *Ant.* xii.413), especially in connecting Jaķim's death to the existing four-fold listing of executionary forms known in the Mishnah.[37] Therefore I would commend caution about claiming that the historical figure of Alcimus himself practiced crucifixion.

What is significant here for early Jewish perceptions of crucifixion is how the narrative portrays crucifixion as a derisive death (hence Jaķim's mocking of Jose). Furthermore, this story indicates that, even in the rabbinic midrashim, crucifixion could be a form of martyr's death for men of renown such as Jose.[38] In this regard this text could be compared to Josephus' treatment of the crucified Maccabean martyrs.[39]

2.3 The 800 Crucified by Alexander Jannaeus

One event, which Josephus considered significant enough to record in both his *Antiquities* and in the *War*, concerns the crucifixion of eight hundred Jews by Alexander Jannaeus (*Bell.* i.97–98; *Ant.* xiii.380). This represents the only instance in Josephus where a person of Jewish descent, who also still held to Jewish customs, crucified others.[40]

---

[36] Stauffer, *Jerusalem*, 124–25; 128–32

[37] Neusner suggests that the Jaķim account is "an echo of one of the several ʿAkiba martyrdom-legends" (*Rabbinic Traditions*, 1:77).

[38] The martyrdom implications of this text are acknowledged, though without argument, in Jan Willem Van Henten and Friedrich Avemarie, *Martyrdom and Noble Death: Selected texts from Graeco-Roman, Jewish and Christian Antiquity* (London/New York: Routledge, 2002), 134–35, 142–44.

[39] See above §2.1; also note *Ass. Moses* below in §3.2.

[40] Alexander's lineage is noted in *Ant.* xiii.320f. Regardless of whether one follows Stauffer's argument (described above in §2.2; see his *Jerusalem*, 124–25) in holding that the high priest Alcimus (whom he identifies with Jaķim of Ẓeroroth) was actually the first Jewish leader to crucify, Josephus' Alcimus account certainly does not give the impression that

Alexander Jannaeus (=Yannai), a Hasmonean king, combined the offices of Jewish king and high priest. According to Josephus, while Alexander frequently fought fierce battles with the neighbours of Judaea, he also spent much of his resources putting down homegrown Jewish rebellions. The first such revolt reported by Josephus occurs at "the festival" (of Tabernacles) where Alexander, while offering the sacrifice in his role as high priest, is pelted with citrons by the crowds. Alexander responds by slaying six thousand of his countrymen (*Ant.* xiii.372–73; *Bell.* i.88–89).[41] Later, after the king of Arabia decisively defeats an advance by Jannaeus, the Jews revolt again, and Alexander slays "fifty thousand" of them (so *Ant.* xiii.376; *Bell.* i.91). When Alexander seeks to appease his Jewish subjects, his offers are rejected. Instead a group of "Jews" (Josephus provides no more detailed identification) turns for assistance to Demetrius III (whom Josephus sarcastically deems "the Unready"). Demetrius' forces initially bring the needed assistance; but, after a brief victory, Demetrius retreats when he hears of six thousand Jews who turn to Jannaeus' side. The Jewish rebels continue to fight, but they are now no match for their king. When Alexander finally gains the upper hand, he brings his captives back to Jerusalem to exact his gruesome retribution:

καὶ πάντων ὠμότατον ἔργον ἔδρασεν· ἑστιώμενος γὰρ ἐν ἀπόπτῳ μετὰ τῶν παλλακίδων ἀνασταυρῶσαι προσέταξεν αὐτῶν ὡς ὀκτακοσίους, τοὺς δὲ παῖδας αὐτῶν καὶ τὰς γυναῖκας ἔτι ζώντων παρὰ τὰς ἐκείνων ὄψεις ἀπέσφαττεν, ὑπὲρ μὲν ὧν ἠδίκητο ἀμυνόμενος, ἄλλως δὲ ὑπὲρ ἄνθρωπον ταύτην εἰσπραττόμενος τὴν δίκην. (*Ant.* xiii.380–81)

...and there he did a thing that was as cruel as could be: while he feasted with his concubines in a conspicuous place, he ordered some eight hundred of the Jews to be crucified, and slaughtered their children and wives before the eyes of the still living wretches. This was the

---

crucifixion was involved (*Ant.* xii.396). Josephus also clearly questions any remaining Jewish allegiances of Tiberius Alexander, the Roman procurator of Jewish descent, who crucified fellow Jews (*Ant.* xx.100, 102; see below in §3.4). Actually, Josephus appears reticent to attribute penal suspension or crucifixion to any Jewish leader other than to Alexander Jannaeus. Thus Josephus does not employ suspension terminology at all when rendering the events of Joshua 8:29; 10:26 and 2 Samuel 4:12 (cf. *Ant.* v.48, 61; vii.52) – see the discussion of these passages in the next chapter. Kuhn ("Die Kreuzesstrafe," 707) calls the Alexander Jannaeus episode "der einzige wirkliche Beleg" that Jewish people themselves practiced crucifixion in Palestine. However, in order to prove this, Kuhn must discount the crucifixions done by Tiberius Alexander, contend against Stauffer's Alcimus thesis, and dispute the crucifixion possibilities in the Temple Scroll, in the Ruth Targum, and in the Simeon ben Shetach traditions.

[41] The *Antiquities* also records that the rebels προσεξελοιδόρησαν δ' αὐτὸν ὡς ἐξ αἰχμαλώτων γεγονότα καὶ τῆς τιμῆς καὶ τοῦ θύειν ἀνάξιον ("reviled him as well for having come from captives and for being unworthy of the office or to sacrifice"; xiii.372) – for Yannai as descended from captives also cf. *b. Qidd.* 66a. The *War* specifies that Jannaeus had to call in non-Jewish mercenaries to quell the uprising.

revenge he took for the injuries he had suffered; but the penalty he exacted was inhuman for all that.

This is actually the more favourable account of these crucifixions, for in the *Antiquities* Josephus seeks to show Alexander's side of the conflict, while in the *War* he is much more terse.[42] Nevertheless, even in the *Antiquities* Josephus finalizes his discussion of all this by noting that Alexander, "as a result of his excessive cruelty," was branded with the savage eponym "θρακίδαν" by his countrymen (xiii.383). Remarkably, in the *War* Josephus prefaces Alexander's mass crucifixion with προύκοψεν δ' αὐτῷ δι' ὑπερβολὴν ὀργῆς εἰς ἀσέβειαν τὸ τῆς ὠμότητος ("so furious was he that his savagery went to the length of impiety").[43]

These, then, are the kinds of harsh judgments that Josephus makes against the actions of Alexander: πάντων ὠμότατον ("cruel as could be"), ὑπὲρ ἄνθρωπον ("inhuman"), even accusing him of ἀσέβειαν. This last (ἀσέβεια – "impiety") labels the whole action as religiously immoral. This could, of course, be solely for the benefit of Josephus' Roman audience; however, one wonders if this does not also betray Josephus' own evaluation of the Jewish legality of the penalty imposed.

Though differing slightly in vividness of reporting, both of Josephus' accounts of this mass crucifixion agree, even in the details. Largely on the basis of Josephus' testimony, most scholars have been inclined to see these crucifixions as representing an actual historical incident. It is otherwise difficult to explain how Josephus, who proudly traces his Hasmonean ancestry and who numbered himself a Pharisee, would have gladly indicted both his ancestry and his affiliation in these sections of his writings.[44]

However, while accepting the accuracy of Josephus' narratives, P.-E. Guillet attempts to argue that ἀνασταυρόω in these passages does not refer to

---

[42] In *Ant.* xiii.381–82 Josephus recalls the ways Alexander had been injured (note ἠδίκητο) – injuries that provoked his gruesome revenge. However, the parallel narrative in *Bell.* i.97 has no such account. Also note that the Jews' venomous reproach to Alexander's call for peace is stronger in *Bell.* i.92 than in *Ant.* xiii.376. For other examples of Josephus' gentler account of Jannaeus in the *Antiquities* one could contrast *Ant.* xiii.320–23 with *Bell.* i.85.

[43] *Bell.* i.97: προύκοψεν δ' αὐτῷ δι' ὑπερβολὴν ὀργῆς εἰς ἀσέβειαν τὸ τῆς ὠμότητος· τῶν γὰρ ληφθέντων ὀκτακοσίους ἀνασταυρώσας ἐν μέσῃ τῇ πόλει γυναῖκάς τε καὶ τέκνα αὐτῶν ἀπέσφαξεν ταῖς ὄψεσι· καὶ ταῦτα πίνων καὶ συγκατακείμενος ταῖς παλλακίσιν ἀφεώρα. "So furious was he that his savagery went to the length of impiety. He had eight hundred of his captives *crucified* in the midst of the city, and their wives and children butchered before their eyes, while he looked on, drinking, with his concubines reclining beside him." The Loeb edition conjectures [ἐν] before ταῖς ὄψεσι; this seems unwarranted based on the manuscripts, but it does not affect Marcus' Loeb translation given above.

[44] This is not to vouchsafe details such as the excessively large rounded numbers. However, the mention of crucifixion, given the intensity of focus on that action, is not a mere detail to Josephus in this incident.

crucifixion, but to "impalement" (to which he finds precedence among Jewish rulers in Num 25:4).[45] But Guillet's conjecture is based on an inadequate understanding of the semantics of ἀνασταυρόω in Josephus' writings. The term certainly means "crucify" everywhere else in the *War* and probably through most of the *Antiquities*; therefore, Josephus' readers could hardly have thought ἀνασταυρόω meant anything different here.[46] More significantly, the *Antiquities* text clearly indicates that the children and wives are slain "before the eyes" of their "still living" (ἔτι ζώντων) crucified father/husbands subsequent to the act of crucifixion itself (after ἀνασταυρῶσαι in the text).[47] Hence, their deaths are represented here by Josephus as prolonged suspensions of the still living victims for purposes of execution.

The context in Josephus' two accounts clearly identifies the eight hundred crucified individuals as Jews who fought against Alexander, but the narratives do not specify by name the exact Jewish group or groups involved.[48] Contemporary scholarship has often considered them Pharisees,[49] an identification that has been crucial in the literature on the Qumran Nahum Pesher.[50] To understand why, we must continue with Josephus' report.

According to Josephus, the end result of Alexander's brutality was that eight thousand of his opponents fled into exile, returning only upon his death (*Bell.* i.98; *Ant.* xiii.383). Conspicuously, when Alexander Jannaeus dies, the Pharisees are numbered among his chief enemies (*Ant.* xiii.400–406); and it is those very Pharisees who seek revenge on the individuals who counseled Alexander to crucify the eight hundred (slaughtering many).[51]

---

[45] P.-E. Guillet, "Les 800 «Crucifiés» d'Alexandre Jannée," *Cahiers du Cercle Ernest Renan* 25 (1977): 11–16. Guillet principally cites the earlier authors Thucydides, Herodotus, and Plato as supporting "impalement" and not crucifixion. However, he is forced to concede that Polybius, Plutarch, and Valerius Maximus (writers closer to the time of Josephus) use the term ἀνασταυρόω to designate "crucifixion" (ibid., 13).

[46] E.g., *Bell.* ii.75, 241, 253, 306–8; iii.321; v.289, 449–51; vii.202 – all of these being analogous instances of leaders who put down insurrections (see further below).

[47] *Ant.* xiii.380–81. A similar idea is also found in his *Jewish War*, where the wives and children are slain "before their eyes" (ταῖς ὄψεσι; *Bell.* i.97).

[48] *Bell.* i.96 calls them τὸ λοιπὸν πλῆθος ("the remaining multitude"), presumably of those οἱ Ἰουδαῖοι (i.92) who had called for Demetrius' help. In the *Antiquities* Josephus is more straightforward in identifying them as οἱ Ἰουδαῖοι (*Ant.* xiii.379).

[49] Often this is just assumed: e.g., Hengel, *Crucifixion*, 84.

[50] See §2.4 below.

[51] So *Bell.* i.113 Διογένην γοῦν τινα τῶν ἐπισήμων, φίλον Ἀλεξάνδρῳ γεγενημένον, κτείνουσιν αὐτοί σύμβουλον ἐγκαλοῦντες γεγονέναι περὶ τῶν ἀνασταυρωθέντων ὑπὸ τοῦ βασιλέως ὀκτακοσίων. ἐνῆγον δὲ τὴν Ἀλεξάνδραν εἰς τὸ καὶ τοὺς ἄλλους διαχειρίσασθαι τῶν παροξυνάντων ἐπ᾽ ἐκείνους τὸν Ἀλέξανδρον· ἐνδιδούσης δ᾽ ὑπὸ δεισιδαιμονίας ἀνῄρουν οὓς ἐθέλοιεν αὐτοί. "Thus they [i.e., the Pharisees] put to death Diogenes, a distinguished man who had been a friend of Alexander, accusing him of having

Also, later in the *Antiquities* narrative, though not in the *War*, Josephus represents Alexander's supposed deathbed conversation with his wife, Queen Alexandra. Alexander suggests that the queen should offer his body to the Pharisees so that they might do with the body as they please – even permitting them "*to dishonour my corpse by leaving it unburied* because of the many injuries they have suffered at my hand, *or in their anger to offer my dead body any other form of indignity*" (*Ant.* xiii.403). This deathbed offer to the Pharisees to allow Alexander's body to remain unburied and suffer "any other form of indignity" could conceivably be an allusive reference to a potential *quid pro quo* retribution for Alexander's crucifixion of the eight hundred men. In other words, the Pharisees, having witnessed the crucifixions performed by Alexander along with the consequential heinous lack of proper burial of the eight hundred, are to be provided opportunity to respond in kind to the body of Alexander.[52] That Josephus can portray Alexander as confident that the Pharisees would reject such an offer could be due in the narrative to Alexander's knowledge that the Pharisee's lust for power would cause them instead to exalt the former king's burial.[53] Or, alternatively, perhaps the careful reader should infer that the Pharisees would be legally opposed to leaving his body unburied.[54] Quite likely both motives may be evidenced in the text. In any case, the Queen follows her husband's counsel. The Pharisees respond by burying and eulogizing the corpse, and by taking up the reigns of power.[55]

In Josephus' estimation the Pharisees are a major political force in Israel at this time. They are known enemies of Jannaeus. And they take violent retri-

---

advised the king to crucify his eight hundred victims. They further urged Alexandra to make away with the others who had instigated Alexander to punish those men; and as she from superstitious motives always gave way, they proceeded to kill whomsoever they would." Also see *Ant.* xiii.410.

[52] Hengel contends that the Pharisees in fact did retaliate by crucifying the supporters of Alexander; see §2.5 below.

[53] Evidence for this might be deduced from the way that the Pharisees not only bury Alexander, but eulogise him (*Ant.* xiii.406). Such eulogies could serve to re-affirm, possibly even to raise, the popular stature of the dynasty, thus helping to confirm the power of Alexandra (who, in Josephus' narrative, has already stated her willingness to honour the Pharisees).

[54] Note the force of the word καθυβρίζειν in "whether they wish to *dishonour* my corpse by leaving it unburied" (*Ant.* xiii.403; cf. *Ant.* v.148; vi.344; xx.116). Evidence of this could also be deduced from the Mishnaic texts on burial practices (cf. *m. Sanh.* vi.5), and from Josephus' own conceptions of the importance of burial (*Ant.* iv.264–65; *Bell.* iv.317). It is also possible that the biblical tradition of honouring the king could play a part in these legal issues regarding burial.

[55] Note in *Ant.* xiii.405 that Alexandra is said to have placed in [the Pharisees] hands "both the matters concerning his corpse and [those concerning] the kingdom" (τά τε περὶ τοῦ νεκροῦ καὶ [τὰ περὶ] τῆς βασιλείας (the bracketed τὰ περὶ is omitted by Niese, though it appears in the Loeb edition and in a majority of manuscripts). Also cf. xiii.401.

bution on those whom they associate with Jannaeus' crucifixion of the eight hundred.[56] However, it should be admitted that Josephus himself nowhere identifies the eight hundred with the Pharisees. In fact, prior to Alexander's death, Pharisees are not mentioned at all in connection with him. Therefore, some have rejected the correlation of these eight hundred with the Pharisees.[57]

Certainly, given the many thousands of rebels operating against Alexander, it would be surprising if all of the eight hundred were Pharisees. Yet, given the way the Pharisees emerge as Alexander's chief opponents, it is not unlikely that at least some of those slaughtered were Pharisees. Thus it is probably best not to "identify" the eight hundred as Pharisees, but rather to admit the strong possibility that at least some crucified rebels would have had such allegiances. Therefore, people roughly contemporaneous with the period may have thought pre-eminently of the Pharisees as those who were crucified (see §2.4 on the Nahum Pesher). The resulting early Jewish perceptions about these crucifixions likely would then have depended upon one's viewpoint of the Pharisaic movement and of the broader rebellion against Alexander – to some these crucified men may have appeared as martyrs, but to others they would resemble criminals or rebels receiving their just due.

Josephus' Alexander Jannaeus narratives therefore represent a Jewish king who, on a massive scale, crucified his own people, albeit rebellious ones. Alexander's action was, according to Josephus, counseled by some of his advisors (*Bell.* i.113). Hence it seems less a momentary irrational act and more of a considered policy. The Pharisees violently opposed those who advocated this impious act. The general perceptions that accrued to such horrible deaths were likely influenced by how a person was related to, or felt about, Alexander and his opponents. Josephus himself believed Alexander's actions to have been inhumane and religiously impious.

2.4 Crucifixion and the Nahum Pesher

The Nahum Pesher, though published many years ago, has remained at the centre of Qumran studies and debates. It was one of the first few sectarian texts to be found that referred to specific historical names and events. It also

---

[56] To connect the Pharisees to Alexander's mass crucifixions, Schiffman further draws attention to rabbinic sources (esp. *m. Sukk.* iv.9 and *b. Qidd.* 61a [*sic*, should be 66a]) that parallel these events; Lawrence H. Schiffman, "Pharisees and Sadducees in *Pesher Nahum*," in *Minhah le-Nahum*, ed. Marc Brettler and Michael Fishbane, JSOTSup 154 (Sheffield: JSOT Press, 1993), 275–79.

[57] C. Rabin, "Alexander Jannaeus and the Pharisees," *JJS* 7 (1956): 3–11. Grabbe, though not denying the possibility that a portion of the eight hundred were Pharisees, has asserted that the standard 800=Pharisees view has not been well argued; see Lester L. Grabbe, "The Current State of the Dead Sea Scrolls: Are There More Answers than Questions?" in *The Scrolls and the Scriptures: Qumran Fifty Years After*, ed. Stanley E. Porter and Craig A. Evans, JSPSup 26 (Sheffield: Sheffield Academic Press, 1997), 58–60.

has a much-discussed reference to crucifixion. Though some initially questioned whether crucifixion was intended in the text, as will be seen below later analysis has confirmed this interpretation.

The following represents a portion of the scroll (4QpNah 3–4 i 1–9) without reconstructed readings, save in line 9 where there is a likely citation of Nahum 2:14 (thus providing some basis for determining probable line length). [58] As will be discussed below, the probable line length is crucial for any reliable reconstruction. Allegro notes that the original column width should be between 13.5 to 16 cm., depending on the length of reconstructed text between fragments 3 and 4 of line 9.[59]

	frag. 4	*frag. 3*
] 1	]מדור לרשעי גוים אשר הלך ארי לבוא60 שם גור ארי[[	
] 2	]טרוס מלך יון אשר בקש לבוא ירושלים בעצת דורשי החלקות	
] 3	]ביד מלכי יון מאנתיכוס עד עמוד מושלי כתיים ואחר תרמס	
] 4	] ארי טורף בדי גוריו ומחנק61 ללביותיו טרף	
] 5	] על כפיר החרון אשר יכה בגדוליו ואנשי עצתו	
] 6	]חורה62 ומעונתו טרפה פשרו על כפיר החרון	
] 7	]מות בדורשי החלקות אשר יתלה אנשים חיים	
] 8	]בישראל מלפנים כי לתלוי חי על העץ [יק]רא הנני אלי[כה	
9	נא[ם יהוה צבאות והבערתי בעשן רובכ]ה וכפידיכה תאכל חרב והכר[תי מארץ ט]רפה	

---

[58] Allegro's *editio princeps* is found in *DJD* 5, pp. 37–42 (plates xii–xiv). His initial publication of the passage is found in J. M. Allegro, "Further Light on the History of the Qumran Sect," *JBL* 75 (1956): 89–95. The text below generally follows Allegro in *DJD* 5. However, I have also incorporated the important textual suggestions made by John Strugnell, "Notes en marge du volume V des «Discoveries in the Judaean Desert of Jordan»," *RevQ* 7 (1970): 204–10. I have also consulted the following other transcribed texts: Maurya P. Horgan, *Pesharim: Qumran Interpretations of Biblical Books*, CBQMS 8 (Washington, DC: Catholic Biblical Association of America, 1979), 47; Gregory L. Doudna, *4Q Pesher Nahum: A Critical Edition*, JSPSup 35 (London: Sheffield Academic Press, 2001), 758; Maurya P. Horgan, "Nahum Pesher (4Q169 = 4QpNah)," in *The Dead Sea Scrolls: Hebrew, Aramaic, and Greek Texts with English Translations*, ed. James H. Charlesworth, vol. 6b: Pesharim, Other Commentaries, and Related Documents (Tübingen: Mohr Siebeck; Louisville: Westminster/John Knox, 2002), 148–49; and Shani L. Berrin, *The Pesher Nahum Scroll from Qumran: An Exegetical Study of 4Q169*, STDJ 53 (Leiden: Brill, 2004), 34.

[59] Allegro, "Further Light," 89.

[60] Allegro originally read לביא (as in the MT); but Strugnell ("Notes en marge," 207) contends the letter at issue is a *waw* (as in line 2). See further Horgan, *Pesharim*, 172; idem, "Nahum Pesher," 148. Recently, both Doudna (*4Q Pesher Nahum*, 111–16) and Berrin (*Pesher Nahum*, 34) follow Allegro, though with different results. The orthographic similarities to לבוא in line 2 have led me to follow Strugnell.

[61] Allegro in *DJD* 5 reads just מחנק. Strugnell ("Notes en marge," 207) argues for ומחנק, as was originally published by Allegro in "Further Light," 90. Doudna (*4Q Pesher Nahum*, 127–28) testifies to the difficulty given the small break in the MS here.

[62] Allegro originally חירה. Strugnell contends for חורה ("Notes en marge," 207), and is followed by Horgan, *Pesharim*, text p. 47; and idem, "Nahum Pesher," 148. Doudna follows Allegro (*4Q Pesher Nahum*, 131–36).

1 [...] dwelling for the wicked ones of the nations. *Where the lion went to enter,*[63] *there the cub*[64] *of the lion...*(Nah 2:12)

2 [... Deme]trios[65] king of Javan, who sought to enter Jerusalem with the counsel of the Seekers-of-Smooth-Things

3 [...] into the hand of[66] the kings of Javan from Antikos until the rise of the rulers of the Kittim; but after(wards) [...][67] will be trampled

4 [...] *Lion tears enough*[68] *for his cubs and strangles prey for his lionesses* (Nah 2:13a)

5 [...] on account of[69] the Angry Young Lion, who would strike with his great ones and men of his counsel

6 [*...and fill*] *cave*[70] *and his lair [with] prey.* (Nah 2:13b)   Its interpretation concerns the Angry Young Lion

7 [...]*mwt* in the Seekers-of-Smooth-Things; who will hang up living men[71]

8 [...] in Israel before, for concerning one hanged alive upon the tree [it] reads, *Behold I am against you,*

9 *say*[*s the LORD of hosts, and I shall burn your abundance*[72] *with smoke*] *and a sword will eat your young lions, and I shall cut off from the earth (its) prey.* (Nah 2:14)

Based on the assumption that the small fragment 3 properly belongs to the right hand of this column, and the probability that line 9 (as reconstructed

---

[63] Understanding the text to read לבוא. If one reads לביא, the result is either a Hiphil infinitive of בוא ("made to enter"), or an alternate Hebrew term for lion or lioness (see Doudna, *4Q Pesher Nahum*, 112–116).

[64] Most translate גור as "cub," though Doudna argues for an infinitive construct – "sojourning" or "dwelling" (*4Q Pesher*, 112).

[65] If the *waw* is read instead as a *yod* then translate "Demetris," as Doudna (*4Q Pesher Nahum*, 758) or Berrin (*Pesher Nahum*, 34). All identify him as a Demetrius (see further below). Horgan ("Nahum Pesher," 149) suggests that the lacuna reads: "*and no one to disturb. Its interpretation concerns Demetrius...*"

[66] On alternative reconstructions of the first word of this line, see Horgan, *Pesharim*, 173.

[67] Horgan (*Pesharim*, 163 and text p. 47) suggests for the beginning of line 4: העיר "the city" (i.e., Jerusalem); thus her translation runs "but afterwards [the city] will be trampled [and will be given into the hand of the rulers of the Kittim]." In her later treatment, Horgan admits, "This proposed restoration is shorter than the lacuna" ("Nahum Pesher," 148n.); however, this may work in her favour, since one would expect space prior to the next citation of Nahum 2:13a in line 4 of the *Pesher*.

[68] בדי could also be translated as "limbs of [his cubs]."

[69] Horgan rightly notes that Allegro's reconstruction [על פשרו ...] "its interpretation concerns" does not ultimately provide enough letters to fill the missing units (*Pesharim*, 175). However, her own suggestion ("The interpretation of it concerns Demetrius, who made war [מלחמה עשה אשר] against the Lion of Wrath"), could be improved since it requires an odd combination of על and עשה (though possibly cf. Judg 20:9; Neh 2:19 – neither close parallels; I could find no such use with מלחמה). She later repeats this suggestion in "Nahum Pesher," 149n.

[70] On the difficulties with חורה see Horgan, *Pesharim*, 175–76.

[71] The central problem here concerns the use of אשר in line seven. Some options will be discussed below. The translation above assumes that אשר begins a relative clause referring to a single individual (other than the Seekers-of-Smooth-Things).

[72] MT has רִכְבָּה "her chariot"; here רובכה as in line 10.

above) is a citation of Nah 2:14 (EVV 2:13), Horgan has calculated the
number of units (i.e., characters) missing in each line.[73] The above text is a
rough attempt, based on the photographs and Horgan's calculations, at
correctly lining up the *right-hand side* of fragment 4 with the appropriate
spacing from fragment 3.[74] This should make more apparent the approximate
number of characters needed for reconstructing the missing text between the
fragments (an important matter discussed below).

Strugnell dates the bookhand to a formal type from the late Hasmonean or
early Herodian periods.[75] If Strugnell is correct, then theories based on a late
date for the composition are necessarily ruled out.[76] Further discussion of the
composition date then moves to historical reconstruction of the second and
first century BCE events the scroll describes, and this has proven to be a matter of some controversy.

As is typical of Qumran *pesharim*, in this excerpt a series of biblical quotations are cited along with their interpretation (which is generally introduced
by פשרו). As is also frequently the case, the *pesher* interpretation is typically
preceded by some blank space to separate it from the biblical passage
(cf. line 6).

The crucial crucifixion passage appears in lines six to eight. That the
phrase in line seven אשר יתלה אנשים חיים ("who will hang up living men")
refers to crucifixion, while initially debated, has now long been the scholarly
consensus.[77] In particular, a similar phrase in the *Sifre* to Deuteronomy
(§221), which is modified in some important manuscripts by "in the manner
which the [Roman] government does," has convinced most that this Hebrew
wording refers to crucifixion (see further below in chapter three §4.7). There

---

[73] Horgan, *Pesharim*, 171.

[74] Unfortunately, given the character widths on the printed Hebrew font employed in this
publication, it was not reasonable above to attempt to line up every character relative to its
exact location in the manuscript itself. Nonetheless, I decided that, due to the need to discuss
the possible text now lost between fragments 3 and 4, the crucial item here was the missing
space between the two fragments.

[75] Strugnell, "Notes en marge," 205. The conclusion appears generally accepted (see e.g.,
Berrin, *Pesher Nahum*, 8) though Doudna argues the "Herodian" script may have developed a
few decades earlier than commonly thought (see *4Q Pesher Nahum*, 675–82).

[76] E.g., Solomon Zeitlin, "The Dead Sea Scrolls: A Travesty on Scholarship," *JQR* 47
(1956–1957): 31–36; Arthur E. Palumbo, "A New Interpretation of the Nahum
Commentary," *FO* 29 (1992–1993): 153–62.

[77] The Wieder and Zeitlin debate was noted in our previous chapter. See N. Wieder,
"Notes on the New Documents from the Fourth Cave of Qumran," *JJS* 7 (1956): 71–72; S.
Zeitlin, "The Phrase יתלה אנשים חיים," *JJS* 8 (1957): 117–18; N. Wieder, "Rejoinder," *JJS*
8 (1957): 119–21. Even Baumgarten, who is reticent about conceding crucifixion in
11QTemple lxiv.6–13, admits this is a reference to crucifixion; see Joseph M. Baumgarten,
"Does *TLH* in the Temple Scroll Refer to Crucifixion?" *JBL* 91 (1972): 478–79. See also the
opinion in Berrin, *Pesher Nahum*, 172–73.

are, however, two important questions that remain: (1) when did these events ostensibly occur, and (2) how did the author perceive the crucifixions?

The timing of the events must be fixed on the basis of the names given. First, in line 2 there is a reference to [ ]טרוס מלך יון. It is generally agreed this must be one Demetrios, king of Javan (= the Greeks). Hence the text states that a Hellenistic Demetrius attempted to enter Jerusalem. Second, line three reads "[into the] hands of the kings of Javan from Antikos until the rise of the rulers of the Kittim." Again, it is agreed that אנתיכוס is properly identified as Antiochus, and that the "Kittim" are the Romans. This verse, by stating two temporal bookends, locates the author's time of writing after the rise of the Romans. Most reconstructions also allow these temporal bookends to define the time during which Demetrius sought to enter Jerusalem. Yet there are two major interpretations concerning Demetrius: (1) the most common view is that Demetrius is Demetrius III Eukairos, who was invited by a massive group of Jewish rebels to help them do battle against Alexander Jannaeus (with the crucifixions here in 4QpNahum being those incidents from Josephus discussed above in §2.3);[78] or (2) Demetrius is Demetrius I Soter (c. 162–150 BCE) who brutally aided the Jewish priest Alcimus in containing Judas Maccabeus[79] (with the crucifixions in lines 7–8 being performed either by Antiochus Epiphanes,[80] or by Alcimus in his execution of his Jewish rivals[81]).

Perhaps identification with the times of Alexander Jannaeus is more probable in view of another Qumran text that refers to Alexander's Queen Salome (4Q322),[82] and in light of the prominence that Josephus gives to his account of Alexander's acts of crucifixion. If correlation with Josephus' histories is attempted, then Alexander Jannaeus is indeed the preferable candidate for the title "Angry Young Lion" in 4QpNahum. As noted above (in §2.2), Josephus does not record Alcimus as engaging in crucifixion. Also, although Josephus does report mass crucifixions under Antiochus Epiphanes (see above §2.1), it

---

[78] Many have advocated for this position, but most recently see Berrin, *Pesher Nahum*, 87–130. Tantlevskij's proposal, however, appears to me too specific; see Igor R. Tantlevskij, "The Reflection of the Political Situation in Judaea in 88 B.C.E. in the Qumran Commentary on Nahum (4QpNah, Columns 1–4)," *St. Petersburg Journal of Oriental Studies* 6 (1994): 221–31.

[79] Rowley contends that, if the "Kittim" are the Romans, this could be from the time in which they first play a rôle in the politics of Israel (i.e., when Judas Maccabeus sent an embassy to the senate). See H. H. Rowley, "4QpNahum and the Teacher of Righteousness," *JBL* 75 (1956): 192. See further Isaac Rabinowitz, "The Meaning of the Key ('Demetrius')-Passage of the Qumran Nahum-Pesher," *JAOS* 98 (1978): 394–99.

[80] So Rowley, "4QpNahum," 192–93.

[81] So Stauffer, *Jerusalem*, 124–25; 128–32.

[82] See Geza Vermes, *The Complete Dead Sea Scrolls in English* (London: Allen Lane, 1997), 56.

is more difficult to understand the Pharisees (the most common modern identification of the "Seekers-of-Smooth-Things" in the Nahum Pesher and in
other Qumran literature) as the specific people whom Antiochus Epiphanes
put to death, especially when compared to Josephus' account of Alexander
Jannaeus (whom Josephus likely implies did crucify Pharisees). Nonetheless,
some scholars are willing to move beyond Josephus' description of the events,
contending that Josephus did not report every crucifixion ever known in
Palestine.[83] Still, the identification with Alexander Jannaeus remains slightly
more probable than the other options.

In any case, for this thesis the most important question concerns the perceptions of crucifixion of the author/community behind the scroll. In large
part this issue revolves around the correct reconstruction of the missing sections of lines seven to eight.

In line seven, one major issue concerns how to understand the אשר clause.
There are two main options: (1) it is the relative pronoun "who" and refers
either to the Seekers-of-Smooth-Things or to the preceding subject of the verb
now missing earlier in line seven; or (2) it introduces a subordinate clause and
can be translated by "when." Both are grammatically possible, though the
employment of אשר as a relative pronoun is by far the most common usage in
the *Pesharim*.

Though not impossible, it is unlikely that the "Seekers-of-Smooth-Things"
form the subject of the אשר clause, despite the proximity of בדורשי החלקות
to אשר. That is to say, it is unlikely that the Seekers-of-Smooth-Things perform the crucifixions in this passage. For one, they would constitute a plural
subject with a singular verb (יתלה; contrast 4QpNah 3–4 ii 2, 8; also iii 7).
For another, אשר clauses in *pesher* interpretations generally identify contemporary individuals with aspects of the prophetic text, and they do so by
referring to non-prefixed nouns placed after phrases such as פשרו על (cf. the
preceding line 6); but the Seekers-of-Smooth-Things in line seven bears a ב
prefix. This prefix connects the Seekers-of-Smooth-Things to a more prominent noun (missing from the extant MS), which would be the more likely
subject of יתלה. Possibly there were two אשר clauses in line seven, with the
first lost to decay of the manuscript (cf. the following lines 11 and 12). Therefore, I see no reason to discount the common understanding that the subject of
יתלה is anyone other than the "Angry Young Lion" in line six.

It thus appears that some single individual (probably the "Angry Young
Lion") has been executing others via crucifixion. Generally, most scholars do
not read the "living men" (אנשים חיים, who were reported crucified in line 7)

---

[83] Doudna argues that crucifixion would certainly have been anticipated to come with the
appearance of the Roman leader Pompey on the scene, and thus he dates the events to prophetic expectation of judgment on the Seekers-of-Smooth-Things projected onto the foreseen
arrival of Pompey (*4Q Pesher Nahum*, esp. pp. 670–72).

as *grammatically equivalent* to the דורשי החלקות ("Seekers-of-Smooth-Things"), though the crucified "living men" could have logically included some Seekers-of-Smooth-Things. However, Doudna has suggested that the noun phrase אנשים חיים functions adverbially to יתלה, that the אשר acts as the direct object of its relative clause, and that אשר refers to the Seekers-of-Smooth-Things – "the Seekers-of-Smooth-Things, whom he will hang up (as) living men."[84] This suggestion is certainly plausible; and it has the advantage of explaining both the proximity of אשר to the בדורשי החלקות, and the lack of direct object marker or prepositional prefix on אנשים חיים. Yet, I am reticent to follow Doudna's proposal given that this requires the antecedent of the relative pronoun אשר to be the phrase בדורשי החלקות even though that phrase bears the ב prefix (see my preceding paragraph). In any case, whether based on a grammatical identification or not, it is certainly plausible to believe that at least some of the crucified were from the ranks of the Seekers-of-Smooth-Things.

The sense of how these crucified individuals are viewed in the *Pesher* comes especially from how one reconstructs line eight. Allegro's original suggestion was[85]:

7 [ ]מ[ות בדורשי החלקות אשר יתלה אנשים חיים

8 [אשר לא יעשה]בישראל[מלפנים כי לתלוי חי עֹל הֹעֵֹץ [יק]רא הנני אלי[כה

7 […] death (?) by the Seekers-after-Smooth-Things, who used to hang (or, hangs) men up alive

8 […which was never done (?)] before in Israel, for it (the Scripture) calls the one hanged alive on the tree – *Behold, I am against* [*thee,*

Others have essentially followed Allegro in proposing some sense of horror by the writer against the actions of the Angry Young Lion.[86]

However, Yigael Yadin caused a significant stir when, on the strength of 11QTemple lxiv.6–13 (which appears to validate suspension as a means of execution), he suggested that the author of 4QpNahum would have been in favour of the Lion of Wrath's (=Angry Young Lion's) actions.[87] Since the Nahum Pesher primarily attacks other Jewish sects (especially "the Seekers-after-Smooth-Things"), Yadin held that it would have been unlikely that the

---

[84] Doudna, *4Q Pesher Nahum*, 390–394. Fitzmyer had anticipated this suggestion is his translation of the passage; see Joseph A. Fitzmyer, "Crucifixion in Ancient Palestine, Qumran Literature, and the New Testament," *CBQ* 40 (1978): 493–513.

[85] Allegro, "Further Light," 91.

[86] E.g., André Dupont-Sommer, "Le commentaire de Nahum découvert près de la Mer Morte (4Q p Nah): traduction et notes," *Sem* 13 (1963): 57, 59, 67; Florentino García Martínez, "4QpNah y la Crucifixión: Nueva hipótesis de reconstrucción de 4Q 169 3–4 i, 4–8," *EstBib* 38 (1979–1980): 221–35.

[87] Y. Yadin, "Pesher Nahum (4Q pNahum) Reconsidered," *IEJ* 21 (1971): 1–12. We shall examine 11QTemple lxiv.6–13 below in chapter three.

Qumranites would then criticize the man who had punished such an enemy sect. Yadin contended that "wrath" in the Bible is always associated with God's anger, and hence the "Lion of Wrath" must be God's instrument. He also noted the difficulties that negative associations with the Lion's actions creates in rendering ‫יק]רא‬ in line 8. Hence Yadin proposed the reconstruction[88]:

‫מות בדורשי החלקות אשר יתלה אנשים חיים‬   ‫אשר   משפט]‬ 7
‫על העץ כי זאת/כן התורה/המשפט]בישראל מלפנים כי לתלוי חי על העץ [יק]רא‬ 8

7 [*Who   sentence of*] *death* ‫בדורשי החלקות‬ *(and) who hangs men alive*
8 [*on the tree as this is the law*] *in Israel as of old since the* hanged one is called alive on the tree.

However, Baumgarten questions Yadin's rationale for this translation.[89] Though the Qumran sectarians opposed the "Seekers-of-Smooth-Things," they also could easily have disapproved of the person who "punished" them (note that gentiles afflict the Seekers-of-Smooth-Things in 4QpNah 3–4 ii 4– 5).[90] Further, God's instruments of wrath in biblical prophecy may themselves be held guilty (cf. Isa 10:5–7); and this could likewise be true of the sectarians' view of the Lion of Wrath. Additionally, Baumgarten argues that ‫חרון‬ ("wrath") is not only used to denote God's anger but human anger as well, and thus ‫חרון‬ can be a negative term at Qumran.[91] Finally, Baumgarten remarks that the connotation of "young lion" in 4QpNah 3–4 i 8–12 develops the negative portrayal of the (Assyrian) lion in Nahum 2:12–14, and this would indicate that divine retribution falls against the "young lion" (i.e., Alexander Jannaeus).[92]

Baumgarten, following this argumentation and having rejected Yadin's contention that 11QTemple proves that the Qumran sect commended crucifixion,[93] has suggested two different reconstructions of line eight[94]:

---

[88] Y. Yadin, "Pesher Nahum," 11–12. Yadin allowed himself some room to maneuver in terms of line length by providing two sets of two options in line 8: (1) ‫כן‬ or ‫זאת‬ and (2) ‫המשפט‬ or ‫התורה‬. Essentially the same meaning (and hence translation) would be preserved following either. Unfortunately, both are too short to be the actual missing characters. In a later publication Yadin goes with [‫כי כן המשפט‬]; see Yigael Yadin, *The Temple Scroll*, 3 + suppl. vols. (Jerusalem: Israel Exploration Society, 1977–1983), 1:378.

[89] Baumgarten, "*TLH* in the Temple Scroll," 479–81.

[90] Ibid., 479. Also, in a related vein, see 1QpHab ix.4–7.

[91] Baumgarten ("*TLH* in the Temple Scroll," 480) cites in this regard the "scorching anger" of the Kittim in 1QpHab iii.2 (*sic.*, properly iii.12) – ‫[וב]חרן אף‬.

[92] See both Baumgarten, "*TLH* in the Temple Scroll," 480; and Joseph M. Baumgarten, "Hanging and Treason in Qumran and Roman Law," *ErIsr* 16 (1982): 13*.

[93] The first chapter of this book examined and rejected Baumgarten's lexical arguments that ‫תלה‬ in 11QTemple lxiv.6–13 cannot be a reference to crucifixion. See further on 11QTemple in the next chapter.

(1) [Such a thing had never] before [been done] in Israel, for he (the Young Lion of Wrath) took "hanged" (Deut 21:23) to mean "alive on a tree."

(2) ... for regarding one who *hangs* a living man upon a tree (Scripture) reads: Behold I am against you, says the Lord of hosts.

Essentially then we have two poles with regard to the viewpoint on the crucifixions by the Lion of Wrath in the Nahum Pesher. Yadin and others argue that the Qumranites thought it a valid punishment, while Baumgarten has become an important voice for the revised original assertion that the Qumranites were horrified at the actions of the Lion of Wrath. How are we to arbitrate between these views?

As Horgan notes, one of the significant difficulties with these early textual reconstructions in lines 7 and 8 is that they are all too short and thus all fail to fill the character space present in the missing right hand of the scroll.[95] Consequentially, no early reconstruction accomplished a full explanation of the whole text. Recent proposals have been more careful here. Nonetheless, each reconstruction must be viewed as somewhat tenuous, since the decision about whether the author of the *Pesher* thought this punishment was appropriate almost necessarily precedes the actual process of reconstruction. What then should we conclude?

Baumgarten appears correct in challenging Yadin's assertion that "wrath" is always a positive concept used only of God; and thus Baumgarten rightly questions Yadin's contention that an instrument of wrath can only be viewed as a positive entity. Indeed, the "Lion" is not represented as a positive figure either in the biblical Nahum or in the *Pesher* itself (cf. the interpretation of Nah 2:14 in lines 10ff.). This supports the conclusion that the actions of the Lion may have been viewed negatively, or at least neutrally. Furthermore, a negative view in the *Pesher* coincides better with Josephus' account of Alexander, although one should not assume that the sectarian author of 4QpNahum shared Josephus' perspective on such events. Certainly one cannot see in the *Pesher* itself any reason to believe the author praised the Angry Young Lion for any other activity. However, while it is likely that the figure who crucifies others was perceived negatively or (at best) neutrally in this text, it is nonetheless notable that someone of Yadin's academic ability could recognize sufficient precedent within Second Temple Jewish literature to conceive of a Jewish community speaking positively of an execution by

---

[94] Note neither translates by itself the whole line (the first omits the last two words, the second omits the first two extant Hebrew words). The first appears in Baumgarten, "TLH in the Temple Scroll," 481. Baumgarten later rejects this first translation in view of the second (which to its detriment requires the passive participle לתלוי to bear an active sense); see Baumgarten, "Hanging," 14*.

[95] Horgan, *Pesharim*, 171.

suspension (his arguments concerning 11QTemple we must examine in chapter three).

A crucial question involves ascertaining how lines seven and eight relate to the יק[רא] ("it reads") at the end of verse eight and to the subsequent quotation of Nahum 2:14 in lines eight through ten. This has proven to be a difficult matter since biblical quotations in the *Pesharim* usually have no introductory verb connecting them with the text preceding the biblical citation. For this reason, some scholars have amended the text here by adding words to complete יקרא.[96] However, the text as it stands most naturally applies the judgment of Nahum 2:14 on the one who is hung on a tree ("for concerning one hanged alive upon the tree [it] reads, *Behold I am against you, says the LORD of hosts*"). This translation implies that the person hung was evidently viewed negatively by the author of the Nahum Pesher.[97]

In conclusion, the Nahum Pesher refers to an act of crucifixion in Palestine somewhere in the second to first century BCE. The probabilities still favour this being a reference to the crucifixions enacted by Alexander Jannaeus, though one must admit both the fragmentary nature of the text and the lack of full scholarly consensus. The crucified victims appear to be theologically indicted by Nahum 2:14 ("behold I am against you says the Lord of Hosts"). In light of the fragmented text, it is disputed whether the one performing the crucifixions met the approval or rejection of the author. Although the Angry Young Lion may be indicted here, quite possibly the author of this *pesher* simply reported the event as evidence of God's opposition to the Seekers-of-Smooth-Things and to their colleagues. Nonetheless, it should be admitted that the interpretation of this text has been frequently debated. The importance of the text requires that it be examined, while the disputes caution us against resting conclusions about ancient Jewish perceptions of crucifixion on this text alone without correlating this passage with other sources.

2.5 Simeon b. Shetach and the Witches of Ashkelon

האיש תולין אותו פניו כלפי־העם והאשה פניה כלפי־העץ דברי־רבי־אליעזר. וחכמים אומרים האיש נתלה ואין האשה נתלית. אמר להם רבי אליעזר והלא מעשה בשמעון בן שטח שתלה שמנים נשים באשקלון. אמרו לו שמנים נשים תלה ואין דנין שנים ביום אחד.

"The man – they hang him with his face towards the people; the woman – her face towards the tree." says Rabbi Eliezer. But the sages say, "The man is hung, but the woman is not hung." Rabbi Eliezer said to them, "But did not Simeon ben Shetach hang eighty women in Ashkelon?" They said to him, "Eighty women he hung, but two are not judged in a single day."

---

[96] E.g., Doudna adds מקולל אל after יקרא to read "For one hanged alive on [a stake is cal]led {'accursed of God'}"; see *4Q Pesher Nahum*, 758–59, and esp. pp. 421–25.

[97] A similar conclusion has been argued in much greater detail by Berrin, *Pesher Nahum*, 165–92.

This fascinating interchange in *m. Sanh.* vi.4 occurs in the midst of the Mishnaic discussion of the law of hanging in Deuteronomy 21:22–23. Several questions arise concerning this law: Who may be hung? How many may be hung at once? And what direction are they hung?[98] Rabbi Eliezer, who is well-known for his appeal to historical precedent, invokes the story of Simeon ben Shetach and his hanging of women.

The *Sifre on Deuteronomy* §221 repeats this rabbinic debate, though it focuses solely on whether women should be hung (the direction of hanging is not mentioned).[99] More important is how the *Sifre* treats Simeon's breach of the rabbinic ruling that only one person a day should be tried in a death penalty case. The *Sifre* adds at the end, "But this was needed of the moment, to teach others by it."[100] In comparison to the Mishnah, the *Sifre* apparently attempts to mitigate the renunciation of Simeon's deviant practice. Simeon, it must be remembered, was one of the *zugot* and highly praised as a predecessor of the Pharisaic and rabbinic tradition.

The narrative in the Mishnah and *Sifre* only provides the bare essentials of the Simeon episode – his name, that eighty women were involved, and that he hung them. Suspension is clearly associated with their execution, but the text does not tell us if death preceded their hangings, or if they were alive for a while during their suspensions. However, two key passages in the Yerushalmi develop this story.

The Yerushalmi narratives in both *y. Ḥag.* ii.2 [77d–78a] and *y. Sanh.* vi.9 [23c–d] recall a basically similar tale, though in each location it is tailored to fit the context and the issues at hand.[101] Both accounts begin with a prolonged introduction about two holy men, one of whom ultimately learns that Simeon b. Shetach stands guilty of having left unfulfilled his commitment to kill the witches in Ashkelon. When Simeon is confronted with his own guilt, he determines to keep his promise by employing a ruse to execute the witches. Simeon, pretending to be a sorcerer, approaches the witches' lair. He convinces these witches that he can supply them with handsome men; and they beg him to do so. Simeon, who has secretly brought with him a man for each

---

[98] These questions, and other rabbinic halakhic treatments of Deuteronomy 21:22–23, are analyzed below in chapter three (§4.7).

[99] Some manuscripts of the *Sifre* do mention a debate later in §221 about the direction of hanging for men *and women*, but the discussion is only on the lips of R. Judah. Though this dispute is not in early important witnesses to the text (and is placed in smaller lettering in Finkelstein's edition, pp. 254–55), it has some plausible connection in comparison to the stoning saying of R. Judah in *t. Sanh.* ix.6 (note R. Judah attributes his tradition there to R. Eliezer).

[100] אלא שהשעה צריכה ללמד בה את אחרים.

[101] *Ḥagigah* is concerned more with the issue of who was *nasi* between Judah b. Tabbai and Simeon b. Shetach, while *Sanhedrin* wishes to develop the explanation behind R. Eliezer's appeal to this story.

sorceress, calls his men out of hiding. He orders the men to lift the witches off the ground, thus causing the witches to lose their magical powers. Then each witch is suspended until dead.

Important to this story is the assumption that the witches must die in a way in which they are no longer in touch with the ground. A well-rehearsed theme in ancient literature on witchcraft is that the sorceress must be in touch with the earth from which she draws her powers.[102] Thus, both versions of the Yerushalmi tale necessitate that these women are actually executed by some form of suspension. They are certainly not hung *post mortem*, and thus, since the *Sifre* (§221) only approves of postmortem suspension, the tales diverge from the procedure sanctioned in the *Sifre* for carrying out the hanging called for in Deuteronomy 21:22–23. Furthermore, because the Yerushalmi narratives employ the term צלב and its cognates, these tales could naturally be understood in antiquity as connecting such executionary suspensions with the kinds of penalties that included crucifixion.

M. Hengel has well noted the many mythical elements in this story: e.g., witchcraft, the suspiciously round number eighty, the visionary context in the introduction, and the setting ("Ashkelon" – enemy territory – hardly a place where a Jewish leader could expect to slaughter eighty women without reprisal).[103] Hengel wishes to go behind these mythological elements in order to determine what historical event inspired this tale. He argues forcefully, based on Simeon b. Shetach's known opposition to Alexander Jannaeus, that this narrative represents an encoded tale about Pharisaic retribution (led by Simeon) on those who had counseled the crucifixion of eight hundred Jews under Jannaeus. These men associated with Alexander were spoken of derisively as "eighty witches." Thus, according to Hengel, the Pharisees retaliated in kind by crucifying the supporters of Alexander.[104]

In evaluating Hengel's thesis, it should be noted that Josephus, our main source for the Pharisaic reaction against Alexander Jannaeus, does not report a crucifixion retaliation by the Pharisees (*Bell.* i.113–14; *Ant.* xiii.410–16). However, this could be attributed either to Josephus' ignorance of specifics, or to his general desire not to associate crucifixion with Pharisaic Jewish leaders.

More troublesome is the manner in which R. Eliezer cites these events to justify a legal point about *women*. If Hengel is correct, then by consequence it

---

[102] See Martin Hengel, *Rabbinische Legende und frühpharisäische Geschichte: Schimeon b. Schetach und die achtzig Hexen von Askalon*, AHAW.PH 1984,2 (Heidelberg: Carl Winter, 1984), 19–20.

[103] Ibid., 41–47. Cf. suggestion in Otto Betz, "Probleme des Prozesses Jesu," in *Aufstieg und Niedergang der Römischen Welt*, ed. Wolfgang Haase, vol. II.25.1 (Berlin/New York: Walter de Gruyter, 1982), 609.

[104] Hengel, *Rabbinische Legende*, 48–57.

must be assumed that probably the true origin of the tale has already been lost by the time of the Mishnah (and possibly by the time of R. Eliezer) such that it has simply become a narrative about suspending women. Alternatively, the point made by R. Eliezer could constitute an inside joke (everyone knows the "witches" were not actually women, but that is the very humour of it all).

Hengel has provided a coherent and well-reasoned scenario to explain the mythical elements that have accrued to this striking tale. But could there be alternative possibilities? For example, one could conceive of Simeon hanging just a few women accused of witchcraft ("eighty" is an exaggeration) in enemy territory, and getting away with it (either because his act went unnoticed, or because the women were not thought worth fighting over). Or "Ashkelon" could mean some despised locale in Israel, though the "women" are still women/witches. Hengel carefully argues the plausibility for his identification of each of the elements in the encoded tale; still, there may well be equally plausible alternatives to his reconstruction.

For this thesis it is not necessary to affirm or deny Hengel's scenario. Rather, in the context of a discussion about ancient Jewish perceptions of crucifixion, it is important to note that later rabbinic tradition could associate an executionary suspension with one of the great *zugot*, who was an esteemed ancestor of Pharisaic and rabbinic tradition. Furthermore, the story certainly varies at several key points from the later officially sanctioned rabbinic procedure by suspending women via mass execution (in all traditions), and by employing suspension as the form of execution (in the Yerushalmi accounts). Clearly, rabbinic traditions that limit the hanging of human bodies to *post mortem* suspension must not have been sufficiently strong to require a re-writing of this tale. And, to the extent that this story corresponds with reality when the mythical elements are removed, it serves as possible historical testimony that the later rabbinic constraints on the exercise of penal suspension were not always in force in earlier periods. Moreover, this narrative associates the execution of purveyors of magic with a penal procedure that was likely understood by many to be in the same sphere of punishment as crucifixion.

3. Crucifixion in the Roman Period

Roman crucifixion was well known to the Jewish people in the imperial provinces. Josephus provides many examples of crucifixions in Palestine, especially during the First Jewish Revolt. Philo notes a remarkable case of government-sponsored persecution in Alexandria. Other literary works corroborate the widespread use of crucifixion by the Romans in Palestine. And one remarkable archaeological find from the outskirts of Jerusalem indicates the use of ossuary reburial in honoring the remains of a crucified man. This section investigates such material remains and literary accounts. Here again the focus continues on ascertaining ancient Jewish perceptions of the cross, rather than on developing a "history of crucifixion" in Palestine.[105]

Hengel contends that the Roman punishment was largely associated with slaves, rebels, and robbers/bandits.[106] Roman citizens, though not in all periods of history truly exempt, generally did not need to fear such a penalty – it was for social classes other than theirs. The penalty was certainly among the worst possible punishments, being specifically treated in several places as the greatest misfortune to befall a man. In Roman literature, barbarian peoples are frequently said to crucify, thus insinuating a kind of barbarous feel to the penalty. Lately, many writers have emphasized the great shame attached to such a penalty – a naked man, beaten and ridiculed, hanging for all to see while he slowly dies, his carcass becoming food for birds. Naturally, these perceptions often are mirrored in the Jewish sources. However, since Jewish revolutionaries, especially in the first century CE, frequently suffered the horrors of the cross, our sources sometimes favour the vantage point of the victims over that of their Roman oppressors.

3.1 Crucifixion in the Time of Varus

We read in Josephus of a mass crucifixion during Varus' governorship of Syria after the death of Herod the Great. While Archelaus (Herod's heir) was away in Rome establishing his claim to the throne, Sabinus (the Roman procurator of Judaea) unwisely sought to contain a minor Jewish uprising

---

[105] One mention of the σταυρός that is not analysed in this chapter concerns the narrative in Dio Cassius (*Roman History* xlix.22.6) of the Roman flogging on a σταυρός of the last Hasmonean Jewish king, Antigonus, around 38–37 BCE. See text in Earnest Cary, *Dio's Roman History*, 9 vols., LCL (Cambridge, Mass.: Harvard; London: Heinemann, 1914–1927), 5:386–389. After Antony's escapades on the eastern frontier, he leaves Gaius Sosius as governor of Syria. Sosius conquers Antigonus in war, leaving the throne now open for Herod, and then he has Antigonus flogged while tied to a cross (τὸν δ᾽ Ἀντίγονον ἐμαστίγωσε σταυρῷ προσδήσας). Yet, in the context of Dio's account, Antigonus is subsequently beheaded (καὶ μετὰ τοῦτο καὶ ἀπέσφαξεν). Though this flogging is called a punishment no other king has suffered by Roman action (ὃ μηδεὶς βασιλεὺς ἄλλος ὑπὸ τῶν Ῥωμαίων ἐπεπόνθει), the death itself apparently was not caused by crucifixion according to Dio. Moreover, Josephus, the one Jewish author who recounts this episode, does not record the use of a σταυρός; rather, he merely reports the event as a beheading (πέλεκυς ἐκδέχεται in *Bell.* i.357; ἀνελεῖν in *Ant.* xiv.490; πελεκίσαι in *Ant.* xv.8). Josephus cites Strabo's *History* (now lost) as a corroborating source (*Ant.* xv.9–10), where Strabo states that Antony's execution of Antigonus constituted the first ever Roman beheading (πελεκίσαι) of a king (also see Plutarch, *Ant.* xxxvi.2, where the death is also described by ἐπελέκισεν). Therefore, save for the fairly remote possibility that Josephus may have wished to downplay any crucifixion overtones in this story (such a claim would require both Dio's account to be accurate, and Josephus to have known about the scourging on the σταυρός), there are no extant Jewish perceptions of crucifixion tied to this event.

[106] Hengel, *Crucifixion*, 46–63 (repr. 138–55).

(and, according to Josephus, to plunder the royal treasury). Sabinus even sent his soldiers to do battle with the Jews inside the Temple precincts, which ultimately resulted in the burning of the Temple porticoes. Eventually Varus had to come to his aide, and, accompanied by two legions plus auxiliaries, conquered the rebellious movement throughout Palestine. After Varus was received in Jerusalem, Josephus narrates (*Bell.* ii.75; cf. *Ant.* xvii.295):

Οὔαρος δὲ κατὰ[107] μοῖραν τῆς στρατιᾶς ἐπὶ τοὺς αἰτίους τοῦ κινήματος ἔπεμψεν περὶ τὴν χώραν, καὶ πολλῶν ἀγομένων τοὺς μὲν ἧττον θορυβώδεις φανέντας ἐφρούρει, τοὺς δ᾽ αἰτιωτάτους ἀνεσταύρωσεν περὶ δισχιλίους.

Varus now detached part of his army to scour the country in search of the authors of the insurrection, many of whom were brought in. Those who appeared to be the less turbulent individuals he imprisoned; the most culpable, in number about two thousand, he crucified.

As is frequently the case in his crucifixion reports in the Roman period, Josephus takes the passionless stance of the observer reporting events. Josephus betrays no sympathy for the lot of the "two thousand." The Romans, whose side Josephus ultimately himself takes in a much more significant revolt, merely act with military precision to put down Jewish rebellion.

However, one could postulate that the relatives and friends of the crucified rebels, as well as those Jews who revolted alongside them, would have taken a much more compassionate stance toward men who, while seeking to rid their nation of Roman hegemony, died such a pitiable death. In fact, in the *Assumption of Moses* we may have other evidence of just such a perspective.

3.2 Crucifixion in the Assumption of Moses

In the *Assumption* (or *"Testament"*) *of Moses*, a clear reference to Herod the Great (the petulant king who reigned for 34 years) is continued with the following narrative (6.7–9):[108]

(7) Et <p>roducit natos <su>ccedentes sibi; breviora tempora do<mi>nabunt.[109] (8) In par<t>es eorum chortis venient et occidentes rex potens qui expugnabit eos (9) et ducet captivos, et partem aedis ipsorum igni incendit, aliquos crucifigit circa coloniam eorum.[110]

(7) And he [the petulant king] will bring forth children who will succeed him. They will rule for shorter periods. (8) Cohorts will come into their territory, and a mighty king from the West, who will defeat them, (9) and lead them off in chains. And he will burn part of their Temple with fire, some he will crucify near their city.

---

[107] According to Niese's edition, the κατά is omitted in four manuscripts; and the Loeb text places it in brackets.

[108] Text and translation are from Johannes Tromp, *The Assumption of Moses: A Critical Edition with Commentary*, SVTP 10 (Leiden: E. J. Brill, 1993), 15–17 (hereafter "Tromp").

[109] Tromp conjectures *do<mi>nabunt* for *donarent*.

[110] The readings *par<t>es*, *chortis*, *qui*, and *ducet* are all conjectured emendations (for *pares*, *mortis*, *quia*, and *ducent* respectively), which Tromp adopts from previous editors of the single extant manuscript.

Assuming for the moment a literary unity to the *Assumption of Moses*, and given that this text follows fast on the heels of a passage concerning Herod, one is encouraged to think that the author was himself writing after Herod's death about specific events immediately subsequent to Herod's demise. The most natural chronology then for "king from the West" would be the time of the Roman legate Varus. While this identification has been questioned, the *Assumption* here has the ring of historical writing – especially the detail that only a portion of the Temple was to be burned. Josephus records both the partial burning of the Temple porticoes under Varus (*Ant.* xvii.261–64), and the captivity and crucifixion of Jewish rebels (*Ant.* xvii.295–98; note that this includes συγγενεῖς ὄντες Ἡρώδου, xvii.298).

In fact, in chapters five to ten of the *Assumption*, at no point is the Second Temple in Jerusalem fully destroyed (contrast *As. Mos.* 3:2 of the first Temple). This provides a strong argument for the book being written before 70 CE. As Tromp acknowledges, the partial burning of the Temple is hard to understand in such a generalized account apart from reference to the time of Varus.[111] However, Tromp contends that, apart from an explanation based on "the author's aspiration to historical precision," this assists the author's literary motif of describing the persecution of chapter six as less than the persecution in chapter eight. Actually, we should note that the fact that a Temple destruction is not mentioned in chapter eight and is mentioned (if only partially) in chapter six, points to the author breaking with his own motif of escalating the destruction between chapters six and eight. Hence the author must have been constrained by historical reality to report in the earlier account an event so significant as the partial destruction of the Temple. Tromp's own dating of the book to a few years after the death of Herod actually favours the argument that the historical events during Varus' rule would have been much in view.[112]

We might ask why the text only mentions "some" (*aliquos*) being crucified, while Josephus numbers two thousand victims of the *crux* under Varus. Tromp correctly emphasizes here the author's desire to contrast the persecution in chapter six with the even harsher events of chapter eight.[113] The author thus underplays his hand on the events of Varus' day, so that he can show that an even worse persecution is around the corner. Hence, after the leadership of Israel by impious men (in chapter seven), the author records in chapter eight:

(1) Et <ci>ta <ad>veniet in eos ultio et ira quae talis non fuit in illis a saeculo usque ad illum tempus in quo suscitavit illis regem regum terrae et potestatem a potentia magna, qui confitentes circumcisionem in cruce suspendit. (2) Nam necantes torquebit, et tradi[di]t duci vinctos in custodiam, (3) et uxores eorum di[i]sdonabuntur gentibus. Et filii eorum pueri

---

111 Tromp, *Assumption*, 204–5.
112 Tromp's dating is found in *Assumption*, pp. 116–17.
113 Ibid., 205.

secabuntur a medicis [pueri] inducere aҫrobis<ti>am illis. (4) Nam illi in eis punientur in tormentis et igne et ferro, et cogentur palam bajulare idola eorum, inquinata quomodọ sunt pariter contin<g>entibus ea. (5) Et a torquentibus illos pariter cogentur intrare in abditum locum eorum, et cogentur stimulis blasfemare verbum contumeliose. Novissime post haec et leges quod habebunt supra altarium suum.

(1) And suddenly revenge and wrath will come over them, such as there will never have been over them since eternity until that time, in which he will raise for them the king of the kings of the earth, and a power with great might, *who will hang on the cross those who confess circumcision*, (2) but who will torture those who deny it. And he will lead them chained into captivity, (3) and their wives will be divided among the gentiles, and their sons will be operated on as children by physicians in order to put on them a foreskin. (4) But they will be punished by torments, and with fire and sword, and they will be forced to carry publicly their idols, that are defiled, just like those who touch them. (5) And they will also be forced by those who torture them to enter into their hidden place, and they will be forced with goads to disgracefully blaspheme the word. Finally, after these things (*sc.* they will be forced to blaspheme) also the laws through the things they will have upon their altar.[114]

This description in chapter eight is often held to represent the persecution under Antiochus IV (see above §2.1).[115] Yet this presents a interpretive difficulty since, in what appears to be a running narrative, the events which apparently refer to Herod the Great and Varus (chapter six) precede those concerning Antiochus Epiphanes (chapter eight). Solutions to this have varied.[116] One possibility is to see here essentially an older (even Maccabean) document into which chapters five to six have clumsily been interpolated by a later redactor.[117] Another possibility is to advocate a post-Herodian date for the document while simultaneously postulating a transpositional error in our sole manuscript copy (chapter eight should be located earlier in the book).[118]

However, a final option has much to commend it: the work can be envisioned as essentially a literary unity (written or compiled shortly after Herod's death) with chapter eight projecting an eschatological persecution that is subsequent to the time of writing but based on previous events in Jewish history. This is not to excise forever the possibility of sources and redaction, but to put

---

[114] Text and translation from Tromp (italics are mine).

[115] So Stauffer, *Jerusalem*, 124.

[116] As is frequently noted, Zeitlin's famous suggestion that the book is from the second century CE is too dependent on the contention that Second Temple Jews did not date events *Anno Mundi*; see Solomon Zeitlin, "The Assumption of Moses and the Revolt of Bar Kokba," *JQR* 38 (1947): 9–12; and the refutation in John J. Collins, "The Date and Provenance of the Testament of Moses," in *Studies on the Testament of Moses*, ed. George W. E. Nickelsburg, Jr., SBLSBS 4 (Cambridge, Mass.: Society of Biblical Literature, 1973), 16n.

[117] So George W. E. Nickelsburg, Jr., "An Antiochan Date for the Testament of Moses," in *Studies on the Testament of Moses*, ed. George W. E. Nickelsburg, Jr., SBLSBS 4 (Cambridge, Mass.: Society of Biblical Literature, 1973), 33–37.

[118] So R. H. Charles, *The Assumption of Moses* (London: Adam and Charles Black, 1897), 28–30 (chapters eight and nine should precede chapter five). Lattey reportedly held that only chapter eight should precede chapter five.

the focus on comprehending the current form of the text. [119] The eschatological thrust of chapter eight is evident in 8:1 (*quae talis non fuit in illis a saeculo usque ad illum tempus* – "such as there will never have been over them since eternity until that time") and on the temporal connection in the next line after 8:1–5 with the eschatological figure of Taxo (9:1, *Tunc illo die*, "then on that day" – though *die* is conjectured).[120] Thus chapter eight takes up general themes of earlier Jewish persecutions (including that of Antiochus IV), but constructs out of them a predictive view of the future.

If this picture is correct, then the *Assumption of Moses* provides early testimony to the crucifixions under Varus (6:8–9). More importantly, it shows that, based on previous Jewish experience, crucifixion was perceived as one of the severe elements to be expected in times of eschatological persecution (8:1). Note here that it is those who stay true to the Jewish faith – those who confess their circumcision – who are crucified.[121] Even those scholars who hold that chapter eight refers specifically to the time of Antiochus Epiphanes (and not to the future) must properly acknowledge that these crucifixions in the *Assumption of Moses* convey the sense of dying for one's allegiance to Judaism. Thus, this text indicates early first century associations of crucifixion with martyrdom, especially as typified by the Maccabean martyrs under Antiochus IV (cf. Josephus in §2.1 above).[122]

---

[119] A similar opinion, known in earlier scholars, is recently found in J. J. Collins, "Date and Provenance," 15–30. Collins concedes use of sources within a unified narrative in John J. Collins, "Some Remaining Traditio-Historical Problems in the Testament of Moses," in *Studies on the Testament of Moses*, ed. George W. E. Nickelsburg, Jr., SBLSBS 4 (Cambridge, Mass.: Society of Biblical Literature, 1973), 38–43. Also see Tromp, 116–17, 120–23. And compare J. Priest, "Testament of Moses (First Century A.D.): A New Translation and Introduction," in *The Old Testament Pseudepigrapha*, ed. James H. Charlesworth, vol. 1 (Garden City, NY: Doubleday, 1983), 920–21.

[120] That Taxo represents an eschatological figure is supported, for example, in J. W. van Henten and F. Avemarie, *Martyrdom and Noble Death*, 80. Unfortunately this work overlooks the martyrdom imagery present in chapter eight of the *Assumption* (though they do see martyrdom in chapters nine and ten).

[121] Tromp (p. 218) is cautious about stating that the word "cross" was in the Greek *Vorlage* of 8:1, since *suspendere in cruce* could conceivably derive from κρεμάζειν ἐπὶ ξύλου or κρεμάζειν ἐπὶ σταυροῦ. Of course, either of these would be appropriate Greek idioms for crucifixion. In any case, the Latin translation is likely correct in conveying the crucifixion sense of the Greek passage given: (1) the probable Roman historical context for the composition, (2) analogous persecution events in Jewish history during the Hellenistic and Roman periods, and (3) the implied heightening in chapter eight of persecution in comparison to chapter 6:8–9 (where the verb *crucifigit* is directly employed).

[122] Goldstein contends that Josephus alludes to the *Assumption of Moses* twice: when he mentions crucifixion in association with Antiochus IV (*Ant.* xii.256) and when he refers to an "ancient saying of inspired men" that the Temple would be burnt (*Bell.* iv.388); see Jonathan A. Goldstein, "The Testament of Moses: Its Content, Its Origin, and Its Attestation in Josephus," in *Studies on the Testament of Moses*, ed. George W. E. Nickelsburg, Jr., SBLSBS

3.3 Crucifixion in Alexandria

Philo's *In Flaccum* records a host of atrocities practiced against the Jews while A. Avillius Flaccus, the prefect of Alexandria and Egypt, colluded with the Alexandrian enemies of Judaism in hopes of impressing the Emperor Gaius. The events are to be dated to the autumn of 38 CE.[123] In Philo's account, after being forcibly evicted from their homes and businesses, the Jews are then subjected to mob beatings, slayings, mass burnings, draggings, and finally, as the culmination of these atrocities, we read (*Flacc.* 72):[124]

καὶ οἱ μὲν ταῦτα δρῶντες ὥσπερ ἐν τοῖς θεατρικοῖς μίμοις καθυπεκρίνοντο τοὺς πάσχοντας· τῶν δ᾽ ὡς ἀληθῶς πεπονθότων φίλοι καὶ συγγενεῖς, ὅτι μόνον ταῖς τῶν προσηκόντων συμφοραῖς συνήλγησαν, ἀπήγοντο, ἐμαστιγοῦντο, ἐτροχίζοντο,[125] καὶ μετὰ πάσας τὰς αἰκίας, ὅσας ἐδύνατο χωρῆσαι τὰ σώματα αὐτοῖς, ἡ τελευταία καὶ ἔφεδρος τιμωρία σταυρὸς ἦν.

And those who did these things as if in theatrical skits were acting like those who were suffering; but friends and relatives of those who had truly suffered, merely because they sympathized with the misfortunes of their family relations, were arrested, scourged, tortured, and, after all these torments, as much as their bodies were able to hold, the last and lurking punishment was a cross.

In contrast to the preceding mob treatment of the Jews, these crucifixions appear to be official acts, since the friends and relatives are "arrested" (ἀπήγοντο).[126] The official Roman context, the scourging preceding the execution, and the use of crucifixion vocabulary all would imply (both in the event itself, and in the minds of later readers of Philo) that this is an account of mass crucifixion. In this context, crucifixion emerges as the most gruesome official penalty that could be applied; and the paragraph forms the narrative climax of the section describing the general persecution of the Jewish

---

4 (Cambridge, Mass.: Society of Biblical Literature, 1973), 47–48. However, in both cases the correspondences between Josephus and the *Assumption of Moses* are not precise; and, assuming Josephus was reading a version of the *Assumption* similar in chapter arrangement to our extant manuscript, Josephus would have needed to read the chapters out of sequence in order to see chapter six as a reference to 70 CE and chapter eight as a reference to Antiochus IV.

[123] So Schürer, *HJPAJC*, 1:391n.; esp. cf. Philo, *Flacc.* 56.

[124] Texts of Philo are from Leopoldus Cohn et al., eds., *Philonis Alexandrini opera quae supersunt*, 7 vols. (Berlin: Georgi Reimer, 1896–1930) [hereafter designated as Cohn-Wendland]. Translation is mine.

[125] ἐτροχίζοντο is missing in a single manuscript (L); see Cohn-Wendland 6:133.

[126] Conceivably ἀπάγω could bear the less technical sense of "lead away," but the context of more official executionary forms, in combination with the comments of *Flacc.* 84–85, would argue for the legal sense of "arrest, bring before a magistrate and accuse" (cf. Liddell-Scott, s.v. ἀπάγω). Contrast the opinion of P. W. van der Horst, who calls this "lynch mob justice"; see Pieter W. van der Horst, *Philo's Flaccus: The First Pogrom: Introduction, Translation, and Commentary* (Leiden: Brill; Atlanta: Society of Biblical Literature, 2003), 167–168.

Alexandrians.[127] Thus, crucifixion stands as the worst atrocity to befall the Jewish populace.[128]

Philo does not record these crucifixions in the parallel sections of the *Legatio ad Gaium* (see 119–37; esp. 132). This could well be because the figure of Flaccus and his official persecution is not emphasized in that work; rather, the Alexandrians and the Emperor Gaius (=Caligula) himself are the foes, and the central issue is the state-instituted worship of Gaius. We see no reason then to discount Philo's testimony that Jews were crucified under Flaccus.[129]

Philo follows this with an account of the horrendous treatment of the Jewish senate (they are scourged, some to death). He then returns to these crucifixions (*Flacc.* 81), pointing out that Flaccus' actions ultimately breached the usual postponement of punishment that accompanies special celebrations. On previous state holidays, the bodies of the crucified were taken down from the crosses for burial (*Flacc.* 83). But Flaccus enacted the contrary, making the crucifixions themselves part of the celebration (*Flacc.* 84):

ὁ δ᾽ οὐ τετελευτηκότας ἐπὶ σταυρῶν καθαιρεῖν, ζῶντας δ᾽ ἀνασκολοπίζεσθαι[130] προσέταττεν, οἷς ἀμνηστίαν ἐπ᾽ ὀλίγον, οὐ τὴν εἰς ἅπαν, ὁ καιρὸς ἐδίδου πρὸς ὑπέρθεσιν τιμωρίας, οὐκ ἄφεσιν παντελῆ. καὶ ταῦτ᾽ εἰργάζετο μετὰ τὸ πληγαῖς αἰκίσασθαι ἐν μέσῳ τῷ θεάτρῳ καὶ πυρὶ καὶ σιδήρῳ βασανίσαι.

But he [=Flaccus] did not order [them] to take down those who had expired on a cross; rather he ordered the living to be crucified – those to whom the season used to give for a little while an incomplete amnesty toward a delay of punishment [yet] not toward a complete discharge. And he did these things after tormenting [them] with blows in the midst of the theatre and torturing [them] with fire and iron.

Again, crucifixion is clearly in view as evidenced by the vocabulary, the Roman context, and especially the indication that some had died on the cross (τετελευτηκότας ἐπὶ σταυρῶν) while living people were being affixed to the cross (ζῶντας δ᾽ ἀνασκολοπίζεσθαι). As above (in *Flacc.* 72), these crucifixions are preceded by beating and torture.

Philo undoubtedly found offensive the lack of burial given to his fellow Jews (note his comments in *Flacc.* 61, 83). He also emphasizes the extreme vulgarity of the celebration (84–85). It is therefore remarkable that Philo

---

[127] *Flacc.* 53–72 (the section is preceded by the destruction of the synagogues, and followed by the persecution of the Jewish senate).

[128] It is intriguing that Philo does *not* state that the crucifixion was inappropriate for the class standing of the Jews in Alexandria (also true in *Flacc.* 81–85; contrast *Flacc.* 78–80 on the kind of scourging employed).

[129] Crucifixion does receive some independent testimony as an official Roman penalty in Alexandria from this period in the form of a papyrus from Oxyrhynchus. See *p. Oxy* 2339 from first-century CE Alexandria (as mentioned in Hengel, *Crucifixion*, 80n).

[130] MS H reads the variant form ἀνασκολωπίζεσθαι; see Cohn-Wendland 6:135.

focuses in the above passage more on the inappropriate way Flaccus practiced crucifixion during a festival celebration rather than on any inherent iniquity in the penalty itself. Repeatedly in this text he indicates that all propriety required here was a temporary amnesty.

Indeed, the rhetorical location of *In Flaccum* 81–85 appears to be ordered to provoke the good Roman citizen to be ashamed that Flaccus would commit such atrocities during the Emperor's birthday (γενεθλιακαῖς αὐτοκράτορος, *Flacc.* 83):

ἤδη τινὰς οἶδα τῶν ἀνεσκολοπισμένων μελλούσης ἐνίστασθαι τοιαύτης ἐκεχειρίας καθαιρεθέντας καὶ τοῖς συγγενέσιν ἐπὶ τῷ ταφῆς ἀξιωθῆναι καὶ τυχεῖν τῶν νενομισμένων ἀποδοθέντας· ἔδει γὰρ καὶ νεκροὺς ἀπολαῦσαί τινος χρηστοῦ γενεθλιακαῖς αὐτοκράτορος καὶ ἅμα τὸ ἱεροπρεπὲς τῆς πανηγύρεως φυλαχθῆναι.

Already I know some individuals among the crucified who were taken down during such a holiday, which was about to arrive, and who were restored to their relatives because they were thought worthy of burial and because they gained the customary rites. For it was necessary that even the dead have the benefit of some good on birthdays of the emperor, and at the same time [it was necessary that] the sacredness of the festal assembly be guarded.

In contrasting Flaccus' practice with other crucifixions he has known, Philo also provides indirect testimony to a more general practice of crucifixion in Alexandria. Apparently, even the Romans believed that leaving the bodies unburied during a festival committed a sacrilegious offense.[131] Thus Philo suggests that "the sacredness of the festal assembly" (τὸ ἱεροπρεπὲς τῆς πανηγύρεως) must be maintained. The Jewish people had an even stronger opposition to leaving suspended human bodies unburied (see the discussion of Deuteronomy 21:22–23 in the next chapter).

This reminds us that Philo mixes in this account his own perceptions of crucifixion alongside those aspects of his description that he believes will provoke his audience. Most likely there is some substantial common ground between Philo and his audience: crucifixion is a gruesome (perhaps the most gruesome) penalty a person can suffer, and the burial of the dead (often denied to victims of the cross) is a matter of proper sobriety (at least during religious festivals). Thus, Philo can justly argue that the Jews were unfairly and horrendously treated since they did nothing to provoke these atrocities. Nevertheless, crucifixion as a mode of punishment still appears in Philo to be an accepted part of society.

One final, but important, comment: Philo does not describe the deaths of his fellow Jewish Alexandrians as martyrdoms *per se*, for they are not suffering for their faith or religious practices. Rather, it is simply their Jewish ancestry in a context of governmentally endorsed racial hatred that brings

---

[131] Outside the sphere of Roman festivals, one is reminded of John 19:31, where early burial of the crucified is assumed prior to a particular Jewish Sabbath on the "Day of Preparation."

them to the *crux*. In short, Philo presents these Jewish crucifixion victims as innocent sufferers for their race.

3.4 Crucifixion in Palestine under the Procurators

With the gradual demise of the Judaean monarchy after Herod the Great, Rome at different periods sent procurators to rule the territory of Judaea. These men regularly engaged in the Roman practice of crucifixion, and thus we hear several reports in Roman Palestine of crucifixion employed against Jews prior to the first Jewish revolt.

The crucifixion of Jesus of Nazareth between two (presumably Jewish) brigands just outside Jerusalem (the Holy City itself!) has made famous the use of crucifixion by Pontius Pilate (procurator 26–36 CE). Pagan writers of the day had little trouble believing in Pilate's action (so Lucian, *Pereg.* 13; cf. Tacitus, *Annals* xv.44.3). And it is difficult to understand how Christians would have proclaimed a *crucified* Messiah and Saviour, unless such a crucifixion had actually occurred. In reporting this event, the New Testament texts provide significant details regarding the procedures employed in crucifixion (e.g., preceded by scourging, the carrying of the *patibulum* by the victim, the use of nails, the posting of a *titulus*, mob derision, etc.). If these NT texts were at all to have been read favourably by contemporaries familiar with crucifixion, it is doubtful that these descriptions could be significantly at odds with the general practice of crucifixion witnessed by others. Indeed, many of these procedures recorded in the NT cohere well with other texts examined in our present study.

The codices of Josephus' *Antiquities* also speak of the crucifixion of Jesus (*Ant.* xviii.64):

καὶ αὐτὸν ἐνδείξει τῶν πρώτων ἀνδρῶν παρ᾽ ἡμῖν σταυρῷ ἐπιτετιμηκότος Πιλάτου οὐκ ἐπαύσαντο οἱ τὸ πρῶτον ἀγαπήσαντες·

When Pilate, upon hearing him [= Jesus] accused by men of the highest standing amongst us, had condemned him to be crucified, those who had in the first place come to love him did not give up their affection for him.[132]

The famous *Testimonium Flavianum* (*Ant.* xviii.63–64) involves so many critical issues that we cannot reasonably treat the whole passage here in suffi-

---

[132] The entire *Testimonium Flavianum* (*Ant.* xviii.63–64) reads: "About this time there lived Jesus, a wise man if indeed one ought to call him a man. For he was one who wrought surprising feats and was a teacher of such people as accept the truth gladly. He won over many Jews and many of the Greeks. He was the Messiah. When Pilate, upon hearing him accused by men of the highest standing amongst us, had condemned him to be crucified, those who had in the first place come to love him did not give up their affection for him. On the third day he appeared to them restored to life, for the prophets of God had prophesied these and countless other marvellous things about him. And the tribe of the Christians, so called after him, has still to this day not disappeared."

cient detail.[133] Nonetheless, if this text of Josephus is viewed with some favour (even if several later scribal interpolations are also postulated),[134] it is certainly possible that Josephus' original text contained the mention of Jesus' crucifixion at the command of Pilate. First, it is notable in this brief text that Pilate is portrayed as the one most responsible for Jesus' crucifixion, whereas one would expect a Christian interpolator (influenced by the Gospels, Acts, and later Christian tradition) to have placed more of the responsibility on the Jews.[135] Second, as should be obvious already from our study of crucifixion, Josephus paints a broad picture of Roman usage of such a penalty, even noting elsewhere crucifixions of specific named individuals by Roman authorities (see esp. *Ant.* xx.102); thus the mention in the *Testimonium* of the crucifixion of Jesus is in keeping with Josephus' themes and terminology. Third, if one assumes that the *Testimonium* was in some form originally to have been included by Josephus in this particular locale in the *Antiquities*,

---

[133] The *Testimonium Flavianum* was quoted by Eusebius in the fourth century (*Hist. Eccl.* i.11; *Dem. Evang.* iii.5.105), but apparently was not known in its current Greek form to Origen in the third century. Note that Origen, who cites other portions of book eighteen of the *Antiquities*, insists that Josephus was not a Christian (see *Contra Celsum* i.47; *Comm. Matthew* x.17 [on Matt 13:58]). The Greek text of the *Testimonium* contains many features that it is hard to imagine a non-Christian, pro-Roman, Jewish author affirming (e.g., εἴγε ἄνδρα αὐτὸν λέγειν χρή – "if indeed one ought to call him a man"; ὁ χριστὸς οὗτος ἦν – "he was the Christ"; ἐφάνη γὰρ αὐτοῖς τρίτην ἔχων ἡμέραν πάλιν ζῶν τῶν θείων προφητῶν ταῦτά τε καὶ ἄλλα μυρία περὶ αὐτοῦ θυμάσια εἰρηκότων "[for] on the third day he appeared to them restored to life, for the prophets of God had prophesied these and countless other marvellous things about him"). However, the Greek text contains some expressions that are unlikely to originate from an early Christian scribe (e.g., σοφὸς ἀνήρ – "a wise man"; εἰς ἔτι τε νῦν τῶν Χριστιανῶν ἀπὸ τοῦδε ὠνομασμένον οὐκ ἐπέλιπε τὸ φῦλον – "and the tribe of the Christians, so called after him, has still to this day not disappeared"). Also, a later reference in the *Antiquities* to James "the brother of Jesus, the so-called Christ" (*Ant.* xx.200) likely refers back to a previous mention in the *Antiquities* of Jesus the [so-called] Christ. For these reasons, some scholars have defended the authenticity of the whole passage, some have postulated that the whole passage was added by Christian scribes, and many others have suggested an authentic core with multiple Christian scribal interpolations. For an extensive historical review of (especially early) scholarly opinions see Alice Whealey, *Josephus on Jesus: The Testimonium Flavianum Controversy from Late Antiquity to Modern Times*, Studies in Biblical Literature 36 (New York: Peter Lang, 2003).

[134] The original-core-with-interpolations approach has much to commend it, for some phrases of dubious authenticity stand immediately alongside others that are unlikely to have originated from a Christian scribe. Furthermore, this argument is especially strengthened when the Greek text is compared with Agapius' recension of Josephus' text, which Pines has shown to have varied from the Greek *Testimonium* at just those places where we would anticipate that a Christian scribe had altered the original – see Shlomo Pines, *An Arabic Version of the Testimonium Flavianum and its Implications* (Jerusalem: Israel Academy of Sciences and Humanities, 1971). On the interpolation theory see especially Schürer, *HJPAJC*, 1:428–441; John P. Meier, "Jesus in Josephus: a modest proposal," *CBQ* 52 (1990): 76–103.

[135] See Meier, "Jesus in Josephus," 95.

then one is left to ask: How does this passage fit in the immediate context? Two answers suggest themselves simultaneously. One is that the mention of σταυρός in the *Testimonium* provides one of the few links between the context of chapter three of *Antiquities* book eighteen and the passage immediately following the *Testimonium* (i.e., the scandal at the Temple of Isis in *Ant.* xviii.65–80, esp. 79). Another is that Josephus' original account of Jesus might likely have portrayed the Jesus movement as yet another in a series of "uprisings" that Pilate needed to squash (cf. *Ant.* xviii.62, 87)[136]; and, in Josephus' understanding of Roman legal procedures, this would have called for the leader of the uprising to be executed on the σταυρός.

Thus, if we were to suppose a basic core of authentic Josephus material in the *Testimonium*, then most likely Josephus also originally would have written about the crucifixion of Jesus by Pontius Pilate. Josephus' own perceptions of this event are difficult to ascertain with certainty, especially given the likelihood of Christian interpolation in the overall *Testimonium*. The immediately preceding context in *Antiquities* appears to indict Pilate for his insensitivity to Jewish religion and customs (*Ant.* xviii.55–62). Yet, the following context records a series of calamities and shameful practices that required harsh Roman legal intervention (*Ant.* xviii.65–87), and it is quite possible that Jesus' actions were originally portrayed by Josephus as an uprising that Pilate believed he needed to quell. The extant text mentions that the action of Pilate against Jesus was approved by the "men of the highest standing among us" (τῶν πρώτων ἀνδρῶν παρ' ἡμῖν); if deemed original, this would indicate that some Jewish leaders favoured the indictment of Jesus.[137] Likely, as with other narratives in Josephus of Jewish figures being crucified, the various perceptions of this event by contemporary Jewish people would have depended upon their different opinions of the figure himself and of his movement.[138] Those who saw Jesus as an admirable person would have viewed such a death with greater shock than those who understood him to be one who fomented opposition to the established order.

Moving on to other events under the procurators of Judaea, and again following Josephus, we learn that the procurator Tiberius Alexander (c. 46–48 CE), who was a Jewish nephew of Philo (but who had given up his ancestral customs, cf. Josephus, *Ant.* xx.100), crucified James and Simon, the sons of Judas the Galilean (*Ant.* xx.102). Judas had led a revolt under

---

[136] This point is also made in Schürer, *HJPAJC*, 1:437–441.

[137] On the authenticity of this phrase, see Schürer, *HJPAJC*, 1:434.

[138] For example, some rabbinic accounts likely also allude to the death of Jesus (e.g., *b. Sanh.* 43a), and later Jewish *Toledoth Jeshu* traditions certainly refer to his execution. On these texts, see below in chapter seven. In that literature certain Jewish opinions about Jesus himself (and likely about the Christian church in general) have demonstrably influenced the descriptions of his form of death.

Quirinius, and presumably his sons James and Simon sought to follow in his footsteps. Josephus supplies no other details, nor does he provide any personal evaluation of the event.

In a similar matter of fact way, Josephus tells of crucifixions ordered by Quadratus (*Ant.* xx.129; *Bell.* ii.241), who as governor of Syria finally intervened in a bloody dispute between Jews, Samaritans, and the forces of the procurator Cumanus. Josephus' account makes clear that, though the Samaritans were fundamentally responsible, and though Cumanus had furthered the catastrophe by accepting a bribe, there were also blameworthy Jewish rebels and bandits. Thus one has a sense of justice being applied (albeit a terrible justice) when both Samaritan and Jewish insurrectionists are crucified. It is interesting to contrast these crucifixions with the "beheadings" we read about just afterwards in Josephus' *War* (ii.242). Likely some people were beheaded rather than being crucified because of their higher class standing.[139] This would add to the sense that typical Roman punishments are being employed.

According to Josephus, Cumanus was succeeded by Felix as procurator (c.52–60 CE).[140] Felix, like his predecessor, employed crucifixion to rid the country of bandits/robbers (λησταί).[141] Although Josephus can be quite critical of Felix, especially in the *Antiquities* (e.g., xx.141–43), I see no reason to think that Josephus portrayed the crucifixions by Felix as anything but a natural attempt to counter banditry.[142] Notice in Josephus' *War* that Eleazar is "plundering the country" (τὴν χώραν λησάμενον – *Bell.* ii.253, following Niese's text), and thus by Felix' actions "the country was cleansed" (καθαρθείσης τῆς χώρας; *Bell.* ii.254). Also note that the *Antiquities*, in a section not mentioning these crucifixions, portrays Felix' daily execution of the λῃστήριοι and γόηται as a military step at containing their infestation (*Ant.* xx.160–61).

While Josephus plays the objective reporter in many of these crucifixion accounts, he makes a more impassioned denunciation of the Florus' actions. Florus, concerning whom Josephus has nothing good to say (cf. *Bell.* ii.277–79; *Ant.* xx.252–58), is portrayed frequently as intentionally fanning the flames of revolt and forcing the Jews to war (esp. *Bell.* ii.283). According to Josephus, after committing many other heinous crimes, Florus orders the Roman soldiers to sack the upper market of Jerusalem, killing and plundering

---

[139] Note that in the parallel account in the *Antiquities*, the number executed differs and the means of death is unspecified, but the executed Doëtus is described as τῶν Ἰουδαίων τις πρῶτος ("someone who is first among the Jews"; *Ant.* xx.130).

[140] On the discrepancies between the accounts of Tacitus and Josephus regarding Cumanus and Felix, see Schürer, *HJPAJC*, 1:459n.

[141] *Bell.* ii.253.

[142] Contrast Schürer (*HJPAJC*, 1:462–63), who may be entirely correct historically to side with Tacitus' assessment of Felix' methods (*Ann.* xii.54.1–4; also cf. *Hist.* v.9.3), but who misses some of the positive ways these actions are viewed by Josephus himself.

the innocent, with the result that many were crucified, even some of the Jewish elite (*Bell.* ii.306–308):

(306) φυγὴ δ᾽ ἦν ἐκ τῶν στενωπῶν καὶ φόνος τῶν καταλαμβανομένων, τρόπος τε ἁρπαγῆς οὐδεὶς παρελείπετο, καὶ πολλοὺς τῶν μετρίων συλλαβόντες ἐπὶ τὸν Φλῶρον ἀνῆγον· οὓς μάστιξιν προαικισάμενος ἀνεσταύρωσεν.[143] (307) ὁ δὲ σύμπας τῶν ἐκείνης ἀπολομένων τῆς ἡμέρας ἀριθμὸς σὺν γυναιξὶν καὶ τέκνοις, οὐδὲ γὰρ νηπίων ἀπέσχοντο, περὶ τριάκοντα[144] καὶ ἑξακοσίους συνήχθη. (308) βαρυτέραν τε ἐποίει τὴν συμφορὰν τὸ καινὸν τῆς Ῥωμαίων ὠμότητος· ὃ γὰρ μηδεὶς πρότερον τότε Φλῶρος ἐτόλμησεν, ἄνδρας ἱππικοῦ τάγματος μαστιγῶσαί τε πρὸ τοῦ βήματος καὶ σταυρῷ προσηλῶσαι, ὧν εἰ καὶ τὸ γένος Ἰουδαῖον ἀλλὰ γοῦν τὸ ἀξίωμα Ῥωμαϊκὸν ἦν.

[306] There ensued a stampede through the narrow alleys, massacre of all who were caught, every variety of pillage; many of the peaceable citizens were arrested and brought before Florus, *who had them first scourged and then crucified.* [307] The total number of that day's victims, including women and children, for even infancy received no quarter, amounted to about six hundred and thirty [*or* 3,600].[145] [308] The calamity was aggravated by the unprecedented character of the Romans' cruelty. For Florus ventured that day to do what none had ever done before, namely, *to scourge before his tribunal and nail to the cross men of equestrian rank,* men who, if Jews by birth, were at least invested with that Roman dignity.

For the first time in Josephus' accounts of Roman crucifixions, the victims of the crosses are clearly innocent sufferers. In addition to his mention of women, children, and infants (in ii.307), we should especially note that it is τῶν μετρίων ("those of moderation", ii.306) who are the ones crucified. However, in addition to the array of innocent victims who face such horrors, Josephus particularly focuses his attention on the social standing of those crucified. It is clear from the remarks of some classical authors that crucifixion was often considered a penalty beneath the dignity of members of the higher Roman socio-economic classes.[146] Perhaps in this connection the crucifixion by Florus of Jewish citizens of Rome touched too close to home for Josephus.[147] Moreover, for Josephus this episode proves Florus' cruelty, and thus serves as an explanatory rationale for subsequent Jewish rebellion.

---

[143] One MS reads ἐσταύρωσεν instead of ἀνεσταύρωσεν (the meanings are equivalent).

[144] Niese (*Flavii Iosephi Opera*, 6:212) indicates that four Greek codices (plus the extant Latin translations) of Josephus read τριάκοντα ("thirty"). Whereas three Greek codices read τρισχιλίους ("three thousand"); and this more expansive number is found in Thackeray's Loeb Classical Library edition.

[145] The translation follows Thackeray's Loeb edition, except for italics and for the words "six hundred and thirty [or 3,600]" where Thackeray reads "three thousand six hundred" – on this textual issue, see the previous note.

[146] Cf. Cicero, *Rab. Post.* 16 (cf. 9–17); *Ver.* v.162–63; see Hengel, *Crucifixion*, 39–45; 51–63. However, Hengel, detecting some legal precedents for crucifixion of Roman citizens for crimes of high treason, notes that these precedents may have applied in *Bell.* ii.308 (*Crucifixion*, 40).

[147] Josephus' own social class may be deduced from his statements in *Vita* 1–7, 414–30 (esp. 423).

3.5 Crucifixion in the Jewish War

Josephus intersperses several narratives of crucifixion in his account of the disastrous Jewish revolt. In the first occurrence, Josephus contrasts the willingness of a Jewish deserter to betray Jotapata (which was then under the command of Josephus) with the strongmindedness of a previously crucified Jewish soldier (*Bell.* iii.320–21):

(320) τῷ δ᾽ ἦν μὲν δι᾽ ὑπονοίας ὁ αὐτόμολος τό τε πρὸς ἀλλήλους πιστὸν εἰδότι τῶν Ἰουδαίων καὶ τὴν πρὸς τὰς κολάσεις ὑπεροψίαν. (321) ἐπειδὴ καὶ πρότερον ληφθείς τις τῶν ἀπὸ τῆς Ἰωταπάτης πρὸς πᾶσαν αἰκίαν βασάνων ἀντέσχεν καὶ μηδὲν διὰ πυρὸς ἐξερευνῶσι τοῖς πολεμίοις περὶ τῶν ἔνδον εἰπὼν ἀνεσταυρώθη τοῦ θανάτου καταμειδιῶν·

(320) Vespasian, knowing the Jews' loyalty to each other and their indifference to chastisement, regarded the deserter with suspicion. (321) For on a former occasion a man of Jotapata who had been taken prisoner had held out under every variety of torture, and, without betraying to the enemy a word about the state of the town, even under the ordeal of fire, was finally crucified, meeting death with a smile.

Crucifixion as the actual cause of death is likely in view, preceded by torture; this can be seen in the sequence of the narrative and in the way that he smiles while being crucified alive.[148] It is hard to definitively vouchsafe the trustworthiness of this account, especially since it falls within Josephus' narrative about his own great military failure. Regardless, it does hold out an ideal of the brave Jewish revolutionary, who refuses to break his loyalty to his comrades, even while he endures the cross.[149]

In contrast, one can compare the crucified man of Jotapata with the last crucifixion account in the *Bellum Judaicum* (vii.196–203). Here the Jews of Machaerus are dismayed at the scourging of Eleazar, their captured Jewish son, who had previously fought bravely to defend the city. The Roman general Bassus, aware of this, decides to see if he cannot impel the populace to relinquish the fortress (*Bell.* vii.202–203):

(202) ὁ μὲν γὰρ προσέταξε καταπηγνύναι σταυρὸν ὡς αὐτίκα κρεμῶν[150] τὸν Ἐλεάζαρον, τοῖς δὲ[151] ἀπὸ τοῦ φρουρίου τοῦτο θεασαμένοις ὀδύνη τε πλείων προσέπεσε, καὶ

---

[148] Assuming the present participle "καταμειδιῶν" represents action concurrent with ἀνεσταυρώθη. For the meaning "smile at, despise" see, Liddell-Scott, s.v. καταμειδιάω.

[149] Cf. *Bell.* iii.151–53; vii.417–19 (concerning faithfulness to the Jewish religion in the face of horrendous tortures and death); and esp. note the response of the Essenes, who smiled and laughed while being tortured during the revolt according to Josephus (*Bell.* ii.152–53). See further Martin Hengel, *The Zealots: Investigations into the Jewish Freedom Movement in the Period from Herod I until 70 A.D.*, trans. David Smith (Edinburgh: T&T Clark, 1989), 259–62.

[150] The manuscripts are fairly evenly divided between reading κρεμῶν and κρεμνῶν (though the translation would be unaffected by this change).

διωλύγιον ἀνῴμωζον οὐκ ἀνασχετὸν εἶναι τὸ πάθος βοῶντες. (203) ἐνταῦθα δὴ τοίνυν Ἐλεάζαρος ἱκέτευεν αὐτοὺς μήτε αὐτὸν περιιδεῖν ὑπομείναντα θανάτων τὸν οἴκτιστον καὶ σφίσιν αὐτοῖς τὴν σωτηρίαν παρασχεῖν τῇ Ῥωμαίων εἴξαντας ἰσχύι καὶ τύχῃ μετὰ πάντας ἤδη κεχειρωμένους.

[202] For he ordered a cross to be erected, as though intending to have Eleazar instantly suspended; at which sight those in the fortress were seized with deeper dismay and with piercing shrieks exclaimed that the tragedy was intolerable. [203] At this juncture, moreover, Eleazar besought them not to leave him to undergo the most pitiable of deaths, but to consult their own safety by yielding to the might and fortune of the Romans, now that all others had been subdued.

Overcome by Eleazar's appeals, especially given his distinguished family connections, the Jewish populace surrenders the fortress.

The horror of crucifixion is displayed here, producing immense consternation in the city. Eleazar, who lacked the fortitude of his countryman mentioned earlier (*Bell.* iii.321), and who is portrayed as a brave but petulant youth, calls for his own release. When Eleazar calls crucifixion θανάτων τὸν οἴκτιστον ("the most pitiable of deaths") it is difficult to determine if Josephus is merely reporting Eleazar's (possibly hyperbolic) pleading, or if this is Josephus' own view of crucifixion. Nonetheless, these words stand in context as an apt description of the penalty that Eleazar fears and that so many of his countrymen underwent. Undoubtedly this fear of crucifixion was rooted in the pain and suffering it engendered. There also might be overtones of avoiding shame and extreme humiliation, especially given the distinguished family lineage of Eleazar and the consequential concern that he not undergo a penalty rarely applied to those of higher class standing. Certainly Josephus represents the immense dread of crucifixion as sufficient to overthrow an entire city.

Indeed, Titus himself employs crucifixion to a similar goal. Thus we learn that Titus orders a captured prisoner to be crucified before the walls of Jerusalem, endeavoring to induce surrender of the city (*Bell.* v.289). That this attempt failed does not prevent Titus from continuing in this strategy as his men capture more and more people who were trying to escape the horrors of famine-stricken Jerusalem (*Bell.* v.449–51):

(449) λαμβανόμενοι δὲ κατ' ἀνάγκην ἠμύνοντο, καὶ μετὰ μάχην ἱκετεύειν ἄωρον ἐδόκει. μαστιγούμενοι δὴ καὶ προβασανιζόμενοι τοῦ θανάτου πᾶσαν αἰκίαν ἀνεσταυροῦντο τοῦ τείχους ἀντικρύ. (450) Τίτῳ μὲν οὖν οἰκτρὸν τὸ πάθος κατεφαίνετο πεντακοσίων ἑκάστης ἡμέρας ἔστι δὲ[152] ὅτε καὶ πλειόνων ἁλισκομένων, οὔτε δὲ τοὺς βίᾳ ληφθέντας ἀφεῖναι ἀσφαλὲς καὶ φυλάττειν τοσούτους φρουρὰν τῶν φυλαξόντων ἑώρα· τό γε μὴν

---

[151] According to Niese's text (*Flavii Iosephi Opera*, 6:596) the elided form of δὲ (i.e., δ᾽) in the Loeb edition is only found in one Greek codex. The same holds for the elided form of (i.e., μήτ᾽) in vii.203.

[152] Again here the Loeb edition has the elided form δ᾽ instead of δέ in Niese (see also in v.451), though in both occasions the majority of MSS read δέ.

πλέον οὐκ ἐκώλυεν τάχ᾽ ἂν ἐνδοῦναι πρὸς τὴν ὄψιν ἐλπίσας αὐτούς,[153] εἰ μὴ παραδοῖεν, ὅμοια πεισομένους. (451) προσήλουν δὲ οἱ στρατιῶται δι᾽ ὀργὴν καὶ μῖσος τοὺς ἁλόντας ἄλλον ἄλλῳ σχήματι πρὸς χλεύην, καὶ διὰ τὸ πλῆθος χώρα τε ἐνέλειπε τοῖς σταυροῖς καὶ σταυροὶ[154] τοῖς σώμασιν.

[449] When caught, they were driven to resist, and after a conflict it seemed too late to sue for mercy. They were accordingly scourged and subjected to torture of every description, before being killed, and then crucified opposite the walls. [450] Titus indeed commiserated their fate, five hundred or sometimes more being captured daily; on the other hand, he recognized the risk of dismissing prisoners of war, and that the custody of such numbers would amount to the imprisonment of their custodians; but his main reason for not stopping the crucifixions was the hope that the spectacle might perhaps induce the Jews to surrender, for fear that continued resistance would involve them in a similar fate. [451] The soldiers out of rage and hatred amused themselves by nailing their prisoners in different postures; and so great was their number, that space could not be found for the crosses nor crosses for the bodies.

The passage testifies to the variety of possible positions on a cross (ἄλλον ἄλλῳ σχήματι – "in different postures"), which could still be identified as "crucifixion." Again, as we have seen so often, scourging and torture precede crucifixion.[155]

Josephus, in accord with his tendency to put Titus in the best possible light, merely states that Titus, though commiserating the lot of the Jewish prisoners, "does not stop" the crucifixions. However, Josephus also delineates Titus' motives: (1) Titus could neither dismiss the prisoners, (2) nor could he afford guards to them, and (3) Titus hoped that such crucifixions might produce a Jewish surrender for fear of a similar fate. These sound like Titus' military rationale for his official sanction of the mass crucifixion of prisoners. So, as he had done earlier (in *Bell.* v.289), Titus apparently ordered the crucifixions as part of an ongoing strategic policy.

That Josephus feels he must mitigate the actions of Titus likely displays either Josephus' own discomfort that his patron crucified so many of his Jewish countrymen, or his fear that others would judge Titus harshly for such a cruel policy. In either case, given Josephus' sponsorship by the Flavians, the inclusion of this event in his narrative makes the historical veracity of these crucifixions almost certain. Yet, as much as possible, Josephus makes sure that the soldiers themselves are held responsible; and they are portrayed as

---

[153] The Loeb text tentatively adds here [ὡς], apparently following the Latin (see Niese, *Flavii Iosephi Opera*, 6:496).

[154] One manuscript omits καὶ σταυροί; the omission appears a likely case of haplography due to *homoioarcton* with the first σταυροῖς.

[155] Here Thackeray's translation obscures the order of events ("They were accordingly scourged and subjected to torture of every description, before being killed, and then crucified opposite the walls"). It is more likely that the προβασανιζόμενοι τοῦ θανάτου πᾶσαν αἰκίαν, while showing that some died in torture (and possibly associating crucifixion with these tortures), does *not* indicate that all who then approached the cross (ἀνεσταυροῦντο) were already dead.

raging and sadistic torturers. This shows that, even in the disciplined ranks of the Roman army (be they here auxiliaries or legionnaires), inhumanity in war was commonplace. Crucifixion here serves as an extremely gruesome reminder of this fact.

Finally, there is one occasion on which Josephus' own compassion for the crucified actually motivated him to action (*Vita* 420):

πεμφθεὶς δ᾽ ὑπὸ Τίτου Καίσαρος σὺν Κερεαλίῳ καὶ χιλίοις ἱππεῦσιν εἰς κώμην τινὰ Θεκῶαν λεγομένην προκατανοήσων, εἰ τόπος ἐπιτήδειός ἐστιν χάρακα δέξασθαι, ὡς ἐκεῖθεν ὑποστρέφων εἶδον πολλοὺς αἰχμαλώτους ἀνεσταυρωμένους καὶ τρεῖς ἐγνώρισα συνήθεις μοι γενομένους, ἤλγησά τε τὴν ψυχὴν καὶ μετὰ δακρύων προσελθὼν Τίτῳ εἶπον. ὁ δ᾽ εὐθὺς ἐκέλευσεν καθαιρεθέντας αὐτοὺς θεραπείας ἐπιμελεστάτης τυχεῖν. καὶ οἱ μὲν δύο τελευτῶσιν θεραπευόμενοι, ὁ δὲ τρίτος ἔζησεν.

Once more, when I was sent by Titus Caesar with Cerealius and a thousand horse to a village called Tekoa, to prospect whether it was a suitable place for an entrenched camp, and on my return saw many prisoners who had been crucified, and recognized three of my acquaintances among them, I was cut to the heart and came and told Titus with tears what I had seen. He gave orders immediately that they should be taken down and receive the most careful treatment. Two of them died in the physicians' hands; the third survived.

This recollection occurs in a series of apologetic statements in the *Vita* about how Josephus did not seek his own gain through his personal standing with Titus; rather, he sought the freedom of his countrymen (i.e., his friends). Josephus' compassion for his former colleagues somehow rings hollow when one notes the multitude he did not (could not?) save. The text reads as a vivid historical memory; and the detail that two of the three died despite his aid increases its believability. It is striking that the toll of crucifixion on the victims' bodies was so significant that death came even with careful medical assistance.[156] Particularly noticeable about the account is how it simply states as background information that "many prisoners" were being crucified – a further indication of the frequency of this practice during the first Jewish revolt.[157]

3.6 The Crucified Man from Givʿat ha-Mivtar

In June 1968 the remains of a crucified man were discovered in an ossuary from northeastern Jerusalem.[158] Tomb 1 from Givʿat ha-Mivtar had twelve

---

[156] Compare the legal possibility that a crucified man may be redeemed off the cross by a Roman matron and still live (*y. Yebam.* 16:3). However, a similar tradition represents the matron redeeming three men as they are still being led out to be crucified (*Midr. Psa.* 45:5).

[157] Note the opinion of Mason concerning this passage: "Josephus' narrative suggests that stretches of the major roads out of Jerusalem were lined with crosses, like the Appian Way outside Rome after Spartacus' revolt of the 70s BCE." In Steve Mason, *Life of Josephus: Translation and Commentary* (Leiden: Brill, 2001), 167.

[158] The following description follows the published report of V. Tzaferis, "Jewish Tombs at and near Givʿat ha-Mivtar, Jerusalem," *IEJ* 20 (1970): 18–32.

loculi for burial, and held a total of eight ossuaries (=Jewish reburial contain-ers). Ossuary number four contained the bones of the crucified man, along with bones from a child.[159]

This ossuary was undecorated aside from guide markings to enable proper placement of the lid and two inscriptions on the side of the ossuary.[160] One inscription, centered, shallow, and more neatly written merely reads יהוחנן ("Jehohanan"). The other is deeper, slightly below the first, and off to one side; it was originally reported to read:

יהוחנן
בן חגקול

The word חגקול is problematic. Naveh suggests that the writer intended to write ז instead of ג, which would yield חזקול – possibly related to יחזקול "Ezekiel" (thus בן חזקול would be "son of Ezekiel").[161] Alternatively, he notes Yadin's verbal suggestion that it may be a corruption of a foreign name (e.g., Αγκολ).[162] Yadin later suggested reading a *heh* and thus הגקול, which he identified with the term העקול – "the bowlegged," referring to the strad-dled position of the crucified victim.[163] However, Yadin's suggestion, as he himself admits, requires an unusual change from ע to ג.[164] Perhaps Naveh's original suggestion, as now revised by Rahmani (who reads חזקיל with a

---

[159] Six of the fifteen ossuaries located in the tombs at Givʿat ha-Mivtar contained bones of both adults and children; N. Haas, "Anthropological Observations on the Skeletal Remains from Givʿat ha-Mivtar," *IEJ* 20 (1970): 40.

[160] This information is from J. Naveh, "The Ossuary Inscriptions from Givʿat ha-Mivtar," *IEJ* 20 (1970): 35. The statement that the second inscription reads "Jehohanan ben Jehohanan" is mistaken in Joseph Zias and Eliezer Sekeles, "The Crucified Man from Givʿat ha-Mivtar: A Reappraisal," *IEJ* 35 (1985): 280.

[161] Naveh, "Ossuary Inscriptions," 35.

[162] Kuhn argued for a Semitic equivalent of ἀγκύλος ("crooked, curved") – referring to his manner of death; see Heinz-Wolfgang Kuhn, "Der Gekreuzigte von Givʿat ha-Mivtar: Bilanz einer Entdeckung," in *Theologia Crucis – Signum Crucis*, ed. Carl Andresen and Günter Klein (Tübingen: J. C. B. Mohr [Paul Siebeck], 1979), 312–16; and Kuhn, "Die Kreuzesstrafe," 714.

[163] Y. Yadin, "Epigraphy and Crucifixion," *IEJ* 23 (1973): 18–20. Yadin believes the first name refers to the father (Jehohanan) who was crucified, and the second refers to his son of the same name who was known by the epithet Jehohanan, son of the "bowlegged one" (i.e., son of the crucified one). Yadin then concludes that crucifixion must have been performed in such a way as to force the legs into a bowlegged position. In addition to the problems men-tioned in the text above, Yadin's proposal suffers from how his proposed crucifixion position varies from the more recent analyses of the victim's bones (see Zias & Sekeles, "Crucified Man," 22–27).

[164] Rahmani also counters that the *ḥet* simply cannot be read as a *heh* when it is compared with the other clear examples of these letters on Jewish ossuaries; cf. L. Y. Rahmani, *A Catalogue of Jewish Ossuaries in the Collections of the State of Israel* (Jerusalem: The Israel Antiquities Authority/The Israel Academy of Sciences and Humanities, 1994), 130 (No. 218).

yodh), remains the most likely (i.e., the inscription reads "Jehoḥanan son of Ezekiel").[165]

On the basis of stone ossuary usage, and especially due to the pottery found in tomb 1, the burials would have likely occurred in the Herodian period, being part of "a vast Jewish cemetery of the Second Temple period."[166] Tzaferis suggests that, since the pottery and ossuary exclude the period of Alexander Jannaeus, and "since the general situation during the revolt of A.D. 70 excludes the possibility of burial," this crucifixion must be dated in the first century CE and before the outbreak of the first Jewish revolt.[167] Although it would indeed be very unlikely that re-burials took place during the siege of Jerusalem (68–70 CE), one can hardly rule out a date afterwards. In any case, on the basis of ossuary usage and pottery dating in the tomb complex, a first century date does appear most reasonable. Thus we have archaeological evidence to suggest, as the literary evidence does, that crucifixion would have been familiar during the early Roman period in Judaea.

Unfortunately, the examination of the skeletons was necessarily cut short by the call for modern reburial. Thus the initial report by Haas on the cruci-fied remains has been questioned in several areas.[168] The following constitutes a brief summary of Haas' conclusions, in light of the revisions suggested in the re-analysis by Zias and Sekeles: The ossuary, in addition to containing the bones of the adult male and the child, also contained a cuboid bone of a third skeleton (probably due to accidental mingling of bones). The right calcaneum (heel) of the adult male was pierced by a large iron nail (there are not however remnants of the left heel, contrary to initial reports). There are remnants of a wooden plaque between the calcaneum and the head of the nail (probably for use in affixing the heel). The bones had been sprinkled with oil, especially near obvious injuries. The revised assessment argues, contrary to Haas, that there was no *coup de grâce* involving the shattering of the shins to hasten death, nor was it necessary to amputate the legs to facilitate removal from the cross. The man was generally healthy (showing no signs of suffering disease, malnutrition, injury, or heavy manual labour), not even having the

---

[165] Rahmani, *Catalogue*, p. 130.

[166] So Tzaferis, "Jewish Tombs," 30. Tzaferis notes of tomb 1 that "the bulk of the pot-tery is to be dated to after the rise of the Herodian dynasty" (ibid., 20). Further, in tomb 1 Tzaferis notes that the inscription on ossuary 1 ("Simon, builder of the Temple") would imply a date during the construction of the Herodian Temple (20 BCE – 70 CE).

[167] Tzaferis, "Jewish Tombs," 31.

[168] Haas' report is found in "Anthropological Observations," 38–59. Critique of Haas' article can especially be found in Zias and Sekeles, "Crucified Man," 22–27. A more popular summary may be found in Joe Zias and James H. Charlesworth, "CRUCIFIXION: Archaeology, Jesus, and the Dead Sea Scrolls," in *Jesus and the Dead Sea Scrolls*, ed. James H. Charlesworth (New York: Doubleday, 1992), 279–80.

cleft palate that was initially suggested. All are agreed that death was produced by crucifixion. While many attempts have been made to determine the
exact form of crucifixion (e.g., whether the arms were tied or pinned, whether
the legs were pinned together or separate), given our current focus on perceptions of crucifixion, this issue is not our principle concern.[169]

Concerning the class status of the crucified man, Tzaferis describes the use
of ossuaries as an expensive luxury.[170] Even if this particular ossuary is not
finely decorated or well-manufactured, when combined with the indications
of the man's generally health, an ossuary burial here likely implies that the
deceased did not belong to the lowest orders of society.[171]

Reburial of bones was very widely practiced in Palestine, and was even
especially recognized in the context of discussions speaking about bodies that
had been suspended (cf. *m. Sanh.* vi.5–6 – though here a Jewish penalty).[172]
Its attestation in the case of this crucified man suggests that the body of the
crucified was shown a degree of sympathy, or at least non-abhorrence. The
bones could receive standard reburial, including burial in a family tomb with
an ordinary inscription.

3.7 Crucifixion in Rabbinic Law and Anecdote

A brief rabbinic connection of Deut 28:66 to crucifixion appears in Proem 1
to Esther Rabbah:

ד"א והיו חייך תלואים לך מנגד זה שהוא נתון בדיוטי של קיסרין ופחדת לילה ויומם
זה שהוא יוצא לידון ולא תאמין בחייך זה שהוא יוצא להצלב

"Another explanation is this: 'Your life will hang in doubt before you' – this applies to one
who is placed in the prison of Caesarea. 'And you will fear night and day' – this applies to
one who is brought forth for trial. 'And you will have no assurance of your life' – this applies
to one who is brought out to be crucified."

---

[169] In addition to the works cited above, also see Yadin, "Epigraphy,"18–22; Vilhelm
Møller-Christensen, "Skeletal Remains from Givʿat ha-Mivtar," *IEJ* 26 (1976): 35–38. If the
Zias/Sekeles revised assessment of the osteological evidence is followed, then it appears the
legs were pinned separately (likely on either side of the vertical cross) and the arms were tied
to the patibulum. Nonetheless, given the variety of positions that could be labeled "crucifixion" in antiquity (see above in chapter one, §§2.1 & 2.2), one should be careful to not gener-
alize too much from this one case.

[170] Tzaferis, "Jewish Tombs," 30.

[171] Also Haas, "Skeletal Remains," 54. Kuhn ("Die Kreuzesstrafe," 713) notes: "In diesen
Zusammenhang paßt der Umstand, daß der Betreffende auf eine privilegierte Weise in einem,
wenn auch bescheidenen Ossuar, d. h. ohne Verzierungen, wiederbestattet wurde."

[172] נתעכל הבשר היו מלקטין את־העצמות וקוברין אותם במקומן – "When the flesh
had wasted away they gathered together the bones and buried them in their own place."
(*m. Sanh.* vi.6 in Danby translation). Text from Samuel Krauss, *Die Mischna: Text,
Übersetzung und ausführliche Erklärung*, vol. IV.4–5: Sanhedrin, Makkot (Giessen: Alfred
Töpelmann, 1933), 204 (where it is listed as *m. Sanh.* vi.8).

This passage, with its references to the Roman administrative center at Caesarea and to the Roman executionary method of crucifixion, would fit the milieu of those Palestinian Amoraim who taught in Caesarea (third-fifth centuries), although it is not impossible that it relates to an earlier time.[173] It also confirms the antecedent likelihood that the penalty of crucifixion was widely familiar among the tannaitic rabbis.

In a similar way, a number of rabbinic legal traditions presuppose the employment of crucifixion by Roman authorities in their day. So some texts mention the dripping blood of a crucified person (*m. Ohol.* 3:5; *t. Ohol.* 4:11; *b. Nid.* 71b), or a crucified man signaling for a writ of divorce (*t. Giṭ.* 7[5]:1; *y. Giṭ.* 7:1 [48c]; *b. Giṭ.* 70b), or the employment of a crucifixion nail in magical charms (*m. Šabb.* 6:10; *y. Šabb.* 6:9 [8c]; *b. Šabb.* 67a).[174] Important testimony in an extra-canonical tractate ordains that a family should cease to reside near their family member's crucified body until its flesh has sufficiently decayed (*Semaḥot* ii.11 [44b]).[175] Further references to crucifixion in an early halakhic midrash evidence the graphic recollection of suffering under the cross (e.g., *Sifre Deut.* §§24, 323). Rabbinic sources can also draw proverbial analogies to the ongoing experience of official crucifixion.[176]

Although these texts do not necessarily correspond to direct experiences the rabbis may have had themselves, in every case they indicate familiarity with crucifixion during the tannaitic period. In that light, two other rabbinic anecdotes are worth examining in detail.

3.7.1 Rabbi Nathan and the Persecuted

Our sources from the Bar Kokhba revolt are sparser, but there is an intriguing passage in the *Mekilta* that may refer to Hadrianic times[177]:

לאוהבי ולשומרי מצותי. לאוהבי זה אברהם אבינו וכיוצא בו ולשומרי מצותי אלו
הנביאים והזקנים. רבי נתן אומר לאוהבי ולשומרי מצותי אלו[178] שהם יושבין בארץ
ישראל ונותנין נפשם על המצות מה לך יוצא ליהרג על שמלתי את בני [ישראל][179] מה

---

[173] Due to the clear official Roman penal context, my translation above represents להצלב as "to be crucified."

[174] These texts are addressed in chapters four (§2) and five (§3)

[175] See below in chapter five, §3.

[176] So *Sifre Deut.* §308. See further the brigandage material in chapter five, §2.

[177] *Mekilta*, Baḥodesh 6 on Exod 20:3–6. Text in Jacob Z. Lauterbach, *Mekilta de-Rabbi Ishmael*, 3 vols. (Philadelphia: Jewish Publication Society of America, 1933–1935), 2:247; and H. S. Horovitz and I. A. Rabin, *Mechilta D'Rabbi Ismael*, Corpus Tannaiticum 3.1(3) (Frankfurt: J. Kauffmann, 1931), p. 227 lines 5–10.

[178] The printed editions add here ישראל, perhaps focusing the discussion only on those of Israelite descent.

[179] MS Oxford 151(2) omits ישראל, included by the printed texts and the Munich MS. On possible motives for its inclusion, see the previous note. Horovitz/Rabin omit. Interestingly, it is also missing from the *Lev. Rab.* and *Midr. Psa.* parallels mentioned below.

לך יוצא לישרף על בתורה שקראתי מה לך יוצא ליצלב[180] על שאכלתי את המצה מה
לך לוקה מאה פרגל[181] על שנטלתי את הלולב. ואומר אשר הכתי בית מאהבי מכות
אלו גרמו לי ליאהב לאבי[182] שבשמים:

Of Them that Love Me and Keep My Commandments. "Of them that love Me," refers to our
father Abraham and such as are like him. "And keep My commandments," refers to the
prophets and the elders. R. Nathan says: "Of them that love Me and keep My commandments," refers to those who dwell in the land of Israel and risk their lives for the sake of the
commandments. "Why are you being led out to be decapitated [slain הרג]?" "Because I circumcised my son to be an Israelite." "Why are you being led out to be burned?" "Because I
read the Torah." *"Why are you being led out to be crucified?"* "Because I ate the unleavened
bread." "Why are you getting a hundred lashes?" "Because I performed the ceremony of the
Lulab." And it says: "Those with which I was wounded in the house of my friends" (Zech.
13.6). These wounds caused me to be beloved of My father in heaven.[183]

The saying is ascribed to Rabbi Nathan, who is reputed to have returned to
Palestine from Babylonia c.145–160 CE. Partly on the strength of that reference, and on the mention of persecution against Jews who circumcise,[184]
many identify this saying with the Hadrianic period.[185] The series of forms of
persecution imply Roman judicial proceedings. That fact, combined with the
vocabulary for suspension (ליצלב), and the likely Hadrianic date, make it
virtually certain that this persecution text includes use of official Roman crucifixion.

Most, however, do not notice the difficulty created by the parallel traditions in *Leviticus Rabbah* and *Midrash Tehillim*.[186] In neither of these

---

[180] For מה לך יוצא ליצלב the Munich MS reads: מה לצלב.

[181] There is some textual variation in מאה פרגל, with the printed editions reading
מאפרגל.

[182] Two textual variants are worth noting in this line: (1) For ליאהב ("to be loved") the
Yalkut reads לאהוב ("to love"); also note *Midrash Ḥakhamim* (לאהב אבי). (2) For לאבי
("my Father") the Oxford MS reads לאביהם ("their fathers"), and Munich MS reads לאבינו
("our fathers"). Both Lauterbach and Horovitz/Rabin prefer לאבי.

[183] Translation from Lauterbach, *Mekilta*, 2:248.

[184] The *Historia Augusta* (Vita Hadrian xiv.2) claims that Hadrian's removal of the
Jewish right to circumcise was the cause for the Bar Kokhba revolt. Similarly, after the revolt,
circumcision is also deemed unlawful under Hadrian until it is permitted again for Jews by
Antoninus Pius. See discussion in Schürer, *HJPAJC*, 1:536–40, 555.

[185] So Jakob Winter and August Wünsche, *Mechiltha: Ein tannaitischer Midrasch zu
Exodus* (Leipzig: J. C. Hinrich, 1909), 213n.; Jacob Neusner, *A History of the Jews in
Babylonia*, 5 vols., SPB (Leiden: E. J. Brill, 1965–1970), 1:78 (dating the saying to just
before Nathan's return to Palestine); Schürer, *HJPAJC*, 1:555 (and n.190). Stauffer also
follows this dating, but he further contends that, insofar as the R. Nathan's saying included
themes from the persecution under Antiochus Epiphanes, his saying must have referred to
various times of persecution from 175 BCE–137 CE (Stauffer, *Jerusalem*, 162n.25). It is
indeed possible that Nathan picks up themes from earlier persecutions, but the vividness of
the account makes it likely he is speaking mostly from contemporary experience.

[186] *Lev. Rab.* xxxii.1 (on Lev 24:10); *Midr. Psa.* on Ps 12:5.

accounts is the ascription to R. Nathan found. Furthermore, the lists of persecutions, and of the corresponding customs that bring persecution, differ in all
three accounts.[187] Most significantly for our study, "crucifixion" as a persecution appears only in the *Mekilta*. Of course, the *Mekilta* represents the earliest
known written version,[188] but the tradition history is probably quite complex.

In terms of dating the traditions, first it is notable that, throughout the different layers of tradition, circumcision maintains its first position. This
implies a specific context of legal opposition to circumcision – which fits the
time of Hadrian well, as was noted above. Second, both *Leviticus Rabbah* and
Midrash Tehillim, though not specifying a rabbi for this tradition, attach this
material to sayings of R. Nehemiah (third generation *Tanna*, disciple of
Akiba, and thus associated with the Bar Kokhba rebellion) – possibly also
insinuating a Hadrianic milieu.

It is conceivable that the *Mekilta* reference to crucifixion belongs to a separate strand of tradition than is evidenced in the midrashim on Leviticus and
Psalms. Alternatively, at some stage later the reference in the *Mekilta* tradition to "crucifixion" was deemed inappropriate by the bearers of tradition
(either because of its heinous associations, or because it had ceased being a
common means of execution/persecution).

Nevertheless, whether one follows a Hadrianic date for the saying or not,
what is clear is that the redactor of the *Mekilta* implies such an association.[189]
Further, this redactor mentions crucifixion as one of the typical deaths that a
Jewish martyr might undergo for keeping the commandments. The marty-
rological context is all the more significant in light of the striking phrase:
"These wounds caused me to be beloved of my Father in heaven."[190]

---

[187] So the *Mekilta* – slaying: circumcising, burning: reading the Torah, crucifixion: eating
מצה, hundred lashes (scourging): performing the Lulab. Whereas *Leviticus Rabbah* – stoning: circumcising, burning: Sabbath-keeping, slaying: eating מצה, scourging: making
Sukkah/performing the Lulab/wearing tephilin/inserting blue thread/performing will of Father
in heaven. *Midrash Tehillim* – slaying: circumcising, stoning: Sabbath-keeping, burning:
eating מצה, scourging: performing will of Father in heaven. However, such a layout simplifies the significant textual issues in, for example, *Leviticus Rabbah* where the order is further
varied in the manuscript tradition (none of which, I am sad to say, support the *Mekilta*).

[188] Following the dating in Stemberger, *Introduction* , 255, 291, 322–23.

[189] In addition to the ascription to R. Nathan, also note the locational reference to "those
who dwell in the land of Israel."

[190] As the footnotes above indicate, various scribes seem to have been uncomfortable with
this phrase, and instead alter it to read, "These wounds cause me to love my Father," or "...to
be loved by the fathers," or something similar. But, in addition to having the strongest support
in the *Mekilta*, this same phrase also appears in the best traditions of *Leviticus Rabbah* and
Midrash Tehillim; so it can hardly be doubted that this is a central motif in the tradition. Perhaps this helps make sense of the association with R. Nehemiah in the later versions, for he
was known for his famous saying, "Beloved are chastenings. For just as sacrifices effect
atonement so sufferings effect atonement" (*Sifre Deut.* 32).

3.7.2 Rabbi Eleazar and the Thieves

R. Eleazar ben Simeon (fourth generation *tanna*[191]) is said to have advised an officer of the Roman government how to detect thieves. The Romans then co-opted his services to find such brigands. The story in the *Bavli* continues[192]:

R. Eleazar, son of R. Simeon, was accordingly sent for, and he proceeded to arrest the thieves. Thereupon R. Joshua, son of Ḳarḥah, sent word to him, "Vinegar, son of wine! How long will you deliver up the people of our God for slaughter!" Back came the reply: "I weed out thorns from the vineyard." Whereupon R. Joshua retorted: "Let the owner of the vineyard himself [God] come and weed out the thorns."

One day a fuller met him [R. Eleazar], and dubbed him "Vinegar, son of wine." Said the Rabbi to himself, "Since he is so insolent, he is certainly a culprit." So he gave the order to his attendant: "Arrest him! Arrest him!" When his anger cooled, he went after him in order to secure his release, but did not succeed. Thereupon he applied to him [the fuller], the verse: *Whoso keepeth his mouth and his tongue, keepeth his soul from troubles.* Then they hanged him, and he [R. Eleazar son of R. Simeon] stood under the gallows and wept. Said they [his disciples] to him: "Master, do not grieve; for he and his son seduced a betrothed maiden on the Day of Atonement." [On hearing this,] he laid his hand upon his heart and exclaimed: "Rejoice, my heart! If matters on which thou [sc. the heart] art doubtful are thus, how much more so those on which thou art certain![193]

Clearly R. Eleazar is represented as colluding with the Romans, with the apparent result that Jewish "thieves" are captured and crucified. The first paragraph cited above may produce an ultimately negative assessment of Eleazar's activities (ending as it does with the retort by R. Joshua). However, that paragraph is preceded in context by a narrative (not quoted above) about Eleazar's wisdom in discovering thieves/brigands. As noted earlier, in Roman Palestine such brigands were typically crucified. The second paragraph above also justifies Eleazar's actions from their results (the man deserved crucifixion anyway).[194] And a final episode in the narrative string (not cited above) further shows that Eleazar is a man whose righteous flesh will not decay. As it stands, then, the whole narrative complex presents R. Eleazar's actions (including his collusion with the Romans!) as wise and righteous.

Assuming that collusion with the Romans would likely not be a populist action,[195] it is possible to conceive of this narrative series being formulated initially in circles positive to Eleazar so as to vindicate his reputation. Alter-

---

[191] See Stemberger, *Introduction*, 79.

[192] *b. B. Meṣ.* 83b.

[193] Soncino translation.

[194] That this is an episode of crucifixion is briefly defended in the first chapter of this book. The Soncino Talmud rightly suggests here that Eleazar's confidence that this man deserved hanging comes from the fact that "the seduction of a betrothed maiden is punished by stoning, and all who are stoned are hung."

[195] However, some second century Jewish patriarchs are thought to have had the favour of the Romans; see Catherine Hezser, *The Social Structure of the Rabbinic Movement in Roman Palestine*, TSAJ 66 (Tübingen: Mohr Siebeck, 1997), 435–49.

natively, the first paragraph cited above may constitute an initial tradition that opposes Eleazar, with the other material being added later by a redactor to vindicate him. Either scenario presumes that it was commonly held that Eleazar colluded with the Romans.[196] Also in either case, it is striking that the very portion of the complex that favours Eleazar also clearly indicates that crucifixion was the result of Eleazar's collusion with the Romans. Such a text must imply that some Jews, at least at the time the tradition was penned, believed crucifixion was at times a deserved penalty; and further it suggests that collusion with the Romans to produce candidates for the cross could also be acceptable in some rabbinic circles.

4. Summary

This brief survey should suffice to demonstrate that Jewish people had long been acquainted with crucifixion and other bodily suspension penalties. In the Hellenistic and Roman periods crucifixion is evidenced in the Diaspora and frequently attested in Palestine, even occasionally at the hands of Jewish leaders. However, the lasting memory of the post-Second Temple generations would have especially been of their many comrades who were hung from the cross before and after the destruction of the Temple.

When we consider the numerous episodes depicted above, it is worth highlighting the specific emphases in individual sources. Philo was a well-bred and highly educated Jew, whose Hellenistically-influenced philosophy fused with his Jewish faith. He recalls vivid scenes of Jewish Alexandrians pinned to crosses for the entertainment of Flaccus and associates. Yet, Philo merely presents them as innocent sufferers rather than as religious martyrs.

The *Nahum Pesher* originates from a religious movement that was opposed to other sects within ancient Judaism. The Pesher records their sectarian impressions as the "Seekers-of-Smooth-Things" (likely referring to Pharisees), after calling for pagan assistance in a bid for control of Jerusalem, are soundly defeated and crucified by the Lion of Wrath (most probably a reference to Alexander Jannaeus). Unfortunately, key phrases are lost in this fragmentary scroll, including phrases that could potentially clarify how these crucifixions were viewed. Attempted reconstructions have read into the Pesher's perspective either abject horror, or some level of affinity with the Lion of Wrath's action. Nonetheless, the scroll most likely indicates that people who are "hung alive upon the tree" are opposed by God himself ("behold I am against you says the Lord of Hosts").

---

[196] This is not surprising, given Eleazar's reputation. On Eleazar see Wilhelm Bacher, *Die Agada der Tannaiten*, 2 vols. (Strassburg: Karl J. Trübner, 1884–1890), 400–407; and more recent bibliography in Stemberger, *Introduction*, 79.

Most likely the *Assumption of Moses* was completed in the early first century, and possibly was authored in Palestine. This work conveys the perspective that God's vindication of his people comes only through the martyrdom of God's righteous remnant (not through their recourse to arms). In this regard, crucifixions are seen both as the plight of Israel's sons when Israel has gone astray, and as an extreme suffering of those martyrs who follow the commandments of Moses.

The rabbis, as conveyors of pious tradition, clearly belonged to a literary and religious elite, but the traditions themselves may incorporate many diverse elements. Thus, the Simeon b. Shetach narratives, especially in their later Talmudic form, incorporate magical and folk elements, giving them a popular feel. Such populist traditions may also be found in the Jose b. Joezer accounts, which record the crucifixion of a rabbinic master, taking such a penalty against God's innocents for granted. On the other hand, the Simeon b. Shetach stories speak of a mass hanging, which in later tradition is almost certainly represented as a mass crucifixion (or at least a mass execution by suspension otherwise at variance with later rabbinic teaching), instigated by a great Pharisee. The rabbis, in transmitting the Simeon traditions, pass over many perplexing issues those traditions could have raised about early Pharisaic legal procedures (e.g., for example here women are hung, they are hung all in one day, and they are executed without a trial). Concerning legal procedures, various rabbinic debates mention crucifixion in examinations of case law (concerning the uncleanness of "mingled blood", the magic use of crucifixion nails, the deathbed enacting of divorce, and the burial of those crucified by the government); these examples show that crucifixion at one point was common enough in Palestine to have necessitated discussion of its legal implications. The rabbis also speak of one of their own (R. Eleazar) joining forces with the Romans to conquer banditry; he detects brigands and hands them over to the Romans for crucifixion. Further, early rabbinic writings associate crucifixion as part of the Hadrianic persecution of those martyrs who continue to practice Judaism. Therefore, in rabbinic sources a variety of perspectives are attached to traditional accounts of crucifixion. Crucifixion can signal the horrible death of innocent sufferers or martyrs, but it can also imply the just recompense for banditry or witchcraft.

Throughout this chapter it has become evident that Josephus provides the greatest number of history-inspired narratives of crucifixion. The majority of Josephus' accounts function as mere reports of acts of crucifixion (especially by Roman soldiers). His detached objectivity here could be explained by several motives: (1) he attempts to follow his own claims of historical accuracy and objectivity (cf. *Bell.* i.9; *Ant.* i.17); (2) he does not wish to overly offend his Roman hosts, above all Titus; and (3) he conceives of crucifixion as simply one of those great brutalities that must be applied in suppressing brigandage and rebellion (and hence there is no reason to incessantly comment on its excess). Most likely a mixture of these motives is to be found in Josephus.

Yet Josephus, as a priestly, upper-class Pharisaic disciple, also finds certain historical events of crucifixion deeply offensive. The impious way in which the Hasmonean Jewish king Alexander Jannaeus crucified fellow Jews (albeit rebellious ones) earns curt and caustic comments from Josephus (*Bell.* i.97–98; *Ant.* xiii.380). Neither does he portray favourably the soldiers who mockingly played at crucifying multitudes of Jews outside the walls of Jerusalem (though Titus is absolved of responsibility; *Bell.* v.449–451). Josephus does not shirk from describing the horror of crucifixion. He himself even breaks down in tears for his crucified comrades. Indeed, crucifixion is so horrible that some battle-hardened Jews will even betray their own city to avoid "the most pitiable of deaths" (*Bell.* vii.202–203), though the bravest Jewish rebels endure even crucifixion with a smile (*Bell.* iii.321). However, for Josephus the true sadism of Florus' implementation of crucifixion was not merely that he *crucified* citizens of moderation, but that he crucified those of *equestrian rank* – clearly the protesting voice of the upper classes (*Bell.* ii.306–308).

As is clear from this last comment, our sources vary in terms of the social status and geographical locations of those passing down the accounts; and this variation can affect their perspectives on crucifixion. However, some general themes do emerge: Crucifixion is almost universally viewed as a horrendous penalty, often being mentioned among the most extreme forms of death. However, in certain cases, such a punishment was so well known that it is taken for granted (e.g., in war, or in dealing with heinous criminals). Nonetheless, a theme in some Jewish texts is that not everyone who goes to the cross merits its prolonged agony – some Jews are "innocent sufferers." Occasionally the suffering of the innocent comes as the direct result of their adherence to the customs of Judaism – they become crucified martyrs. This is strikingly evidenced when Josephus and the *Assumption of Moses* agree in portraying the Maccabean martyrs as crucified. The cross, then, is the ultimate torment not only for the bandit and the rebel, but also for the innocent and the martyr.

Chapter Three

Biblical Suspension Texts and Jewish Tradition

This chapter addresses passages from the Hebrew Bible that speak of the bodily suspension of a person (either before or after death). Actual crucifixion is probably not in view in the Hebrew Bible itself. Rather, the significance of these texts for this study ultimately stems from their influence in later Jewish thought where they appear either explicitly or implicitly to inform perceptions of crucifixion.

Specifically, below are examined later Jewish traditions associated with passages in the Hebrew Bible that contain: the phrase תלה [אתו] על עץ, the causative *binyanim* of the Hebrew verb יקע, or the Aramaic verb זקף. Some brief text-critical notes are made to determine forms of these texts present in Jewish antiquity. Nevertheless, this chapter primarily seeks to illuminate how early Jewish interpretations of these passages manifest ancient Jewish perceptions of crucifixion and suspension.

One could rightly inquire why this chapter follows in the sequence it does; after all, the Hebrew Bible itself refers to an era that preceded the material in the previous chapter. However, here we are less concerned with the reported historical events, and more interested in the reception of these biblical episodes in Second Temple and rabbinic Judaism. To the extent that the Hebrew biblical authors intended to invoke memories of penalties that paralleled widespread ancient Near Eastern practices, it is quite possible that the OT suspension penalties imitate those forms depicted in Assyrian reliefs (such as the Lachish materials in the British Museum discussed in the next section). Thus the OT authors themselves could very well be referring to public impalements on tall stakes; and these impalements either would have been performed *post mortem*, or they would have produced immediate death. However, Jewish readers in the Second Temple era began understanding these texts in light of the various suspension penalties practiced in their own day.

The previous chapter strongly indicates that Jewish people, living during the rise of Hellenism and under the empire of the Romans, witnessed frequent crucifixions – numbering at times in the hundreds or thousands. Therefore, one should not be surprised in this period that biblical stories were increasingly retold by employing the crucifixion imagery so prevalent in the Hellenistic and Roman world. Note that in this era authors were also summarizing famous stories from pagan antiquity with crucifixion vocabulary. Thus the death of Polycrates of Samos, who (according to Herodotus) was horribly executed and then attached *post mortem* to a stake, was later understood to be an act of executionary suspension[1]; and Lucian repeatedly represents the myth of Prometheus, tethered to a rock and devoured daily by an eagle, as an act of crucifixion (Lucian, *Prometheus*).

Septuagint scholars have employed the term "actualization" to refer to the activity of translating passages with terms and phrases that bring the biblical text into a cultural sphere more contemporary to the time of the translator.[2] Hence, when a Greek translator of the book of Esther (departing from his normal literalistic translation of the Hebrew "hung on a tree") suddenly utilizes the term σταυρόω to speak of Haman's demise, the translator "actualizes" the text. In doing so, not only does he signal that he himself views the biblical story in light of suspension practices in his own day, but he also constrains the future readers of his translation to understand the story to refer to "crucifixion-like" events. As shall be shown inductively below, this practice of employing technical suspension/crucifixion vocabulary to render biblical narratives is far from limited to the Greek translation of Esther. In fact, most biblical texts involving human bodily suspension are actualized by at least some Jewish translators and interpreters. Further, beyond mere actualization of vocabulary, several key treatments of these biblical episodes shift or omit words from the biblical text, thus effectively heightening the sense that some Jewish people in the Second Temple and Rabbinic eras understood these narratives as referring to crucifixion.[3] The procedure in this chapter is to

---

[1] Herodotus' sequence of verbs (in *Hist.* iii.125) informs us that the pinning to the stake (using the verb ἀνασταυρόω) occurred after Polycrates death, though the focus remained on the hanging (ἀνακρεμάμενος). Later tradition focused so much on the suspension that it would appear to the casual reader to be an act of crucifixion – see possibly Lucian, *Cont.* 14 (taking the Hermes reference to ἀνασκολοπισθήσεται to refer to means of death, with the Charon response a summary of many means of executing people like Polycrates); and Philo, *Prov.* ii.24–25 (with the death expressed by προσηλοῦτο and later summarized by κρεμάμενος). See further Hengel, *Crucifixion*, 24n.

[2] This includes such scholars as Seeligmann, Hanhart, Koenig, and van der Kooij. See e.g., A. van der Kooij, "Isaiah in the Septuagint," in *Writing and Reading the Scroll of Isaiah*, ed. C. G. Broyles and C. A. Evans, vol. 2 (Leiden: Brill, 1997), 513–529. The term "actualization" has been understood either (1) to refer to a translation/interpretation of the biblical text through the lens of a later interpreter's cultural assumptions; or, more specifically, (2) to designate a Jewish translation/interpretation which claims that a biblical text predicts (or parallels) certain contemporary events (cf. the *pesherim* literature at Qumran). It is the former, more broad, understanding that is intended in this chapter, since most Jewish traditions in this chapter merely manifest a tendency toward assimilating the suspension penalty into the current culture of the translator (the biblical text is generally not held to predict contemporary events).

[3] A brief summary of these biblical episodes, with a focus to how the biblical texts have been "actualized" in favor of crucifixion, can be found in David W. Chapman, "Crucifixion, Bodily Suspension, and Jewish Interpretations of the Hebrew Bible in Antiquity," in *Beyond*

examine initially the original suspension texts from the Hebrew Bible, and then to focus on how the penalties in these texts came to be understood in Second Temple and rabbinic Judaism. Summaries are provided for longer sections. In order to indicate the cultural framework in which the original biblical texts were written, it is important to first place them within the context of the ancient Near East.

1. Suspension in the Ancient Near East

Old Testament texts on human bodily suspension should be viewed against their ancient Near Eastern background. Further, Greek and Roman authors frequently understood such ANE bodily suspension penalties (particularly those in Persia) to be in continuity with crucifixion.

Early testimony to post-mortem suspension of dangerous thieves can be found in Hammurabi's Code.[4] In another place the Code decrees that a woman who has her husband killed should be "impaled" (whether ante- or post-mortem is debatable).[5] One Ugaritic text indicates the use of *post mortem* suspension (subsequent to throwing the forcibly inebriated person down from a high place and stoning him) to punish a blasphemer who had brought pestilence on the people.[6] A related penalty of impalement is later recorded in the Middle Assyrian Laws for the woman who procures an abortion – her body is specifically to be left unburied.[7] This Assyrian law could be contrasted with the OT command to bury a suspended body within the day (Deut 21:22–23). Likewise, one could compare the penalty recorded in Ezra 6:11 (suspension outside one's own house for anyone altering the royal edict) to a stele inscription from the time of Sennacherib that requires the suspension before one's own house for building a dwelling that encroaches upon the royal road.[8]

---

the Jordan: Studies in Honor of W. Harold Mare, ed. Glenn A. Carnagey, Sr. et al. (Eugene, Oreg.: Wipf & Stock, 2005), 37–48.

[4] §§21, 227. For discussion of the crucial verb see G. R. Driver and John C. Miles, *The Babylonian Laws*, 2 vols., Ancient Codes and Laws of the Near East (Oxford: Clarendon Press, 1952/55), 2:158–59; cf. also 1:108–9, 424–25.

[5] §153. See discussion in Driver and Miles, *Babylonian Laws*, 1:313–14; 2:230.

[6] The text is discussed in David M. Clemens, *Sources for Ugaritic Ritual and Sacrifice: Volume 1: Ugaritic and Ugarit Akkadian Texts*, AOAT 284/1 (Münster: Ugarit-Verlag, 2001), 1038–1040. Clemens argues that this is an instance of impalement rather than crucifixion (despite an occasional translation to the contrary by the text's editor, Arnaud), though Clemens admits that the plural mention of wood (and the singular reference to the criminal) may complicate this analysis. I am grateful to my colleague Robert Vasholz for this reference.

[7] Tablet A, §53; cf. G. R. Driver and John C. Miles, *The Assyrian Laws*, Ancient Codes and Laws of the Near East (Oxford: Clarendon Press, 1935), 115–18; 420–21.

[8] English translation in Daniel David Luckenbill, *Ancient Records of Assyria and Babylonia*, 2 vols. (Chicago: University of Chicago, 1926–1927), 2:195 (§476). For this text I

Apart from these legal texts, there are reliefs and inscriptions from ninth-to seventh-century Assyria that provide repeated testimony to impalement and bodily suspension of conquered foes in battle.[9] Indeed it becomes a common boast of Assyrian kings that they have taken captive the inhabitants of a town and suspended/impaled its leaders.[10] The Assyrians also practiced such executions in their most distant territories, as when bodily suspension was employed against rebellious Egyptian vassals of the Assyrian king Ashurbanipal.[11]

This Assyrian practice of mutilating and suspending the bodies of conquered peoples also is testified later among the Medes and Persians in the famous trilingual Behistûn (= Bisitun) Inscription of Darius the Great.[12] The text of this monumental inscription, apparently including the reference to the suspended rebel vassals, was copied and widely distributed. It was even known by the Jewish community in fifth century BCE Elephantine.[13]

Studies often associate the inception of crucifixion in antiquity with the Persians; and indeed sources frequently testify to acts of suspension under Persian rule. However, it should be noted that: (1) this testimony is largely found in later Greek and Latin sources (thus stemming from a Hellenistic viewpoint of history), (2) as remarked in chapter one, the terminology employed by these sources is rarely sufficient in itself definitively to

---

am indebted to Richard Neville. For hanging before one's own house also cf. Hammurabi's Code §§21 & 227 (noted above).

[9] For reliefs cf. ANEP 362 (conquest of Dabigu by Shalmaneser III), 368 (=AoBAT 132; Tiglath-Pileser III relief from Nimrûd), 373 (= AoBAT 141; Sennacherib conquest of Lachish).

[10] See Luckenbill, *Records*, 2:294–95, 324 (=§§773, 844); also 1:279 (§776 of the Annals of Tiglath-Pileser III); 1:281 (§783, in the Nimrûd Slab Inscription, c.734 BCE); and 1:284 (§789, in the Nimrûd Tablet, 728 BCE). For the Tiglath-Pileser material, I am indebted to Leslie McFall. For further examples see under "*zaqāpu*" and "*zaqīpu*" in *CAD*, vol. 21.

[11] So in the Rassam Cylinder and in Cylinder B; see Luckenbill, *Records*, 2:294–95 (§773 = ANET[3] p. 295) and 2:324 (§844).

[12] See L. W. King and R. C. Thompson, *The Sculptures and Inscription of Darius the Great on the Rock of Behistûn in Persia* (London: Harrison & Sons, 1907), pp. 35–39 (Persian §§32–33), 121–25 (Susian §§25–26), 181–83 (Babylonian §§26–27). Revised Babylonian text in Elizabeth N. Voigtlander, *The Bisitun Inscription of Darius the Great: Babylonian Version*, Corpus Inscriptionum Iranicarum II.1 (London: Lund Humphries, 1978), 27–29, 57–58.

[13] Unfortunately the Elephantine MS is fragmentary at the crucial point, but editors typically suggest that the bodily suspension boast had been transmitted with the whole text. See reconstructed line iii.35 in A. Cowley, *Aramaic Papyri of the Fifth Century B.C.* (Oxford: Clarendon Press, 1923), pp. 253, 258, 263 (Cowley hypothesizes the text read צלבת). And, more recently, see column vii, lines 47–49 in Bezalel Porten and Ada Yardeni, *Textbook of Aramaic Documents from Ancient Egypt*, 4 vols. (Winona Lake: Eisenbrauns, 1986–1993), 3:68–69 (Porten suggests the text in line 48 reads בזקיפא). Stauffer (*Jerusalem*, 123–24) emphasized the importance of the Elephantine papyri in this connection.

determine that "crucifixion" was employed as opposed some other form of human bodily suspension, and (3) other ancient peoples in Europe, Egypt, and Asia were said to crucify as well.[14] Nevertheless, it is apparent from the testimony of the Behistûn inscription and elsewhere that Persians frequently employed bodily suspension in the context of execution. Jewish knowledge of this Persian practice can easily be witnessed in Ezra 6:11 and in the book of Esther (e.g., 2:23; 5:14; 6:4; 7:9–10; 8:7; 9:13–14; 9:25).

As already mentioned, Greek and Latin authors frequently asserted that the ancient (albeit barbaric) Persian civilization practiced crucifixion. The tendency among prominent Hellenistic authors to envision Persian executionary practices as involving crucifixion may also have influenced Jewish perceptions of Persian history as well as Jewish understandings of their own narratives of that period (cf. the later Esther interpretations examined below).

The point of this brief discussion is to underline the fact that Jewish people knew among their neighbours an extended history of human bodily suspension long before Greek and Roman hegemony. The Hebrew Bible represents Israelites as practicing such suspensions themselves (Deut 21:22; Josh 8:29; 10:26; possibly 2 Sam 4:12), as benefiting from such penal legislation by others (Ezra 6:11; Esther 7:9–10; 8:7; 9:13–14; 9:25), and even as suffering from such penalties (2 Sam 21:12; Lam 5:12). However these same biblical texts also indicate that the common ancient Near Eastern practice of bodily suspension was not, in fact, adopted uncritically by all Israelites, for prolonged exposure of the body was sometimes expressly opposed (since the suspended body was connected with the curse of God).[15] Finally, the Hellenistic tendency to associate crucifixion with some ancient Near Eastern empires may also have influenced Jewish perceptions of these empires and perhaps even Jewish perceptions of Jewish history.

2. Joseph and the Baker (Genesis 40–41)

In Genesis 40, Joseph interprets dreams by the imprisoned chief butler and the chief baker. To the baker he pronounces (Gen 40:19):

בְּעוֹד שְׁלֹשֶׁת יָמִים יִשָּׂא פַרְעֹה אֶת־רֹאשְׁךָ מֵעָלֶיךָ וְתָלָה אוֹתְךָ עַל־עֵץ וְאָכַל הָעוֹף אֶת־בְּשָׂרְךָ מֵעָלֶיךָ

"Within yet three days Pharaoh will lift up your head from upon you, and he will hang you on a tree, and the birds will eat your flesh from upon you."

---

[14] On these three points cf. Martin Hengel, *Crucifixion in the Ancient World and the Folly of the Message of the Cross*, trans. John Bowden (London & Philadelphia: SCM Press & Fortress Press, 1977), 22–25 (repr. 114–17).

[15] So Deut 21:22–23; cf. Josh 8:29; 10:26.

If the first מֵעָלֶיךָ ("from upon you") is included, then the phrase יִשָּׂא פַרְעֹה אֶת־רֹאשְׁךָ מֵעָלֶיךָ ("Pharaoh will lift up your head from upon you") would probably refer to Pharaoh calling for a beheading of the baker.

The Hebrew text form of this verse is well represented with only one significant variant. Two Hebrew MSS (according to *BHS*) and the Vulgate omit the first מֵעָלֶיךָ. Several scholars (including the editors of *BHS*) prefer to follow the omission of the first מֵעָלֶיךָ, noting both that its absence would maintain the parallelism with "lift up your head" elsewhere in Genesis 40 (cf. vv. 13, 20), and that its omission provides an easier reading in this context.[16]

Nevertheless, the textual evidence strongly favours including the first מֵעָלֶיךָ for at least three reasons: (1) The Hebrew testimony for omission is extremely sparse.[17] (2) The Vulgate is not merely missing the first "from upon you" but also the second; hence, it is probable that Jerome's omission stems from a desire to smooth out the text for his Latin readers rather than from a variant Hebrew text. (3) Other attested early versions most likely stem from Hebrew texts reading the first מֵעָלֶיךָ.[18] Note that the Septuagint, Old Latin, and Peshiṭta translations render the phrase "lift up your head" idiomatically elsewhere in chapter forty when it is without מֵעָלֶיךָ in the Hebrew (e.g., 40:13 – Pharaoh "will remember your leadership" in the LXX; also cf. 40:20). However, these same translations in verse 19 are so indebted to a Hebrew

---

[16] Several scholars suggest that a scribe inserted the first מֵעָלֶיךָ in verse 19 on analogy with the second; e.g., Arnold B. Ehrlich, *Randglossen zur hebräischen Bibel*, 7 vols. (Leipzig, 1908–1914), 1:204; Hermann Gunkel, *Genesis*, trans. Mark E. Biddle, Mercer Library of Biblical Studies (Macon, Ga.: Mercer University Press, 1997), 414; John Skinner, *A Critical and Exegetical Commentary on Genesis*, 2nd ed., ICC (Edinburgh: T. & T. Clark, 1930), 463; Claus Westermann, *Genesis 37–50: A Commentary*, trans. John J. Scullion (Minneapolis: Augsburg, 1986), 72; Nahum M. Sarna, *Genesis*, JPS Torah Commentary (Philadelphia: Jewish Publication Society, 1989), 279–80; Victor P. Hamilton, *The Book of Genesis*, 2 vols., NICOT (Grand Rapids: Eerdmans, 1990–1995), 2:483. The omission of מֵעָלֶיךָ is also recommended by *BHK*.

[17] The two Hebrew manuscripts *BHS* lists omitting מֵעָלֶיךָ are presumably those numbered 18 and 674 (the latter from 1474 CE) in Johannes B. De-Rossi, *Variae Lectiones Veteris Testamenti*, 4 + suppl. vols. (Parma: Ex Regio Typographeo, 1784–1798), 1:36. However, it is worth noting De-Rossi's own assessment of this testimony: "*Sed ut abest superius v.13, nonnisi incuria amanuensium ad hunc vers. animum intendentium omissum puto.*" The Samaritan Pentateuch MSS also include מעליך. Finally, when remarking on the only readable (though fragmentary) text of Genesis 40:19 from Qumran, the editors of the text suggest that, although not preserved in the fragments, the inclusion of מעליך would be required by the line length of line 1 (*sic*, actually line 2) in 4QGen^e (=4Q5) frag. 4 i 5 (in *DJD* XII, p. 49).

[18] E.g., LXX ἀπὸ σοῦ [in all but a few Medieval MSS]; OL *abs te*; and Peshiṭta ܡܢܟ – all three translating as "from you." The targumim also assume a מֵעָלֶיךָ Hebrew *Vorlage*: *Tg. Neof.* reads מעילוך ("from upon you"); *Tg. Onq.* simplifies to מינך ("from you"); *Tg. Ps.-J.* clarifies the reading with מעילוי גופך ("from upon your body"). The Samaritan Targum also includes מן עליך ("from upon you").

מֵעָלֶיךָ that they render the clause literally with the idea of "he will lift your head *from you*" in verse 19 (also cf. *Tg.Ps.-J.* and *Tg. Onq.*).[19] Thus, we conclude that the מֵעָלֶיךָ is original, and that it was well known in early translation traditions.

Crucial to this study is the fact that the idea of "hanging on a tree" is well documented in all the manuscripts and versions.[20] In fact, the one variant of note in this regard comes from the Samaritan Pentateuch, which attaches an article to "tree," thus reading "and he will hang you on *the* tree" (ותלא אתך על העץ).[21]

The sequence within the MT text of 40:19 appears to imply death by beheading (or perhaps beheading subsequent to some other means of execution) followed by the *post mortem* suspension of the body (with the resulting feeding of the birds).[22] Some commentators, emending the text to exclude the first מֵעָלֶיךָ ("from upon you") in verse 19, understand "lift up your head" to signify "summon" and the subsequent suspension (וְתָלָה) to be the means of death (generally seen as equivalent to ANE impalement).[23]

---

[19] See further John William Wevers, *Notes on the Greek Text of Genesis*, SBLSCS 35 (Atlanta: Scholars Press, 1993), 668, 672–73 (also noting the genitive in LXX 40:19 ἔτι τριῶν ἡμερῶν); and David Marcus, "'Lifting up the Head': On the Trail of a Word Play in Genesis 40," *Prooftexts* 10 (1990): 23–24.

[20] Also present in 4QGen[e] (= 4Q5); and suggested by the editors of *DJD* XII in their transcription of 4QGen[c] (= 4Q3; though here only the ל of על is certain).

[21] The Samaritan Pentateuch will often include an article where the MT does not; see Rudolf Macuch, *Grammatik des samaritanischen Hebräisch*, Studia Samaritana 1 (Berlin: Walter de Gruyter, 1969), 484ff.

[22] So Ibn Ezra, loc. cit.. See further: Franz Delitzsch, *A New Commentary on Genesis*, trans. Sophia Taylor, 2 vols. (Edinburgh: T. & T. Clark, 1888–1889), 2:291–92; A. Dillmann, *Genesis: Critically and Exegetically Expounded*, trans. Wm. B. Stevenson, 2 vols. (Edinburgh: T. & T. Clark, 1897), 2:364; E. A. Speiser, *Genesis*, AB 1 (Garden City, NY: Doubleday, 1964), 307–8; also (hesitatingly) Gerhard von Rad, *Das erste Buch Mose: Genesis*, 10th ed., ATD 2/4 (Göttingen: Vandenhoeck & Ruprecht, 1976), 304. In contrast, D. Marcus argues that the Hebrew phrase "lift up your head from you" is roughly the equivalent of the English "off with his head" – i.e., it represents vaguely a call to execution without specifying means; see Marcus, "Lifting up the Head," 18. Also note that Rashbam took the phrase to signify the standing up of the body for the purpose of hanging; see Martin I. Lockshin, *Rabbi Samuel ben Meir's Commentary on Genesis: an Annotated Translation*, Jewish Studies 5 (Lewiston, NY: Edwin Mellen, 1989), 277. It should be admitted that any implied order of executionary measures hinges on how one understands the syntax of the *waw*-conjunction on וְתָלָה. On the feeding of the birds, see further in this section; also cf. 4Q385a 15 i 3–4 mentioned in the appendix of this book.

[23] This argument draws strength from the parallel text in 40:13, where it is also said to the chief-butler, "Pharaoh will lift up your head"; and note a similar parallel in 40:20, where the idea of "summoning" works quite well. Note likewise 2 Kgs 25:27 and Jer 52:31. Also adduced are Akkadian parallels to "lift your head" with the meaning "summon." The argument is well developed by G. R. Driver, review of *Ancient Israel's Criminal Law: A New Approach to the Decalogue*, by Anthony Phillips, In *JTS* n.s., 23 (1972): 161; also see

However, as noted above, the textual witness strongly supports including the first מֵעָלֶיךָ;[24] and this text representing מֵעָלֶיךָ must have been well known among the early translators of Genesis.[25]

However, the two other references in this Genesis narrative to the death of the baker neglect any "beheading" elements, and they instead telescope the events of the execution of the baker into the single phrase "and him he hung" (e.g., וְאֹתוֹ תָלָה in Genesis 41:13; cf. וְאֵת שַׂר הָאֹפִים תָּלָה in 40:22).[26] The versions also support the MT in these summary references to suspension.[27] Thus, although beheading is clearly implied in one verse, the crucial penalty emphasized in the overall Genesis narrative is the bodily suspension of the chief baker.[28]

2.1 Philo and the Chief Baker

In Jewish traditions, crucifixion language is often employed in rendering this narrative. So Philo speaks of the episode using ἀνασκολοπίζω (*Jos.* 96–98;

Hamilton, *Genesis*, 2:483. However, the phrase "lifting the head" does permit wider reference than is implied by Driver, et al.; see E. A. Speiser, "Census and Ritual Expiation in Mari and Israel," *BASOR* 149 (1958): 20–21; and Marcus, "Lifting," 21. Related interpretations, also dependent on omission of מֵעָלֶיךָ, can be found in: Anthony Phillips, *Ancient Israel's Criminal Law: A New Approach to the Decalogue* (Oxford: Basil Blackwell, 1970), 27 ("take up a case"); Westermann, *Genesis*, 77 (Pharaoh turns personally to him during an audience); Sarna, *Genesis*, 279–80 ("call to account").

[24] The inclusion of מֵעָלֶיךָ also works on a literary level. It is often held that there is a word play here between the "lifting of the head" in vv. 13, 19, and 20; e.g., see Delitzsch, *Genesis*, 2:291; Walter Brueggemann, *Genesis*, IBC (Atlanta: John Knox, 1982), 321. But this word play is made all the more clear with the מֵעָלֶיךָ; see Dillman, *Genesis*, 2:364; D. Marcus, "Lifting," 18–19.

[25] As noted earlier; see the LXX, OL, Peshitta, and all targumic traditions. Also note the themes of beheading and hanging in Philo, *Jos.* 96, 98; *Som.* ii.213 (see below §2.1).

[26] In 40:20, both the butler and baker's heads are lifted, and the language apparently continues the word play implied by 40:19. Hence, it is possible that a reference to beheading also is assumed in 40:20 in preparation for 40:22. In any case, 41:13 clearly telescopes the incident.

[27] The LXX and Syriac versions exhibit the suspension clauses in Genesis 40:22; 41:13 with no significant variants. While the Old Latin also supports the LXX in Genesis 41:13, some OL manuscripts do not include *suspendit* in Genesis 40:22. Unlike the MT, the LXX has a passive rendering of וְאֹתוֹ תָלָה in Genesis 41:13 (ἐκεῖνον δὲ κρεμασθῆναι), but Wevers attributes this to the translator's attempt to solve the dilemma in his Hebrew text of the grammatical subject of תָלָה (also note a similar translational alteration in the preceding clause) – see Wevers, *Notes on Genesis*, 680–81. The omitted subject of the Hebrew sentence in 41:13 is striking enough that Rashi labels it an example of מקראות קצרים (i.e., "elliptical sentences") and spells out the subject (= Pharaoh) in his commentary.

[28] Rather than a variant text-form in Genesis 40:19, this is the likely explanation of why Josephus in *Ant.* ii.72–73 omits the idea of beheading when he encapsulates the means of execution with ἀνασταυρόω (see below).

Som. ii.213) and προσηλόω (*Som.* ii.213) in addition to κρεμάννυμι and ἀνακρεμάννυμι (*Jos.* 156). For example, Philo recounts the biblical narrative in *De Josepho* 93–98, with the crucial passages reading:

[96] τὰ τρία κανᾶ σύμβολον τριῶν ἡμερῶν ἐστιν· ἐπισχὼν ταύτας ὁ βασιλεὺς ἀνασκολοπισθῆναί σε καὶ τὴν κεφαλὴν ἀποτμηθῆναι κελεύσει καὶ καταπτάμενα ὄρνεα τῶν σῶν εὐωχηθήσεται σαρκῶν, ἄχρις ἂν ὅλος²⁹ ἐξαναλωθῇς.

[98] ...τῶν κατὰ τὸ δεσμωτήριον εὐνούχων ὑπομνησθεὶς ἀχθῆναι κελεύει καὶ θεασά-μενος τὰκ τῆς τῶν ὀνείρων διακρίσεως ἐπισφραγίζεται, προστάξας τὸν μὲν ἀνασκολο-πισθῆναι τὴν κεφαλὴν ἀποτμηθέντα,³⁰ τῷ δὲ τὴν ἀρχὴν ἣν διεῖπε πρότερον ἀπονεῖμαι.³¹

[96] The three baskets are a symbol of three days; upon reaching these, the king will com-mand you to be crucified and your head to be cut off, and the attacking birds will feast on your flesh, until you wholly are consumed.
[98] ...[the king], remembering the eunuchs in the prison, commanded them to be brought, and beholding them he confirmed the judgment of the dreams, ordering the one to be cruci-fied, his head being cut off, but to the other to be assigned the office that he held before.

Beyond Philo's explicit use of crucifixion terminology (ἀνασκολοπισθῆναι), one striking feature of this text is the way it employs and revises the Septuagint understanding of "lift up the head." Where the LXX renders this phrase in 40:20 idiomatically with "remember the office" (ἐμνήσθη τῆς ἀρχῆς, cf. 40:13), so similarly does Philo (ὑπομνησθεὶς in *Jos.* 98; cf. ὑπομνησθήσεται in 92). Where the LXX has literally conveyed the idea of "lift your head from you" in 40:19, Philo has the head being cut off. However, Philo reverses the order of "lifting your head from you" and "hang you on a tree" (especially noticeable in *Jos.* 96), likely implying that the suspension precedes the beheading.³² The mention of "attacking birds," while also indebted to the LXX of Genesis 40:19, would remind Philo's contemporaries of the scavenger birds often associated with crucifixion.

In *De Josepho* 151–56, Philo further treats this episode, presenting an interpretation that he has "heard" (cf. 151). In this understanding the hung "baker" represents the one who provides food for the body (whose mind is allegorically "Pharaoh"). When the entity represented by the "baker" fails to provide proper sustenance, he receives back his due:

[156] τελευτὴ γὰρ ἔπεται σιτίων σπάνει· οὗ χάριν καὶ ὁ περὶ ταῦτ᾽ ἐξαμαρτὼν εἰκότως θνῄσκει κρεμασθείς, ὅμοιον κακὸν ᾧ διέθηκε παθών· καὶ γὰρ αὐτὸς ἀνεκρέμασε καὶ παρέτεινε τὸν πεινῶντα λιμῷ.

---

²⁹ While an adjective in the Cohn-Wendland text, some MSS have the adverb ὅλως.

³⁰ Many manuscripts (A, B, E, M) read ἀποτμηθῆναι ("to be cut off"; agreeing with *Jos.* 96), while one manuscript (F, followed here by Cohn/Wendland) reads ἀποτμηθέντα.

³¹ One MS ἀποδοῦναι, others ἀπολαβεῖν.

³² Colson's translation of *Jos.* 98 ("ordering one to be beheaded and impaled"; in *Philo*, LCL 5:189) is unlikely to have been Philo's intent in light of how this reverses the sequence of infinitives in *Jos.* 96, as well as the order of the verbs in *Jos.* 98. On this matter the trans-lations of Yonge and Laporte are preferable.

[156] For death follows lack of bread-food, on account of which the one who errs greatly concerning these things also properly dies by being hung, a similar evil to which he treated the sufferer, for indeed he had hung up and stretched the famished man with hunger.

Notably the central penalty in this passage involves the suspension of the baker. Indeed, if we properly understand the participle κρεμασθείς as conveying instrumentality ("by being hung"), then such suspension is the means of death.

Philo, himself, offers a different interpretation in *De Somniis* ii.205–14. Here the "head" in the dream is understood allegorically as "mind," whereas the baker is a "belly-slave" who provides for the intemperate Pharaoh. The three baskets represent past, present and future dimensions of pleasure that the mind contemplates; but the birds represent unforeseen (though apparently God-ordained) events that devour the inventions of pleasure (= baskets). So Philo opines (*Som.* ii.213):

περισυληθείς[33] οὖν ὁ νοῦς ὧν ἐδημιούργησεν, ὥσπερ τὸν αὐχένα ἀποτμηθεὶς ἀκέφαλος καὶ νεκρὸς ἀνευρεθήσεται, προσηλωμένος ὥσπερ οἱ ἀνασκολοπισθέντες τῷ[34] ξύλῳ τῆς ἀπόρου καὶ πενιχρᾶς ἀπαιδευσίας.

The mind, therefore, stripped of the things it fabricated, like one who was severed at the neck, will be discovered headless and a corpse, nailed like those crucified to the tree of poor and needy lack of training.

This passage, clearly denoting people affixed to "the tree" (employing προσηλόω and ἀνασκολοπίζω), exemplifies the way Philo has wed crucifixion terminology to his interpretation of the baker's execution.[35] "Lack of training" (ἀπαιδευσίας), a term known in classical philosophical discourse, likely indicates that the mind here has received neither proper instruction nor practice in discipline; and thus such a mind partakes of "foolishness."

In this passage Philo again refers to the idea of a suspended beheaded corpse. Does this reverse the order of suspension and then decapitation found above in *Jos.* 96–98? Not necessarily, for this vivid imagery pictures the total results of the punishment that the mind receives without taking the reader sequentially through the allegorical executionary process. In any case, it is clear that Philo connects beheading with crucifixion imagery; and Philo can use such imagery to depict the punishment of the mind that is in want of proper philosophical outlook. A similar Philonic metaphorical use of crucifixion can be found in *De Posteritate Caini* 61 (see below in chpt. 5, §1).

---

[33] MS A reads περισυλληφθείς, but Mangey argues for περισυληθείς and Cohn-Wendland agree.

[34] MS A reads αὐτῷ (i.e., "crucified to *his* tree"). Mangey suggests αὖ τῷ ("crucified *moreover to the* tree"). Cohn-Wendland reads τῷ (as above), though also conjecturing σταυρῷ τῷ ("crucified to a cross, the tree of…").

[35] This is standard Philonic terminology for crucifixion (as noted by Hengel, in *Crucifixion*, p. 24) – see esp. *Flacc.* 83–85; *Post.* 61.

2.2 Josephus and the Chief Baker

Josephus likewise employs crucifixion terminology in his rendering of Genesis 40. *Antiquities* ii.72–73: reads:

[72] ...λέγει δύο τὰς πάσας ἔτι τοῦ ζῆν αὐτὸν ἔχειν ἡμέρας· τὰ γὰρ κανᾶ τοῦτο σημαίνειν· [73] τῇ τρίτῃ δ᾽ αὐτὸν ἀνασταυρωθέντα βορὰν ἔσεσθαι πετεινοῖς οὐδὲν ἀμύνειν αὑτῷ δυνάμενον. καὶ δὴ ταῦτα τέλος ὅμοιον οἷς ὁ Ἰώσηπος εἶπεν ἀμφοτέροις ἔλαβε· τῇ γὰρ ἡμέρᾳ τῇ προειρημένῃ γενέθλιον τεθυκὼς ὁ βασιλεὺς τὸν μὲν ἐπὶ τῶν σιτοποιῶν ἀνεσταύρωσε, τὸν δὲ οἰνοχόον τῶν δεσμῶν ἀπολύσας ἐπὶ τῆς αὐτῆς ὑπηρεσίας κατέστησεν.

[72] ...[Joseph] told him that he had in all but two days yet to live (the baskets indicated that), [73] and that on the third day he would be crucified and become food for the fowls, utterly powerless to defend himself. And in fact this all fell out just as Joseph had declared to both of them; for on the day predicted the king, celebrating his birthday with a sacrifice, crucified the chief baker but released the butler from his bonds and restored him to his former office.[36]

Note that Josephus twice represents the suspension of the baker with ἀνασταυρόω in ii.73. A few lines later, in the narrative recapitulation of this event (*Ant.* ii.77; cf. Gen 41:13), Josephus refers to the baker's death with σταυρόω.[37]

Furthermore, Josephus omits the whole clause (present in the MT, LXX, etc.) that states, "Pharaoh will lift up your head from you."[38] Concerning this omission one possibility is that Josephus, like Rashbam in his commentary from almost a millennium later, saw the "lifting of the head from you" as an elevation of the whole person (head and body together) in preparation for the suspension on the tree; thus the entire execution could be described with the word ἀνασταυρόω. Another option is that Josephus, possibly aware that Genesis 41:13 and 40:22 emphasizes the suspension element of the execution, telescopes the event (either due to his conscious choice, or due to his lack of closely reading the text) into a death by suspension. In any case, by removing the apparent reference in Genesis to beheading prior to his suspension, Josephus actually increases the death by crucifixion aspects of his narrative.[39]

---

[36] Translation by Thackeray, LCL 4:199.

[37] ὅτι τε σταυρωθείη κατὰ τὴν αὐτὴν ἡμέραν ὁ ἐπὶ τῶν σιτοποιῶν (ii.77; "that the chief of the bakers was crucified on the same day").

[38] Since the whole clause is omitted, Josephus does not provide independent evidence in the text critical question (mentioned earlier) surrounding whether the first מֵעָלֶיךָ in the MT of Genesis 40:19 is an addition to the Hebrew text. Rather, as noted above, not only does the textual evidence indicate that the מֵעָלֶיךָ is original, but the evidence most pertinent to the Second Temple period (esp. the LXX and 4QGen^e frag. 4 i 5) suggests that Josephus was in all probability working with a Greek or Hebrew text that could be construed to imply the beheading of the baker.

[39] So also Thackeray in *Josephus*, LCL 4:199. Contrast Nodet, who contends in his edition "il est moins complexe d'admettre que FJ suit l'héb"; see Étienne Nodet, ed., *Flavius*

It is also noteworthy that the baker, subsequent to ἀνασταυρωθέντα, is described by Josephus as: βορὰν ἔσεσθαι πετεινοῖς οὐδὲν ἀμύνειν αὐτῷ δυνάμενον ("to be food for birds, unable to defend himself"; ii.73). In the MT and LXX he is merely prophesied to be "food for birds," with no mention of his incapacity to self-defense. Josephus' wording likely implies that the baker must be still alive while suspended in order to be able (not) to defend himself.[40] Again this serves to indicate a protracted death on a σταυρός.

2.3 Targumim and the Chief Baker

In rendering Genesis 40:19 the targumim employ צלב and its cognate noun. The underlining in the texts below highlights targumic variations and expansions.

(*Tg. Onq.*) בסוף תלתה יומין יעדי פרעה ית רישך מינך ויצלוב יתך על צליבא וייכול עופא ית בסרך מינך

(*Tg. Neof.*) לסוף תלתא יומין ירים פרעה ית ראשך מעילוך ויצלב יתך על צליבה[41] ויאכל עופא ית בשרך מעלווי ראשך[42]

(*Tg.Ps.-J.*) בסוף תלתא יומין יעדי בסייפא ית רישך מעילוי גופך ויצלוב יתך על קיסא ויכול עופא ית בישרך מינך

(*Tg. Onq.*) At the end of three days Pharaoh will <u>remove</u> your head from you, and he will <u>suspend</u> you on the <u>cross</u>,[43] and the birds will eat your flesh from you.

(*Tg. Neof.*) Toward the end of three days Pharaoh will lift your head from upon you, and he will <u>suspend</u> you on a <u>cross</u>, and the birds will eat your flesh from upon your <u>head</u>.

(*Tg. Ps.-J.*) At the end of three days Pharaoh will <u>remove by the sword</u> your head from upon <u>your body</u>, and he will <u>suspend</u> you on the tree, and the birds will eat your flesh from you.

Josèphe, Les Antiquités Juives, 2+ vols. (Paris: Les Éditions du Cerf, 1990–present), vol. 1b, p. 84. Yet, the very point is that Josephus cannot be following the Hebrew when he omits the whole "lifting your head" clause. Where a few later Hebrew manuscripts omit the מֵעָלֶיךָ ("from upon you"), Josephus does not even read the universally testified "Pharaoh will lift up your head" (present in all manuscripts of the MT and the LXX).

[40] On the idea of birds eating the flesh of the crucified compare: Euripides *Electra* 897–98 (of the dead body of Aegisthus); Pliny, *Nat. Hist.* xxxvi.107; Lucian *Prom.* 2, 4, 9; *Sacr.* 6 (of the still living Prometheus).

[41] צליבה: margin קיסה ("tree" for "gallows").

[42] מעילווי ראשך: margin [מע[לווך ("from upon you" for "from upon your head").

[43] "The cross" translates צליבא (also cf. *Tg. Neof.*), which is a common translation for this noun, and which allows it to be viewed distinctly from the more neutral קיסא ("the tree" in *Tg. Ps.-J.*). However, this admittedly does bias the translation to a crucifixion reading. Certainly, צליבא technically designates a device intended for penal bodily suspension, though both death by crucifixion and a *post mortem* suspension (such as is likely here) can occur on a צליבה (see discussion in chapter one, §2.3.1). "Cross" thus should be understood here to mean "a device employed for public penal bodily suspension." Similar comments could be made on subsequent translations of צליבה in the targumim below.

The targumim to Genesis 40:22 and 41:13 also employ צלב.[44] Here in 40:19 each targum implies that beheading preceded suspension (a conclusion heightened in *Tg. Ps.-J.* with בסיפא "by the sword," and also in *Tg. Onq.* with יעדי "will remove"). This illustrates that a post-mortem suspension is intended. Nonetheless, while a modern reader might tend to distinguish sharply such a penalty from crucifixion, the vocabulary used here (צליבא/צלב) had a strong association with crucifixion. As noted in chapter one, crucifixion formed a subset of human bodily suspension, and this vocabulary (צליבא/צלב) could be comfortably applied to designate any such suspension. Therefore, though the targumim here indicate post-mortem suspension, this biblical episode likely may have been connected by those hearing the targumim with many such suspension penalties (including with crucifixion).

2.4 Summary

In the MT and early versions, Joseph's interpretation of the baker's dream indicates that the baker will be executed by beheading and subsequent bodily suspension (Gen 40:19). However the most emphasized aspect of his execution is his "hanging" (Gen 40:23; 41:13). This incident, especially with its mention of carrion birds, easily lent itself to later depiction employing suspension terminology with crucifixion overtones. So Philo employs ἀνασκολοπίζω in speaking of this episode, even implying that the beheading occurred after the suspension. Josephus considers it a case of ἀνασταυροῦν and σταυροῦν, and he omits altogether the aspects of beheading, thus almost certainly indicating crucifixion. The targumim maintain the beheading aspects of the narrative (most emphasized in *Tg. Ps.-J.*) and the order implied in the MT; however, the use in the targumim of the technical human suspension term צלב and its cognates likewise shifts the whole episode well within the range of ancient human bodily suspensions (among which crucifixion was included). Thus we have strong attestation in the first century, and continued indications in the targumic era, of possible crucifixion associations with the death of the chief baker.

3. Moses and the Leaders (Numbers 25:4)

In Shittim the women of Moab lure the Israelites to follow Baal; and the Lord responds in Numbers 25:4:

---

[44] See *Tg. Onq.*, *Tg. Neof.*, and *Tg. Ps.-J.* on Gen 40:22 and 41:13; as well as a Cairo Genizah targumic text on Gen 41:13 in Michael L. Klein, *Genizah Manuscripts of Palestinian Targum to the Pentateuch*, 2 vols. (Cincinnati: Hebrew Union College, 1986). So also the Samaritan Targum on these verses (except for MS A in 40:19).

וַיֹּאמֶר יְהוָה אֶל־מֹשֶׁה קַח אֶת־כָּל־רָאשֵׁי הָעָם וְהוֹקַע אוֹתָם לַיהוָה נֶגֶד הַשָּׁמֶשׁ וְיָשֹׁב חֲרוֹן אַף־יְהוָה מִיִּשְׂרָאֵל

And the LORD said to Moses, "Take all the leaders of the people, and execute them unto the LORD in front of the sun; and the heat of the anger of the LORD may turn from Israel."

Moses then summons the judges of Israel and commands them to slay the idolaters (v. 5). The narrative shifts to Phinehas' zealous spearing of Zimri and his Midianite consort. Phinehas' action results in the appeasement of God's wrath, in the subsequent lifting of the plague, and in the announcement of perpetual priesthood on Phinehas' house.

In Numbers 25:4 cited above, the most natural referent of אוֹתָם ("them") is the preceding group of רָאשֵׁי הָעָם ("the leaders of the people").[45] However, this would have Moses executing all the Israelite leadership – a surprising thought, made even less probable in the MT context by how Moses immediately instructs the judges of Israel (almost certainly "leaders") to slay others who are guilty (Num 25:5). Some suggest emendations to the MT here,[46] or postulate clumsy redactional seams.[47] However it is clear that the Septuagint, (as well as the Old Latin and the Vulgate) renders a Hebrew text similar to the MT, indicating that such a text was in wide circulation.[48] The targumic versions appear to be attempts to mitigate this same Hebrew syntax (by having Moses summon the leaders in order to commission them to execute the offenders). Interestingly, the Samaritan Pentateuch on 25:4 removes the problem altogether, also replacing the difficult word הוֹקַע:[49]

---

[45] So George Buchanan Gray, *A Critical and Exegetical Commentary on Numbers*, ICC (Edinburgh: T. & T. Clark, 1903), 383; Jacob Milgrom, *Numbers*, JPS Torah Commentary (Philadelphia: Jewish Publication Society, 1990), 213; Timothy R. Ashley, *The Book of Numbers*, NICOT (Grand Rapids: Eerdmans, 1993), 517. An Amoraic debate between R. Judan and R. Nehemiah took opposing views on whether the leaders are included in אוֹתָם (*Num. Rab.* xx.23; see below).

[46] For רָאשֵׁי הָעָם *BHS* lists two such proposals: רִשְׁעֵי ה' ("the wicked of the people") or הָרְשָׁעִים ("the wicked ones").

[47] So Gray, *Numbers*, 383 (apparently considering 25:4 to be from J and other material from E; see, p. 381); also cf. Martin Noth, *Numbers: A Commentary*, trans. James D. Martin, OTL (London: SCM Press, 1968), 197–98; J. de Vaulx, *Les Nombres*, SB (Paris: J. Gabalda et Cie, 1972), 299. In contrast Milgrom (*Numbers*, 476–77) argues against such a disparity in source material.

[48] Wevers contends that, since the majority of LXX MSS do not read "all" (παντας) in front of τοὺς ἀρχηγούς, the LXX translator perhaps envisioned only some of the leaders being so punished; see John William Wevers, *Notes on the Greek Text of Numbers*, SBLSCS 46 (Atlanta: Scholars Press, 1998), 421. For the textual point see John William Wevers, *Text History of the Greek Numbers* (Göttingen: Vandenhoeck & Ruprecht, 1982), 135. However, manuscripts of Philo do indicate that his LXX text read παντας (*Som.* i.89).

[49] While 4QNum^b often supports the Samaritan text of Numbers, here in Numbers 25:4 (= 4QNum^b 31–33 i 10–12 [in column 18]) the scroll, though quite fragmentary, apparently corroborates the MT by including remnants of [וה]וקע in line 11; see *DJD* 12, pp. 237–38.

וַיֹּאמֶר יהוה אֶל מֹשֶׁה אֲמֹר וַיַּהַרְגוּ אֶת הָאֲנָשִׁים הַנִּצְמָדִים לְבַעַל פְּעוֹר וְיָשֹׁב חֲרוֹן אַף
יהוה מִיִּשְׂרָאֵל

And the LORD spoke to Moses, <u>saying, "And they shall slay the men who are yoked to Baal Peor;</u>[50] and the heat of the anger of the LORD may turn from Israel."

Given the substantial external evidence in favour of the text of the MT, and the difficult nature of this verse in the MT itself, it is reasonable to postulate that the Samaritan reading represents a paraphrastic attempt to clarify the meaning of its Hebrew *Vorlage*.

Concerning הוּקַע in the MT, the survey of the *hiphil* of יקע above in chapter one concluded that the exact meaning of the term is rather elusive. The variety of versional renderings of this passage indicates that this was also true for ancient Jewish readers: Aquila reads ἀνάπηξον (lit. "to fix, transfix; impale or crucify"[51]) and Symmachus, κρέμασον ("to hang" – suggesting connection with other OT bodily suspension narratives). The Peshiṭta has the men being "spread out" (ܪܘܣ) in front of the sun. The general theme to these renderings involves the idea of public exposure (often by suspension).

The Septuagint employs παραδειγμάτισον ("to make an example of") to render וְהוֹקַע. This either refers to a public execution,[52] or to a public chastisement of the leaders (possibly involving torture, or maybe merely a "dressing down") before calling for the execution of the actual offenders.[53] Philo understands the LXX to refer to exposure to the sun and to God (*Som.* i.88–91). The Old Latin "*ostenta*," also conveys the idea of making an example of the leaders, quite possibly due to dependence on the LXX.[54]

Significantly, some Second Temple authors omit discussing this verse. For example, Josephus does not record God's command to Moses in Numbers 25:4; instead he has Moses assembling the people to endeavour to bring them to repentance (*Ant.* iv.142–44). The author of the *Liber Antiquitatum Biblicarum* omits mentioning altogether God's command and the

---

[50] Or possibly, "they shall slay the yoked men before Baal Peor."

[51] Cf. Liddell-Scott, s.v. ἀναπηγνὺμι. On impalement and crucifixion indicated by ἀναπήγνυμι cf. Plutarch, *Art.* 17.

[52] Such a use of παραδειγματίζω may be seen in LXX Dan 2:5 (= MT הַדָּמִין תִּתְעַבְדוּן) – a similar Hebrew phrase is rendered with διαμελισθήσεται ("he will be dismembered") in LXX Dan 3:96 [= MT 3:29].

[53] Cf. other LXX uses of παραδειγματίζω: Jer 13:22; Ezek 28:17; Esth C22 [= 4:17q = 14:11] (here said of Haman). Salvesen contends that παραδειγμάτισον suggests public humiliation rather than death; see Alison Salvesen, *Symmachus in the Pentateuch*, JSS Monograph 15 (Manchester: University of Manchester, 1991), 139. Dorival (comparing LXX with Polybius) likewise sees here "châtiment public," perhaps involving torture; see Gilles Dorival, *La Bible Alexandrie: Les Nombres* (Paris: Les Éditions du Cerf, 1994), 460.

[54] Dorival believes the Peshiṭta ܪܘܣ also conveys the sense of the LXX; see Dorival, *Nombres*, 460. However, though the semantic ranges of the Greek and Syriac may overlap here, they are not equivalent.

plague.[55] However, as we shall see, some important targumic and rabbinic traditions parallel Aquila and Symmachus when they employ the language of suspension in reference to this verse.

3.1 Targumim and Numbers 25:4

In contrast to the fairly vague language of Targum Onqelos, the Palestinian targumim (Neofiti, Pseudo-Jonathan, and the Fragment tradition) all apply suspension terminology in rendering this verse:

(*Tg. Onq.*) ‏ואמר יוי למשה דבר ית כל רישי עמא ודון וקטול דחייב קטול קדם יוי
‏לקביל שמשא ויתוב תקוף רוגזא דיוי מישראל

(*Tg. Neof.*) ‏ואמר ייי למשה דבר ית כל ראשי עמא ואקים יתהון בסנהדרין קדם ייי
‏ויהוון דיינין כל מן דמתחייב קטלה יצלבון[56] יתיה על צליבה וקברין ית נבלתהון עם
‏מטמעי שמשא בכדן יחזור תקוף רוגזה דייי מן ישראל

(*Tg. Ps.-J.*) ‏ואמר ייי למשה סב ית כל רישי עמא ומני יתהון דיינין וידונון דינין דקטולין
‏ית עמא דטעו בתר פעור ותצלוב יתהון קדם מימ[רא] דייי על קיסא קבל שמשא
‏בקרי*צתא* ועם מטמוע שימשא תחית יתהון ותקברינון ויתוב תקוף רוגזא דייי
‏מישראל[57]

(*Frg. Tg.* MS440) ‏ואמר מימרא דייי למשה סב ית כל רישי עמה ואוקים יתהון סנהדרין
‏קדם ייי ויהוון צלבין כל מן דמתחייב למתקטלא ועם מעלי[58] שמשא יהון מחתין
‏נבלתיה וקברין בכן[59] יחזור תקוף רוגזא דייי מן ישראל

(*Tg. Onq.*) And the LORD said to Moses, "Take all the leaders of the people, and pass judg-ment, and execute those who are liable to the death penalty before the LORD in front of the sun; and the strength of the anger of the LORD will turn from Israel."

(*Tg. Neof.*) And the LORD said to Moses, "Take all the leaders of the people, and appoint them in a Sanhedrin before the LORD, and let them be judges. Everyone who is liable to the death penalty they shall suspend on a cross, and bury their corpses with the sinking of the sun. In this manner the strength of the anger of the LORD will retract from Israel."

(*Tg. Ps.-J.*) And the LORD said to Moses, "Take all the leaders of the people, and appoint them judges, and let them judge capital cases – the people who went astray after Peor. And

---

[55] Cf. *Bib. Ant.* xviii.14; and see Howard Jacobson, *A Commentary on Pseudo-Philo's Liber Antiquitatum Biblicarum*, 2 vols., AGJU 31 (Leiden: E. J. Brill, 1996), 1:611.

[56] Interlineal variants in the Neofiti MS read ‏[למת]קטלה‏ ("to be killed") for ‏קטלה‏ and ‏וצלבין‏ ("and suspending") for ‏יצלבון‏.

[57] Text from Alexandro Diez Macho et al., eds., *Biblia Polyglotta Matritensia IV: Targum Palaestinense in Pentateuchum*, 5 vols. (Madrid: Consejo Superior de Investigaciones Científicas, 1977–1988). Throughout this book this edition is preferred to (though checked with) Ginsburger's edition. Asterisks indicate individual letters are supplied from MS mar-ginal note.

[58] MS110 ‏מטמע‏ ("sinking") for ‏מעלי‏ ("departing"); see *Tg. Neof.* and cf. *Tg. Ps.-J.* On ‏מעלי שמשא‏ meaning "sunset" see Marcus Jastrow, *A Dictionary of the Targumim, the Talmud Babli and Yerushalmi, and the Midrashic Literature*, 2 vols. (New York: Pardes, 1950), s.v. ‏מְעָלָה‏. Unless noted, MS110 follows MS440 except for minor orthography.

[59] MS110 reads ‏נבילתהון מחתין‏ for ‏נבלתיה‏; ‏מחתין‏; and MS110 reads ‏ובכן‏ for ‏בכן‏.

you shall suspend them before the Memra of the LORD on the tree opposite the sun at day-break; but with the sinking sun you shall lower them and you shall bury them. And the strength of the anger of the LORD will turn from Israel."

(*Frg. Tg.*) And the Memra of the LORD said to Moses, "Take all of the leaders of the people, and appoint them a Sanhedrin before the LORD. And let them suspend everyone who is liable to the death penalty; but with the departing sun let them lower their corpses and bury [them]. After this the strength of the anger of the LORD will retract from Israel."

The complex textual history of these targumic traditions makes it difficult to pronounce on exact connections between them. However, some common elements are evident. In each Palestinian targum the purpose of summoning the leaders is to make them judges, which certainly was not explicit in the Hebrew original. Such a tradition likely also underlies Onqelos, especially given the way Onqelos orders only those people slain who are guilty (קְטוֹל דְחַיָּיב וּקְטוֹל). Thus, the targumim solve the problem of who is to be executed in the MT וְהוֹקַע אוֹתָם ("and execute them").

While Onqelos (using the somewhat generic קְטַל) does not mention the means of execution, the Palestinian targumim agree that it involves צלב ("suspend"). In each case the verb צלב is not preceded by any other executionary means, leaving quite open the possibility that this is the method of death. Note also that *Targum Neofiti* employs the noun צליבה (translated above as "cross") rather than a more generic word for tree.[60]

All the Palestinian targumim explicitly tie this execution back to the legislation from Deuteronomy 21:22–23, which requires burial on the same day for the one who is suspended.[61] There are further verbal connections in the targumim (including here also Onqelos) between their treatments of Numbers 25:4 and Deuteronomy 21:22–23: especially the term חייב along with the idea of executing those who are "guilty (of a crime worthy) of execution."

Baumgarten has argued that the connections drawn in the targumim between Numbers 25:4 and Deuteronomy 21:22–23 indicate that these targumim conceived of the punishment in accordance with traditional rabbinic legislation. And, since the rabbinic legislation rejects crucifixion as a punishment, Baumgarten contends that references to crucifixion must also be absent in the targumim on Numbers.[62] However, Baumgarten fails to note that, unlike the rabbinical legislation on execution, there is nothing in these texts to indicate the suspension (צלב) is *post mortem* (contrast *Tg. Ps.-J.* on Lev 24:23 and on Deut 21:22–23). On the contrary, the natural way to read the

---

[60] On this translation of צליבה, see comments above on *Tg. Onq.* on Gen 40:19.

[61] Possibly the idea of "opposite the sun" in Numbers 25:4 helped suggest that the burial was before sunset; so Louis Ginzberg, *The Legends of the Jews*, trans. Henrietta Szold & Paul Radin; index by Boaz Cohen, 7 vols. (Philadephia: Jewish Publication Society, 1909–1938), 7:135 (n.790).

[62] Baumgarten, "Hanging," 8*–9*.

MT of Numbers 25:4 is that הוקע is the means of death (this is clearly recognized by *Tg. Onq.* with קטל); and, in the same way, צלב is likely also the means of execution in the Palestinian targumim. Any form of execution via suspension breaks with the traditional rabbinic fourfold means of execution,[63] and it also departs from rabbinic limitations on Deuteronomy 21 as a *post mortem* penalty.[64] Hence the Palestinian targumim on Numbers 25:4 vary, at least in some measure, from the so-called rabbinic norm.

Three important consequences come with this: (1) These Palestinian targumim then contravene the spirit of rabbinic tradition by indicating that suspension (in some *ante mortem* form) is here a means of death – one sanctioned by God and enacted by a Sanhedrin or judicial body. (2) Though there is flexibility in the semantic range of צלב such that it need not designate crucifixion (which is why it is translated above as "suspend"),[65] a person in a Graeco-Roman context reading or hearing the Palestinian targumim could easily have conceived of crucifixion as the likely means of death. (3) Deuteronomy 21:22–23 is here thought to apply to a death penalty enacted by *ante mortem* suspension.

3.2 Rabbinic Writings and Numbers 25:4

Rabbinic support for aspects of the targumic exegesis exists as early as *Sifre Numbers* 131:

ויאמר ה' אל משה קח את כל ראשי העם והוקע אותם לה' נגד השמש ⟨אמר לו הושב ראשי העם⟩ דיינים ויהיו צולבים את החטאים נגד השמש.[66]

And the Lord said to Moses, "Take all the leaders of the people, and execute them unto the LORD in front of the sun..." [Num 25:4]. He said to him, "Bring back the leaders of the people as judges and let them suspend those sinners in front of the sun."

---

[63] The Mishnah prescribes stoning, burning, beheading, and strangling (*m. Sanh.* vii.1). See discussion in chapter one, §3.

[64] As was mentioned in chapter 1 (§3) and is further noted in this chapter (§4.7), the rabbinic argument against the legality of crucifixion contended that death *precedes* hanging in Deuteronomy 21:22 (see e.g., *Sifre Deut.* 221; *b. Sanh.* 46b). Therefore, several key passages in the extant rabbinic legislation, while opposing the Roman practice of crucifixion, also consequentially required all penal suspensions to be *post mortem*.

[65] Also note that *Targum Pseudo-Jonathan* on Numbers 25:8 (paralleling extant rabbinic haggadah) increases the impalement aspects of the Phinehas account, which could possibly signal the executionary form intended in this Targum on Numbers 25:4.

[66] The text is from H. S. Horovitz, ed., *Siphre ad Numeros adjecto Siphre zutta: Cum variis lectionibus et adnotationibus*, Corpus Tannaiticum III.3 (Leipzig: Gustav Fock, 1917), p. 172. The most notably textual variant is that some manuscripts omit the bracketed section (i.e., "He said to him, 'Bring back the leaders of the people...'"). Such a shorter and more difficult reading could be understood to be somewhat ambiguous with regard to the fate of "the leaders of the people," but it likely also would imply that these leaders were viewed "as judges" (דיינים).

The *Sifre* thus conveys both the idea that Moses congregated the leaders in order to commission them,[67] and the notion that וְהוֹקַע involves suspension (צוּלבים) opposite the sun.

The Bavli, from the lips of Amoraim, spells out how some deduced that וְהוֹקַע meant suspension (*b. Sanh.* 34b–35a):

דיני נפשות דנין ביום וכו': מנהני מילי אמר רב שימי בר חייא אמר קרא והוקע אותם
לה' נגד השמש א"ר חסדא מניין להוקעה שהיא תלייה דכתיב והוקענום לה' בגבעת
שאול בחיר ה' וכתיב ותקח רצפה בת איה את השק ותטהו לה אל הצור בתחלת קציר

"*Judge capital cases in the day, etc.*" [= *m. Sanh.* 4:1]. From what words is this said? R. Shimi bar Ḥiyya said: "Scripture says, 'And execute [וְהוֹקַע] them unto the LORD in front of the sun.'" R. Ḥisda said: "From where is it that הוֹקעה is hanging? Where it is written, 'And we will hang them [וְהוֹקענוֹם] unto the Lord in Gibeah of Saul, the chosen of the Lord.' [2 Sam 21:6] And it is written, 'And Rizpah the daughter of Aiah took sack cloth, and spread it out for herself unto the rock, at the beginning of the barley harvest' [2 Sam 21:10]."

Here Numbers 25:4 provides halakhic support (via "in front of the sun") to the Mishnaic injunction that death penalty cases must be tried before nightfall. The sun must still be up in order for such people to be punished "in front of the sun." The question naturally arises: what was the penalty in Numbers 25:4? Thus R. Ḥisda (third generation Babylonian Amora) argues that, since הוקע also appears in 2 Samuel 21 in a context of prolonged bodily exposure (given that Rizpah had to guard the bodies from carrion birds from the beginning of harvest until the rains), so too הוקע in Numbers 25:4 must imply prolonged suspension.[68] What is conveniently overlooked here is that, to the degree that Numbers 25:4 serves as a precedent for Jewish legal procedure, analogous arguments would imply the potential for accepting suspension as a legitimate capital penalty.

In *Num. Rab.* xx.23 [Vilna 88b], third generation Amoraim continue the debate as to whether the leaders were executed:

ויאמר ה' אל משה קח את כל ראשי העם והוקע אותם ר' יודן אמר ראשי העם תלה על
שלא מיחו בבני אדם רבי נחמיה אמר לא תלה ראשי העם אלא אמר לו הקב"ה למשה
הושיב להן ראשי סנהדריות ויהיו דנים כל מי שהלך לפעור׃ אמר מי מודיען אמר לו
אני מפרסמן כל מי שטעה סר מעליו והשמש זורחת עליו בתוך הקהל ויהיו הכל
יודעין מי שטעה ויתלו אותו תדע לך שהוא כן ויאמר משה אל שופטי ישראל הרגו איש
אנשיו וגו':

The Lord said to Moses, "Take all the leaders of the people and execute (וְהוֹקַע) them..." [Num 25:4]. R. Judan said, "He hung the leaders of the people because they had not tried to prevent the sons of man." Rabbi Nehemiah said, "He did not hang the leaders of the people; but the Holy One, blessed be He, said to Moses, 'Appoint for them heads of Sanhedrins, and

---

[67] This is further assumed later in this context of the *Sifre*. Also see *y. Sanh.* 10:2 [28d] (=10,2/33 in the Schäfer/Becker *Synopse*), though here the guilty are slain (הורגים), not explicitly suspended. Similarly see *b. Sanh.* 35a (attributed to Rab).

[68] Rashi on Numbers 25:4 repeats this same argument for הוקע meaning תליה.

they shall judge everyone who went to Peor.' [Moses] said, 'Who will make [them] known?' [The Lord] said to him, 'I will present them. Whoever erred, the cloud will depart from upon him and the sun will shine upon him in the midst of the congregation, so that all will know who erred.[69] And they will hang him [ויתלו אותו].' You know this because, 'And Moses said to the judges of Israel, "Each, slay men, etc." [Num 25:5]'"

Note that suspension ("hanging" – תלה) is the assumed means of execution. Salvesen mistakenly asserts, "…R. Nehemiah denied that the word [הוקע] meant 'to hang'; it meant 'to seat', הושב, and referred to assembling a sanhedrin to try the people who had followed Baal of Peor."[70] Rather, suspension is the assumed penalty throughout this passage. This is evident in both R. Judan's statement ("he hung the leaders of the people" – ראשי העם תלה) and in R. Nehemiah's paraphrase of the final command of the Lord ("and they will hang him" – ויתלו אותו). The dispute here does not concern the method of execution ("hanging" – תלה), which is assumed by all parties, but the referent of the biblical "them" (אותם). The question is: who are the ones to be hung (the "them")? R. Judan argues that the leaders were executed ("hung"). Whereas R. Nehemiah contends, in agreement with the *Sifre* and the targumim cited above, that Moses assembled the leaders as judges (understood implicit in the OT קה), and then hung the guilty people who went after Baal Peor.

3.3 Summary

In the Hebrew text of Numbers 25:4 the Lord commands Moses to execute the ones responsible for Israel being lured to idolatry. The actual method of execution is a means of some debate among early translators and Jewish commentators. The Hebrew text by itself could be understood to imply the execution of the leaders of Israel. However, two prominent developments occur in the rabbinic period: (1) the leaders are not generally thought to be executed, rather they are summoned to help with the judgment of Israel; and (2) the method of execution is often held to involve a death via *ante mortem* suspension.

While the Septuagint translated the key executionary term (וְהוֹקַע) with a fairly vague notion of making a public example (παραδειγμάτισον) of the criminals, Symmachus implied that the execution was a matter of "hanging" (κρέμασον), and Aquila possibly understood it as "impalement" or "crucifixion" (ἀνάπηξον). More interesting is the manner in which the Rabbis openly argue that the Lord's command to execute such heretics involved death via suspension (on analogy with 2 Samuel 21). Moreover, the Pales-

---

[69] The departing cloud and revealing sun seem to be interpretations of the MT נֶגֶד הַשָּׁמֶשׁ ("in front of the sun") – so explicitly in Rashi on Numbers 25:4 (relying on "a haggadic midrash").

[70] Salvesen, *Symmachus*, 138–39.

tinian targumim consistently understood the execution as an official judicial action involving what is most probably death by suspension (צלב). This departure from the Mishnaic approved rabbinic death penalties was noted above. To the degree that a penal suspension was in view here, deaths produced by suspension (including, but not necessarily limited to, crucifixion) could have been associated with the judgment that rightly falls on those who pursue false gods (such as Baal Peor). The linking of this passage in the Palestinian targumim with Deuteronomy 21 provides a helpful bridge to our next section.

4. The Law of Hanging and Burial (Deuteronomy 21:22–23)

(22) וְכִי־יִהְיֶה בְאִישׁ חֵטְא מִשְׁפַּט־מָוֶת וְהוּמָת וְתָלִיתָ אֹתוֹ עַל־עֵץ (23) לֹא־תָלִין נִבְלָתוֹ עַל־הָעֵץ כִּי־קָבוֹר תִּקְבְּרֶנּוּ בַּיּוֹם הַהוּא כִּי־קִלְלַת אֱלֹהִים תָּלוּי וְלֹא תְטַמֵּא אֶת־אַדְמָתְךָ אֲשֶׁר יְהוָה אֱלֹהֶיךָ נֹתֵן לְךָ נַחֲלָה

(22) And when there is in a man a sin bearing a judgment of death, and he is executed, and you hang him on a tree, (23) his corpse shall not spend the night on the tree, but you shall surely bury him in that day, for a curse of God is the one who is hung, and you shall not defile your land, which the Lord your God gives to you as an inheritance.

Apart from the differences in the versions noted below, the principal variations in the Hebrew manuscripts involve the existence of the *waw* on the initial וְכִי in verse 22,[71] and whether the עֵץ at the end of verse 22 is articular.[72] Reading the *waw* on וְכִי at the beginning of the verse may serve to link the legislation of 21:22–23 with that of the stubborn and rebellious son (21:18–21)[73] – a connection followed by Josephus and possibly others.[74]

---

[71] Concerning the omitted *waw* BHS lists Kennicott manuscripts, the Samaritan Pentateuch, a LXX codex (the Göttingen LXX edition here refers to the 8th c. uncial V) and the Vulgate.

[72] BHS records that a Hebrew manuscript and the Samaritan Pentateuch include the article, as do several Medieval Septuagint minuscules. The targumim and the Peshiṭta employ emphatic forms. Note that the Samaritan Pentateuch, in the one other pentateuchal parallel to וְתָלִיתָ אֹתוֹ עַל־עֵץ (Gen 40:19, see §2 above), also reads the articular הָעֵץ. The evidence appears to support omission of the article in verse 22, with the addition of the article either due to a specific kind of wooden device being understood by the scribe/translator or due to an analogy with הָעֵץ in verse 23. Also, one Hebrew manuscript and some Septuagintal minuscules omit the article in verse 23 on הָעֵץ; this is plausibly explained as a scribal assimilation to the anarthrous עֵץ in verse 22.

[73] Surprisingly, modern commentators have not to my knowledge observed that, though כִּי frequently begins a legal statement in Deuteronomy (especially in chapters 12–26), with a *waw* וְכִי usually links a legal statement with some preceding legislation either in contrast (Deut 14:24; 15:21; 19:11; 23:23 [EVV 23:22]) or in simple addition (15:13; 18:6, 21; in these a note of contrast might still be detected). The situation is more complicated in the LXX, where "ἐὰν δὲ..." occurs more frequently (I located 63 occurrences). Note also the

Otherwise, the nature of the offenses included in חֵטְא מִשְׁפַּט־מָוֶת ("a sin bearing a judgment of death")[75] is not specified in the text; and this apparently led to later Jewish speculation concerning who merited such a penalty (see below).

Of significant interest is the order implied by וְהוּמָת וְתָלִיתָ אֹתוֹ עַל־עֵץ ("and he is executed, and you hang him on a tree"). It is most probable that the sequence of verbs indicates that the person is executed first and then hung after death. It is nonetheless conceivable that the *waw* on וְתָלִיתָ ("and you hang [him]") does not imply sequence but apposition (i.e. that the means of execution and the hanging are the same), and this may explain some early renderings of the phrase.[76]

Understanding verse 22 to supply (via כִּי with imperfect) either the protasis of a conditional or the temporal situation assumed (cf. GKC §§159bb, 164d), then verse 22 apparently describes the conditions for the actual commandment in verse 23 – the central concern being that the corpse not "spend the night" on the tree. Under this reading, it is merely assumed that the Hebrews will judge people who merit execution and suspension, but the point of verse 23 is to provide a limitation on the practice of human bodily suspension (bodies are to be buried in the same day they are suspended). One could think of this as a restriction on the kind of widespread ancient Near Eastern suspension penalty mentioned above in the first section of this chapter. However, it should be noted that, though this is the standard understanding (and may be favoured on the basis of the lack of *waw* at the beginning of verse 23), it is technically possible for the apodosis of the conditional to be read in either of the two perfect consecutive clauses in verse 22 (cf. GKC §159bb), thus mandating the penalty of bodily suspension (note 11QTemple lxiv.6–8; 9–11 below).[77]

The discourse relationship between each of the clauses in verse 23 (with וְלֹא...כִּי...כִּי...לֹא־תָלִין) is rather complex. The second clause (...כִּי־קָבוֹר) is related to the first causally ("*because* you shall bury him") or adversatively ("*but* you shall bury him").[78] Either sense works here, though perhaps given the negative command in clause one and the natural contrast with it in clause

---

structural parallelism produced by כִּי־יִהְיֶה לְאִישׁ (Deut 21:18) and וְכִי־יִהְיֶה בְאִישׁ (Deut 21:22).

[74] Josephus, *Ant.* iv.264; cf. the comment attributed to Ben ʿAzzai (second generation Tanna) in *Deut. Rab.* vi.4 (*Ki Teṣe*).

[75] The חֵטְא is in apposition to מִשְׁפַּט־מָוֶת, with the latter delimiting the kind of offense in view (a capital crime); see S. R. Driver, *A Critical and Exegetical Commentary on Deuteronomy*, 3rd ed., ICC (Edinburgh: T. & T. Clark, 1902), 248.

[76] Especially the Peshitta and the treatment in the Temple Scroll (see below).

[77] Thus, although the above translation is more likely, one could conceivably translate verse 22 as "And *if* there is in a man a sin bearing a judgment of death, *then* he shall be executed, and you shall hang him on a tree." Verse 23 then would begin a new sentence.

[78] Cf. GKC §§158b, 163a.

two, an adversative force fits best.[79] The third clause ("for a curse of God…") is most easily understood as providing the grounds (i.e., causal כִּי) for the legislation of the first two clauses.[80]

Some modern translations punctuate this third clause as parenthetical, with the fourth clause (beginning with וְלֹא) continuing the command force of the first two,[81] thus indicating that the possible pollution in clause four stems from corpse impurity in clause two. Otherwise, if clause three is not parenthetical, then the idea of "you shall not pollute" likely arises from the third clause (i.e., from the "curse of God"), indicating that the presence of the curse of God in the midst of Israel defiles her land. A closely related Deuteronomic admonition to not pollute the land occurs in Deuteronomy 24:4. Here the divorced woman who has been "defiled" cannot be remarried to her first husband, for this would be an abomination before the Lord, and "you shall not bring guilt on the land, which the Lord your God is giving you as a possession."[82] Though both the verb for "bring guilt" on the land and the word for "land" differ from those in 21:23, the structures of 21:22–23 and 24:4 are quite parallel.[83] Following this parallel, in both cases the pollution apparently arises from what such a situation does in God's sight (render an abomination in 24:4; provide a curse in 21:23 – both are כִּי clauses) in light of the sin to be avoided (not remarrying the defiled in 24:4; not leaving the corpse unburied in 21:23). If this parallel is followed, then the pollution in Deuteronomy 21:23 (clause four) would result from the "curse of God" (clause three), which itself is the cause deduced for the command to bury a suspended person (clause two). Hence, the translation above does not render the third ("curse of God") clause as parenthetical, and instead implies that the defilement on the land issues from the "curse of God."

One of the most complex interpretive issues in verse 23 involves the type of genitive reflected in קִלְלַת אֱלֹהִים ("a curse of God") construct. Is it a subjective genitive ("cursed by God") or an objective one ("one who curses

---

[79] So the LXX and Peshiṭta.

[80] The LXX, OL, and Peshiṭta assume causality.

[81] E.g., the New American Standard version reads: "…but you shall surely bury him on the same day (for he who is hanged is accursed of God), so that you do not defile your land which the LORD your God gives you as an inheritance." Olson has argued that, if a chiasm is read in chapter 21 – whereby verses 1–9 (about what to do if a slain body is found lying in the land [בָּאֲדָמָה]) parallels 22–23 – then this proves the emphasis in 21:22–23 is on corpse impurity; see Dennis T. Olson, *Deuteronomy and the Death of Moses*, OBT (Minneapolis: Fortress Press, 1994), 96–97. However, the legislation of 21:1–9 focuses not on the lack of burial, but on cleansing Israel of bloodguilt from murder when they are innocent. Furthermore, the internal members of the supposed chiasm appear even less convincing.

[82] וְלֹא תְחַטִּיא אֶת־הָאָרֶץ אֲשֶׁר יְהוָה אֱלֹהֶיךָ נֹתֵן לְךָ נַחֲלָה

[83] The final clause is precisely the same, as is the structure of כִּי…לֹא followed by the command not to pollute/bring guilt on the land.

God")?[84] Each of these options may be further subdivided based on whether the cursing is produced prior to the suspension or as a result of the suspension. Thus a subjective genitive could either imply that the guilty person is hung to display that the curse of God resides on them as the result of their sin;[85] or it could indicate that, when somebody is hung, they are (as the result of being so suspended) cursed by God.[86] An objective genitive could suggest either that they are hung because they blasphemed God ("cursed him"),[87] or that the person, being made in the image of God, becomes a reproach to God's image by being hung.[88] In the history of interpretation each of these positions has been held, with Christian interpreters tending to opt for some form of subjective genitive (possibly under the influence of the LXX and Gal 3:13) and rabbinic interpreters most often (though not exclusively) siding with the objective genitive.

4.1 Greek and Latin Traditions on Deuteronomy 21:22–23

The Septuagint contains a careful rendition of the Hebrew text:

(22) ἐὰν δὲ γένηται ἔν <u>τινι</u> ἁμαρτία κρίμα θανάτου καὶ ἀποθάνῃ καὶ κρεμάσητε αὐτὸν ἐπὶ ξύλου (23) οὐκ ἐπικοιμηθήσεται τὸ σῶμα αὐτοῦ ἐπὶ τοῦ ξύλου <u>ἀλλὰ</u> ταφῇ θάψετε αὐτὸν ἐν τῇ ἡμέρᾳ ἐκείνῃ <u>ὅτι κεκατηραμένος ὑπὸ</u> θεοῦ <u>πᾶς</u> κρεμάμενος <u>ἐπὶ ξύλου</u> καὶ οὐ μιανεῖτε τὴν γῆν ἣν κύριος ὁ θεός σου δίδωσίν σοι ἐν κλήρῳ

(22) And if there is in <u>someone</u> a sin bearing a judgment of death, and he is executed, and you [plural] hang him on a tree, (23) his body shall not lay[89] on the tree, <u>but</u> you [pl.] shall surely bury him in that day, <u>for everyone</u> who hangs <u>on a tree has been cursed by</u> God, and you [pl.] shall not defile the land, which the Lord your God gives to you in inheritance.

---

[84] See Moshe J. Bernstein, "כי קללת אלהים תלוי (Deut 21:23): A Study in Early Jewish Exegesis," *JQR* 74 (1983): 21–45.

[85] While the LXX, OL and Vulgate clearly render a subjective genitive, it is difficult to say with certainty into which sub-category they fit (LXX ὅτι κεκατηραμένος ὑπὸ θεοῦ πᾶς κρεμάμενος ἐπὶ ξύλου; OL *quoniam maledictus a Deo est omnis qui suspensus fuerit in ligno;* Vulgate *quia maledictus a Deo est qui pendet in ligno*). Cf. 11QTemple lxiv.12.

[86] This may be the sense of *Tg. Neof.* (לִיט קדם יהוה כל דצליב), which in any case renders a subjective genitive.

[87] The objective genitive interpretation is implied in Symmachus (ὅτι διὰ βλασφημίαν θεοῦ ἐκρεμάσθη), the Peshiṭta (ܡܛܠ ܕܡܨܚܐ ܐܠܗܐ), and many rabbinic traditions mentioned in §4.7 below.

[88] This idea may lie behind *m. Sanh.* vi.5 (R. Meir's statement), *Tg. Ps.-J.* Deut 21:23, and especially R. Meir's parable in *t. Sanh.* ix.7 and *b. Sanh.* 46b.

[89] For ἐπικοιμάομαι Liddell-Scott designates "fall asleep after or over [a thing]; fall asleep; overlay"; Friedrich Rehkopf, *Septuaginta-Vokabular* (Göttingen: Vandenhoeck & Ruprecht, 1989), p. 117 – "daraufschlafen"; J. Lust et al., *A Greek-English Lexicon of the Septuagint*, 2 vols. (Stuttgart: Deutsche Bibelgesellschaft, 1992/1996), 1:171 – "to overlay, to lay upon." Cf. 3 Kgdms 3:19; 1 Esdr 5:69. Aquila reads οὐκ αὐλισθήσεται ("shall not pass the night").

The most overt interpretive elements of this translation concern its treatment of the Hebrew phrase כִּי־קִלְלַת אֱלֹהִים תָּלוּי.[90] The Septuagint understands the genitive אֱלֹהִים in the construct קִלְלַת אֱלֹהִים to be a subjective genitive (God delivers the curse, hence the person is cursed ὑπὸ θεοῦ). The noun קִלְלַת ("curse") is considered the activity God has done and is rendered as a participle (κεκατηραμένος). The Hebrew participle תָּלוּי states the category of person under discussion ("one hung"); and the LXX translation affirms it as a universal truth that everyone (πᾶς) hung in this manner is so cursed. The addition of ἐπὶ ξύλου ("on a tree") after πᾶς κρεμάμενος ("everyone who hangs") is in keeping with the mention of a "tree" in the context of verse 22; but, given the universal slant of the LXX ("all who hang"), it also serves to limit the curse to those who are hung in this penal fashion.

Other notable features of the LXX concern how it construes the clausal connections of the Hebrew text. So the וְכִי at the beginning of verse 22 is translated as the beginning of a conditional (ἐὰν δέ – "and if"). The protasis of the conditional continues until the end of the verse (the two successive καί conjunctions in verse 22 most likely continuing the protasis, with an epexegetical reading of either καί being unlikely).[91] In verse 23 the LXX renders the first Hebrew כִּי adversatively (ἀλλά – "but") and the second causatively (ὅτι – "for"). Also, the LXX translates the second person commands as plural throughout, in contrast to the singular verbs in the MT.

Thus a person reading the Septuagint would likely understand verse 22 to be the conditional, with verse 23 constituting the command to bury the body (in contrast to prolonged exposure). The reason given for burying the body is that the body bears a curse from God (as is clear from the fact that it was suspended in this penal fashion); and this curse could defile the land given to Israel by God.

Hexaplaric fragments indicate that Aquila, Symmachus and Theodotion opted for different interpretations of the קִלְלַת אֱלֹהִים construct in Deuteronomy 21:23. Symmachus reads ὅτι διὰ βλασφημίαν θεοῦ ἐκρεμάσθη ("because he was hung on account of blasphemy of God"). Here the Hebrew construct is understood as an objective genitive – the person "cursed God" and thus must be a blasphemer. This appears indebted to the common rabbinic

---

[90] The Hebrew text that the LXX translators used for this passage was likely similar to the current MT text. This appears reasonable given the near uniformity in the Hebrew textual traditions (see above), and the fact that all the versional traditions (save possibly the switch in clausal order in verse 22 of the Peshiṭta) can be explained as rendering a similar Hebrew text. The LXX even supports the BHS edition in the two slight textual variations found in some Hebrew manuscripts (namely, as mentioned above, the inclusion of the conjunction at the beginning of verse 22, and the anarthrous עֵץ at the first mention of "tree").

[91] See also Wevers on the use of the conditional and on the clausal structure of the LXX passage in John William Wevers, *Notes on the Greek Text of Deuteronomy*, SBLSCS 39 (Atlanta: Scholars Press, 1995), 346.

understanding of Deuteronomy 21:23 (see below, also cf. Josephus, *Ant.* iv.202). In contrast to Symmachus and the LXX, both Aquila and Theodotion render the Hebrew literally with κατάρα θεοῦ κρεμάμενος ("a curse of God is the one hung"). The Greek original of Symmachus, Aquila and Theodotion is known primarily from these few Greek Hexaplaric fragments, which focus on the קִלְלַת אֱלֹהִים construct.[92] However, Jerome also penned a Latin translation of the whole of verses 22–23 from these early Greek translators.[93]

"The Three" on Deuteronomy 21:22–23 in Jerome's
Commentariorum in Epistolam ad Galatas, book II (on Gal 3:14)

Aquila	Symmachus	Theodotion
[22] Et cum fuerit in viro peccatum in[1] iudicium mortis, et occisus fuerit, et suspenderis eum super lignum,	[22] Si autem fuerit homini peccatum ad iudicium mortis, et occisus fuerit, et suspenderis eum super lignum,	[22] Et quia erit in viro peccatum in[1] iudicium mortis, et morietur, et suspendes eum in ligno,
[23] non commorabitur morticinium eius super lignum, sed sepeliens sepelies eum in die illa, quia maledictio Dei est, qui suspensus est: et non contaminabis humum tuam quam Dominus Deus tuus dabit tibi haereditatem.	[23] non pernoctabit cadaver ipsius super lignum, sed sepultura sepelies eum[1] in die ipsa, quia propter blasphemiam Dei suspensus est et non contaminabis terram tuam quam Dominus Deus tuus dabit tibi ad haereditatem.	[23] non dormiet morticinium eius super lignum, quia sepultura sepelies eum in die ipsa, quia maledictio Dei est suspensus: et non contaminabis adama[2] tuam quam Dominus Deus tuus dederit tibi haereditatem.
[1]*Al.* et	[1]*Al.*. illud	[1]*Al. tacet* in [2]*Al.* adamam (Jerome notes that this is a Semitic word)

To the extent that Jerome's translation accurately represents the Greek originals,[94] it appears that (though there are some other minor differences between

---

[92] Two other Greek words (οὐκ αὐλισθήσεται – "shall not pass the night") are also preserved in some sources from Aquila's translation of verse 23; see Field, *Origenis Hexaplorum* on Deut 21:22–23.

[93] Jerome, *Comm. Gal.* ii (on Gal 3:13–14; in Migne, *PL* 26, 386C–387B). Field provides an attempted retroversion of Jerome's Latin back into Greek (*Origenis Hexaplorum*, 1:304–5).

[94] In order to appraise how carefully Jerome's translations reflect the original Greek texts, one can compare his Latin renditions of the extant Greek Hexaplaric fragments and one can also study his Latin translation of the corresponding LXX text of Deuteronomy 21:22–23 (this also appears in his *Comm. Gal.* ii on Gal 3:13–14). His Latin translation of the LXX text reads: "[22] Si autem fuerit in aliquo peccatum et iudicium mortis, et mortuus fuerit, sus-

the translations of Symmachus, Aquila and Theodotion[95]) the major point of contention was indeed the meaning of the קִלְלַת אֱלֹהִים construct.[96]

Not surprisingly, the Old Latin traditions largely follow the LXX,[97] especially in interpreting כִּי־קִלְלַת אֱלֹהִים תָּלוּי as *quoniam maledictus a Deo est omnis qui suspensus fuerit in ligno* ("because all who were hung on a tree are cursed by God").[98] The most important difference in the Old Latin concerns the beginning of verse 23, where it has telescoped the first two Hebrew clauses (which were also fully represented in the LXX) into one phrase ("but also by a burial you bury him that day").[99]

Jerome's Vulgate likewise continues the subjective genitive interpretation of קִלְלַת אֱלֹהִים with *maledictus a Deo* ("cursed by God").[100] However, in

penderitis eum in ligno, [23] non dormiet corpus illius super lignum, sed sepelientes sepelietis eum in die illa; quia maledictus a Deo omnis qui pendet in ligno: et non contaminabis terram tuam quam Dominus Deus tuus dabit tibi in haereditatem." Jerome appears to have accurately translated the Hexaplaric and LXX renditions of קִלְלַת אֱלֹהִים. Also he has carefully differentiated between the renderings of תָּלִין by Aquila (αὐλισθήσεται; *commorabitur*) and the LXX (ἐπικοιμηθήσεται; *dormiet*), correctly preserving the connotations of "sleep" possible in the latter. Further, his Septuagint translation appears to follow the text as it is preserved today, diverging from modern critical editions principally in adding *et* between *peccatum* and *iudicium mortis* (v. 22) and in omitting a conjunction before *suspenderitis* (v. 22) – this latter omission creating the most significant syntactic disparity. He also is somewhat loose with his tenses (cf. *dabit* in v. 23) and plurals (cf. the switch to singular *contaminabis* in v. 23). Thus it appears that in word choice Jerome closely parallels his texts, but he is occasionally loose in some syntactic matters.

[95] Aside from vocabulary divergences, especially note the rendering of the opening כִּי of v. 22 (LXX and Sym. *si autem*; Aq. *et cum*; Theo. *et quia*).

[96] Jerome himself emphasizes this as the central interpretive issue, and he also cites an Ebionite translation (ὅτι ὕβρις θεοῦ ὁ κρεμάμενος [my corrected diacritics] – "an outrage towards God is the one hung"), the *Dialogue of Jason and Papiscus* (λοιδορία θεοῦ ὁ κρεμάμενος – "a reproach of God is the one hung") and an unnamed Hebrew source (*quia contumeliose Deus suspensus est* – "because God has been hung in an insulting way"). Each of these supports an objective genitive translation (though in different ways).

[97] Old Latin Deut 21:22–23 (from Sabatier): [22] *Si autem fuerit in aliquo delicto ita ut judicium mortis sit, & morietur & suspendetis eum in ligno*: [23] *sed & sepultura sepelietis eum ipsa die: quoniam maledictus a Deo est omnis qui suspensus fuerit in ligno: & non inquinabitis terram, quam Dominus Deus tuus dabit tibi in forte.*

[98] There is a change in tense of the participle κρεμάμενος to *suspensus fuerit*. But the LXX affinities are obvious in the causative interpretation (*quoniam*) of the whole clause, the universalizing (*omnis*) of it to all hung on the tree (*in ligno*), and particularly the rendering of the person as cursed by God (*a Deo*).

[99] The OL traditions also saw need in verse 22 to define the relationship between the sin and the judgment of death (*delicto ita ut judicium mortis fit*).

[100] The Vulgate on Deut 21:22–23: [22] *Quando peccaverit homo quod morte plectendum est et adiudicatus morti adpensus fuerit in patibulo* [23] *non permanebit cadaver eius in ligno sed in eadem die sepelietur quia maledictus a Deo est qui pendet in ligno et nequaquam contaminabis terram tuam quam Dominus Deus tuus dederit tibi in possessionem.* Also note the inclusion of *in ligno* after *pendet* (in keeping with the LXX).

other respects it frequently parts with the LXX.[101] Given the history of the Christian association of Deuteronomy 21 with the crucifixion of Jesus, it is not surprising that Jerome specifies that the tree employed for suspension is a *patibulo*, and that he implies that the person is hung alive (v. 22).[102]

Concluding this discussion of the Greek and Latin versions, one observes that they largely follow the Hebrew text, with any variations from the Masoretic tradition being best explained as interpretive elements from the translator. Thus, when each version translates the opening Hebrew clause in verse 22 (beginning with וְכִי), they betray whether they think it to indicate a conditional ("if" – LXX, Old Latin, and apparently Symmachus) or a temporal clause ("when" – Vulgate and apparently Aquila and Theodotion). The principal variation among the translators concerns the proper understanding of קִלְלַת אֱלֹהִים ("curse of God"). While Aquila and Theodotion render that Hebrew construct with a highly literal Greek equivalent, the other translations are more willing to paraphrase. Symmachus understands the clause to indicate blasphemy; but the Septuagint, Old Latin, and Vulgate all translate the passage to indicate that the hung person has been cursed by God.

4.2 The Peshiṭta on Deuteronomy 21:22–23

(22) ܘܐܢ ܚܝܒ ܓܒܪܐ ܚܠܦ ܚܛܗܐ ܕܕܝܢܐ ܕܡܘܬܐ. ܘܢܙܕܩܦ ܥܠ ܩܝܣܐ ܘܢܬܩܛܠ. (23) ܠܐ
ܬܒܘܬ ܫܠܕܗ ܥܠ ܩܝܣܐ. ܐܠܐ ܬܩܒܪܘܗܝ، ܒܝܘܡܐ ܗܘ. ܡܛܠ ܕܗܘ ܕܡܨܚܐ ܠܐܠܗܐ ܙܩܝܦ.
ܘܠܐ ܬܛܡܐ ܐܪܥܟ ܕܝܗܒ ܠܟ ܡܪܝܐ ܐܠܗܟ ܝܪܬܘܬܐ ∴

(22) And if a man is condemned on account of a sin bearing the judgment of death, and he is hung on the tree and he is killed, (23) his corpse shall not spend the night on the tree, but you [pl.] shall bury him in that day, because one who reviles God is hung, and you shall not defile your land, which the Lord your God gave to you [as] a possession.

The principle matter of interest here is that the Peshiṭta has reversed the order of the Hebrew clauses in 21:22 from those in the Masoretic Text (וְהוּמָת וְתָלִיתָ אֹתוֹ עַל־עֵץ – "and he is executed, and you hang him on a tree") to produce the idea that the suspension precedes (and presumably causes) the death ("and he is hung on the tree and he is killed").[103] The testimony of the Peshiṭta with regard to Jewish tradition here might be thought dubious since the translation is passed down through Christian sources.[104]

---

[101] For example, note the temporal clause beginning v. 22 (*quando*, cf. LXX ἐὰν δέ); *homo* as subject in that same clause; the omission of the emphatic repetition ταφῇ θάψετε (cf. *sepelietur*) in v. 23; and especially the lack of a universalizing adjective in v. 23 (contrast LXX πᾶς).

[102] *et adiudicatus morti adpensus fuerit in patibulo*; cf. Salvesen, *Symmachus*, 155.

[103] The Syriac clauses are transposed back, in accordance with the Hebrew, in the relatively early MS 9a1 and in its 17th c. successors. However, the main manuscript tradition supports the order of the reading here, which also represents the *lectio difficilior*.

[104] So Salvesen (*Symmachus*, 154–55) insinuates that the Peshiṭta, like the Vulgate, is indebted to Galatians 3:13.

However, many believe Jewish tradition (if not an original Jewish Syriac translation) underlies much of the Peshiṭta, especially in the Pentateuch.[105] And in this passage it is worth noticing that ܐ̈ܠܗܐ ܨܚ̈ܝܐ ("who reviles God") in 21:23 implies that a blasphemer is hung, which is not the traditional Christian interpretation (contrast Galatians 3:13), but which follows a more typical rabbinic exposition. Also, that the person is "condemned" or "guilty" (ܚܝܒ) is reminiscent of the targumic construction in Deuteronomy 21:22, which also employs guilt terminology (חובת דין דקטול).[106]

4.3 The Temple Scroll and Deuteronomy 21:22–23

One of the most discussed texts related to Deuteronomy 21:22–23 is 11QTemple lxiv.6–13 (underlining indicates divergences from Deut 21):

6	כי...
7	יהיה איש רכיל בעמי[107] ומשלים את עמי לגוי נכר ועושה רעה בעמי
8	ותליתמה[108] אותו על העץ וימות על פי שנים עדים ועל פי שלושה עדים
9	יומת והמה יתלו אותו העץ כי יהיה באיש חטא[109] משפט מות ויברח אל
10	תוך הגואים ויקלל את עמי ,את[110] בני ישראל ותליתמה גם אותו על העץ
11	וימות ולוא תלין נבלתמה על העץ כי קבור תקוברמ(ה)[111] ביום ההוא כי

---

[105] For a brief survey of the modern debate over Peshiṭta origins (especially of the Pentateuch) see Peter B. Dirksen, "The Old Testament Peshitta," in *Mikra: Text, Translation, Reading and Interpretation of the Hebrew Bible in Ancient Judaism and Early Christianity*, ed. Martin Jan Mulder, CRINT II.1 (Assen/Maastricht: Van Gorcum; Philadephia: Fortress, 1988), 261–85. For a summary of arguments for Jewish roots see Sebastian P. Brock, "The Peshitta Old Testament: Between Judaism and Christianity," *CNS* 19 (1998): 483–502. For an extensive reconstruction of development see M. P. Weitzman, *The Syriac Version of the Old Testament: An Introduction*, University of Cambridge Oriental Publications 56 (Cambridge: Cambridge University Press, 1999), 206–62 (on Deut 21:22–23 also note pp. 98, 159).

[106] *Tg. Onq.* Deut 21:22–23; cf. also *Tg. Ps.-J.* and *Tg. Neof.*

[107] בעמו ("his people") in Yadin's edition, but בעמי ("my people") in Qimron's; see Yigael Yadin, *The Temple Scroll*, 3 + suppl. vols. (Jerusalem: Israel Exploration Society, 1977–1983); Elisha Qimron, *The Temple Scroll: A Critical Edition with Extensive Reconstructions*, JDS (Beer Sheva: Ben-Gurion University, 1996). This is true of all 4 occurrences of עמ(ו)י in lines 7 and 10. Puech's transcription of 4Q524 reads עמו in lines 2 & 4 (cf. 11QTemple lxiv.10); see Émile Puech, *Qumrân Grotte 4, XVIII: Textes Hébreux (4Q521–4Q528, 4Q576–4Q579)*, DJD 25 (Oxford: Clarendon Press, 1998). It is very difficult to distinguish י and ו in the plates of both 11QTemple [= 11Q19] and 4Q524.

[108] תמה- is a long form of the 2nd person masculine plural afformative; see Elisha Qimron, *The Hebrew of the Dead Sea Scrolls*, HSS 29 (Atlanta: Scholars Press, 1986), §310.11 (p. 43).

[109] The א was added to the scroll later.

[110] 11QTemple has a *waw* inserted (ואת) after the text was written; it is best explained as an "explicative *waw*"; so Yadin, *Temple Scroll*, 2:290. But the *waw* is missing in 4Q524.

[111] The ה of the 3rd person plural suffix was erased after it was written; see Yadin, *Temple Scroll*, 2:291. Both forms of the suffix are known at Qumran; see Qimron, *Hebrew*, §322.18 [p. 62].

מְקֻלְלֵי אלוהים ואנשים תלוי עַל הֵעֵץ ולוא תטמא את הֵאדמה אשר אנוכי   12

נותן לכה נחלה   13

(6–7) If a man will be a slanderer[112] against my people and surrenders[113] my people to a foreign nation and does evil against my people, (8) then[114] you [plural] shall hang him on the tree and he shall die[115] – on the mouth of two witnesses and on the mouth of three witnesses (9) he shall be put to death, and they shall hang him [on] the tree. If there is in a man a sin bearing a judgment of death and he has fled to (10) the midst of the nations and he has cursed my people [and] the sons of Israel, then you [pl.] shall also hang him on the tree, (11) and he shall die.[116] And their corpse shall not spend the night on the tree, but you shall surely bury them in that day, for (12) those[117] who are hung on the tree have been cursed of God and men, and you shall not defile the land, which I (13) give to you as an inheritance.

---

[112] In Biblical Hebrew רכיל appears 6 times as "slanderer" (Lev 19:16; Jer 6:28; 9:3; Ezek 22:9; Prov 11:13; 20:19; in Proverbs some translations read "gossip"). See especially Lev 19:16: לֹא־תֵלֵךְ רָכִיל בְּעַמֶּיךָ לֹא תַעֲמֹד עַל־דַּם רֵעֶךָ ("You shall not walk as a slanderer against [or 'among'] your people; you shall not stand on account of the blood of your neighbour"). Also note 1QS vii.15–17 [17–19 in some editions]; 1QH[a] xiii.25 [= v.25 in E. L. Sukenik, ed., *The Dead Sea Scrolls of the Hebrew University* (Jerusalem: The Magnes Press, 1955)].

[113] Reading וּמַשְׁלִים as a Hiphil participle from שָׁלַם ("consummate, surrender completely, make peace"). See Y. Yadin, "Pesher Nahum (4Q pNahum) Reconsidered," *IEJ* 21 (1971): 6; also see Yadin, *Temple Scroll*, 2:289.

[114] Grammatically the apodosis of the conditional in lines 6–7 could be located: (1) here, (2) beginning with וימת (line 8), (3) beginning with והמה (line 9), or (4) suspended until after the second conditional in line 9 (...כי יהיה באיש) and thus presumably beginning with ולוא תלין... in line 11 (as in most commentaries on Deut 21:22–23). Of these (2) and (3) are unlikely given that bodily suspension would then be present both in the protasis complex and in the apodosis. And (4) is questionable since it requires both conditionals to work syndetically, yet there is no *waw* conjunction on כי in line 9. Given that (1) is the best option in line 8, then the apodosis in the parallel conditional in lines 9–11 would also most likely begin with the ותליתמה in line 10. Thus ...ולוא תלין in line 11 (note the *waw* not in Deut 21:23) introduces a decree in addition to the conditional commands in lines 6–11 (though logically dependent on them). Although it was noted above (in the discussion of the Masoretic Hebrew text of Deut 21:22–23) that this is a less probable way of understanding the syntax of Deuteronomy 21:22–23 itself (requiring verse 22 to be one conditional command, and verse 23 to be a separate decree), it is nevertheless possible to read the biblical text in a similar fashion. Therefore, this aspect of the Temple Scroll could be based on exegesis of Deuteronomy.

[115] It is possible to read וימת על פי שנים עדים as one clause and not two (i.e., "and he shall die on the mouth of two witnesses"). However, the similar phraseology in Deuteronomy 17:5–6; 19:15 (where על פי שנים עדים begins a new clause) and the parallel in 11QTemple lxiv.10–11 (ותליתמה גם אותו על העץ וימת, though here וימת is a non-consecutive *waw*) naturally cause one to consider וימת as a clause to itself. Also cf. 11QTemple lxiv.5–6 (ורגמוהו כול אנשי עירו באבנים וימות).

[116] Point וְיָמֻת (Qal with non-conversive *waw*); cf. lxiv.6.

[117] Though תלוי here, as in the biblical text, is singular, the participle מקוללי is plural and continues the plural sense of line 11. Bernstein notes two possible translations and favours the second: "accursed of God and man is the one hanged on the tree" or "it is the accursed of God and men who is hanged on the tree"; see Moshe J. Bernstein, "*Midrash*

The immediately surrounding context of this passage in the Temple Scroll involves a rewriting of Deuteronomy chapters 21–22; this follows the sequence of Deuteronomy with only occasional brief interpolations. This passage forms the exception by augmenting the text of Deuteronomy 21:22–23 with two significant insertions (see lines 6–9 and lines 9–10; other divergences are also marked above by underlining). The interpretive motive for these insertions would likely be to clarify the specific crimes meriting the penalty of suspension, thus interpreting the Hebrew Bible's חֵטְא מִשְׁפַּט־מָוֶת ("sin bearing a judgment of death"). The essential result of these insertions is to specify the two types of criminals who are punishable by a death of hanging: (1) the person who betrays God's people to a foreign nation (lines 6–9);[118] and (2) a man, deserving the death penalty, who curses God's people while in a foreign nation.[119] The plural references ('their'/'them') in lines 11 and 12 then apply the burial legislation of Deuteronomy 21:23 to both these cases.[120] One notes that the basic structure of Deuteronomy 21:22–23 remains, although the material of 21:22 is essentially repeated twice in lines 6–11 to facilitate the delineation of the two types of criminals.

When Yadin first published this text, he drew two other conclusions based on comparison with Deuteronomy 21:22–23. First, this text twice reverses the MT order וְהוּמָת וְתָלִיתָ אֹתוֹ עַל־עֵץ ("and he is put to death and you hang him on a tree" in Deut 21:22) to read ותליתמה אותו על העץ וימת ("and you hang him on the tree and he dies" in lines 8, 10–11); the Temple Scroll thus implies a sequence of hanging and then death (i.e., hanging as the means of death).[121] Second, the MT phrase קִלְלַת אֱלֹהִים ("curse of God") is rendered

---

Halakhah at Qumran? 11QTemple 64:6–13 and Deuteronomy 21:22–23," *Gesher* 7 (1979): 153–54; and Bernstein, "כי קללת אלהים תלוי," 42. Both are grammatically possible, and Bernstein does not provide significant evidence supporting one over the other.

[118] It is difficult to determine the relationship between the three clauses that define the first crime. They can create a sequence of three aspects of the crime, or the first *waw* may be explicative (such that clauses two and three explain the kind of slander – one which produces national betrayal and destruction), or the second *waw* may describe the effect of the previous clause(s). It is even possible, though less likely, that each *waw* should be taken to mean "or." A similar *waw* conundrum exists in the threefold description of the second crime.

[119] Yadin first held that he defects to another nation and curses God's people because the death sentence had been passed on him (Yadin, "Pesher Nahum," 7); but later Yadin rejects this in favour of seeing the flight to the enemy as the sin deserving the death penalty (Yadin, *Temple Scroll*, 1:374 – calling for an explicative *waw*). Bernstein concurs with Yadin's later assessment because: (1) "a change of death penalty for an additional offense sounds rather peculiar," and (2) on the basis of a parallel assessment of the clausal structure of crimes one and two; see Bernstein, "Midrash Halakhah," 149.

[120] This seems the most likely explanation for the switch from (MT) תִּקְבְּרֶנּוּ and נִבְלָתוֹ to תקוברמ(ה) and נבלתמה in the Temple Scroll; cf. Yadin, *Temple Scroll*, 2:291. See additionally the גם ("also") in line 10.

[121] Yadin, "Pesher Nahum," 9; cf. *Temple Scroll*, 1:374–78.

מקוללי אלוהים ואנשים ("having been cursed of God and men"); this appears
to imply a subjective genitive (i.e., "cursed by God") and also incorporates
derision by men.[122] Yadin went on to postulate that the two crimes specified
in this expansion of Deuteronomy 21:22–23 are so precise as to have developed out of actual historical events, which he claimed were likely related to
the suspension of the "seekers of smooth things" in the Nahum Pesher (identified by Yadin and others with the crucifixion of the eight hundred by
Alexander Jannaeus).[123]

However, other scholars have disputed Yadin's conclusions. Three such
challenges are especially worth consideration: (1) Baumgarten's argument
that crucifixion is not implied here. (2) Bernstein's contention that this passage is not intended as a halakhic commentary on Deuteronomy 21:22–23. (3)
And Schwartz' assertion that the Temple Scroll here does not rightly imply
that the person is himself "cursed of God and men."

Baumgarten adduces lexical arguments, and potential parallels with Roman
sources, in order to show that תלה as a death penalty in the Temple Scroll
must refer to "hanging on a noose" and *not* to crucifixion. In the first chapter
(§2.2) we discussed Baumgarten's various lines of reasoning. His lexical
arguments were found to be insufficient due to the semantic range of תלה
(which can indeed embrace crucifixion as well as other forms of suspension).[124] However, this same lexical range does not by itself make it possible
to clearly limit this passage to convey only death by crucifixion. With that in
mind, in affirming that bodily suspension was the means of death in the
Temple Scroll, this *could* very well have included crucifixion on a cross,
though the method employed cannot be definitively determined on the basis
of lexis alone.[125] Apart from which specific executionary suspension form

---

[122] Yadin, "Pesher Nahum," 7–8. In a later publication Yadin holds that, while the phrase
clearly suggests a subjective genitive, it also simultaneously supports an objective understanding of the phrase insofar as the guilty man has "cursed" his people (= Israel) in line 10,
cf. *Temple Scroll*, 1:379. Therefore, the author may have deliberately interpreted the
קִלְלַת אֱלֹהִים construct in Deuteronomy 21:23 to imply both an objective and subjective
genitive.

[123] On Alexander's deed see above in chapter two (§2.3).

[124] Kuhn has further suggested that, in contrast to the widespread testimony to crucifixion
in the fourth to first centuries C.E., there is no definitive evidence in that period for execution
upon a noose; see Heinz-Wolfgang Kuhn, "Die Bedeutung der Qumrantexte für das
Verständnis des Galaterbriefes aus dem Münchener Projekt: Qumran und das Neue
Testament," in *New Qumran Texts and Studies: Proceedings of the First Meeting of the
International Organization for Qumran Studies, Paris 1992*, ed. George J. Brooke and
Florentino García Martínez, STDJ 15 (Leiden: E. J. Brill, 1994), 180. This line of argument is
worth further examination, but the lexical argument alone appears sufficient to undermine
Baumgarten's thesis.

[125] So Yadin, noting Baumgarten's opposition to crucifixion as the mode of death, writes:
"…I do have doubts whether the members of the sect differentiated between hanging alive –

was intended, this passage remains very pertinent to this study, both because it conveys a distinctive Jewish understanding of this important biblical text, and because it reveals sectarian Jewish impressions about the kind of people whom they believe merited suspension as a means of execution. If one views crucifixion as a specific form of execution within a broader range of bodily suspension penalties, then the concepts associated with such suspensions in general (especially as means of execution) may well have carried over to crucifixion more narrowly defined.

M. Bernstein contends that this passage in the Temple Scroll, unlike the laws that surround it, is not an example of *midrash halakhah* but is an interpolation of legal material that did not originate in "exegesis" of Deuteronomy 21:22–23.[126] Rather, according to Bernstein each of the two crimes, which are closely related, could not have originated from an understanding of Deuteronomy 21, from its context, or from Scripture at all. The first crime, though drawing on the language of Leviticus 19:16, clearly cannot be developed from that passage (which does not mention the death penalty, let alone witnesses); furthermore, the language of ומשלים...ועושה (which continues to specify this crime) is unbiblical. Likewise the scroll's depiction of the second crime, though starting with the language of Deuteronomy 21:22, quickly departs from this into concerns possibly influenced more by ancient history than by the biblical text. Because the passage only *replaces* Deuteronomy 21:22–23 in the Temple Scroll, Bernstein contends that "no clarification of the meaning of the biblical text was ever intended by the author"; and thus from this passage we cannot learn much about what the author, or the sect, thought about Deuteronomy 21:22–23 itself (p. 160).

Bernstein's treatment, thorough as it is, suffers from both too tight a definition of "exegesis"[127] and from a discounting of the strong continuities

---

that is, at the end of a rope – and crucifixion." See Yadin, *Temple Scroll*, 1:378n. Others have been more definitive that crucifixion is in view here. In addition to materials cited in chapter one above, see: J. Massyngberde Ford, "'Crucify him, crucify him' and the Temple Scroll," *ExpTim* 87 (1975–1976): 275–78; Otto Betz, "The Death of Choni-Onias in the Light of the Temple Scroll from Qumran," in *Jerusalem in the Second Temple Period*, ed. A. Oppenheimer et al. (Jerusalem: Yad Izhak Ben-Zvi, 1980), 84–97 (English summary, p. v); with German version in Otto Betz, "Der Tod des Choni-Onias im Licht der Tempelrolle von Qumran: Bemerkungen zu Josephus Antiquitates 14,22–24," in *Jesus Der Messias Israels: Aufsätze zur biblischen Theologie*, WUNT I.42 (Tübingen: Mohr [Siebeck], 1987), 59–74; Otto Betz, "Jesus and the Temple Scroll," in *Jesus and the Dead Sea Scrolls*, ed. James H. Charlesworth (New York: Doubleday, 1992), 83–87; and Émile Puech, "Die Kreuzigung und die altjüdische Tradition," *Welt und Umwelt der Bibel* 9 (1998): 73–75.

[126] Bernstein, "Midrash Halakhah," 145–66.

[127] Note the statement: "We must distinguish, however, between exegesis which reflects a serious attempt to comprehend the biblical text and exegesis which superimposes meaning upon the text rather than deriving meaning from it." (Bernstein, "Midrash Halakhah," 159) It appears Bernstein only designates the former as *midrash halakhah*.

between the Temple Scroll passage and Deuteronomy. Bernstein never strictly defines his criteria for assessing "exegesis" and "*midrash halakhah*", though it seems to involve: (1) a dependency on the root text (here Deut 21:22–23), (2) a clear lineage of interpretive links with other biblical passages (any unbiblical material seems to count against *midrash halakhah*), and (3) the further requirement that any halakhic law must necessarily fit only at the location of the text being exegeted in the Temple Scroll.[128] One wonders if rabbinic halakhic works could qualify as *midrash halakhah* under these terms. Even if the text is considered an interpolation, problems remain concerning why the redactor chose to situate this text here in the very place in the Temple Scroll where one would expect a quotation of Deuteronomy 21:22–23 (given the sequence of passages quoted from Deuteronomy chapters 21 and 22 in this portion of the Temple Scroll). If an interpolation, it appears the redactor saw a close relation between his material and that of Deuteronomy 21:22–23. In any case, readers of the text who were at all familiar with the corresponding section in Deuteronomy could not help but view the two as related. More importantly, the text of Deuteronomy 21:22–23 is substantially at the center of these lines in the Temple Scroll, and the additional material, though its ancestry may at times be obscure, seems to be directed primarily at one central issue – defining which "sins bearing a judgment of death" merit suspension on the tree. And this issue is one that has confounded exegetes, including halakhic exegetes (cf. *Sifre Deut.* 221) over the centuries.

Contrary to Bernstein, D. Schwartz[129] has argued that the "commentator" who wrote the Temple Scroll, in seeking to understand the meaning of כִּי־קִלְלַת אֱלֹהִים in Deuteronomy 21:23, turned to the legislation against cursing God in Exodus 22:27 (אֱלֹהִים לֹא תְקַלֵּל וְנָשִׂיא בְעַמְּךָ לֹא תָאֹר – "you shall not curse God, and a leader over your people you shall not curse"), which also combines קלל with אלהים. Then, according to Schwartz, the commentator linked this with Leviticus 19:16 (לֹא־תֵלֵךְ רָכִיל בְּעַמֶּיךָ – "you shall not walk as a slanderer against your peoples"), due to the "common topic" of "evil speech" and the similarity with בְעַמְּךָ ("over your people" or "against your people"). From Leviticus 19:16 then he deduced the first crime in 11QTemple lxiv.6–8 of slandering (i.e., revealing national secrets). And from Exodus 22:27 he deduced the second crime in lines 9–10 of cursing the nation (i.e., cursing אֱלֹהִים and cursing the people).

Concerning this reconstruction Schwartz admits two difficulties, to which he responds. First, the second crime in the Temple Scroll does not appear to

---

[128] Such assumptions are particularly evident in Bernstein, "Midrash Halakhah," pp. 159–60.

[129] Daniel R. Schwartz, "'The Contemners of Judges and Men' (11Q Temple 64:12)," in *Studies in the Jewish Background of Christianity*, WUNT 60 (Tübingen: J. C. B. Mohr [Paul Siebeck], 1992), 81–88.

refer to the cursing of אֱלֹהִים (normally translated as "God"; rather, it involves fleeing to other nations. However, Schwartz contends, if one understands אֱלֹהִים as referring to "judges" (instead of designating "God"), then the person can be understood as reviling אֱלֹהִים (i.e., the "judges") by that person fleeing from his death sentence.[130] Second, if מקולל is taken as *puʿal* then the person in line 12 *is cursed* (passive) by אֱלֹהִים and men rather than having actually *cursed* them (active, as is required in Schwartz's account). However, Schwartz suggests that מקולל is not in *puʿal* but either in *piʿel* (with the *waw* being either a *mater lectionis* or "a figment of Qumran pronunciation") or in *polel*; in both cases (*piʿel* or *polel*) this would imply that the person has himself actively cursed the judges and men.

While others had noted the parallels with Leviticus 19:16 and Exodus 22:27, Schwartz's synthesis is quite innovative. However, it suffers from what amounts to the central claim, namely that the construct in מקולל אלוהים ואנשים should be read as an objective genitive ("the hung man curses judges and men"). As noted above, this requires that the מקולל *not* be in the *puʿal* form, but rather that it be a form of the *piʿel* or *polel*, despite what most other scholars have assumed. Yet, Schwartz himself inadvertently points to a significant counter-example to his thesis: 4QpPsᵃ (= 4Q171) 1–10 iii 9–12.[131] This text is based on Psalm 37:22, and reads ומקוללו where the MT has וּמְקֻלָּלָיו (*puʿal*). While Schwartz contends that here is another example of a *polel* form of קלל, in fact the text can most easily be read as following the Masoretic pointing with the *puʿal* being signaled in *plene* form by the additional *waw*.[132] This is all the more likely as ומקוללו in line 9 of 4QpPsᵃ is parallel with the *puʿal* [ו]מבורכ (= MT

---

[130] For אֱלֹהִים as "judges", Schwartz refers broadly to studies of rabbinic literature and to Exod 22:8, 9, 11 (presumably he means MT Exod 22:7, 8, 10). Yet, concerning the Exodus citations: both verses in Exod 22:7–8 principally have the articular form הָאֱלֹהִים (though, on the strength of הָאֱלֹהִים earlier in 22:7–8, the word is used without the article later in verse 8); and 22:10 appears an inaccurate citation (the word being יהוה).

[131] So in 4QpPsᵃ 1–10 iii 9: כיא מבורכ[ו יר[שו ארץ ומקוללו יכ]רתו; "for those who are blessed of him shall inherit land, but those who are cursed of him shall be cut off"; this reconstructed text is from *DJD* V, p. 44; also followed by Maurya P. Horgan, *Pesharim: Qumran Interpretations of Biblical Books*, CBQMS 8 (Washington, DC: Catholic Biblical Association of America, 1979), text p. 53; and see Maurya P. Horgan, "Psalm Pesher 1 (4Q171 = 4QpPsᵃ = 4QPs 37 and 45)," in *The Dead Sea Scrolls: Hebrew, Aramaic, and Greek Texts with English Translations*, ed. James H. Charlesworth, vol. 6b: Pesharim, Other Commentaries and Related Documents (Tübingen: Mohr Siebeck; Louisville: Westminster/ John Knox, 2002), 14 (where she reads ומקוללו).

[132] The omission of the *yôdh* of the 3ms suffix is a frequent trait of Qumran Hebrew – so Horgan (*Pesharim*, 218) compares it with 4QpPsᵃ 1–10 ii 5 (בהירו). On this see Qimron, *Hebrew*, §322.141 (p. 59). Alternatively, Strugnell reads ומקולליו in each location (which gives the same sense); see John Strugnell, "Notes en marge du volume V des «Discoveries in the Judaean Desert of Jordan»," *RevQ* 7 (1970): 214.

מִבְּדָכָיו).[133] Thus, not only does a *polel* of קלל remain unattested in Hebrew literature, but also the DSS themselves provide an instance (as does the MT) of a similar *pu'al* participle from קלל.

In summary, 11QTemple lxiv.6–13 is naturally read as an attempt at defining what kinds of people merit the penalty of Deuteronomy 21:22–23. Moreover, the two conditionals in lines 6–9 and 9–11 both require execution by suspension to be applied to the two kinds of criminals so described. The biblical basis for delineating these two crimes remains obscure, and perhaps there is merit in following Yadin's suggestion that historical events must have suggested these crimes as "sins bearing a judgment of death." The text most likely renders the OT קִלְלַת אֱלֹהִים as a subjective genitive (God curses the hung person), and freely brings in the derision of people along with the cursing by God (מקוללי אלוהים ואנשים – "cursed of God and men").[134] Therefore, this text provides a significant witness that at least some Jewish people saw suspension as a viable means of execution, and that they found biblical warrant for their view in Deuteronomy 21:22–23.

4.4 Philo and Deuteronomy 21:22–23

Philo explicitly treats Deuteronomy 21:22–23 twice. *De Specialibus Legibus* iii.83–209 contains a Philonic exposition of the pentateuchal legislation that relates to the Sixth Commandment (= Philo's seventh) against murder. In iii.151–52 Philo writes:

(151) ἐπεὶ δ᾽ ὅρον οὐκ ἔχουσιν οἱ πονηροὶ τὰς φύσεις τοῦ πλημμελεῖν, ἀλλ᾽ ἀεὶ μεγαλουργοῦσι προσυπερβάλλοντες καὶ τὰς κακίας ἐπιτείνουσι καὶ διαίρουσι πρὸς τὸ ἄμετρον καὶ ἀπερίγραφον, μυρίους μὲν θανάτους, εἴπερ οἷόν τε ἦν, ὥρισεν ἂν κατ᾽ αὐτῶν ὁ νομοθέτης· ἐπεὶ δὲ τοῦτ᾽ οὐκ ἐνεδέχετο, τιμωρίαν ἄλλην προσδιατάττεται κελεύων τοὺς ἀνελόντας ἀνασκολοπίζεσθαι. (152) καὶ τοῦτο προστάξας ἀνατρέχει πάλιν ἐπὶ τὴν αὑτοῦ φιλανθρωπίαν, ἡμερούμενος πρὸς τοὺς ἀνήμερα εἰργασμένους, καί φησι· μὴ ἐπιδυέτω ὁ ἥλιος ἀνεσκολοπισμένοις, ἀλλ᾽ ἐπικρυπτέσθωσαν γῇ πρὸ δύσεως καθαιρεθέντες. ἦν γὰρ ἀναγκαῖον τοὺς ἅπασι τοῖς μέρεσι τοῦ κόσμου πολεμίους μετεωρίσαντας εἰς τοὐμφανὲς ἐπιδείξασθαι μὲν αὐτοὺς ἡλίῳ καὶ οὐρανῷ καὶ ἀέρι καὶ ὕδατι καὶ γῇ κολασθέντας, πάλιν δὲ εἰς τὸν νεκρῶν χῶρον ὑποσῦραί τε καὶ καταχῶσαι, ὅπως μὴ τὰ ὑπὲρ γῆν μιαίνωσι.

(151) And, since evil-doers do not limit their natures to offend, but they always perform immense things by exceeding [the bounds], and their wickedness they heighten and determine beyond any measure and limit, the lawgiver (if indeed it was possible) would on the one hand appoint myriads of deaths against them; but, since this was not possible, He ordained besides another punishment, commanding those who took human life to be crucified. (152) And, after

---

[133] Though Schwartz cites M. Horgan favourably on this passage, Horgan points ומקוללו as *pu'al*; see Horgan, *Pesharim*, 197 & 217.

[134] It is intriguing that, just like the LXX (the other great early exponent of the subjective genitive interpretation), the Temple Scroll in line 12 also clearly delimits the extent of those designated as "hung" (תלוי) by adding "on the tree" (על העץ).

ordering this, He hastens again to his philanthropy, being subdued toward those who had worked savage acts; and He says, "Do not let the sun set upon those who have been crucified, but let them be concealed in the earth, having been taken down before sunset." For it was necessary to raise up the enemies with respect to all the parts of the cosmos, in order that they on the one hand be displayed publicly to sun and heaven and air and water and earth as punished,[135] and again to drag [them] down to the place of the dead and also to bury [them], in order that they not defile the things above the earth.

Though the language employed differs from the Septuagint (with the exception of μιαίνω), Philo clearly refers to Deuteronomy 21:22–23. This is evident in the reference to suspension, and it is especially manifest in the need to bury the suspended bodies within the day in order to avoid defilement.

There are several notable elements in Philo's interpretation of Deuteronomy 21. First, the crime concerned is murder.[136] Second, like the author of the Temple Scroll, Philo understands Deuteronomy 21:22 to be a God-given command (κελεύων, also note προσδιατάττεται and προστάξας) to execute the guilty through suspension. Third, the punishment meted out to these criminals is crucifixion (ἀνασκολοπίζω).[137] Fourth, such punishment involves the public display of the crucified before all elements of the cosmos.[138] Fifth, the burial is required in order to prevent pollution of things above ground (this likely implies that Philo saw the body itself as bearing a kind of pollution, likely one connected to the curse of God in Deuteronomy 21:23). Sixth and finally, following on what was said earlier, the Deuteronomic command to bury the hung person especially concerns the burial of crucifixion victims.

---

[135] It is also possible for the comma to appear before κολασθέντας, allowing one to maintain the μὲν...δέ construct (though the placement of the δέ is admittedly then somewhat peculiar). This would result in the following translation: "...and again that [one] drag down *those who were punished* to the place of the dead..."

[136] "Murder" is evident in the context of the discussion of the sixth commandment, in the immediate context (which speaks of the death penalty for murderers; cf. iii.150 & 153), and in the employment of τοὺς ἀνελόντας in iii.151. Also compare the many other instances of ἀναιρέω in *Spec. Leg.* book III. Admittedly, ἀναιρέω can permit other interpretations (possibly cf. iii.42, 116); however, in this context "those who take human life" is most probable for ἀνελόντας, and murder is the most common meaning of ἀναιρέω in *Spec. Leg.* book III – referring to taking a human life by my count 27 times in *Spec. Leg.* iii.85–168. This count is based on Günter Mayer, *Index Philoneus* (Berlin: Walter de Gruyter, 1974).

[137] "Crucifixion" is the best translation given: (1) the fact that ἀνασκολοπίζω is the only term used to describe this execution (note that no other means of death precedes the suspension in this context); (2) the way such a criminal would have been expected to be executed in Philo's day; and (3) the way ἀνασκολοπίζω is used elsewhere in Philo's vocabulary (cf. *Flacc.* 83–84). A contrasting view, without argumentation, is found in Cécile Dogniez and Marguerite Harl, *La Bible D'Alexandrie: Le Deutéronome*, vol. 5 (Paris: Les Éditions du Cerf, 1992), 248.

[138] This is perhaps reminiscent of Numbers 25:4 (where the person is punished "in front of the sun").

In *De Posteritate Caini* 26, Philo provides an allegorical application of Deuteronomy 21:22–23. The context contends that only those people who draw near to the unwavering God will be stable, whereas those who forsake God in favour of creation will have a life without rest and quietness (as described in Deuteronomy 28:65–66, "your life shall hang before your eyes").

(25) ...καὶ ἔστιν αὐτῷ ὅπερ ἔφη ὁ νομοθέτης, πᾶσα ἡ ζωὴ κρεμαμένη, βάσιν οὐκ ἔχουσα ἀκράδαντον, ἀλλὰ πρὸς τῶν ἀντισπώντων καὶ ἀντιμεθελκόντων ἀεὶ φορουμένη πραγμάτων. (26) οὗ χάριν ἐν ἑτέροις "κεκατηραμένον ὑπὸ θεοῦ τὸν κρεμάμενον ἐπὶ ξύλου" φησίν (Deut 21:23), ὅτι, θεοῦ δέον ἐκκρέμασθαι, ὁ δὲ ἀπηώρησεν ἑαυτὸν σώματος, ὅς ἐστιν ἐν ἡμῖν ξύλινος ὄγκος, ἐπιθυμίαν ἐλπίδος ἀντικαταλλαξάμενος, ἀγαθοῦ τελείου μέγιστον κακόν. ἐλπὶς μὲν γὰρ τῶν ἀγαθῶν οὖσα προσδοκία ἐκ τοῦ φιλοδώρου θεοῦ τὴν διάνοιαν ἀρτᾷ, ἐπιθυμία δὲ ἀλόγους ἐμποιοῦσα ὀρέξεις ἐκ τοῦ σώματος, ὃ δεξαμενὴν καὶ χώραν ἡδονῶν ἡ φύσις ἐδημιούργησεν. (27) οὗτοι μὲν οὖν ὥσπερ ἀπ᾽ ἀγχόνης τῆς ἐπιθυμίας ἐκκρεμάσθωσαν.

(25)...And, wherefore, it is for him the Law-giver said, "all his life hangs," (Deut 28:66) since it does not have an unshaken foundation, but, from being drawn in a contrary direction and dragged in a different way, it is always born along by circumstances. (26) On account of which in different words He says, "...the one who hangs on a tree has been cursed by God" (Deut 21:23, cf. LXX). For it is necessary to be hung upon God, but this one hangs down from his own body, which is in us as a wooden mass, receiving desire in exchange for hope – the greatest evil for perfect good. For hope on the one hand, being the expectation of good things, fastens the intention on the bountiful God; but desire which produces unreasoning yearning [fastens the intention] on the body, which nature fabricated as the receptacle and the proper place of pleasures. (27) These, therefore, are hung as from the halter of desire.

This cites the subjective genitive understanding of קִלְלַת אֱלֹהִים ("curse of God") from the Septuagint of Deuteronomy 21:23 (κεκατηραμένον ὑπὸ θεοῦ – "has been cursed by God"), though without the universalizing πᾶς ("all") of the LXX (and in the accusative case). However, Philo also assumes that the man has rejected God (and is thus suspended on the unstable pleasures of the body). Though not explicitly tied to an understanding of "curse of God," it nevertheless appears that the person who rejects (even despises) God is in turn cursed by God.

The last sentence (from *Post.* 27) may signal the kind of hanging Philo has in view, namely a hanging upon a "halter" (ἀγχόνη). This indicates that Philo imagines the person hung as on a noose, which is an unclean death frequently associated with suicide.[139] While not here speaking of crucifixion, later in this Philonic treatise a similar analogy is made of the person crucified and pinned to the tree (*Post.* 61).[140] This fact, combined with the crucifixion application of Deuteronomy 21:23 in *Spec. Leg.* iii.151–52, shows that Philo could envi-

---

[139] For suicide associated with the ἀγχόνη see: *Spec. Leg.* iii.161; *Mut.* 62 (the latter, along with *Aet.* 20–21, speaks of such a death as unclean – see chapter 1 §3). For similar allegorical usage also see *Quis Her.* 269; *Praem.* 151.

[140] On this text see the discussion of Philonic allegory in chapter 5 §1.

sion both suspension on the noose and crucifixion as partaking of similar associations. Also noteworthy, given the way the verses are often joined in the Church Fathers, is Philo's connecting Deuteronomy 21:22–23 with Deuteronomy 28:66 (both mention "hanging").[141]

In summary, the two overt citations of Deuteronomy 21:22–23 in Philo move in different directions. On the one hand, a short allusion to Deuteronomy 21:23 appears connected (via the word κρεμάννυμι – "hang") to an allegorical exposition of Deuteronomy 28:66. In that citation the "cursed by God" understanding of the Septuagint is cited, but the action envisioned appears to be suspension on a noose. Philonic allegory will receive fuller treatment in chapter five below, and in those texts similar allegorical categories are employed in contexts where crucifixion is more specifically understood. On the other hand, in his explicit treatment of the laws of Deuteronomy (*Spec. Leg.* iii.151–52), Philo views the Deuteronomy passage as a command from God both to crucify murderers publicly and then to bury them. Their criminal nature necessitates the most extreme penalty possible, but God's philanthropy requires him to curtail prolonged suspension.

4.5 Josephus and Deuteronomy 21:22–23

Josephus explicitly refers to Deuteronomy 21:22–23 in *Antiquities* iv.264–65:

(264) ᾧ δ᾽ ἂν οἱ λόγοι καὶ ἡ παρ᾽ αὐτῶν διδασκαλία τοῦ σωφρονεῖν τὸ μηδέν εἶναι φανῶσιν, ἐχθροὺς δ᾽ ἀσπόνδους αὐτῷ ποιῇ τοὺς νόμους τοῖς συνεχέσι κατὰ τῶν γονέων τολμήμασι, προαχθεὶς ὑπ᾽ αὐτῶν τούτων ἔξω τῆς πόλεως τοῦ πλήθους ἑπομένου καταλευέσθω καὶ μείνας δι᾽ ὅλης τῆς ἡμέρας εἰς θέαν τὴν ἁπάντων θαπτέσθω νυκτός. (265) οὕτως δὲ καὶ οἱ ὁπωσοῦν ὑπὸ τῶν νόμων ἀναιρεθῆναι κατακριθέντες. θαπτέσθωσαν δὲ καὶ οἱ πολέμιοι καὶ νεκρὸς μηδὲ εἰς ἄμοιρος γῆς κείσθω περαιτέρω τοῦ δικαίου τιμωρίαν ἐκτίνων.

(264) But the youth with whom these words and the lesson in sobriety conveyed by them appear to pass for naught and who makes for himself implacable enemies of the laws by continuous defiance of his parents, let him be led forth by their own hands without the city, followed by the multitude, and stoned to death; and, after remaining for the whole day exposed to the general view, let him be buried at night. (265) Thus shall it be too with all who howsoever are condemned by the laws to be put to death. Let burial be given even to your enemies; and let not a corpse be left without its portion of earth, paying more than its just penalty.[142]

The context in *Antiquities* iv.257–65 involves Josephus' rendering of the laws of Deuteronomy 21:10–14, 18–23. Here Josephus is undoubtedly referring to Deuteronomy 21:22–23; this is apparent not merely from context but also in the legislation to bury the corpses as night. Despite the allusion to Deuteron-

---

[141] For Fathers see below in chapter 7. For the reference to Deuteronomy 28:66, see further below in §10.

[142] Translation by Thackeray, LCL 4, 603.

omy 21:22–23, Josephus refrains from speaking of the Jews as "hanging" anyone – they merely expose people's bodies for common view (εἰς θέαν τὴν ἀπάντων) before burial. The suspension is clearly *post mortem*, given that the person is "stoned to death" (καταλευέσθω).

An intriguing facet of Josephus' account is that he runs together the stoning of the stubborn and rebellious son (Deut 21:18–21) with the legislation concerning the hanging of executed corpses (Deut 21:22–23).[143] This may be due to an interpretive strategy analogous to the rabbinic procedure of דָּבָר הַלָּמֵד מֵעִנְיָינוֹ ("argument from the context")[144] and focused on the death penalty connection. The interlacing of the two pericopes in Deuteronomy may also have been assisted by the conjunction at the beginning of Deuteronomy 21:22 (in both the MT and the LXX). Nevertheless, Josephus also indicates here in *Antiquities* iv.265 that all those who are deserving of the death penalty are to receive similar treatment (note especially the ὁπωσοῦν).

The burial of the dead was a significant facet of Judaism in this period,[145] though this would also have been a theme familiar to Graeco-Roman readers.[146] Here Josephus broadens the sentiment of the Deuteronomic law to mandate that all who are executed must be buried. This passage (iv.264–65) does not directly refer to the issue of what "curse of God" in Deuteronomy 21:23 means; however, the notion that the unburied corpse "pays more than its just penalty" (περαιτέρω τοῦ δικαίου τιμωρίαν ἐκτίνων) may imply, if taken as an aside on Deuteronomy 21:23, that the corpse was cursed.

Josephus more directly interprets the Deuteronomic "curse of God" in *Antiquities* iv.202:

Ὁ δὲ βλασφημήσας θεὸν καταλευσθεὶς κρεμάσθω δι' ἡμέρας καὶ ἀτίμως καὶ ἀφανῶς θαπτέσθω.

"But the one who blasphemed God, having been stoned, let him be hung for a day, and let him be buried dishonourably and obscurely."

In this section of the *Antiquities* Josephus has launched into a topical rendering of the Mosaic Law, here focusing on blasphemy. In this brief sentence Josephus apparently fused Deuteronomy 21:22–23 with other pentateuchal laws (notably Leviticus 24:16 on the stoning of the blasphemer). Deuteronomy 21:22–23 is clearly present in this fusion, as evidenced both by the "hanging" of the corpse and by the need to bury that corpse by the end of the day. Of great interest here is how this legal fusion came about.

---

[143] Cf. *Deut. Rab.* vi.4 (*Ki Teṣe*).

[144] One of Hillel's seven *middoth* (cf. *t. Sanh.* 7.11).

[145] Cf. Tobit 1:18–19, 2:4–8; 12:12–14; *m. Sanh.* vi.5 (esp. cf. *b. Sanh.* 46a [Mishnah], 46b [Gemara]).

[146] Thus Thackeray, in part due to his theory of Josephus' pro-Sophocles assistant, points to parallels in Sophocles *Ajax* 1326 and *Ant.* 1071; see H. St. J. Thackeray, *Josephus*, LCL 4 (London: Heinemann, 1978), 603n.

It is quite likely, especially in light of parallels elsewhere in rabbinic Judaism, that the "curse of God" construct in Deuteronomy 21:23 had been interpreted by Josephus as "one who curses God," i.e., as a "blasphemer."[147] Thus one could translate Deuteronomy 21:23 as "his body shall not spend the night on the tree, but you shall bury him, because the hanged man is a blasphemer..." From this Josephus inferred that the blasphemer ought to be hung for a day. While most modern interpreters view the whole verse of Deuteronomy 21:22 as conditional (hanging is optional; but, if practiced, then Deut 21:22–23 limits its application), Josephus *requires* hanging of the blasphemer.[148] That Josephus also demands that the person executed by stoning should be buried "dishonourably and obscurely" may find its parallel in the special graveyards for use by the Beth Din (i.e., the judicial court) described in the rabbinic literature.[149]

In sum, Josephus apparently read the "hanging upon the tree" of Deuteronomy 21:22–23 as a punishment, subsequent to the actual death by stoning, of the blasphemer (from the Deuteronomic "curse of God") or of the stubborn and rebellious son (by context with Deut 21:18–22). He may potentially have allowed the suspension of others who suffer the death penalty (*Ant.* iv.265). However, in his exposition of the Mosaic Law, Josephus keeps crucifixion (as a form of execution) away from being endorsed by the biblical text. Both passages analyzed above presume that the person is first stoned to death before being suspended.

Nevertheless, Deuteronomy 21:22–23 likely lies behind another passage in Josephus. In *Bellum Judaicum* iv.317 the Idumaeans, who murdered the chief priests Ananus and Jesus, are additionally censured for their burial practices:

προῆλθον δὲ εἰς τοσοῦτον ἀσεβείας, ὥστε καὶ ἀτάφους ῥῖψαι, καίτοι τοσαύτην Ἰουδαίων περὶ τὰς ταφὰς πρόνοιαν ποιουμένων, ὥστε καὶ *τοὺς ἐκ καταδίκης ἀνεσταυ-ρωμένους* πρὸ δύντος ἡλίου καθελεῖν τε καὶ θάπτειν.

They actually went so far in their impiety as to cast out the corpses without burial, although the Jews are so careful about funeral rites that even malefactors who have been sentenced to crucifixion are taken down and buried before sunset.[150]

Burial before sunset, in accordance with Deuteronomy 21:23, is incumbent even for the crucified. It is possible to argue that, much as Tobit buried any Israelite he could find, so burial rites are to be accorded to all (the crucified person being an extreme example). However, why would the ἀνεσταυρωμένος come to Josephus' mind when he thinks of burial, except

---

[147] So Bernstein, "כי קללת אלהים תלוי," 27–28.

[148] This also appears true of Josephus' reading in *Ant.* iv.264–65. Cf. above Philo, *Spec. Leg.* iii.151–52; 11QTemple lxiv.6–13. Also see some rabbinic treatments of Deuteronomy 21 below.

[149] Cf. *m. Sanh.* vi.5; *t. Sanh.* ix.8–9.

[150] Translation by Thackeray, LCL 3, 93.

that this person has been essentially "hung on the tree" and thus best exemplifies the commandment from Deuteronomy 21:23 to bury the malefactor?

4.6 Targumim on Deuteronomy 21:22–23

(*Tg. Onq.*) [22] וארי יהי בגבר חובת דין דקטול ויתקטיל <u>ותצלוב</u> יתיה על <u>צליבא</u>
[23] לא תבית נבילתיה על <u>צליבא</u> ארי <u>מקבר</u> תקבריניה ביומא ההוא ארי <u>על דחב</u>
<u>קדם יוי אצטליב</u> ולא תסאיב ית ארעך דייי אלהך יהיב לך אחסנא

(*Tg. Neof.*) [22] וארום יהווי בגברא <u>סדר</u> חובת דין דקטולין ויתקטל <u>ותצלבון</u> יתיה על
קיסה [23] לא תבית נבלתיה על קיסה ארום מקבר תקברון יתיה ביומה ההוא ארום
<u>ליט קדם ייי כל דצליב</u> ולא תסאבון ית ארעכון דייי אלהכון יהיב <u>לכן</u> אחסנה

(*Tg. Ps.-J.*) [22] וארום <u>אין</u> יהוי בגבר חובת דין קטול <u>ויתחייב</u> ויתקטיל <u>אטלות אבנין ובתר כדין</u>
<u>יצלבון</u> יתיה על קיסא [23] לא תבית ניבלת <u>גושמיה</u> על קיסה ארום מקבר תקברוניה
ביומה ההוא ארום <u>קילותא קדם אילקא למצלוב גבר אלהן חובוי גרמו ליה ומן בגלל</u>
<u>דבריוקנא דייי אתעבד ותקברוניה עם מטמוע שימשא דלא יקילון בריתא ביה ולא</u>
<u>תטנפון בנבילתהון דחייביא ית ארעכון דייי אלקכון יהיב לכן</u>

(*Frg. Tg.* MS440)[151]   [22] על <u>ע</u>ין : <u>ותצלבון</u> יתיה על קייסא

(*Tg. Onq.*) [22] And if there is in a man a sin bearing a judgment of death, and he is executed, and you <u>suspend</u> him on <u>the cross</u>, [23] his corpse shall not spend the night[152] on the <u>cross</u>, but you [pl.] shall surely bury him in that day, because <u>on account of his having sinned before the LORD he was suspended</u>; and you shall not defile your land, which the LORD your God <u>will</u> give to you as an inheritance.

(*Tg. Neof.*) [22] And if there is <u>arranged</u> in <u>the</u> man a sin bearing a judgment[153] of death<u>s</u>, and he is executed, and you [pl.] <u>suspend</u> him on a tree, [23] his corpse shall not spend the night on <u>a</u> tree,[154] but you [pl.] shall surely bury him in that day, because cursed [participle] <u>before the LORD</u> is <u>everyone who is suspended</u>,[155] and you [pl.] shall not defile your [pl.] land, which the LORD your [pl.] God <u>will</u> give to you [pl.] as an inheritance.

---

[151] Similarly, with mere orthographic variation, MS264 reads ותצלבון יתיה על קיסא (as does apparently the Nürnberg-Stadtbibliothek MS).

[152] The translation above understands תבית in the unpointed consonantal text of the Targum as *pe'al* (rendering "his corpse shall not spend the night") – this is certainly possible and is in keeping with the normal Masoretic understanding of the Hebrew. However, if one follows the pointing in Sperber's text of Onqelos, then the verb (תָבֵית) is *aph'el*, implying "you shall not keep his corpse overnight." Similar possibilities arise in interpreting the תבית in Neofiti and Pseudo-Jonathan, though see the footnote on this below.

[153] Neofiti margin reads: בגברא חובה <u>סדר</u> דין ("in a man a sin <u>arranged</u> [for] a judgment").

[154] As noted a couple footnotes above, this could be pointed *aph'el*, as in Sperber's edition of *Tg. Onq* ("you shall not keep his corpse overnight"). However, without such pointing it is more natural to read נבלתיה (which bears no direct object marker) as the subject of the *pe'al* תבית ("his corpse shall not spend the night"). This then parallels the Masoretic understanding of the Hebrew text of Deuteronomy 21:23. Also note "you" throughout is plural, whereas the *aph'el* would require second person *singular*. So also in *Tg. Ps.-J.*

[155] Neofiti margin: בזיו [בזין?] [leg?] יקר שכינתיה דייי אצלב [מצלב] [leg ולא תס']. McNamara and Maher (ET in Díez Macho, *Neophyti 1*) translates as: "(for) contempt (?) of

(*Tg. Ps.-J.*) [22] And if <u>indeed</u> there is in a man a sin bearing a judgment of death, <u>and he is convicted [to] a casting of stones [= a stoning]</u>, and <u>after this they suspend</u> him on the tree; [23] the corpse <u>of his body</u> shall not spend the night on a tree, but you [pl.] shall surely bury him in that day, because <u>it is a disgrace before the Lord to suspend a man, unless his sins caused it. And because in the image of the LORD he was made</u>, you [pl.] shall bury him <u>with the setting of the sun, so that the creatures will not treat him improperly</u>; and you [pl.] shall not defile <u>with the corpses of the guilty</u> your [pl.] land, which the LORD your [pl.] God <u>will</u> give to you [pl.].

(*Frg. Tg.*) [22] *On a tree:* And you [pl.] shall <u>suspend</u> him on <u>the</u> tree.

All targumim render the Hebrew חֵטְא מִשְׁפַּט־מָוֶת ("a sin bearing a judgment of death") with a parallel Aramaic construction חובת דין דקטול ("a sin bearing a judgment of death"). However, Pseudo-Jonathan, in keeping with much rabbinic teaching, specifies that the capital crime must be one punishable by stoning (cf. *m. Sanh.* vi.4).

All of the targumim also employ צלב as the verb of suspension. As noted in chapter one above, this verb is only used of human penal bodily suspension; thus it is a more technical word than the Hebrew תלה ("hang") or its Aramaic equivalent תלא. Further, while most of these targumim refer to the device for suspension with the more generic word for "tree" (קיסה), Onqelos designates the suspension device with the more technical term צליבא. In order to maintain the lexical difference between קיסא and צליבא, the latter has been translated above as "cross" (though this should not be interpreted to assume that an *ante mortem* crucifixion is necessarily implied).

However, all these Aramaic traditions also maintain the Hebrew word order in verse 22, implying that צלב was not the means of death.[156] Targum Pseudo-Jonathan goes so far as to specify in verse 22 that the suspension occurs *after* (ובתר כדין) the stoning. Nevertheless, the צליבא/צלב word group does embrace the terms typically used in describing crucifixions. Therefore, while these interpretive traditions either maintain the Hebrew word order, or actually distance these verses from implying execution via crucifixion (especially Pseudo-Jonathan), they do employ the group of terms that would be used for the sphere of penalties of which crucifixion was one. This may indicate that, while the rabbis could debate whether the Deuteronomic passage necessitated crucifixion, practically speaking a person who had already been crucified might popularly be deemed to be associated with the "curse of God" mentioned in Deuteronomy 21.

The greatest diversity among the targumim concerns how each renders the Hebrew construct קִלְלַת אֱלֹהִים ("curse of God"). For example, Onqelos avoids the Hebrew terminology of cursing almost altogether, instead focusing

---

the glory of the Shekinah of the Lord is one crucified (*or:* 'hanged') and you shall not defile…"

[156] See Baumgarten, "*TLH* in the Temple Scroll," 474.

on the hung man's sinfulness as the reason for his suspension. If this stems from an actual interpretation of the Hebrew Bible (rather than a mere replacement of a difficult phrase), then possibly the meturgeman assumed an objective genitive in the Hebrew (implying blasphemy), but broadened it to include other sins "before the Lord." Hence, one might suggest that he employed the broad term דחב ("of having sinned") from חוב ("to incur guilt, to sin") in verse 23 rather than more specific blasphemy terminology; and he thus arrived at the paraphrase "on account of his having sinned before the Lord". Furthermore, this use of חוב in verse 23 of Onqelos was likely chosen to connect with the חובת ("sin") in verse 22 (חובת דין דקטול – "a sin bearing a judgment of death").

The text of Neofiti follows the subjective genitive understanding of the Hebrew קִלְלַת אֱלֹהִים ("curse of God") by stating that all those who are suspended are "cursed before the Lord" (ליט קדם ייי). The curse thus rests on the suspended person, rather than falling on God. However, we should note that the margin of Neofiti varies from the text itself, by indicating the criminal has sought to defile the Shekinah of the Lord; this shows that at least one reader of the Neofiti text believed instead that an objective genitive was the correct interpretation.[157] Intriguingly, Neofiti also here emphasizes the universal possibilities of the Hebrew participle תָּלוּי by employing כל ("all") in כל דצליב ("everyone who is suspended"). Thus in both the subjective genitive interpretation and in the universal application of the participle, Neofiti parallels the interpretation of the Septuagint (see above). This indicates that, despite the tendency in the rabbinic period to view this as a text referring to blasphemers (see below), the interpretive tendencies previously manifest in the Septuagint on verse 23 continued within prominent Jewish circles well into the rabbinic period (at least in Palestine).

Pseudo-Jonathan is quite expansive in just the section where the Masoretic Text has קִלְלַת אֱלֹהִים. This targum emphasizes the disgrace that comes in suspending a person, acceptable only because he is guilty. And it connects the need for burial with how the man bears the "image of God" – a link reminiscent of a parable attributed to R. Meir (*t. Sanh.* ix.7; see below §4.7). But, unlike Meir's parable, here the concern is that this man, who is created in God's image, will be treated shamefully by the wildlife – likely referring to his flesh being devoured, though the verb that is employed (קלל) could also connote "to curse."[158] Pseudo-Jonathan then appears to understand the genitive both ways: a prolonged suspension produces the danger of a "cursing" of

---

[157] See Bernstein, "כי קללת אלהים תלוי," 34–35. The marginal text (along with a translation) can be found above in our translational footnote on this clause in Neofiti.

[158] Note that the animals molesting the bodies of the suspended is a theme met in the Genesis 40 traditions examined above, and also in 2 Samuel 21 (see §6 below). This theme is also known in several ancient crucifixion accounts.

the man by ravenous beast and fowl; but this also becomes a disgrace (קילותא – again note the use of a cognate of קלל/קיל) before God (likely due to God's image being put to shame).[159]

In sum, the targumim on Deuteronomy 21:22–23 all employ technical Aramaic terminology to refer to penal human bodily suspension. While Onqelos and Neofiti simply follow the Hebrew word order, Pseudo-Jonathan specifies that this penalty is a *post mortem* punishment preceded by stoning. However, the main contribution of these traditions is to attempt to determine the meaning of the Hebrew "curse of God" construct. In this regard, the departure in Onqelos from the biblical wording may imply an objective genitive understanding (as does the margin of Neofiti even more clearly). The main text of Neofiti manifests a subjective genitive viewpoint. Pseudo-Jonathan, our most expansive targum on these verses, apparently includes both a subjective and an objective genitive view.

4.7 Rabbinic Writings and Deuteronomy 21:22–23

Early rabbinic interpretations of the Deuteronomy passage seek to carefully delineate the boundaries of the legislation. The Mishnah (*m. Sanh.* vi.4), though mentioning the dissenting voice of R. Eliezer, states that the Sages teach: after being stoned to death, the naked male blasphemer or idolator[160] is hung by tying his hands to a pole sunk into the ground; the man is then immediately untied and buried. The hanging of the blasphemer or idolator is an assumed aspect of their execution. In *m. Sanh.* vi.4 only a portion of this teaching is directly ascribed to Deuteronomy 21:22–23:

ומתירין אותו מיד. ואם לן עובר עליו בלא תעשה. שנאמר לא־תלין נבלתו על העץ כי־
קבור תקברנו כי קללת אלהים תלוי וגו' כלומר מפני מה זה תלוי. מפני שבירך את־
השם ונמצא שם שמים מתחלל

And they untie him immediately; but if not, then on account of him a negative command is transgressed – as it is said, "his corpse shall not spend the night on the tree, but you shall surely bury him, for a curse of God is the one who is hung, etc." That is to say: why was this person hung? Because he blessed [= cursed] the Name [= God], and the Name of Heaven was found profaned.

As also noted in *Sifre Deuteronomy* 221, the negative command is in the first clause of Deuteronomy 21:23 ("his corpse shall not spend the night"), whereas a positive command is in the second ("you shall surely bury"). For present purposes, two items are especially noteworthy in this Mishnaic passage: First, in order not to violate the negative command לא־תלין ("shall

---

[159] An alternative explanation is found in Bernstein, "כי קללת אלהים תלוי," pp. 30, 32–33.

[160] In *b. Sanh.* 45b–46a blasphemy and idolatry are explicitly treated as separate transgressions, both of which are encompassed in Deuteronomy 21:22–23.

not spend the night") in Deuteronomy 21:23, the body must be removed "immediately."[161] Second, the Hebrew construct קללת אלהים ("curse of God") in Deuteronomy 21:23 is clearly understood as an objective genitive – the person is thus considered a blasphemer (one who curses God). This Mishnah, however, also presents the dissenting voice of Rabbi Eliezer (second generation Tannaite) arguing that *all* those who are stoned are hung (including both men and women); he based this on the precedent established by Simeon b. Shetah, who hung the "witches" in Ashkelon (for this incident see above in chapter 2, §2.5).[162]

In *m. Sanh.* vi.5 there is also a rather curious attempt, attributed to Rabbi Meir, to understand Deuteronomy 21:23:

אמר רבי מאיר בזמן[165] שאדם מצטער. שכינה מה הלשון[164] אומרת כביכול.[163] קלני מראשי קלני מזרועי. אם כן המקום מצטער על דמם של רשעים שנשפך. קל וחמר על דמם של צדיקים

Rabbi Meir said, "When a man suffers [the penalty of the law][166] what expression does the *Shekinah* say, as if this was possible? 'I am lighter than my head, I am lighter than my arm.'[167] If thus the Existence [= God] suffers on account of the blood of wicked men which is poured out, how much more on account of the blood of righteous men."

As in a parable also attributed to Meir in the Tosefta (noted below), here the קללת in the Deuteronomic קללת אלהים ("curse of God") is something projected onto God (probably the equivalent of an objective genitive), and hence God suffers. While in the Hebrew Bible קללת is clearly a noun ("a curse"), here Meir employs instead the cognate verb קלל. The *piʿel* of קלל means "to curse," but the *qal* form of the verb קלל can refer to something "being light." So, not only has Meir switched from the nominal form to a verbal cognate, but he has also switched from the most analogous *binyan* of that verb (*piʿel*) to one less likely (*qal*) in order to have God say, "I am lighter (קַלֵּנִי) than my head/arm." This switch from noun to verb (and also essentially within verbal *binyanim*) caused consternation in the Talmudic commentaries on Rabbi

---

[161] On this use of מיד see M. H. Segal, *A Grammar of Mishnaic Hebrew* (Oxford: Clarendon Press, 1927), 241. The manuscripts of *Sifre Deut.* 221 (aside from citations of the *Sifre* in the Yalqut and in MHG) record the same statement, omitting the מיד, but indicating that the whole punishment is accomplished before dusk. The process is most clearly delineated in *b. Sanh.* 46b.

[162] For R. Eliezer's dissent see *m. Sanh.* vi.4 (cf. *b. Sanh.* 46a), *Sifre Deut.* 221, and (with Gemara) *y. Sanh.* vi.9 [23c]. The prevailing opinion that only men are to be hung is affirmed again (without reporting any dissent) in *m. Sota* iii.8.

[163] כביכול ("as if it were possible") is omitted in both Talmuds.

[164] In those manuscripts where שכינה as a reference to God is omitted הלשון "the tongue" stands as a euphemism for God.

[165] Mishnah in *b. Sanh.* 46a reads בשעה in place of בזמן.

[166] As suggested in Jastrow, *Dictionary*, s.v. צער.

[167] I.e., "my head is heavy, my arm is heavy."

Meir's interpretation (cf. *y. Sanh.* vi.10 [23d]; *b. Sanh.* 46b), although it does seems to be a basic, if construed, word play based on an objective genitive interpretation.

Sifre Deuteronomy 221 elaborates on the Mishnaic injunctions concerning penal suspension found in *Sanh.* vi.4, and it also connects them more fully to the text of Deuteronomy. So וְתָלִיתָ אֹתוֹ ("and you shall hang *him*") is cited to show that, while the man is hung, his clothes are not (i.e., he is hung naked), because clothes are not included in אֹתוֹ (him). From similar proof it is shown that false witnesses unmasked at his trial are not hung (they are not "him") despite meriting death; also the court should not suspend two persons in one day (the "him" is singular). Similarly, that a woman is not hung is substantiated by the use of אִישׁ ("man") and not אִשָּׁה ("woman") in Deuteronomy 21:22 (וְכִי יִהְיֶה בְאִישׁ – "and when there is in a *man*").[168] It is worth noting again that Simeon ben Shetaḥ's simultaneous suspension of eighty female witches in Ashkelon departs from several of these rabbinic halakhic deductions, as R. Eliezer points out in his minority dissent. Further, while the Mishnah (*Sanh.* vi.5) without Scripture proof permits a body to remain unburied overnight in order to more fully prepare a proper burial, the *Sifre* finds warrant for this since the Deuteronomic command requires only the burial of the one hung "on the tree"; Deuteronomy 21:22–23 is thus deemed to be applicable only in situations in which the corpse is disgraced by being suspended.[169]

Other injunctions are also noted in the *Sifre* that are not in the Mishnah. So כִּי־קָבוֹר תִּקְבְּרֶנּוּ ("you shall surely bury it") is cited to show that the "tree" used for suspension is to be buried with the person – presumably understanding the masculine singular antecedent of the pronominal suffix on תִּקְבְּרֶנּוּ ("you shall bury *it*") to refer to the עֵץ ("tree").[170]

In keeping with Mishnaic teaching, the blasphemer (objective genitive) interpretation of קִלְלַת אֱלֹהִים ("curse of God") is also found twice in this *piska* of the *Sifre* – once following the wording of the Mishnah, and once providing biblical support to the view of the Sages (also stated in both Talmuds) that all who blaspheme are hung.

Finally the *Sifre* states that Deuteronomy 21:22 limits the kind of hanging that can be employed:

---

[168] Cf. *b. Sanh.* 46a.

[169] So also *b. Sanh.* 47a. The influence of Deuteronomy 21:22–23 on burial practices in general, beyond its specific application to cases concerning capital crimes, can also be seen, for example, in: *Mek.* Nezikin iv [Lauterbach, 3:39]; also note *y. Nazir* vii.1 [55d].

[170] Also in *b. Sanh.* 46b. Others have inferred that the ground for this argument comes from the emphatic nature of קָבוֹר תִּקְבְּרֶנּוּ (so the notes to the Soncino Hebrew-English Talmud, *loc. cit.*). However, contrast *t. Sanh.* ix.8 ("The sword with which he is slain, the cloth with which he is strangled, the stone with which he is stoned, and the tree on which he is hung – all of them require immersion; but they do *not* bury them with him.").

יכול יהו תולים אותו חי כדרך שהמלכות עושה תלמוד לומר והומת ותלית אותו על עץ.

One might think that they will hang him alive, as in the manner that the [Roman] government does; so Scripture says, "…and he was put to death, and you hung him on a tree."

While some texts do not read שהמלכות עושה כדרך ("as in the manner which the [Roman] government does"), there is substantial support for this phrase, and thus it is included in Finkelstein's edition.[171] Its inclusion would indicate more specifically that crucifixion is being rejected, since crucifixion was at that time the typical mode of public execution by suspension. In any case, the *Sifre* here definitely opposes suspension as a means of execution, based on the order of verbs in Deuteronomy 21:22.[172] A related injunction is found in *b. Sanh.* 46b:

תנו רבנן אילו נאמר חטא ותלית הייתי אומר תולין אותו ואחר כך ממיתין אותו כדרך
שהמלכות עושה תלמוד לומר והומת ותלית ממיתין אותו ואח"כ תולין אותו

The Rabbis taught, "If it were to say, 'He sinned, and you hanged [him],' then I would have said, 'They hang him and afterwards they put him to death, as in the manner which the [Roman] government does.' Scripture says, 'And he is put to death and you hang [him].' [So] they put him to death and afterwards they hang him."

The Bavli cites this argument as an ancient *baraita*, although it employs different terminology than in the *Sifre*. Nonetheless, the meaning and argumentation is the same. Here crucifixion is clearly rejected (note the *post mortem* suspension argument, and especially עושה שהמלכות כדרך – "as in the manner which the [Roman] government does").

Tosefta Sanhedrin ix.6–7 relates two sets of Tannaitic traditions not recorded in either the Mishnah or *Sifre*:

וכשתולין אותו אחד קושר ואחד מתיר כדי לקיים בו מצות תלייה

(ix.6) And when they hang him, one ties and one merely unties, to carry out with regard to him the commandment of hanging.

Note that here the suspension of the person is actually considered to be a מצוה ("commandment").[173] This text itself provides a specific methodology to the idea, found above in the Mishnah and *Sifre*, that the period of hanging

---

[171] The phrase is found in MS Rome (Assemani 32), MS Berlin (Acc. Or. 1928, 328), and in excerpts of *Sifre Deuteronomy* in *Midrash Ḥakhamim* and in the *Midrash ha-Gadol*, etc. It is omitted in MS Oxford (Neubauer 151), MS London (Margoliouth 341, Add 16406), and in the Venice edition. For such a phrase cf. *m. Sanh.* vii.3.

[172] For the phrase תולים אותו חי cf. 4QpNah 3–4 i 8; and note the Zeitlin and Wieder debate about this phrase (mentioned in chapter 1 §2.3.1).

[173] The same procedure, along with the statement that this fulfils the "commandment of hanging," appears in *b. Sanh.* 46b. Compare this with the impetus to see hanging as commanded in Deuteronomy 21 in 11QTemple, Philo and Josephus (see above). Also note instances where hanging is appended to biblical examples of stonings: e.g., *Sifre Num.* 114 on Numbers 15:32–35; also *Tg. Ps.-J.* Lev 24:23.

is to be short. Apparently the time of suspension is to be quite brief, such that the untying immediately follows (or perhaps is simultaneous with) the tying of the victim to the tree. The Tosefta continues (in ix.7):

היה ר' מאיר אומ' מה תלמ' לומר כי קללת אלהים תלוי לשני אחים האומים דומין זה לזה אחד מלך על כל העולם כולו ואחד יצא לליסטייא לאחר זמן נתפס זה שיצא לליסטיא והיו צולבין אותו על הצלוב והיה כל עובר ושב או' דומה שהמלך צלוב לכך נאמר כי קללת אלהים תלוי:

R. Meir would say, "What Scripture teaches – 'because a curse of God is the one who is hung' – is like two brothers who were twinlike, this one was like the other. One was king over all the whole world, but the other went out to the brigands. After time, this one who went out to the brigands was arrested. And they crucified him on the cross. And everyone who passed to and fro would tell the rumour that the king was crucified. Therefore, it is said, '…because a curse of God is the one who is hung.'"

On the lips of the third generation Tanna, renowned for his parables, is a story that defines the import of the "curse of God" in Deuteronomy 21:23. It assumes an objective genitive (God is defamed); but, unlike other rabbinic renderings here, it is not the hung person who curses/blasphemes God, rather the act of hanging curses/defames God by identification with the victim. The one brother, who is "king of the whole world," appears a fairly certain allusion to God himself.[174] Though not actually stated in the passage, apparently Meir's parable hinges on mankind being created in God's image and likeness (cf. above *Tg. Ps.-J.* on Deut 21:23).[175] That the parable concerns crucifixion is evident not just from the language employed (צלב and הצלוב), but also from the term ליסטייא (the equivalent of Greek ληστής, "robber, bandit or brigand"),[176] since λησταί were crucified in Roman times.[177] It is, of course, striking that R. Meir could associate a parable about crucifixion with Deuteronomy 21:23.[178]

---

[174] See discussion in Børge Salomonsen, *Die Tosefta Seder IV: Nezikin (Sanhedrin – Makkot)* (Stuttgart: W. Kohlhammer, 1976), 150: "Die Worte מלך על כל העולם כולו stören. Vielleicht sind sie bloß eine Überspitzung, die nicht zu interpretieren ist; es wäre aber auch möglich, daß „ein König über die ganze Welt" Gott hieße."

[175] Possibly this parable of R. Meir should be compared with Jerome's "Hebrew" source, who taught Jerome an alternate understanding of the "curse of God" construct in Deuteronomy 21 (*Comm. Gal.* ii on Gal 3:13–14; in Migne, *PL* 26, 387B): "*Dicebat mihi Hebraeus qui me in Scripturis aliqua ex parte instituit, quod possit et ita legi*: quia contumeliose Deus suspensus est." – "A Hebrew, who partly instructed me in the Scriptures to some extent, said to me that it is also possible to be read thus: 'because God has been hung in an insulting way.'"

[176] Samuel Krauss, *Griechische und Lateinische Lehnwörter im Talmud, Midrasch und Targum*, 2 vols. (Berlin, 1898–1899), 2:315–16.

[177] See further below in chapter 5, §2.

[178] Travers Herford's suggestion is not convincing that R. Meir developed this parable based on the stories of Jesus in the Gospels; see R. Travers Herford, *Christianity in Talmud and Midrash* (London: Williams & Norgate, 1903), 86–88. Rather, the impetus more likely stems from the history of identifying crucifixion with someone "hung on a tree."

This story also appears as a *baraita* in *b. Sanh.* 46b. The whole concept is basically the same as in the Tosefta, but with numerous differences of detail (noted with underline):

תניא אומר ר"מ <u>משלו משל</u> למה הדבר דומה לשני אחים <u>תאומים בעיר אחת</u> אחד
<u>מינוהו</u> מלך ואחד יצא לליסטות <u>צוה המלך ותלאוהו</u> כל <u>הרואה אותו אומר</u> המלך
<u>תלוי צוה המלך והורידוהו</u>

It is taught: R. Meir said, "<u>They tell a parable</u>, 'To what is this matter similar? To two brothers <u>in one city</u> who were twinlike. One <u>of them</u> was a king, but the other went out to a brigand's <u>life. The king commanded and they hanged him.</u> All <u>who saw him said, "The</u> king is being hung!" The king commanded and they took him down.'"

The most significant of these differences include: (1) the less direct attribution of this parable to Meir (משלו – "they tell a parable"), (2) the omission of the universal reign of the king, (3) the use of תלא rather than צלב to depict the suspension, (4) the fact that the king himself here commands the suspension and taking down of his brother, and (5) a different phrasing of what the populace said. However, despite these divergences, the narrative arc of the parable and its main point remain the same.

In the Bavli version of the parable, the suspension is designated with ותלאוהו and תלוי rather than the Tosefta's צולבין אותו על הצלוב. Halperin contends that this indicates that later rabbinic authors could substitute תלה for צלב.[179] However, his argument assumes both that the Tosefta form of this narrative is earlier than the one in the Bavli, and that the Bavli form intentionally revises the parable in the Tosefta. While the Tosefta as a whole is generally considered earlier than the Bavli, modern scholars debate the date of its redaction and do not rule out later scribal interpolations. Moreover, although we might be willing to stipulate the greater antiquity of the Tosefta text, the version in the Bavli may not be a direct recension of the Tosefta account (especially give the many significant differences in wording). These two accounts could have common origins in the traditions about R. Meir, but they likely also evidence separate oral or literary lineages. Most likely the Bavli form is influenced by the desire to conform Meir's parable to the term תלוי found in the Hebrew of Deuteronomy 21:23 itself. Nevertheless, even in the Bavli the context of brigandage likely implies that crucifixion was the mode of suspension (note no other means of death is mentioned or implied).

This quick review of early rabbinic accounts on Deuteronomy 21:22–23 has led to a number of observations. The rabbis sought to understand and delimit the circumstances under which the Deuteronomic text was executed. The accepted punishment in the Mishnah and in the *Sifre* required a very short, *post mortem*, naked suspension of the stoned male blasphemer/idolator. Among other matters, this displays the frequent application of an objective

---

[179] Halperin, "Crucifixion," 39–40 (see above in chapter 1, §2.3.1).

genitive understanding of "curse of God" – the person has "cursed God." However, in two separate traditions, R. Meir follows the objective genitive in a slightly different direction: the "curse" rests on God because the suspended man, who images God, is himself viewed as cursed. Although the rabbis are at times careful to distinguish this penalty from sanctioning the Roman practice of crucifixion, Rabbi Meir's famous parable (in both its recensions) is predicated on an overt *de facto* connection between the crucified person and the "curse of God" found in Deuteronomy.

4.8 Summary

In the Hebrew Bible, Deuteronomy 21:22–23 limits the practice of *post mortem* suspension of executed criminals – they are to be buried the day they are hung to prevent profanation of the promised land. The text is ambiguous in its pronouncement that the hung person is a "curse of God" (the genitive here could be subjective or objective, i.e., "cursed by God," or "a cursing to God").

Although the likely intent of the Hebrew text of Deuteronomy 21:22 is to provide the conditional protasis for verse 23, it is possible to read verse 22 in such a way that the hanging of the executed person is viewed as a command. Certainly, the Temple Scroll, Philo, Josephus, Targum Pseudo-Jonathan, and many rabbinic passages understood (each in their own way) the suspension of the person as a necessary, rather than an optional, element of the execution.

In keeping with Deuteronomy 21:23, the duty of burial is consistently asserted in ancient Jewish literature,[180] with some rabbinic texts even requiring that the person be hung only momentarily on the tree. However, as will be observed further below, certain rabbinic traditions recognized biblical exceptions to this requirement for burial of suspended bodies – at least in the suspension of Haman and his sons, and in the case of the sons of Saul.[181] Furthermore, despite the general influence of Deuteronomy 21:23 on Jewish burial rites, some rabbis argued that this text did not apply to non-suspended corpses when the relatives need an extra day to provide proper burial.[182]

The "curse of God" construct in Deuteronomy 21:23 received various interpretations in early Jewish literature. The earliest extant view (being witnessed in the Septuagint and Old Latin texts, as well as in the Temple

---

[180] In addition to the texts mentioned above, a possible reference to the biblical duty to bury a suspended body might be seen in 4Q385a 15 i 3–4. See the discussion and caveats in the appendix at the end of this book.

[181] Concerning 2 Samuel 21 see *b. Yeb.* 79a; *y. Sanh.* vi.9 [23c–d]; *y. Qidd.* iv.1 [65b]; *Num. Rab.* viii.4 (all discussed below in §6.2). For the targumic admission that the hanging of Haman is incompatible with Deut 21:23, see below in §8.3. Also note *Śemaḥot* ii.9 [44b] (where the rabbis legislate that the family should not steal the body of crucified person; see below in chapter five, §3).

[182] So *Sifre Deut.* 221; *b. Sanh.* 47a.

Scroll and later in Targum Neofiti) is that the hung person is cursed by God. Yet the most common rabbinic view (also witnessed in Josephus, Symmachus and the Peshiṭta) is that this person has cursed God by being a blasphemer. An alternative reading of the objective genitive can also be witnessed (especially as attributed to R. Meir) – namely that those hung, though not themselves cursing God, nonetheless in some way bring defamation upon the Lord in whose image they were created. In one of the more complex Jewish expositions, *Targum Pseudo-Jonathan* simultaneously combines this alternative form of the objective genitive alongside a subjective understanding.

While Deuteronomy 21:22 speaks broadly of a "sin bearing a judgment of death," ancient Jewish writers disputed the specific offence required for a person to merit suspension. Philo applies the verse to those who take human life. Josephus, at one point drawing on the context of Deuteronomy 21, indicates that a rebellious son was to suffer *post mortem* hanging. The Temple Scroll directs the legislation both at the person who betrays Israel to a foreign power and at the person who escapes to another nation and curses Israel. Generally the rabbis (and Josephus in one passage), in keeping with their interpretation of "curse of God" as a reference to blasphemy, declare that the law concerns only blasphemers and idolators. However, at least one dissenting rabbinic voice (R. Eliezer) claimed that the command included all criminal acts that warrant death by stoning (also possibly cf. *Tg. Ps.-J.* on Deut 21:22). Thus we witness a diversity of views as to the various types of crimes that merit bodily suspension.

The word order of Deuteronomy 21:22 in the Hebrew text (and in the LXX) could imply that hanging on a tree comes after death (a central conclusion of some rabbinic treatments and of *Targum Pseudo-Jonathan*). Nevertheless, the Peshiṭta reverses these clauses, thus likely indicating that it perceived the suspension to precede (even to cause) the execution. This order (suspension then death) is all the more prominent within the Qumran *Temple Scroll*. The first-century Jewish philosopher Philo (employing the term ἀνασκολοπίζω) actually asserts that the Lawgiver in Deuteronomy 21 ordained capital punishment via suspension/crucifixion. Additionally, other texts from Jewish antiquity implicitly tie crucifixion to Deuteronomy 21:22–23. So, though Josephus is quite cautious not to connect the Deuteronomic text with crucifixion in his legal treatments, still he remarks that Jews are careful to bury victims of the cross before nightfall. Similarly, a parable attributed to R. Meir assumes that there is an inherent analogy between a crucified twin of the king and the person (created in God's image) hung in accordance with Deuteronomy 21.

Thus a number of Jewish interpreters in widespread contexts (e.g., in Greek and in Hebrew, in the Diaspora and in Palestine) overtly linked Deuteronomy 21:22–23 to death by suspension (and even to crucifixion itself). Other texts, while not identifying the passage with crucifixion, use the very human penal suspension terminology that could also be applied to death on the cross (e.g. צלב and cognates); and these passages, apart from sanctioning crucifixion, may nevertheless indicate that all those suspended (including even the crucified corpse) could be viewed to have invoked *de facto* the "curse of God." In light of this, one can better understand how, in frequent early Christian witness to Jewish anti-Christian polemic, the ancient Jewish position assumed that the curse of Deuteronomy 21:22–23 applied to those who are crucified (see chapter 7, §6).

5. "Hanging on the Tree" in the Deuteronomic History

Twice in Joshua people are "hung on the tree." In the first account, the army of Israel attacks Ai, destroys the city, slays the inhabitants, and presents the still living king of Ai to Joshua. After the city is razed the narrative records (Joshua 8:29):

וְאֶת־מֶלֶךְ הָעַי תָּלָה עַל־הָעֵץ עַד־עֵת הָעָרֶב וּכְבוֹא הַשֶּׁמֶשׁ צִוָּה יְהוֹשֻׁעַ וַיֹּרִידוּ אֶת־נִבְלָתוֹ
מִן־הָעֵץ וַיַּשְׁלִיכוּ אוֹתָהּ אֶל־פֶּתַח שַׁעַר הָעִיר וַיָּקִימוּ עָלָיו גַּל־אֲבָנִים גָּדוֹל עַד הַיּוֹם הַזֶּה

But he hung the king of Ai on the tree until the evening time; and, as the sun was setting, Joshua commanded and they took down his corpse from the tree. And they flung it into the opening of the gate of the city.[183] And they erected over him a great heap of stones, [which stands] until this day.

Later in Joshua 10, after the five kings who attacked Gibeon are defeated by Israel under Joshua's leadership, the five are found hidden in the cave at Makkedah. Joshua has them executed and suspended (Joshua 10:26–27):

(26) וַיַּכֵּם יְהוֹשֻׁעַ אַחֲרֵי־כֵן וַיְמִיתֵם וַיִּתְלֵם עַל חֲמִשָּׁה עֵצִים וַיִּהְיוּ תְּלוּיִם עַל־הָעֵצִים עַד־
הָעָרֶב: (27) וַיְהִי לְעֵת בּוֹא הַשֶּׁמֶשׁ צִוָּה יְהוֹשֻׁעַ וַיֹּרִידוּם מֵעַל הָעֵצִים וַיַּשְׁלִכֵם אֶל־הַמְּעָרָה
אֲשֶׁר נֶחְבְּאוּ־שָׁם וַיָּשִׂמוּ אֲבָנִים גְּדֹלוֹת עַל־פִּי הַמְּעָרָה עַד־עֶצֶם הַיּוֹם הַזֶּה:

(26) And Joshua struck them afterwards, and he put them to death,[184] and he hung them on five trees; and they were hanging on the trees until the evening. (27) And it happened at the time the sun was setting, Joshua commanded and they took them down from upon the trees. And they flung them into the cave where they [= the kings] had hid themselves. And they placed great stones over the mouth of the cave, [which remain] until this selfsame day.

These two passages from Joshua are closely related, both in subject matter and in vocabulary. The principal difference between them is that the word order in Joshua 10:26 strongly implies that the five kings are put to death prior to hanging (in agreement with Deuteronomy 21:22), while the actual means of death is left open in Joshua 8:29.

---

[183] LXX has them "casting him into the trench" (ἔρ[ρ]ιψαν αὐτὸν εἰς τὸν βόθρον).

[184] LXX telescopes וַיַּכֵּם...וַיְמִיתֵם with καὶ ἀπέκτεινεν αὐτούς ("and he killed them").

Both texts clearly agree with the admonition in Deuteronomy 21:22–23 to bury suspended bodies within the day. In fact, when compared with the text of Deuteronomy, these two passages more explicitly state a time of burial (namely just at sunset).[185] Furthermore, whereas Deuteronomy 21:22 does not specify which types of capital crimes merit hanging, here those leaders opposing the Israelites during time of war are suspended in victory. This shifts the concept of hanging from a legal capital punishment to the grim realities of military conquest. Of course, as was noted at the beginning of this chapter (§1), suspension of conquered kings is a common theme in ANE literature. In Joshua, the striking variation from ANE norms was not in the suspension of such conquered kings, but in the burial accorded to them in the day of conquest (whereas it appears that other ANE armies left the victims to decompose publicly). The theme of military suspensions would also have been familiar to readers of Greek and Roman literature, although later Hellenistic and Roman accounts often associated such events with crucifixion.[186]

Remarkably, the Septuagint understands the "tree" (הָעֵץ) in Joshua 8:29 to be a ξύλον δίδυμον ("forked tree"), which may more fully indicate the kind of suspension the translator envisaged.[187] Certainly later Christian interpreters of the LXX could see a reference to crucifixion here, as when Jerome's Vulgate renders it with *de cruce* ("from the cross").[188]

Aside from these two passages in Joshua, there are three other incidents in the books of Samuel in which a person was said to have been hung. In the first, while Absalom attempts to escape David's men, he is caught by his hair in an oak tree and "hangs" there (2 Sam 18:10) until Joab spears him.[189] Obviously no intentional punishment is implied in Absalom's suspension, though some traditions associated with this passage are still of interest.[190]

Second, in 1 Samuel 31:1–13 Saul is injured during a battle with the Philistines; and, after he commits suicide, the Philistines cut off his head and (in 1 Sam 31:10) "fastened his dead body to the wall of Beth-shan"

---

[185] Cf. LXX ἕως ἑσπέρας ("until evening").

[186] See e.g., Hengel, *Crucifixion*, 46, 73–74, 76.

[187] *Tg. Jon.* reads צלב על צליבא.

[188] See further Jacqueline Moatti-Fine, *La Bible Alexandrie: Jésus (Josué)* (Paris: Les Éditions du Cerf, 1996), 138–39.

[189] 2 Samuel 18:10 (MT): הִנֵּה רָאִיתִי אֶת־אַבְשָׁלֹם תָּלוּי בָּאֵלָה ("Behold I saw Absalom hanging in an oak."); LXX, Peshitta, and *Tg. Jon.* also support "hanging." In 2 Samuel 18:9, the MT phrase is: וַיֻּתַּן בֵּין הַשָּׁמַיִם וּבֵין הָאָרֶץ ("and he was set between heaven and earth"). However, instead of וַיֻּתַּן ("and he was set") as found in the Masoretic Hebrew text of 18:9, the LXX ([ἀν]εκρεμάσθη), Peshitta (ܘܐܬܬܠܝ), and Targum Jonathan (ואתלי) would support an original Hebrew reading ויתל ("and he was hung") as in 4QSamᵃ [=4Q51] xlvii(C) 14; see Edward D. Herbert, *Reconstructing Biblical Dead Sea Scrolls: A New Method Applied to the Reconstruction of 4QSamᵃ*, STDJ 22 (Leiden: Brill, 1997), 171. So also P. Kyle McCarter, Jr., *II Samuel*, AB 9 (Garden City, New York: Doubleday, 1984), 401.

[190] See our brief discussion in the footnotes of chapter seven.

(וְאֶת־גְּוִיָּתוֹ תָּקְעוּ בְּחוֹמַת בֵּית שָׁן). While suspension is here only implied,[191] a retrospective mention of this event in 2 Samuel 21:12 refers to Saul's body as being "hanged" (cf. אֲשֶׁר תְּלָוּם שָׁם הַפְּלִשְׁתִּים – "where the Philistines hanged them").[192]

Third, when David learns that Rechab and Baanah have slain Saul's son Ish-bosheth, he has them both killed, orders their hands and feet removed, and demands his men "hang them beside the pool at Hebron" (2 Sam 4:12).[193]

5.1 Josephus and Hanging in the Deuteronomic History

Of all the five texts surveyed above, Josephus applies crucifixion terminology only to the suspension of Saul's body. Thus in *Antiquities* vi.374, the Philistines, having just stumbled on the corpses of Saul and his sons, cut off their heads and enact the following *post mortem* insult:

καὶ τὰς μὲν πανοπλίας αὐτῶν ἀνέθηκαν εἰς τὸ Ἀστάρτειον ἱερόν, τὰ δὲ σώματα ἀνεσταύρωσαν πρὸς τὰ τείχη τῆς Βηθσὰν πόλεως, ἣ νῦν Σκυθόπολις καλεῖται.

And their [= Saul's and his sons'] full suits of armour they set up as a votive in the temple of Astarte, but their bodies they crucified to the walls of the city of Bethsan, which now is called Scythopolis.

Although Josephus employs his typical crucifixion terminology (ἀνεσταύρωσαν), the context in the *Antiquities* indicates that these bodies are already corpses prior to their decapitated "crucifixions." This serves as a reminder that, not only is the Greek terminology more flexible than our English equivalents, but also Josephus was likely less concerned to delineate a particular methodology of executionary punishment when he employed the term ἀνασταυρόω and more interested in associating any suspension of the human body with the same class of penalty as crucifixion. Josephus' employment of ἀνασταυρόω is noteworthy here in that the bodies are suspended onto something other than a σταυρός.[194] However, this could be compared to Lucian's dialogue *Prometheus*, where Lucian repeatedly portrays the great Titan Prometheus as crucified to the rock wall of a mountain.

---

[191] *Targum Jonathan*, however, employs the Aramaic term צלב ("suspend") for the Hebrew תקע ("fasten"). Further, the LXX renders תקע with καταπήγνυμι ("stick fast, plant firmly"), a Greek word that can be used in crucifixion contexts (see chapter 1, §2.2) – so also to a certain extent with the Syriac ܡܚ.

[192] The Qere on 2 Samuel 21:12 (תְּלָאוּם – "[the Philistines] hanged them") is an orthographical variant based on תלא rather than תלה. Cf. esp. Targum Jonathan דְּצַלְבוּנִן; also Peshiṭṭa ܙܩܦܘ ܐܢܘܢ; whereas the LXX merely reads ἔστησαν αὐτούς – "they made them stand" (though uncials M & N κρεμασάντων αὐτούς "hanging them"). On crucifixion connotations, cf. Josephus, *Ant.* vi.374 (below).

[193] MT וַיִּתְלוּ עַל־הַבְּרֵכָה בְּחֶבְרוֹן; LXX ἐκρέμασαν; Peshiṭṭa ܘܨܠܒܘ; and *Tg. Jon.* וּצְלָבוּ.

[194] From Polybius it can be inferred that crucifixions were often done *before* the walls of a city (*Hist.* x.33.8; cf. i.86.4–7).

This Josephus account appears based largely on 1 Samuel 31:9–10, except for the way Saul's sons are also maltreated (in the MT only Saul's body is mentioned). Concerning the biblical basis for the inclusion of Saul's sons in Saul's own bodily suspension, it is notable that three of his sons are mentioned as slain in 1 Samuel 31:8 (MT); but, perhaps more significantly, both Saul and his son Jonathan were said to be "hung" in Beth-shan in the Hebrew of 2 Samuel 21:12. Josephus' narrative appears to have combined the information from the context of 1 Samuel 31 with that from 2 Samuel 21. Thus the underlying reason for Josephus' employment of crucifixion terminology could be indebted to the connotations arising from a combination of the Hebrew terms for "fastened" (1 Sam 31:10) and "hung" (2 Sam 21:12). Alternatively, if the tradition Josephus was utilizing cannot be traced back to the Hebrew text, then the next most likely reason for Josephus' use of ἀνασταυρόω would be the influence of the Septuagint word κατέπηξαν ("stick fast") in its treatment of 1 Samuel 31:10 (= LXX 1 Kgdms 31:10).

Quite remarkably, given his fairly consistent employment of crucifixion terminology in other biblical texts mentioning suspension,[195] Josephus does *not* speak of Joshua or David crucifying their opponents. Thus, Josephus does not at all mention the execution of the king of Ai in *Antiquities* v.48; indeed, the whole account is much more tame than the Hebrew or Septuagintal text (cf. Josh 8:29). Similarly, Josephus merely records that Joshua "took" the five kings and "punished all" (*Ant.* v.61; contrast Josh 10:26). Admittedly, in *Antiquities* vii.52 Josephus renders David's command (2 Samuel 4:12) to kill, mutilate and suspend the bodies of Ish-bosheth's murders with πᾶσαν αἰκίαν αὐτοὺς αἰκισάμενος διεχρήσατο ("having inflicted every kind of torture on them, he put them to death"). This language is indeed quite strong,[196] yet αἰκία and αἰκίζω usually can still be differentiated from crucifixion terminology in reference to manner of death.[197]

In other cases Josephus is happy to paraphrase biblical human bodily suspension narratives with σταυρός/crucifixion terminology (e.g. the baker in Genesis, Haman in Esther, and the king's decree from Ezra). Yet, the Deuteronomic history accounts can be distinguished from the rest because in each of the Deuteronomic history cases (aside from the Philistine treatment of the body of Saul) it is a *Jewish* agent who brings about the suspension punish-

---

[195] Cf. the Josephus' accounts of the material from Genesis 40 & 41 (above) and of the Esther narratives (see below).

[196] Cf. *Ant.* xi.330; xiii.232; xv.71, 358; xvi.389; xvii.64; also *Bell.* i.35, 57–58, 269, 593; ii.152, 312, 448; iv.329, 652; v.103; vii.272, 369, 373, 384; *Vita* 147. This terminology in one other context possibly refers to the crucifixion of a dead body (*Ant.* xiii.403); but note the flexibility in *post mortem* αἰκία implied in comparison with *Bell.* i.325.

[197] Cf. *Bell.* v.449 where προβασανιζόμενοι τοῦ θανάτου πᾶσαν αἰκίαν precedes the ἀνεσταυροῦντο; also note the implications of *Ant.* x.115; xv.289; *Bell.* ii.246; iii.321; iv.385; vii.450; *C. Ap.* i.191.

ment. Therefore, Josephus' refusal to render these cases as instances of crucifixion could be his attempt to attenuate before a Roman audience harsh historical activities of the Jewish nation; but it could also be due to Josephus' own sensitivity against implying that crucifixion was biblically permissible at the hands of Jewish people (particularly at the command of biblical heroes). Perhaps both motives could be adduced. Note that throughout the Joshua accounts Josephus minimizes the Israelite activity of exterminating all non-Jewish inhabitants in the promised land; however, in *Antiquities* vii.52, given the nefarious murder of Ish-bosheth, Josephus allows the severe nature of David's kingly justice to come through (cf. *Ant.* vii.161). Yet, even in the punishment of Ish-bosheth's murderers, Josephus still refuses to employ the more obvious ἀνασταυρόω in his rendering of the biblical text.

5.2 Targum and Hanging in the Deuteronomic History

The targumic tradition, as is typically true of pentateuchal targumim in cases of human suspension, renders all these instances of hanging with צלב except 2 Samuel 18:9–10. This is even true in 1 Samuel 31:10, where the Hebrew תקעו ("fastened") is conveyed by צלבו (cf. דצלבונון in *Tg.* 2 Sam 21:12). That the Targum to 2 Samuel 18:9–10 employs תלי (rather than צלב) is the exception that proves the rule, for Absalom does not suffer a capital (or post-mortem) penalty, but is merely accidentally suspended alive by his hair (so also *b. Soṭa* 10b; *Num Rab* ix.24).

Especially notable is the use of the phrase צלב על צליבא in the Targum on Joshua 8:29, where the combination verb and noun, alongside a lack of any other means of execution, might easily have connoted crucifixion to the early reader.[198] However, this should not be pressed too far, since similar phraseology appears to indicate a post-mortem penalty in the Targum on Joshua 10:26.[199]

5.3 Summary

By matter of a quick summary, one notes that there are a few passages in the books of Joshua and Samuel that mention the hanging of men in association with their deaths. Joshua twice is said to demand the suspension of conquered kings (in Joshua 10:26–27 this is most likely *post mortem*); and in both cases, even though these are military executions, he complies with the burial requirement known from Deuteronomy 21:22–23. While the Septuagint

---

[198] Cf. Leivy Smolar et al., *Studies in Targum Jonathan to the Prophets and Targum Jonathan to the Prophets*, Library of Biblical Studies (New York: KTAV, 1983), 98.

[199] ומחנון יהושע בתר כן וקטלנון וצלבנון על חמשה צליבין והוו צליבין על צליבא עד רמשא ("And Joshua destroyed them afterwards, and he slew them and suspended them on five crosses; and they were suspended on the crosses until evening.") A similar statement could be made for the Targum on 1 Sam 31:10, 2 Sam 4:12, and 2 Sam 21:12.

renders Joshua 8:29 with ξύλον δίδυμον ("forked tree") and early Christian authors could understand this as a crucifixion, Josephus plays down these passages significantly by sensitively avoiding discussion of the particulars. The targumic traditions continue their common Aramaic translational procedure by applying צלב and cognates to these human bodily suspensions.

The targumic application of צלב is also found in the instances of human suspension in the books of Samuel.[200] In the Hebrew text these involve: the "fastening" (1 Sam 31:10) and "hanging" (2 Sam 21:12) of the body of Saul, and the suspension at David's command of the bodies of the murderers of Ish-bosheth (2 Sam 4:12). Josephus' reticence to apply crucifixion terminology to the Davidic command (regarding the murderers of Ish-bosheth) is all the more striking given his willingness to speak of the Philistines crucifying the dead bodies of Saul and his sons (*Ant.* vi.374).

6. The Death of Saul's Seven Sons (2 Samuel 21)

Apart from the Deuteronomic history accounts that explicitly mention the "hanging" of people, there is one other text in this corpus that deserves special mention since it has been associated in post-biblical Jewish tradition with penal human bodily suspension. In 2 Samuel we read that David, who has learned that a famine in Israel is due to Saul's action of putting the Gibeonites to death, agrees to the Gibeonite terms for exacting their revenge on Saul's family (2 Sam 21:6, 9–10):

(6) יֻתַּן־לָנוּ[201] שִׁבְעָה אֲנָשִׁים מִבָּנָיו וְהוֹקַעֲנוּם לַיהוָה בְּגִבְעַת שָׁאוּל בְּחִיר יְהוָה. וַיֹּאמֶר הַמֶּלֶךְ אֲנִי אֶתֵּן:...

(9) וַיִּתְּנֵם בְּיַד הַגִּבְעֹנִים וַיֹּקִיעֻם בָּהָר לִפְנֵי יְהוָה וַיִּפְּלוּ שְׁבַעְתָּיִם[202] יָחַד וְהֵם[202] הֻמְתוּ בִּימֵי קָצִיר בָּרִאשֹׁנִים תְּחִלַּת[203] קְצִיר שְׂעֹרִים: (10) וַתִּקַּח רִצְפָּה בַת־אַיָּה אֶת־הַשַּׂק וַתַּטֵּהוּ לָהּ אֶל־הַצּוּר מִתְּחִלַּת קָצִיר עַד נִתַּךְ־מַיִם עֲלֵיהֶם מִן־הַשָּׁמָיִם וְלֹא־נָתְנָה עוֹף הַשָּׁמַיִם לָנוּחַ עֲלֵיהֶם יוֹמָם וְאֶת־חַיַּת הַשָּׂדֶה לָיְלָה:

(6) "Let seven men from his [= Saul's] sons be given to us, and we will execute them unto the LORD in Gibeah of Saul, the chosen of the LORD." And the king said, "I will give [them]."...

(9) And he gave them into the hand of the Gibeonites, And they executed them on the mountain before the LORD; and the seven [of them] fell together. But they were put to death in the first days of harvest, [at] the beginning of the barley harvest. (10) And Rizpah the daughter of Aiah took sackcloth, and spread it out for herself unto the rock, from the beginning of harvest

---

[200] The hanging of Absalom by his own hair (2 Sam 18:9–10) was shown to vary from typical penal suspension, and thus even the targumim use תלי in speaking of his hanging.

[201] Qere: יִתֶּן־לָנוּ. Variant Qere: ונתתם.

[202] For שְׁבַעְתָּיִם the Qere is שְׁבַעְתָּם ("seven *of them*"); for וְהֵם the Qere is וְהֵמָּה ("but they" – minor morphological change).

[203] Qere: בִּתְחִלַּת ("*at* the beginning").

until water was poured upon them from heaven. And she did not permit the fowl of the heavens to rest upon them by day, nor the beasts of the field by night.

Among these seven sons of Saul were two sons of Rizpah. Rizpah's actions convinced David to bury the bones of these seven men (21:13) along with reburying Saul and Jonathan. All this being done, God "granted entreaty for the land" (21:14).

The context clearly provides an extended time of exposure (21:10 – from the beginning of the barley harvest until the rains), but the method of execution is not fully clear. The verb יקע (see chapter 1, §2.3.3) appears here three times (21:6, 9, 13). As in Numbers 25:4 the versions seem at odds to comprehend its meaning. Hence the early extant Greek translations employ three different translational equivalents: ἀνάπηξον ("transfix"; Aquila on 2 Sam 21:6, 9), κρέμασον ("hang"; Symmachus on 2 Sam 21:6), and ἐξηλίασαν ("set out in the sun"; LXX 2 Kgdms 21:9; also 21:6, 13 and cf. 21:14 [in many mss.]). Notably, both Aquila and Symmachus are utilizing the same vocabulary they do in rendering Numbers 25:4 (see above in §3). The Peshiṭta translates the penalty with two different Syriac terms: ܘܗܒܚܘ ("slayed, sacrificed"; Peshiṭta 2 Sam 21:9; cf. 21:6), ܘܐܬܩܛܠ ("killed"; Peshiṭta 2 Sam 21:13). *Targum Jonathan* employs צלב ("suspended, crucified"; *Tg. Jon.* 2 Sam 21:6, 9, 13). Josephus avoids describing the mode of execution altogether, only quickly mentioning that David gave the sons of Saul to the Gibeonites for retribution/punishment (πρὸς τιμωρίαν, *Ant.* vii.296; cf. ἐκόλασαν in vii.297).

Thus one can see that, even in antiquity, there was no clear agreement on the exact death penalty implied in 2 Samuel 21. Nonetheless, at least some of the versions assume some prolonged bodily suspension (Symmachus, *Targum Jonathan*, also probably Aquila); and these very translations apply the same terminology they (or their translational analogs) use in Numbers 25:4.[204] Both the connection with Numbers 25 and the suspension terminology can be witnessed in various rabbinic traditions.

6.1 Targum and the Sons of Saul

Yet, before moving to the rabbinic traditions we should note that, whereas with the suspension terms in Symmachus and Aquila we do not have complete extant texts, in *Targum Jonathan* there is more material for study. The mention of birds who would "rest" on the slain provides a natural connection between this passage and Genesis 40:19 (see above); and this connection is improved in *Targum Jonathan*, which renders יקע by צלב (also found in all

---

[204] This was noted above with Symmachus and Aquila. Of course, the matter is more complex for *Targum Jonathan*, since this particular targum does not include the Pentateuch. However, the widespread use of צלב in all the targumim on Numbers 25:4 would bear out this same likely connection available to the Aramaic reader.

targumim on Genesis), thus bringing the key verbs in both passages into agreement among the various targumic traditions. Thus the various Aramaic traditions would provide potential mental connections not only with Numbers 25:4 but also with Genesis 40:19.

This targumic designation of the form of execution with צלב is, as noted earlier, the common way of indicating human bodily suspension (both in the Pentateuch and in the Former Prophets). Given the lack of other contextual indicators in this passage concerning means of death, the term צלב in the Targum would naturally imply the mode of execution; and it is plausible that crucifixion associations would accrue to such a rendering. Further, the mention of carrion birds,[205] and the prolonged time of suspension, would heighten the possibility that ancient readers/hearers of *Targum Jonathan* could likely have associated these deaths with the executionary suspension forms prevalent in late antiquity.

6.2 Rabbinic Writings and the Sons of Saul

The targumic rendering of these executions with צלב appears to presume an ongoing interpretation of these deaths as involving suspension. In fact, there is record of just such a discussion in the Bavli in *b. Sanh.* 34b–35a (cited above in §3.2) where the Rizpah account, which clearly involved prolonged exposure, is said to prove that those deaths that employ the *hiphil* and *hophal* of יקע must have involved hanging (תלייה). As this Bavli passage also indicates, explicit connections (based on יקע) were drawn between Numbers 25:4 and 2 Samuel 21.

At several other junctures in rabbinic literature the account of David, the Gibeonites, and the sons of Saul receives expansive treatment in many overlapping traditions (for example, *y. Sanh.* vi.9 [23c–d]; *y. Qidd.* iv.1 [65b–c]; *Num. Rab.* viii.4). Among other issues these passages specify the dates of the sons' hanging (16th of Nisan until 17th of Marḥeshvan) – an extended time of seven months.

This creates the most interesting conundrum for the rabbis: how do these verses relate to the command to bury the hung person in Deuteronomy 21:23? One answer is that the rule of law had changed for Saul's sons, since Saul had killed proselytes (this apparently assumes that the Gibeonites, whom Saul had put to death, were proselytes). In fact, it is said that this decision to execute Saul's sons resulted in an increase in proselytes.[206] A related idea is found in *b. Yeb.* 79a, which portrays travelling Gentiles so overwhelmed at the rigourous justice of Israel (since these princes were hung for the sake of mere proselytes) that the gentiles themselves wish to join Israel.

---

[205] Carrion birds are often said to peck at the crucified; e.g., Pliny, *Nat. Hist.* xxxvi.107; Lucian *Prom.* 2, 4, 9; *Sacr.* 6 (of the still living Prometheus).

[206] *y. Qidd.* iv.1 [65b–c]; *Num. Rab.* viii.4; cf. *y. Sanh.* vi.9 [23d].

A second attempt to reconcile this practice with the command to bury (Deut 21:23) comes in the form of the statement that, "Greater is the sanctification of the Name than the profanation of the Name." In this approach Deuteronomy 21:23 refers to the profanation of the divine Name, while 2 Samuel 21 refers to the sanctification of His Name (and thus apparently trumps the requirements of Deuteronomy 21).[207] In the Yerushalmi R. Eliezer b. Jacob[208] contrasts in a somewhat analogous way the strictness of the rules that one shall not blaspheme (with its punishment in Deut 21:22–23) with the rule that one shall not disgrace the name (exemplified in the punishment on Saul's house in 2 Samuel 21).[209]

None of these are particularly convincing legal explanations of how 2 Samuel 21 could so contravene Deuteronomy 21, but they do prove that the issue was an important one for the rabbis. As is examined below (§8.4) similar issues arise in the Esther narratives concerning the death of Haman. In fact, the hanging of the sons of Saul and the suspension of Haman and his sons are compared with one another in some targumic traditions.[210] During the time these rabbis were seeking to justify a biblical episode that they conceived as a prolonged (seven months!) penalty of hanging (during which the bones rotted and birds preyed on the bodies), in those same years the Roman government was visibly crucifying criminals on trees for prolonged periods.

7. Princes are Hung (Lamentations 5:12–13)

Toward the end of Lamentations there appears a communal lament that focuses on the atrocities Israel has endured. Among other afflictions, it mentions the fate of Israel's leaders and children (Lam 5:12–13):

(12) שָׂרִים בְּיָדָם נִתְלוּ פְּנֵי זְקֵנִים לֹא נֶהְדָּרוּ

(13) בַּחוּרִים טְחוֹן נָשָׂאוּ וּנְעָרִים בָּעֵץ כָּשָׁלוּ

(12) Princes were hung by their hand; faces of elders were not honoured.
(13) Young men carried the mill,[211] and young lads staggered over the wood.

---

[207] In *y. Qidd.* iv.1 [65b] (= Schäfer, *Synopsis* 4,1/13) this is attributed to R. Abba bar Zimina (אבא בר זמינא = 4th c. Palestinian Amora); but *y. Sanh.* vi.9 [23d] (= Schäfer, *Synopsis* 6,9/15) reads בא בר זמינא; different still in *Num. Rab.* viii.4. However, in all places the saying is delivered "in the name of R. Hoshayah."

[208] Probably third generation Tannaite, though possibly first generation.

[209] *y. Sanh.* vi.9 [23c] (= 6,9/8 in Schäfer *Synopsis*); note that this is translated under *y. Sanh.* vi.7 in Neusner's English translation.

[210] Note the discussion of *Tg. Esth II* 9:24 below in §8.3. There Esther justifies the prolonged exposure of Haman and his sons on the precedent of Saul's sons.

[211] The meaning of this clause is debated, so compare: Delbert R. Hillers, *Lamentations: A New Translation with Introduction and Commentary*, 2nd ed., AB 7a (New York:

The context of 5:11–14 concentrates on the horrors that women and men faced in the exilic period. After speaking of the rape of the women in 5:11, the two verses above mention in descending social order the fate of the men (a similar order is reiterated in 5:14). The Hebrew perfect verbs are translated above with the English simple past; however, many modern interpreters (going back to Lam 5:1) understand these as current afflictions for the writer.[212]

For present purposes the key issues concern the kinds of sufferings to befall the princes and the young lads. In both cases the kinds of sufferings implied revolve in part around the use of the prepositional prefix בְּ (*beth*). Regarding the princes in verse 12, they are said to be hung, but in what manner? And was this a mode of death? The *beth* ("by") on בְּיָדָם ("by their hand") in verse 12 could either indicate instrument (i.e., the princes are hung from their own hands), or it could designate agency (i.e., the princes are hung by the "hand" of their enemy).[213] The issue then is whose "hand" is involved – the princes' or the enemy's? Of these two options, given that "hand" is singular in Hebrew and also is used of the adversaries in 5:8, it is more likely that the Hebrew implies that the princes are hung at the hand (singular) of their enemy.[214] However, some early versions render the "hand" בְּיָדָם as plural. This is especially true in the Old Greek reading ἄρχοντες ἐν χερσὶν αὐτῶν ἐκρεμάσθησαν ("leaders by their hands were hung"); but is also found in the Peshitta translation ܐܬܬܠܝܘ ܒܐܝܕܝܗܘܢ ܪܘܪܒܢܐ ("princes by their hands were hung").[215] The use of the plural "hands" here likely indicates that at least some early translators understood the princes as being suspended from their own hands. If this form of suspension were thought to be the means of death for the princes, then, to a Jewish reader in Graeco-Roman antiquity, crucifixion (as a form of execution where the victim is suspended by their hands) would have been an obvious mode of death for these princes.

In a similar exegetical/syntactical conundrum, as one seeks to determine the fate of the young lads in the last clause of verse 13, the principle difficulty has to do with the function of the *beth* in בְּעֵץ (translated above as "over the wood"). While most commentators are inclined to envision here the young

---

Doubleday, 1992), 158–59; Johan Renkema, *Lamentations*, trans. Brian Doyle, Historical Commentary on the Old Testament (Leuven: Peeters, 1998), 611–13.

[212] Cf. esp. Renkema, *Lamentations*, 609–10.

[213] The ambiguity is noted, for example, in Iain W. Provan, *Lamentations*, New Century Bible Commentary (Grand Rapids: Eerdmans, 1991), 131; also see William D. Reyburn, *A Handbook on Lamentations*, UBS Handbook Series (New York: United Bible Societies, 1992), 138.

[214] So also Hillers, *Lamentations*, 158.

[215] Peshitta text from Bertil Albrektson, *Studies in the Text and Theology of the Book of Lamentations: With a Critical Edition of the Peshitta Text*, Studia theologica Lundensia 21 (Lund: CWK Gleerup, 1963), 53–54. Cf. Vulgate *principes manu suspensi sunt.*

men as staggering *under* the weight of the wood they are forced to carry,[216] the *beth* with the verb כָּשַׁל would likely convey the sense of *over* the wood.[217] Hillers, therefore, suggests emending בָּעֵץ to בְּעֶצֶב ("from hard work"), but he is without manuscript support.[218] Most interesting for this thesis is that, while the better manuscripts of the Septuagint preserve the rendering "and young men were weakened by wood,"[219] the so-called Lucianic recension manuscripts (as well as the margin of the Syro-Hexapla) understand this as "young men were crucified upon wood."[220] The crucifixion interpretation in the Lucianic manuscripts may conceivably be traced to Christian influence, but similar interpretations are also known from Jewish treatments.

7.1 The Targum and the Lament

(12) רברבנין בידיהון אצטליבו אפי סביא לא סברו[221]

(13) רובין ריחיא נטלו וטליא[222] בצליבת קיסא תקלו

---

[216] Compare Symmachus in the Syro-Hexapla: ܐܘ̈ܠܕ̈ܐ ܬܚܝܬ ܩܝܣܐ (which is re-translated into Greek by Field in his *Origenis Hexaplorum* 2:761: καὶ τοὺς παίδας ὑπὸ ξύλον ἐποίησαν). Apparently Symmachus takes the *beth* on בָּעֵץ as "under" (ܬܚܝܬ); a less likely alternative would be that Symmachus took the *beth* as "by" (thus ὑπὸ ξύλου), but was mistranslated in the Syriac of the Syro-Hexapla as if Symmachus' Greek read ὑπὸ ξύλον.

[217] Cf. Ehrlich, *Randglossen*, 7:53–54. Also cf. Vulgate (noted below).

[218] Hillers, *Lamentations*, 159. No variants are listed in *BHS*, nor in De Rossi's *Variae Lectiones*, iii.246 (or supplement p. 130). More significantly, all the versions clearly read "wood" (see below). 5Q6 (= 5Q*Lamentations*) vi.2 is unfortunately missing the relevant fragment (see *DJD* III, p. 177; and *Planche* xxxviii [note column numberings of V and VI are accidentally reversed in the plates]).

[219] LXX: καὶ νεανίσκοι ἐν ξύλῳ ἠσθένησαν. Compare the Peshiṭta: "and youths stumbled against the trees" (ܘܥ̈ܠܝܡܐ ܒܩܝܣ̈ܐ ܐܬܬܩܠܘ).

[220] Lucianic recension (in Ziegler, Göttingen LXX): ἐπὶ ξύλοις ἐσταυρώθησαν (also note Field, *Origenis Hexapla*, 2:761; and Field's supplement in that volume "Auctarium," p. 55). Possibly cf. Jerome's Vulgate: *et pueri in ligno corruerunt* ("and young men fell on the tree").

[221] The edition used is that of Étan Levine, *The Aramaic Version of Lamentations* (New York: Hermon Press, 1976). For סברו ("they did [not] honour") MS Salonika reads אתהדרו ("were [not] honoured"). Sperber, who relies on a single manuscript tradition, also prints אתהדרו; see Alexander Sperber, *The Bible in Aramaic: Based on Old Manuscripts and Printed Texts*, 4 vols. (Leiden: Brill, 1959–1973), vol. 4.1, p. 149. This is in agreement with the Yemenite tradition; so the edition of Albert van der Heide, *The Yemenite Tradition of the Targum of Lamentations: Critical Text and Analysis of the Variant Readings*, SPB 32 (Leiden: E. J. Brill, 1981), p. 37*. A transcription of Codex Vaticanus Urbanus Hebr. 1 (which agrees with the text above) and a new English translation is available in Christian M. M. Brady, *The Rabbinic Targum of Lamentations: Vindicating God* (Leiden: Brill, 2003), 154, 166.

[222] For רובין ("young men") MS Salonika and Sperber's edition read ורבין ("and youths"); also the Yemenite tradition with variants (Van Der Heide, 38*). For וטליא ("and young boys") MS Salonika and the Yemenite tradition read עולימיא ("youths"), so also Sperber's edition.

12 Princes were crucified by their hands; the faces of the elders they did not honour.
13 Young men carried the millstones, and young boys stumbled against the crucifying of the tree.

The Targum to Lamentations employs the verb צלב in verse 12 and its cognate in verse 13, thus clearly indicating that the princes and young boys were suspended. Such terminology could also permit a crucifixion interpretation of their fates within a culture in which the cross was a common mode of punishment.[223] This crucifixion interpretation is all the more likely in the Targum on 5:12 given that the suspension is by the hands (בידיהון, plural as in the LXX and Peshiṭta). This conjures up the image of the princes' hands being pinned or tied to the צליבא. The verb תקל ("stumbled") in verse 13b can also connote "to fail" (see Jastrow, s.v.), and thus graphically illustrates the final moments on the cross at the collapse of the young boys.[224]

7.2 Rabbinic Writings and the Lament

This text receives treatment in Lamentations Rabbah (v.12):[225]

שרים בידם נתלו פני זקנים לא נהדרו. אפיטרופא הוה עליל לקרתא וצייר על שורי
קרתא ותלי להון, והוו סביא אתיין ומפייסן ליה עליהון, ולא הוה מקבל עליהון, לקיים
מה שנאמר שרים בידם נתלו פני זקנים לא נהדרו :

"Princes were hung by their hand; faces of elders were not honoured." The administrator would come to a town and besiege the walls of the city. And he hung them.[226] And the elders[227] came and [sought to] appease him on their account; but he would not accept [their attempts to appease him] on their account. This validates what is said: "Princes were hung by their hand; faces of elders were not honoured."

The textual evidence varies here, but the traditions all imply that the "administrator" would hang the princes upon entering the town. Intriguingly the word for "administrator" (אפיטרופא = ἐπίτροπος) is also used of Roman administrators (procurators and proconsuls), and thus Jastrow suggests that here a

---

[223] So Levine in the commentary to his *Aramaic Version of Lamentations*, pp. 187–88.

[224] Levine (*Aramaic Version of Lamentations*, p. 189) also takes the Targum on 5:13b as a reference to crucifixion.

[225] The text is from Salomon Buber, *Midrasch Echa Rabbati: Sammlung agadischer Auslegungen der Klagelieder* (Wilna, 1899), 157. For a fifth century date of origin and comments on the complicated issues concerning the text of *Lam. Rab.*, see Günter Stemberger, *Introduction to the Talmud and Midrash*, trans. Markus Bockmuehl, 2nd ed. (Edinburgh: T & T Clark, 1996), 284–86.

[226] The Wilna ed. (60d) reads והוה נסיב טבי דקרתא ותלי להון ("And he would take the best of the city and hang them."). For the first clause Sokoloff suggests: וצאיר כל טבי קרתא ("and held all the prominent people of the city"); see Michael Sokoloff, *A Dictionary of Jewish Palestinian Aramaic of the Byzantine Period*, Dictionaries of Talmud, Midrash and Targum 2 (Ramat-Gan, Israel: Bar Ilan University Press, 1990), p. 461a, s.v. צור.

[227] Wilna ed. בני אנש סבין (literally, "sons of a man of the elders").

Roman proconsul is intended.[228] Indeed, the taking of the city in this passage is strongly reminiscent of the events of the Jewish revolts, especially in the Buber text where the walls are besieged before the leaders are hung.[229] In fact, multiple other passages in *Lamentations Rabbah* likely refer to the Jewish revolts against the Romans.[230] Certainly, if a Roman context is intended by the midrash, then the "hanging" by the אפיטרופא likely refers to crucifixion.

When it comes to the last clause of Lamentations 5:13, *Lamentations Rabbah* only makes one brief remark:

ונערים בעץ כשלו. אמר ר' יהושע בן לוי שלש מאות מצאו[232] חרוזים בטלה אחד[231]

"And young lads staggered over the wood." Rabbi Joshua b. Levi said, "They found three hundred strung up in one hanging."[233]

This eminent Palestinian Amora (first half 3rd c.) is said to have interpreted the "staggering over the wood" of the young lads in Lamentations as a reference to these lads having been strung up. While the Vilna edition has them all hanging from one branch, which would tell against crucifixion (and which also sounds very implausible), the stringing up of the boys is in keeping with the death by suspension in the Targum, and thus may point to an ongoing association in the rabbinic period of death by suspension with Lamentations 5:13b. Further, Yose ben Yose, an author of *piyyuṭim* in the Amoraic period, also evokes Lamentations 5:13b in what may be a covert reference to Jewish suffering under the banner of the Christian cross. It would naturally have been easier for Yose to do this in a poetic context if there was already an ongoing association of crucifixion with this brief text.[234]

---

[228] Jastrow, *Dictionary*, s.v. אפיטרופא; cf. Daniel Sperber, *A Dictionary of Greek and Latin Legal Terms in Rabbinic Literature*, Dictionaries of Talmud, Midrash and Targum 1 (Ramat-Gan: Bar-Ilan University Press, 1984), 56–59 (esp. 58).

[229] Cf. Josephus, *Bell*. v.289, 449–51; vii.202–3.

[230] References to the Jewish revolts are elsewhere known in this midrash, for example, in *Lam. Rab*. i.5; i.16; ii.2; iv.19; also *Petiḥta* 12; i.12; iii.4–6; iii.10–12; iii.22–24; iii.58–60; v.5.

[231] For בטלה אחד the Wilna edition has בשוכה אחת ("in one limb [of a tree]").

[232] Wilna: שלש מאות תינוקות נמצאו ("three hundred boys were found").

[233] The word בטלה is problematic. Context argues against בַּטָלָה ("vanity") or טָלֶה ("lamb"). This translation assumes Jastrow's possibility (not in Sokoloff's *Dictionary of Jewish Palestinian Aramaic*) of טלה meaning "to hang on, to patch, line" (see Jastrow, *Dictionary*, s.v. טלי) – though admittedly Jastrow assumes a strange consonantal shift from *taw* in תלה.

[234] See William Horbury, "Suffering and messianism in Yose ben Yose," in *Suffering and Martyrdom in the New Testament*, ed. William Horbury and Brian McNeil (Cambridge: Cambridge University Press, 1981), 153–54. Less definite is the punishment implied by *Pesiqta Rabbati* xxxiii.13, which considers the youths as "smitten [or punished] by the tree," (ולקו בעץ) and briefly contrasts their fate with the eschatological hope that they will have long life (like that of a tree, cf. Isa 65:22).

In any case, there are some hints in *Lamentations Rabbah* that Lamentations 5:12–13 could be understood in light of Roman executionary practices against Jewish people. When combined with the fairly overt suspension/crucifixion language of the targumic tradition, it becomes possible to consider whether the crucifixion connotations in some of the Greek and Syriac traditions (especially overt in the Lucianic recension) may have some rabbinic corollaries. However, since we possess few early Jewish expositions of this biblical text, it is difficult to fully assess the prior antiquity of these traditions.

8. The Hanging of Mordecai and Haman (Esther)

וּבְבֹאָהּ לִפְנֵי הַמֶּלֶךְ אָמַר עִם־הַסֵּפֶר יָשׁוּב מַחֲשַׁבְתּוֹ הָרָעָה אֲשֶׁר־חָשַׁב עַל־הַיְּהוּדִים עַל־
רֹאשׁוֹ וְתָלוּ אֹתוֹ וְאֶת־בָּנָיו עַל־הָעֵץ

But, when she [Esther] came before the king, he said with the written decree: "His [Haman's] evil plan which he devised against the Jews will return on his own head." And they hung him and his sons on the tree.

This citation from Esther 9:25 comes in the middle of the book's explanation for the origins of the festival of Purim. Its clear theme concerns the divine reversal of fortune on the enemies of the Jewish nation (especially on the person of Haman). Haman had wished to "hang Mordecai" (so Esth 5:14; 6:4; 7:9) and had prepared a special "tree" (usually translated as a "gallows") fifty cubits high for that purpose. However, Haman himself is hung on the tree (7:9–10; 8:7; 9:25) and his sons face a similar fate (9:13–14, 25). All of these verses employ essentially the same suspension language evidenced in the citation above (i.e., וְתָלוּ אֹתוֹ עַל־הָעֵץ).[235] This penalty is also mentioned in Esther 2:23 where the eunuchs Bigthan and Teresh, who plotted to kill the king, are "hung on a tree" – an episode which provides not merely a later crucial testimonial for Mordecai (who discovered their plot), but also a literary premonition of the death of Haman, who is thus numbered among the king's worse enemies.[236] Haman had desired the wholesale slaughter of the Jewish people (Esth 3:6–15); and the text above (Esth 9:25) shows that the hanging of Haman was viewed, not merely as a reversal of the penalty he wished to inflict on Mordecai, but also as a just recompense for Haman's plotting against the Jewish people.

The precise mode of death that Haman suffers in this narrative is an issue much debated by the commentators. It should be noted that Haman's sons are first slain (הרג, Esth 9:7–10), and thus their hanging is portrayed as *post*

---

[235] None of the textual variants are of great concern.
[236] This "literary premonition" is also noted in *Esth. Rab.* vii.3.

mortem (Esth 9:13–14). However, when it comes to the planned demise of Mordecai and the execution of Haman, most agree that "hanging" here is the actual method of execution, rather than a mere *post mortem* suspension.[237] Some suggest that it was a form of impalement, others that it was a hanging from the neck, and others that it was crucifixion.[238] It is possible that crucifixion dates back to this early period, but impalement is known to have been a longstanding penalty in the ANE and so is slightly to be preferred.[239] The language of the text however is flexible enough to permit any of these possibilities. In contrast, ancient Jewish translations and interpretations often sought to specify more exactly the mode of death.

8.1 The Greek Traditions and Haman

εἶπεν δὲ Βουγαθαν εἰς τῶν εὐνούχων πρὸς τὸν βασιλέα ἰδοὺ καὶ ξύλον ἡτοίμασεν Αμαν Μαρδοχαίῳ τῷ λαλήσαντι περὶ τοῦ βασιλέως καὶ ὤρθωται ἐν τοῖς Αμαν ξύλον πηχῶν πεντήκοντα εἶπεν δὲ ὁ βασιλεύς σταυρωθήτω ἐπ᾽ αὐτου. (Esth 7:9 LXX)

And Bougathan, one of the eunuchs, said to the king, "Behold, Haman also prepared a tree for Mordecai, who spoke concerning the king; and a tree fifty cubits high was raised up[240] in Haman's property." And the king said, "Let him be crucified on it."

As early as the Greek versions of Esther, the term σταυρόω is employed to describe the penalty imposed on Haman. This term is evident in the quotation above from the LXX (i.e., the B-text) of Esther 7:9 (σταυρωθήτω ἐπ᾽ αὐτου – "let him be crucified upon it").[241] Moreover, σταυρόω is found in *both* the A and B texts of the "addition" E18 (=16:18 =Rahlfs 8:12^r) – "...διὰ τὸ

---

[237] E.g., Frederic W. Bush, *Ruth, Esther*, WBC 9 (Dallas: Word, 1996), 373.

[238] Jerome's Vulgate tends to apply crucifixion language throughout these texts (see below in chapter seven).

[239] See ANE evidence above in the opening section of this chapter. A different opinion in Carey A. Moore, *Esther*, AB 7b (Garden City, New York: Doubleday, 1971), 31; Gillis Gerleman, *Esther*, BKAT 21 (Neukirchen-Vluyn: Neukirchener Verlag, 1973), 86.

[240] The sense of the aorist middle ὤρθωται is likely passive here, though a passive form for ὀρθόω did exist in Greek.

[241] While the B-text (LXX) reads εἶπεν δὲ ὁ βασιλεύς Σταυρωθήτω ἐπ᾽ αὐτοῦ ("And the king said, 'Let him be crucified on it'"), the corresponding A-text (i.e., L 7:13 in Hanhart; 8:13 in Clines) renders this same basic idea as καὶ εἶπεν ὁ βασιλεύς Κρεμασθήτω ἐπ᾽ αὐτῷ ("And the king said, 'Let him be hung on it'"). Clearly, apart from the word-shift in the verb, these two phrases are quite similar, although in general the A-text (the so-called Lucianic recension, or L in Hanhart's edition) differs significantly in this section (L 7:12–21) from the B-text. For the texts see Robert Hanhart, ed., *Esther*, Septuaginta VIII,3 (Göttingen: Vandenhoeck & Ruprecht, 1966). Also note the A-text appears (without apparatus) along with a translation in David J. A. Clines, *The Esther Scroll: The Story of the Story*, JSOTSup 30 (Sheffield: JSOT Press, 1984), 238–39. Intriguingly, the Old Latin (text in Sabatier, 2:815) does not follow the LXX (B-text) here in employing clear crucifixion terminology (see Esth 7:9: *suspendatur super illud Aman, & uxor eius, & decem filii eius* – note that the OL also brings the hanging of the sons forward to this verse in the narrative).

αὐτὸν τὸν ταῦτα ἐξεργασάμενον πρὸς ταῖς Σούσων πύλαις ἐσταυρῶσθαι σὺν τῇ πανοικίᾳ…" ("…because the man himself [=Haman] who
caused these things was crucified at the gates of Susa along with his whole
household").[242]

In Esther 7:9 the B-text likely translates a Hebrew text-form similar to the
Masoretic תְּלֻהוּ עָלָיו with the Greek Σταυρωθήτω ἐπ᾽ αὐτοῦ.[243] As can be
seen even in the following verse (7:10), generally the translator of the B-text
(LXX) is content to render the Hebrew word for "hang" (תלה) with a virtually equivalent Greek word (κρεμάζω). Hence in Esther 7:10 the phrase
וַיִּתְלוּ אֶת־הָמָן עַל־הָעֵץ (lit. "and they hung Haman on the tree") is translated
fairly literally with καὶ ἐκρεμάσθη Αμαν ἐπὶ τοῦ ξύλου ("and Haman was
hung on the tree").[244] Yet, Esther 7:9 shows that it was also possible for the
Greek translator of the B-text to encapsulate the whole Hebrew concept of a
person "hung on a tree" by employing the verb σταυρόω ("crucify").[245] Such
an interpretation also must have influenced the narrative expansion in E18.

---

[242] The B-text of E18 is cited above. As is often the case in the Greek Additions to Esther,
the A-text (numbered L 7:28 in Hanhart; 8:28 in Clines) essentially agrees with the B-text
(though with the noticeable omission of σὺν τῇ πανοικίᾳ). Note that, whereas in Esther 7:9–
10 the "tree" is said to be on Haman's property, here in the Additions to Esther the place of
execution is at the gates of the city – a public venue and a common locale for ancient
executionary suspensions.

[243] The textual relationship of the B-text (= LXX) to the other extant Hebrew and Greek
texts is a matter of some discussion, but most recent authors hold that the B-text, apart from
the Additions, represents a somewhat free rendering of some Hebrew text very similar to the
Masoretic Text form. See the Esther commentaries by Gerleman (p. 39), Moore (p. lxi), and
Bush (p. 278). And especially refer to Linda Day, *Three Faces of a Queen: Characterization
in the Books of Esther*, JSOTSup 186 (Sheffield: Sheffield Academic Press, 1995), 15–18;
and Clines, *Esther Scroll*, 69 (note his chart on p. 140).

[244] Elsewhere in the LXX of Esther κρεμάννυμι + ἐπὶ τοῦ ξύλου generally renders
תלה + עַל־הָעֵץ; e.g., 5:14 (cf. the A-text of L 5:23); 6:4; 8:7. Sometimes the Greek translator
apparently omitted rendering עַל־עֵץ, presumably implying it through the mere use of
κρεμάννυμι; see 2:23; 9:13 (though some texts in 9:13 supply ἐπὶ τοῦ ξύλου, as does the
Hexaplaric recension); and 9:25 (also cf. the A-text of L 6:7 and L 7:12 in Hanhart). Shifts in
the person and voice of the verb are fairly common from the Hebrew to the Greek.

Here it is worth reemphasizing that κρεμάζω ἐπὶ τοῦ ξύλου appears elsewhere in the Old
Greek OT (see Gen 40:19; Deut 21:22–23 (2x); Josh 8:29; Josh 10:26; 1 Esdras 6:31
[EVV 32]). In each of these LXX instances (aside from 1 Esdras 6:31 and the second occurrence in Deut 21:23) the Greek phrase parallels the MT עַל־הָעֵץ [אֹתוֹ] תָּלָה (an expression
that only occurs in these verses in the MT and in the Esther texts noted above). Thus there
had been a long history of literalistic Greek translations of these Hebrew suspension texts,
making all the more significant the translator's choice to use σταυρόω in Esther 7:9.

[245] Although the Hebrew phrase in Esther 7:9 is technically "hang him on it," it is reasonable to assume that the translator naturally understood the עָלָיו ("on it") in תְּלֻהוּ עָלָיו
("hang him on it") to refer back to הִנֵּה־הָעֵץ ("behold the tree") previously in the verse (cf.
5:14 in the B-text and the MT). Thus the translator interpreted the concept of a person "hung
on a tree" with σταυρόω.

Given that there is no other indication in Esther 7:9 (Greek B-text) or E18 as to how the execution of Haman was performed, then it is likely that σταυρόω would be the implied means of death. While some have contended that the "tree" which Haman erects is too high (fifty cubits!) for use in crucifixion,[246] in actuality tall crosses were known in the Roman period.[247] Certainly, during the late Hellenistic and the Roman eras, readers of these Greek texts of Esther would naturally have assumed this σταυρόω execution terminology to refer to executionary forms common in their own day (particularly crucifixion).

Further, the A-text ("Lucianic" recension), at variance with the MT, adds crucifixion imagery at 7:14 (cf. MT 6:11). In that verse, when Haman is called upon to honour Mordecai with robe and horse, he is required to do such reverence to Mordecai "just like in that day he [= Haman] had decided to crucify him" (καθότι ἐκείνῃ τῇ ἡμέρᾳ ἐκεκρίκει ἀνασκολοπίσαι αὐτόν).

8.2 Josephus and Haman

Josephus, like the Greek recensions, also freely employs crucifixion terminology in his paraphrase of the Esther narratives. The relationship of Josephus' account to the extant Greek versions is complex, though most agree that he had something akin to one or both of our Greek versions in front of him.[248] In fact, at neither of the two locations just discussed (Esther 7:9 [LXX]; or E18 [= L 7:28]) does Josephus' wording replicate precisely that of either Greek recension (*Ant.* xi.267, 280), though perhaps his wording is closest in his E18 parallel in *Antiquities* xi.280.[249] Nevertheless, like the Greek recensions of

---

[246] So Bush, *Esther*, 414. Josephus states 60 cubits (*Ant.* xi.246).

[247] E.g., Suetonius, *Galba*, ix.1 (in LCL); see further Hengel, *Crucifixion*, 40–41 (and note 5).

[248] Moore argues that the Josephus "paraphrase" of the Greek version of Esther (including, as Josephus does, additions B, C, D and E) provides a *terminus ad quem* for the initial Greek translation of Esther; see Carey A. Moore, ed., *Studies in the Book of Esther*, LBS (New York: Ktav, 1982), p. lxiii. Dorothy is more specific in seeing the primary Greek text influencing Josephus as the Lucianic recension (A-text), though he does not deny that Josephus may have had access to other recensions; see Charles V. Dorothy, *The Books of Esther: Structure, Genre and Textual Integrity*, JSOTSup 187 (Sheffield: Sheffield Academic Press, 1997), 335. Feldman claims that Josephus clearly used a Greek text, but allows that he may also have had access to an Aramaic targum (cf. *Ant.* xi.273–83 and *Tg. Esth II* 8:12); see Louis H. Feldman, "A Selective Critical Bibliography of Josephus," in *Josephus, the Bible, and History*, ed. Louis H. Feldman and Gohei Hata (Leiden: E. J. Brill, 1989), pp. 354–55, 366; and Louis H. Feldman, *Studies in Josephus' Rewritten Bible*, JSJSup 58 (Leiden: Brill, 1998), 526n.

[249] The sense of the passage is largely paralleled between Josephus and the Greek texts of Esther, though specific verbal parallels are most apparent in the following phrases in L 7:28 (= B-text E17–18): (1) καλῶς οὖν ποιήσατε [B-text Sinaiticus ποιήσετε] μὴ προσέχοντες [B-text προσχρησάμενοι], where Josephus himself reads οἷς ποιήσετε καλῶς μὴ προσ-

these two verses, Josephus does indeed employ crucifixion terminology at both these locations in his Esther account.[250] Moreover, Josephus inserts σταυρός when he adds a narrative detail not paralleled in the Hebrew or in the Greek versions (*Ant.* xi.261).[251] And most interesting of all, Josephus also utilizes crucifixion terminology in his Esther narrative in at least two places where the ancient Greek versions do not (*Ant.* xi.208, 246; cf. Esther 2:23; 5:14).[252]

Thus, as above in the case of the baker in Genesis 40–41, Josephus renders "hanging someone on a tree" using ἀνασταυρόω ("crucify") and similar terminology.[253] Again, as noted above, one cannot be absolutely certain that Josephus has a slow lingering death on a *crux* in mind by using this terminology. But we have moved into a word group with a semantic field that certainly would allow Josephus' contemporaries a "crucifixion" interpretation of Haman's death. And this is terminology that Josephus himself frequently employs in contexts that are clear cases of crucifixion.[254] Further, this inclination to use words that can designate crucifixion is continued in other Jewish paraphrases of the Esther narratives, especially in the two Targums to Esther that magnify this trend.

8.3 Targumim and Haman

The two main targumim to Esther (*Rishon* and *Sheni*) occasionally employ the verbs זקף and תלי in speaking of the execution of Haman and the suspension of his sons.[255] This shows that the meturgeman was not constrained to use the

---

έχοντες; and (2) πρὸς ταῖς Σούσων πύλαις ἐσταυρῶσθαι, where Josephus reads πρὸ τῶν πυλῶν τῶν ἐν Σούσοις ἀνεσταύρωσα μετὰ τῆς γενεᾶς. Interestingly, Josephus' μετὰ τῆς γενεᾶς evidences a conceptual parallel only in the B-text (σὺν τῇ πανοικίᾳ).

[250] "ὁ δὲ βασιλεὺς ἀκούσας οὐκ ἄλλῃ τιμωρίᾳ περιβάλλειν ἔκρινε τὸν Ἀμάνην ἢ τῇ κατὰ Μαρδοχαίου νενοημένῃ, καὶ κελεύει παραχρῆμα αὐτὸν ἐξ ἐκείνου τοῦ σταυροῦ κρεμασθέντα ἀποθανεῖν." (*Ant.* xi.267). "...καὶ τὸν ταῦτα κατ᾽ αὐτῶν μηχανησάμενον πρὸ τῶν πυλῶν τῶν ἐν Σούσοις ἀνεσταύρωσα μετὰ τῆς γενεᾶς..."(*Ant.* xi.280).

[251] Σαβουχάδας δὲ τῶν εὐνούχων εἷς ἰδὼν τὸν σταυρὸν ἐν τῇ Ἀμάνου οἰκίᾳ πεπηγότα... (*Ant.* xi.261).

[252] Esther 5:14 = L 5:23–24. Esther 2:23 is not paralleled in the A-text. In rendering these verses, while Josephus uses the aorist of ἀνασταυρόω, the Greek versions here both employ the aorist of κρεμάννυμι, which is more in literal keeping with the וַיִּתָּלוּ... עַל־עֵץ of the MT.

[253] It may also be of interest here to remember that Josephus, following linguistic usage evident elsewhere in Greek, can also speak of someone as "hung" (κρεμάννυμι) on a σταυρός (*Ant.* xi.267; *Bell.* vii.202).

[254] See the many instances from Josephus reported above in chapter 2, §2.

[255] Grossfeld has suggested that *Targum Sheni* was composed at least by the seventh century, and possibly as early as the fourth century; and he contends that *Targum Rishon* is from some time between 500–700 CE. See Grossfeld's fullest discussion in Bernard Grossfeld, *The Two Targums of Esther: Translated, with Apparatus and Notes*, The Aramaic Bible 18 (Edinburgh: T & T Clark, 1991), 19–21, 23–24. See also his general summary in Bernard

technical executionary suspension terminology from צלב. So the Hebrew statement יִתְלוּ עַל־הָעֵץ ("let them hang [the ten sons of Haman] on the tree")[256] from Esther 9:13 is rendered in *Targum Rishon* (*Tg. Esth I* 9:13) with יזדקפון על קיסא ("let them be lifted up on the tree"), although the corresponding text in *Targum Sheni* (*Tg. Esth. II* 9:13) does refer more specifically to the executionary device in its יתלין על צליבא ("let them hang [the sons] on the cross").

However, both these targumim most often render the Hebrew "hanging" verses with צלב and its cognates. This is true in *Targum Rishon* on 2:23; 5:14; 6:4; 7:9, 10; 8:7; 9:14, 25. And it is likewise the case in *Targum Sheni* on 2:23; 5:14; 7:9, 10; 8:7; 9:14, 24, 25. Additional sections, which expand the targumim beyond the Hebrew text, also employ this terminology.[257]

In some cases, the targumim actually expand on the implication that Haman's death was actually caused by his suspension. An interesting example is the extensive addition in *Tg. Esth II* 5:14 where no mode of execution is deemed by Haman's wife possible for Mordecai save hanging/crucifixion (since biblical history records that Jewish figures have escaped from all other means of execution) – the clear assumption is that צלב is a mode of execution.[258] Another expansive passage of note is in *Tg. Esth II* 7:10, where Mordecai is himself commissioned by the king to carry out Haman's execution, and Haman begs for a more respectable death than by the צליבא.[259] Thus, while the Hebrew text implies that Haman actually dies by executionary suspension (i.e., by being "hung on the tree"), the targumim in places heighten this impression and provide a technical vocabulary for such a death. This certainly would connect Haman's demise with the sphere of penalties among which crucifixion was the most common in Roman antiquity.

Grossfeld, *The Targum Sheni to the Book of Esther: a critical edition based on MS. Sassoon 282 with critical apparatus* (New York: Sepher-Hermon, 1994), ix–x; and contrast his earlier view in Bernard Grossfeld, *The First Targum to Esther: According to the MS Paris Hebrew 110 of the Bibliotheque Nationale* (New York: Sepher-Hermon Press, 1983), iv–v. The word searches in this section were made much easier by Grossfeld's production of a concordance to *Targum Sheni* in his edition of the same, and through Bernard Grossfeld, *Concordance of the First Targum to the Book of Esther*, SBLAS 5 (Chico, Calif.: Scholars Press, 1984).

[256] A text also known in rabbinic tradition, cf. *b. Meg.* 15b; 16b.

[257] Note twice in "The Deed of Sale of Haman" from 3:2 of MS Paris Heb. 110 (text in Grossfeld, *First Targum*, 14–16, 49–52; idem, *Targum Sheni*, 76–77; translation in idem, *Two Targums*, 141–42). Also this terminology appears in *Targum Rishon* 2:1 (the princes who advised the king to kill Queen Vashti are ordered to die by suspension); and 7:6 (Esther tells the king of Haman's plot). Both targumim on 9:14 expand the biblical episode in order to delineate the distance between each cross of the crucified sons of Haman.

[258] A shorter version of this occurs in *Tg. Esth I* 5:14; also see *Esth. Rab.* ix.2 (mentioned below in §8.4); further rabbinic parallels in Grossfeld, *First Targum*, 152–53.

[259] The passage also contains a debate among the trees of the earth as to which should be used for Haman's crucifixion (contrast *Esth. Rab.* ix.2).

Remarkably, various traditions in the targumim acknowledge that the prolonged hanging of Haman contravenes Deuteronomy 21:23. The explanation
is alternatively found either in contrasting Haman's hanging with that of the
sons of Saul (*Tg. Esth II* 9:24),[260] or in viewing these suspensions as a reversal of the hanging of Saul's bones by the Amalekites in 1 Samuel 31 (as in
some MSS of Targum Rishon to 9:25).[261]

Intriguingly, a brief expansion in *Tg. Esth I* 7:9 adds to the original text of
Esther an almost verbatim Aramaic citation of Ezra 6:11, but here applying it
to Haman's death (עלוי יתמחי וזקיף ביתיה מן אע יתנסח), "a beam shall be
pulled up from his house, and being raised up he shall be smitten on it").[262]
Notably, in context this זקף terminology is used interchangeably with צלב.
Further allusions to Ezra 6:11 in reference to Haman's death are also else-
where apparent in manuscripts of the Esther targumim.[263] For more on
Ezra 6:11 see section nine below.

8.4 Rabbinic Writings and Haman

Though the most interesting rabbinic treatments of Haman's demise are found
in midrashim that are dated later than the period under study, a brief summary
is still in order. Many midrashic texts employ צלב and its cognates in speaking of Haman's planned death for Mordecai, and of Haman's own demise.[264]
At least one of these passages likely implies a death by crucifixion, as is clear
in its mentioning (alongside the צליבא) the ropes and especially the nails
(מסמרים) that Haman planned to utilize (*Esth. Rab.* x.5). In that text Haman

---

[260] Text in Grossfeld, *Targum Sheni*, 72–73; translation in idem, *Two Targums*, 192.
Since Saul's sons were publicly displayed (for months) merely because their father killed the
Gibeonite *proselytes*, how much more so should Haman be suspended beyond a single day. In
this *Qal wa-ḥomer* argument, the logic apparently hinges on the fact that Haman sought to
slaughter *Israel* itself, not mere proselytes; however, note that in *y. Sanh.* vi.9 [23d] there is a
contrast involving the purity of motive in becoming a proselyte.

[261] Text and translation in Grossfeld, *First Targum*, p. 196. The Amalekites are taken as
forerunners of Haman's race.

[262] See Grossfeld, *First Targum*, 29, 170–171; also in idem, *Two Targums*, 78. Cf. *PRE*
50.

[263] Note the expansive addition ("Deed of Sale of Haman") in the 15thc. MS Paris
Heb. 110 in 3:2 of both targumim (see Grossfeld, *First Targum*, 15; idem, *Targum Sheni*, 80;
cf. translation in apparatus of idem, *Two Targums*, 141). Also note the Cairo Geniza fragment
on Esther 5:14 in Cambridge University Library T-S B 11.52 folio 1v, lines 11–12; in Rimon
Kasher and Michael L. Klein, "New Fragments of Targum to Esther from the Cairo Geniza,"
HUCA 61 (1990): 93; text also in Grossfeld, *Targum Sheni*, 80. This Geniza fragment almost
certainly refers to crucifixion, as the mention of "nails" makes clear (1v, lines 17–18). Also
note לזקיפא in *Tg. Esth II* 2:7.

[264] E.g., *Gen. Rab.* xxx.8; *Exod. Rab.* xx.10; *Lev. Rab.* xxviii.6; *Esth. Rab.* Proem 1; ii.14;
iii.15; vii.3, 10, 11; ix.2; x.5, 15; *Pes. Rab.* xix.2. Such terminology is also known in the later
Esther midrashim (e.g., *Aggadat Esther*).

bemoans to Mordecai: "Stand and dress. Last night I was working to prepare for him [*sic*] the cross [צליבא], but the Holy One was preparing for him the crown. I was preparing for you ropes and nails [חבלים ומסמרים], but the Holy One was preparing for you the clothing of kings. I, when [I was just about to be] asking from the king [for permission] to crucify you on the cross [למיצליב יתך על צליבא], he rather said to me to give you a ride you on the horse. Stand and dress." [265]

As can also be seen in that passage, a typical theme in rabbinic traditions concerns that of God's sovereign reversal: those about to be hung (Mordecai), hang their opponents (i.e., Haman); thus see *Exod. Rab.* xx.10; also *Gen. Rab.* xxx.8; *Esth. Rab.* x.15; and *Pes. Rab.* xix.2. In *Leviticus Rabbah* Mordecai even appears as the archetypical rabbi teaching his committed disciples, who stand by him although he faces crucifixion (*Lev. Rab.* xxviii.6).

As in the Targumim on Esther 5:14, one reads in *Esth. Rab.* ix.2 that Haman's wife counsels sending Mordecai to the cross, "for we have not found one from his people who escaped from it." Travers Herford has suggested that this is a covert polemical reference to Jesus' execution,[266] but the narrative makes sense quite apart from any veiled reference to Jesus (and this is all the more true in the targumim in their additions to 5:14). Nonetheless, there are moments in the rabbinic and targumic treatments of Haman's death that it appears some connection to Jesus' crucifixion might be implied.[267]

8.5 Summary

Executionary bodily suspension recurs throughout the book of Esther – first in the execution of the king's eunuchs, then in the planned death of Mordecai, and finally in the execution of Haman and his sons. With regard to Haman's sons, the penalty is likely post-mortem, but elsewhere suspension appears to be the means of death.

Later, especially during Hellenistic and Roman hegemony, such a death was naturally associated with executionary forms contemporary to the readers (almost certainly including crucifixion). The earliest indications of this appear

---

[265] My translation of *Esth. Rab.* x.5 incorporates "cross" and "crucify" given the use of both ropes and nails. One might conceivably argue that the "nails" were used to build the "gallows" (as some translate צליבא) on which Mordecai was to be hung from the neck with the "rope." However, note in context three matters: (1) more than one rope is mentioned here (rather than only one, which is all that would be required to hang Mordecai from the neck); (2) both ropes and nails are paralleled syntactically in the text, likely implying parallel usage; and (3) Haman's original plan in the three-stage narrative progresses from a constructed צליבא to the use of ropes and nails to the suspension of Mordecai (it seems to me in this progression that the ropes and nails are both prepared in order to affix Mordecai to the צליבא).

[266] See Herford, *Christianity in Talmud*, 87–88.

[267] See below in chapter seven, §4.

in the Greek versions of Esther. And, by the first century, Josephus frequently refers to the deaths with technical suspension terminology – indeed, the same terminology he utilizes when speaking of crucifixions under the Romans. It would certainly have been difficult for a contemporary of Josephus to read his *Antiquities* without perceiving Haman's death to be equivalent to the crucifixions common in the first-century Roman world.

Similarly the targumim and rabbinic references frequently employ technical suspension vocabulary, with some targumic traditions portraying this as the means of death. And in one rabbinic tradition there is even reference to the ropes and nails of the cross. Some traditions in the targumim struggle to explain how the prolonged suspension of Haman relates to the command to bury in Deuteronomy 21:23. Also, the targumim connect Haman's execution in Esther with the king's decree in Ezra 6:11.

9. A King's Decree (Ezra 6:11)

וּמִנִּי שִׂים טְעֵם דִּי כָל־אֱנָשׁ דִּי יְהַשְׁנֵא פִּתְגָמָא דְנָה יִתְנְסַח אָע מִן־בַּיְתֵהּ וּזְקִיף יִתְמְחֵא עֲלֹהִי וּבַיְתֵהּ נְוָלוּ יִתְעֲבֵד עַל־דְּנָה

"And a decree was issued by me that for every man who alters this command, a beam shall be pulled up from his house, and being raised up he shall be smitten on it, and his house will be made as a dunghill on account of this."

The decree here concerns the king's command that his governors permit, and even assist, the rebuilding of the Temple of Jerusalem. The central difficulty in understanding the kind of penalty envisioned here comes in interpreting (וּזְקִיף יִתְמְחֵא עֲלֹהִי). The participle זְקִיף likely indicates suspension of the person,[268] while the *ithpeʿel* of מחא normally would imply "[let him] be smitten."[269] The problem concerns how these two verbal forms work together, and thus what kind of penalty they demand. One possibility is that the person is raised up and then "impaled" (i.e., smitten) on the beam (אָע).[270] Another option is that the person is raised upon the pole and then flogged.[271] Finally, some scholars actually have suggested that this phraseology might imply

---

[268] So BDB 1091b glosses this verb as "raise, lift up"; but Koehler and Baumgartner suggest "gepfählt" (note that later זקף can also imply "crucify" in rabbinic Aramaic; see chapter 1, §2.3.2).

[269] So BDB 1099b, which glosses the verb as "let him be smitten (nailed)"; K-B glosses as "an den Pfahl geschlagen werden."

[270] E.g., BDB 1091b. Also F. Charles Fensham, *The Books of Ezra and Nehemiah*, NICOT (Grand Rapids: Eerdmans, 1982), 90–91. Commentators often appeal to ANE texts and artifacts that imply impalement as a typical penalty (esp. *ANEP* 362, 368, 373); see further above in section one of this chapter.

[271] Cf. H. G. M. Williamson, *Ezra, Nehemiah*, WBC 16 (Waco: Word Books, 1985), 69, 72, 83.

crucifixion.[272] In my opinion, the exact methodology intended by the Hebrew here is frankly difficult to determine, and the ANE pictorial analogs would suggest some form of implalement. However, the Jewish traditions associated with this text are fascinating.

The corresponding text in the Greek of 1 Esdras 6:31 [EVV 32] indicates that the punishment for disobeying Darius' law involves being "hung" on a beam from the lawbreaker's own house (ληµφθῆναι ξύλον ἐκ τῶν ἰδίων αὐτοῦ καὶ ἐπὶ τούτου κρεµασθῆναι).[273] Probably, the author of 1 Esdras understood the text as either impalement or crucifixion (hence ξύλον... κρεµασθῆναι without reference to smiting). The Old Greek of Ezra in 2 Esdras 6:11 (καθαιρεθήσεται ξύλον ἐκ τῆς οἰκίας αὐτοῦ καὶ ὠρθωµένος παγήσεται ἐπ᾽ αὐτοῦ) renders the MT more literally; it implies that, having been raised, the person (depending upon the Greek manuscript) is either "fixed on the beam" (if the verb is πήγνυµι) or "smitten/beaten on it" (if the verb is πλήσσω).[274]

9.1 Josephus and the Darius/Cyrus Decree

In contrast to Ezra 6:1–12 (cf. 1 Esdras 6:22–33 [EVV 23–34]), Josephus provides two accounts of the decree of "Cyrus" (one a first person letter from Cyrus, *Ant.* xi.12–18; and one which is read to Darius from the ὑπόµνηµα Κύρου, xi.99–103). In both locations Josephus understands the command in Ezra 6:6–12 to come from Cyrus, while in Ezra and 1 Esdras it originates with the edict of Darius (cf. Ezra 6:12; 1 Esdras 6:33).

Significantly, Josephus' two versions both employ ἀνασταυρόω to depict Cyrus' decree.[275] This is comparable to 1 Esdras in understanding the essential penalty as bodily suspension. But by specifying "crucifixion," it maintains also the intensity of fixing/smiting known in 2 Esdras and in the Hebrew text.

9.2 Rabbinic Writings and the King's Decree

As was briefly noted in §8.3 above, the death sentence language of this royal decree is frequently related to the execution of Haman in rabbinic Esther

---

[272] Here possibly Myers (referring to Herodotus *Hist.* iii.159), though he translates the text "let him be impaled on it"; see Jacob M. Myers, *Ezra, Nehemiah*, AB 14 (New York: Doubleday, 1965), 48, 52.

[273] One fifteenth-century manuscript reads κρεµάσθη. For text, see Robert Hanhart, ed., *Esdrae liber I*, Septuaginta 8,1 (Göttingen: Vandenhoeck & Ruprecht, 1974).

[274] The correctors to Vaticanus read πληγήσεται (hence also the text of the Cambridge edition), while the text itself of Vaticanus has πληγῆς ἔσται (minuscule 55 reads πληγή ἔσται). Hanhart (in the Göttingen LXX) follows Alexandrinus, et al. in reading παγήσεται.

[275] τοὺς δὲ παρακούσαντας τούτων καὶ ἀκυρώσαντας ἀνασταυρωθῆναι βούλοµαι (*Ant.* xi.17); and τοὺς δὲ παραβάντας τι τῶν ἐπεσταλµένων συλληφθέντας ἐκέλευσεν ἀνασταυρωθῆναι (xi.103). Both locations render the single narrative represented in Ezra 6:11 [= 2 Esdras 6:11] and in 1 Esdras 6:31 [EVV 32].

literature. This is true in the Esther Targumim,[276] occasionally even at the expense of narrative flow.[277] And further examples appear in medieval midrashic works.[278] It is a reasonable postulate that the uniting of the Ezra text with the Esther literature is due both to the common suspension motif (זקף in Ezra and תלה in Esther), and also to how both the king's decree and the Esther narrative could be viewed as a gentile governmental vindication of God's people Israel against their post-exilic opponents.

10. Expansions of Other Biblical Passages

The biblical texts covered so far in this chapter have mostly had some basis (either explicit or reasonably inferred) for asserting in the Hebrew text that they refer to human bodily suspension. Outside of the traditions associated with these passages, there are some sporadic Jewish traditions that also connect crucifixion with other biblical episodes.

For example, one might examine a brief expansive addition to 1 Samuel 5 in Pseudo-Philo's *Liber Antiquitatum Biblicarum* (55:3). Here the Philistines have captured the Ark of the Covenant, and placed it in the temple to Dagon. The next day Dagon's image is found lying on its face. That morning the Philistines crucify (*crucifigentes*) the priests of Dagon. Along with several other details in this narrative,[279] the mention of the crucifixion of the priests does not appear to be based on the Hebrew text, or on its expansion in the Old Greek. Probably we should not make too much of this single association of crucifixion with this story in Samuel. However, it does show this author's tendency to actualize this text by expanding it to include penalties known later, and it also indicates a willingness in this author to think of Israel's (and God's) enemies meeting a just (if gruesome) end on the cross at the hands of their own countrymen.[280]

---

[276] This is explicitly done via citation in the Esther Targum fragments from the Cairo Geniza on Esther 5:14 (Cambridge Univ. Library MS T-S B 11.52 [= B 12.21] folio 1v, lines 11–12) – see Kasher and Klein, "New Fragments," 93. Cf. this with the less overt quotation/reference in *Tg. Esth I* 7:9 (cited above in §8.3). Also see the extensive addition to *Tg. Esth I & II* at 3:2 in MS Paris Heb. 110 (see bibliography in §8.3 above).

[277] So in *Tg. Esth I* 7:9–10 the inserted Ezra material calls for Haman to be executed on a beam taken from his own house; but this stands alongside the original Esther material where Haman is executed on the gallows, which he had already built for Mordecai.

[278] Cf. esp. *PRE*, chpt. 50; for other midrashim see Grossfeld, *First Targum to Esther*, 170–71.

[279] For example, the *LAB* adds the mention of the hands and feet of Dagon lying before the Ark to the first morning after the Ark was in the temple of Dagon (this likely incorporates material otherwise associated with the second day in the Hebrew and Greek Bible).

[280] It is also interesting to contrast this application of crucifixion in Pseudo-Philo with the author's tendency otherwise to avoid using crucifixion language.

It also should be noted that earlier (in §4.4 concerning *De Posteritate Caini* 26) we observed how Philo associated the hanging of Deuteronomy 28:66 with Deut 21:22–23.[281] Though Deut 28:66 does speak of "hanging" (תָּלְאִים), it does so in a fairly metaphorical way: "...and your life will be hanging before you, and you shall fear by night and by day, and you will not trust in your life".[282] Philo picks up on that metaphor of fear, but also connects the text of Deut 28:66 with Deut 21 via the use of "hanging." Of course, in this particular section of *De Posteritate Caini* Philo does not explicitly connect these two Deuteronomic texts with crucifixion, though he does link crucifixion to Deut 21:22–23 elsewhere.[283]

More substantially, a short rabbinic saying connects Deuteronomy 28:66 to crucifixion in Proem 1 to Esther Rabbah. This was already noted in chapter two (§3.7), but it is worth re-quoting:

ד"א והיו חייך תלואים לך מנגד זה שהוא נתון בדיוטי של קיסרין ופחדת לילה ויומם
זה שהוא יוצא לידון ולא תאמין בחייך זה שהוא יוצא להצלב

"Another explanation is this: 'Your life will hang in doubt before you' – this applies to one who is placed in the prison of Caesarea. 'And you will fear night and day' – this applies to one who is brought forth for trial. 'And you will have no assurance of your life' – this applies to one who is brought out to be crucified."

In chapter two it was remarked that this likely tapped into rabbinic memories of the Roman administrative center in Caesarea, including its prison and the judgments that were rendered there (involving crucifixion). Here we should observe that this (fairly late) rabbinic text exposits Deuteronomy 28:66 clause-by-clause, and that it applies the sense of "fear" and "hanging" in that biblical passage to the expectation of a death-penalty being exacted on the cross.

Lastly, it will be observed later in chapter 5 that the Pharaoh of the Exodus, as one of the great enemies of Israel, is at times compared with a crucified brigand.[284] In these texts, Pharaoh is said to have boasted that he will destroy Israel (and/or Moses) like a brigand boasts that he will kill the king's son. Implicitly the brigand receives his own just reward for his

---

[281] The passage in *De Posteritate Caini* 26 reads: "(25)...And, wherefore, it is for him the Law-giver said, 'all his life hangs,' [Deut 28:66] since it does not have an unshaken foundation, but, from being drawn in a contrary direction and dragged in a different way, it is always born along by circumstances. (26) On account of which in different words He says, 'the one who hangs on a tree has been cursed by God' [Deut 21:23, cf. LXX]."

[282] וְהָיוּ חַיֶּיךָ תְּלֻאִים לְךָ מִנֶּגֶד וּפָחַדְתָּ לַיְלָה וְיוֹמָם וְלֹא תַאֲמִין בְּחַיֶּיךָ: The Septuagint renders this fairly literally, only incorporating the idea of "before your eyes" (ἀπέναντι τῶν ὀφθαλμῶν σου) where the Hebrew reads "before you" (לְךָ מִנֶּגֶד).

[283] For evidence, see above in §4.4.

[284] See below in chapter five (§2) on *Mekilta* (*de-Rabbi Ishmael*) *Shirata* 7 (cf. *Mekilta de-Rabbi Shimon bar Yohai* xxxiii.1); also *Exod. Rab.* ix.4. And compare somewhat more remotely *PRK* xi.2.

actions/boasts (i.e., he himself is crucified). Of the examples cited in this chapter, this association of crucifixion with Pharaoh is perhaps most removed from the biblical text itself, but such a recurring application (at least in rabbinic works) should be noted as another attempt to weave the later Jewish experience of crucifixion into haggadic expositions of the biblical text.

In this brief section of this lengthy chapter we have observed that some Jewish expositors occasionally apply crucifixion imagery to biblical passages otherwise not clearly associated with bodily suspension. However, these applications are not sufficiently well attested in other Jewish literature to suggest that such interpretations stem from widespread early Jewish tradition. Yet, perhaps we should observe that some early Christian authors also applied Deuteronomy 28:66 to the cross.[285] Nonetheless, it is certainly noticeable that some Jewish authors could employ crucifixion in vivid ways to speak of the punishment of those who oppose Israel's God; and this theme should be connected with other aspects of our larger study.

11. Chapter Summary

Jewish society likely knew the punishment of *post mortem* bodily suspension from before the Davidic monarchy. They would have heard of, and possibly witnessed, impalements under the great ANE dynasties. And their own narratives of biblical history indicate that they adopted, with some modifications, these practices from their neighbours.

Several times in the Masoretic Text there occur references to the suspension of a person hung on a tree. Deuteronomy 21:22–23 provides a legal limitation on such penalties (hung persons are to be buried within the day). Examples of Joshua's decrees in the text of Joshua 8:29 and 10:26–27 are in accord with this Deuteronomic command to bury the suspended corpses; however, these episodes in Joshua do not concern capital crimes, rather they represent the results of conquest in war (also cf. 2 Sam 4:12). Other biblical suspension episodes take place in non-Palestinian venues – such as the execution of the chief baker in Genesis 40–41 (involving beheading and the graphic depiction of birds pecking at the deceased) and the royal recompense upon Haman in the book of Esther. In addition to these texts, there are a few instances in the Hebrew Masoretic Text where a death by suspension is either indicated (Ezra 6:11) or has been inferred by Jewish interpreters from the

---

[285] For example, in the Christian dialogue tradition, Deut 28:66 is cited in *Dialogue of Athanasius and Zacchaeus* 36; *Dialogue of Simon and Theophilus* ii.4 [= Harnack vi.22]; *Dialogue of Timothy and Aquila* 24.4; 53.8. On these texts see William Varner, *Ancient Jewish-Christian Dialogues* (Lewiston, N.Y.: Edwin Mellen, 2004), pp. 40–41, 114–115, 194–195, 268–269. Also see Melito, *Peri Pascha* 61.

context (e.g., Lamentations 5:12–13; and all the instances of the *hiphil* and *hophal* of יקע in Numbers 25:4 and 2 Samuel 21).

The intent of this chapter has been to illustrate how early Jewish interpretation developed each of these biblical texts – often incorporating technical suspension terminology and concepts. As was noted in the chapter introduction, this is not a claim that crucifixion was originally intended in the Hebrew Bible. Rather, these biblical texts were "actualized" by later readers, and over time these ancient penalties were associated with the kinds of human bodily suspensions common in later eras (including crucifixion). Indeed, by the first century, several of these biblical anti-heroes had become exemplars of death by crucifixion. So the baker in Genesis 40 appears in Philo as crucified and then beheaded. And Josephus, who entirely removes beheading from the narrative, depicts the execution simply with (ἀνα)σταυρόω. Haman's death is similarly depicted with σταυρόω and ἀνασκολοπίζω in the Greek versions of Esther; and Josephus expands the use of crucifixion language in his Esther account. Josephus also understands the decree in Ezra 6:11 to indicate crucifixion, and he employs matching terminology with regard to the suspension of the dead body of Saul (implying perhaps not as rigorous a disjunction between *post mortem* suspension and crucifixion as is assumed by some modern interpreters).

Similarly, in each of these episodes at least some of the targumim employ צלב and its cognates. No other biblical texts are rendered in the targumim with צלב terminology.[286] Hence this word group (consisting of צלב and its cognates) retains its technical usage to designate the bodily suspension of an executed person. Such language certainly overlaps with Greek technical vocabulary for human bodily suspension (e.g., σταυρόω and ἀνασκολοπίζω), and thus the targumim represent later renderings that connect well with the first-century interpretations of Philo and Josephus. Further, although in Genesis 40 the targumim maintain the order of beheading followed by suspension, no such prior means of execution is involved in Esther. Indeed, the rabbinic accounts also often employ technical suspension language in reference to Haman, even in at least one location mentioning the nails that he planned to use in pinning Mordecai to the cross. In the targumim and rabbinic literature, the hanging of the Jewish princes in Lamentations 5:12 is also rendered as an instance of their execution via suspension by the conquering Gentile army (as too the boys in Lam 5:13); these verses in Lamentations thus acquire striking significance in midrashic developments under the repeated conquest and hegemony by the Roman Empire. In sum, some targumic and rabbinic texts appear to assume suspension was the means of death in these biblical events, while other such texts do not. Yet, all these

---

[286] For validation of this claim, see the indices to the various targumim mentioned in the bibliography at the end of this book.

biblical episodes frequently are technically designated as instances of human bodily suspension. Thus, the kinds of perceptions associated with these texts likely informed Jewish thoughts more broadly about bodily suspension penalties (including crucifixion) in later eras.

The targumic and rabbinic accounts additionally argue that the executionary biblical texts that utilize יקע in the MT (Num 25:4 and 2 Sam 21) are instances of suspension. Indeed, the suspension of the sons of Saul in 2 Samuel 21, much like the prolonged crucifixion of Haman, created a tension with the Deuteronomic legislation in Deuteronomy 21:23. This tension the rabbis sought to alleviate by appeal to various benefits that accrued from these prolonged hangings.

As was noted in the summary concerning Deuteronomy 21:22–23 traditions, this text was often taken to *mandate* suspension of certain criminals. In a few key statements, the rabbinic and targumic literature sought to distinguish the post-mortem penalty implied in this text from crucifixion as practiced by the Romans. However, there are indications that at least some Jewish literature from a variety of historical contexts betrays the assumption that executionary suspension (if not crucifixion) was necessitated by Deuteronomy 21 (e.g., 11QTemple lxiv.6–13; Philo, *Spec. Leg.* iii.151–52; and the Peshitta). Further texts signal that, apart from direct legal applications, crucifixion could nevertheless be associated with Deuteronomy 21 (e.g., Josephus, *Bell.* iv.317; *t. Sanh.* ix.7; *b. Sanh.* 46b). Another key factor in the exposition of Deuteronomy 21:23 concerns the kind of genitive implied in קִלְלַת אֱלֹהִים. While the view represented in the older sources, and also present in the rabbinic period, was that those hung were themselves cursed (LXX, OL, 11QTemple, *Tg. Neof.*), an objective genitive rendition is commonly found in most rabbinic interpretations, especially with reference to blasphemy (also Josephus, Symmachus and the Peshitta). The central rabbinic view thus called for blasphemers to be stoned and then hung. But there is evidence for others to also merit suspension in Philo, Josephus, the Temple Scroll, and even within rabbinic circles.

This chapter has surfaced the oft-overlooked point that all the biblical passages that refer to some form of penal suspension are, at least occasionally, rendered in early Jewish literature with technical terminology that locates them within the specific sphere of human bodily suspension penalties – a range of penalties that in the Hellenistic and Roman periods included crucifixion. This is especially true of biblical passages employing תלה with עַל-(ה)עֵץ. Thus is less surprising in this period that a Hebrew phrase such as תלה עַל-(ה)עֵץ can (in the Qumran scrolls and in rabbinic literature) clearly indicate ante-mortem executionary procedures (including crucifixion).[287]

---

[287] In connection with Deut 21:22–23 see: 11QTemple lxiv.6–13; *b. Sanh.* 46b; and *Sifre Deut.* §221. See also 4QpNah 3–4 i 6–8 (treated above in chpt. 2, §2.4).

Further the targumic and rabbinic literature explicitly connects many of these passages with the legislation limiting penal suspension in Deuteronomy 21:22–23. Thus the Palestinian targumim all bring Numbers 25:4 in line with Deuteronomy 21. Also the Esther targumim on the suspension of Haman, as well as the rabbinic discussions of the hanging of Saul, attempt to explain how these texts relate to Deuteronomy 21:23. Thus these passages partook in antiquity of similar associations arising from lexical and thematic connections.

Broadly stated then, these texts provided in antiquity a host of biblical exemplars of suspended (even crucified) people. With the possible exception of the princes and the boys in Lamentations 5:12–13, these executionary suspension recipients are basically negative personalities – the baker, the Israelite idolaters following after Baal, the conquered enemies of Israel, and even the sons of Saul (perhaps guilty by association with their father's actions). Most notably Haman, who attempts to suspend the righteous Mordecai and to destroy the Jewish race, himself faces "the tree" (even "the cross" in several ancient traditions). And Deuteronomy 21:22–23 could be understood to associate such suspensions with either (depending on how the ancient reader understood the קִלְלַת אֱלֹהִים construct) the blasphemy and defiling of God, or the cursing of the one who is hung. Such biblical texts were actualized in Jewish antiquity to refer to contemporary experiences of human bodily suspension, and thus these passages often appear explicitly or implicitly to have informed ancient Jewish perceptions of crucifixion.

Chapter Four

Crucifixion in Symbology and Magic

This chapter investigates the extent to which Jewish magical traditions incorporated crucifixion symbols and artifacts. These can rightly be divided into two areas of inquiry.

The first question concerns the use of cross-shaped lines in Jewish burial traditions and in magical texts. Budge labels two crossed lines as "one of the oldest amuletic signs in the world, perhaps even the oldest."[1] However, Budge also rightly cautions against identifying these early "crosses" with crucifixion itself and with symbols of Christianity. Nonetheless, emblems of cross-shaped marks are known in Jewish magic epigrams, and some have associated such designs with crucifixion. Should these marks indeed be connected with crucifixion symbolism?

The second area of investigation involves the employment of crucifixion artifacts in ancient magical charms. Both Jewish and pagan sources evidence overt links between articles used in crucifixion (especially nails) and magic. Does the evidence here provide any clues as to how crucifixion was conceived by Jewish people in the ancient world?

1. The Sign of the Cross-Mark

A complex matter for interpretation concerns the use of cross-shaped signs on Jewish tombstones and ossuaries. Erich Dinkler has suggested that the cross symbol, which could be a variant spelling for the Hebrew letter *taw*, represents the "sign of Yahweh." This sign, he argues, was first mentioned in the Bible in connection with Cain and later linked with the blood smear on the door at Passover and with the eschatological mark in Ezekiel 9:3–6. Dinkler contends that this "sign of the cross" was believed to protect from demonic malevolence, and he associates this sign with a symbol for crucifixion itself.[2]

---

[1] E. A. Wallis Budge, *Amulets and Talismans* (New York: University Books, 1961), 336.

[2] Erich Dinkler, "Zur Geschichte des Kreuzsymbols," *ZTK* 48 (1951): 148–72; also reprinted in Erich Dinkler, *Signum Crucis: Aufsätze zum Neuen Testament und zur Christlichen Archäologie* (Tübingen: J. C. B. Mohr [Paul Siebeck], 1967), 1–25. He returned to this argument in Erich Dinkler, "Kreuzzeichen und Kreuz – Tau, Chi und Stauros," *JAC* 5 (1962): 93–112 (see esp. 93–99); also reprinted in *Signum Crucis*, 26–54.

A related argument, though understanding the ossuary evidence as Christian, appears in the work of Jack Finegan.[3]

On the other hand, Goodenough cautions that the principle interpretive evidence for Dinkler (the single mention in Ezekiel of the *taw* as the "sign of Yahweh") provides little basis for such a far ranging analysis.[4] However, Goodenough, noting the use of the cross as a symbol in magical amulets and magic books, does argue that in the ancient world the cross shape was part of a host of straight-line magical symbols that also found use as tokens of eschatological protection in Jewish thought.[5]

Subsequent to Goodenough's work, later publications have provided further evidence of crossed-line shapes in magical texts.[6] Nevertheless, it is

---

[3] Jack Finegan, *The Archeology of the New Testament: The Life of Jesus and the Beginning of the Early Church* (Princeton: Princeton University Press, 1969), 220–60 (esp. 220–31; 234–53). A condensation of some of this material appears in Jack Finegan, "Crosses in the Dead Sea Scrolls: A Waystation on the Road to the Christian Cross," *BARev* 5 (1979): 41–49.

[4] Erwin R. Goodenough, *Jewish Symbols in the Greco-Roman Period*, 13 vols., Bollingen Series 37 (New York: Pantheon Books, 1953–1968), 1:131–32. Yet, Goodenough appears more inclined to follow Dinkler's analysis in 7:177–78.

[5] Goodenough, *Jewish Symbols*, 1:132 (cf. plates 225–29 in vol. 3); for uses of the cross motif in Jewish magic: see 2:254.

[6] Note the following examples: Joseph Naveh and Shaul Shaked, *Amulets and Magic Bowls: Aramaic Incantations of Late Antiquity* (Jerusalem: Magnes Press/Leiden: E. J. Brill, 1985) Bowls 1, 4; Geniza texts 6, 7, 8; Joseph Naveh and Shaul Shaked, *Magic Spells and Formulae: Aramaic Incantations of Late Antiquity* (Jerusalem: Magnes Press, 1993), Amulet 27, Geniza texts 11, 15, 18 (MS pp. 1, 6, 8, 15, 17), 23, 29; Lawrence H. Schiffman and Michael D. Swartz, *Hebrew and Aramaic Incantation Texts from the Cairo Genizah: Selected Texts from Taylor-Schechter Box K1*, Semitic Texts and Studies 1 (Sheffield: Sheffield Academic Press, 1992), TS K1.168, TS K1.169 [NB both TS K1.127 and TS K1.137 are also published in this volume]; Peter Schäfer and Shaul Shaked, eds., *Magische Texte aus der Kairoer Geniza*, 2 vols., TSAJ 42 & 64 (Tübingen: J. C. B. Mohr [Paul Siebeck], 1994–1997), vol. 1: T.-S. NS 322.10; T.-S. K 1.157; Or. 1080.5.4; Or. 1080.15.81; vol. 2: T.-S. NS 322.50; T.-S. K 1.163. This listing is not intended to be complete, only suggestive. It also includes those shaped like an X rather than a + (on which note my comments below). Further, some manuscripts of the *Sepher ha-Razim* also bear cross marks alongside strings of other magical characters; but these MSS occasionally differ, so the symbolic tradition may not bear the antiquity accorded the text of the book as a whole. See Mordecai Margalioth, *Sepher ha-Razim: A Newly Recovered Book of Magic from the Talmudic Period* (Jerusalem: American Academy for Jewish Research, 1966), pp. 83, 94, and esp. p. 86; also Michael A. Morgan, *Sepher Ha-Razim: The Book of the Mysteries*, SBLTT 25 (Chico, Calif.: Scholars Press, 1983), pp. 46, 52, 63. Possibly one should take into account W. S. McCullough, *Jewish and Mandaean Incantation Bowls in the Royal Ontario Museum*, Near and Middle East Series 5 (Toronto: University of Toronto Press, 1967), bowl D (which, though in Mandaic, McCullough believes to be strongly influenced by Jewish bowls, even possibly written by a Jew). For some other possible Jewish uses of the cross motif, see Goodenough, *Jewish Symbols*, 1:155, 212–13, 222–23, 236–37, 277; 2:84. Multiple point crosses are also described in Goodenough 1:163, 169, 171–72; however, related symbols are called "stars" with reference to a possible Christian text in Naveh & Shaked, *Amulets*, 56.

indeed a leap to move from crossed lines etched on an ossuary (or more care-fully inscribed on an amulet, magic bowl, or literary text) to an identification of those lines with the cross of crucifixion. Certainly persuasive is the identi-fication of some occurrences of crossed-line symbols with the palaeo-Hebraic character for *taw* (i.e., X). Especially remarkable is the appearance of the palaeo-Hebraic *taw* in later Qumran Hebrew in the horoscopic/magical text 4Q186 (= 4QCryptic).[7] Also suggestive are some literary examples that Goodenough cites concerning the religious imagery of such a *taw* symbol.[8]

However, this connection of magical crossed-line symbols with *taw*, providing as it does an adequate explanation by itself of the symbol's development, actually distances these examples from any originally intended connection with crucifixion. In fact, the only hard evidence that has been cited heretofore for a connection between the *taw* and crucifixion is mentioned in Tertullian and is later found on the lips of a Jewish-Christian reported in Origen.[9] These likely represent a Christian reinterpretation of Jewish teachings on the *taw* mark. Therefore, so far we lack any definitive connec-tion between magical crossed lines (and/or the *taw*) and crucifixion in Judaism itself.

In recently published Geniza documents (albeit ones from late antiquity) one indeed notices that crossed lines often occur as symbols in magical texts.[10] However, we also observe that these cross-shaped symbols appear: (1) very often in a string of different straight- (and curved-) line magical char-acters, (2) usually with circles at the end of each line segment, and (3) often in the shape of an X (though admittedly also in the shapes of T and +). Each of these factors distances these "cross shapes" from a crucifixion cross.

Notably, in the one Geniza text that includes several of these crossed-line symbols and simultaneously the Aramaic term for the crucifixion cross (צלוב), there appears to be no connection between the symbols (which are

---

[7] See *DJD* V, 88–91 (esp. plate 31). For other examples of palaeo-Hebraic *taw* with two crossed lines from the Hasmonean period see Richard S. Hanson, "Paleo-Hebrew Scripts in the Hasmonean Age," *BASOR* 175 (1964): 26–42.

[8] Esp. *CD-B* xix.9–12 (citing the תו mark in Ezek 9:4 as the protecting emblem when the Messiah of Aaron and Israel comes); Origen, *Selecta in Ezechielem* 9 [Migne, *PG*, vol. 13, 800d–801a] (Aquila and Theodotion translate תו in Ezek 9:3–6 as the Greek Θαυ [*sic* not Ταυ as is sometimes alleged], while a Jewish-Christian says this refers to the cross and is to be placed on Christian foreheads); Tertullian, *Adversus Marcionem* iii.22.5–6 [Kroymann, *CCL*, 1:539] (Tertullian translates תו in Ezek 9:4 as Tau of the Greeks, which he claims is the form of a cross); *b. Hor.* 12a; *b. Ker.* 5b (both talmudic texts compare the shape of the anointing of the priest to a *chi*). On these texts also see Finegan, *Archeology*, 223–26. A fuller list is provided, but without separating between *taw* and the cross, in Pau Figueras, *Decorated Jewish Ossuaries* (Leiden: E. J. Brill, 1983), 106–7.

[9] These references were noted in the previous footnote: Origen, *Selecta in Ezechielem* 9; and Tertullian, *Adv. Marc.* iii.22.5–6.

[10] See the references to Geniza materials noted above.

earlier in the document) and the crucifixion term.[11] It might also merit mention that at least some Jewish early medieval anti-Christian polemic connects the crucifixion cross with *ṣade* rather than *taw*.[12] Such connection with *ṣade* likely had a dual appeal over any supposed connection with *taw*: (1) its shape conforms closer than *taw* to that of a crucifixion cross (true at least since the pre-Hellenistic spread of Aramaic orthography into Hebrew); and (2) the main Hebrew and Aramaic word grouping for crucifixion (i.e., צלב and cognates) begins with a *ṣade*. For these many reasons it is unlikely that there were overt Jewish crucifixion references in the crossed-line symbols in ancient magical texts; rather, these symbols, to the extent that their origin can be traced, appear more rightly to be associated simply with *taw*.

Finally, returning to the issue of cross-shaped etchings on ancient Jewish ossuaries, these are often more problematic than Dinkler allows. Some scholars have argued that the clearest examples on ossuaries are Christian marks, thus bearing no implications for the study of Judaism.[13] And, even when such crossed lines are considered as coming from a Jewish hand, their religious/magical intention has been called into question. This is especially true of the more lightly etched marks, which could instead have provided alignment reference points for use in applying later inscriptions to an unfinished ossuary.[14]

Therefore, as the data currently stands, there is little definitive evidential value for ancient Jewish perceptions of crucifixion in these magical crossed-line symbols, be they on ossuaries or in magical texts. However, given the popularity of the crossed-line magical symbol in antiquity, it is not surprising to find *Christian* amulets and magic objects from late antiquity incorporating

---

[11] The text, T-S Arabic 44.44, is discussed more fully below. See Naveh & Shaked, *Magic Spells*, 220–22 (text 23) and especially plate 69. In light of probable Jewish opposition to Christian symbolic use of the cross, one could ask whether these later magical texts manipulate ancient emblems in order to downplay any overt connection to crucifixion. However, the symbolic representations in these Geniza texts appear quite traditional; and the use of the צלוב in the magical formula of this Geniza text indicates that no similar hypothetical rejection of Christianity inhibited that particular traditional use of the cross.

[12] See the *Midrash ha-ʾOtiot* version B as translated in Pau Figueras, "A Midrashic Interpretation of the Cross as a Symbol," *LASBF* 30 (1980): 160. Figueras (on p. 161) dates the pertinent passage somewhere between the fourth to seventh centuries CE.

[13] E.g., Finegan believes them to be Jewish Christian (*Archeology*, 237–49). In a more nuanced fashion, Rahmani holds some cross marks to be later Christian additions to the Jewish ossuaries; see L. Y. Rahmani, *A Catalogue of Jewish Ossuaries in the Collections of the State of Israel* (Jerusalem: The Israel Antiquities Authority/The Israel Academy of Sciences and Humanities, 1994), p. 20 (on the Jesus ossuary from the Mount of Offence).

[14] E.g., Rahmani, *Catalogue*, pp. 19–20; see his No. 114 on pp. 106–7 (= Talpioth Ossuary No. 8 – central chalk crosses "seem to be in preparation for additional ornamentation"); for further possible examples of cross-shaped alignment markers see his Nos. 118; 568; 747; 829; and, most controversially, No. 841.

traditional and modified cross-shapes with likely reference to Jesus' crucifixion.[15]

2. The Crucifixion Nail

The principle early evidence for Jewish use of crucifixion articles in magic
comes from a brief mention in the Mishnah (*Šabb.* vi.10):

יוצאין בביצת החרגול ובשן של שועל ובמסמר הצלוב משו' רפואה. דברי ר' יוסי ור'
מאיר אומר אף בחול אסור משום דרכי האמורי:

They may go out [on the Sabbath] with the egg of a ḥargol [= a kind of locust], and with a
tooth of a fox, and with the nail of the cross for the sake of healing – so says Rabbi Yose. But
Rabbi Meir says even in an ordinary day it is forbidden, because of the "ways of the
Amorite."

Here Tannaitic rabbis disagree about the permissibility of certain magical
charms for healing. Most likely, especially given the reported debate between
Akiba's famous students R. Meir and R. Yose ben Ḥalafta,[16] the practices
cited represent common magical practice in some sectors of ancient Judaism.
The Mishnah apparently favours the second view that such charms violate the
biblical injunction against practicing pagan magic (i.e., the "ways of the
Amorite").[17] The use of nails in crucifixion is widely known.[18] Although the

---

[15] Christian amulets with crosses are mentioned in Goodenough, *Jewish Symbols*, vol. 2,
pp. 223, 231, 238. Also see Naveh & Shaked, *Amulets*, Amulet 32 (discussion p. 108 – in
Christian Palestinian Aramaic), Bowl 26 (discussion pp. 140–41); idem, *Magic Spells*, Bowl
17.

[16] The manuscripts vary, some omit Yose's name and read "so R. Meir, but the sages
say..." (so also Albeck's edition and Bavli manuscripts); the Yerushalmi knows a tradition
with the names of Yose and Meir reversed (*y. Šabb.* 6:9 [8c]). The above text agrees with
Abraham Goldberg, *Commentary to the Mishna Shabbat: Critically Edited and Provided with
Introduction, Commentary and Notes* (Jerusalem: Jewish Theological Seminary of America,
1976). See also Wilhelm Nowack, *Schabbat (Sabbat): Text, Übersetzung und Erklärung
Nebst einem textkritishen Anhang*, Die Mischna: Text, Übersetzung und ausführliche
Erklärung II.1 (Gießen: Alfred Töpelmann, 1924), 64–66.

[17] This is all the more the case if the variant ("but the sages say") discussed in the previous footnote is read as in the Bavli. However, note that some Rabbi's believed the injunction
against following the "ways of the Amorite" did not apply in cases of healing remedies
(*b. Šabb.* 67a; *y. Šabb.* 6:9 [8c]). A fuller early listing of such "ways" can be found in
t. Šabb. 6–7. See Giuseppe Veltri, *Magie und Halakha: Ansätze zu einem empirischen
Wissenschaftsbegriff im spätantiken und frühmittelalterlichen Judentum*, TSAJ 62 (Tübingen:
J.C.B. Mohr [Paul Siebeck], 1997), 93–183.

[18] See chapter 2 §1. E.g., note the use of a nail in pinning the body of the crucified man
found at Givʻat ha-Mivtar (see chapter 2 §3.6). As a consequence it is likely that crucifixion
nails are intended, for example, in *Tg. Esth II* 5:14 where Haman employs both carpenters to
make the cross for Haman and smiths to forge the iron (וקיינאי דמתקנין דפרזל). Likely

reported authorities here are second century, the long legacy of Jewish magic, and the basic conservative nature of magical traditions, makes it likely that such a use of a crucifixion nail pre-dates the Rabbinic authorities cited.[19]

The Babylonian and Jerusalem Talmuds, commenting on this Mishnaic passage, differ as to what illnesses required the carrying of a crucifixion nail – the Bavli says it combats an inflammation (דעבדי לזרפא; *b. Šabb.* 67a), while the Yerushalmi more specifically says it is good for a spider's bite (טב לעכביתא; *y. Šabb.* 6:9 [8c]).[20] Possibly, such a nail had several magical uses. So, a much later text from the Cairo Geniza apparently employs crucifixion nails in a love potion:[21]

17 לאהבה   כאתם (איצא)[22]
18 כד מסמ((א))ר[23] מן כשבה מצלוב ואעמל מנה כאתם
19 ואיצא אכר[24] פצה ואנקש עליה אורי בלע תלע
20 פאדא ארדת תעמל בה מא   הלע אוריה[25]

(17) For love. [blank] A seal, again.
(18) Take a nail from the wood of someone crucified, and make of it a seal.
(19) Again, another one, of silver, and engrave on it (*magic words*).[26]
(20) If you wish, you can make with it what you will.

The magical use of a crucifixion nail is also known in Pliny the Elder (23/24–79 CE) to combat quartan fever (a type of malaria).[27] Lucan (39–65 CE), in a flowery section where he both abhors witchcraft and simultaneously speaks of

---

also note the phrase "the smiths who were preparing nails to be set in the gallows (cross)" in the Geniza fragment of Targum Esther in Cambridge University Library T-S B 11.52 folio 1v, lines 17–18, in Rimon Kasher and Michael L. Klein, "New Fragments of Targum to Esther from the Cairo Geniza," *HUCA* 61 (1990): 93; translation from p. 103.

[19] Jewish religion is connected with a branch of magic in Pliny, *NH* xxx.2.11; Jewish magicians and exorcists are also encountered in Acts 13:6; 19:13–14. On the conservatism of magical traditions see: P.S. Alexander in Schürer, *HJPAJC*, vol. 3.1, 344.

[20] Jastrow (עכוביתא, s.v.): thistle sting or a spider's bite.

[21] T-S Arabic 44.44 (2/17–20); text number 23 in Naveh and Shaked, *Magic Spells*, 220–22 (the translation is theirs). The last line ("make with it what you will") is reminiscent of the ring made from a crucifixion nail in Lucian, *Philops.* 17 (see below).

[22] This is the editors' suggestion for איא (cf. line 19).

[23] The bracketed א is a very small character above the second מ.

[24] The editors suggest that this is a corruption of כד or of <ה>אבר "needle."

[25] The editors believe that these two words belong at the end of the previous line.

[26] The editors choose not to attempt to translate this series of "magic words."

[27] Pliny, *N.H.* xxviii.11.46: *iidem in quartanis fragmentum clavi a cruce involutum lana collo subnectunt, aut spartum e cruce, liberatoque condunt caverna quam sol non attingat.* "These also wrap up in wool and tie round the neck of quartan patients a piece of a nail taken from a cross, or else a cord taken from a crucifixion, and after the patient's neck has been freed they hide it in a hole where the sunlight cannot reach." Text and translation by W. H. S. Jones in H. Rackham et al., *Pliny Natural History*, 10 vols., LCL (London: Heinemann/Cambridge, Mass.: Harvard University Press, 1938–1962), 8:34–35. Also noted in Veltri, *Magie*, 95–96.

its efficacy, mentions parts of the cross among other artifacts witches gather from the dead for use in magic.[28] Lucian (second century CE) speaks ironically of the protection from spirits provided by a "ring made from the iron of crosses" sold by an Arab.[29] The testimony of these Roman authors makes it all the more likely that the carrying of a crucifixion nail was an established magical remedy early in the Roman period.

Since the texts themselves do not indicate why a crucifixion nail could be thought to produce healing, attempts to understand the rationale here inevitably involve some speculation. It has certainly been suggested that this follows the tendency in folk magic to employ as charms articles associated with violent deaths.[30] In any case, it is interesting that some sectors of Judaism (even rabbinic Judaism) did not consider it improper to handle crucifixion nails. And, more importantly, some Jews believed that healing properties and love potions could be associated with articles employed in crucifixion. Of course, the healing properties intended here are immediate and physical; they are neither eschatological nor spiritual, and they bear no lasting impact on a person's relationship to the deity.

3. Summary

This chapter opposes the claim that cross marks on ancient ossuaries and tombs definitively represented (non-Christian) Jewish magical tokens associ-

---

[28] Lucan, *Bell.* vi.543–49: *Laqueum nodosque nocentes/ Ore suo rumpit, pendentia corpora carpsit/ Abrasitque cruces percussaque viscera nimbis/ Volsit et incoctas admisso sole medullas./ Insertum manibus chalybem nigramque per artus/ Stillantis tabi saniem virusque coactum/ Sustulit, et nervo morsus retinente pependit.* "She breaks with her teeth the fatal noose, and mangles the carcass that dangles on the gallows, and scrapes the cross of the criminal; she tears away the rain-beaten flesh and the bones calcined by exposure to the sun. She purloins the nails that pierced the hands, the clotted filth, and the black humour of corruption that oozes over all the limbs; and when a muscle resists her teeth, she hangs her weight upon it." Text and translation in J. D. Duff, *Lucan*, LCL (London: William Heinemann/Cambridge, Mass.: Harvard University Press, 1928), 342–45.

[29] Lucian, *Philops.* 17: καὶ μάλιστα ἐξ οὗ μοι τὸν δακτύλιον ὁ Ἄραψ ἔδωκε σιδήρου τοῦ ἐκ τῶν σταυρῶν πεποιημένον καὶ τὴν ἐπῳδὴν ἐδίδαξεν τὴν πολυώνυμον; "especially since the Arab gave me the ring made of iron from crosses and taught me the spell of many names." Text and translation in A. M. Harmon et al., *Lucian*, 8 vols., LCL (London: William Heinemann/Cambridge, Mass.: Harvard University Press, 1913–1967), 3:346–47. It is perhaps of interest that later in this same treatise Lucian testifies to the belief that the ghosts of those who die violently, including those crucified (ἀνεσκολοπίσθη), walk the earth (*Philops.* 29) – does this help explain why a talisman from a crucifixion nail can ward off spirits?

[30] So Wilhelm Nowack in his edition of tractate *Shabbat* for the Gießen Mishnah, p. 66n. Cf. the text from Lucan mentioned in an earlier note (*Bell.* vi.543–549).

ated with crucifixion. It also finds no direct evidence that the crossed-line symbols employed on Jewish magical texts and amulets should be connected with early Jewish perceptions of crucifixion. However, these crossed-line symbols in ancient Judaism (some of which may have been explicitly connected with the palaeo-Hebraic *taw*) likely were combined with crucifixion imagery in some sectors of early Christianity. In this regard, the occasional Jewish practice unintentionally provided symbolism that later could be attached to the crucifixion cross by Christians. Similar use of Jewish symbolism shall be met again in the next chapter in a further discussion of the various phenomena there deemed "latent symbolism."

Nevertheless, Jewish magic (like forms of magic known more broadly in the Roman world) did make use of some crucifixion objects in certain magical charms and formulae. That some Jewish people would carry a crucifixion nail shows that objects associated with crucifixion were not inevitably deemed unclean. Moreover, such a practice would indicate that pieces of the crucifixion cross, like other emblems of violent death, might be thought to promote physical healing and have other magical properties.

Chapter Five

Crucifixion in Imagery, Proverb and Case Law

Since crucifixion was so well known in antiquity, inevitably it was employed to some effect for illustrations in ancient literature – both Jewish and pagan.[1] Below are discussed some images of crucifixion that were used by Philo, and others that were applied in rabbinic aphorisms, narratives and case law. Finally, in an extended sense, some other Jewish customs and haggadic references could be thought to have incorporated the imagery of crucifixion.

1. Philonic Allegory

Philo, a master of word pictures, utilizes crucifixion images in several allegorical expositions. Earlier (in chapter three) some instances of Philonic allegory were encountered in his treatments of Genesis 40:19 (*Som.* ii.213; cf. *Jos.* 156) and Deuteronomy 21:23 (*Post.* 25–26). A theme in these expositions is that the crucified or suspended man metaphorically represents the person who has centered his life on bodily pleasures. Another instance of this theme in Philo occurs in *De Posteritate Caini* 61, where Philo comments on the names found in Numbers 13:22.

ἑρμηνεύεται δὲ ὁ μὲν Ἀχειμὰν ἀδελφός μου, ὁ δὲ Σεσεὶν ἐκτός μου, ὁ δὲ Θαλαμεὶν κρεμάμενός τις· ἀνάγκη γὰρ ψυχαῖς ταῖς φιλοσωμάτοις ἀδελφὸν μὲν νομίζεσθαι τὸ σῶμα, τὰ δὲ ἐκτὸς ἀγαθὰ διαφερόντως τετιμῆσθαι· ὅσαι δὲ τοῦτον διάκεινται τὸν τρόπον, ἀψύχων ἐκκρέμανται καὶ καθάπερ οἱ ἀνασκολοπισθέντες ἄχρι θανάτου φθαρταῖς ὕλαις προσήλωνται.

And "Acheiman" is interpreted "my brother"; and "Sesein" [is interpreted] "outside me"; and "Thalamein" [is interpreted] "someone hanging." For it is necessary for souls which love the body that the body be considered a "brother," and that "external" good things have been preeminently esteemed; and, as many [souls] as are disposed in this condition, these "hang" from soulless things, and, just as those who have been crucified, they are nailed to perishable materials until death.

The vivid picture that arises from *Post.* 61 is that the following of bodily pursuits fastens the soul to perishable realities as to a cross. Crucifixion is indi-

---

[1] See, e.g., Martin Hengel, *Crucifixion in the Ancient World and the Folly of the Message of the Cross*, trans. John Bowden (London & Philadelphia: SCM Press & Fortress Press, 1977), 66–68; 81–83 (repr. 158–60; 173–75).

cated here by ἀνασκολοπίζω (which Philo clearly uses of crucifixion in *Flacc.* 72, 83–84), by the notion of being "nailed" (προσηλόω),[2] and by the reference to a period of hanging nailed to the cross "until death" (ἄχρι θανάτου).[3]

Etymological analysis underlies every juncture of Philo's allegorical interpretation, with the crucifixion connection being based on Θαλαμείν [MT תַלְמָי]⁴ interpreted as "someone hanging."[5] Significantly, Philo moves from bodily "hanging" to crucifixion by nailing to a tree. This, along with his expositions of Genesis 40:19 and Deuteronomy 21:23, strongly indicates that Philo associates "crucifixion" with "hanging [on a tree]."

Philo's allegory here is slightly different than in previous cases. As in *Som.* ii.213 (see above: chpt. 3, §2.1) Philo equates with the crucified body any soul (or mind) committed to serving bodily pursuits. However, in *Som.* ii.213 the "tree" (= cross) is "lack of education" (ἀπαιδευσία), whereas in *Post.* 61 above it is "perishable materials" (φθαρταῖς ὕλαις).[6] This latter analogy more closely resembles Philo's exposition of Deuteronomy 21:23 in *Post.* 26–27 (see chpt. 3, §4.4), where the person, who ought to hang on God, hangs instead upon the pleasures of his own body (which is a ξύλικος ὄγκος, "wooden mass"). However, in *Post.* 27 the person, rather than being crucified, is suspended on a halter (ἀγχόνη). In fact, the suspension of the soul (on a halter or on a cross) forms a theme in several Philonic works.[7] Probably the foundational *analogy* for Philo lies in bodily suspension, while the *imagery* (halter or cross) can vary since both represent bodily suspension. This further testimony confirms that Philo associated crucifixion with other forms of bodily suspension. In this regard, Philo in Alexandria manifests a viewpoint very similar to that of Josephus.

Certainly, Philo is an author who does not shirk from applying crucifixion imagery (and the vivid horror it entailed) to drive home his point. Such usage

---

[2] Cf. Philo, *Som.* ii.213; also likely cf. Philo, *Prov.* ii.24; and note the brief discussion of Greek words for crucifixion (including προσηλόω) above in chapter 1, §2.2.

[3] Hengel (*Crucifixion*, 67; repr. 159) compares this text to analogies in Seneca (*Dial.* 7.19.2–3; in *De Vita Beata*), who also compares bodily desires to the cross.

[4] The Greek and Latin MSS of Num 13:22 exhibit a great variety of renderings of תַלְמָי. See the textual apparatus to the Göttingen LXX on Numbers 13:22.

[5] Philo likely understood the Hebrew name to be derived from תלה ("he hung"); so R. Arnaldez, *De Posteritate Caini*, Les oeuvres de Philon d'Alexandrie 6 (Paris: Cerf, 1972), 79n.

[6] Note the word play on ὕλη, which can mean both "wood" and (esp. in philosophy) "matter/materials."

[7] For further instances of suspension of the soul on a halter see: *Quis Her.* 269; *Praem.* 151. Such a death is considered unclean in *Aet.* 20–21; *Mut.* 62 (see above chpt. 1, §3). Also note the Polycrates account in Philo, *Prov.* ii.24–25 = Eusebius, *Praep.* viii.14.24–25; see text in Karl Mras, *Eusebius Werke Achter Band: Die Praeparatio Evangelica*, 2 vols., GCS 43,1 (Berlin: Akademie-Verlag, 1954), 1:468–69.

also provides indirect corroboration of the author's (and the audience's) own awareness of the ongoing practice of crucifixion in their day.

2. The Crucified Brigand

A recurring theme in rabbinic narratives is that of the crucified brigand. Robbers, bandits, and rebels were frequently crucified in the Roman period (and before).[8] Such individuals are often designated as ληστής (Hebrew לִיסְטֵס [pl. לִיסְטִים]; Aramaic לִיסְטָאָה; cf. Latin *latro*).[9] These terms can designate both individuals who use violence to steal as well as those criminals who band together in groups – perhaps "brigand" is the best English equivalent.[10] From the clans of brigands frequently come the ranks of rebels, and this added greater impetus to Roman attempts at suppression.[11] Crucifixion became a chief tool in these efforts. Thus, where Roman brigand terminology and terms for human bodily suspension coincide, it is highly likely that "crucifixion" is the form of execution intended.[12]

Some instances have already been mentioned in previous chapters. Josephus provides an account of how Felix crucified an "incalculable number" of brigands (λησταί, *Bell.* ii.253). The Bavli represents Rabbi Eleazar as cooperating with the Roman authorities in trapping such brigands

---

[8] See above in chapter 2, §1. Also see Hengel, *Crucifixion*, 47–50 (repr. 139–42); Martin Hengel, *The Zealots: Investigations into the Jewish Freedom Movement in the Period from Herod I until 70 A.D.*, trans. David Smith (Edinburgh: T&T Clark, 1989), 30–33.

[9] For the Hebrew and Aramaic terminology see Samuel Krauss, *Griechische und Lateinische Lehnwörter im Talmud, Midrasch und Targum*, 2 vols. (Berlin, 1898–1899), 2:315–16; Daniel Sperber, *A Dictionary of Greek and Latin Legal Terms in Rabbinic Literature*, Dictionaries of Talmud, Midrash and Targum 1 (Ramat-Gan: Bar-Ilan University Press, 1984), 106–10.

[10] On the range of usage cf. Hengel, *Zealots*, 24–25, 35–36; also see rabbinic references to brigands in ibid., 34–41. For present purposes, the term "brigand" also has the benefit of being less associated with the complex issues of the sociological causation of "banditry" prominent in, for example, Richard A. Horsley, "Josephus and the Bandits," *JSJ* 10 (1979): 42–63; Richard A. Horsley and John S. Hanson, *Bandits, Prophets, and Messiahs: Popular Movements in the Time of Jesus* (Minneapolis: Winston Press, 1985), 48–87 (Horsley himself actually uses the terms brigand and bandit interchangeably); also cf. Brent D. Shaw, "Tyrants, Bandits and Kings: Personal Power in Josephus," *JJS* 44 (1993): 176–204.

[11] In fact, Hengel argues that one could only become an official enemy of Rome (*hostes*) by a legal declaration of war, otherwise rebellious activists simply went by the term *latrones* (= λησταί); see, Hengel, *Zealots*, 31–32 (cf. p. 29 noting the difficulty of deciding whether robbers or "Zealots" are intended in specific instances using ληστής). Kuhn tends to view such crucified *Räuber* as executed political rebels, especially in his analysis of Palestine from the arrival of Pompey to the Jewish War; see Kuhn, "Die Kreuzesstrafe," 724–727.

[12] Therefore, in this section צלב and its cognates shall be translated as directly indicating crucifixion.

(*b. B. Meṣ.* 83b). Also, Rabbi Meir draws an analogy to Deuteronomy 21:23 where, after the twin brother of the king joins a band of brigands (לסטים), he is caught and crucified, thus bringing a popular curse on the countenance of the king (*t. Sanh.* ix.7; *b. Sanh.* 46b). As in Meir's parable, the crucified לסטים occur in other rabbinic narratives.

One earlier reference, albeit not associated with an attributed authority, comes from the Tannaitic midrash *Mekilta de-Rabbi Ishmael* (*Shirata* 10)[13]:

יי ימלוך אימתי תבינהו בשתי ידיך. משל למה הדבר דומה ללסטים שנכנסו לפלטין של
מלך בזזו נכסיו והרגו פמליא של מלך והחריבו פלטרין של מלך לאחר זמן ישב עליהן
המלך בדין תפש מהם הרג מהם צלב מהם וישב בפלטין שלו ואחר כך נתודעה מלכותו
בעולם לכך נאמר מקדש יי כוננו ידיך יי ימלוך לעולם ועד.

"The LORD will reign." (Exod 15:18) When? [When] you [= God] will build it [= the Temple] with your two hands. To give a parable, to what is this matter compared? To brigands who entered the palace of a king, plundered his property, slew the king's *familia* and destroyed the king's residence. After a time, the king sat over them in judgment – he imprisoned some of them,[14] he slew some of them, he crucified some of them – and he dwelt in his palace. And afterwards his reign was made known in the world. Thus it is said: "The sanctuary, O LORD, your hands established. The LORD will reign forever and ever." (Exod 15:17–18)

In this commentary, the citation of Exodus 15:18 that initiates the question ("when will God reign?") is taken as a reference to God's re-establishment of his Temple. The analogy of God with a king is a natural one, especially given the verb מלך in Exodus 15:18 ("the Lord *reigns*"); and the opposition of לסטים to kings forms a motif in rabbinic stories.[15] In the analogy, the king's victory over the לסטים provides opportunity for him to crucify some. This three-part judgment of the לסטים (imprisonment, slaying, crucifying) is reminiscent of Roman practice as reported by Josephus (e.g., *Bell.* ii.75, 241–42; *Ant.* xx.129–31). Again, it is natural that the "king" would crucify his opponents. However, it is notable that this analogy puts God as the analog of the king who crucifies.

There is variant form of this saying reported to have been in the *Mekilta de-Rabbi Shimon bar Yohai* (*MRS*).[16] The arc and central points of the parable

---

[13] The text follows Jacob Z. Lauterbach, *Mekilta de-Rabbi Ishmael*, 3 vols. (Philadelphia: Jewish Publication Society of America, 1933–1935), 2:79–80 (lines 42–49). Cf. H. S. Horovitz and I. A. Rabin, *Mechilta D'Rabbi Ismael*, Corpus Tannaiticum 3.1(3) (Frankfurt: J. Kauffmann, 1931), p. 150 (lines 11–14) on [*Beshallah*] *Shirata* 10.

[14] This is a partitive use of מן; thus מהם (literally "[some] from them") should be translated "some of them."

[15] See Hengel, *Zealots*, 37–38.

[16] *MRS* xxxvi.2 according to the text and translation in: W. David Nelson, *Mekhilta de-Rabbi Shimon bar Yohai* (Philadelphia: Jewish Publication Society, 2006), 157. The *MRS* is no longer extant except in fragmentary manuscripts and in citations found within later works (especially the *Midrash ha-Gadol*). This passage is reported to have come from Ms. Firkovich II A 268 (so Nelson, p. 155).

are the same between the two competing forms of the *Mekilta*. The principal differences between these two versions are that in the *MRS*: (1) the brigands specifically capture only the king's servants (rather than the broader group of *familia*); (2) the brigands seize, slay, crucify and burn the servants; (3) the king returns to seize, slay, crucify and burn the brigands; and (4) the Exodus text is only cited once. Here in the *MRS* the parable exactly parallels the actions of the king with those of the brigands.[17] This adds a neat literary structure to the form in the *Mekilta de-Rabbi Shimon*. It also closely parallels the experience of the Roman persecution of the Jewish people (i.e., the Romans, who captured, slew, crucified and burned the Jewish revolutionaries) with the expected eschatological recompense upon God's enemies. God again is the analog of the king who will crucify his opponents.

The *Mekilta de-Rabbi Ishmael* cites a related analogy in *Shirata* 7. In the midrashic context, Pharaoh personally declares the five boasts the "enemy" declares in Moses' song from Exodus 15:9. Against these the Holy Spirit juxtaposes statements of Pharaoh's own demise. Then this parable follows[18]:

מושלו משל למה הדבר דומה ללסטים שהיה עומד ומנאץ אחר פלטרין של מלך אומר
אם אמצא את בן המלך אני תופשו והורגו וצולבו[20] וממית אותו מיתות חמורות[19] כך
היה פרעה הרשע עומד ומנאץ בתוך ארץ מצרים אמר אויב ארדוף אשיג וגו' ורוח
הקדש מלעגת עליו ואומרת נשפת ברוחך

To give a parable, to what is this matter compared? To a brigand[21] who was standing and threatening behind a king's palace, saying: "If I find the king's son, I shall seize him, and slay him, and crucify him, and make him die most severe deaths." So also was wicked Pharaoh standing and threatening in the midst of the land of Egypt: "An enemy said: 'I will pursue, I will overtake, etc.'" [Exod 15:9] But the Holy Spirit mocks him and says: "You blew with Your wind…" [Exod 15:10 – in reference to God's Red Sea destruction of Pharaoh's army].

The implicit conclusion to the parable is that, like wicked Pharaoh, the tables are turned on the boastful brigand and he is himself seized and crucified. The conclusion need not be spoken because people in the author's day would

---

[17] The king: תפס מהן והרג מהן וצלב מהן ושרף מהן ("he seized some of them, and slew some of them, and crucified some of them, and burned some of them"). Whereas the brigands are said to have: תפסו מעבדין והרגו מהן וצלבו מהן ושרפו מהן ("they seized some of [his] servants, and slew some of them, and crucified some of them, and burned some of them").

[18] Lauterbach, 2:57–58 (lines 57–63); cf. Horovitz/Rabin, p. 141 (lines 1–3) on [*Beshallaḥ*] דויהי 7.

[19] For וממית אותו מיתות חמורות ("and make him die most severe deaths"), Horovitz/Rabin reads וממיתו מיתה חמורה ("and make him die a most severe death"). In either case the essential meaning remains the same, though, if the singular is read, likely a certain death would be implied – perhaps even more clearly epexegetic to crucifixion.

[20] The Horovitz/Rabin text reads "וצו בו" (p. 141, l. 2) in the edition I used; this must be a printer's error (there are signs of a missing letter in the original printing). Cf. Lauterbach, the Venice edition (16d) and Weiss' Vienna edition of 1865 (p. 49a).

[21] The noun is plural, but the sense throughout is singular.

expect such brigands to be crucified, and because Pharaoh's own analogous destruction was well known. Remarkably, in another later haggadic passage Pharaoh boasts that he will "crucify" Moses.[22] Of the four elements in the brigand's boast quoted above (seize, slay, crucify, make die most severe deaths), the last two (possibly the last three) appear to escalate the rhetoric beyond a quick means of execution.[23] This is reminiscent of some of the hyperbolic language used by Graeco-Roman authors in reference to crucifixion.[24] It is also interesting to note that the verb for "threaten" (נאץ) used in the parable can bear, in contexts referring to God, the connotation of "blaspheme."[25] As mentioned repeatedly above in chapter three, "hanging on a tree" can be associated with the death of blasphemers (via Deut 21:22–23).

Another parable, from a slightly later source, speaks of the dangers of an evil woman who demands that her husband do things beyond his power (*Eccl. Rab.* vii.37 [21c] on Eccl 7:26).[26] The woman in this parable is jealous of the wealth of a neighbouring brigand, and she insists that her husband join with that brigand. The beleaguered husband does so, and the following ensues:

נפק בההוא ליליא נפק ליסטאה ותקין תזקיטא בתריהון ۰ דין דהוה חכים שביליא ערק
ואישתזיב ۰ ודין לא הוה חכים שביליא איתצייד ואיצטלב ۰ וקרון עלוי לקיש לסטים[27]
בכיר לצלובים:

He [= the husband] went out in that night, the brigand went out [i.e., with his gang], but the sergeant arranged [to go out] after them. This one [i.e., the brigand] who recognized the paths fled, and he was saved. But this one [who] did not recognize the paths [i.e., the husband] was caught, and he was crucified. And they applied to him [the proverb], "The latest of the brigands is the first of the crucified."

---

[22] *Exod. Rab.* ix.4. Also note the way the drowning of Pharaoh can be treated as a reversal similar to the hanging of Haman (*Exod. Rab.* xx.10; *PRK* xi.2; *Midr. Pss.* xxii.15).

[23] Alternatively, the string could be individual items of ranting without highlighting one means of death over another. Or one could argue that, since the first of these four items (תופשו) is not an executionary form ("seize him"), the items are in order of performance; and thus צולבו (translated above as "crucify him") comes sequentially after הורגו ("slay him"), implying that the suspension is *post mortem*. However, the last member in the series (וממית אותו מיתות, "and make him die most severe deaths"), shows that the order of verbs cannot be purely sequential. Nevertheless, the variant form attributed to the *Mekilta de-Rabbi Shimon bar Yohai* (xxxiii.1) adds "I will burn him" (ושורפו אני) after "I will crucify him"; see text and translation in Nelson, *Mekhilta de-Rabbi Shimon*, 144.

[24] Recall Josephus, *Bell.* vii.203 (θανάτων τὸν οἴκτιστον; "the most pitiable of deaths"); cf. multiple Graeco-Roman instances of such hyperbolic language in Hengel, *Crucifixion*, 7–10.

[25] See Jastrow, s.v.

[26] A range of dates from the sixth to the eighth century are often given for the *Midrash Qohelet*; see Günter Stemberger, *Introduction to the Talmud and Midrash*, trans. Markus Bockmuehl, 2nd ed. (Edinburgh: T & T Clark, 1996), 318.

[27] Jastrow (p. 170) suggests ללסטים.

The text continues an ongoing association of crucifixion with the punishment of brigands. It is possible that the concluding proverb is a traditional saying, in which case it would antedate the above story.

One fascinating proverbial adage about crucifixion is ascribed to Rabbi Samuel, son of Naḥman (third generation Palestinian *Amora*). It appears in two slightly different contexts. In Esther Rabbah, Queen Vashti refuses to appear naked before the king; this becomes the launching point for the following rabbinic statements (*Esth. Rab.* iii.14 [7d] on Esth 1:12):[28]

ר' שמעון בר אבא אמר בשם רבי יוחנן אין הקדוש ברוך הוא דן את הרשעים בגיהנם
אלא ערומים ומה טעם דכתיב (תהלים ע"ג) בעיר צלמם תבזה ∘ אמר ר' שמואל בר
נחמן הן דליסטאות מקפח תמן מצטלב ∘

R. Simeon bar Abba said in the name of Rabbi Johanan: Is it not so that the Holy One, blessed be He, punished the wicked ones in Gehinnom only naked? And what is the sense of the Scriptures (Psalms 73[:20]), "In waking[29] you will despise their image." R. Samuel bar Naḥman said, "Where the brigands rob, there he is crucified."

R. Samuel's brief proverb that the locale of crucifixion is that of the crime coheres well with established Roman legal procedure.[30] Two further statements (not quoted above) follow after these two sayings; and all four are apparently affirmed as true, and as creating a kind of composite statement about the ultimate state of Israel's enemies. What editorial connection lies behind linking the sayings of R. Simeon and R. Samuel? Two links are possible: (1) crucifixion involves suspending the person naked, just as the wicked are said to be punished in Gehenna, or (2) the mention of Gehinnom in R. Simeon's adage reminds one of R. Samuel's statement because of an intrinsic Gehinnom link. The context of nakedness in *Esth. Rab.* iii.14 (also present in a citation, not quoted above, of R. Nathan immediately after R. Samuel's crucifixion maxim) suggests that the first link is at play.

However, it is possible that both linkages lie in the background, and the second receives support from a citation in the *Pesikta de-Rab Kahana* (suppl. ii.2).[31] After referring to R. Samuel's argument that Gehenna (= Gehinnom) is set in Jerusalem (where the nations will be judged), the *PRK* again cites this esteemed Palestinian *Amora*[32]:

---

[28] The first half of *Esther Rabbah* appears to be early sixth century (thus Stemberger, *Introduction*, 319).

[29] M. Simon, in the Soncino translation, suggests "nakedness" rather than "waking."

[30] Cf. Hengel, *Crucifixion*, 48n (repr. 140n).

[31] Stemberger (*Introduction*, 295) dates the *PRK* to the fifth century (as opposed to Zunz's date of AD 700), although he allows for subsequent fluidity in transmission of the text.

[32] Bernard Mandelbaum, *Pesikta de Rav Kahana: According to an Oxford Manuscript with variants from all known manuscripts and genizoth fragments and parallel passages with commentary and introduction*, 2nd ed., 2 vols. (New York: Jewish Theological Seminary of America, 1987), 2:453 (lines 19–21). Translation is mine. Also see translation of *PRK* suppl. ii.2 in William G. (Gershon Zev) Braude and Israel J. Kapstein, *Pesikta de-Rab Kahana:*

א"ר שמואל בר' נחמני במקום שקיפח הליסטים שם צולבין אותו, מן ירושלים קפחו
ושבו לפיכך יצלבו בירושלם,

R. Samuel bar Naḥmani said: "In the place where the brigands rob, there they crucify him.
From Jerusalem they [the nations] robbed and then returned; therefore they will be crucified
in Jerusalem."

After this statement, there appropriately follows a citation of Zechariah 14:1.
In the broader context there is an explicit link (via Jerusalem) between Gehinn-
nom and R. Samuel's brigand proverb – the rabbi connected Gehinnom (in
the environs of Jerusalem) with his contention that Jerusalem, despoiled by
the nations, will be the site of the nations' demise. As noted in the previous
paragraph, this Gehinnom connection may be at play in the compiler's citation of R. Samuel's similar proverb in the Esther Rabbah text,[33] though there
the context of nakedness cannot rightly be ignored.

In any case, in this *PRK* application of R. Samuel's striking proverb, the
most fascinating point is that God's eschatological recompense on the nations
clearly involves their mass *crucifixion* in Jerusalem. While perhaps implicit in
the Esther Rabbah report of Samuel's proverb (and a concept found in
Mek. Shirata 10, noted earlier), here in the *PRK* this mass eschatological
crucifixion image is strikingly present.

Another passage in the *Pesikta de-Rab Kahana* (xi.2) would imply that
God works through his own people to enact such eschatological recompense,
so that the people who were crucified return to crucify their executioners[34]:

אמרו לאלהים מה נורא מעשיך ברוב עוזך יכחשו לך אויביך. א"ר יוחנן אמרו לפעלה
טבה אישר. מה נורא מעשיך, מה דחילין אינון מנגנייה דידך, הנהרגין הורגין את
הורגיהן, הנצלבין צולבין את צולביהן, המשתקען משקעין את משקעיהן, הפה שאמר
כל הבן הילוד היארה תשליכוהו הושלך לים, מרכבות פרעה וחילו ירה בים שאר
קיטעה דכבת קמייה.

Say to God, "How your works are feared; by your great might your enemies cringe before
you." (Ps 66:3) R. Yohanan said, "They said to a good worker, 'Be strong.'" "How your
works are feared." (Ps 66:3) How awe-inspiring are the contrivances of your hand. Those
who are slain slay their executioners; those who are crucified crucify their crucifiers; those
who are drowned drown those who drowned them. The mouth that said, "Every son who is
born, you shall throw them in the river," (Exod 1:22) was thrown to the sea. "The chariots of
Pharaoh and his army were thrown in the sea." (Exod 15:4). The remainder portion [of the
passage] is as before.

Although this does not speak of a brigand, it fits with the thrust of previous
passages. God vindicates his oppressed people, and the Exodus serves as a

---

R. Kahana's compilation of discourses for Sabbaths and festal days (Philadelphia: Jewish
Publication Society of America, 1975; London: Routledge & Kegan Paul, 1975), 463.

[33] The wording of R. Samuel's proverb varies between *Esth. Rab.* and *PRK*, though the
essence is the same.

[34] Text in Mandelbaum, *Pesikta de Rav Kahana*, 1:177–178.

great reminder of this. Between the exposition of Psalm 66:3 and the Exodus references, there are three examples of villains who meet their own chosen means of execution – the executioner, the crucifier and the one who drowns others. Pharaoh's demise clearly ties into the saying that "those who are drowned drown those who drowned them." This would explain why "the one who drowns" is the last villain listed, since that reference leads into the statement about Pharaoh. Why then mention the executioner and the crucifier? With memories of the Roman Empire at hand, it is hard to imagine these as referring to anything other than an eschatological hope that God would recompense Rome as he had Pharaoh. However, a similar saying is placed on the lips of R. Eliezer the son of R. Jose the Galilean in the *Midrash Tehillim* (*Midr. Ps.* 22:15), and there the "crucifier" passage is applied retrospectively to Haman, who himself was crucified on his own cross.[35] Nevertheless, perhaps even here the encouragement to the ancient Jewish readers would have been that: Just as God has worked to bring recompense on Israel's foes in the past, so he shall do so in the future.

In light of these fairly strong depictions of God as one who favours the crucifixion of the crucifier, it is only appropriate that we end on another citation from the (relatively late) rabbinic work *Midrash Tehillim*:[36]

בנוהג שבעולם אם יכה אדם בנו של אפרכוס או בנו של מלך, נוטלין את ראשו,
ושורפין אותו, או צולבין אותו, אבל הקב"ה אינו כן, אלא כעל גמולות כעל ישלם, חמה
לצריו גמול לאויביו, לכך נאמר את גמולך שגמלת לנו, וכן יש בספר ירמיה תשיב להם
גמול ה' כמעשה ידיהם,

In the custom of those in the world, if a man strikes the son of a governor or the son of a king, then they remove his head, and burn him or crucify him. But the Holy One, blessed be He,

---

[35] Braude's translation reads: "Of this it is written *Say unto God: 'How terrible are thy works?'* (Ps. 66:3), a verse that R. Eliezer the son of R. Jose the Galilean interpreted as follows: How terrifying are Thy works! For they that were to be slain, slew those who would have slain them; and they that were to be hanged, hanged those who would have hanged them [הנצלבין צולבין את צולביהן] – 'those who are crucified crucify their crucifiers']; and they that were to be drowned, drowned those who would have drowned them; and they that were to be burned, burned those who would have burned them; and they that were to be cast into the lions' den, cast into it those who would have cast them. And the instances? [Then follow the examples: Pharaoh (drowned), Nebuchadnezzar (furnace), Persians and Medes (Daniel lions' den), and Haman (crucified)...] The wicked Haman was up all night preparing a gallows fifty cubits high to hang Mordecai on; but in the morning Haman himself and his sons were hanged thereon, as is said *They hanged Haman on the gallows that he had prepared for Mordecai* (Esther 7:10), and as is also said *The king... commanded... that he and his sons should be hanged on the gallows* (Esther 9:25)." Translation in William G. Braude, *The Midrash on Psalms*, 2 vols., Yale Judaica 13 (New Haven: Yale University Press, 1959), 1:309–311.

[36] *Midr. Psa.* 121:3. Translation may be found in Braude, *Midrash on Psalms*, 2:299. Translation below is mine. Stemberger (*Introduction*, 323) dates the redaction of the second half of the *Midrash Tehillim* (on Pss 119–150) to the thirteenth century (or possibly earlier).

does not do thus. But "according to rewards accordingly he will repay– wrath to his foes, recompense to his enemies" (Isa 59:18). Thus it is said, "[Daughter of Babylon, who is devastated, blessed will be the one who repays you] with your recompense which you paid to us" (Ps 137:8) And thus there is in the book of Jeremiah, "You, Lord, will return to them recompense according to the work of their hands." (Lam 3:64).

This passage assures the reader that the eschatological recompense of God is not excessive, but is in keeping with the injury received. The government leaders may be so angry at a slight injury to one of their children that they may go to extreme measures to judge the perpetrator – even crucifying them (apparently *post mortem*). God, however, only returns just recompense to his enemies. The passages from Isaiah, Psalms and Lamentations are connected by *gezerah shewa* (each containing גמול), with all citations being drawn from passages addressing the recompense to be rendered to Israel's gentile opponents. In this case, this means that God equitably will devastate Babylon as she has devastated God's people.

In sum, each of these rabbinic texts displays ongoing Jewish awareness of brigands being crucified by the authorities. The texts above are largely haggadic developments from both *Tannaim* and *Amoraim*. No sympathy is shown from any of these rabbis to the brigands. Rather, the brigands' wickedness is assumed, and their crucifixions appear to be a fitting consequence of their actions. In one instance a story/proverb of brigandage serves to warn of the dangers of the ensnaring woman. However, generally narratives and aphorisms about brigandage and crucifixion are employed to speak of eschatological reversal, especially to portray God's victorious recompense on Pharaoh and the nations.

3. Rabbinic Case Law

The repeated mention of crucifixion in rabbinic case law is in some ways reminiscent of rabbinic proverbial imagery. Here crucifixion serves as the extreme case by which one can test the application of rabbinic legal principles. Earlier chapters have addressed rabbinic law as it relates to Deuteronomy 21:22–23, where the officially recorded rabbinic opinion insists that Jewish *post mortem* suspension ought to be distinguished from Roman crucifixion methods.[37] The previous chapter also discussed how rabbinic case law dealt with the magical use of crucifixion nails, associating such practices with the disavowed "ways of the Amorite."[38] In addition to these, there are a few other occasions where crucifixion is referenced in rabbinic halakhah.

---

[37] Especially *Sifre Deut.* 221; *b. Sanh.* 46b. See above in chapter 3, §4.7.

[38] This halakhah is found in *m. Šabb.* 6:10; *y. Šabb.* 6:9 [8c]; *b. Šabb.* 67a. See above in chapter 4, §2.

For example, the dripping blood of a crucified person becomes a case study for discussing purity legislation (*m. Ohol.* 3:5):

איזהו דם תבוסה. צלוב שדמו שותת ונמצא תחתיו רביעית דם. טמא. אבל המת שדמו
מנטף ונמצא תחתיו רביעית דם טהור. רבי יהודה אומר לא כי. אלא השותת. טהור.
והמנטף. טמא :

What counts as 'mixed blood'? [Concerning] one who was crucified, whose blood flows out, and under whom was found a quarter [of a *log*] of blood, [that blood] is unclean. But [concerning] the corpse, whose blood drips, and under whom was found a quarter [of a *log*] of blood, [that blood] is clean. Rabbi Judah says: It is not so, but [the blood] that flows out is clean, and [the blood] that drips is unclean.

This discussion (also cf. *t. Ohol.* 4:11; *b. Nid.* 71b) concerns under what circumstances blood from a cadaver renders the ground beneath it unclean. The measurement "*log*" [= לוג] equaled the contents of six eggs; a רביעית is a fourth of a לוג. A quarter-*log* of blood from a dead person renders a dwelling unclean. However, the rabbis also considered unclean the blood from a dead person that was "mixed" with his or her own blood while he or she was still alive (cf. *m. Ohol.* 2:2). Crucifixion fits into the category of mixed blood because a person bleeds while both alive and dead in the same place.

According to *m. Ohol.* 3:5, the great tannaitic rabbis were not all in agreement about what proportions of blood (blood from the person while living or while dead) constituted a full quarter-*log* of mixed blood. The Mishnah favors Rabbi Akiba's position that mixed blood constitutes one-eighth-*log* of both blood in life and blood in death (i.e., if half the blood is from a dead person, it is enough to constitute a quarter-*log* together). There are dissenting opinions from both R. Ishmael (you need a quarter-*log* of each) and R. Eleazar son of R. Judah.

In the passage cited above, R. Judah presumes that blood drips out of a dead body, and gushes out of one who is still alive. Thus he argues that dripping blood is of greater concern. However, the other opinion (which is either the majority opinion, or that of R. Eleazar)[39] apparently contends that the discrete drops of blood from a dripping corpse each count as disconnected events that individually do not satisfy the "quarter-*log*" requirement; whereas flowing blood, since it consists of one continuous stream, can provide enough blood at one time to achieve the quarter-*log* (this is clarified in *t. Ohol.* 4:11). Interestingly, the Tosefta and the Bavli (*t. Ohol.* 4:11; *b. Nid.* 71b) both portray R. Judah as arguing for virtually the opposite position concerning the

---

[39] Blackman suggests that this is R. Eleazar's view, continuing the statement that is attributed to R. Eleazar in the immediately preceding clause. Blackman also suggests that R. Eleazar is the disciple of Judah, rather than his son. See Philip Blackman, *Mishnayoth*, 2nd ed., 7 vols. (New York: Judaica Press, 1964), 6:214. However, most other translators assume that Eleazar is Judah's son, and thus either a second-or a fourth-generation Tanna; see Stemberger, *Introduction*, 75, 80.

impurity of dripping blood from a crucified victim as he does in the Mishnah (with Judah's position in the Mishnah being attributed by the Tosefta and the Bavli to R. Simeon). In this alternative rendering, R. Judah contends that one does not know whether the drop of blood that is associated with death has yet fallen to the ground; since the final drop of death might still remain on the cross, the dripping blood is considered clean by R. Judah.

From the standpoint of this present study, a few matters are worth observing. First, this bit of case law assumes that the form of death represented by the word צלוב involves a prolonged bloody death, for a person so executed can be presumed to have bled both while alive and while dead. This coheres well with the argument that death via a צליבה refers to death by crucifixion, and it reminds us just how gruesome crucifixion could be. Second, there is nothing in itself in the blood of a crucified person that renders that blood any more impure than blood from some other cadaver. The question that arises in this discussion stems not from the act of crucifixion *per se*, but from the mingling of blood of life and blood of death. Third, crucifixion here serves as a particularly good test event for determining exactly what legally should be meant by "mixed blood"; that is, crucifixion can make for interesting case law.

Another place where crucifixion enters into halakhic discussions concerns the standards required for accepting a writ of divorce (*t. Giṭ.* 7[5]:1):

היה צלוב ומגוייד ורמז לכתוב גט לאשתו כותבין ונותנין לה כל זמן שיש בו נשמה

[If] there was one being crucified and bleeding to death, and he gestures [to them] to write a writ of divorce to his wife. They write and give [it] to her, as long as there is breath in him.

The matter here concerns under what circumstances a man's non-verbal consent may be sufficient to enact a divorce. The immediately following case involves a person who is so ill that he cannot speak (they must test him three times). Yet, by the time of the Talmuds (esp. *b. Giṭ.* 70b), the tradition is that the man must both gesture *and speak* (ורמז ואמר כתבו גט לאשתי).[40] In the talmudic Gemara, this passage is invoked concerning debates over whether the person has to remain conscious and clear-headed in order for the writ to be enforced. There in the Talmuds, it appears that a person in such a state may be thought to have drifted in and out of consciousness.

One interpretive issue in the Tosefta concerns the use of the *waw* on ומגוייד. The Neusner translation understands this as "or," but the more natural reading would be "and"; thus, the person here is thought to be bleeding to death while being crucified. Note how this would be consistent with the *Oholoth* traditions just discussed above. However, both Talmudic traditions later render the connection with או instead of the *waw*; this clearly indicates that two different deaths (crucifixion *or* bleeding to death) are in view among

---

[40] Cf. *y. Giṭ.* 7:1 [48c], which has the same clause, except it reads לאשתו.

later interpreters (*y. Giṭ.* 7:1 [48c]; *b. Giṭ.* 70b). The Bavli even reverses the order of clauses to read "and they saw him bleeding to death or being cruci-fied on the cross."[41]

This case law indicates: First, a person dying via צלוב could be thought to remain conscious for at least part of the process, and this would indicate a prolonged death, such as was common with crucifixion. Second, it is possible that, in the earliest form of the tradition, this death also was thought to pro-duce much bleeding. Third, a person crucified could still be considered capable (both mentally and morally) of enacting a major legal procedure.

The tractate *Yebamoth* concerns itself, in part, with determining under what circumstances a woman may remarry, given the evidence of her hus-band's death. The Mishnah discusses crucifixion as one case example (*m. Yeb.* 16:3):

אין מעידין אלא עד שתצא נפשו, ואפילו ראוהו מגויד, וצלוב, והחיה אוכלת בו.

They do not witness [his death] except until his soul departs, even if they saw him bleeding to death, and being crucified, and the wild beast eating him.

This case assumes that one might see a person in such a state and anticipate that death will soon inevitably follow; yet, potentially the person could still survive. Death must absolutely be assured before the wife can remarry, so conclusive evidence must be presented for her husband's demise. Merely seeing a person in the process of crucifixion is not sufficient to assure his having expired. This would certainly indicate that crucifixion is in view in this passage (וצלוב), since the person is hung with a view to a prolonged lin-gering death.[42] Therefore, this passage presupposes the hypothetical possibility that one might be taken down from the cross and live (cf. Josephus, *Vita* 420–421). The Gemara of the Palestinian Talmud supplies a possible reason such a crucified person might survive: A Roman matron might redeem him from the cross before he has died.[43]

---

[41] In *b. Giṭ.* 70b: ראוהו מגויד או צלוב על הצליבה – "they saw him bleeding to death or being crucified on the cross." In this context in the Bavli, the cutting open of the person seems more important than crucifixion, for the tradition here is used to prove R Judah's statement (in the name of R. Samuel) that a man who has "two passages" cut can still gesture for a writ of divorce.

[42] The Mishnah cited in the Jerusalem Talmud further designates the impending death as "being crucified on the cross" (וצלוב על הצליב; *y. Yeb.* 16:3)

[43] *y. Yeb.* 16:3: וצלוב על הצלוב אומר אני מטרונא עברה עליו ופדאתו – "And [con-cerning] he who is crucified on the cross, I say the matron came upon him and redeemed him." Josephus (*Vita* 420) records having asked for three crucified friends to be removed from the cross and to receive medical care – one does survive, though two perish (see chpt. 2, §3.5). Cf. *Midr. Psa.* 45:5: in a parable a Roman matron redeems three men on their way to being crucified (שלשה יוצאין ליצלב – "three were going out to be crucified"), in a reversal of disposition they later end up carry the standards of the king; however, note in the text that these men do not yet appear to have been pinned to their crosses.

Again here, most English translations treat these three modes of death in *m. Yeb.* 16:3 as discrete case situations by rendering the *waw* with "or" ('bleeding to death, *or* being crucified, *or* the wild beast eating him').[44] This is certainly possible, but one might wonder if the more natural understanding of the *waw*-sequence is to describe a single extreme case during which a person is bleeding alive on a cross, while facing wild beasts. Such a scenario is certainly consistent with some ancient depictions of crucifixion. This would also explain the otherwise inconsistent statement in the Tosefta and in the Bavli that one does not accept death testimony when a person is crucified, but one does accept death testimony when a person was bleeding to death (even apart from actually witnessing the departing of the soul).[45] However, the Yerushalmi, despite containing a Mishnaic text where the modes of death are connected by the *waw*-sequence, still treats these as discrete forms of death in its Gemara.[46]

In another example of crucifixion in rabbinic case law, an extra-canonical tractate ordains that the family should cease to reside near the crucified body until its flesh has sufficiently decayed (*Semaḥot* ii.11 [44b]).[47]

מי שהיה בעלה צלוב עמה בעיר, אשתו צלובה עמו בעיר, אביו ואמו צלובין עמו – לא
ישרה באותה העיר אלא אם כן היתה עיר גדולה כאנטוכיא. לא ישרה בצד זה, אבל
ישרה בצד אחר. עד מתי הוא אסור? עד שיכלה הבשר, ואין הצורה ניכרת בעצמות

[A wife] whose husband was crucified[48] in her city,[49] [a man] whose wife is crucified in his city, [a person] whose father and his mother are crucified [in] his [city] – [such a person]

---

[44] So the translations by Danby, Blackman, and Neusner.

[45] See *t. Yeb.* 14:4: נצלב אין מעידין עליו נתגייר מעידין עליו – "[If] he was crucified, they do not witness concerning him; [if] he were bleeding to death, they witness concerning him." However, an opposing view is immediately stated by R. Simeon b. Eleazar concerning one who is bleeding to death, since Simeon believes such a person can be healed and live. This same debate is recounted in *b. Yeb.* 120b, which notes that the majority view (i.e., accepting the witness about a man who is bleeding to death) comes with Tannaitic authority (רבנן דתניא).

[46] *y. Yeb.* 16:3. A person can face a sword and live, or a matron can redeem the crucified, or a person attacked by a wild beast may survive by being shown mercy from heaven.

[47] Text in Dov Zlotnick, *The Tractate Mourning*, Yale Judaica (New Haven: Yale University Press, 1966), p. 4 (text pagination) – pointing removed. The translation is mine. In the Rabbinowitz (Soncino) translation this is listed as "Rule 13"; see J. Rabbinowitz, "Ebel Rabbathi Named Masseketh Semahoth: Tractate on Mourning," in *The Minor Tractates of the Talmud*, ed. A. Cohen, vol. 1 (London: Soncino, 1965), 334. Stemberger (*Introduction*, 229) follows Zlotnick in suggesting a fairly early date for the tractate (even as early as the third century).

[48] Rabbinowitz ("Ebel Rabbathi," 334) translates צלוב as "impaled," even though he acknowledges that this passage envisions a penalty enacted by the Roman authorities during which a person would be suspended for view.

[49] עמו בעיר – literally "with him in the city"; i.e., "in her city." A similar idiom is also found in the next two clauses.

should not dwell in that city, unless a city as large as Antioch. He [whose family member was crucified] should not dwell within this border; rather, [such a] mourner should dwell within another border.[50] Until when is this forbidden? Until the flesh was consumed, and there is not the form [of the person] remembered in the bones.

This tractate (also known as *Ebel Rabbati* – 'Great Mourning') depicts the laws of burial. It is likely that this legislation is designed to remove the immediate family from the shame associated with crucifixion, especially since the crucified victims still would have been suspended for public view.[51] In a city as large as Antioch, one could potentially remain anonymous; but in any other smaller town the family might have been connected to the victim. When the person can no longer be identified (even their skeleton no longer betrays family resemblance), the family can hope to return. One interesting feature of this text concerns the assumption that both men and women may face the cross; hence, a man's wife or a person's mother might be crucified. It would be nice to know for what reason such people were pinned to the cross, and here I am inclined to speculate that this was connected with the crucifixion of brigands (since this would bring greater shame on the family than a crucified Jewish nationalist),[52] yet we must admit that the text does not overtly address this.

Just a few lines earlier in this tractate there is another passage that likely implies that the family of the crucified person should not attempt to steal the body off the cross (*Śemaḥot* ii.9 [44b]):[53]

הרוגי מלכות, אין מונעין מהן מכל לכל דבר. מאימתי מתחילין להן למנות? משעת שנתיאשו מלשאול, אבל לא מלגנוב. כל הגונב, הרי זה שופך דמים, ולא כשופך דמים בלבד – אלא כעובד עבודה זרה, ומגלה עריות, ומחלל שבתות

[Concerning] those executed by a government – there shall not be a withholding from them of any matter [i.e., of any funeral rite]. When do they begin to count their death? From the time they give up hope from asking [for the corpse], but not from stealing [the corpse].[54] Everyone who steals [the corpse], such a person is [like] one who sheds blood – and not only like one

---

[50] This is understood by both Zlotnick and Rabbinowitz to indicate that, if the mourning family lives in a city as large as Antioch, then they should move to a new section of the city. See Zlotnick, *Tractate Mourning*, 36; Rabbinowitz, "Ebel Rabbathi," 334.

[51] A similar opinion is found in Zlotnick, *Tractate Mourning*, 105. Rabbinowitz oddly suggests ("Ebel Rabbathi," 334): "On seeing him, people will recall the impaling of his relative, and that would be a slight on the memory of the victim."

[52] Another possibility is that the text does address families of crucified Jewish rebels, in which case this rabbinic ruling may be designed to release them from mourning rites in order to escape family detection by the Romans. Nevertheless, the avoidance of the shame of the cross seems to me the more likely explanation.

[53] Text in Zlotnick, *Tractate Mourning*, 4 (text) – pointing removed. This is called "Rule 11" in Rabbinowitz, "Ebel Rabbathi," 333.

[54] Zlotnick follows Lieberman in suggesting that the item to be stolen here is the body of the executed victim (Zlotnick, *Tractate Mourning*, 104). This certainly coheres with the context of the passage.

who sheds blood, but also as like one who serves foreign idols, and one who uncovers nakedness, and one who profanes Sabbaths.

The word for "executed" (הרוגי) is fairly nondescript, in that it does not necessarily spell out the form of execution, though it often can be used to designate execution by the sword. Such executions in this historical context are clearly ones carried out by the Roman government. More importantly, central to this passage is the assumption that the victim's body may be very difficult to reclaim (although it could potentially be stolen). In this sense, whether this text directly applied to crucifixion (as to bodies publicly exposed for extended times by the government) or whether it would simply apply *a minori ad maius* to crucifixion (via *qal wa-ḥomer*; lesser-to-greater), it is probable that this passage stems from rabbinic desire to discourage the stealing of bodies from Roman execution devices. The concern is so great here that such a person is compared to the most heinous defilers of Jewish religion – the murderer, the idolater, the adulterer, and the Sabbath-breaker (all these directly disobey the Ten Commandments).[55] This could be thought to speak to the thief's own personal moral status (note that theft also coheres with the allusions to the Ten Commandments).[56] However, it seems more likely that the person here, by attempting to steal from the Roman government a body that is being held for official posthumous punishment, actually could imperil the whole Jewish community under Roman rule. This would explain why the passage then goes on (immediately after the text cited above) to parallel this person, who seeks to steal the corpse of a execution victim, with one who seeks to steal past customs (הגונב את המכס) and with one who seeks to steal past the *ḥerem* (הגונב את החרם).[57] In each case, these actions, as acts against the government, could bring sanction on the whole Jewish community. There-

---

[55] Rabbinowitz ("Ebel Rabbathi," 334) attempts to explain away the text as a scribal error: "This sentence is repeated from the last clause of Rule 9 and has no relevance to the present context." The clause Rabbinowitz mentions in his Rule 9 [= Zlotnick ii.7] is omitted altogether in the text reprinted by Zlotnick.

[56] In a related sense, Zlotnick (*Tractate Mourning*, 104) quotes favourably from Naḥmanides: "When fleeing, they put their lives in danger, and at times came close to profaning the Sabbath and worshipping idols." Despite Naḥmanides' great wisdom, this seems quite a reach: How is it that they come close to worshipping idols? Why is adultery invoked in the text?

[57] There is a strong parallel in the passage between "stealing the body," "stealing past customs" and "stealing past the *ḥerem*." Each of these is compared (with identical wording) to the murderer, the idolator, the adulterer, and the Sabbath-breaker. The exact meaning of (*ḥerem*) is in doubt, but Zlotnick (*Tractate Mourning*, 104) suggests that it refers to the *ḥaramin* of *m. Ned.* 3:4, where it likely refers to official tax-gatherers (or "confiscators") – "They may vow to executioners ['murderers' in Blackman's translation], and to confiscators (ולחרמין), and to tax-collectors that it is the heave-offering (תרומה), even though it is not the heave-offering, [or] that they belong to the king's household, even though they do not belong to the king's household."

fore, the rabbis forbid the stealing of the corpse (even for purposes of burial) in the strongest possible terms.[58]

In any case, it should be noted that here in the text of *Semaḥot* the family should engage in the typical public mourning-rites for a person executed by the Romans (even without access to the corpse). This can be contrasted with those executed by Jewish rabbinic courts, since such a person is not to be publicly mourned by the family at all (*Šem.* ii.6; cf. *m. Sanh.* vi.6).

Summary. Rabbinic case law employs crucifixion on several occasions in order to investigate the ramifications of traditional rabbinic halakhah. When taken together, these passages clearly indicate that tannaitic rabbis were well aware of the tendency for the Roman government to execute criminals on the cross. These discussions also testify to how such an executionary form involved a prolonged bloody death suspended (צלוב) on a cross (צליבה). A crucified person could remain conscious long enough to signal legally binding decisions. It was even hypothetically possible that a crucified person could be brought down from the cross (before having expired) and still live. Women potentially faced crucifixion as did men. Crucified victims (like others executed by the Romans) are to be mourned (unlike those executed by the Sanhedrin), though one certainly should not anger the Roman government by attempting to steal the body.

The blood of the crucifixion victim is no more or less impure than that of a typical cadaver; and his or her corpse is to be given the same burial rights (when this is practical). Also, the crucified person is still considered trustworthy enough legally to accept his call for a writ of divorce. Thus, in light of the occasional application of the "curse of God" statement to the crucified victim (in keeping with Deut 21:22–23, see above in chapter 3, §4), it is important in these applications of case law to note that the crucified person has not been so defiled by his or her form of execution as to be rendered more impure than any other dying person, or more untrustworthy. Nevertheless, given the shame associated with a publicly crucified person, one rabbinic tradition instructs families of these victims in most cases to move from their own city until the body is unrecognizable.

4. Latent Imagery and Crucifixion

By "latent image" is meant a conception that was not necessarily formally recognized in connection with crucifixion by Jewish people in antiquity, but

---

[58] One might contrast this with opposing perspectives from other Jewish literature, such as Tobit 1:16–20. Tobit, out of great religious devotion, buries the bodies of fellow Jews executed by Sennacherib, even to the point where Tobit's own property was confiscated in punishment, and he was hunted down for execution.

that could later be used by early Christians as a (pre-)figuration of the cross. While there are several of these in the stock-in-trade of early Christian authors, two deserve particular note because of their claim to Jewish ancestry (traced below) and the attention they have received in recent scholarship.

4.1 The Binding of Isaac

ויקח אברהם את עצי העולה [וישם על יצחק בנו] כזה שטוען צלובו בכתפו

"And Abraham took the wood of the burnt-offering [and he placed it on Isaac his son]" (Gen 22:6) – as one who bears his cross on his shoulder. (*Gen. Rab.* lvi.3)

The *ʿAqedah* (binding of Isaac) has long played a special role in Judaism, as witnessed in antiquity on the murals of ancient synagogues and in literature from the period. Notably, while *Bereshit Rabbah* grants significant space to the midrash of this biblical episode, on the exposition of Gen 22:6a the Midrash gives only four brief Hebrew words (כזה שטוען צלובו בכתפו; "as one who bears his cross on his shoulder") before speeding on to talk about the knife that was employed (cf. Gen 22:6b).[59]

The bracketed portion (וישם על יצחק בנו; "and he placed it on Isaac his son") is missing in many major manuscripts, although it is present in the important Vatican manuscript.[60] Without this phrase, one might conclude that Abraham was the one bearing the wood as if a cross. However, even if the bracketed text referring to Isaac is not deemed original, in keeping with standard rabbinic procedure the short allusion to Genesis 22:6 would have intentionally brought to mind the whole biblical passage, including the reference to Isaac. Moreover, other parallel rabbinic traditions focus on Isaac as the one carrying the wood (see below).

This analogy in *Bereshit Rabbah* is tantalizingly short, and the context provides no clue (aside from the mention of wood) as to why some rabbis could compare the *ʿAqedah* to crucifixion. Nor is this saying attributed to any rabbi, which could help to date this tradition. Of course, it is well known that criminals executed on Roman crosses could be asked to bear their own

---

[59] The *Bereshit Rabbah* is often understood to be among the oldest of the works collected in the *Midrash Rabbah*. Hence Stemberger has argued for an early fifth-century date (*Introduction*, 279).

[60] J. Theodor and Ch. Albeck, *Bereschit Rabba*, 3 (+ 2 Register) vols. (Berlin: M. Poppelauer, 1912–1936), 2:598. All the major MSS cited by them omit the bracketed material (though the modern edition of *Yalqut Shimoni* 100 [on Gen 22:6] contains it). However, MS Vatican 60 does include the longer text; see *Midrash Bereshit Rabba: Codex Vatican 60 (Ms. Vat. Ebr. 60): A Previously Unknown Manuscript, Recently Established as the Earliest and Most Important Version of Bereshit Rabba*, (Jerusalem: Makor, 1972), p. 209 [=105a]. The published Geniza fragments do not cover this portion of the text; cf. Michael Sokoloff, *The Geniza Fragments of Bereshit Rabba: Edited on the Basis of Twelve Manuscripts and Palimpsests* (Jerusalem: Israel Academy of Sciences and Humanities, 1982), 137.

implement of pain and death to the place of execution,[61] so the analogy is quite apt.

Kessler has remarked how unusual it is that this text, when compared to other pericopes in midrashic literature, appears without elucidating interpretation.[62] He suggests that this may be due to concerns about Christian reaction or censorship. Kessler also postulates that the popularity of Genesis Rabbah may have made this brief text too well known to permit easy deletion of such a controversial statement.[63]

In the later compilation *Pesiqta Rabbati* (31:2), the crucifixion analogy reappears with further development. In context, "Zion" is portrayed as attempting to excuse its failings since its children, fathers, and women were only following the bad examples of the nations around them. God replies that good examples were known from the patriarchs:[64]

אברהם שאמרתי לו להביא את יצחק בנו ולא עיכב ויצחק היה טעון עצים כאדם שטען
את הצלוב שלו ושרה כשבאו המלאכים לבשרה והניח כל שפחותיי[65] ולשה ועשת' עוגו',
יצחק בנו של אברהם טעון עצים לבוא להתקרב לפניי ואתם הבנים מלקטי' עצים לע"ז

Abraham, when I said to him to bring Isaac his son, did not hesitate. And Isaac was carrying sticks of wood as a man who carries his cross. And Sarah, when the messengers came to bear good tidings, she made all her handmaids rest, and she kneaded and made cakes. Isaac, the son of Abraham, carries sticks of wood to go to be sacrificed before Me. But you, [your] sons gather sticks of wood[66] to serve strange gods.

The passage then concludes with a further contrast (not cited above) between righteous Abraham and Sarah versus the people of Zion. The reference to Isaac carrying the wood forms part of the whole midrashic structure, thus it likely goes back to the earliest recension of this pericope in *Pesiqta Rabbati*. In Jewish tradition Isaac often stands out as a righteous figure in the ʿ*Aqedah*,

---

[61] Cf. Hengel, *Crucifixion*, 25 (repr. 117).

[62] See Edward Kessler, *Bound by the Bible: Jews, Christians and the sacrifice of Isaac* (Cambridge: Cambridge University Press, 2004), 113–114. Originally this argument appeared in Edward Kessler, "A Study of the Relationship between Judaism and Christianity in the First Six Centuries CE through an Analysis of Jewish and Christian Interpretations of Genesis 22:1–14" (PhD diss., University of Cambridge, 1999), 98.

[63] Kessler, *Bound by the Bible*, 114.

[64] The text here follows the *editio princeps* (53d–54a) as it is recorded in Rivka Ulmer, *Pesiqta Rabbati: A Synoptic Edition of Pesiqta Rabbati Based upon all Extant Manuscripts and the Editio Princeps*, 3 vols., South Florida Studies in the History of Judaism (Atlanta: Scholars Press [vols. 1–2]; Lanham, Maryland: University Press of America [vol. 3], 1997–2002), 2:735 (Ulmer lists this as *Pesiqta Rabbati* 31 §6). As reported in Ulmer there is no substantial variation (other than orthography) between this text and manuscripts Parma 3122 (184-b) and JTS 8195 (199–200). An English translation can also be found in William G. Braude, *Pesikta Rabbati: Discourses for Feasts, Fasts, and Special Sabbaths*, 2 vols., Yale Judaica 18 (New Haven: Yale University Press, 1968), 2:603. The translation here is mine.

[65] MS Parma 3122 (184b) adds עמדה והיא – "and she [Sarah] was standing."

[66] This is understood in the manuscripts as a reference to Jeremiah 7:18.

thus it is not surprising that he is viewed so here.[67] Since Isaac carries the wood, he is clearly the analog of the man about to be crucified.

Interestingly, there is an alternative version of this midrashic tradition found in the Buber edition of *Midrash Tanḥuma* (Wayyera 46):

ויקח אברהם [את עצי העולה וישם על יצחק בנו]. למה היה יצחק דומה למי שהיה יוצא לישרף ועציו על כתפיו[68]

"And Abraham took [the wood of the burnt-offering and he placed it on Isaac his son]" (Gen 22:6) To what was Isaac compared? To one who was going out to be burnt – and his wood on his shoulders.

As in *Pesiqta Rabbati* (and possibly in *Gen. Rab.*), here the focus is clearly on Isaac and his carrying of the wood. The unique feature of this tradition is that, where the two texts mentioned earlier have Isaac carrying wood as someone might carry a *cross*, here Isaac is compared to a person about to be executed by *burning*. In one sense, of course, this analogy is more straightforward, since Abraham's sacrifice was to be a burnt offering (העולה). However, Kessler has argued that the *Midrash Tanḥuma Buber* text represents an emendation of the *Genesis Rabbah* version, with the deletion of the צלוב indicating "Christian influence" requiring censorship to avoid "either unwarranted internal or external attention."[69]

It is indeed tempting to speculate that the original idea of crucifixion, so overt in *Genesis Rabbah* (a text often paralleled in both recensions of *Midrash Tanḥuma*) and continued in the *Pesiqta Rabbati*, has been altered in this version. Possibly the above analogy was simply conceived as more appropriate in its later sermonic context (crucifixion no longer being practiced). Or possibly it was intentionally altered – out of abhorrence of the practice of crucifixion itself, or out of concern over later Christian censors, or out of opposition to Christian analogies between Isaac and the crucified Jesus. Here one experiences the difficulty of interpreting this literature *vis-à-vis* potential Christian influence: that Isaac carries wood as a man to his own burning makes full sense on its own in light of the Jewish emphasis on Isaac as a burnt offering. Beyond that (*pace* Kessler), if a parallel crucifixion tradition is being revised, this does not need to be accounted for with reference to Christianity, though such a background remains possible.

All of these passages on the ʿAqedah and crucifixion come centuries after the origins of Christianity, with the earliest text being in current transcription

---

[67] Cf. Louis H. Feldman, "Josephus as a Biblical Interpreter: The ʿAQEDAH," *JQR* 75 (1985): esp. 234–45; Kessler, *Bound by the Bible*, 100–107.

[68] Salomon Buber, *Midrasch Tanchuma: Ein Agadischer Commentar zum Pentateuch von Rabbi Tanchuma ben Rabbi Abba* (Wilna: Wittwe & Gebrüder, 1885), pp. 113–14 (= 57a–b). The bracketed portion of the text is apparently supplied by Buber and is not to be found in his MSS.

[69] Kessler, *Bound by the Bible*, 114; Kessler, "Study," 99.

no more ancient than the fifth century.[70] Rabbinic traditions, of course, often serve to pass on genuinely older material, and this is especially true of the Palestinian midrash in *Bereshit Rabbah*. However, dating such individual traditions is remarkably tricky. And thus it is difficult to speak on the possible antiquity of the ʿ*Aqedah*/crucifixion analogy. Some have suggested that it predates the Christian use of the ʿ*Aqedah* as a prefigurement of Christ. On the other hand, others have proposed that the Jewish association of the ʿ*Aqedah* with the cross arose out of Jewish contact with Christian concepts.[71] In either event, it would be surprising if any crucifixion traditions linked to Isaac could have been transmitted for long by rabbis in an increasingly Christian society without some recognition of the Christian appropriation of similar concepts.[72]

Recent years have witnessed significant discussion concerning the Jewish development of the ʿ*Aqedah*. When did the ʿ*Aqedah* begin to take on its important significance for Jewish thought? At what point were redemptive connotations to be found in the development of the legend? How soon was it connected with the Passover traditions?[73] We have the space here neither to develop this debate nor to examine the central evidence. Nevertheless, even if a relatively early date were granted to the central traditions embedded in Jewish ʿ*Aqedah* legends, the explicit crucifixion texts treated above still are later than the formation of early Christianity. Perhaps the most cautious way to approach these Jewish crucifixion traditions found in midrash on the ʿ*Aqedah* is to recognize that, once a connection was made between crucifixion and the bearing of the wood to the place of Isaac's *Bindung*, there was sufficient resonance with this connection within certain circles in ancient Judaism that this analogy took hold of the haggadic imagination (even in the context of increasing Christian power in society).

---

[70] As noted above, Stemberger dates *Genesis Rabbah* to the early fifth century. He also holds that the *Pesiqta Rabbati* and *Midrash Tanḥuma* both represent traditions with highly complicated redaction histories (but with possible early recensions in the sixth to seventh centuries, and in the fifth century respectively). Stemberger, *Introduction*, 279, 302, 305–6.

[71] E.g., P. R. Davies and B. D. Chilton, "The Aqedah: A Revised Tradition History," *CBQ* 40 (1978): 539.

[72] See chapter 7 (§9) for Christian use of the ʿ*Aqedah*.

[73] Chilton and Davies view all expiatory significance in the binding of Isaac as a post-Temple phenomenon; see Davies and Chilton, "Aqedah," 514–36; Philip R. Davies, "Passover and the Dating of the Aqedah," *JJS* 30 (1979): 59–67; Bruce D. Chilton, "Isaac and the Second Night: a Consideration," *Bib* 61 (1980): 78–88. Others maintain that ʿ*Aqedah* traditions were well known previously in Judaism; see the responses to Davies and Chilton in, for example, Robert Hayward, "The Present State of Research into the Targumic Account of the Sacrifice of Isaac," *JJS* 32 (1981): 292–306; C. T. R. Hayward, "The Sacrifice of Isaac and Jewish Polemic Against Christianity," *CBQ* 52 (1990): 292–306; Geza Vermes, "New Light on the Sacrifice of Isaac from 4Q225," *JJS* 47 (1996): 143–46. For a review of positions cf. Lukas Kundert, *Die Opferung/Bindung Isaaks*, 2 vols., WMANT 78 & 79 (Neukirchen-Vluyn: Neukirchener Verlag, 1998), 1:7–28.

4.2 The Paschal Lamb

Joseph Tabory of Bar-Ilan University has succinctly but strongly argued that Justin Martyr correctly informs us that the paschal lamb was roasted and dressed as if attached to the cross.[74] Justin's report reads (*Dial.* xl.3)[75]:

Τὸ γὰρ ὀπτώμενον πρόβατον σχηματιζόμενον ὁμοίως τῷ σχήματι τοῦ σταυροῦ ὀπτᾶται· εἰς γὰρ ὄρθιος ὀβελίσκος διαπερονᾶται ἀπὸ τῶν κατωτάτω μερῶν μέχρι τῆς κεφαλῆς, καὶ εἰς πάλιν κατὰ τὸ μετάφρενον, ᾧ προσαρτῶνται καὶ αἱ χεῖρες τοῦ προβάτου.

For the lamb, which is roasted, is roasted and dressed up in the form of the cross. For one spit is transfixed right through from the lower parts up to the head, and one across the back, to which are attached the legs of lamb.

Tabory essentially contends that, while Justin could not have eyewitnessed the form of roasting in the Jerusalem Temple (having been born too late), it is likely that during his youth in Shechem he witnessed the ancient Samaritan method of roasting the paschal lamb. This method, which appears to have diverged from modern Samaritan practice, likely paralleled the ancient Jerusalem procedure.

Tabory's support for this includes: (1) Despite sanctioned Mishnaic practice (*m. Pes.* vii.1), a *baraita* in the Jerusalem Talmud contends that the spit should be inserted in the direction Justin mentions (*y. Pes.* vii.1 [34a]).[76] (2) Evidence from ancient Jewish paschal ovens indicates that the lamb would have been inserted in them with the spit vertical, as a man would be hung on a pole. (3) A second pole could be used in flaying the lamb before inserting the spit (*m. Pes.* v.9);[77] and comparison with modern Samaritan practice (likely of great antiquity) indicates that, when both the pole and the spit are in place, the effect created would be the appearance of a lamb skewered to a cross.

Tabory remarks that rabbinic tradition required the use of a wood spit, thus further producing an analog of the cross.[78] Further, just as the crucified man (who carries his cross to the place of execution) was first attached to the horizontal pole and then the vertical shaft, so too the lamb was first flayed on the horizontal pole and then skewered on the vertical spit. Tabory also notes that

---

[74] Joseph Tabory, "The Crucifixion of the Paschal Lamb," *JQR* 86 (1996): 395–406.

[75] Translation: ANF, 1:215 (following Tabory); text: Miroslav Marcovich, ed., *Iustini Martyris Dialogus cum Tryphone*, PTS 47 (Berlin: Walter de Gruyter, 1997), 137.

[76] The *baraita* reads: .אית תניי תני תוחבו מבית נקובתו עד שהוא מגיע לתוך פיו Tabory's translation: "There is a Tanna who teaches, 'They insert from the buttocks until it reaches the midst of the mouth.'"

[77] The Mishnah describes this practice as an "alternate procedure" (Tabory's words) when there are no hooks available from which to suspend the lambs for flaying. Tabory's claim that the animals were suspended by their legs for flaying can also be supported from *m. Tam.* iv.2.

[78] See Tabory, "Paschal Lamb," 398n (drawing on *m. Pes.* vii.1). The spit was wooden to avoid cooking the meat with a metal rod (since the meat must be roasted) – cf. *Mek.* Pisḥa 6; *y. Pes.* vii.1 [34a]; *b. Pes.* 74a.

the paschal lamb wore its own cleaned entrails on its head, much like a crown
– thus providing yet another comparison between the crucified Jesus and the
roasted paschal lamb.[79] Finally, Tabory connects this head-up vertical position of the paschal lamb to the portrayal in the Beit Alpha mosaic of the ram
that took Isaac's place on the altar, contending that the roasting of the paschal
lamb influenced the portrayal of the ram in Jewish art on the *'Aqedah*.

Tabory's argumentation on the whole is persuasive. His most difficult task
involves establishing a head-up vertical position for the roasting of the lamb.[80]
Even here his argumentation is substantial. But it is worth noting that, while
the head-up position is necessary in order to verify the detail that Justin supplies about the direction of inserting the spit, the analogy with the cross really
only requires the employment of two poles.[81]

Tabory is careful not to fully suggest that this cruciform roasting technique
was an intentional pre-Christian mimicry of crucifixion, though he allows
implications to stand that cause one to wonder how far he is willing to go.
Certainly, the Jewish materials involved so far in the discussion do not provide support for an intentional connection of the paschal lamb with the
crucifixion cross.

However, although it is improbable that they developed the roasting technique in mimicry of crucifixion, in light of the frequency of execution by
crucifixion in the Roman period (and before), it is conceivable that such an
analogy may have struck non-Christian as well as Christian Jews. At the very
least, the roasting of the paschal lamb represents a latent image that later
could be exploited by Justin as an analog of the cross of Jesus.

4.3 Summary: Latent Imagery

Thus in the binding of Isaac and in the roasting of the paschal lamb there are
Jewish traditions that could be understood to parallel the plight of the crucified person. Of these two, the binding of Isaac is particularly striking in that,
even after Christianity could be considered a rival to Judaism, an analogy
with crucifixion still captured the imagination of some rabbis. However,
unlike other Jewish traditions discussed in this thesis, we lack firm evidence
that any Jewish people themselves conceived of such crucifixion analogies
prior to the origins of Christianity. The Isaac analogy is only found in later

---

[79] Cf. *y. Pes.* vii.1 [34a].

[80] Note the disagreement over the interpretation of the relevant passages in the traditional
commentaries. See the notes of Bokser and Schiffman in Jacob Neusner, et al., *The Talmud of
the Land of Israel: A Preliminary Translation and Explanation*, 35 vols. (Chicago: University
of Chicago Press, 1982–1994), 13:547 (note 6).

[81] Consider that some Christian traditions can portray Peter as crucified upside down (the
question here is not the accuracy of such a tradition, but that this can still be considered a
death on a cross).

rabbinic sources. And concerning the paschal lamb imagery, we must admit that a Christian apologist is the only extant ancient author to have noted the parallel with crucifixion and the direction of the lamb roasting. Nevertheless, at the very least, these traditions formed latent images – images that already had some resonance within Jewish life and thought, and that could be employed by others who sought to explain the import of the crucified messiah from Nazareth.

Chapter Six

Perceptions of Crucifixion in Ancient Jewish Communities: A Summary

The previous chapters indicate that Jewish people in the Second Temple and early rabbinic periods frequently witnessed acts of crucifixion. Crucifixion itself could take different forms, and it was likely considered to function within the broader sphere of *ante-* and *post-mortem* human bodily suspension penalties. In such an environment, Jewish sources evidence various views concerning the act of crucifixion, and concerning the people who faced such a harsh death. The perceptions these materials betray can be summarized firstly in tendencies detectable in individual writers or bodies of writings, and secondly in themes discernible throughout the literature.

1. Literary Sources

A few brief comments should be made concerning individual tendencies in sub-groups of the literature.

1. *Philo*, in an historical report, lists crucifixion as one of the most excruciating outrages of Flaccus against the Alexandrian Jews (*Flacc.* 72). However, Philo does not make the victims into martyrs; and, in order to win the reader to his position, Philo relies on Flaccus' breach of the traditional clemency offered on imperial birthdays rather than indicting crucifixion as an unacceptable penalty (*Flacc.* 83–85). Elsewhere, Philo simply assumes crucifixion to be a background part of society, repeatedly employing the cross as one of his illustrative metaphors – often in conjunction with an allegorical treatment of pentateuchal κρεμάννυμι [αὐτὸν] ἐπὶ ξύλου texts.[1] In such allegorical expositions crucifixion served, for example, as a vivid warning against the dangers of giving oneself over to bodily desire. Philo also believed crucifixion to be God's ordained punishment for those who take human life, drawing on Deuteronomy 21:22–23 (*Spec. Leg.* iii.151–52, possibly referring to brigands).

2. *Josephus*, as noted in chapter 2, often merely reports crucifixion events without condemning the crucifiers *per se* (especially in his Roman accounts).

---

[1] See chapter 3, §§ 2.1 & 4.4 (concerning Gen 40 and Deut 21) and chapter 5, §1.

The exceptions appear when the appropriate class boundaries are not upheld (*Bell.* ii.306–8), or when Roman soldiers exhibit too much lust for cruelty (e.g., *Bell.* v.449–51). Nevertheless, Josephus readily recognized the harshness of the penalty, as evidenced by his attitude to the punishment of his own friends (*Vita* 420–21) as well as witnessed in his depictions of other scenes (esp. *Bell.* vii.201–3 – θανάτων τὸν οἴκτιστον, "the most pitiable of deaths").[2] There are also martyrological overtones in some of Josephus' pre-Roman crucifixion accounts (esp. *Ant.* xii.255–56, where Jewish families are crucified under Antiochus Epiphanes for following their ancestral customs).

Like Philo, Josephus renders some key biblical "hanging on a tree" texts by employing crucifixion terminology (especially concerning the stories of the baker from Genesis 40 and of Haman in Josephus' Esther account). However, Josephus is more circumspect than Philo in attaching crucifixion associations to Deuteronomy 21:22–23 (save indirectly in *Bell.* iv.317). Also, Josephus never allows a biblical Jewish protagonist to commit an act of crucifixion (noticeably omitting suspension episodes involving Joshua or David). Finally, Josephus soundly condemns the actions of the one Jewish leader (Alexander Jannaeus) who does crucify.[3] Thus, while Josephus does not denounce crucifixion as a Roman activity, he also appears quite reticent to admit the same as an acceptable Jewish punishment. In this regard, Josephus' attitudes mirror those of the rabbis.

3. *Targumim and rabbinic literature* represent large and diverse bodies of works, yet it is useful to summarize some trends in these materials as well. The targumim employ the term צלב (and its cognates) for all biblical episodes of human penal suspension (especially in rendering those Hebrew texts that employed תלה על העץ or הוקע). Because of its focused application in this literature, צלב and its cognates served as specialized technical vocabulary for human bodily suspension; and thus such a term employed in the targumim conceptually brings these biblical episodes well into the realm of penalties that included crucifixion in antiquity. However, sometimes the targumic traditions also seek to conform those biblical texts to rabbinic teaching about *post-mortem* suspension (including the rabbinic rejection of *ante-mortem* suspension).[4]

Rabbinic discussions of case law were certainly influenced by the ongoing Jewish experience of crucifixion during the era of Roman rule. In such discussions crucifixion served as the extreme case for a number of legal issues. In such law, crucifixion nails are mentioned with regard to their use as magical tokens; yet, while these magical applications are rejected by some rabbis

---

[2] Also see *Bell.* iii.320–21, where crucifixion is the capstone of a series of tortures.

[3] See the discussion in chapter 2, §2.3.

[4] E.g., *Tg. Ps.-J.* on Lev 24:23 and on Deut 21:22–23 (for similar tendencies cf. *Tg. Neof.* and *Tg. Ps.-J.* on Num 25:4).

(and associated with the "ways of the Amorite"), this rejection appears to be due more to a disavowal of magical practices in general than to a simple abhorrence of the nail from a cross (see chpt. 4). From other discussions of case law it appears that the bodies and blood of crucified corpses are not considered any more or less impure than other cadavers (though shame and grief could require the family to leave their own town while the body of a relative still decays on the cross).[5]

Rabbinic tradition formally disdained crucifixion as a Jewish penalty, while it accepted it as a Roman one.[6] In fact, although there was occasionally the acknowledgment that crucifixion may have been applied unjustly against Jews,[7] many rabbinic accounts involving crucifixion apparently viewed the Roman application of the penalty as a just punishment for evil men.[8] In a few key sayings, rabbinic teachers even drew analogies to an eschatological "crucifixion" of God's brigand-like Gentile opponents.[9] In a similar vein, an intriguing story concerning R. Eleazar actually divulges that this Tannaitic rabbi handed over Jewish brigands to the Roman cross.[10] Finally, in juxtaposition with standard rabbinic practice, the great Pharisee Simeon ben Shetach was portrayed as suspending witches alive.[11] Perhaps this indicates that, at different eras in history, there was more diversity in practice than is reflected in the recorded rulings about acceptable methods of execution.

Of course, these few voices (Philo, Josephus, and the targumic and rabbinic literature) all likely represent elite perspectives (though from disparate social and geographic locations), and they cannot rightly be thought to provide in and of themselves a broad-based picture of perceptions of crucifixion among Jewish people in antiquity. Fortunately, other references also demonstrate Jewish reflection about crucifixion; and all this material can be correlated to give some greater sense of the whole. So, in order to provide a more adequate summary, certain general themes should be mentioned.

---

[5] See esp. chapter 5, §3. The crucifixion cases reported concern the impurity of "mixed blood" beneath a cross, the ability to accept legal decisions from a person on the cross, the question of when death can be assured to the wife (who wishes remarriage), and the mourning rites required for such victims. Also note the case law concerning crucifixion nails employed in magic (in chapter 4, §2).

[6] For rabbinic opposition to crucifixion as a legitimate application of Deut 21:22–23, see esp. *Sifre Deut.* 221; cf. *b. Sanh.* 46b; *Midr. Tannaim* 132.7 (cf. above chapter 3, §4.7). Nonetheless, this makes it all the more remarkable that crucifixion is connected with Deuteronomy 21:22–23 in an allegory attributed to Rabbi Meir (*t. Sanh.* ix.7; *b. Sanh.* 46b).

[7] E.g., *Mek.* Baḥodesh 6 on Hadrianic times (above in chapter 2, §3.7.1) and also the account of the death of Jose ben Joezer (in chapter 2, §2.2).

[8] Note especially the rabbinic texts on brigandage in chapter five.

[9] Esther Rabbah (iii.14 [7d] on Esth 1:12); *Pesikta de-Rab Kahana* (suppl. ii.2); see above in chapter 5, §2.

[10] In *b. B. Meṣ.* 83b – analysed above in chapter 2, §3.7.2.

[11] As discussed in chapter 2, §2.5.

2. Themes

In collating general Jewish perceptions about crucifixion, one must pay careful attention to the periods and locales in history in which those perceptions are evidenced. The more broadly attested a certain category, the more likely that it represents an overarching perception. With this in mind, the following themes should be considered.

1. *The Crucified Brigand* was a common figure in Judaea and Galilee in the late Second Temple period. Josephus frequently testifies to brigandage in this period, also mentioning an instance of mass crucifixion of brigands (*Bell.* ii.253). Roman policy, not limited to Judaea, often called for the crucifixion of such brigands. Such an empire-wide policy likely led to a common association of the cross with brigands and rebels. Thus, the rabbinic anecdotes and proverbs (noted in chapter five) about brigands facing the cross assume, by their very aphoristic nature, that the reader/hearer would recognize the brigand-on-the-cross motif as a common Jewish experience. One of the striking features about some of the rabbinic parables is that, on several occasions, they place God in the rôle of king/avenger who will punish via crucifixion the allegorical "brigand" (usually a reference to Gentile usurpers). Outside these parabolic contexts, the Bavli represents the controversial Rabbi Eleazar ben Simeon as colluding with the Romans in an attempt to suppress brigandage by recommending evildoers to the cross (*b. B. Meṣ.* 83b). Thus, in the late Second Temple and early rabbinic periods there is evidence that Jewish people, like others in the Graeco-Roman world more broadly, would have connected "crucifixion" with the death of brigands. There is also evidence that at least some of the populace favoured such strong governmental suppression of brigandage.[12]

2. *The Crucified Rebel*, in a related sense, also formed part of the backdrop of Graeco-Roman life in the more remote provinces. In the works of Josephus, a repeated correlation occurs between crucifixion and rebellion in Palestine. This is true even prior to the revolt of 66–73CE (note the account of Varus in *Bell.* ii.75; *Ant.* xvii.295), but it is especially evident in Josephus' recollections of that great rebellion. Remarkably, especially given the numbers of people so executed in the first Jewish revolt (and the likely continued use of the penalty in the later revolts), Jewish written sources other than Josephus provide few if any explicit links between crucifixion and Jewish rebels. Yet, because of the frequent use of this death penalty against insurrectionists during the late Second Temple period, it is quite likely that crucifixion was associated with rebellion and Jewish revolutionary movements.

In such a context, how a Jewish person viewed the victim of the cross would have been greatly influenced by one's stance on the legitimacy of

---

[12] Josephus displays a disdain for brigands similar to that found in rabbinic sources.

militant Jewish nationalism. In contrast to Jews who were Roman sympa-
thizers, one can imagine that the family, friends, and fellow partisans of the
crucified rebel had a much different picture of his suffering. Also, to the
extent that Jewish nationalism was connected with particular social, economic
and religious groups, the views of the cross within those groups likely were
marked by their experiences of the Roman practice.

3. *The Crucified Martyr* was a person cruelly executed by the authorities
because of his or her intense commitment to the ideals of Judaism. Such a
person may not be far removed in the popular imagination from the crucified
nationalist rebel.[13]

However, an explicit connection between martyrdom and crucifixion is
most clearly met in the *Assumption of Moses* (8:1–3), where the mere
following of Jewish religion, apart from any revolutionary objectives, is
persecuted cruelly on the cross. This likely hearkens back to the plight of the
Maccabean martyrs, though it treats them only typically and projects comparable associations onto contemporary persecutions in the early first century CE
(cf. *As. Mos.* 6:8–9). Josephus indicates a similar linking of the death of the
Maccabean martyrs with crucifixion (*Ant.* xii.255–56). His added testimony,
the significance of which in this connection seems not to be widely noted,
may point to a broader belief in the first century that these celebrated martyrs
were hung on the cross.

Further, comments attributed to Rabbi Nathan from Hadrianic times also
identify crucifixion with contemporary persecutions against those practicing
ancestral Jewish religion.[14] Thus, in the first and second centuries, there exists
important evidence that the cross could be associated with martyrdom.[15]

4. *The Innocent Sufferer* on the cross is known in pericopes from Philo,
Josephus, and rabbinic writings.[16] In these instances, the deaths of the
crucified are projected neither as a testimony to the Jewish religion nor as
moving the God of Israel to vindicate his people. Nonetheless, these victims
are considered blameless and undeserving of such a fate. Of course, the line
between martyr and innocent sufferer is a fine one, but the distinction pro-

---

[13] Cf. Martin Hengel, *The Zealots: Investigations into the Jewish Freedom Movement in
the Period from Herod I until 70 A.D.*, trans. David Smith (Edinburgh: T&T Clark, 1989),
259–62. Hengel elsewhere mentions only a single set of traditions about a comparably crucified pagan martyr (M. Atilius Regulus), who died at the hands of the Carthaginians; see
Martin Hengel, *Crucifixion in the Ancient World and the Folly of the Message of the Cross*,
trans. John Bowden (London & Philadelphia: SCM Press & Fortress Press, 1977), 64–66
(= reprint pp. 156–58).

[14] *Mek.* Baḥodesh 6; on this see chapter 2, §3.7.1.

[15] From a later period of rabbinic tradition, recall that undesignated traditions about Jose
ben Joezer, one of the first *zugot*, imply that he suffered crucifixion innocently, possibly as a
result of his esteemed Jewish practice (*Gen. Rab.* lxv.22; *Midr. Psa.* 11:7).

[16] E.g., Philo, *Flacc.* 72, 83–85; Josephus, *Bell.* ii.306–8. Also see previous note.

vides a way of conceptualizing recollections of the many people who were crucified simply because they were being maltreated, apart from suffering on account of Jewish observances and without making proper *testimonia*. A biblical example of this may be found in the princes in Lamentations 5:12 who are "hung" – later traditions imply that their suspension was the means of execution. Naturally, in such deaths, the executing authorities are made out as the evildoers, although presumably the authorities and their collaborators viewed these events differently.

5. *Biblical Exemplars* of the cross occur in Jewish translations and interpretations of several Old Testament narratives. In particular, the biblical phrase תלה על העץ was associated with crucifixion and related bodily suspension penalties.[17] As observed in chapter three, the evidence of this association in biblical texts comes as early as the Second Temple period – from the Greek translations of Haman's execution in Esther (also found in Josephus) to the crucified baker of Genesis 40 in Philo and Josephus.[18] Additionally, some Jewish traditions (especially Josephus) associated crucifixion with the edict of the king in Ezra 6:11.

The targumim employ צלב and its cognates in their renderings of human penal suspension in these same biblical texts. This is true of all the narrative passages discussed in chapter three that have an extant targum, including both those MT passages which "hang" (using תלה) people on trees and those texts which employ the *hiphil* or *hophal* of יקע as an executionary form. As noted in chapter one, while Aramaic צלב cannot be limited to "crucify," it certainly often allows such an understanding. Indeed, צלב always appears in the targumim and in extant rabbinic literature as a technical term for human bodily suspension associated with death; and it frequently indicates crucifixion in such literature. Thus, it would have been easy for the hearers of the targumim to have continued the already well-defined identification of some biblical episodes with crucifixion (esp. concerning Haman, as evidenced in the Greek translations and in Josephus); and it is quite conceivable that such hearers imagined a similar penalty in other passages (such as those concerning the suspended princes and children in Lamentations 5:12–13). Further, such identifications endure in the rabbinic writings, especially with regard to Haman.[19] Nevertheless, on other occasions employing צלב, the targumim may seek to highlight the *post-mortem* nature of the biblical suspension[20]; yet, even here, the connotations associated with bodily suspen-

---

[17] In addition to the material in chapter 3, note also chapter 1, §2.3.1, and the discussion of Philo, *Post.* 61 in chapter 5, §1.

[18] Also cf. the language employed concerning the body of Saul and his sons in Josephus, *Ant.* vi.374.

[19] Also cf. *Sifre Num.* 131; *Lam. Rab.* v.12–13.

[20] E.g., *Tg. Ps.-J.* on both Gen 40:19 and Deut 21:22.

sion in those passages may have influenced perceptions of any penal bodily suspension (including those performed *ante-mortem* on the cross).

In this regard, we can properly speak of the actualization of the OT text. While the deaths of these biblical figures clearly involved suspension in the Hebrew Bible, such a suspension usually was not depicted in the OT as the likely means of execution. Yet, on analogy with the contemporary experience of their Jewish communities, later Jewish authors naturally associated these deaths with the types of penal suspension practiced in their own day. And thus, for generations of Jewish people, these biblical accounts became exemplars of suspended people (including those who had been crucified).

It is important to remember the negative nature of most biblical exemplars who underwent suspension (save presumably Lam 5:12–13). No one wished his son to grow up to be like the baker of Genesis 40–41, or the king of Ai in Joshua. Worst by far was Haman, the very man who sought the destruction of the entire Jewish race. Therefore, one is especially struck by the great wealth of tradition associating Haman with crucifixion.

6. *Deuteronomy 21:22–23*, as another biblical text speaking of someone "hung on a tree," was also connected (at least as early as the Temple Scroll) with death by suspension; and some Jewish authors even related this text explicitly to crucifixion. This is true in spite of rabbinic traditions that intentionally distance this Deuteronomy passage from Roman crucifixion.[21] Here we move the discussion from Jewish traditions concerning biblical exemplars to those about biblical legislation.

Some Jewish texts imply that Deuteronomy 21:22–23 mandated execution by suspension, thus linking this OT commandment with the kind of *ante-mortem* executionary form to which crucifixion belonged.[22] Furthermore, various intertestamental and rabbinic passages indicate that a person crucified by the Roman government could be considered to be in the same category as the "hung man" of Deuteronomy 21. Hence, given the rabbinic opposition to crucifixion as a legitimate application of Deuteronomy 21:22–23, R. Meir's analogy of Deuteronomy 21:23 with the crucifixion of a brigand (*t. Sanh.* ix.7; *b. Sanh.* 46b) could well be the tip of the conceptual iceberg in terms of popular awareness that the crucified person was very much like the suspended person of Deuteronomy 21. A similar point might be made with regard to Josephus' allusion to Deuteronomy 21 in *Bell.* iv.317, since Josephus elsewhere appears careful to distance crucifixion from Deut 21:22–23 (despite his otherwise frequent use of crucifixion terminology when speaking of a biblical person hung on a tree).

---

[21] See the discussion of Deuteronomy 21 in chapter three.

[22] Deut 21:22–23 is interpreted to mandate a form of execution in: 11QTemple lxiv.6–13 (here quite possibly crucifixion); Philo, *Spec. Leg.* iii.151–52 (most probably crucifixion); and the Peshiṭta rendering.

In this regard, the multiple interpretations of the "curse of God" construct
(קִלְלַת אֱלֹהִים) in Deut 21:23 create at least two key potential associations
with crucifixion. Rabbinic interpretation codified in the Talmud (also supported by Josephus, Symmachus, and the Peshiṭta) applies this text to the
blasphemer (as one who "curses God"). On the other hand, the more ancient
tradition (being witnessed in the LXX, Old Latin, and known as late as
Targum Neofiti[23]) envisions קִלְלַת אֱלֹהִים as a reference to the suspended
person being cursed by God.[24] To the extent that this slogan ("curse of God")
was found in the popular imagination about crucifixion, the label of "blasphemer" or that of "accursed" may have been associated with the memory of
the crucified.[25]

7. *The Crucified Magician* receives some evidence from the encounter of
Simeon ben Shetach with the witches of Ashkelon. Witchcraft was subject to
the death penalty both in the Pentateuch (e.g., Exod 22:18) and in Roman law.
The Yerushalmi indicates that the suspension of witches was a necessary
means of death in order to disable their magical powers (which supposedly
came from contact with the ground). However, it also seems likely that the
sorceress who uses the name of God in witchcraft should be considered a
blasphemer, and therefore deserves hanging (though classically this should
follow after stoning; cf. *m. Sanh.* vi.4; vii.4, 11). Even given the popular folk-
story form of the later expansions of this tale about Simeon, it is difficult to
know how pervasive was such a concept testified here in the Mishnaic story
and in the Palestinian Gemara.

8. *Crucifixion Nails and Magical Healing* are mentioned together in a
recurring Mishnaic tradition (see chapter four). There is also further evidence
of crucifixion nails used as charms in later Jewish practice, as well as in
pagan magic. This is similar to ancient magical applications of other
implements involved in violent deaths. Thus, crucifixion objects could be
employed in Jewish folk religion (especially to produce physical healing).

9. *The Shamefulness and Horror of the Cross* are implied in many ancient
Jewish accounts, although explicit shame terminology is rare. In this regard,
the dread of the cross, undoubtedly associated in part with the painfulness of

---

[23] Also likely testified in 11QTemple lxiv.12, where the suspended person is cursed by
both God and men (מקוללי אלוהים ואנשים תלוי על העץ).

[24] As noted in chapter 3, *Targum Neofiti* on Deuteronomy 21:23 manifests the same
application of this verse as the LXX to the cursing of all those hung on the tree. This indicates
that such a view did not quickly perish after the penning of the Septuagint, but was still found
well into the rabbinic era.

[25] Nonetheless, it should be remembered that, whether or not the crucified person was
deemed to have been cursed, in rabbinic case law this does not affect the question of the
purity of his shed blood, or the burial of his corpse, or the mourning rites that can be observed
(see chapter 5, §3; also note the ossuary reburial granted the crucified man at Givat ha-
Mivtar).

such a death, also could be due to the social implications of being suspended naked to public view. Hence, Josephus portrays the young Eleazar as one who calls his impending crucifixion "the most pitiable of deaths" (*Bell.* vii.203). The immediate family of a crucified person is directed in rabbinic case law to leave town until the body can no longer be recognized (*Śem.* ii.11), plausibly due to avoiding the shame and the personal pain of seeing one's family member so punished. Additionally, rabbinic aphorisms and parables involving crucifixion frequently level derision at the brigand's manner of death (cf. chapter 5, §2). Even the vulgar jesting of Jaķim at the execution of Jose b. Joezer presumes the horrible cruelty of such a death (cf. chapter 2, §2.2).

Some modern authors have seen shame as the central underlying thought associated with crucifixion in the ancient world.[26] This study suggests that other associations were more frequently verbalized. Nevertheless, at times shame does appear consciously associated with crucifixion – alongside recognition of the painfulness and horror of this gruesome death. Still, the honourable death of a Jewish patriot or a martyr appears in no way mitigated by the fact that such a death took place on a cross (cf. Josephus, *Bell.* iii.321).[27]

10. Finally, certain *latent images* within Jewish thought and practice could bear overtones that connected key Jewish traditions with the cross.[28] Thus, while the roasting technique employed for the paschal lamb in all probability did not develop as a conscious mimicry of the cross, nonetheless the image of the paschal lamb prepared in a cruciform manner for roasting likely still would have been striking to the ancient Jewish observer who had witnessed frequent crucifixions. And, though it is difficult to assess the antiquity in the ʿ*Aqedah* traditions of the rabbinic comparison of Isaac carrying his own wood to a person bearing his own cross, certainly the haggadic statement that Isaac bore his wood as a man does a cross implies that crucifixion associations, even in the context of a growing Christian presence in society, found resonance with Jewish understandings of this key patriarchal episode.

3. Crucifixion in Jewish Literature and the Roman World

This list of general themes, of course, finds correspondence with the larger Graeco-Roman context. As is readily recognized, some of these conceptual

---

[26] See, for example, Jerome H. Neyrey, "Despising the Shame of the Cross: Honor and Shame in the Johannine Passion Narratives," *Semeia* 68 (1996): 113–37 (esp. 113–15); Jerome H. Neyrey, *Honor and Shame in the Gospel of Matthew* (Louisville: Westminster/John Knox, 1998), 139–62 (esp. 139–40).

[27] For the Graeco-Roman world more broadly cf. the material in Hengel, *Crucifixion*, 47n.5 (repr. 139n.); also cf. ibid., 64–66 (repr. 156–58).

[28] For the working definition of "latent image" see the introduction to chapter 5, §4.

categories are not distinctly Jewish (e.g., crucified bandits and rebels, the shame of the cross). However, the Hebrew Bible in translation and interpretation provided biblical exemplars of crucifixion and some possibilities for halakhic and haggadic discussion of the practice of the penalty. Thus, especially in those perceptions that were rooted in the understanding of the Hebrew Bible, conceptions of the cross could take on different dimensions in ancient Judaism than in their surrounding context. Moreover, the Jewish experience of collective suffering at the hands of Roman authorities marked Jewish perceptions of crucifixion in ways that differed from those in many other sectors of the Roman world. Thus, although ancient Jewish views often overlapped with those of the world about them, there were also distinctly Jewish perceptions of the cross in antiquity.

It remains then to briefly suggest how these Jewish perceptions of crucifixion (at times in continuity with the broader Roman world) may be reflected in early Jewish polemic and in early Christian thought.

Part Two

Ancient Jewish Perceptions of Crucifixion
and the Cross of Christ

Chapter Seven

Jewish Perceptions of Jesus' Crucifixion
and the Early Church

While proclaiming a crucified Messiah, early Christians, conscious of their relationship with Jewish communities, inevitably interacted with Jewish perceptions of the cross. This chapter seeks to show that at least some of the perceptions detected already in ancient Judaism were applied by Jewish people to Jesus' crucifixion. The chapter also investigates some of the ways these perceptions impacted the literature of early Christianity. This dual focus (on both Jewish and Christian views of Jesus' crucifixion) allows us to integrate the data from both sides and thus to observe Jewish and Christian interaction concerning Jesus' crucifixion from the rise of Christianity until the close of the Babylonian Talmud.[1]

Specifically, what we shall observe is that the sparse data indicates some polemical use in Judaism of negative concepts of crucifixion against the followers of the crucified Jesus. More widely evidenced in the existing sources is the Christian reaction. From Christian literature, one observes several Christian approaches to the existing Jewish perceptions of crucifixion. Some Jewish views of the cross were so negative as to require immediate and forceful rejection in order for the Christian kerygma to establish itself. Other ideas, while inherently negative, could be molded as insights into the divine logic of the crucified Saviour. Still other impressions were more favourable to a crucified person, and thus could shed light on the meaning of the cross of Jesus, even providing positive points of contact for proclaiming the gospel of the Crucified.

Of course, it is notoriously difficult to determine whether any single Christian concept can be traced back to Judaism alone as opposed to the larger Graeco-Roman milieu. In fact, such a disjunction often represents a false dichotomy, especially since Jewish thought frequently encompassed

---

[1] The focus below in Christian literature primarily concerns the New Testament and Christian writings before the Council of Nicaea, though occasionally, later sources are brought in to support the earlier trends or to show, via contrast, the lack of earlier Christian interaction with certain Jewish perceptions of the cross. Also, the sparsity of Jewish texts that clearly interact with early Christianity has made it at times necessary to infer trajectories from later Jewish works (including later *adversus Christianos* sources). See further the next note on the use of *adversus Iudaeos* literature.

concepts endemic within its own Graeco-Roman context (witness, for example, the case of the 'crucified brigand'). Thus, the observed parallels between Judaism and Christianity below may not in all cases represent a purely linear development; and their origins in the history of ideas may be quite complex. Nonetheless, to find Christian parallels to Jewish views, one can focus on early material or on texts that claim to portray actual discussions or refutations of Jewish positions (e.g., *adversus Iudaeos* literature).[2] Such a literary focus can help increase the probability that actual Jewish influence can be traced.

Further, in some cases, later Jewish *adversus Christianos* literature betrays application of standard concepts of crucifixion in its evaluation of the crucified Jesus. If both Jewish and Christian polemic can be shown to debate related views of crucifixion, then this too may be evidence of ancient Jewish categories in discussion. In this regard, M. Simon has well pointed out that the crucifixion of Jesus, combined with the messianic and divine claims Christians attached to him, was at the core of ancient Jewish and Christian debate.[3]

The categories below are taken from the summary of Jewish perceptions of crucifixion in the previous chapter. Early Christians certainly drew on other concepts from Judaism and the OT as they sought to understand the meaning of their crucified Messiah. No attempt has been made here to be comprehensive in the assessment of all early Christian notions about the cross, and only a representative sample of primary sources (and secondary discussion of those sources) is provided. Nonetheless, the goal is to take up the material from the previous inductive study of crucifixion in Jewish life and thought, and then to observe the possible influence of these categories on early Jewish and Christian interaction about the cross of Jesus. It is hoped that such an overview helps to illustrate how Jewish pre-conceptions about crucifixion were applied to Jesus by Jews and Christians in antiquity.

1. The Crucified Brigand

Given the close association in both Jewish and Graeco-Roman literature of crucifixion with the execution of brigands (including violent rebels), it is hardly remarkable that Jesus was connected by certain later Roman authors

---

[2] Harnack and others have questioned the degree to which Jewish opinion is reflected in *adversus Iudaeos* literature. The literature on this topic is now quite extensive, but a reasonable evaluation of the evidence can be found in the helpful summary and critique of positions in James Carleton Paget, "Anti-Judaism and Early Christian Identity," *ZAC* 1 (1997): 195–225. Carleton Paget focuses especially on Miriam S. Taylor, *Anti-Judaism and Early Christian Identity: A Critique of the Scholarly Consensus*, SPB 46 (Leiden: E. J. Brill, 1995).

[3] Marcel Simon, *Verus Israel: A study of the relations between Christians and Jews in the Roman Empire (135–425)* (Oxford: Oxford University Press, 1986), 157–63 (esp. 158–59).

with brigandage.[4] Even some modern authors contend that Jesus was a revolutionary "Zealot" calling for violent, national revolt; or at least that he was sympathetic with contemporary religious insurrectionists.[5]

While the evidence that the actual, historical Jesus was a violent Zealot remains quite scant,[6] the impression created by some of his teachings, and by his gathering a band of disciples (including one explicitly labeled a "Zealot," Luke 6:15; Acts 1:13), could have permitted ancient observers of the Jesus movement to label him an insurrectionist.[7] Indeed, it is possible that the Jewish historian Josephus actually had concluded just that.[8] And this label had all the more force when connected with Jesus' crucifixion amidst brigands.

Therefore, it would not be surprising if some Jewish opponents of early Christianity played off these brigandage associations (especially in connection with crucifixion), although, admittedly, the direct evidence for this comes from the third century and later (and largely from Christian sources). For example, the pagan author Celsus, in the context of speaking of Jesus' crucifixion, attributed to a Jew the charge that Jesus could be compared to λῃσταί ('brigands'; Origen, *Contra Celsum* ii.44).[9] Pionius in the *Martyrium*

---

[4] Cf. William Horbury, "Christ as brigand in ancient anti-Christian polemic," in *Jesus and the Politics of His Day*, ed. Ernst Bammel and C. F. D. Moule (Cambridge: Cambridge University Press, 1984), 183–95.

[5] Survey of contemporary opinion in E. Bammel, "The revolution theory from Reimarus to Brandon," in *Jesus and the Politics of His Day*, ed. Ernst Bammel and C. F. D. Moule (Cambridge: Cambridge University Press, 1984), 11–68.

[6] On some of the key Gospel texts (e.g., Matt 10:34ff.; Luke 12:51–53; Mark 8:27ff.; Luke 22:35–38; etc.) note the articles by Black, Catchpole and Lampe in Ernst Bammel and C. F. D. Moule, eds., *Jesus and the Politics of His Day* (Cambridge: Cambridge University Press, 1984). Also David Hill, "Jesus and Josephus' 'messianic prophets'," in *Text and Interpretation*, ed. Ernest Best and R. McL. Wilson (Cambridge: Cambridge University Press, 1979), 150–52. Eisler was inclined to view the portrait of Jesus as a brigand to be more accurate than the Gospels; see Robert Eisler, *ΙΗΣΟΥΣ ΒΑΣΙΛΕΥΣ ΟΥ ΒΑΣΙΛΕΥΣΑΣ*, 2 vols. (Heidelberg: Carl Winters, 1929). However, Horbury rightly points out that the "crime of the crucified has been made to fit his punishment" ("Christ as Brigand," 193; and cf. 189–93).

[7] This material is emphasized with connection to Jesus' execution in Kuhn, "Die Kreuzesstrafe," 725–26, 732–36.

[8] See the discussion of the *Testimonium Flavianum* (*Ant.* xviii.63–64) in chapter two, §3.4. There it was suggested that, if one follows the theory that the *Testimonium* contains an original core from Josephus (expanded by Christian interpolations), then its current context in the *Antiquities* would imply that Josephus' original narrative concerning Jesus likely spoke of the Jesus movement as another "uprising" that required suppression by Pilate.

[9] Text in Paul Koetschau, ed., *Origenes Werke, Zweiter Band: Gegen Celsus; Die Schrift vom Gebet*, 2 vols., GCS 2 & 3 (Leipzig: J. C. Hinrichs, 1899), p. 166. Translation in *ANF* 4:448 – "But since this Jew of Celsus compares Him [=Jesus] to robbers, and says that 'any similarly shameless fellow might be able to say regarding even a robber and murderer whom punishment had overtaken, that such an one was not a robber, but a god, because he predicted to his fellow-robbers that he would suffer such punishment as he actually did suffer'..." The question of the veracity of Celsus' Jewish source is complex, at times this material seems to

Pionii (13:3) is reputed to have warned that the Jews say Ὁ Χριστὸς ἄνθρωπος ἦν καὶ ἀνεπαύσατο ὡς βιοθανής ('Christ was a man and he died as a criminal').[10] Similarly, in the likely post-Constantinian *Martyrium Cononis* iv.6–7, the term βιοθανής ('criminal') is applied to Jesus in the context of Jews who speak ill of Jesus' ancestry and crucifixion (and who have written accounts of him).[11] In fact, censored passages from the Talmud, as well as later Jewish *adversus Christianos* anti-gospels (known as the *Toledoth Jeshu* texts), also contain brigandage overtones in their treatment of Jesus.[12] This later Jewish material may increase the probability that earlier Christian literature (both in the Christian *Martyria*, and in Origen's account of Celsus' Jewish source) portray some authentic early Jewish accusations of brigandage associated with Jesus' execution.

In the New Testament literature, Matthew and Mark readily admit the brigandage connotations of crucifixion by specifically mentioning that Jesus' comrades on the cross were δύο λησταί ('two brigands'; Matt 27:38; cf. Mark 15:27). Luke and John are more circumspect in this regard, with Luke merely calling them κακοῦργοι ('criminals'; Luke 23:32–33, 39), and with John referring to them even more abstractly (John 19:18 – καὶ μετ'

---

concur with later Jewish writings, and in other cases Origen himself seems to query whether Celsus accurately represented Jewish opinion. On this issue see: N. R. M. De Lange, *Origen and the Jews: Studies in Jewish-Christian Relations in Third-Century Palestine*, UCOP 25 (Cambridge: Cambridge University Press, 1976), 66, 68–73. Without attempting to defend the accuracy of all references to Celsus' Jewish source, this particular tradition coheres well with what one might expect a Jewish person to think regarding claims of a crucified Messiah.

[10] See Herbert Musurillo, *The Acts of the Christian Martyrs*, OECT (Oxford: Clarendon Press, 1972), 152. Musurillo suggests a date for the *Martyrium Pionii* at the end of the third century due to its language, anti-Semitic rhetoric, and incorporation of Decian and post-Decian persecution imagery (ibid., xxviii–xxix). Eusebius' reference to this work in his *Church History* (iv.15.46–47) indicates that the document must be pre-Constantinian. Gero also contends that this *adversus Iudaeos* section in the *Martyrium* is pre-Constantinian; see Stephen Gero, "Jewish Polemic in the Martyrium Pionii and a 'Jesus' Passage from the Talmud," *JJS* 29 (1978): 166. Certainly in its current form this brief statement does not likely provide an exact quote from a Jewish person (since it would be surprising for a Jewish non-Christian to call Jesus Ὁ Χριστὸς). However, Pionius' statement makes considerable sense as an indirect recording of common Jewish reasons for rejecting Jesus (whom the Christian author prefers to call Ὁ Χριστὸς). This is true concerning the Jewish assertion both of Jesus' non-deific status ('Christ was a man' – with his humanity perhaps most fully exhibited by his mortality) and of Jesus' means of execution being that similar the common criminal.

[11] Musurillo, *Acts of the Christian Martyrs*, 188–90. Musurillo considers the work post-Constantinian, and he holds the events it describes to refer to the Decian persecution, though with little historical accuracy (ibid., xxxiii).

[12] E.g., in the uncensored manuscripts of *b. Sanh.* 43a "Jeshu" is referred to as a "revolutionary" (בר הפוכי – literally a 'son of destruction,' or possibly 'son of perversity'), who was hung on the eve of Passover; see translation and text in R. Travers Herford, *Christianity in Talmud and Midrash* (London: Williams & Norgate, 1903), 83, 406. On the debates surrounding this text, see notes in the next section.

αὐτοῦ ἄλλους δύο; "and two others with him").[13] Yet, even John indirectly testifies to associations of brigandage with crucifixion since Jesus on the cross took the place of Barabbas, who was a λῃστής ('brigand'; John 18:40).

However, in a strikingly standardized Jesus logion, all three Synoptic Gospels portray Jesus in the garden retorting: ὡς ἐπὶ λῃστὴν ἐξήλθατε μετὰ μαχαιρῶν καὶ ξύλων – "have you come out with swords and clubs as upon a brigand?"[14] The usage of this logion by the Evangelists appears to undermine, ironically and intentionally, any association of Jesus with brigandage.[15] Furthermore, the passivist response of Jesus to his captors also is heightened in the Matthean and Lucan contexts by their individual treatments of the cutting-off-the-ear incident, where Jesus (rather than calling for open revolt) actually heals the only person injured during his capture (Matt 26:51–54; Luke 22:50–51; contrast Mark 14:47).[16] Hence, whether from a general awareness of Jewish and Graeco-Roman associations of brigandage with crucifixion, or from actual early anti-Christian polemic, the Evangelists already appear sensitive to the possible perception of Jesus as a brigand (especially in his apprehension and Roman crucifixion). The possibility that Jesus was a violent brigand, they subtly dismiss.

Later authors, faced with more overt accusations of Jesus acting as a brigand, had to be firmer in their rejection of them. Origen refutes the charge from

---

[13] Cf. Mark 15:7, where Barabbas is among the στασιασταί ('those who stir up sedition'). Also note John 18:30, where the Jews call Jesus a κακὸν ποιῶν ('doer of evil').

[14] Matt 26:55; Mark 14:48; Luke 22:52. This phrase is elsewhere alluded to as early as the *Martyrium Polycarpi* 7:1, where Polycarp's pursuers come upon him with arms "as upon a brigand" (ὡς ἐπὶ λῃστήν; the exact wording of Matt 26:55 and parallels). The allusion seems intentional in light of *Mart. Pol.* 6:2 (where Polycarp becomes a 'sharer with Christ' in his manner of death).

[15] So also E. Bammel, "The trial before Pilate," in *Jesus and the Politics of His Day*, ed. Ernst Bammel and C. F. D. Moule (Cambridge: Cambridge University Press, 1984), 445n. See also R. T. France, *The Gospel of Mark: A Commentary on the Greek Text*, NIGTC (Grand Rapids: Eerdmans; Carlisle: Paternoster, 2002), 594–95. Nolland is less confident about the ironical implications, though he allows the possibility; see John Nolland, *The Gospel of Matthew: A Commentary on the Greek Text*, NIGTC (Grand Rapids: Eerdmans; Bletchley: Paternoster, 2005), 1115. On this passage also see the helpful comments in Raymond E. Brown, *The Death of the Messiah: From Gethsemane to the Grave: A Commentary on the Passion Narratives in the Four Gospels*, 2 vols., ABRL (New York: Doubleday, 1994), 1:283–84.

[16] Among others, Evans argues that the disciple who attacked the high priest's servant should be identified throughout the four Gospels; see Craig A. Evans, *Mark 8:27–16:20*, WBC 34b (Nashville: Thomas Nelson, 2001), 424–25. Brown is less confident of making such details agree, though he acknowledges that all four Gospels refer to the same incident; see Brown, *Death of the Messiah*, 265–281. Donald Senior, in his "Passion Series," has repeatedly emphasized how this scene in the four Gospels is consistent with Jesus' repudiation of violence; see e.g., Donald Senior, *The Passion of Jesus in the Gospel of Matthew* (Collegeville, Minn.: Michael Glazier, 1985), 84–89.

Celsus' Jewish source by countering that: (1) such an association of God (i.e., Jesus) with the death of transgressors was foretold; (2) a murderer (i.e., Barabbas) was released instead of the innocent Jesus; (3) Jesus' own pious followers have suffered similar unjust persecutions; and (4) Jesus' death was an unjust act of impious men (*Contra Celsum*, ii.44.). Pionius is said to have contested the Jewish criminal allegations against Jesus by asking: What other criminal has had such faithful disciples, and what criminal's name is similarly powerful enough to expel demons and to perform wonders still displayed in the church?[17] It is striking that neither Origen's nor Pionius' response over-laps substantially with the other, thus making it likely that Origen and the author of the *Martyrium Pionii* were working with independent traditions.

In summary, there is evidence that some Jewish people in antiquity opposed Jesus as a crucified brigand. Certainly, many Jewish people would have resonated with pagan views of the crucified Jesus (consider especially Celsus), who likewise typically thought of crucified individuals as criminals. Christians, naturally, sought to counter such charges through a variety of counter-arguments, and there may even be indications of sensitivity to such charges as early as the time of the Gospels.

2. The Crucified Magician

Early Christianity believed Jesus was God's messenger who worked miracles throughout his ministry. The opponents of Christianity countered that Jesus performed his works by "magic."[18] Indeed, the charge of magic was lodged

---

[17] See *Martyrium Pionii* xiii.4–7. Musurillo's translation reads (*Acts of the Christian Martyrs*, 153): "For you have also heard that the Jews say: Christ was a man, and he died a criminal. But let them tell us, what other criminal has filled the entire world with his disci-ples? What other criminal had his disciples and others with them to die for the name of their master? By what other criminal's name for so many years were devils expelled, and are still expelled now, and will be in the future? And so it is with all the other wonders that are done in the Catholic Church. What these people forget is that this criminal departed from life at his own choice."

[18] M. Smith contends that the evidence of these opponents may well have been closer to the reality of the historical Jesus than the miracle-working portrait of the Gospels; see Morton Smith, *Jesus the Magician* (London: Victor Gollancz, 1978). Smith's collection of pagan and Jewish evidence that associates Christ (and his followers) with magic provides a helpful sup-plement to the sources cited here, but his incautious treatment of the date and historical value of these sources weighs heavily against his thesis – cf. Sean Freyne, review of *Jesus the Magician*, by Morton Smith, In *CBQ* 41 (1979): 658–661. Also see the (at times overstated) rejection of Smith's thesis by Graham H. Twelftree, *Jesus the Exorcist: A Contribution to the Study of the Historical Jesus*, WUNT II/54 (Tübingen: J. C. B. Mohr [Paul Siebeck], 1993), 190–207. A much more constructive approach to similar material can be found in Graham N. Stanton, "Jesus of Nazareth: A Magician and a False Prophet Who Deceived God's People?"

by both pagan and Jewish opponents.[19] Thus, while Justin Martyr presents counterarguments against charges of magic in his *First Apology* (xxx.1), which claims a pagan audience,[20] Justin also notes Jewish charges of magic associated with Jesus in his *Dialogue with Trypho the Jew* (69.7).[21] Indeed, Justin alleges that Jesus was received in this fashion by his Jewish contemporaries: "But though they saw such works, they asserted it was magical art. For they dared to call Him a magician, and a deceiver of the people."[22] Similarly, although Origen notes pagan accusations of magic against Jesus (*Contra Celsum* i.6 and i.68),[23] he also records Celsus' contention that a Jew would have accused Jesus of learning magic in Egypt.[24] The *Martyrium Pionii* even states that Jewish opponents of Christianity asserted Jesus had made a magical use of the cross itself.[25]

According to the Justin passage just cited, Jewish opponents of Jesus were said to combine the allegation that he was a magician with the idea that he was a "deceiver of the people" (*Dial.* 69.7). There are striking parallels to these allegations in the Talmud itself, where the accusation is made that a person called "Jeshu" actually "practiced magic and led astray Israel."[26] The most famous of these reads (*b. Sanh.* 43a):

---

in *Jesus of Nazareth: Lord and Christ: essays on the Historical Jesus and New Testament Christology*, ed. Joel B. Green and Max Turner (Grand Rapids: Eerdmans, 1994), 164–80.

[19] On Jewish accusations of Jesus performing magic, see also Simon, *Verus Israel*, 341. Further texts can be found in Walter Bauer, *Das Leben Jesus im Zeitalter der neutestamentlichen Apokryphen* (Tübingen: J. C. B. Mohr [Paul Siebeck], 1909), 465.

[20] See text in Miroslav Marcovich, ed., *Iustini Martyris apologiae pro christianis*, PTS 38 (Berlin: Walter de Gruyter, 1994), 76.

[21] Text in Miroslav Marcovich, ed., *Iustini Martyris Dialogus cum Tryphone*, PTS 47 (Berlin: Walter de Gruyter, 1997), 191.

[22] Translation in *ANF* 1:233.

[23] Text in Koetschau, *Gegen Celsus*, vol. 1, pp. 59 [21ff.] & 122 [17ff.].

[24] Origen, *Contra Celsum* i.28 (Koetschau, *Gegen Celsus*, 1:79). Also compare (without the attribution to a Jew) *Contra Celsum* i.38 (Koetschau 1:89).

[25] *Martyrium Pionii* 13.8–9 (Musurillo, *Acts of the Christian Martyrs*, 152–155): "Again they assert that Christ performed necromancy or spirit-divination with the cross [μετὰ τοῦ σταυροῦ]." This is perhaps reminiscent of the use of crucifixion nails and cords in magic (see chapter four, §2). Pionius counters that no (Christian or even Jewish) Scripture says this of Christ, and that only wicked men make such allegations.

[26] Cf. the *baraita* in *b. Sanh.* 43a (in uncensored MSS); also see *b. Sanh.* 107b ("And a teacher said, 'Jeshu ha-Noṣri practiced magic and lead astray Israel.'"). Note here that *b. Sanh.* 107b is in a context that discusses only the second charge (i.e., leading astray, though it also fits a charge of idolatry). This might indicate that the dual-charge tradition existed independently of the Bavli narrative, and was a typical encapsulation of Jesus' activities – he both "practiced magic" and "led astray." These rabbinic passages are debated by modern scholars concerning whether they refer to Jesus; so, for example, contrast Travers Herford with Johann Maier. See Travers Herford, *Christianity in Talmud and Midrash*, 35–41, 51–54, 78–86; and Johann Maier, *Jesus von Nazareth in der talmudischen Überlieferung*, ErFor 82 (Darmstadt: Wissenschaftliche Buchgesellschaft, 1978), 127–29, 198, 219–43. Note also the

And it is tradition: On the eve of Pesaḥ they hung Jeshu [the Nazarene]. And the crier went forth before him forty days (saying), '[Jeshu the Nazarene] goeth forth to be stoned, because he hath practised magic and deceived and led astray Israel. Any one who knoweth aught in his favour, let him come and declare concerning him.' And they found naught in his favour. And they hung him on the eve of Pesaḥ. Ulla says, 'Would it be supposed that [Jeshu the Nazarene] a revolutionary, had aught in his favour?' He was a deceiver, and the Merciful hath said (Deut. xiii.8) *Thou shalt not spare, neither shalt thou conceal him.* But it was different with [Jeshu the Nazarene], for he was near to the kingdom.[27]

The tradition indicates that Jeshu was stoned as well as hung (תלאוהו לישו –
"they hung Jeshu"), though the latter penalty is clearly the more important, since it is repeated in the text. To the extent that this was connected with Jesus, who was well known to have been crucified, then there appears both an attempt to connect his death with proper rabbinic death penalty practice (stoning then hanging) while not loosing the connection between his cruci-fixion and being "hung [ותלאוהו] on the eve of Passover." Observe that in this passage, the charge of magic is connected with the penal bodily suspen-sion of Jeshu. Note that the narrative reads that the official court charge against Jeshu was "because he practiced magic, and deceived and lead astray Israel" (על שכיסף והיסית והידיח את ישראל). While a charge of sorcery could naturally arise as a counter to the Christian image of Jesus as God's miracle worker, it is also possible that the crucifixion of Jesus may have rein-forced the association of Jesus with magic, at least in the minds of some later Jewish polemicists against Christianity.

It indeed appears that one might associate crucifixion with the death of a magician in antiquity. For example, in the context of dealing with pagan and Jewish claims of magic against Jesus, Origen allows that magicians (skilled in γοητεία) are made to die comparable "wretched deaths" to that of Jesus.[28] In the previous chapter, it was noted that the incident involving Simeon ben Shetach, who hung women/witches, betrays a possible association of witch-

---

review of Maier's general program in David Goldenberg, "Once More: Jesus in the Talmud," *JQR* 73 (1982): 78–86. On these texts and others see Stanton, "Jesus: A Magician?" 166–71. Also cf. with caution D. Neale, "Was Jesus a *Mesith*? Public Response to Jesus and His Ministry," *TynBul* 44 (1993): 89–101.

[27] Translation in Travers Herford, *Christianity in Talmud and Midrash*, 83. The Hebrew text (which was censored in some talmudic MSS) is accessible in Travers Herford, *Christianity in Talmud and Midrash*, 406 (discussion, p. 83ff.); and in Hermann L. Strack, *Jesus die Häretiker und die Christen nach den ältesten jüdischen Angaben*, Schriften des Institutum Judaicum in Berlin 37 (Leipzig: J. C. Hinrichs, 1910), 1 (discussion on pp. 18*–19*). Maier, believes the passage originally referred to a magician named Ben Pandera rather than Jesus; cf. Maier, *Jesus von Nazareth*, 219–37. A helpful summary of Maier's argumentation can be found in Kuhn, "Die Kreuzesstrafe," 666–69. For a refutation of Maier's position see William Horbury, "The Benediction of the *Minim* and Early Jewish-Christian Controversy," *JTS* 33 (1982): 55–58 (repr. 104–107).

[28] Origen, *Contra Celsum* ii.44 (Koetschau, *Gegen Celsus*, p. 166 [17–19]).

craft with blasphemy and its punishment in crucifixion. This evidence is admittedly sparse and somewhat late, since it was first recorded in the Mishnah without reference to the women being witches, and since explicit connection to witchcraft is only found later in the Palestinian *Gemara*. However, with some caution one can compare the suspended death of magic workers in the Simeon accounts with the tradition cited above from the Babylonian Talmud (*Sanh* 43a), where Jeshu, who practiced magic and led astray Israel, is hung (the context implying this suspension occurred after he was stoned). A similar tradition is found in some medieval texts of the Jewish counter-gospels known as the *Toledoth Jeshu*.[29] In fact, some earlier *Toledoth Jeshu* manuscripts portray Jesus as first hung on the cross and then stoned while he was still on the cross, on account of his magical use of the divine Name along with other seditions.[30] Further, in an earlier period, Chrysostom portrays Jewish opponents as answering the question "Why did you crucify the Christ?" by replying, "As being one who leads astray and practices magic."[31]

Given the number of disparate places Jewish assertions of Jesus as a magician appear in Christian *adversus Iudaeos* literature, combined with the later Jewish *adversus Christianos* testimony of the Bavli and the *Toledoth Jeshu* manuscripts, one might suggest that this magical charge against Jesus portrays an authentic early Jewish response to Christianity (and a Jewish retort that could be connected with Jesus' death by crucifixion).

As previously noted, the Mishnaic form of execution for the sorcerer (as for the one who led people astray) was stoning (e.g., *m. Sanh.* vii.4, 11). Both *b. Sanh* 43a and the *Toledoth Jeshu* traditions appear to combine the known fact of Jesus' crucifixion with the rabbinically sanctioned penalty (i.e., stoning) for his actions. While hanging is only prescribed in the Mishnah for the blasphemer and idolator (*m. Sanh.* vi.4; in both cases notably preceded by

---

[29] Note Schwager XI.59 folio 95a §5; this can be found in William Horbury, "A Critical Examination of the Toledoth Jeshu" (Ph.D. diss., University of Cambridge, 1971), 188. In this text, Jesus performs magic and blasphemes before Queen Helen. Also note later in this manuscript that Jesus is commanded to be stoned and hung (folio 95b–96a, in Horbury, "Critical Examination," 192–93). Some post-Medieval *Toledoth Jeshu* manuscripts also portray Jesus as bringing spells from Egypt, especially as having inserted a parchment of the name of God into his flesh; see Horbury, "Critical Examination," 239–40.

[30] E.g., MS T.-S. Loan 87 folio 2ʳ (transl. by Horbury, "Critical Examination," 86). In the same manuscript, John is crucified (1ᵛ 30–32, Horbury, "Critical Examination," 84) and two of Jesus' five disciples are likewise stoned upon a cross (1ʳ 5–10, Horbury, "Critical Examination," 77–78). On the death of Jesus in this text, see Hillel I. Newman, "The Death of Jesus in the *Toledot Yeshu* Literature," *JTS* n.s. 50 (1999): 59–79 (with an abbreviated translation on 63–64). Newman suggests that the Aramaic of this text might suit the seventh century or earlier (with traditions at least pertinent to late antiquity).

[31] Κἂν ἐρωτήσῃς αὐτούς, Διὰ τί ἐσταυρώσατε τὸν Χριστόν; λέγουσιν, Ὡς πλάνον καὶ γόητα ὄντα. Chrysostom, *Expositio in Psalmum* VIII.3 (*PG* 55.110).

stoning), the extension of the suspension penalty to one who lead astray Israel and practiced magic apparently was conceivable for the authors behind these Jewish texts about Jesus.

Turning briefly to Christian responses to such allegations, the Gospels at times appear to be sensitive to the charge that Jesus was a magician.[32] This is particularly evident when Jewish opponents of Jesus assert that he "casts out the demons by the ruler of the demons," who is identified as Beelzebul (Mark 3:22 and parallels; cf. Matt 10:25; John 8:48). Such a charge is associated with the Pharisees (Matt 9:34; 12:24), with the scribes (Mark 3:22), and with Jesus' opponents more broadly (Luke 11:15–16; John 8:48). In response, each of the Synoptic Gospels records Jesus' counter-argument that it makes no logical sense for Beelzebul to fight against his own demonic forces (Mark 3:22–27; Matt 12:22–29; Luke 11:14–23). Indeed, the Gospels caution that any allegation that Jesus was a demon-empowered miracle worker constitutes grave spiritual error (John 8:48–56), even to the point of committing unforgivable blasphemy against the Holy Spirit (Mark 3:28–30; Matt 12:20–32).[33] Certainly, it is reasonable to suppose that, among the ancient opponents of the Jesus movement, such an accusation of demonic magic empowering Jesus' miracles would have continued long after Jesus' death. In that case, perhaps the Gospels intentionally pass down these narratives as a way of dispelling such allegations.

However, it should be noted that the Gospels do not explicitly report anyone connecting the charges of Jesus' demonic magic with his execution on the cross.[34] Nevertheless, such a linking of Jesus' death with magic was indeed

---

[32] See Smith, *Jesus the Magician*, 21–44; and Twelftree, *Jesus the Exorcist*, 198–99. Both overstate their cases, though in opposite directions (see note on both Smith and Twelftree above).

[33] Focusing on the Marcan account, commentators typically connect Jesus' saying about the blasphemy of the Holy Spirit with the Pharisee's rejection of Jesus' miraculous signs and proclamation of the kingdom (see esp. ὅτι in Mark 3:30): e.g., Walter Grundmann, *Das Evangelium nach Markus*, 4th ed., THNT 2 (Berlin: Evangelische Verlagsanstalt, 1968), 85; William L. Lane, *The Gospel According to Mark*, NICNT (Grand Rapids: Eerdmans, 1974), 144–46. Cranfield cogently argues that Mark 3:28–30 was not originally a separate saying from the narrative of 3:22–27; C. E. B. Cranfield, *The Gospel According to Saint Mark*, CGTC (Cambridge: Cambridge University Press, 1977), 139. One can compare the "unforgivable" nature of this sin to rabbinic sayings that certain sins immediately indicate a loss of position in the world to come; so Morna Hooker, *The Gospel According to Saint Mark* (London: A & C Black, 1991), 117. One question concerns whether βλασφημίαι here implies blasphemy against God and God's Spirit (so most commentators), or whether it is used in the more generic sense of "slanderous speech" – the latter view is upheld by France, *Mark*, 175–76; contrast C. S. Mann, *Mark*, AB 27 (Garden City, N.Y.: Doubleday, 1986), 256.

[34] Smith's repeated examples (*Jesus the Magician*, 33, 38–43) concerning the "son of God" texts and John 18:28 (κακὸν ποιῶν) are particularly unconvincing in that he fails to recognize the Jewish context of the former and the generic terminology of the latter (so too with his discussion of ὁ πλάνος in Matt 27:63 – cf. Twelftree, *Jesus the Exorcist*, 201–3).

known in some patristic writings. The Fathers vehemently reject such a link.[35] Their principal counter-argument is to reassert that Jesus' wondrous acts were true miracles, resulting in the healing of the lame, the blind and the deaf, and even effecting the raising of some from the dead (a miracle all believers will receive in the end).[36] Thus, when facing such allegations, the Fathers did their best to disassociate Jesus' crucifixion from notions of magic.

3. The Crucified Blasphemer

The New Testament writings note that blasphemy was a charge lodged by the Jewish populace and leaders against Jesus and his followers.[37] The Matthean and Marcan passion narratives even portray blasphemy as the crucial criminal allegation arising from the Sanhedrin hearing of Jesus – an allegation sufficient to require Jesus' death (Matt 26:65; Mark 14:63).[38] Consequently, Jesus is led away to Pilate to be judged (on other counts) and crucified.

However, according to rabbinic *halakah*, Jewish execution for blasphemy properly required stoning first and then hanging (blasphemy along with idolatry being the two offenses rabbinic authorities agreed merited suspension).[39] Of course, the Gospels present the occasional threat of stoning against Jesus; and often such a threat explicitly results from accusations of blasphemy.[40] What is more, later Jewish accounts of Jesus' death sometimes read

---

[35] Again note Origen, *Contra Celsum* ii.44 (where allegations against Jesus of brigandage and magic appear side by side). In addition to his response concerning brigandage cited in the previous section, Origen says: "For no one can point to any acts of a sorcerer which turned away souls from the practice of the many sins which prevail among men, and from the flood of wickedness (in the world)." Translation in *ANF* 4:448.

[36] Such is the argument of Justin, *Dialogue* 69.

[37] Matt 9:3; 26:65; Mark 2:7; 14:64; Luke 5:21; John 10:33,36; Acts 6:11 (cf. 26:11; 1 Tim 1:13). Cf. Hermann Wolfgang Beyer, "†βλασφημέω, †βλασφημία, †βλάσφημος," in *Theological Dictionary of the New Testament*, ed. Gerhard Kittel, trans. Geoffrey W. Bromiley, vol. 1 (Grand Rapids: Eerdmans, 1964), 621–25.

[38] A significant contribution to the study of the authenticity and meaning of the Marcan account may be found in Darrell L. Bock, *Blasphemy and Exaltation in Judaism and the Final Examination of Jesus: A Philological-Historical Study of the Key Jewish Themes Impacting Mark 14:61–64*, WUNT II/106 (Tübingen: Mohr Siebeck, 1998), see esp. pp. 184–237. Bock's conclusions I find quite compelling, though I would differ with his usage of 11QTemple lxiv.6–13 on p. 208.

[39] For stoning and hanging see *m. Sanh.* vi.4; cf. *Sifre Deut* 221; *Tg. Ps.-J.* Deut 21:22. Stoning for blasphemy is commanded in Lev 24:10–16. The death of blasphemers in this era (without description of means) can be found in Josephus, *Bell.* ii.145.

[40] So John 8:59; 11:8; and esp. 10:31–39 in a clear context of blasphemy. Luke likewise illustrates an attempt to stone Jesus by throwing him off a cliff (Luke 4:29; following the procedure known from rabbinic *halakhah*, cf. *m. Sanh.* vi.4). On such stonings for blasphemy cf. Josephus, *Ant.* xx.200 and Acts 7:58.

the order of stoning followed by crucifixion onto his execution, with "hanging" encapsulating the whole executionary process. This is especially true in *b. Sanh.* 43a, where stoning is mentioned, but where the stress is on the *hanging* of Jeshu before the Passover – as if the reference to hanging encapsulates the whole execution[41]

Jerome briefly lists those who understood the "curse of God" reference in Deuteronomy 21:22–23 to concern a person who profanes God.[42] These include both the heterodox Jewish Christian sect of the Ebionites, and the *Dialogue of Jason and Papiscus.* Unfortunately Jerome does not inform us how the Ebionites employed this text; nor does he indicate whether in this early *Dialogue* it was the character of the Jewish antagonist or of the Christian apologist who is said to connect Deuteronomy 21 to the death of the blasphemer. However, Jerome does provide some verification of Christian awareness of the association in Judaism of crucifixion with blasphemy. In the Christian material considered here, the earlier Gospels form the clearest Christian awareness of a Jewish connection between the charge of blasphemy and Jesus' crucifixion.

4. Biblical Exemplars and the Crucified Jesus

Early Christians readily admitted that Jesus "hung on a tree" (e.g., Gal 3:13; Acts 5:30; 10:39). As was shown earlier, the Hebrew verb for "hung" often was used for crucifixion (e.g., 4QpNah 3–4 i 7; *Sifre Deut.* 221), and it is even likely that the phrase "hung on a tree" in some Jewish literature signified a means of executionary suspension (11QTemple lxiv.6–13). This phrase echoes the terminology of Deuteronomy 21:22–23 (which will be treated further in its own section below). Moreover, as was discussed in chapter three, the Hebrew Bible employs the phrase "hung on a tree" in order to describe the executionary suspensions of several Old Testament figures; and Second Temple and rabbinic treatments of these OT narratives often actualized those suspension accounts in order to conform them to later Jewish experiences of penal bodily suspension and crucifixion.

However, only occasionally did the Church Fathers associate such OT exemplars with crucifixion; and even more rarely, if ever, were these biblical characters understood as types of Christ. This is not wholly surprising, given

---

[41] Even if one postulates a later insertion of stoning materials in *b. Sanh.* 43a as Horbury does (see earlier note), the point remains for the passage as finally redacted. Note also the *Toledoth Jeshu* texts in the preceding section, which portray Jesus' magic as resulting from his misuse of the divine Name, and which portray Jesus as both stoned and crucified.

[42] Jerome, *Comm. Gal.* ii (on Gal 3:13–14; in Migne, *PL* 26, 387B). Jerome also provides our main source concerning Symmachus, Aquila and Theodotion on this passage (see above in chapter 3, §4.1). Also see the discussion of Deut 21:22–23 in §5 of this chapter.

the poor reputation of most OT figures hung on trees (e.g., the chief baker, the king of Ai, and Haman).[43] In fact, none of these exemplars appears explicitly connected with Jesus in the New Testament.[44] Nevertheless, there are a few strands of later Christian tradition worth observing (even though most have no certain direct rootedness in interaction with Jewish perceptions). Most importantly, the spectre of a crucified Haman appears to lie behind some early Christian and Jewish polemical interactions.

1. *Jerome's Vulgate* almost invariably renders in crucifixion language the Hebrew executionary suspension texts mentioned in chapter three. This is most overt when he employs *crux* terminology, but he also can use the word *patibulum*, which may connote crucifixion: Gen 40:19 *ac suspendet te in cruce* (40:22 *in patibulo*; 41:13 *in cruce*); Num 25:4 *et suspende eos contra solem in patibulis*; Deut 21:22 *et adiudicatus morti adpensus fuerit in patibulo* (cf. *in ligno* twice in 21:23); Josh 8:29 *regem quoque eius suspendit in patibulo… et deposuerunt cadaver eius de cruce*; Josh 10:27 *ut deponerent eos de patibulis* (*stipites* in 10:26); 2 Sam 21:6 *dentur nobis septem viri de filiis eius et crucifigamus eos Domino in Gabaath Saul*; 2 Sam 21:9 *qui crucifixerunt illos in monte coram Domino* (cf. 21:13 *qui adfixi fuerant*); Esth 5:14 *placuit ei consilium et iussit excelsam parari crucem* (earlier in the verse referred to as a *trabs* on which Mordechai *adpendatur*); Esth 6:4 *iuberet Mardocheum adfigi patibulo* (other *in patibulo* references in Esth 2:23 and 7:10); Esth 8:7 *et ipsum iussi adfigi cruci*; Esth 9:25 *denique et ipsum et filios eius adfixerunt cruci* (cf. 9:13–14 *in patibulis*). Jerome appears quite methodical in his usage, not translating any other verses with either *crux* or *patibulum*, nor failing (save in Lam 5:12)[45] to reference with these terms a person suspended on a tree. One wonders why Jerome opted for such translations (thus actualizing the text with crucifixion terms). Whether he was aware of Jewish interpretations of these passages is certainly worth further study. Given Jerome's consistent translation of these suspension passages into crucifixion language, it is all the more striking that other Church Fathers rarely drew crucifixion analogies from these biblical exemplars of executionary suspensions.

2. *The suspended baker* in Genesis 40–41 is depicted as hanging in the miniatures of the 5th c. Cotton Genesis.[46] Contrast Origen, who likens the

---

[43] With the possible exception of the princes in Lam 5:12 (discussed above in chpt. 3, §7).

[44] It should be remarked that A. T. Hanson, drawing on the LXX and *Tg. Ps.-J.*, suggests that Num 25:1–5 lies behind Col 2:14–15 (and likely also Heb 6:6); see Anthony Tyrrell Hanson, *Studies in Paul's Technique and Theology* (London: SPCK, 1974), 1–12. Yet, while the parallels Hanson draws are striking, they are not fully compelling.

[45] Lam 5:12–13 *principes manu suspensi sunt… et pueri in ligno corruerunt.*

[46] Connected with a twelfth-century Christian church mosaic in Venice and reported in Kurt Weitzmann and Herbert L. Kessler, *The Cotton Genesis: British Library Codex Cotton Otho B. VI*, The Illustrations in the Manuscripts of the Septuagint (Princeton: Princeton

Pharaoh's execution of the baker, which he represents as a *decapitation*, to the kind of evil Herod perpetrated in beheading John the Baptist. Noticeably Origen's analogy is connected neither to crucifixion nor to Jesus.[47] Otherwise, crucifixion analogies to the suspended baker attributed to Christians are few and rather late.[48]

3. *The king of Ai* is said by Ambrose to be crucified as in the "ancient curse" (presumably referring to Deut 21:22–23). However, while Ambrose draws a moral lesson out of this, he makes no mention of any parallel between the king's crucifixion and that of Jesus.[49] On the other hand, Origen reverses the more natural crucifixion-typology by understanding Joshua as the type of Jesus (note that both names are the same in Greek) rather than the king of Ai. Meanwhile, in Origen the crucified king of Ai, who is hung ἐπὶ ξύλου διδύμου ('on the split tree,' following the LXX), represents *diabolus* (= the devil), who is crucified by Christ along with his principalities and powers (*Hom. Josh.* viii.3; cf. Col 2:14–15).[50]

4. *Haman*, who in the book of Esther is suspended on a tree/cross, is the one biblical exemplar of crucifixion to receive repeated mention in Christian antiquity.[51] From the fourth century on, some Latin authors make casual reference to the crucifixion of Haman.[52] Jerome even speaks of the Esther narra-

---

University Press, 1986), pp. 213–14 (figures 419–20). See also Kurt Weitzmann, "Zur Frage des Einflusses jüdischer Bilderquellen auf die Illustrationen des Alten Testamentes (mit 10 Tafelabbildungen)," in *Mullus*, ed. Alfred Stuiber and Alfred Hermann, Jahrbuch für Antike und Christentum, Ergänzungsband 1 (Münster: Aschendorffsche Verlagsbuchhandlung, 1964), 409–11 (plate 17). A slightly erroneous summary is found in Gabrielle DeFord, "Beheaded, Crucified, Impaled or Hanged?" *BRev* 14.2 (1998): 51.

[47] Origen, *Comm. Matt.* x.22. Cf. *Hom. Lev.* viii.3 with text in Marcel Borret, *Origène Homélies sur le Lévitique*, 2 vols., SC 286 & 287 (Paris: Cerf, 1981), 2:16–17.

[48] Cf. the twelfth-century mosaic (see note above). The thirteenth-century Jewish polemical anthology *Nizzahon Vetus* §25 records that the Christians argue the hanged baker was a type of Christ; see David Berger, *The Jewish-Christian Debate in the High Middle Ages: A critical edition of the NIZZAHON VETUS with an introduction, translation, and commentary*, Judaica Texts and Translations 4 (Philadelphia: Jewish Publication Society of America, 1979), 58–59.

[49] Ambrose, *Epistulae Extra Collectionem Traditae* 1.24 (= *Maur.* 41.24); for text see Otto Faller and Michaela Zelzer, eds., *Sancti Ambrosii Opera, Pars Decima: Epistulae et Acta*, 4 vols., CSEL 82 (Vienna: Hölder-Pichler-Tempsky, 1968–1996), 3:158–59 (301–3); translation in *NPNF* second series, vol. 10, p. 449.

[50] For the whole context see *Homilies on Joshua* viii.1–7. Text in W. A. Baehrens, *Origenes Werke, Sechster Band: Homilien zum Hexateuch in Rufins Übersetzung*, 2 vols., GCS 29 & 30 (Leipzig: J. C. Hinrichs, 1920–1921), 336–45; French translation available in Annie Jaubert, *Origène Homélies sur Josué*, SC 71 (Paris: Cerf, 1960).

[51] See the valuable study, to which I am often indebted in this section: T. C. G. Thornton, "The Crucifixion of Haman and the Scandal of the Cross," *JTS* n.s., 37 (1986): 419–426.

[52] So Ambrose, *Offic.*, iii.21.124. Text in Maurice Testard, *Saint Ambroise: Les Devoirs*, 2 vols. (Paris: Société d'Édition «Les Belles Lettres», 1984/1992), 2:140. Translation in

tives in the context of Deuteronomy 21:23 and Galatians 3:13. However, for Jerome, it is not Haman who is the potential analog of Christ, but *Mordecai*, who, though innocent, is destined for the cross because of Haman's evil schemes.[53]

Most importantly, crucifixion associations with Haman elsewhere in the early Church almost always appear in polemical contexts with Judaism.[54] For example, Roman/Christian legal texts suggest not only that Jewish people in late antiquity continued the traditional association of Haman's death with crucifixion, but also that Jews also consequently connected Jesus' manner of execution with Haman's demise. So the Theodosian Code[55]:

IMPP. HONOR(IUS) ET THEOD(OSIUS) AA. ANTHEMIO P(RAEFECTO) P(RAETORI)O
Iudaeos quodam festivitatis suae sollemni Aman ad poenae quondam recordationem incendere et sanctae crucis adsimulatam speciem in contemptum Christianae fidei sacrilega mente exurere provinciarum rectores prohibeant, ne iocis suis fidei nostrae signum inmisceant, sed ritus suos citra contemptum Christianae legis retineant, amissuri sine dubio permissa hactenus, nisi ab inlicitis temperaverint.
DAT. IIII KAL. IUN. CONSTANT(INO)P(OLI) BASSO ET PHILIPPO CONSS.

THE TWO EMPERORS AND AUGUSTI HONORIUS AND THEODOSIUS TO ANTHEMIUS PRAEFECTUS PRAETORIO
The governors of the provinces shall prohibit the Jews from setting fire to Aman in memory of his past punishment, in a certain ceremony of their festival, and from burning with sacrilegious intent a form made to resemble the saint cross in contempt of the Christian faith, lest

---

NPNF second series, vol. 10, p. 87 (where it is numbered iii.21.123). See further, Thornton, "Haman," 422n.

[53] Jerome, *Comm. Gal.* ii (on Gal 3:13–14; in Migne, *PL* 26, 388A). In this sense Jerome also compares Jesus with the three whom Nebuchadnezzar threw into the furnace (Dan 3:20), with Eleazar and the Maccabean martyrs (2 Macc 6:27ff.), and especially with Naboth whom Jezabel arranged executed on the false charge of blasphemy (1 Kings 21:8–16).

[54] Outside polemical contexts, contrast, for example, the mere talk of Haman's suspension (ἐκρεμάσθη – 'hung,' rather than using 'crucified') in Hippolytus, *Comm. Daniel* iii.30. See text in G. Nath. Bonwetsch and Hans Achelis, *Hippolytus Werke Erster Band: Exegetische und homiletische Schriften*, GCS 1 (Leipzig: J. C. Hinrichs, 1897), p. 178. French translation in *SC* 14, p. 162. Hippolytus appears to quote either Esther 5:14 or 7:9–10, but the wording is not an exact citation (it appears closest to the B-text of 7:9–10, in which case he willfully omits Σταυρωθήτω). Also note (Ps.?)-Hippolytus, *Chronicon* §685 (*Aman autem suspensus est*); text in Adolf Bauer and Rudolf Helm, *Hippolytus Werke Vierter Band: Die Chronik*, 2nd ed., GCS 46 (Leipzig: J. C. Hinrichs, 1955), p. 110. Similarly, note Rufinus' Latin translation of Origen, *Princ.* iii.2.4 (*quidem eius Aman suspendi iuberet*); text in Paul Koetschau, ed., *Origenes Werke, Fünfter Band: De Principiis [ΠΕΡΙ ΑΡΧΩΝ]*, GCS 22 (Leipzig: J. C. Hinrichs, 1913), p. 251.

[55] *CTh* xvi.8.18. Text in Th. Mommsen and Paul M. Meyer, *Theodosiani libri XVI cum constitutionibus Sirmondianis et Leges novellae ad Theodosianum Pertinentes*, 2 vols. (Berlin: Weidmann, 1954), vol. 1/2, 891. Translation and notes in Amnon Linder, *The Jews in Roman Imperial Legislation* (Detroit: Wayne State University Press, 1987), 236–38 (#36). The final line places the legislation on 29 May 408 (so Linder, p. 238).

they mingle the sign of our faith with their jests, and they shall restrain their rites from ridiculing the Christian Law, for they are bound to lose what had been permitted them till now unless they abstain from those matters which are forbidden.
GIVEN ON THE FOURTH DAY BEFORE THE CALENDS OF JUNE AT CONSTANTINOPLE, IN THE CONSULATE OF BASSUS AND PHILIPPUS.

This decree from the Theodosian Code is reiterated in the Justinian Code, which records: "The Jews should not put on fire the figure of the cross in the form of Aman, or they shall forfeit those religious matters that they were previously granted."[56] The imperial legislators apparently believed that certain Jewish rites during the festival of Purim (which commemorates the victory over Haman and other anti-Semites) involved the burning of the cross (probably to be understood as an effigy of Haman).[57] These legislators understood this as an act critical of Christianity.

Further evidence exists of Christian belief in Jewish celebration of Haman's crucifixion. Thus, a later Byzantine Christian baptismal formula for Jewish converts imprecates those who nail Haman to wood in the shape of the cross, burning him in effigy and thus exposing Christians to maledictions. That formula reads: "I next curse those who keep the festival of the so-called Mordecai on the first Sabbath of the Christian fasts (= Lent), nailing Haman to wood and then mixing with him the emblem of a cross and burning them together, subjecting Christians to all kinds of imprecations and a curse."[58] Socrates, in his *Historia Ecclesiae*, also famously alleged that Jews in their merry-making once affixed a boy to a cross. It has been argued that this (dubious) allegation must have been connected somehow with Purim celebrations and with the Christian view of those celebrations as reflected in the Christian laws concerning Purim and in baptismal formulae.[59]

---

[56] *CJ* i.9.11: Οἱ Ἰουδαῖοι μὴ ἐν σχήματι τοῦ Ἀμᾶν τὸν τύπον τοῦ σταυροῦ καιέτωσαν. ἐπεὶ καὶ τῆς ἐπιτετραμμένης αὐτοῖς θρησκείας στεροῦνται. Text and translation in Amnon Linder, *The Jews in the Legal Sources of the Early Middle Ages* (Detroit: Wayne State University Press, 1997), 48 (#65).

[57] Purim festivals have long been noted for their revelries (cf. *b. Meg.* 7b – ordaining drunkenness). See bibliography in Linder, *Jews in Roman Imperial Legislation*, p. 238.

[58] The translation is from Thornton ("Haman," 424), who also provides the following corrected text (the original text appears in the appendix to the Clementine Recognitions in *PG* 1, 1457C): ἀναθεματίζω μετὰ τούτων καὶ τοὺς τὴν ἑορτὴν τελοῦντας τοῦ λεγομένου Μαρδοχαίου κατὰ τὸ πρῶτον Σάββατον τῶν Χριστιανικῶν νηστειῶν καὶ ξύλῳ δῆθεν τὸ Ἀμᾶν προσηλοῦντας, εἶτα μιγνύντας αὐτῷ τὸ σταυροῦ σημεῖον, καὶ συγκατακαίοντας [*PG* συγκατατάιοντας], ἀραῖς τε παντοίαις καὶ ἀναθέματι τοὺς Χριστιανοὺς ὑποβάλλοντας. Juster discusses this and other baptismal formulae for Jewish converts in Jean Juster, *Les Juifs dans l'Empire Romaine: Leur condition juridique, économique et sociale*, 2 vols. (Paris, 1914), 1:114–19.

[59] Socrates, *HE*, vii.16.1–5; text in Günther Christian Hansen, ed., *Sokrates Kirchengeschichte*, GCS, n.f. 1 (Berlin: Akademie Verlag, 1995), 361; translation in *NPNF* series 2, vol. 2, p. 161. This account has rightly been viewed with skepticism in light of the frequency in that period of anti-Semitic Christian charges of "blood libel" against Jews.

In light of this scattered (but unified) Christian evidence, it is fascinating to read that a later medieval Jewish perspective, found in the Cairo Genizah targumic fragments on Esther, does indeed indirectly associate the cross in the book of Esther with the Christian church:[60]

> The House of Israel were gathered and sat before him [Mordecai], saying, 'You caused them, the House of Israel, all of this trouble, for if you had risen before Haman and bowed down to him, then all of this oppression would not have come upon us.' Mordecai responded and said to them, to Israel, 'The garment that the wicked Haman was wearing had two crosses [צְלִיבִין] embroidered on it, one on its front and one on its back; and if I were to rise and bow down to him, I would in effect be practicing idolatry. And you know that anyone who practices idolatry [will be destroyed] from this world and from the world to come.'

Here Haman's apparel likely parallels that of Christian priests, whose robes bore crosses on the front and back. Thus, there appears in this Jewish targumic text an indirect charge of idolatry at the worship of the [Christian] cross. Yet, Haman's clothes also make an ironic point, since his death later in the targum occurs on the cross (צְלִיבָא).

In this context, the fifth-century dialogue by Evagrius, *Altercatio Simonis et Theophili*, places on the lips of its Jewish antagonist this interesting argument against the messianic status of Jesus:[61]

> *Simon Iudaeus dixit*: Aestuo vehementer cogitatione potuisse Christum tam maledictam et ludibriosam sustinere passionem, si tamen vera sunt, quae dicitis, a patribus nostris crucis patibulo esse suffixum. Scimus plane Aman maledictum a patribus nostris pro merito suo esse crucifixum, qui genus nostrum petierat in perditionem, in cuius morte pereuoluto[62] anno gratulamur et sollemnia votorum facta[63] celebramus, quod a patribus tradita accepimus.

Nevertheless, regardless of the legitimacy of Socrates' charge, the idea appeared to Socrates plausible enough. This must be due to a common Christian notion that Jewish Purim celebrations tended toward drunken excess, and that such celebrations could employ crucifixion imagery. Among others, Thornton ("Haman," 424) draws this connection between the Socrates account and Christian views of Purim celebrations.

[60] Cambridge University Library T-S B 12.21 folio 1v, lines 1–7. Text and translation in Rimon Kasher and Michael L. Klein, "New Fragments of Targum to Esther from the Cairo Geniza," *HUCA* 61 (1990): 95, 105. Kasher and Klein remark that this manuscript is from the eleventh or twelfth century (on p. 91).

[61] *Altercatio Simonis et Theophilis*, ii.4. Text in Edward Bratke, ed., *Scriptores ecclesiastici minores saeculorum IV. V. VI., Fasciculus I: Evagrii Altercatio legis inter Simonem Iudaeum et Theophilum Christianum*, CSEL 45 (Vindobonae: F. Tempsky/Lipsiae: G. Freytag, 1904), p. 25. This translation is mine. A new edition with Harnack's text and a new translation is conveniently found in William Varner, *Ancient Jewish-Christian Dialogues* (Lewiston, N.Y.: Edwin Mellen, 2004), pp. 112–113 (Varner, following Harnack, labels the text as vi.22). On this dialogue see A. Lukyn Williams, *Adversus Judaeos: A Bird's-Eye View of Christian Apologiae until the Renaissance* (Cambridge: Cambridge University Press, 1935), 298–305.

[62] Varner reads *peracta revoluto* instead of *perevoluto* (*Dialogues*, p. 112).

[63] Varner (*Dialogues*, pp. 112–13) here reads *votorum festa* (which he understands as 'festivals of prayers') rather than *votorum facta* ('with the fixed deed of offerings'). Varner

Simon the Jew said: I am powerfully agitated by the thought that it is possible for the Christ to endure such a cursed and derisive passion (if nevertheless the things which you say are true), being fastened by our fathers upon the patibulum of a cross. We clearly know Haman the cursed was crucified by our fathers for his due reward – he who attempted to bring our race into destruction, in whose death we rejoice as the year comes round and we celebrate with the fixed deed of offerings, because we received [this] as handed down from the fathers.

According to Evagrius' Jewish antagonist Simon, the curse of Jesus' crucifixion is made all the more substantial when it is shown that Jesus' punishment was the same as that of Haman "the cursed." Simon insists that one of the striking similarities between Jesus and Haman is not just that they were both crucified, but that they were both deemed worthy of such a cursed death "by our fathers."[64] He argues that this death of Haman is what brings festivity on the annual celebration (i.e., Purim) commended by the fathers. After the passage cited above, Simon then refers to Absalom the parricide, who was hung in the tree (2 Sam 18:9), as a further example of such a curse. Finally, in a climactic concluding flourish, Simon cites Deuteronomy 21:23 as definitive evidence that Jesus' crucifixion proves that he was cursed (see further below).

The citation of Deuteronomy 21:23 here in this dialogue follows the Christian text of Galatians 3:13 rather than the MT or even the LXX; and this illustrates that one must be cautious about affirming the details in Evagrius' *Altercatio* as actual historical Jewish polemic. However, Simon's employment of crucifixion motifs is in keeping with Jewish interpretive traditions about Haman's death (chapter 3, §8 above). It also would align well with the Haman/Christ analogy reported in Jewish anti-Christian Purim activities, which were outlawed (as noted above) in the roughly contemporary Theodosian and Justinian codes. More interesting is the reaction of Evagrius' character Theophilus the Christian, who counters that these curses and exemplars are not applicable to Christ, since Christ was without sin.[65] Note here

---

also understands the following clause to begin with *quae* ('which,' referring to the festivals) rather than *quod* ('because').

[64] An interesting translation dilemma concerns whether to understand the second use of *a patribus nostris* ('by our fathers') as adverbial to *maledictum* ('the cursed'), which precedes "by our fathers," or as adverbial to the verb *esse crucifixum* ('was crucified'), which follows. The difference would concern whether Haman was merely *cursed* by their Jewish ancestors (as Varner reads in *Dialogues*, p. 113), or whether Haman was understood as actually *crucified* by the ancestors. I have followed the latter translation because: (1) the ablative of personal agent naturally would be used with the passive verb; (2) the crucifixion is represented as a just act to be lauded (*pro merito suo* – 'for his due reward'); and (3) this clause then parallels the use of *a patribus nostris* in the previous clause. Thus Evagrius makes his Jewish interlocutor suggest that, just as his Jewish ancestors crucified Jesus, so his ancestors had rightly crucified Haman.

[65] *Altercatio*, ii.4 (Bratke, *Evagrii Altercatio*, p. 26; lines 11ff.). See Varner, *Dialogues*, pp. 112–113 (listed as vi.22).

that Theophilus does not dispute the crucifixion of Haman; rather, he attempts to prove that the despicable Haman is not a true exemplar of the sinless crucified Jesus.

The evidence thus points to an occasional acknowledgment, especially in later Church Fathers, that Haman was crucified. However, partly in light of supposed Jewish use of this analogy, Haman's death is not taken up as a type of Christ.[66] Instead, any continuity between the deaths of Haman and Jesus are rejected, and Jewish acts that could conceivably signal such associations are outlawed.

5. *Summary*: While a few later Church Fathers occasionally admitted that crucifixion associations could be connected to the executionary suspensions of some OT characters, the fact that the Bible treated these individuals negatively generally required that these OT figures be rejected as exemplars of the crucified Christ. On the other hand, their brutal deaths could occasionally be mentioned in the context of moralizing examples. Most importantly, Jewish polemic, especially in connection with Purim traditions, appears occasionally to have picked up on the parallels between Jesus' crucifixion and Haman's death. This would help explain why the Christian rejection of Haman as a type of Christ is especially caustic.

5. The Curse of the Cross

During his heated denouncement of an apparently heterodox Jewish-Christian theology, the Apostle Paul quotes Deuteronomy 21:22–23 in Galatians 3:13:

Χριστὸς ἡμᾶς ἐξηγόρασεν ἐκ τῆς κατάρας τοῦ νόμου γενόμενος ὑπὲρ ἡμῶν κατάρα, ὅτι γέγραπται· ἐπικατάρατος πᾶς ὁ κρεμάμενος ἐπὶ ξύλου,

Christ redeemed us from the curse of the law, becoming a curse for us; for it is written, 'Cursed is everyone who hangs on a tree.'

---

[66] Particularly unconvincing is Aus' attempt to connect the Gospels' account of the release of Barabbas with the Esther narratives; see Roger David Aus, *Barabbas and Esther and Other Studies in the Judaic Illumination of Earliest Christianity*, South Florida Studies in the History of Judaism 54 (Atlanta: Scholars Press, 1992), 1–27. Early in that chapter Aus draws some interesting parallels between the Gospels and the Esther traditions; yet, significant problems include: (1) Aus' tendency to combine discrete and unparalleled traditions in various Jewish documents without regard to their date, to their distribution, or to whether these disparate traditions have ever been seen together, (2) an assumption that, when NT Gospel texts make OT allusions, such NT texts are necessarily unhistorical, (3) a stretched and implausible connection between Barabbas and the brief mention of Barnabazos, whom Josephus names as Mordecai's informant, (4) a failure to recognize that Barabbas is viewed negatively in the Gospels while Mordecai's informant presumably would have been viewed positively by Josephus (and any that knew such a tradition), and (5) a lack of analysis of early Christian interpretations of the Gospels and of Esther to confirm (or to deny) his thesis.

Neither the Hebrew nor the LXX is actually cited here. Instead, Paul paraphrases the text of Deuteronomy 21:23 in a way that parallels the cursing
language of Deuteronomy 27:26 as cited in Galatians 3:10 (ἐπικατάρατος
πᾶς).[67] His paraphrase generally follows the early interpretation of Deuteronomy 21:23 found in the LXX – both envisage the "curse of God" (אֱלֹהִים
קְלָלַת) in Deuteronomy to be God's cursing of all people who are hung on the
tree (subjective genitive).[68] Paul's argument contends that only faith in Christ
can provide justification, since the crucifixion curse on Christ (3:13) serves as
a viable exchange for the curse otherwise residing on those who are under law
(3:10).[69] It is in order to signal that connection between the two curses in

---

[67] The principle difference between Deuteronomy (both in the MT and in the LXX) and
Galatians concerns the lack of explicit reference to God in Paul's paraphrase; see F. F. Bruce,
The Epistle to the Galatians: A Commentary on the Greek Text, NIGTC (Grand Rapids:
Eerdmans, 1982), 165–66. Paul emphasizes, as does the LXX, a universal sense (πᾶς) in the
participle κρεμάμενος ('hung'; cf. merely תָּלוּי in the MT); and also Paul specifies like the
LXX that such hanging occurs ἐπὶ ξύλου ('on a tree') in continuity with previous phraseology in 21:22–23. In contrast to the language used in the LXX, Paul employs ἐπικατάρατος
for "cursed" rather than κεκατηραμένος (LXX), thus enabling him to parallel this text with
his citation of Deuteronomy 27:26 found earlier in Galatians 3:10.

[68] Also cf. *Tg. Neof.* Deut 21:23 (דִצְלִיב כל ייי קדם לִיט). There is little actual func-
tional difference between the perfect participle in the LXX (κεκατηραμένος) and the
adjective in Paul (ἐπικατάρατος). The omission of ὑπὸ θεοῦ here is likely necessitated in
order to create the parallel wording with Galatians 3:10.

[69] Much ink has been spilled attempting to understand the nature of this "viable
exchange." The debate is too lengthy, and the topic not sufficiently relevant, to enter into
fully here. "Vicarious substitution" is supported in Ronald Y. K. Fung, *The Epistle to the
Galatians*, NICNT (Grand Rapids: Eerdmans, 1988), 150; cf. J. B. Lightfoot, *The Epistle of
St. Paul to the Galatians* (Reprint. Grand Rapids: Zondervan, 1957), 139; and see Kjell Arne
Morland, *The Rhetoric of Curse in Galatians: Paul Confronts Another Gospel* (Atlanta:
Scholars Press, 1995), 221–24 (who prefers to call this "expiation"). "Interchange" of bless-
ing and curse via participation in Christ is suggested by M. D. Hooker, "Interchange in
Christ," *JTS* n.s. 22 (1971): 349–52 (reprint 13–16); also Bruce, *Galatians*, 168. The refer-
ence to Deut 27:26 in Gal 3:10 may refer to a "covenant breaker" (Bruce, *Galatians*, 164; cf.
Morland, *Rhetoric of Curse*, 51–64) or to one who is set outside of the covenant promise (J.
D. G. Dunn, *The Theology of Paul's Letter to the Galatians* [Cambridge: Cambridge University Press, 1993], 86) – in either case, for Paul the Messiah takes upon himself that role. That
the Messiah's work is "for us" (ὑπὲρ ἡμῶν) probably refers to both Jewish people under the
law (Gal 4:5) and to Gentiles, since Gentiles join in those: who are "all" under a curse
(Gal 3:10; note here πᾶς and πᾶσιν), who are explicitly included in those receiving benefits
from Christ's work (εἰς τὰ ἔθνη in Gal 3:14), and who are elsewhere treated as under law in
Paul (cf. Rom 2:14f.); see Bruce, *Galatians*, 166–167. Dunn famously contended that the
"curse of the Law" is a curse upon all those who "restrict the grace and promise of God in
nationalistic terms, who treat the law as a boundary to mark the people of God off from the
Gentiles..."; see James D. G. Dunn, "Works of the Law and the Curse of the Law (Galatians
3.10–14)," *NTS* 31 (1985): 536 (reprint 228–229, also 237–241). In contrast, one might well
consider Donaldson's assertion that the "curse of the Law" brings bondage to sin and to the
powers of this age because the law produces transgressions in its sinful adherents; see T. L.

Galatians 3:10 and 3:13 that Paul conforms his paraphrase of Deuteronomy 21:23 to the language of Deuteronomy 27:26 in Galatians 3:10.

For present purposes, the crucial assumption in Paul's argument is that the cursing of Deuteronomy 21:23 (in the sense of the subjective genitive supported by the LXX[70]) applies to the crucified person and hence to Jesus. Some have contended this hearkens back to what Paul would have believed prior to his conversion experience.[71] Certainly, Paul as a converted Jewish follower of Jesus reverses the negative associations, which such a curse would have, into a positive understanding of the work of Christ on the cross.[72]

Max Wilcox contends explicit allusions to Deuteronomy 21:22–23 may be found wherever the NT employs the language of "hanging on a tree." In particular, such allusions occur in the Petrine kerygma of Acts 5:30 and 10:39 (both κρεμάσαντες ἐπὶ ξύλου) as well as in the statements of Acts 13:29 (ἀπὸ τοῦ ξύλου) and 1 Pet 2:24 (ἐπὶ τὸ ξύλον).[73] Such an allusive use of the Deuteronomic text is certainly possible; however, given the general association of crucifixion with "hanging on the tree" in Semitic examples of the period, it seems more likely that these NT texts merely employ a standard Semitism of the age.[74] To establish a definite allusion to Deut 21:22–23 it

---

Donaldson, "The 'Curse of the Law' and the Inclusion of the Gentiles: Galatians 3.13–14," *NTS* 32 (1986): 94–112 (esp. 104–105).

[70] The lack of inclusion of "by God" in his citation of Deut 21:22–23 should not be taken to imply that the "curse of the Law" came not from God, but from the Law itself (whereas God only blesses). For this view, see J. Louis Martyn, *Galatians*, AB 33a (New York: Doubleday, 1997), 324–328. On the contrary, Paul is well aware that the Law itself comes from the hand of God (Rom 7:22; 8:7; 1 Cor 9:9, 21; Gal 3:21).

[71] E.g., Martin Hengel and Anna Maria Schwemer, *Paul Between Damascus and Antioch*, trans. John Bowden (London: SCM Press, 1997), 99–100. Also see the fuller treatment in Martin Hengel and Anna Maria Schwemer, *Paulus zwischen Damaskus und Antiochien: Die unbekannten Jahre des Apostels*, WUNT I.108 (Tübingen: Mohr Siebeck, 1998), 164–65.

[72] Recent analyses of Paul's argument Galatians 3:13 also draw on the importance of Jewish (esp. Qumran) interpretations of Deuteronomy 21:22–23. See esp. Heinz-Wolfgang Kuhn, "Die Bedeutung der Qumrantexte für das Verständnis des Galaterbriefes aus dem Münchener Projekt: Qumran und das Neue Testament," in *New Qumran Texts and Studies: Proceedings of the First Meeting of the International Organization for Qumran Studies, Paris 1992*, ed. George J. Brooke and Florentino García Martínez, STDJ 15 (Leiden: E. J. Brill, 1994), 178–82 (summary on 171–72).

[73] Max Wilcox, "'Upon the Tree' – Deut 21:22–23 in the New Testament," *JBL* 96 (1977): 90–94. Wilcox is followed by others; for example, see John T. Carroll and Joel B. Green, *The Death of Jesus in Early Christianity* (Peabody, Mass.: Hendrickson, 1995), 171–172; George J. Brooke, *The Dead Sea Scrolls and the New Testament* (Minneapolis: Fortress, 2005), 99–100 (here one certainly need not go as far as Brooke in suggesting that the NT authors were using a "text type" of Deuteronomy similar to 11QTemple lxiv).

[74] Cf. 4QpNah 3–4 i 6–8; 11QTemple lxiv.6–13; and the tendency, frequently discussed above (esp. in chapter 3), to render biblical תלה אותו על [ה]עץ texts with crucifixion terminology. Semitisms, of course, are plentiful in Acts, as Wilcox himself has recognized in

would be helpful to have more explicit connections between these NT texts and Deuteronomy 21, but these are largely lacking.[75] This is not, however, to preclude the impact of Deuteronomy 21 (often via Paul) on later Christian writers (especially those outside a Semitic context) who speak of Jesus "suspended on a tree."[76]

Nonetheless, these texts corroborate the view (asserted above in chapter three) that "hanging on a tree" could designate "crucify" in multiple Semitic contexts. Quite likely, a similar Semitism for crucifixion on the ξύλον ('tree/wood') lies behind the metaphorical saying of Jesus, who, while being led to the cross, turns to the daughters of Jerusalem and instructs them not to weep for him, but rather to cry for their own children, saying, "if they do these things with the moist wood [ἐν τῷ ὑγρῷ ξύλῳ], what will happen with the dry?" I wonder, given the proverbial nature of some of Jesus' most elusive eschatological imagery in Luke (e.g., 18:37), if the saying is intended to reference the mass crucifixions of Jewish revolutionaries and λῃσταί/ κακοῦργοι (23:32–33; cf. 22:52) leading up to, and during, the Jewish Revolt (cf. 21:20–24; 23:28–30).[77]

Another possible NT allusion to Deuteronomy 21:23 has been found in the Jewish desire to bury the corpses of Jesus and other crucified victims (esp. John 19:31).[78] However, though general Jewish traditions on the need for burial may be traced in part back to Deuteronomy 21, the Johannine text actually relates the Jewish desire for burial more to the solemnity of the Passover Sabbath (cf. also John 19:42), and thus John does not make explicit allusion to Deuteronomy 21:23.[79] The Joseph of Arimathea traditions in the

---

Max Wilcox, *The Semitisms of Acts* (Oxford: Clarendon Press, 1965), see esp. pp. 34–35 (which contain his treatment of Deut 21:22).

[75] Wilcox ("Upon the Tree," 92–93) is most convincing regarding Acts 13:28–30, but the connections could be nothing more than superficial resemblances save for the mention of ξύλον, which is part of the Semitism.

[76] E.g., Melito, *De fide* (see SC 123, p. 242, line 35); Origen, *Comm. Matt.* 142 (GCS 38, p. 295, line 23); Origen, *Gen. Hom.* ii.4 (GCS 29, p. 33, line 8). See also notes below.

[77] Luke 23:31. Such a reference in 23:31 to the cross has also been suggested by Joseph A. Fitzmyer, *The Gospel According to Luke*, 2 vols., AB 28 (Garden City: Doubleday, 1981–1985), 2:1498–99. However, Nolland argues that the metaphor trades on imagery of fire and wood, though he cannot ascertain exactly what that fire/wood metaphor means; see John Nolland, *Luke*, 3 vols., WBC 35 (Dallas: Word, 1989–1993), 3:1138.

[78] The NA[27] OT citation apparatus suggests an allusion here to Deuteronomy 21:23. Modern commentators also reference Deut 21 to explain the desire for burial; e.g., Brown, *Death of the Messiah*, 2:1174; Donald Senior, *The Passion of Jesus in the Gospel of John* (Collegeville, Minn.: Michael Glazier, 1991), 120–21. Perhaps one should contrast this with Revelation 11:9–10 (where the dead bodies of the two prophets are left unburied for three and a half days before rising again).

[79] This is also the opinion of Judith M. Lieu, "Reading in Canon and Community: Deuteronomy 21.22–23, A Test Case for Dialogue," in *The Bible in Human Society*, ed. M. Daniel Carroll et al., JSOTSup 200 (Sheffield: Sheffield Academic Press, 1995), 325–26.

Synoptics also speak of his laudable desire to bury Jesus. While Mark attributes this to the day of his death being the day of preparation for the Sabbath (Mark 15:42; cf. John 19:31), Matthew and Luke omit such a mention (Matt 27:58; Luke 23:52). So, Matthew and Luke may be indebted to a general sense of need to bury the dead, although, again here, the Deuteronomic text could only very inferentially be in the background. However, by the time of the (likely second-century) *Gospel of Peter*, the burial of Jesus is considered to be necessitated "in the Law," which commands the executed person be buried before sundown: "And Herod said, 'Brother Pilate, even if no one had asked for him, we would bury him, since also the Sabbath dawns. For it is written in the Law, *let not the sun set on the one who has been put to death.*'" (*Gos. Pet.* ii.5).[80]

Outside the NT, many early Christian authors refer to Deuteronomy 21 while speaking about the cross. Often their comments are overtly indebted to Paul's allusion in Galatians 3:13.[81] Sometimes however, especially in earlier works, the use of Deuteronomy 21:22–23 appears to be different from that found in Paul. So the second century *Dialogue of Jason and Papiscus,* by Aristo of Pella, apparently contained a reference to Deuteronomy 21:23 in the form λοιδορία θεοῦ ὁ κρεμάμενος ('a reproach of God is the one hung'). However, Jerome, our source for this knowledge, does not inform us whether it is the Jewish character or the Christian who cites the verse in this dialogue.[82] In the same source, Jerome notes that Deuteronomy 21:23 was

----

[80] Greek text of ii.5: καὶ ὁ Ἡρῴδης ἔφη· «Ἀδελφὲ Πειλᾶτε, εἰ καὶ μή τις αὐτὸν ᾐτήκει, ἡμεῖς αὐτὸν ἐθάπτομεν, ἐπεὶ καὶ σάββατον ἐπιφώσκει. Γέγραπται γὰρ ἐν τῷ νόμῳ ἥλιον μὴ δῦναι ἐπὶ πεφονευμένῳ.» Text in M. G. Mara, *Évangile de Pierre*, SC 201 (Paris: Cerf, 1973), p. 42 (comments pp. 86–87, 128). See also *Gos. Pet.* v.15 (Mara, *Évangile de Pierre*, p. 48). In neither ii.5 nor v.15 does the Greek correspond to the LXX of Deut 21:23, but the allusion is almost certainly here (though note also Josh 8:29; 10:27). One could compare the much later tradition in some *Toledoth Jeshu* texts that Jesus, knowing that the Jews would have to bury his body in accordance with Deuteronomy 21:23, made (false) predictions that he would no longer be found on the cross – see, for example, MS T.-S. Loan 87 folio 2ʳ lines 7–8, 11–25 (from transl. by Horbury, "Critical Examination," 86–88, cf. pp. 106–9, 192–93).

[81] E.g., Irenaeus, *Contra Haer.* iii.18.3 (cf. iv.10.2; v.18.1,3); Tertullian, *Adv. Marc.* iii.18.1; v.3.9–10; *Adv. Prax.* 29.3–4; *De fuga* 12.2; Eusebius, *Dem.* i.10.23; Epiphanius, *Pan.* lxvi.79.6–10.

[82] See Jerome, *Comm. Gal.* ii (on Gal 3:13–14; in Migne, *PL* 26, 387B). "*Memini me in Altercatione Jasonis et Papisci, quae Graeco sermone conscripta est, ita reperisse:* λοιδορία θεοῦ ὁ κρεμάμενος, *id est,* maledictio Dei qui appensus est." – "I am reminded in the *Dialogue of Jason and Papiscus,* which has been written as a Greek discussion, that thus I discovered: λοιδορία θεοῦ ὁ κρεμάμενος, that is, 'a reproach of God is he who has been hung.'" This text is also noted in I. C. Th. Otto, *Corpus Apologetarum christianorum saeculi secundi,* 9 vols. (Ienae: Hermann Dufft, 1857–1879), 9:357. Skarsaune has argued that this *Dialogue* was Justin's "recapitulation source" of *testimonia*; see Oskar Skarsaune, *The Proof from Prophecy: A Study in Justin Martyr's Proof-Text Tradition: Text-Type, Provenance, Theological Profile,* NovTSup 56 (Leiden: E. J. Brill, 1987), 234–42 (esp. 238). However, at

known among the law-oriented, Christian heretical sect of the Ebionites in the form ὕβρις θεοῦ ὁ κρεμάμενος ('an outrage towards God is the one hung').[83] Jerome also cites a "Hebrew" person (possibly a Jewish-Christian) who taught him that verse 23 should be translated as if God himself has been hung in an insulting manner.[84] This last understanding (that of Jerome's Hebrew source) differs from the others by explicitly identifying the victim with God[85]; naturally, this might have some attraction among Christians, who understood Jesus as the crucified God incarnate. In any case, all of these translations Jerome cites support an objective-genitive understanding of קִלְלַת אֱלֹהִים in Deuteronomy 21:23 (cf. the discussion of blasphemer above) in contrast to the Septuagint and to Paul.

The text in the *Epistle of Barnabas* 5:13 ('for it was necessary that He should suffer on a tree') does not appear to be arguing from Deuteronomy 21:22–23, since the context (5:13b–14) supplies the prophetic proof texts – a melding of Psalms and Isaianic citations.[86] More promisingly, the mention in *the Epistle of Barnabas* (7:7, 9) of the typological curse on the scapegoat may indeed be an allusion to Paul's reference to Deuteronomy 21 in Galatians 3:13 (since both 7:7 and 7:9 read ἐπικατάρατος).[87] However, the

---

least for Deuteronomy 21:23, Skarsaune's claim is predicated on the assumption that Aristo himself affirmed (presumably via the mouth of the Christian and not the Jew) this as the correct translation/interpretation of the verse. Jerome, however, does not provide enough information to verify this assumption.

[83] Jerome, *Comm. Gal.* ii (on Gal 3:13–14; in Migne, *PL* 26, 387B): "*Haec verba Ebion ille haeresiarches Semichristianus, et Semijudaeus ita interpretatus est*, ὅτι ὕβρις θεοῦ ὁ κρεμάμενος, *id est*, quia injuria Dei est suspensus." [My corrected Greek diacritics.] – "These words Ebion, that semi-Christian and semi-Jewish heresiarch, has interpreted thus, ὅτι ὕβρις θεοῦ ὁ κρεμάμενος, 'because an insult of God is the one hung.'" For ὕβρις plus genitive in the sense of "outrage towards" see Liddell-Scott, s.v.

[84] Ibid. "*Dicebat mihi Hebraeus qui me in Scripturis aliqua ex parte instituit, quod possit et ita legi*: quia contumeliose Deus suspensus est." – "A Hebrew, who partly instructed me in the Scriptures to some extent, said to me that it is also possible to be read thus: 'because God has been hung in an insulting way.'"

[85] For such a direct statement of God being hung, compare the parable of the twins by R. Meir quoted above in chapter 3 (§4.7).

[86] Contrast Wilcox, "Upon the Tree," 85; and Martin C. Albl, *"And Scripture Cannot be Broken": The Form and Function of the Early Christian Testimonia Collections*, NovTSup. 96 (Leiden: Brill, 1999), 155. On the quotation in *Barnabas* 5:13b see Hans Windisch, *Die Apostolischen Väter III: Der Barnabasbrief*, HNT (Tübingen: J. C. B. Mohr [Paul Siebeck], 1920), 332; Pierre Prigent and Robert A. Kraft, *Épître de Barnabé*, SC 172 (Paris: Cert, 1971), 113–14n.; Ferdinand R. Prostmeier, *Der Barnabasbrief*, Kommentar zu den Apostolischen Vätern 8 (Göttingen: Vandenhoeck & Ruprecht, 1999), 250n.

[87] This *Barnabas* passage makes a common Christian typological use of the scapegoat of Leviticus 16:7–10, applying it to the sin-removing work of Christ. Note that, while the Leviticus text mentions no curse on the scapegoat, *Barnabas* adds this detail, employing the same word for curse (ἐπικατάρατος) as is found in Galatians 3:13, where it depicts the work of Christ. So *Barn.* 7:9: "Listen: 'the first goat is for the altar, but the other is accursed [τὸν

author of *Barnabas* shies away from any overt discussion of the Deuteronomic text.

In the Fathers, the earliest extant, overt reference to the curse of Deuteronomy 21:23 appears on the lips of the Jew Trypho in Justin's *Dialogue*. For Justin's Jewish protagonist, the shamefulness of the cross can be proven from the statement in the law: "Cursed is the one crucified" (ἐπικατάρατος γὰρ ὁ σταυρούμενος ἐν τῷ νόμῳ λέγεται εἶναι; *Dial*. 89.2).[88] Trypho reiterates this challenge a few sentences later and speaks of the "death cursed in the law."[89] Trypho's appeal in *Dialogue* 32 to "the last curse contained in law" also likely concerns Deuteronomy 21:23.[90]

Justin, as the Christian apologist in the *Dialogue*, is slow to directly address Trypho's challenge; and he first adduces typological exemplars of Christ's crucifixion (90–91). When Justin finally tackles Trypho's appeal to Deuteronomy 21 (*Dial*. 94.5), he initially declares that, while the Law does pronounce a curse against crucified people, no such curse lies against Christ![91] This comes as quite a surprise to those steeped in Paul's argument in Galatians 3:13, which apparently affirms that Christ did bear a curse.[92] Justin, however, then hastens on to parallel Paul's usage in Galatians, arguing that all are under a curse for having failed to keep the law perfectly (95.1; cf. Gal 3:10, Deut 27:26), but that Christ took up this curse (95.2; cf. Gal 3:13) for every race of man (cf. Gal 3:14). Thus, Justin is not only aware of Paul's

---

δὲ ἕνα ἐπικατάρατον],' and note that the one that is accursed is crowned [τὸν ἐπικατάρατον ἐστεφανωμένον], because then 'they will see him' on that day with the long scarlet robe 'down to the feet' on his body, and they will say, 'Is not this he whom we once crucified and rejected and pierced and spat upon?'" Text and translation in Kirsopp Lake, *The Apostolic Fathers*, 2 vols., LCL (Cambridge, Mass.: Harvard University Press, 1912), 366–367.

[88] Like many other references to Deut 21:23 in the Fathers, Justin's text appears influenced by the form found in Gal 3:13 (note the similar use of ἐπικατάρατος). This may cause one to question the authenticity of this challenge as truly coming from Jewish lips; however, Justin may still represent a real Jewish question, albeit in Christian Greek form. The authenticity issue is addressed further below.

[89] *Dial*. 90.1: εἰ δὲ καὶ σταυρωθῆναι καὶ οὕτως αἰσχρῶς καὶ ἀτίμως ἀποθανεῖν διὰ τοῦ κεκατηραμένου ἐν τῷ νόμῳ θανάτου, ἀπόδειξον ἡμῖν· ἡμεῖς γὰρ οὐδ' εἰς ἔννοιαν τούτου ἐλθεῖν δυνάμεθα. "But whether both to be crucified and to die thus shamefully and dishonourably via the death which has been cursed in the law, prove this to us; for we are unable to arrive at the thought of this."

[90] *Dial*. 32.1: οὗτος δὲ ὁ ὑμέτερος λεγόμενος Χριστὸς ἄτιμος καὶ ἄδοξος γέγονεν, ὡς καὶ τῇ ἐσχάτῃ κατάρᾳ τῇ ἐν τῷ νόμῳ τοῦ θεοῦ περιπεσεῖν· ἐσταυρώθη γάρ. "But this so-called Christ of yours has become dishonourable and disreputable, such that he even fell into the last curse in the law of God, for he was crucified."

[91] *Dial*. 94.5 οὐκ ἔτι δὲ καὶ κατὰ τοῦ Χριστοῦ τοῦ θεοῦ κατάρα κεῖται. "...but even yet a curse does not lie against the Christ of God..." Cf. *Dial*. 111.2.

[92] Contrary to the opinion of Ernest De Witt Burton, *A Critical and Exegetical Commentary on the Epistle to the Galatians*, ICC (Edinburgh: T. & T. Clark, 1921), 172; see Hooker, "Interchange in Christ," 349 (repr. 13).

argument, but integrates it into his own. However, Justin only speaks of Christ "taking up" or "receiving" this curse (ἀναδέχομαι in 95.2), not "becoming" a curse (contrast γενόμενος ὑπὲρ ἡμῶν κατάρα in Gal 3:13).[93] Then, he proceeds to the first full-fledged citation in his *Dialogue* of Deuteronomy 21:23 (*Dial.* 96.1; following the wording of Gal 3:13). But here, Justin claims that it actually applies to the cursing of the Christians in synagogues and to their deaths as martyrs (*Dial.* 96.1–3; cf 95.4).

On the one hand, Justin's response represents a rhetorical *tour-de-force* as he sidesteps Trypho's argument, explains Christian salvation from this curse, and then turns the passage against Trypho and the Jewish synagogue. However, Justin's argumentation also illustrates his own discomfort with the curse in Deuteronomy 21:23. Unlike Paul, he cannot affirm that the curse specifically applied to Christ, so he cautiously refers to Christ as "taking up" the curse before hastening on to give a wholly different (and less than convincing) argument that the text ultimately pertains to the cursing of Christian believers. In this regard, if Justin's use of Deuteronomy 21:22–23 in this dialogue should be attributed to a *testimonia* collection, then Skarsaune would surely be correct to claim that the collection itself must have represented opposition to the application of Deuteronomy 21:23 to Christ.[94] However, if the appeal to Deuteronomy 21:23 represents a live Jewish argument against Christianity in Justin's day, then Justin's attempt to side-step the text may be driven by real apologetic concerns.[95]

Other *contra Iudaeos* literature also consistently represents the Jewish party raising the issue of Deuteronomy 21:23. So, in a section of disputed provenance in Tertullian's *Adversus Iudaeos*, the author portrays Jews as contending both that the passion of Christ was not predicted in Scripture, and that the kind of death (*genus mortis*) Jesus suffered was accursed in keeping

---

[93] Note also the circumlocution Justin employs in 95.2: ὡς κεκατηραμένου – "as having been cursed."

[94] Skarsaune, *Proof*, 218–20. Skarsaune argues that *Dial.* 94.5 represents this "recapitulation source" in its rejection of the application of Deuteronomy 21:23 to Christ. Yet, Skarsaune also contends that Justin fully affirmed Paul's reasoning in 95.1f., thus creating a tension between 94.5 (even though already muted by Justin from his source) and 95.1f. The argument in 95.4–96.2 is "an after-thought, added to give polemical sting to the whole discussion." However, Skarsaune does not address himself to the crucial difference between Paul's wording γενόμενος ὑπὲρ ἡμῶν κατάρα and Justin's lesser ἀναδέχομαι. If this is taken into account, then the argument in 95.1–3 does appear a muted version of Paul's, and there seems less difference between the Christ, who was not cursed but took up the curses of others, and God, who commanded that the brazen serpent be suspended as a sign to salvation, but who remained blameless (*Dial.* 94.5, cf. 94.1–3; also note Christ is again said not to be cursed in 111.2).

[95] Of course, both possibilities could be true: in the midst of a live interaction with Jewish claims, Justin may have drawn on a *testimonia* tradition that opposed any consideration that Jesus had been cursed.

with Deuteronomy 21:23 (cited according to Gal 3:13).[96] The author, however, counters that Christ was not cursed for any sin in himself, but was exposed to such a death so that the prophecies that the messiah would be reviled might come true (*Adv. Iud.* x.2–5).

An interchange similar to the argument found in the manuscripts of Tertullian is also found in the *Dialogue of Timothy and Aquila*. Here yet again, the Jew (Aquila) initiates discussion of the text and derides the Christian for proclaiming as God the one accursed.[97] Timothy responds by saying that Christ was not accursed (οὐχ ἵνα αὐτὸς γένηται κατάρα), but that he came to destroy the curse of Adam written in the Law (Gen 3:17–19).[98]

As mentioned earlier, the *Altercatio Simonis et Theophili* likewise portrays its Jewish antagonist (Simon) as putting forth the Deuteronomic text (again in the form of Gal 3:13) in order to say that Jesus was cursed. In this regard, Simon also draws an analogy to Haman's cursed death via crucifixion. Theophilus the Christian responds to the challenge in a manner reminiscent of the Tertullian text, emphasizing the sinlessness of Christ and citing a string of proof texts showing prophetically that people would revile the Christ.[99]

In the *Dialogue of Athanasius and Zacchaeus* the Christian (Athanasius) actually introduces Deut 21:23 (quoting the form found in Gal 3:13), though the Jewish representative immediately seizes upon the opportunity to suggest

---

[96] Tertullian, *Adv. Iud.* x.1; see Hermann Tränkle, *Q. S. F. Tertulliani Adversus Iudaeos: mit Einleitung und kritischem Kommentar* (Wiesbaden: Franz Steiner, 1964), p. 26 (18–21). The latter portion of this treatise (including chapter 10) is judged by some to be a later addition to Tertullian's original work. Further, especially since Harnack, it has often been held that the author was not truly in contact with Jewish opposition, but in this work was furthering Tertullian's teaching of Christian doctrine (especially against the Marcionites, cf. *Adv. Marc.* i.11.8–9; iii.18.1; v.3.9–10). Tränkle provides a discussion of these issues, and those of possible sources (pp. xi–lxxxviii); also see discussion in Heinz Schreckenberg, *Die christlichen Adversus-Judaeos-Texte und ihr literarisches und historisches Umfeld (1.-11.Jh.)*, Europäische Hochschulschriften xxiii.172 (Frankfurt: Peter Lang, 1999), 216–25 (and note his extensive bibliography).

[97] *Dialogue of Timothy and Aquila* 24.5; see Robert G. Robertson, "The Dialogue of Timothy and Aquila: A Critical Text, Introduction to the Manuscript Evidence, and an Inquiry into the Sources and Literary Relationships" (Th.D. Diss., Harvard University, 1986), p. xlix; cf. Varner, *Dialogues*, 194–195. Lawrence Lahey has produced an edition of the Short Recension (hereafter *SR*) of this work; in that recension the passage appears at *SR* xix.1 (Lahey's numbering); see Lawrence Lanzi Lahey, "The Dialogue of Timothy and Aquila: Critical Greek Text and English Translation of the Short Recension with an Introduction including a Source-critical Study" (PhD, University of Cambridge, 2000), 166–167. The citation of the Deuteronomic text is again in the form of Galatians 3:13.

[98] *Dial. Tim. & Aq.* 24.6–8 (citation 24.8; Robertson pp. xlix–l); *SR* xix.3–8; Varner, *Dialogues*, 194–195.

[99] *Altercatio* ii.4 (Bratke, *Evagrii Altercatio*, 26.3ff.). See text and translation in Varner, *Dialogues*, 112–115 (where he cites the passage as vi.22, following Harnack).

that this means Jesus was cursed.[100] However, Athanasius dismisses the passage as indicating merely that the Lord (who is led to slaughter as a man, and took the sin of the world as God) would be reckoned with transgressors.[101]

Thus the Christian *adversus Iudaeos* literature (especially the dialogues) frequently records mention of Deuteronomy 21:23 in early Jewish/Christian disputes. As a possible legacy of such debates, the *Didascalia Apostolorum* even contends that the curse of Deuteronomy 21:23 was written to blind those [esp. Jews] who follow the "Second Legislation."[102]

The question is: Does this Christian portrait authentically represent early Jewish polemic as well as Christian response? A definite answer is not possible since the comparable Jewish *adversus Christianos* material, which also does attest to the polemical use of Deuteronomy 21:22–23, does not clearly antedate the medieval period. Yet, Jewish polemic from the Middle Ages does make extensive use of Deuteronomy 21. Thus the "earliest surviving [9th c.] Jewish polemical treatise criticizing Christian doctrines," *Qiṣṣat Mujādalat al-Usquf,* says (§104): "Now if Jesus was crucified, his body then, according to you, is cursed, because it is written in the Torah...[followed by a citation of Deut 21:23]."[103] Other medieval Jewish *adversus Christianos* works make similar assertions.[104] Note that such arguments (which assume a subjective

---

[100] Earlier the issue for Zacchaeus the Jew was just this: Ἀπο τῆς παλαιᾶς με διαθήκης πεῖσον, ὅτι δεῖ αὐτόν σταυρωθῆναι – "persuade me from the Old Covenant that it was necessary for him to be crucified" (*Dialogue of Athanasius and Zacchaeus* 37). Certainly, *Athanasius and Zacchaeus* must be used with caution since some have suggested that it was really a work of missionary catechism (and not an account of actual dialogue). Even Varner (*Dialogues,* 17–19), who is otherwise quite optimistic about real Jewish and Christian encounter being represented in the dialogue tradition (ibid., 286–88), follows Andrist in this regard. However, two points might be sustained: (1) Even if deemed missionary catechesis, this work still could interact with real potential Jewish objections to Christianity likely to be encountered in missionary endeavors; and (2) it seems from my reading that many of the questions that Zacchaeus the Jew proposes in the course of the *Dialogue* are more pointed, more closely tied to a close awareness of OT scripture, and less predictable than might be expected from an artificial intra-Christian document.

[101] *Dialogue of Athanasius and Zacchaeus* 41–42. Text and translation in Varner, *Dialogues,* 44–45.

[102] *Didascalia Apostolorum* 26; see R. Hugh Connolly, *Didascalia apostolorum: the Syriac version translated and accompanied by the Verona Latin fragments* (Oxford: Clarendon, 1969), pp. 222, 230, 233 (and note Connolly's comments on p. lxi). In the *Didascalia,* the "Second Legislation" is the reassertion of the law in Deuteronomy, and this Second Legislation results in the blinding of the people against Christian truth.

[103] See the translation and discussion in Daniel J. Lasker and Sarah Stroumsa, *The Polemic of Nestor the Priest: Qiṣṣat Mujādalat al-Usquf and Sefer Nestor Ha-Komer,* 2 vols. (Jerusalem: Ben-Zvi Institute, 1996), 1:72, 157 (cf. §180 on p. 87 with discussion p. 168).

[104] Thus examine the related *The Polemic of Nestor the Priest,* in *ibid.,* pp. 119, 128 (§§104, 180). Further note the usage of Deuteronomy in the *Nizzahon Vetus* (§50, see Berger,

genitive in the 'curse of God' of Deut 21:23) prevail despite the general rabbinic application of Deuteronomy 21:23 to the blasphemer (which requires an objective genitive interpretation of Deut 21:23).

Clearly medieval Jewish polemical literature freely applies this text to pronounce a curse on the crucified Jesus. This Jewish medieval evidence, combined with earlier Jewish material associating Deuteronomy 21:22–23 with crucifixion in general (chapter 3, §4 above) and with the consistent early Christian portrayal that commonly introduces such an argument from the Jewish literary interlocutor, makes it fairly probable that a reference to the curse of Deuteronomy 21:23 was employed in actual Jewish *adversus Christianos* polemic in antiquity.[105]

In any case, since early Christian sources often assert that Jewish biblical exegesis associated Deuteronomy 21:22–23 with crucifixion, this demonstrates that at least some Christian authors were conscious that they were countering a possible Jewish perception that Jesus was cursed on the cross. Most Christian authors after Paul, especially in polemical contexts, reject the notion that Christ was cursed, but follow Paul at least so far as to accept that Jesus' crucifixion was the means of removing the general curse on all sinful people – a curse that is found in the law.[106]

Jewish-Christian Debate, 75, 262); and in the *Basle Nizzahon*, on which see the synopsis in William Horbury, "The Basle Nizzahon," *JTS* n.s. 34 (1983): 508. On these works, see also the description in Samuel Krauss, *The Jewish-Christian Controversy from the Earliest Times to 1789*, ed. William Horbury, vol. 1, TSAJ 56 (Tübingen: J. C. B. Mohr, 1995), 246–47. Already above the *Toledoth Jeshu* tradition was mentioned that claims Jesus knew that the Jews would have to bury his body in accordance with Deuteronomy 21:23 – see, for example, MS T.-S. Loan 87 folio 2^r lines 7–8, 11–25 (from transl. by Horbury, "Critical Examination," 86–88, cf. pp. 106–9, 192–93). It might be easier for some readers to locate a related tradition that can be found in a more widely-circulated English edition of the *Toledoth Jeshu* in Hugh J. Schonfield, *According to the Hebrews* (London: Duckworth, 1937), 51 (I note this reference without endorsing Schonfield's program of connecting the *Toledoth* to the lost *Gospel of the Hebrews*).

[105] Our argumentation here coheres with at least two of the criteria Lahey has suggested for judging the authenticity of Jewish arguments in Christian *contra Iudaeos* literature: "Similar material reflected in Jewish *contra Christianos* literature" and "well argued objections from the Jewish side." See Lawrence Lahey, "Jewish Biblical Interpretation and Genuine Jewish-Christian Debate in the Dialogue of Timothy and Aquila," *JJS* 51 (2000): 285. To these we might add: "Attempts from the Christian in the *contra Iudaeos* work to sidestep or mitigate the issue."

[106] Augustine reports an intriguing attempt by some to say that Judas Iscariot was actually the person who was cursed as he "*hung* on the tree" (and not Jesus who was "*nailed*" to a tree). Augustine rightly observed that this is incompatible with Gal 3:13, which Augustine interpreted to mean that the God-man Jesus, in his mortal body, received the curse of a mortal death, and that this action itself cursed death. See Eric Plumer, *Augustine's Commentary on Galatians: Introduction, Text, Translation, and Notes*, OECT (Oxford: Oxford University Press, 2003), 158–63.

6. Shame, Horror and the Cross

The shamefulness and humiliation of the cross of Christ is readily admitted in several NT passages. So the author of the book of Hebrews, likely a representative of Hellenistic Jewish-Christianity, speaks of Jesus as intentionally enduring the cross and "disdaining the shame" (Heb 12:2; αἰσχύνης καταφρονήσας).[107] Jesus here becomes a model of endurance to be followed by the believer (cf. Heb 13:13). Elsewhere, however, those who "fall away" are said to be re-crucifying the Son of God, and thus, "making a spectacle" of him (Heb 6:6; παραδειγματίζοντας – cf. Num 25:4 LXX).[108] In the Pauline corpus, the humility of Jesus, which is to be imitated by the believer, receives its final and most sensational expression in his death on the cross (Phil 2:8). And in the Gospels the shameful and horrendous nature of Jesus' death is also emphasized, receiving some of the most explicit descriptions of crucifixion in ancient literature.[109]

This connection with shame and humiliation continued to be acknowledged in the early church Fathers. To give one example, Melito of Sardis, in a homily known for its anti-Jewish fervor (and likely speaking to an audience in contact with Judaism), emphasizes the shamefulness of the naked Christ held up for derision on the cross.[110]

As the few examples above indicate, early Christians used the sense of shame that memories of Jesus' cross evoked in order to motivate fellow Christians both to emulate Jesus' humble endurance and to avoid the kind of apostasy that holds Jesus up to further ridicule.

On the other hand, Trypho, Justin's literary Jewish interlocutor, also focuses on the shame of the cross. However, he presents it as a central reason why he cannot accept the veracity of Jesus' messianic claims.[111] Similarly,

---

[107] On the author of Hebrews as a Hellenistic Jewish-Christian see, for example: William L. Lane, *Hebrews*, 2 vols., WBC 47 a&b (Dallas: Word Books; Nashville: Thomas Nelson, 1991), 1:xlix–li. On the shame language in Hebrews see F. F. Bruce, *Epistle to the Hebrews*, NICNT (Grand Rapids: Eerdmans, 1964), 352–353; Lane, *Hebrews*, 2:413–414.

[108] Given our earlier study of Numbers 25:4 (in chapter 3, §3) and the Old Greek interpretation of והוקע with παραδειγμάτισον, it is tempting to suggest an allusion (or an 'echo') here of Num 25:4 LXX in Hebrews 6:6. Also of possible interest is the application of παραδειγματίζω to the expected demise of Haman in the *Additions to Esther* (Esther 14:11 = 4:17q). However, the verb παραδειγματίζω occurs many other times in the Septuagint manuscripts (also see Jer. 13:22; Ezek. 28:17; Dan. 2:5), and it was likely common enough Greek to suggest caution here.

[109] E.g., Matt 26:67–68; 27:27–31, 39–44 and parallels.

[110] Melito, *Peri Pascha* 96–97. See edition by Stuart George Hall, ed., *Melito of Sardis On Pascha and Fragments*, OECT (Oxford: Clarendon Press, 1979), p. 54.

[111] *Dial.* 32.1 (ἄτιμος καὶ ἄδοξος – 'dishonoured and disreputable'); 89.2 (ἄτιμως… σταυρωθῆναι – 'to be crucified dishonourably'); 90.1 (αἰσχρῶς καὶ ἄτιμως ἀποθανεῖν – 'to die shamefully and dishonourably'). These were all cited more fully in the previous section.

note the charge of shame associated with the cross by the Jewish figure Zacchaeus in the *Dialogue of Athanasius and Zacchaeus* (36): Οὐκ αἰσχύνῃ δεσπότου καὶ θεοῦ, καὶ δυνάμεως καὶ σοφίας σταυρὸν λέγων; ('Is it not a shame speaking about a cross in reference to the Master and God and Power and Wisdom?')[112] Significantly, in the context of Justin's *Dialogue*, the shamefulness of the cross functions almost as an extension of the curse said to reside on the crucified in Deuteronomy 21:22–23.[113]

Admittedly, the concepts of shame and horror associated with crucifixion are part and parcel of the general perception of the cross in antiquity (and thus not specifically Jewish) – even conceivably inherent in the perception of any naked, prolonged, public, tortuous execution. Nevertheless, the association of the shame of the cross with the curse of Deuteronomy 21:23, if original to actual conversation with Jews, provides an extra Jewish component to such perceptions, and an additional dimension to the connotations of the humility of Christ.

7. The Innocent Sufferer

The Gospels frequently emphasize the motif of Jesus as the innocent sufferer. For example, in Jesus' hearing before the Sanhedrin, the Gospels portray the difficulty of finding any substantial charge against Jesus until he makes his "Son of Man" pronouncement (see Matt 26:59–66; Mark 14:55–64; cf. John 18:19–23; omitted in Luke 22:66–71). Though finally giving into the demand for Jesus to be crucified, Pilate can find no real case against him (Luke 23:4, 14–25 [esp. 23:14–16, 22]; John 18:29–19:16 [esp. 18:38; 19:4, 6, 12]; cf. Matt 27:18–19; Mark 15:10, 14). In the Matthean account, Pilate even washes his hands of the matter (Matt 27:24–25),[114] and Judas claims to have sinned in betraying innocent blood (Matt 27:4). In Luke, Jesus' innocence is stated in the very hour of his crucifixion by the criminal next to him (Luke 23:41). NT texts outside the Gospels also portray the innocence of Jesus,[115] often in contexts that speak of Jesus' vicarious suffering and death.[116]

---

[112] Following the text and translation in Varner, *Dialogues*, 40–41.

[113] Each of these aforementioned texts from Justin also contains a citation of Deuteronomy 21:23 on the lips of Trypho.

[114] The complexity of the meaning of this hand-washing has various explanations, with it being possible from within a Graeco-Roman context, but theologically significant given OT washing symbolism; see e.g., Brown, *Death of the Messiah*, 1:831–39; also Senior, *Passion of Jesus in the Gospel of Matthew*, 116–19; Nolland, *Matthew*, 1176–78.

[115] E.g., Heb 4:15; 7:26; 1 John 3:5. Also cf. John 7:18; 8:46.

[116] E.g., 1 Pet 2:22 (citing Isa 53:9); 1 Pet 3:18. Likely cf. Acts 4:27 ('*holy*' servant Jesus'); 2 Cor 5:21; Heb 7:26–27. Also note Jesus as the pure sacrificial lamb in 1 Pet 1:19.

Some Jewish traditions of this period certainly portrayed innocent Jewish people facing the cross (see chpt. 5 above), so there were first-century cultural analogies to the idea that Jesus mounted the cross as an innocent sufferer. It is likely also that Jesus' execution could have been seen to be in continuity with Jewish deaths at the hands of Roman soldiers in the first century (and probably in the second century as well). Thus the proclamation of the early church in its Jewish milieu may have had this point of contact with the Jewish listener. Admittedly, the extant literature of early Christian apologetic does not frequently overtly draw on such contemporary analogies. Christian writings instead tend to focus on biblical examples of innocent sufferers, and especially on the general claim that the Jewish nation persecuted the (innocent) prophets. But the innocence of Jesus is frequently reasserted in *adversus Iudaeos* works – first as a reproach against the Jewish people who called for his execution,[117] but also as a means of circumventing Jewish appeals to biblical texts such as Deuteronomy 21:23.[118]

8. Crucifixion and Martyrdom

In the NT corpus, martyrdom, in the sense of the persecution and death of one who witnesses the work of God, is especially found in the book of Revelation.[119] The Apocalypse even calls Jesus a μάρτυς (Rev 1:5; cf. 3:14), ultimately emphasizing both his role as a faithful and true witness of the things of God and as the slain lamb, who died on the cross in his witness. Crucifixion, as was shown in previous chapters, could be a form of martyr's death in contemporaneous Jewish literature. In a similar way, Matthew portrays Jesus, while he was intoning against his hypocritical audience, as announcing that they will kill, torture, persecute and even "crucify" (σταυρώσετε) the prophets, wise men and scribes who are sent out (Matt 23:34).[120]

In light of this connection between crucifixion and martyrdom, one might well ask whether Jesus elsewhere was viewed as a martyr, especially in his crucifixion. Indeed, some have suggested that early Christian soteriological reflection on the cross of Jesus (especially as represented by the Apostle Paul)

---

[117] E.g., Melito, *Peri Pascha* 74 (Hall, *Melito*, pp. 40–41).

[118] Note the insistence that Deuteronomy 21:23 is inapplicable to Jesus based on Jesus' innocence in Tertullian, *Adversus Iudaeos* x.1; and in the *Altercatio Simonis et Theophili* ii.4 [= vi.22 Harnack] (both discussed in section five above).

[119] See Rev 2:13; 6:9; 12:11; 17:6. Cf. Richard Bauckham, *The Theology of the Book of Revelation*, New Testament Theology (Cambridge: Cambridge University Press, 1993), esp. 73–88; Hermann Strathmann, "μάρτυς, etc.," in *Theological Dictionary of the New Testament*, ed. Gerhard Kittel, trans. Geoffrey W. Bromiley, vol. 4 (Grand Rapids: Eerdmans, 1967), 474–508.

[120] Contrast Luke 11:49, which does not mention "crucify."

centers on his death as a martyr.[121] However, martyrdom was not the only positive category associated with Jesus' crucifixion. For example, it is striking that the Revelation of John, the NT book with the most explicit martyr associations applied to Jesus, also frequently refers to him as the slain "lamb" (among many other christological titles). This notion of the slain lamb implies that OT sacrificial categories significantly influenced the author's understanding of Jesus' death. Thus, in the book of Revelation, while martyrdom may be a component element in the perceived significance of Jesus' crucifixion, it should not be emphasized to the exclusion of other equally (if not more) important categories. Similar points could be made for other New Testament books that employ possible martyrological categories regarding Jesus – these often appear connected with (and even subsidiary to) Old Testament sacrificial imagery.

Nonetheless, Jesus' courageous facing of the cross becomes an archetype of the Christian way of confronting persecution. Jesus' own logion, "Take up your cross, and follow me,"[122] was in the post-apostolic period frequently associated with martyrdom.[123] And martyrs were thought to follow in Jesus' footsteps as they faced their tormentors.[124] A few Christian martyrological

---

[121] See esp. David Seeley, *The Noble Death: Graeco-Roman Martyrology and Paul's Concept of Salvation*, JSNTSup 28 (Sheffield: JSOT Press, 1990); John Downing, "Jesus and Martyrdom," *JTS* n.s. 14 (1963): 279–293; Sam K. Williams, *Jesus' Death as a Saving Event: the Background and Origin of a Concept*, HDR 2 (Missoula: Scholars Press, 1975); John S. Pobee, *Persecution and Martyrdom in the Theology of Paul*, JSNTSup 6 (Sheffield: JSOT Press, 1985); Stephen Anthony Cummins, *Paul and the Crucified Christ in Antioch: Maccabean Martyrdom and Galatians 1 and 2*, SNTSMS 114 (Cambridge: Cambridge University Press, 2001); and the writings of J. W. Van Henten. Some of the strongest statements in Jewish literature regarding the salvific efficacy of a martyr's death can be found in 4 Maccabees (esp. 6:28–29; 17:21–22), which weds OT cultic categories with martyrdom themes, though in the midst of a highly philosophical reinterpretation of Jewish life. On the Maccabean martyr tradition, see esp. Jan Willem Van Henten, *The Maccabean Martyrs as Saviours of the Jewish People: A Study of 2 and 4 Maccabees*, Supplements to the Journal for the Study of Judaism 57 (Leiden: Brill, 1997).

[122] Matt 16:24; Mark 8:34; Luke 9:23. Cf. Matt 10:38; Luke 14:27. On possible interpretations see W. D. Davies and Dale C. Allison, *A Critical and Exegetical Commentary on the Gospel According to Saint Matthew*, 3 vols., ICC (Edinburgh: T & T Clark, 1988–1997), 222–23.

[123] Patristic materials on these verses are gathered in Maria Ko Ha Fong, *Crucem tollendo Christum sequi: Untersuchung zum Verständnis eines Logions Jesu in der Alten Kirche*, Münsterische Beiträge zur Theologie 52 (Münster: Aschendorff, 1984). Kuhn suggests ongoing *imitatio* in suffering is closer to the saying's intent than onetime martyrdom; see H.-W. Kuhn, "σταυρός, σταυρόω," in *Exegetical Dictionary of the New Testament*, ed. Horst Balz and Gerhard Schneider, vol. 3 (Grand Rapids: Eerdmans, 1993), 269.

[124] See recently: B. Dehandschutter, "Example and Discipleship: Some Comments on the Biblical Background of the Early Christian Theology of Martyrdom," in *The Impact of Scripture in Early Christianity*, ed. J. Den Boeft and M. L. Van Poll-Van De Lisdonk, Supplements to Vigiliae Christianae 44 (Leiden: Brill, 1999), 24–26.

accounts even have their victims nailed to the cross.[125] These martyrologies thus could have continued in Christianity the association witnessed in Judaism between the cross and martyrdom.

9. Latent Imagery: The Crucified Sacrifice

Early patristic usage indicates that a whole variety of OT images were employed in defending the concept of the crucified Christ. Justin is not alone when he finds parallels to the cross in such images as the tree of life, the horns in the blessing of Joseph, the hands of Moses held out in prayer, the serpent held high by Moses, and many other OT images.[126] Also many OT texts were said to presage the crucifixion of Jesus,[127] including the supposed statement in Ps 96:10 [LXX 95:10; missing in most MSS] that "God reigned from the tree."[128] However, of these many images, two should be briefly discussed on the basis of our previous findings on latent images in chapter five.

First, in a development remarkably similar to rabbinic *haggadah* on the binding of Isaac (examined above in chapter five, §4.1), the manuscripts of Tertullian's *Adversus Iudaeos* portray Isaac's bearing of the wood to the place of his sacrifice in Genesis 22 as a type of Christ carrying his cross to the place of his crucifixion.[129] Prior to this treatise, in a paschal homily Melito refers to

---

[125] So traditions on the martyrdoms of SS. Peter (perhaps influenced by John 21) and Andrew. See Peter's death in Eusebius, *Hist. Eccl.* ii.25; iii.1; also note the traditions collected in the various manuscripts of the *Acts of Andrew* with translation in Wilhelm Schneemelcher, ed., *New Testament Apocrypha*, trans. R. McL. Wilson, 2nd revised ed., 2 vols. (Cambridge: James Clarke & Co./Louisville: Westminster/John Knox, 1991–1992), 2:146–51; and the *Acts of Peter* 35 (6)–39 (10) in Schneemelcher, 2:314–17. Despite occasional scholarly assertions to the contrary, Blandina is *not* put forth as crucified in Eusebius' narrative of her martyrdom (*Hist. Eccl.* v.1.41–42); cf. Hugh Jackson Lawlor and John Ernest Leonard Oulton, *Eusebius Bishop of Caesarea: The Ecclesiastical History and the Martyrs of Palestine*, 2 vols. (London: SPCK, 1927–1928), 2:157 (on v.1.41).

[126] E.g., Justin, *Dial.* 86.1–6; 90.3–91.4; 97.1–4; 111.1–2; 112.2. Often postulated is a collection of tree *testimonia*, see Albl, *Scripture Cannot be Broken*, 155–57.

[127] Pride of place would go to Isaiah 53 and to Psalm 22; cf. Justin, *Dial.* 98.1–106.4; *Dialogue of Athanasius and Zacchaeus* 38–40. Also intriguing is the "hanging" connection drawn between crucifixion and Deut 28:66, which is known as early as Melito, *Peri Pascha* 61; this connection is also found in the dialogue tradition: *Dialogue of Athanasius and Zacchaeus* 36; *Dialogue of Simon and Theophilus* ii.4 [= Harnack vi.22]; *Dialogue of Timothy and Aquila* 24.4; 53.8 (on these see Varner, *Dialogues*, pp. 40–41, 114–115, 194–195, 268–269).

[128] See J. Duncan M. Derrett, "Ο ΚΥΡΙΟΣ ΕΒΑΣΙΛΕΥΣΕΝ ΑΠΟ ΤΟΥ ΞΥΛΟΥ," *VC* 43 (1989): 378–92.

[129] (Ps.?-)Tertullian, *Adv. Iud.* x.6 *Itaque imprimis Isaac, cum a patre hostia duceretur lignum[que] ipse sibi portans, Christi exitum iam tunc denotabat in victimam concessi a patre lignum passionis suae baiulantis.* "Accordingly, to begin with, Isaac, when led by his

Isaac as one who is "similarly bound" (ὁμοίως φονευόμενον) like Christ, and who carries his wood like the cross of Christ.[130] This homily contains a strong anti-Jewish section, possibly due to Melito's contact with Jews in Sardis. In an intriguing variation on this theme, Irenaeus claims that Christians take up the cross like Isaac took up the wood.[131]

Even prior to the patristic era, a few NT texts allude to the ʿAqedah.[132] And Romans 8:32 sets up what some have considered to be an analogy between God and Abraham (ὅς γε τοῦ ἰδίου υἱοῦ οὐκ ἐφείσατο – 'who indeed did not spare his own son').[133] However, in the NT texts, there is no explicit reference to any analogy between Isaac's wood and Christ's cross. Of course, many have contended that an intricate awareness of Isaac typology lies behind such brief texts as Romans 8:32.[134] And it does seem that the early church was developing the Abraham/Isaac typology.[135]

Still, it remains difficult to determine with certainty whether in the NT period Christians already clearly envisioned the Isaac narrative as a prefigurement of Jesus' crucifixion.[136] It is, nonetheless, clear that by the time

---

father as a victim, and himself bearing his own 'wood,' was even at that early period pointing to Christ's death; conceded [as He was] as a victim by the Father; carrying [as He did] the 'wood' of His own passion." Transl. follows *ANF* 3:165 (brackets mine to indicate material in the published translation not actually in the text). As noted earlier, this section of Tertullian's work is considered by some to have been added by a later redactor.

[130] Melito, *Peri Pascha*, 59, 69 (Hall, *Melito*, pp. 32, 36); also cf. frag. 15 (p. 83 line 21 in Hall); for the general typology see *catena* fragments 9–11 (Hall, pp. 74–77).

[131] Irenaeus, *Contra Haer.* iv.5.4. See Adelin Rousseau et al., *Irénée de Lyon. Contre les hérésies*, 9 vols., SC (Paris: Cerf, 1965–1982), vol. 100/2, p. 434.

[132] See esp. James 2:21–23; Heb 11:17–19. Allusions have also been hypothesized in John 8:56–58; see e.g., Lukas Kundert, *Die Opferung/Bindung Isaaks*, 2 vols., WMANT 78 & 79 (Neukirchen-Vluyn: Neukirchener Verlag, 1998), 1:215–27.

[133] Cf. Heb 11:17. Some possibilities here are developed in James Swetnam, *Jesus and Isaac: A Study of the Epistle to the Hebrews in the Light of the Aqedah*, AnBib 94 (Rome: Biblical Institute Press, 1981), 86–129.

[134] For example, see the classic essays by Hans Joachim Schoeps, "The Sacrifice of Isaac in Paul's Theology," *JBL* 65 (1946): 385–92; Roy A. Rosenberg, "Jesus, Isaac, and the 'Suffering Servant'," *JBL* 84 (1965): 381–88; J. Edwin Wood, "Isaac Typology in the New Testament," *NTS* 14 (1968): 583–589. This view is challenged by Davies and Chilton (see notes in chapter 5, §4.1 above) and by Seeley (*Noble Death*, 59–66). Further bibliography in Kundert, *Opferung/Bindung*, vol. 1.

[135] Summarized in Geza Vermes, "Redemption and Genesis XXII: The Binding of Isaac and the Sacrifice of Jesus," in *Scripture and Tradition in Judaism: Haggadic Studies*, SPB 4 (Leiden: E. J. Brill, 1961), 218–27; and emphasized, for example, in Jon D. Levenson, *The Death and Resurrection of the Beloved Son: The Transformation of Child Sacrifice in Judaism and Christianity* (New Haven: Yale University Press, 1993), 200–232. Also see Edward Kessler, *Bound by the Bible: Jews, Christians and the sacrifice of Isaac* (Cambridge: Cambridge University Press, 2004), 130–135.

[136] Levenson, among others, views the paschal lamb as the connecting link between Jesus/pascha/Isaac (so Levenson, *Death and Resurrection*, 206–19). The possibilities here are

the rabbinic texts themselves connect the bearing of the wood in the *'Aqedah* with crucifixion,[137] many of the church Fathers had long viewed Isaac's wood as analogous to the cross of Jesus of Nazareth.

Second, as is readily apparent from early in the NT period, the paschal lamb was seen as a type of Christ's sacrifice. Paul proclaims, "for also our paschal lamb, Christ, was sacrificed" (καὶ γὰρ τὸ πάσχα ἡμῶν ἐτύθη Χριστός – 1 Cor 5:7).[138] The NT is replete with lamb imagery attached to Jesus,[139] much of which, with strong emphasis on *the* lamb, likely refers to the important paschal lamb.[140] Further, the church Fathers frequently draw explicit connections between Jesus and the paschal lamb.[141]

The origins of this connection can, in large part, be traced back to the timing and location of Jesus' execution.[142] However, as noted in chapter five (§4.2), Justin claims that the Jewish roasting of the paschal lamb was in the form of a cross (*Dial.* 40.3). He uses this as additional proof that Jesus was the antitype of the pascha. If Justin is correct about the form of roasting in his day, then such a paschal analogy with Jesus' crucifixion could have appeared all the stronger to those conversant with ancient Jewish practice.

To the extent that these images of the crucified Messiah (i.e., Jesus as the analog of the sacrificed son, or of the paschal lamb) met with some reception among Jewish respondents to the Christian message, this may indicate the

---

intriguing, but the point remains that the cross itself is not overtly connected to an Isaac typology in the NT. On this see Brown, *Death of the Messiah*, 2:1435–1444.

[137] Again here note *Gen. Rab.* lvi.3; *Pesiq. Rab.* xxxi.2; and see the discussion of these passages earlier in chapter five, §4.1.

[138] Of course, the context of this passage is not soteriological, but the fact that Paul could make such a swift appeal to paschal typology shows that such connections were clearly in development (*pace* Seeley, *Noble Death*, 30–33). Cf. Jesus' death in John 19:36, with its likely appeal to the paschal lamb in Exod 12:46 or Num 9:12.

[139] E.g., John 1:29, 36. Frequently in the Apocalypse (e.g., Rev 5:6ff.; 6:1, 16; 8:1; 12:1; 13:8 and often in chapters 7, 14–17, 21–22). Note the connection produced with the lamb of Isa 53:7 in Acts 8:32.

[140] Strongly affirmed by Levenson, *Death and Resurrection*, 208–209.

[141] Such a connection forms the basis of Melito's *Peri Pascha*, which includes a forceful attack on contemporary Jews. Many different *Pascha* sermons were frequently distributed in early Christianity; and for a listing of Greek sermons on the *Pascha* cf. Mauritus Geerard et al., eds., *Clavis Patrum Graecorum*, 5 + Suppl. vols., CChr (Turnhout: Brepols, 1983–1998), 5:150. Other *adversus Iudaeos* works also employ paschal typology; e.g., Justin, *Dial.* 40.1–3; 111.3–4; Tertullian, *Adv. Iud.* x.18–19; Aphrahat, *Demon.* xii.

[142] So, for example, Matt 26:2: οἴδατε ὅτι μετὰ δύο ἡμέρας τὸ πάσχα γίνεται, καὶ ὁ υἱὸς τοῦ ἀνθρώπου παραδίδοται εἰς τὸ σταυρωθῆναι – "You know that after two days the Passover comes, and the Son of Man is betrayed in order to be crucified." The timing relative to Passover is complicated by the Synoptic and Johannine differences; nevertheless, both the Synoptics and John's Gospel locate Jesus' death close to the Passover event. Furthermore, as early as Justin, the Jerusalem locale of Jesus' crucifixion was explicitly tied to Passover tradition (*Dial.* 40.1–2).

presence of a latent image of the cross within Judaism. While these Jewish images may not necessarily have been formally recognized in connection with crucifixion before Jesus' death, still the resonance was sufficiently strong that later they could be understood as a (pre-)figuration of the cross. Certainly, other latent images might be suggested, and it would be a worthwhile process to cull through the NT and early Christian writings, in order to see if any other analogies and types found there have some claim to actual Jewish ancestry.[143]

10. Conclusion

ἡμεῖς δὲ κηρύσσομεν Χριστὸν ἐσταυρωμένον, Ἰουδαίοις μὲν σκάνδαλον, ἔθνεσιν δὲ μωρίαν... (1 Cor 1:23)

"But we preach Christ crucified – to Jews a stumbling block, and to Gentiles foolishness..."

In this passage, Paul testifies to the difficulties he encountered in his Christian proclamation of the crucified Christ – wisdom-seeking Gentiles considered his gospel of the crucified as foolishness and miracle-seeking Jews found it cause for stumbling. Paul, however, contends that his proclamation is the wisdom of God (1 Cor 1:24). Of course, Paul would not have simply assumed that varying reaction to the gospel had a purely intellectual cause, for he recognized the work of God's Spirit (e.g., 1 Cor 2:4). Yet, there were certainly many negative Jewish perceptions of the cross that indeed would have made Jesus' death appear scandalous to first-century Jews. Nonetheless, we have noted in ancient Jewish literature that while the most obvious perceptions of crucifixion were such as to produce a *scandalon* for the proclamation of the gospel, there were also some views that could have aided the Christian understanding of the cross as the wisdom of God.

In analyzing documents from early Jewish and Christian controversies, certain Jewish notions concerning Jesus' crucifixion emerge. Of course, these documents are relatively sparse from the period under discussion, and most early testimony necessarily derives from Christian sources, which often evidence anti-Jewish biases. Thus, careful use of such sources must be encouraged. However, by now, two points should be evident concerning the views of Jesus' crucifixion placed in the mouths of Jewish antagonists in

---

[143] One possible such image, which Dr. Schwemer has suggested to me, concerns the death of Isaiah the prophet, who was sawn in two with a wooden saw in later tradition; see for example, *Liv. Pro.* 1:1; *Ascen. Isa.* 1:9; 5:11–14; Justin, *Dial.* 120.5; cf. Heb. 11:37. On this text see Anna Maria Schwemer, *Studien zu den frühjüdischen Prophetenlegenden Vitae Prophetarum: Einleitung, Übersetzung und Kommentar*, 2 vols., TSAJ 49–50 (Tübingen: J. C. B. Mohr [Paul Siebeck], 1995–1996), 1:107–115; Anna Maria Schwemer, *Historische und legendarische Erzählungen: Vitae Prophetarum*, JSHRZ I.7 (Gütersloh: Gütersloher Verlagshaus, 1997), 561–63.

Christian *adversus Iudaeos* literature. First, these views that associate Jesus' crucifixion with brigandage, magic, blasphemy and certain OT texts often are consistent with long-standing Jewish perceptions of the cross evidenced before, during and after the death of Jesus. Therefore, these long-standing Jewish perceptions (studied earlier in chapters two through six) may heighten the historical plausibility of some of these early Christian reports of Jewish opposition to a crucified messiah. Second, many (if not most) early Christian allegations of Jewish opposition to a crucified Jesus have analogues in later, avowedly Jewish, *adversus Christianos* literature. Thus one often can go beyond mere Christian testimony about Jewish polemic, and can actually correlate such polemic with trajectories in later Jewish literature. This later evidence also increases the probability of accuracy in at least some of the paralleled early Christian reports of Jewish polemic. Nonetheless, the ramifications of these two points do not constitute an argument for a wholesale acceptance of early Christian accounts of Jewish polemic; these two points are limited to Jewish perceptions of crucifixion, and to how those perceptions appeared to have been applied in antiquity to Jewish rejection of the crucified Jesus.

In this regard, we can now summarize some Jewish views of the crucified Jesus. The charge of brigandage, which sounded somewhat plausible due to Jesus attracting a band of followers and to him delivering a countercultural message, appeared at times attached to Jesus' execution. Similarly, crucifixion imagery may have magnified allegations of Jesus engaging in both magic and blasphemy (since blasphemers and magicians were considered by some to deserve executionary suspension). In some Jewish circles, apparently associations were made between Jesus and the figure of Haman (envisioned as the crucified arch-enemy of Judaism), whose demise was annually celebrated. To many, it must have seemed outrageous that the messiah would have died such a shameful and horrible death. Finally, and perhaps most significantly, in early Jewish and Christian controversy, Jesus' crucifixion could be connected to the curse of Deuteronomy 21:22–23. Certainly, there were many reasons for a Jewish person to have disputed the church's claim that Jesus was the crucified messiah.

Part of the challenge for the early Church required defending its gospel against those who would oppose its crucified Saviour. In doing so, Christians rejected some traditional views of the crucified person, insisting that these were inapplicable to Jesus (e.g., associations of crucifixion with brigandage, magic, blasphemy and negative biblical examples such as Haman). Alternatively, Christians also could transform negative impressions of the cross into more positive concepts (as when Paul envisions the curse in Deuteronomy 21:23 in the context of a soteriological exchange, or when the author of Hebrews invokes the shame of the cross to motivate his audience to endurance). Finally, early Christians championed other more positive perceptions of the cross (e.g., those associated with the innocent sufferer and martyr, and with images of sacrifice).

This is not an attempt to explain the whole Christian kerygma simply on the basis of perceptions of crucifixion in Jewish antiquity. An examination of early Christian writings will show that many dimensions of Christian reflection on the cross of Jesus are beyond the purview of this thesis. Nonetheless, it is hoped that the reader is by now convinced of the importance of studying ways that Jewish perceptions of crucifixion did impact the early Christian proclamation of the Good News.

As was mentioned in the preface, this book has limited aims. It has sought to investigate thoroughly extant ancient Jewish references to crucifixion. Yet, certainly more could be done with later (medieval) Jewish literature, and perhaps in the process of such further study some overlooked earlier Jewish passages may arise. Also, the focus of this last chapter has been largely restricted to literature that claims some level of Christian and Jewish interaction concerning the cross of Christ. The work of this final chapter could thus be expanded in multiple ways: More early or medieval Christian and Jewish polemical literature could be analyzed. Early Jewish-Christian responses to Jewish preconceptions of crucifixion could be further examined (perhaps arguing that Jewish-Christians would most have remained in contact with early expressions of Judaism). And the analysis could be broadened to encompass general early Christian texts in order to determine the influence of long-standing Jewish perspectives of crucifixion on Christianity (apart from certifiable events of Christian and Jewish interaction). In any case, the limited goal for this concluding chapter has been to investigate the impact of Jewish perceptions of the cross on both ancient Jewish and Christian views of Jesus through the analysis of literature that has a reasonable likelihood of recalling at least some actual Jewish and Christian interaction.

By laying out, in a fairly comprehensive way, Jewish perceptions of crucifixion, this study has sought to advance scholarship on ancient views of the cross, and particularly to further current research on the study of crucifixion in Judaism in antiquity. Beyond that, this book has intended to suggest a few verifiable ways that early Christians were influenced by these Jewish perceptions. If it indeed has been established in a limited (but demonstrable) way that such Jewish views impacted Christian understanding of the cross, then this conclusion can serve as a launching point for further studies on the influence of Jewish perceptions of the cross upon early Christian thought.

To summarize, in this book an attempt has been made to focus on Jewish perceptions and their Christian corollaries. The classic discussions of crucifixion have rightly pointed to the categories of shame and horror, and the associations with brigandage and rebellion, especially in the Gentile world. We have found that Jewish literature also clearly attests to these categories. Moreover, for the ancient Jewish person, the Tanakh provided (often negative) exemplars of crucifixion, as well as legislation that proclaimed the suspended man a curse of God. Nevertheless, in complement to these negative associations, there remained more positive perceptions of the cross in early Judaism, such as those involving the death of an innocent sufferer or martyr, as well as latent sacrificial images.

Early Christianity displays clear awareness of most (if not all) these perceptions, and molded them within a commitment to the proclamation of the crucified Christ. Thus early Christian literature on the cross exhibits, to a greater degree than is commonly recognized, a reflection upon the various Jewish perceptions of the cross in antiquity.

Appendix

Two Fragmentary Qumran Texts

Some scholars have connected two texts found at Qumran with crucifixion. Unfortunately, both passages are so fragmentary as to obscure their relevance for this study.

4Q385a 15 i 3–4

One of these fragmentary texts has been variously called Pseudo-Ezekiel or Pseudo-Jeremiah. Originally listed with the 4Q385 fragments, now Devorah Dimant, the editor of *DJD* 30, labels it 4Q385a (frag. 15, col. i):[1]

]וֹ		1
אלי]הֹם אשֹר לֹא הקשיבו		2
]תֹלוי על העץ ועוף		3
]וֹ אמת אל תותירו	השמים]	4
תֹ]אֹ]ואמרהֹ[לֹל[ ] [		5
]לשון נפֹשם		6

1.]
2. to th]em because they did not listen
3.]hung upon the tree and the birds
4. [of heaven   ] truth. Do not leave over
5.] [ ] [ ] and I said [t]he
6.]the tongue of their throat

Line 3 likely mentions someone "hung on the tree." It should be observed from the plates that the ת on תֹלוי ("hung") is not at all clear.[2] However, given

---

[1] The text and translation here follows the transcription of Devorah Dimant, *Qumran Cave 4 XXI: Parabiblical Texts, Part 4: Pseudo-Prophetic Texts*, DJD 30 (Oxford: Clarendon, 2001), 150–51 (and plate v). Dimant also testifies to the confusion over this text by noting that it was originally designated as fragment 7. It is reported as fragment 10 of 4Q385 by García Martínez and Tigchelaar, who also provide a transcription and translation; see Florentino García Martínez and Eibert J. C. Tigchelaar, eds., *The Dead Sea Scrolls Study Edition*, 2 vols. (Leiden: Brill, 1997–1998), 2:770–71. The García Martínez and Tigchelaar transcription largely agrees with Dimant, with the exceptions occurring immediately after the bracketed missing text in line 1 (ה instead of ו), in line 2 (י instead of ה), and in line four (omitting the speculative ו).

[2] Also there is space at the end of line 3 of the manuscript after ועוף. Although the end of line 3 lines up with the end of the column on line 4, that space is filled in lines 2 and 6.

עַל הָעֵץ ("on the tree"), it is natural to read תלוי as preceding that prepositional phrase. This ties into the repeated use of תלה על (ה)עץ in the OT and
in other Jewish literature (see esp. above in chapter three). Therefore, the
bodily suspension of a person is most probably in view.

Dimant suggests השמים ("of heaven") must have stood at the beginning of
line 4, based on other references to "birds of heaven" in Hebrew literature
(Jer 7:33; 15:3; Ezek 29:5; 32:4).[3] More importantly, there is a likely parallel
to Genesis 40:19, where the hung baker's body was also afflicted by birds
(see above in chapter 3, §2), though the clausal structure is a bit different.[4] If
the Genesis 40:19 parallel is followed, then the "of heaven" (השמים) suggestion is not necessary since this is not found in Gen 40:19; and its omission
would provide more space to mention the activity of the birds (presumably
involving eating the flesh of the suspended victim) and more space to transi-
tion to the known words now found in line 4.

The אל תותירו ("do not leave over...") in line 4 has been thought to be an
allusion to Deuteronomy 21:23 ("his corpse shall not spend the night on the
tree, but you shall surely bury him in that day").[5] And line 2 ("because they
did not listen") has been considered an admonition not heeded by the Israelites. The first person "I said" in line 5 then would likely be a statement from
God.[6] Hence, line 4 would be an instruction by God to the Israelites.[7]

One could thus speculate that this text reminds the Israelites to practice the
legislation of Deuteronomy 21:22–23. However, it should certainly be admitted that, though plausible, this speculation relies on a great deal of inference.
The text is highly fragmentary, making it difficult at times even to determine
who is speaking.[8] It is not clear what the broader context of this passage is.
And it is not even certain what other fragmentary 4Q texts this small fragment
should be associated with.[9] Therefore, I would caution against inferring too
much from this scrap of text from the Judaean desert.

---

[3] Dimant, *DJD* 30, 151. A similar suggestion is found in García Martínez and Tigchelaar,
DSS Study Edition, 2:770–771.

[4] Genesis 40:19: וְתָלָה אוֹתְךָ עַל־עֵץ וְאָכַל הָעוֹף אֶת־בְּשָׂרְךָ מֵעָלֶיךָ – "...and he will
hang you on a tree, and the birds will eat your flesh from upon you." Note that the last clause
in Gen 40:19 begins with the verb (וְאָכַל), whereas 4Q385a 15 i 3 begins its possibly parallel
clause with וְעוֹף. On Genesis 40:19, see above in chapter 3, §2.

[5] Dimant, *DJD* 30, 151.

[6] Dimant (*DJD* 30, p. 152) calls וָאֹמְרָה a first singular long imperfect (either real or
inverted), and she refers to similar occurrences in Dan 9:4; 10:16, 19; 12:8; Ezra 8:28; 9:6;
Neh 5:7; 13:9 (to which we could also add Gen 46:31); also see 4Q385 2.9, 4Q389 2.4.

[7] Ibid., 151–52.

[8] For example, Dimant readily admits to an alternative interpretation of וָאֹמְרָה in line 5,
namely that the verb could refer to Jeremiah speaking in the first person (p. 152). This slight
change could dramatically alter the interpretation of the whole fragment.

[9] Note the debates among various scholars as to whether this fragment belongs with the
4Q385 "Pseudo-Ezekiel" texts or with the "Apocryphon of Jeremiah" fragments.

4Q541 24 ii

The work labeled 4Q541 has been variously designated as an Apocryphon of Levi or Apocryphon of Aaron. This document has attracted substantial scholarly attention because of the way it appears to anticipate a suffering messianic figure (see especially 4Q541 9 i 2–7). Émile Puech, the *DJD* editor of this work, has also suggested that it refers to crucifixion in fragment 24, column ii 4–5.[10] His transcription and translation read (*DJD* 31: 252–253):

```
1      [מ]                                    ] [
2  א[ל] תתאבל בשׂק[ן־ן] על [ ] ואל ת[עבד שגיאן די לא להוין
3  מ[פ]ר̇ׄיקן או שגיאן[ ]מׄ̇ס[תרן ]ב[למ]ה די להוי[ן שגיאן מגליאן ואׄ[ל] צׄ[דיקא יבריככה]
4  בקר ובעי ודע מא יונא בעה ואל תמחולהי ביד שחפא ותׄלׄיׄא כׄ[די]ן[ ]אל תדן]
5  וצצא אל תׄקׄרוב בה ותקים לאבוכה שם חדוא ולכול אחיכה יסוד מׄׄבׄחן
6  ת[צ]{ו}א ותחזה ותחדה בנהיר עלמא ולא תהוה מן שנאא        *vacat*
```

2 'Ne] fais pas de deuil avec des sacs [sur …]et ne [commet]s pas [de fautes qui ne seraient pas

3 ra]chetées, qu'elles soient des fautes ca[chées]au[ssi bien que si elles étaien]t des fautes dévoilées, et le *Di[eu] j[uste te bénira*(?).]

4 Cherche et demande et sache ce que demande l'agitateur, et ne le *repousse/l'affaiblis* pas au moyen d'épuisement/*bâton* et de pendaison/crucifixion comme [*pein*]e [(capitale) ne *prononce pas*(?)]

5 et de *clou* n'approche pas de lui. Et tu établiras pour ton père un nom de joie, et pour tous tes frères une fondation éprouvée

6 tu feras surgir. Et tu verras et tu te réjouiras dans la lumière éternelle et tu ne seras pas quelqu'un de l'ennemi.'

The transcription above, as well as a close analysis of the plates, indicates that the text is very uncertain in most of lines 2 and 3, and at the end of line 4. In particular, the ו and ת on ותׄלׄיׄא in line 4 are not clearly visible in the plates.

While others have been willing to follow Puech on his crucifixion identification in this text (if at times only tentatively),[11] the crucifixion reference here is by no means certain. In order to highlight some of the key interpretive

---

[10] Émile Puech, *Qumrân Grotte 4, XXII: Textes Araméens Première Partie (4Q529–4Q549)*, DJD 31 (Oxford: Clarendon Press, 2001), 254–256 (see especially his use of "pendaison/crucifixion" in line four, but also his reference to a "*clou*" ["nail"] in line 5). In his earlier edition, Puech merely translated ותׄלׄיׄא in line 4 as "pendoir/pendaison(?)", but he still suggested the possibility of crucifixion in light of the "clou" in line 5; see Émile Puech, "Fragments d'un apocryphe de Lévi et le personnage eschatologique. 4QTestLévi[c-d](?) et 4QAJa," in *The Madrid Qumran Congress*, ed. Julio Trebolle Barrera and Luis Vegas Montaner, vol. 2 (Leiden: Brill, 1992), 475–478 (esp. 478). Also see his mention of this text in Émile Puech, "Die Kreuzigung und die altjüdische Tradition," *Welt und Umwelt der Bibel* 9 (1998): 75.

[11] E.g., Johannes Zimmermann, *Messianische Texte aus Qumran: Königliche, priesterliche und prophetische Messiasvorstellungen in den Schriftfunden von Qumran*, WUNT II.104 (Tübingen: Mohr Siebeck, 1998), 264–266; George J. Brooke, *The Dead Sea Scrolls and the New Testament* (Minneapolis: Fortress, 2005), 148–151 (esp. 149).

issues, one could compare and contrast Puech's rendering with the translation by García Martínez and Tigchelaar[12]:

1 [...] ... [...] ... [...] *2* Do [n]ot mourn for [him...] and do not [...] *3* [And] God will establish many [...] many [...] will be revealed, and [...] *4* Examine, ask and know what the dove has asked; and do not punish it by the sea-mew and [...] ... [...] *5* do not bring the night-hawk near it. And you will establish for your father a name of joy, and for your brothers you will make a [tested] foundation *6* rise. You will see and rejoice in eternal light. And you will not be of the enemy. *Blank*

Most substantially, this translation reads "night-hawk" in line 5 where Puech reads *clou* ("nail"), and the García Martínez/Tigchelaar translation does not make a reference to suspension in line 4 since they are not certain about the first two letters of זׄתׄלׄיׄא. Similarly, other translators exhibit a variety of alternatives for rendering lines four and five.[13]

The key issues for any crucifixion identification in this passage have principally to do with two words: זׄתׄלׄיׄא in line four and צצא in line five.[14] The first, as we have already noted, is reconstructed from a fragmentary patch of text where the first two letters are uncertain.[15] The second word (צצא) has been variously interpreted, for example, to mean a "nail" (Puech), a "frontlet" ("Stirndiadem") of a priest's garb (Beyer), or some form of bird ("night-hawk" in García Martínez and Tigchelaar). This variety of renderings for צצא is due to different possible definitions of this rare word based on known Aramaic (and other related Semitic) vocabulary. Puech connects צצא to the meaning "nail" via an analogy to Syriac *ṣeṣ'*, arguing that in this manuscript it is improbable that צצא is a defective form of ציצא (meaning "diadème, émeraude, ou autruche/vautour"), which others have argued (*DJD* 31, 255). Even if צצא is understood to mean "nail," it is not certain whether this Qumran text truly refers to crucifixion, let alone exactly how the author of this passage perceived of such a punishment.[16]

---

[12] García Martínez and Tigchelaar, *DSS Study Edition*, 2:1081.

[13] Thus Vermes reads: "Search and seek and know what is sought by the dove and do not smite one who is exhausted with consumption and troubles..." Translation in Geza Vermes, *The Complete Dead Sea Scrolls in English* (London: Allen Lane, 1997), 527. In his earlier translation, García Martínez originally rendered the text in a way closer to Puech's crucifixion interpretation: "*4* Examine, ask and know what the dove has asked; and do not punish one weakened because of exhaustion and from being uncertain a[ll...] *5* do not bring the nail near him." See Florentino García Martínez, *The Dead Sea Scrolls Translated*, trans. Wilfred G. E. Watson (Leiden: Brill, 1994), 270.

[14] Puech also correlates these two key words with שחטפא in line 4, which he understands as a "*bâton*" ("rod") used as an implement of punishment.

[15] This is represented by לׄיׄ[...]ז in García Martínez and Tigchelaar, *DSS Study Edition*, 2:1080. Beyer also omits the ת. Even more uncertain is any possible parallel to תׄלׄלׄ in the highly fragmentary text earlier in 4Q524 (2 ii 1) – for text, see Puech, *DJD* 31, 231.

[16] A related point is made in John J. Collins, "Asking for the Meaning of a Fragmentary Qumran Text: The Referential Background of 4QAaron A," in *Texts and Contexts: Biblical*

At best, one must acknowledge that current scholarship disagrees about whether this text refers to crucifixion.[17] Moreover, the fragmentary nature of the text makes is difficult to tease out with any certainty any perceptions of crucifixion, even if they were there.

Texts in their Textual and Situational Contexts, ed. Tord Fornberg and David Hellholm (Oslo: Scandinavian University Press, 1995), 585–586. Collins states, "It is not certain that there is any reference to a nail here at all. If we assume, however, that the text does refer to crucifixion, there is still no question of a messianic figure being crucified. Rather, the person addressed in the text is told not to afflict the weak by crucifixion... There is certainly no prediction here of a figure who will be subjected to suffering, only an admonition against afflicting the weak."

[17] For a helpful summary of key issues in this passage see Martin Hengel with the collaboration of Daniel P. Bailey, "The Effective History of Isaiah 53 in the Pre-Christian Period," in *The Suffering Servant: Isaiah 53 in Jewish and Christian Sources*, ed. Bernd Janowski and Peter Stuhlmacher, trans. Daniel P. Bailey (Grand Rapids: Eerdmans, 2004), 110–115.

Bibliography

1. Primary Sources

Translations in the thesis are my own unless noted, but the published translations listed below were also consulted. Where possible, the primary LXX text consulted was that of the Göttingen edition (otherwise from the Cambridge edition). The OL text follows the *Vetus Latina* series (otherwise Sabatier).

Albeck, Chanoch. *Shishah Sidre Mishnah*. 6 vols. Jerusalem: Bialik Institute, 1952–58.

Babbitt, Frank C., et al. *Plutarch's Moralia*. 16 vols. LCL. Cambridge, Mass.: Harvard University Press, 1927–1969.

Baehrens, W. A. *Origenes Werke, Sechster Band: Homilien zum Hexateuch in Rufins Übersetzung*. 2 vols. Griechischen christlichen Schriftsteller 29 & 30. Leipzig: J. C. Hinrichs, 1920–1921.

Basore, John W. *Seneca Moral Essays*. 3 vols. LCL. Cambridge, Mass.: Harvard, 1965.

Bauer, Adolf, and Rudolf Helm. *Hippolytus Werke Vierter Band: Die Chronik*. 2nd ed. Griechischen christlichen Schriftsteller 46. Leipzig: J. C. Hinrichs, 1955.

Beer, G., O. Holtzmann, K. H. Rengstorf, L. Rost, and et al, eds. *Die Mischna: Text, Übersetzung und ausführliche Erklärung*. 42+ vols. Gießen: Alfred Töpelmann/ Berlin: Walter de Gruyter, 1912–present.

Berger, David. *The Jewish-Christian Debate in the High Middle Ages: A critical edition of the NIZZAHON VETUS with an introduction, translation, and commentary*. Judaica Texts and Translations 4. Philadelphia: Jewish Publication Society of America, 1979.

Berrin, Shani L. *The Pesher Nahum Scroll from Qumran: An Exegetical Study of 4Q169*. STDJ 53. Leiden: Brill, 2004.

Biblia Sacra iuxta Latinam Vulgatam versionem ad codicum fidem, cura et studio monachorum Abbatiae pontificiae Sancti Hieronymi in Urbe Ordinis Sancti Benedicti edita. 18 vols. Rome: Typis Polyglottis Vaticanis/Libreria Editrice Vaticana, 1926–1995.

Blackman, Philip. *Mishnayoth*. 2nd ed. 7 vols. New York: Judaica Press, 1964.

Bonwetsch, G. Nath., and Hans Achelis. *Hippolytus Werke Erster Band: Exegetische und homiletische Schriften*. Griechischen christlichen Schriftsteller 1. Leipzig: J. C. Hinrichs, 1897.

Borret, Marcel. *Origène Homélies sur le Lévitique*. 2 vols. Sources chrétiennes 286 & 287. Paris: Cerf, 1981.

Bratke, Edward, ed. *Scriptores ecclesiastici minores saeculorum IV. V. VI., Fasciculus I: Evagrii Altercatio legis inter Simonem Iudaeum et Theophilum Christianum*. Corpus scriptorum ecclesiasticorum Latinorum 45. Vindobonae: F. Tempsky/Lipsiae: G. Freytag, 1904.

Braude, William G. *The Midrash on Psalms*. 2 vols. Yale Judaica 13. New Haven: Yale University Press, 1959.

———. *Pesikta Rabbati: Discourses for Feasts, Fasts, and Special Sabbaths*. 2 vols. Yale Judaica 18. New Haven: Yale University Press, 1968.

Braude, William G. (Gershon Zev) and Israel J. Kapstein. *Pesikta de-Rab Kahana: R. Kahana's compilation of discourses for Sabbaths and festal days.* Philadelphia: Jewish Publication Society of America, 1975; London: Routledge & Kegan Paul, 1975.

Brooke, Alan England, Norman McLean, and Henry St. John Thackeray, eds. *The Old Testament in Greek.* London: Cambridge University Press, 1906–1940.

Broshi, Magen, ed. *The Damascus Document Reconsidered.* Jerusalem: Israel Exploration Society, 1992.

Buber, Salomon. *Midrasch Echa Rabbati: Sammlung agadischer Auslegungen der Klagelieder.* Wilna, 1899. Reprint, Hildesheim: Georg Olms, 1967.

____. *Midrasch Tanchuma: Ein Agadischer Commentar zum Pentateuch von Rabbi Tanchuma ben Rabbi Abba.* Wilna: Wittwe & Gebrüder, 1885.

____. *Midrasch Tehillim (Schocher Tob).* Wilna: Wittwe & Gebrüder, 1891.

Cary, Earnest. *Dio's Roman History.* 9 vols. LCL. Cambridge, Mass.: Harvard; London: Heinemann, 1914–1927.

Charles, R. H. *The Assumption of Moses.* London: Adam and Charles Black, 1897.

Charlesworth, James H., ed. *The Old Testament Pseudepigrapha.* 2 vols. New York: Doubleday, 1983–1985. Cited notes and translations appear individually by translator in the General Bibliography.

Clemens, David M. *Sources for Ugaritic Ritual and Sacrifice: Volume 1: Ugaritic and Ugarit Akkadian Texts.* AOAT 284/1. Münster: Ugarit-Verlag, 2001.

Cohn, Leopoldus, Paulus Wendland, Sigofredus Reiter, and Ioannes Leisegang, eds. *Philonis Alexandrini opera quae supersunt.* 7 vols. Berlin: Georgi Reimer, 1896–1930. Critical edition consulted for Greek text.

Colson, F. H., G. H. Whitaker, J. W. Earp, and Ralph Marcus. *Philo.* 10 (+ 2 suppl.) vols. Loeb Classical Library. Cambridge, Mass.: Harvard University Press, 1929–1962.

Connolly, R. Hugh. *Didascalia apostolorum: the Syriac version translated and accompanied by the Verona Latin fragments.* Oxford: Clarendon, 1969.

Cowley, A. *Aramaic Papyri of the Fifth Century B.C.* Oxford: Clarendon Press, 1923. Reprint, Osnabrück: Otto Zeller, 1967.

Danby, Herbert. *The Mishnah.* London: Oxford University Press, 1933.

De-Rossi, Johannes Bern. *Variae Lectiones Veteris Testamenti.* 4 vols. + suppl. Parma: Ex Regio Typographeo, 1784–1798.

Díez Macho, Alejandro. *Neophyti 1: Targum Palestinense MS de la Biblioteca Vaticana.* 6 vols. Textos y Estudios 7–11, and 20. Madrid-Barcelona: Consejo Superior de Investigaciones Científicas, 1968–1979.

Díez Macho, Alexandro, L. Díez Merino, E. Martinez Borobio, and Teresa Martinez Saiz, eds. *Biblia Polyglotta Matritensia IV: Targum Palaestinense in Pentateuchum.* 5 vols. Madrid: Consejo Superior de Investigaciones Científicas, 1977–1988.

Dimant, Devorah. *Qumran Cave 4 XXI: Parabiblical Texts, Part 4: Pseudo-Prophetic Texts.* DJD 30. Oxford: Clarendon, 2001.

Discoveries in the Judean Desert, 27+ vols. Oxford: Clarendon Press, 1955–present. Also see individual volumes listed in bibliography.

Doudna, Gregory L. *4Q Pesher Nahum: A Critical Edition.* JSPSup 35. London: Sheffield Academic Press, 2001.

Driver, G. R., and John C. Miles. *The Assyrian Laws.* Ancient Codes and Laws of the Near East. Oxford: Clarendon Press, 1935.

____. *The Babylonian Laws.* 2 vols. Ancient Codes and Laws of the Near East. Oxford: Clarendon Press, 1952/55.

Duff, J. D. *Lucan.* LCL. London: William Heinemann/Cambridge, Mass.: Harvard University Press, 1928.

Elliger, K., and W. Rudolph, eds. *Biblia Hebraica Stuttgartensia*. 4th ed. Stuttgart: Deutsche Bibelgesellschaft, 1990.

Epstein, I., ed. *Hebrew-English Edition of the Babylonian Talmud*. New ed. 30 vols. London: Soncino, 1967–1989.

Faller, Otto, and Michaela Zelzer, eds. *Sancti Ambrosii Opera, Pars Decima: Epistulae et Acta*. 4 vols. Corpus scriptorum ecclesiasticorum Latinorum 82. Vienna: Hölder-Pichler-Tempsky, 1968–1996.

Field, Fridericus. *Origenis Hexaplorum quae supersunt*. 2 vols. Oxford: Clarendon Press, 1875. (Also compared to apparatus of Göttingen LXX).

Finkelstein, Louis. *Sifre on Deuteronomy*. New York: Jewish Theological Seminary of America, 1969. Originally published as *Siphre ad Deuteronomium: H. S. Horovitzii schedis usus cum variis lectionibus et adnotationibus*. Berlin, 1939.

Freedman, H., and Maurice Simon, eds. *Midrash Rabbah*. 10 vols. 2nd ed. London: Soncino Press, 1951.

García Martínez, Florentino. *The Dead Sea Scrolls Translated*. Translated by Wilfred G. E. Watson. Leiden: Brill, 1994. Originally published as *Textos de Qumrán*. Madrid: Editorial Trotta, 1992.

García Martínez, Florentino, and Eibert J. C. Tigchelaar, eds. *The Dead Sea Scrolls Study Edition*. 2 vols. Leiden: Brill, 1997–1998.

Ginsberger, M. *Pseudo-Jonathan (Thargum Jonathan ben Usiël zum Pentateuch). Nach der Londoner Handschrift (Brit. Mus. add. 27031)*. Berlin: S. Calvary & Co., 1903. Reprint, New York: Hildesheim, 1971.

Goldberg, Abraham. *Commentary to the Mishna Shabbat: Critically Edited and Provided with Introduction, Commentary and Notes*. Jerusalem: Jewish Theological Seminary of America, 1976.

Grossfeld, Bernard. *The First Targum to Esther: According to the MS Paris Hebrew 110 of the Bibliotheque Nationale*. New York: Sepher-Hermon Press, 1983.

_____. *The Targum Sheni to the Book of Esther: a critical edition based on MS. Sassoon 282 with critical apparatus*. New York: Sepher-Hermon, 1994. A KWIC concordance is appendixed to this edition.

_____. *The Two Targums of Esther: Translated, with Apparatus and Notes*. The Aramaic Bible 18. Edinburgh: T & T Clark, 1991.

Hall, Stuart George, ed. *Melito of Sardis On Pascha and Fragments*. Oxford Early Christian Texts. Oxford: Clarendon Press, 1979.

Hammer, Reuven. *Sifre: A Tannaitic Commentary on the Book of Deuteronomy*. Yale Judaica 24. New Haven: Yale University Press, 1986.

Hanhart, Robert, ed. *Esdrae liber I*. Septuaginta 8,1. Göttingen: Vandenhoeck & Ruprecht, 1974.

_____. *Esther*. Septuaginta VIII,3. Göttingen: Vandenhoeck & Ruprecht, 1966.

Hansen, Günther Christian, ed. *Sokrates Kirchengeschichte*. Griechischen christlichen Schriftsteller, n.f. 1. Berlin: Akademie Verlag, 1995.

Harmon, A. M., K. Kilburn, and M. D. Macleod. *Lucian*. 8 vols. LCL. London: William Heinemann/Cambridge, Mass.: Harvard University Press, 1913–1967.

Heide, Albert van der. *The Yemenite Tradition of the Targum of Lamentations: Critical Text and Analysis of the Variant Readings*. Studia post-Biblica 32. Leiden: E. J. Brill, 1981.

Hoffmann, D. *Midrasch Tannaïm zum Deuteronomium*. 2 vols. Berlin: M. Poppelauer, 1908–1909.

Horgan, Maurya P. "Nahum Pesher (4Q169 = 4QpNah)." In *The Dead Sea Scrolls: Hebrew, Aramaic, and Greek Texts with English Translations*, edited by James H. Charlesworth, vol. 6b: Pesharim, Other Commentaries, and Related Documents, 144–55. Tübingen: Mohr Siebeck; Louisville: Westminster/John Knox, 2002.

_____. *Pesharim: Qumran Interpretations of Biblical Books.* CBQMS 8. Washington, DC: Catholic Biblical Association of America, 1979.

_____. "Psalm Pesher 1 (4Q171 = 4QpPsᵃ = 4QpPs 37 and 45)." In *The Dead Sea Scrolls: Hebrew, Aramaic, and Greek Texts with English Translations*, edited by James H. Charlesworth, vol. 6b: Pesharim, Other Commentaries, and Related Documents, 6–23. Tübingen: Mohr Siebeck; Louisville: Westminster/John Knox, 2002.

Horovitz, H. S., ed. *Siphre ad Numeros adjecto Siphre zutta: Cum variis lectionibus et adnotationibus.* Corpus Tannaiticum III.3. Leipzig: Gustav Fock, 1917.

Hyman, D., D. N. Lerrer, and I. Shiloni, eds. *Yalqut Shimʿoni al ha-Torah le Rabbenu Shimʿon ha-Darshan.* 9 vols. Jerusalem: Mossad Harav Kook, 1973–1991.

Jaubert, Annie. *Origène Homélies sur Josué.* Sources chrétiennes 71. Paris: Cerf, 1960.

Kappler, Werner, ed. *Maccabaeorum liber I.* Septuaginta 9,1. Göttingen: Vandenhoeck & Ruprecht, 1990.

King, L. W., and R. C. Thompson. *The Sculptures and Inscription of Darius the Great on the Rock of Behistûn in Persia.* London: Harrison & Sons, 1907.

Klein, Michael L. *The Fragment-Targums of the Pentateuch: According to their Extant Sources.* 2 vols. Analecta Biblica 76. Rome: Biblical Institute Press, 1980.

_____. *Genizah Manuscripts of Palestinian Targum to the Pentateuch.* 2 vols. Cincinnati: Hebrew Union College, 1986.

Koestermann, Erich, Stephanus Borzsák, and Kenneth Wellesley, eds. *Cornellii Taciti libri qui supersunt.* 2 vols (in 5 parts). Bibliotheca scriptorum Graecorum et Romanorum Teubneriana. Leipzig: Teubner, 1965–1986.

Koetschau, Paul, ed. *Origenes Werke, Fünfter Band: De Principiis [ΠΕΡΙ ΑΡΧΩΝ].* Griechischen christlichen Schriftsteller 22. Leipzig: J. C. Hinrichs, 1913.

_____. *Origenes Werke, Zweiter Band: Gegen Celsus; Die Schrift vom Gebet.* 2 vols. Griechischen christlichen Schriftsteller 2 & 3. Leipzig: J. C. Hinrichs, 1899.

Krauss, Samuel. *Die Mischna: Text, Übersetzung und ausführliche Erklärung.* Vol. IV.4–5: Sanhedrin, Makkot. Giessen: Alfred Töpelmann, 1933.

Lahey, Lawrence Lanzi. "The Dialogue of Timothy and Aquila: Critical Greek Text and English Translation of the Short Recension with an Introduction including a Source-critical Study." PhD, University of Cambridge, 2000.

Lake, Kirsopp. *The Apostolic Fathers.* 2 vols. LCL. Cambridge, Mass.: Harvard University Press, 1912.

Lasker, Daniel J. and Sarah Stroumsa. *The Polemic of Nestor the Priest: Qiṣṣat Mujādalat al-Usquf and Sefer Nestor Ha-Komer.* 2 vols. Jerusalem: Ben-Zvi Institute, 1996.

Lauterbach, Jacob Z. *Mekilta de-Rabbi Ishmael.* 3 vols. Philadelphia: Jewish Publication Society of America, 1933–1935.

Le Déaut, R., and J. Robert. *Targum des Chroniques (Cod. Vat. Urb. Ebr. 1).* 2 vols. Analecta Biblica 51. Rome: Biblical Institute Press, 1971.

Les oeuvres de Philon d'Alexandrie. 36 vols. Paris: Éditions du Cerf, 1961–1988. Cited individual volumes listed by translator in the General Bibliography.

Levine, Étan. *The Aramaic Version of Lamentations.* New York: Hermon Press, 1976.

_____. *The Aramaic Version of Ruth.* Analecta Biblica 58. Rome: Biblical Institute Press, 1973.

Linder, Amnon. *The Jews in Roman Imperial Legislation.* Detroit: Wayne State University Press, 1987.

_____. *The Jews in the Legal Sources of the Early Middle Ages.* Detroit: Wayne State University Press, 1997.

Luckenbill, Daniel David. *Ancient Records of Assyria and Babylonia.* 2 vols. Chicago: University of Chicago, 1926–1927.

Macleod, M. D. *Luciani Opera.* 4 vols. Scriptorum classicorum bibliotheca Oxoniensis. Oxford: Oxford University Press, 1972.

Mandelbaum, Bernard. *Pesikta de Rav Kahana: According to an Oxford Manuscript with variants from all known manuscripts and genizoth fragments and parallel passages with commentary and introduction.* 2nd ed. 2 vols. New York: Jewish Theological Seminary of America, 1987.

Mara, M. G. *Évangile de Pierre.* Sources chrétiennes 201. Paris: Cerf, 1973.

Marcovich, Miroslav, ed. *Iustini Martyris apologiae pro christianis.* Patristische Texte und Studien 38. Berlin: Walter de Gruyter, 1994.

____. *Iustini Martyris Dialogus cum Tryphone.* Patristische Texte und Studien 47. Berlin: Walter de Gruyter, 1997.

Margalioth, Mordecai. *Sepher ha-Razim: A Newly Recovered Book of Magic from the Talmudic Period.* Jerusalem: American Academy for Jewish Research, 1966.

Margulies, Mordecai. *Midrash Wayyikra Rabbah: A Critical Edition Based on Manuscripts and Genizah Fragments with Variants and Notes.* 5 vols. Jerusalem: Louis M. and Minnie Epstein Fund of the American Academy for Jewish Research, 1953–1960.

McCullough, W. S. *Jewish and Mandaean Incantation Bowls in the Royal Ontario Museum.* Near and Middle East Series 5. Toronto: University of Toronto Press, 1967.

McNamara, Martin (project director). *The Aramaic Bible.* Edinburgh: T & T Clark, 1987–. Cited individual volumes listed according to translator in the General Bibliography.

Midrash Bereshit Rabba: Codex Vatican 60 (Ms. Vat. Ebr. 60): A Previously Unknown Manuscript, Recently Established as the Earliest and Most Important Version of Bereshit Rabba. Jerusalem: Makor, 1972.

Mommsen, Th. and Paul M. Meyer. *Theodosiani libri XVI cum constitutionibus Sirmondianis et Leges novellae ad Theodosianum Pertinentes.* 2 vols. Berlin: Weidmann, 1954.

Morgan, Michael A. *Sepher Ha-Razim: The Book of the Mysteries.* SBLTT 25. Chico, Calif.: Scholars Press, 1983.

Mras, Karl. *Eusebius Werke Achter Band: Die Praeparatio Evangelica.* 2 vols. Griechischen christlichen Schriftsteller 43,1. Berlin: Akademie-Verlag, 1954.

Musurillo, Herbert. *The Acts of the Christian Martyrs.* OECT. Oxford: Clarendon Press, 1972.

Naveh, Joseph and Shaul Shaked. *Amulets and Magic Bowls: Aramaic Incantations of Late Antiquity.* Jerusalem: Magnes Press/Leiden: E. J. Brill, 1985.

____. *Magic Spells and Formulae: Aramaic Incantations of Late Antiquity.* Jerusalem: Magnes Press, 1993.

Nelson, W. David. *Mekhilta de-Rabbi Shimon bar Yohai.* Philadelphia: Jewish Publication Society, 2006.

Nestle, E., and K. Aland, eds. *Novum Testamentum Graece.* 27th ed. Stuttgart: Deutsche Bibelgesellschaft, 1993.

Neusner, Jacob. *Sifre to Deuteronomy: An Analytical Translation.* 2 vols. Brown Judaic Studies 98, 101. Atlanta: Scholars Press, 1987.

____. *Sifre to Numbers: An American Translation and Explanation.* 2 vols. Brown Judaic Studies 118–119. Atlanta: Scholars Press, 1986.

____. *The Tosefta: Translated from the Hebrew.* 6 vols. New York: KTAV, 1977–1986.

Neusner, Jacob, et al. *The Talmud of the Land of Israel: A Preliminary Translation and Explanation.* 35 vols. Chicago Studies in the History of Judaism. Chicago: University of Chicago Press, 1982–1994. NB: In this thesis Yerushalmi *pereq* and verse numbers accord with that of Leiden MS and the *editio princeps* (persons using J. Neusner's translations and aids will need to make the occasional conversion).

Niese, Benedictus. *Flavii Iosephi Opera*. 7 vols. Berlin: Weidmann, 1887–1895.

Nixon, Paul. *Plautus*. 5 vols. LCL. Cambridge: Harvard University Press, 1916–1938.

Nodet, Étienne, ed. *Flavius Josèphe, Les Antiquités Juives*. 2+ vols. Paris: Les Éditions du Cerf, 1990–present.

Nowack, Wilhelm. *Schabbat (Sabbat): Text, Übersetzung und Erklärung Nebst einem textkritishen Anhang*. Die Mischna: Text, Übersetzung und ausführliche Erklärung II.1. Gießen: Alfred Töpelmann, 1924.

Perrin, Bernadotte. *Plutarch's Lives*. 11 vols. LCL. Cambridge, Mass.: Harvard University Press, 1914–1926.

Plumer, Eric. *Augustine's Commentary on Galatians: Introduction, Text, Translation, and Notes*. OECT. Oxford: Oxford University Press, 2003.

Porten, Bezalel and Ada Yardeni. *Textbook of Aramaic Documents from Ancient Egypt*. 4 vols. Winona Lake: Eisenbrauns, 1986–1993.

Priest, J. "Testament of Moses (First Century A.D.): A New Translation and Introduction." In *The Old Testament Pseudepigrapha*, edited by James H. Charlesworth, vol. 1, 919–34. Garden City, NY: Doubleday, 1983.

Prigent, Pierre, and Robert A. Kraft. *Épître de Barnabé*. Sources chrétiennes 172. Paris: Cerf, 1971.

Puech, Émile. "Fragments d'un apocryphe de Lévi et le personnage eschatologique. 4QTestLévi^{c-d}(?) et 4QAJa." In *The Madrid Qumran Congress*, edited by Julio Trebolle Barrera and Luis Vegas Montaner, vol. 2, 449–501, 674–81. Leiden: Brill, 1992.

____. *Qumrân Grotte 4, XVIII: Textes Hébreux (4Q521–4Q528, 4Q576–4Q579)*. DJD 25. Oxford: Clarendon Press, 1998.

____. *Qumrân Grotte 4, XXII: Textes Araméens Première Partie (4Q529–4Q549)*. DJD 31. Oxford: Clarendon Press, 2001.

Qimron, Elisha. *The Temple Scroll: A Critical Edition with Extensive Reconstructions*. Judean Desert Series. Beer Sheva: Ben-Gurion University, 1996.

Rabbinowitz, J. "Ebel Rabbathi Named Masseketh Semahoth: Tractate on Mourning." In *The Minor Tractates of the Talmud*, edited by A. Cohen, vol. 1, 325–400. London: Soncino, 1965.

Rackham, H., W. H. S. Jones, and D. E. Eichholz. *Pliny Natural History*. 10 vols. LCL. London: Heinemann/Cambridge, Mass.: Harvard University Press, 1938–1962.

Rahmani, L. Y. *A Catalogue of Jewish Ossuaries in the Collections of the State of Israel*. Jerusalem: The Israel Antiquities Authority/The Israel Academy of Sciences and Humanities, 1994.

Robertson, Robert G. "The Dialogue of Timothy and Aquila: A Critical Text, Introduction to the Manuscript Evidence, and an Inquiry into the Sources and Literary Relationships." Th.D. Diss., Harvard University, 1986.

Rousseau, Adelin, Louis Doutreleau, Bertrand Hemmerdinger, and Charles Mercier. *Irénée de Lyon. Contre les hérésies*. 9 vols. Sources chrétiennes 100, 152, 153, 210, 211, 263, 264, 293, 294. Paris: Cerf, 1965–1982.

Sabatier, Petri, ed. *Bibliorum Sacrorum Latinae Versiones Antiquae*. 3 vols. Rheims: Reginald Florentain, 1743–49.

Salomonsen, Børge. *Die Tosefta Seder IV: Nezikin (Sanhedrin – Makkot)*. Stuttgart: W. Kohlhammer, 1976.

Schäfer, Peter and Hans-Jürgen Becker, eds. *Synopse zum Talmud Yerushalmi*. 5+ vols. Texte und Studien zum Antiken Judentum 31,33,35,47,67. Tübingen: J. C. B. Mohr (Paul Siebeck), 1991–1998. Where not available, citations follow Krotoshin edition.

Schäfer, Peter and Shaul Shaked, eds. *Magische Texte aus der Kairoer Geniza.* 2 vols. TSAJ 42 & 64. Tübingen: J. C. B. Mohr [Paul Siebeck], 1994–1997.

Schiffman, Lawrence H. and Michael D. Swartz. *Hebrew and Aramaic Incantation Texts from the Cairo Genizah: Selected Texts from Taylor-Schechter Box K1.* Semitic Texts and Studies 1. Sheffield: Sheffield Academic Press, 1992.

Schneemelcher, Wilhelm, ed. *New Testament Apocrypha.* Translated by R. McL. Wilson. 2nd revised ed. 2 vols. Cambridge: James Clarke & Co./Louisville: Westminster/John Knox, 1991–1992. Originally published as *Neutestamentliche Apokryphen.* Revised ed. Tübingen: J. C. B. Mohr [Paul Siebeck], 1989–1990.

Schwemer, Anna Maria. *Historische und legendarische Erzählungen: Vitae Prophetarum.* JSHRZ I.7. Gütersloh: Gütersloher Verlagshaus, 1997.

Sepher Midrash Rabbah. 2 vols. Wilna ed. (Jerusalem reprint).

Septuaginta: Vetus Testamentum Graecum Auctoritate Academiae Scientiarum Gottingensis editum. Göttingen: Vandenhoeck & Ruprecht, 1931–present.

Sokoloff, Michael. *The Geniza Fragments of Bereshit Rabba: Edited on the Basis of Twelve Manuscripts and Palimpsests.* Jerusalem: Israel Academy of Sciences and Humanities, 1982.

Sperber, Alexander. *The Bible in Aramaic: Based on Old Manuscripts and Printed Texts.* 4 vols. Leiden: Brill, 1959–1973.

Sukenik, E. L., ed. *The Dead Sea Scrolls of the Hebrew University.* Jerusalem: The Magnes Press, 1955.

Tal, Abraham. *The Samaritan Targum of the Pentateuch: A Critical Edition.* 3 vols. Texts and Studies in the Hebrew Language and Related Subjects 4–6. Tel-Aviv: Tel-Aviv University, 1980–1983.

Talmud Yerushalmi. Krotoshin, 1866. The *Synopse* by Schäfer and Becker (above) has generally been preferred.

Tertulliani Opera. 2 vols. Corpus Christianorum, Series Latina 1 & 2. Turnholt: Brepols, 1954.

Testard, Maurice. *Saint Ambroise: Les Devoirs.* 2 vols. Collection des Universités de France. Paris: Société d–Édition «Les Belles Lettres», 1984/1992.

Thackeray, H. St. J., Ralph Marcus, Allen Wikgren, and Louis H. Feldman. *Josephus.* 10 (originally 9) vols. Loeb Classical Library. Cambridge, Mass.: Harvard University Press/ London: William Heinemann, 1926–1965.

Theodor, J., and Ch. Albeck. *Bereschit Rabba mit kritischem Apparat und Kommentar.* 3 (+ 2 Register) vols. Berlin: M. Poppelauer, 1912–1936.

Tränkle, Hermann. *Q. S. F. Tertulliani Adversus Iudaeos: mit Einleitung und kritischem Kommentar.* Wiesbaden: Franz Steiner, 1964.

Tromp, Johannes. *The Assumption of Moses: A Critical Edition with Commentary.* SVTP 10. Leiden: E. J. Brill, 1993.

Ulmer, Rivka. *Pesiqta Rabbati: A Synoptic Edition of Pesiqta Rabbati Based upon all Extant Manuscripts and the Editio Princeps.* 3 vols. South Florida Studies in the History of Judaism. Atlanta: Scholars Press [vols. 1–2]; Lanham, Maryland: University Press of America [vol. 3], 1997–2002.

Varner, William. *Ancient Jewish-Christian Dialogues.* Lewiston, N.Y.: Edwin Mellen, 2004.

Vermes, Geza. *The Complete Dead Sea Scrolls in English.* London: Allen Lane, 1997.

Vetus Latina: Die Rest der Altlateinischen Bibel. Freiburg: Herder, 1951–present.

Vetus Testamentum Syriace Iuxta Simplicem Syrorum Versionem. Leiden: E. J. Brill, 1977–present.

Voigtlander, Elizabeth N. *The Bisitun Inscription of Darius the Great: Babylonian Version.* Corpus Inscriptionum Iranicarum II.1. London: Lund Humphries, 1978.

von Gall, August Freiherr, ed. *Der Hebräische Pentateuch der Samaritaner.* Giessen: Alfred Töpelmann, 1918.

Winter, Jakob, and August Wünsche. *Mechiltha: Ein tannaitischer Midrasch zu Exodus.* Leipzig: J. C. Hinrich, 1909. Reprint, Hildesheim: Georg Olms, 1990.

Yadin, Yigael. *The Temple Scroll.* 3 vols + suppl. Jerusalem: Israel Exploration Society, 1977–1983.

Yonge, C. D., transl. *The Works of Philo: Complete and Unabridged.* New Updated ed. Peabody, Mass.: Hendrickson, 1993.

Ziegler, Joseph. *Isaias.* Septuaginta. Göttingen: Vandenhoeck & Ruprecht, 1939.

Zlotnick, Dov. *The Tractate Mourning.* Yale Judaica. New Haven: Yale University Press, 1966.

Zuckermandel, M. S. *Tosephta: Based on the Erfurt and Vienna Codices.* 2nd ed. Jerusalem: Bamberger & Wahrmann, 1937.

2. Concordances and Indices Consulted

Allenbach, J., et al. *Biblia Patristica: Index des citations et allusions Bibliques dans la littérature patristique.* 6 (+ suppl.) vols. Paris: Éditions du Centre National de la Recherche Scientifique, 1975–1995.

Borbone, P. G., and K. D. Jenner, eds. *The Old Testament in Syriac According to the Peshitta Version: Part 5 Concordance.* Vol. 1 Pentateuch. Vetus Testamentum Syriace. Leiden: Brill, 1997.

Clarke, E. G., W.E. Aufrecht, J.C. Hurd, and F. Spitzer. *Targum Pseudo-Jonathan of the Pentateuch: Text and Concordance.* Hoboken: Ktav, 1984.

Even-Shoshan, Abraham, ed. *A New Concordance of the Old Testament.* Jerusalem: Kiryat Sefer/Grand Rapids: Baker, 1989. Introduction by John Sailhamer.

Fischer, Bonifatius, ed. *Novae concordantiae Bibliorum Sacrorum iuxta Vulgatam versionem critice editam.* 5 vols. Stuttgart-Bad Cannstatt: Frommann-Holzboog, 1977.

Grossfeld, Bernard. *Concordance of the First Targum to the Book of Esther.* SBL Aramaic Studies 5. Chico, Calif.: Scholars Press, 1984. For the concordance to Targum Sheni see B. Grossfeld above in texts consulted.

Hatch, Edwin, and Henry A. Redpath. *A Concordance to the Septuagint and the Other Greek Versions of the Old Testament.* 3 vols. Oxford: Clarendon Press, 1897/1906.

Hyman, Aaron. *Torah Hakethubah Vehamessurah.* Revised and enlarged by Arthur B. Hyman. 2nd ed. 3 vols. Tel-Aviv: Dvir, 1979.

Kasovsky, Chayim Yehoshua. *Thesaurus Mishnae.* Emended ed. 4 vols. Jerusalem: Massadah, 1956–1960.

Kasowski, Chaim Josua. *Thesaurus Thosephthae: Concordantiae Verborum quae in sex Thosephthae ordinibus reperiuntur.* 6 vols. Jerusalem: Jewish Theological Seminary of America, 1932–1961.

Kasowski, Chaim Josua, and Biniamin Kasowski. *Thesaurus Talmudis: Concordantiae Verborum quae in Talmude Babylonico Reperiuntur.* 42 vols. Jerusalem: Ministry of Education and Culture and The Jewish Theological Seminary of America, 1954–1989.

Kassovsky, Ḥaim Joshua. אוצר התרגום קונקורדנציא לתרגום אנקלוס. 5 vols. Jerusalem: Kiriath Moshe, 1933–1940.

Kaufman, Stephen A., Michael Sokoloff, and with the assistance of Edward M. Cook. *A Key-Word-in-Context Concordance to Targum Neofiti.* Publications of the Comprehensive Aramaic Lexicon Project 2. Baltimore: John Hopkins University Press, 1993.

Kiraz, George Anton. *A Computer-Generated Concordance to the Syriac New Testament.* 6 vols. Leiden: E. J. Brill, 1993.

Kosovsky, Biniamin. *Otzar Leshon Hatannaim: Concordantiae verborum quae in Mechilta d'Rabbi Ismael reperiuntur.* 4 vols. Jerusalem: Jewish Theological Seminary of America, 1965–1969.

———. *Otzar Leshon Hatannaim: Concordantiae verborum quae in Sifra aut Torat Kohanim reperiuntur.* 4 vols. Jerusalem: Jewish Theological Seminary of America, 1967–1969.

———. *Otzar Leshon Hatannaim: Thesaurus "Sifrei" Concordantiae verborum quae in "Sifrei" Numeri et Deuteronomium reperiuntur.* 5 vols. Jerusalem: Jewish Theological Seminary of America, 1971–1974.

Kosovsky, Moshe. *Concordance to the Talmud Yerushalmi (Palestinian Talmud).* 6+ vols. Jerusalem: The Israel Academy of Sciences and Humanities and the Jewish Theological Seminary of America, 1979–present.

Mayer, Günter. *Index Philoneus.* Berlin: Walter de Gruyter, 1974.

Moor, Johannes C. de, et al., eds. *A Bilingual Concordance to the Targum of the Prophets.* 14+ vols. Leiden: E. J. Brill, 1995–present.

Reider, Joseph, and Nigel Turner. *An Index to Aquila.* Vetus Testamentum, Supplements 12. Leiden: E. J. Brill, 1966.

Rengstorf, Karl Heinrich, ed. *A Complete Concordance to Flavius Josephus.* 4 vols. Leiden: E. J. Brill, 1973–83.

Strothmann, Werner, Kurt Johannes, and Manfred Zumpe. *Konkordanz zur Syrischen Bibel: Der Pentateuch.* 4 vols. Göttinger Orientforschungen Reihe 1, Syriaca 26. Wiesbaden: Otto Harrassowitz, 1986.

Strothmann, Werner, Kurt Johannes, and Manfred Zumpe. *Konkordanz zur Syrischen Bibel: Die Propheten.* 4 vols. Göttinger Orientforschungen Reihe 1, Syriaca 25. Wiesbaden: Otto Harrassowitz, 1984.

3. General Bibliography

Albl, Martin C. *"And Scripture Cannot be Broken": The Form and Function of the Early Christian Testimonia Collections.* NovTSup. 96. Leiden: Brill, 1999.

Albrektson, Bertil. *Studies in the Text and Theology of the Book of Lamentations: With a Critical Edition of the Peshitta Text.* Studia theologica Lundensia 21. Lund: CWK Gleerup, 1963.

Alcalay, Reuben. *The Complete Hebrew-English Dictionary.* Tel-Aviv/Jerusalem: Massadah, 1965.

Allegro, J. M. "Further Light on the History of the Qumran Sect." *JBL* 75 (1956): 89–95.

Alonso Schoekel, Luis. *Diccionario Bíblico hebreo-español.* Valencia: Institución San Jerónimo, 1990–1993.

Arnaldez, R. *De Mutatione Nominum.* Les oeuvres de Philon d'Alexandrie 18. Paris: Cerf, 1964.

———. *De Posteritate Caini.* Les oeuvres de Philon d'Alexandrie 6. Paris: Cerf, 1972.

Arnaldez, R., and J. Pouilloux. *De Aeternitate Mundi.* Les oeuvres de Philon d'Alexandrie 30. Paris: Cerf, 1969.

Ashley, Timothy R. *The Book of Numbers.* NICOT. Grand Rapids: Eerdmans, 1993.

Aus, Roger David. *Barabbas and Esther and Other Studies in the Judaic Illumination of Earliest Christianity.* South Florida Studies in the History of Judaism 54. Atlanta: Scholars Press, 1992.

Bacher, Wilhelm. *Die Agada der Tannaiten.* 2 vols. Strassburg: Karl J. Trübner, 1884 – 1890.

Bammel, Ernst. "Crucifixion as a Punishment in Palestine." In *Judaica: Kleine Schriften I,* WUNT I.37, 76–8. Tübingen: J. C. B. Mohr (Paul Siebeck), 1986. Originally published in *The Trial of Jesus,* ed. Ernst Bammel (London: SCM Press, 1970), 162–165.

_____. "The revolution theory from Reimarus to Brandon." In *Jesus and the Politics of His Day,* edited by Ernst Bammel and C. F. D. Moule, 11–68. Cambridge: Cambridge University Press, 1984.

_____. "The trial before Pilate." In *Jesus and the Politics of His Day,* edited by Ernst Bammel and C. F. D. Moule, 415–51. Cambridge: Cambridge University Press, 1984.

Bammel, Ernst, and C. F. D. Moule, eds. *Jesus and the Politics of His Day.* Cambridge: Cambridge University Press, 1984.

Barrois, A.-G. *Manuel d'Archéologie Biblique.* 2 vols. Paris: A. et J. Picard, 1939/1953.

Bauckham, Richard. *The Theology of the Book of Revelation.* New Testament Theology. Cambridge: Cambridge University Press, 1993.

Bauer, Walter. *Das Leben Jesu im Zeitalter der neutestamentlichen Apokryphen.* Tübingen: J. C. B. Mohr (Paul Siebeck), 1909. Reprint, Darmstadt: Wissenschaftliche Buchgesellschaft, 1967.

Baumgarten, Joseph M. "Does *TLH* in the Temple Scroll Refer to Crucifixion?" *JBL* 91 (December 1972): 472–81.

_____. "Hanging and Treason in Qumran and Roman Law." *ErIsr* 16 (1982): 7*–16*.

Ben-Ḥayyim, Z. *The Literary and Oral Tradition of Hebrew and Aramaic Amongst the Samaritans.* 5 vols. Jerusalem: Bialik Institute, 1957–77.

Ben-Sasson, Haim Hillel. "Blood Libel." In *EncJud,* vol. 4, 1120–8. Jerusalem: Keter Publishing House, 1972.

Ben-Yehuda, Elieser, and Naphtali H. Tur-Sinai. *Thesaurus Totius Hebraitatis et Veteris et Recentioris* [= מלון הלשון העברית]. 16 vols. Jerusalem: Hemda, 1908–1959.

Bernstein, Moshe J. "*Midrash Halakhah* at Qumran? 11QTemple 64:6–13 and Deuteronomy 21:22–23." *Gesher* 7 (1979): 145–66.

Bernstein, Moshe J. "כי קללת אלהים תלוי (Deut 21:23): A Study in Early Jewish Exegesis." *JQR* 74 (1983): 21–45.

Betz, Otto. "The Death of Choni-Onias in the Light of the Temple Scroll from Qumran." In *Jerusalem in the Second Temple Period,* edited by A. Oppenheimer, U. Rappaport, and M. Stern, 84–97 (English summary, p. V). Jerusalem: Yad Izhak Ben-Zvi, 1980.

_____. "Jesus and the Temple Scroll." In *Jesus and the Dead Sea Scrolls,* edited by James H. Charlesworth, 75–103. New York: Doubleday, 1992.

_____. "Probleme des Prozesses Jesu." In *Aufstieg und Niedergang Der Römischen Welt,* edited by Wolfgang Haase, vol. II.25.1, 565–647. Berlin/New York: Walter de Gruyter, 1982.

_____. "Der Tod des Choni-Onias im Licht der Tempelrolle von Qumran: Bemerkungen zu Josephus Antiquitates 14,22–24." In *Jesus Der Messias Israels: Aufsätze zur biblischen Theologie,* WUNT I.42, 59–74. Tübingen: Mohr [Siebeck], 1987.

Beyer, Hermann Wolfgang. "†βλασφημέω, †βλασφημία, †βλάσφημος." In *TDNT,* edited by Gerhard Kittel, translated by Geoffrey W. Bromiley, vol. 1, 621–5. Grand Rapids: Eerdmans, 1964.

Blinzler, Josef. "The Jewish Punishment of Stoning in the New Testament Period." In *The Trial of Jesus,* edited by Ernst Bammel, SBT II.13, 147–61. London: SCM Press, 1970.

Bock, Darrell L. *Blasphemy and Exaltation in Judaism and the Final Examination of Jesus: A Philological-Historical Study of the Key Jewish Themes Impacting Mark 14:61–64.* WUNT II/106. Tübingen: Mohr Siebeck, 1998.

Brady, Christian M. M. *The Rabbinic Targum of Lamentations: Vindicating God*. Leiden: Brill, 2003.

Brock, Sebastian P. "The Peshitta Old Testament: Between Judaism and Christianity." *Cristianesimo nella storia* 19 (October 1998): 483–502.

Brockelmann, Carl. *Grundriss der vergleichenden Grammatik der semitischen Sprachen*. 2 vols. Berlin: Von Reuther & Reichard, 1908/1913.

____. *Lexicon Syriacum*. Edinburgh: T. & T. Clark/Berlin: Reuther & Reichard, 1895.

Brooke, George J. *The Dead Sea Scrolls and the New Testament*. Minneapolis: Fortress, 2005.

Brown, Francis, S. R. Driver, and Charles A. Briggs. *The Brown-Driver-Briggs Hebrew and English Lexicon: with an appendix containing the Biblical Aramaic*. New ed. Peabody, Mass.: Hendrickson, [1996].

Brown, Raymond E. *The Death of the Messiah: From Gethsemane to the Grave: A Commentary on the Passion Narratives in the Four Gospels*. 2 vols. ABRL. New York: Doubleday, 1994.

Bruce, F. F. *The Epistle to the Galatians: A Commentary on the Greek Text*. NIGTC. Grand Rapids: Eerdmans, 1982.

____. *Epistle to the Hebrews*. NICNT. Grand Rapids: Eerdmans, 1964.

Brueggemann, Walter. *Genesis*. IBC. Atlanta: John Knox, 1982.

Büchler, Adolf. "Alcimus." In *Jewish Encyclopedia*, edited by Isidore Singer, vol. 1, 332–33. New York: Funk and Wagnalls, 1901.

Budde, Karl. *Die Bücher Samuel*. KHC 8. Tübingen: J. C. B. Mohr, 1902.

Budge, E. A. Wallis. *Amulets and Talismans*. New York: University Books, 1961. Originally published as *Amulets and Superstitions*. London, 1930.

Burke, D. G., and H. E. Dosker. "Cross; Crucify." In *ISBE*, edited by Geoffrey W. Bromiley, Fully rev. ed., vol. 1, 825–30. Grand Rapids: Eerdmans, 1979.

Burton, Ernest De Witt. *A Critical and Exegetical Commentary on the Epistle to the Galatians*. ICC. Edinburgh: T. & T. Clark, 1921.

Bush, Frederic W. *Ruth, Esther*. WBC 9. Dallas: Word, 1996.

Caneday, Ardel. "Redeemed from the Curse of the Law: the Use of Deut 21:22–23 in Gal 3:13." *Trinity Journal* 10 (1989): 185–209.

Carleton Paget, James. "Anti-Judaism and Early Christian Identity." *Zeitschrift für antikes Christentum* 1 (1997): 195–225.

Carroll, John T. and Joel B. Green. *The Death of Jesus in Early Christianity*. Peabody, Mass.: Hendrickson, 1995.

Chapman, David W. "Crucifixion, Bodily Suspension, and Jewish Interpretations of the Hebrew Bible in Antiquity." In *Beyond the Jordan: Studies in Honor of W. Harold Mare*, edited by Glenn A. Carnagey, Sr., Glenn A. Carnagey, Jr., and Keith N. Schoville, 37–48. Eugene, Oreg.: Wipf & Stock, 2005.

Chilton, Bruce D. "Isaac and the Second Night: a Consideration." *Bib* 61 (1980): 78–88.

Clines, David J. A., ed. *The Dictionary of Classical Hebrew*. 4+ vols. Sheffield: Sheffield Academic Press, 1993–present.

____. *The Esther Scroll: The Story of the Story*. JSOTSup 30. Sheffield: JSOT Press, 1984.

Cohn, Haim. *The Trial and Death of Jesus*. New York: Ktav, 1977.

____. משפטו ומותו של ישו הנוצר. Tel Aviv: Dvir, 1968.

Cohn, Haim Hermann. "Crucifixion." In *EncJud*, vol. 5, 1133–5. Jerusalem: Keter, 1972.

Collins, John J. "Asking for the Meaning of a Fragmentary Qumran Text: The Referential Background of 4QAaron A." In *Texts and Contexts: Biblical Texts in their Textual and Situational Contexts*, edited by Tord Fornberg and David Hellholm, 579–90. Oslo: Scandinavian University Press, 1995.

____. "The Date and Provenance of the Testament of Moses." In *Studies on the Testament of Moses*, edited by George W. E. Nickelsburg, Jr., SBLSBS 4, 15–32. Cambridge, Mass.: Society of Biblical Literature, 1973.

____. "Some Remaining Traditio-Historical Problems in the Testament of Moses." In *Studies on the Testament of Moses*, edited by George W. E. Nickelsburg, Jr., SBLSBS 4, 38–43. Cambridge, Mass.: Society of Biblical Literature, 1973.

Costaz, Louis. *Dictionnaire Syriaque-Français/Syriac-English Dictionary/Qamus Siryani 'Arabi*. 2nd ed. Beirut: Dar El-Machreq, [1986?].

Cranfield, C. E. B. *The Gospel According to Saint Mark*. CGTC. Cambridge: Cambridge University Press, 1977.

Cummins, Stephen Anthony. *Paul and the Crucified Christ in Antioch: Maccabean Martyrdom and Galatians 1 and 2*. SNTSMS 114. Cambridge: Cambridge University Press, 2001.

Davies, Philip R. "Passover and the Dating of the Aqedah." *JJS* 30 (1979): 59–67.

Davies, P. R., and B. D. Chilton. "The Aqedah: A Revised Tradition History." *CBQ* 40 (1978): 514–46.

Davies, W. D., and Dale C. Allison. *A Critical and Exegetical Commentary on the Gospel According to Saint Matthew*. 3 vols. ICC. Edinburgh: T & T Clark, 1988–1997.

Day, Linda. *Three Faces of a Queen: Characterization in the Books of Esther*. JSOTSup 186. Sheffield: Sheffield Academic Press, 1995.

De Lange, N. R. M. *Origen and the Jews: Studies in Jewish-Christian Relations in Third-Century Palestine*. UCOP 25. Cambridge: Cambridge University Press, 1976.

de Vaulx, J. *Les Nombres*. SB. Paris: J. Gabalda et Cie, 1972.

de Vaux, Roland. *Ancient Israel: Its Life and Institutions*. Translated by John McHugh. London: Darton, Longman & Todd, 1961.

DeFord, Gabrielle. "Beheaded, Crucified, Impaled or Hanged?" *Bible Review* 14.2 (April 1998): 50–1.

Dehandschutter, B. "Example and Discipleship: Some Comments on the Biblical Background of the Early Christian Theology of Martyrdom." In *The Impact of Scripture in Early Christianity*, edited by J. Den Boeft and M. L. Van Poll-Van De Lisdonk, Supplements to Vigiliae Christianae 44, 20–6. Leiden: Brill, 1999.

Delitzsch, Franz. *A New Commentary on Genesis*. Translated by Sophia Taylor. 2 vols. Clark's Foreign Theological Library 37. Edinburgh: T. & T. Clark, 1888–1889.

Derrett, J. Duncan M. "Ο ΚΥΡΙΟΣ ΕΒΑΣΙΛΕΥΣΕΝ ΑΠΟ ΤΟΥ ΞΥΛΟΥ." *VC* 43 (1989): 378–92.

Dhorme, Paul. *Les Livres de Samuel*. Ebib. Paris: J. Gabalda, 1910.

Díez Merino, Luis. "El suplicio de la cruz en la literatura Judia intertestamental." *Studii Biblici Franciscani Liber Annuus* 26 (1976): 31–120.

____. "La crocifissione nella letteratura ebrea antica (Periodo intertestamentale)." In *La Sapienza Della Croce Oggi: Atti del Congresso internazionale Roma, 13–18 ottobre 1975*, vol. 1: La Sapienza Della Croce Nella Rivelazione e Nell'Ecumenismo, 61–8. Torino: Leumann, 1976.

____. "La crucifixión en la antigua literatura judía (Periodo intertestamental)." *Estudios Eclesiásticos* 51 (1976): 5–27.

Dillmann, A. *Genesis: Critically and Exegetically Expounded*. Translated by Wm. B. Stevenson. 2 vols. Edinburgh: T. & T. Clark, 1897.

Dinkler, Erich. "Kreuzzeichen und Kreuz – Tau, Chi und Stauros." *JAC* 5 (1962): 26–54.

____. "Zur Geschichte des Kreuzsymbols." *ZTK* 48 (1951): 148–72.

Dirksen, Peter B. "The Old Testament Peshitta." In *Mikra: Text, Translation, Reading and Interpretation of the Hebrew Bible in Ancient Judaism and Early Christianity*, edited by

Martin Jan Mulder, CRINT II.1, 255–97. Assen/Maastricht: Van Gorcum; Philadephia: Fortress, 1988.

Dogniez, Cécile, and Marguerite Harl. *La Bible D'Alexandrie: Le Deutéronome*. Vol. 5. Paris: Les Éditions du Cerf, 1992.

Donaldson, T. L. "The 'Curse of the Law' and the Inclusion of the Gentiles: Galatians 3.13–14." *NTS* 32 (1986): 94–112.

Dorival, Gilles. *La Bible Alexandrie: Les Nombres*. Paris: Les Éditions du Cerf, 1994.

Dorothy, Charles V. *The Books of Esther: Structure, Genre and Textual Integrity*. JSOTSup 187. Sheffield: Sheffield Academic Press, 1997.

Downing, John. "Jesus and Martyrdom." *JTS* n.s. 14 (1963): 279–93.

Driver, G. R. Review of *Ancient Israel's Criminal Law: A New Approach to the Decalogue*, by Anthony Phillips. In *JTS* n.s., 23 (1972): 160–64.

Driver, S. R. *A Critical and Exegetical Commentary on Deuteronomy*. 3rd ed. ICC. Edinburgh: T. & T. Clark, 1902.

____. *Notes on the Hebrew Text and the Topography of the Books of Samuel*. 2nd, rev. and enlarged ed. Oxford: Clarendon, 1913.

Drower, E. S., and R. Macuch. *A Mandaic Dictionary*. Oxford: Clarendon, 1963.

Dunn, James D. G. *The Theology of Paul's Letter to the Galatians*. Cambridge: Cambridge University Press, 1993.

____. "Works of the Law and the Curse of the Law (Galatians 3.10–14)." *NTS* 31 (1985): 523–42.

Dupont-Sommer, André. "Le commentaire de Nahum découvert près de la Mer Morte (4Q p Nah): traduction et notes." *Sem* 13 (1963): 55–88.

Ehrlich, Arnold B. *Randglossen zur hebräischen Bibel*. 7 vols. Leipzig, 1908–1914. Reprint, Hildesheim: Georg Olms, 1968.

Eisler, Robert. *ΙΗΣΟΥΣ ΒΑΣΙΛΕΥΣ ΟΥ ΒΑΣΙΛΕΥΣΑΣ*. 2 vols. Heidelberg: Carl Winters, 1929.

Elgvin, Torleif. "The Messiah who was Cursed on the Tree." *Themelios* 22 (April 1997): 14–21.

Evans, Craig A. *Mark 8:27–16:20*. WBC 34b. Nashville: Thomas Nelson, 2001.

Falk, Ze'ev W. *Introduction to Jewish Law of the Second Commonwealth*. 2 vols. AGJU 11. Leiden: E. J. Brill, 1972–1978.

Feldman, Louis H. *Josephus and Modern Scholarship (1937–1980)*. Berlin: Walter de Gruyter, 1984.

____. "Josephus as a Biblical Interpreter: The *'AQEDAH*." *JQR* 75 (1985): 212–52.

____. "A Selective Critical Bibliography of Josephus." In *Josephus, the Bible, and History*, edited by Louis H. Feldman and Gohei Hata, 330–448. Leiden: E. J. Brill, 1989.

____. *Studies in Josephus' Rewritten Bible*. JSJSup 58. Leiden: Brill, 1998.

Fensham, F. Charles. *The Books of Ezra and Nehemiah*. NICOT. Grand Rapids: Eerdmans, 1982.

Figueras, Pau. *Decorated Jewish Ossuaries*. Leiden: E. J. Brill, 1983.

____. "A Midrashic Interpretation of the Cross as a Symbol." *Studii Biblici Franciscani Liber Annuus* 30 (1980): 159–66.

Finegan, Jack. *The Archeology of the New Testament: The Life of Jesus and the Beginning of the Early Church*. Princeton: Princeton University Press, 1969.

____. "Crosses in the Dead Sea Scrolls: A Waystation on the Road to the Christian Cross." *BARev* 5 (November/December 1979): 41–49.

Fitzmyer, Joseph A. "Crucifixion in Ancient Palestine, Qumran Literature, and the New Testament." *CBQ* 40 (1978): 493–513.

____. *The Gospel According to Luke*. 2 vols. AB 28. Garden City: Doubleday, 1981–1985.

Fong, Maria Ko Ha. *Crucem tollendo Christum sequi: Untersuchung zum Verständnis eines Logions Jesu in der Alten Kirche.* Münsterische Beiträge zur Theologie 52. Münster: Aschendorff, 1984.

Ford, J. Massyngberde. "'Crucify him, crucify him' and the Temple Scroll." *ExpTim* 87 (1975–76): 275–8.

France, R. T. *The Gospel of Mark: A Commentary on the Greek Text.* NIGTC. Grand Rapids: Eerdmans; Carlisle: Paternoster, 2002.

Freyne, Sean. Review of *Jesus the Magician*, by Morton Smith. *CBQ* 41 (1979): 658–61.

Fulda, Hermann. *Das Kreuz und die Kreuzigung: Eine antiquarische Untersuchung.* Breslau: Wilhelm Koebner, 1878.

Fung, Ronald Y. K. *The Epistle to the Galatians.* NICNT. Grand Rapids: Eerdmans, 1988.

García Martínez, Florentino. "4QpNah y la Crucifixión: Nueva hipótesis de reconstrucción de 4Q 169 3–4 i, 4–8." *EstBib* 38 (1979–1980): 221–35.

Geerard, Mauritus, F. Glorie, and J. Noret, eds. *Clavis Patrum Graecorum.* 5 + Suppl. vols. CChr. Turnhout: Brepols, 1983–1998.

Gerleman, Gillis. *Esther.* BKAT 21. Neukirchen-Vluyn: Neukirchener Verlag, 1973.

Gero, Stephen. "Jewish Polemic in the Martyrium Pionii and a 'Jesus' Passage from the Talmud." *JJS* 29 (1978): 164–8.

Gesenius, Wilhelm, and Udo Rüterswörden. *Hebräisches und Aramäisches Handwörterbuch über das Alte Testament.* Edited by Rudolf Meyer and Herbert Donner. 18th ed. 2+ vols. Berlin: Springer, 1987+.

Ginzberg, Louis. *The Legends of the Jews.* Translated by Henrietta Szold & Paul Radin; index by Boaz Cohen. 7 vols. Philadephia: Jewish Publication Society, 1909–1938.

Glare, P. G. W., ed. *Oxford Latin Dictionary.* Oxford: Oxford University Press, 1968–1982.

Goldenberg, David. "Once More: Jesus in the Talmud." *JQR* 73 (1982): 78–86.

Goldin, Hyman E. *Hebrew Criminal Law and Procedure: Mishnah: Sanhedrin – Makkot.* New York: Twayne, 1952.

Goldstein, Jonathan A. *I Maccabees: A New Translation with Introduction and Commentary.* AB 41. Garden City, NY: Doubleday, 1976.

_____. "The Testament of Moses: Its Content, Its Origin, and Its Attestation in Josephus." In *Studies on the Testament of Moses*, edited by George W. E. Nickelsburg, Jr., SBLSBS 4, 44–52. Cambridge, Mass.: Society of Biblical Literature, 1973.

Goodenough, Erwin R. *Jewish Symbols in the Greco-Roman Period.* 13 vols. Bollingen Series 37. New York: Pantheon Books, 1953–1968.

Grabbe, Lester L. "The Current State of the Dead Sea Scrolls: Are There More Answers than Questions?" In *The Scrolls and the Scriptures: Qumran Fifty Years After*, edited by Stanley E. Porter and Craig A. Evans, JSPSup 26, 54–67. Sheffield: Sheffield Academic Press, 1997.

Gray, George Buchanan. *A Critical and Exegetical Commentary on Numbers.* ICC. Edinburgh: T. & T. Clark, 1903.

Grundmann, Walter. *Das Evangelium nach Markus.* 4th ed. THNT 2. Berlin: Evangelische Verlagsanstalt, 1968.

Guillet, P.-E. "Les 800 «Crucifiés» d'Alexandre Jannée." *Cahiers du Cercle Ernest Renan* 25 (1977): 11–6.

Gunkel, Hermann. *Genesis.* Translated by Mark E. Biddle. Mercer Library of Biblical Studies. Macon, Ga.: Mercer University Press, 1997. Originally published as *Genesis.* 3rd ed. Göttingen: Vandenhoeck & Ruprecht, 1910.

Haas, N. "Anthropological Observations on the Skeletal Remains from Givʿat ha-Mivtar." *IEJ* 20 (1970): 38–59.

Halperin, David J. "Crucifixion, the Nahum Pesher, and the Rabbinic Penalty of Strangulation." *JJS* 32 (1981): 32–46.

Hamilton, Victor P. *The Book of Genesis*. 2 vols. NICOT. Grand Rapids: Eerdmans, 1990–1995.

Hanson, Anthony Tyrrell. *Studies in Paul's Technique and Theology*. London: SPCK, 1974.

Hanson, Richard S. "Paleo-Hebrew Scripts in the Hasmonean Age." *BASOR* 175 (October 1964): 26–42.

Harris, Zellig S. *A Grammar of the Phoenician Language*. AOS 8. New Haven: American Oriental Society, 1936.

Hayward, C. T. R. "The Sacrifice of Isaac and Jewish Polemic Against Christianity." *CBQ* 52 (1990): 292–306.

Hayward, Robert. "The Present State of Research into the Targumic Account of the Sacrifice of Isaac." *JJS* 32 (1981): 127–50.

Heinemann, Joseph. "Early Halakhah in the Palestinian Targumim." *JJS* 25 (February 1974): 114–22.

____. "The Targum of Ex. XXII,4 and the Ancient Halakha." *Tarbiz* 38 (March 1969): 294–6. (In Hebrew).

Hengel, Martin. *The Cross of the Son of God*. Translated by John Bowden. London: SCM Press, 1986.

____. *La crucifixion dans l'antiquité et la folie du message de la croix*. Translated by Albert Chazelle. Lectio divina 105. Paris: Cerf, 1981.

____. *Crucifixion in the Ancient World and the Folly of the Message of the Cross*. Translated by John Bowden. London & Philadelphia: SCM Press & Fortress Press, 1977.

____. "Mors turpissima crucis: Die Kreuzigung in der antiken Welt und die 'Torheit' des 'Wortes vom Kreuz'." In *Rechtfertigung*, edited by Johannes Friedrich, Wolfgang Pöhlmann, and Peter Stuhlmacher, 125–84. Tübingen: J. C. B. Mohr [Paul Siebeck]/Göttingen: Vandenhoeck & Ruprecht, 1976.

____. *Rabbinische Legende und frühpharisäische Geschichte: Schimeon b. Schetach und die achtzig Hexen von Askalon*. AHAW.PH 1984,2. Heidelberg: Carl Winter, 1984.

____. *The Zealots: Investigations into the Jewish Freedom Movement in the Period from Herod I until 70 A.D.* Translated by David Smith. Edinburgh: T&T Clark, 1989. Originally published as *Die Zeloten: Untersuchungen zur Jüdischen Freiheitsbewegung in der Zeit von Herodes I. bis 70 n. Chr.* 2nd ed. Leiden: E. J. Brill, 1976.

Hengel, Martin, and Anna Maria Schwemer. *Paul Between Damascus and Antioch*. Translated by John Bowden. London: SCM Press, 1997.

Hengel, Martin, and Anna Maria Schwemer. *Paulus zwischen Damaskus und Antiochien: Die unbekannten Jahre des Apostels*. WUNT I.108. Tübingen: Mohr Siebeck, 1998.

Hengel, Martin with the collaboration of Daniel P. Bailey. "The Effective History of Isaiah 53 in the Pre-Christian Period." In *The Suffering Servant: Isaiah 53 in Jewish and Christian Sources*, edited by Bernd Janowski and Peter Stuhlmacher, translated by Daniel P. Bailey, 75–146. Grand Rapids: Eerdmans, 2004.

Herbert, Edward D. *Reconstructing Biblical Dead Sea Scrolls: A New Method Applied to the Reconstruction of 4QSam^a*. STDJ 22. Leiden: Brill, 1997.

Herford, R. Travers. *Christianity in Talmud and Midrash*. London: Williams & Norgate, 1903.

Hewitt, Joseph William. "The Use of Nails in the Crucifixion." *HTR* 25 (1932): 29–45.

Hezser, Catherine. *The Social Structure of the Rabbinic Movement in Roman Palestine*. TSAJ 66. Tübingen: Mohr Siebeck, 1997.

Hill, David. "Jesus and Josephus' 'messianic prophets'." In *Text and Interpretation*, edited by Ernest Best and R. McL. Wilson, 143–54. Cambridge: Cambridge University Press, 1979.

Hillers, Delbert R. *Lamentations: A New Translation with Introduction and Commentary*. 2nd ed. AB 7a. New York: Doubleday, 1992.

Hirsch, Emil G. "Crucifixion." In *The Jewish Encyclopedia*, vol. 4, 373–4. New York/London: Funk and Wagnalls, 1903.

Hoftijzer, J., and K. Jongeling. *Dictionary of the North-West Semitic Inscriptions*. 2 vols. HdO I.21. Leiden: E. J. Brill, 1995.

Hooker, Morna. *The Gospel According to Saint Mark*. London: A & C Black, 1991.

_____. "Interchange in Christ." *JTS* n.s. 22 (1971): 349–61.

Horbury, William. "The Basle Nizzahon." *JTS* n.s. 34 (1983): 497–514.

_____. "The Benediction of the *Minim* and Early Jewish-Christian Controversy." *JTS* 33 (1982): 19–61.

_____. "Christ as brigand in ancient anti-Christian polemic." In *Jesus and the Politics of His Day*, edited by Ernst Bammel and C. F. D. Moule, 183–95. Cambridge: Cambridge University Press, 1984.

_____. "A Critical Examination of the Toledoth Jeshu." Ph.D. diss., University of Cambridge, 1971.

_____. "Suffering and messianism in Yose ben Yose." In *Suffering and Martyrdom in the New Testament*, edited by William Horbury and Brian McNeil, 143–82. Cambridge: Cambridge University Press, 1981.

Horsley, Richard A. "Josephus and the Bandits." *JSJ* 10 (1979): 37–63.

Horsley, Richard A., and John S. Hanson. *Bandits, Prophets, and Messiahs: Popular Movements in the Time of Jesus*. Minneapolis: Winston Press, 1985.

Horst, Pieter W. van der. *Philo's Flaccus: The First Pogrom: Introduction, Translation, and Commentary*. Leiden: Brill; Atlanta: Society of Biblical Literature, 2003.

Jacobson, Howard. *A Commentary on Pseudo-Philo's Liber Antiquitatum Biblicarum*. 2 vols. AGJU 31. Leiden: E. J. Brill, 1996.

Jastrow, Marcus. *A Dictionary of the Targumim, the Talmud Babli and Yerushalmi, and the Midrashic Literature*. 2 vols. New York: Pardes, 1950. Reprint, New York: Judaica Press, 1971.

Juster, Jean. *Les Juifs dans l'Empire Romaine: Leur condition juridique, économique et sociale*. 2 vols. Paris, 1914. Reprint, New York: Burt Franklin, 1974.

Kapelrud, Arvid S. "King and Fertility: A Discussion of II Sam 21:1–14." In *Interpretationes ad Vetus Testamentum Pertinentes Sigmundo Mowinckel Septuagenario Missae*, 113–22. Oslo: Land og Kirke, 1955.

Kasher, Rimon, and Michael L. Klein. "New Fragments of Targum to Esther from the Cairo Geniza." *HUCA* 61 (1990): 89–124.

Kessler, Edward. *Bound by the Bible: Jews, Christians and the sacrifice of Isaac*. Cambridge: Cambridge University Press, 2004.

_____. "A Study of the Relationship between Judaism and Christianity in the First Six Centuries CE through an Analysis of Jewish and Christian Interpretations of Genesis 22:1–14." PhD diss., University of Cambridge, 1999.

Koehler, Ludwig and Walter Baumgartner. *The Hebrew and Aramaic Lexicon of the Old Testament*. Leiden: E. J. Brill, 1994–2000.

Kooij, A. van der. "Isaiah in the Septuagint." In *Writing and Reading the Scroll of Isaiah*, edited by C. G. Broyles and C. A. Evans, vol. 2, 513–29. Leiden: Brill, 1997.

Krauss, Samuel. *Griechische und Lateinische Lehnwörter im Talmud, Midrasch und Targum*. 2 vols. Berlin, 1898–1899. Reprint, Hildesheim: Georg Olms, 1964.

_____. *The Jewish-Christian Controversy from the earliest times to 1789*. Edited by William Horbury. Vol. 1. TSAJ 56. Tübingen: J. C. B. Mohr, 1995.

Kuhn, Heinz-Wolfgang. "Die Bedeutung der Qumrantexte für das Verständnis des Galater-
briefes aus dem Münchener Projekt: Qumran und das Neue Testament." In *New Qumran
Texts and Studies: Proceedings of the First Meeting of the International Organization for
Qumran Studies, Paris 1992*, edited by George J. Brooke and Florentino García Martínez,
STDJ 15, 169–221. Leiden: E. J. Brill, 1994.

____. "Der Gekreuzigte von Giv'at ha-Mivtar: Bilanz einer Entdeckung." In *Theologia
Crucis – Signum Crucis*, edited by Carl Andresen and Günter Klein, 303–34. Tübingen: J.
C. B. Mohr [Paul Siebeck], 1979.

____. "Die Kreuzesstrafe während der frühen Kaiserzeit: Ihre Wirklichkeit und Wertung in
der Umwelt des Urchristentums." In *Aufstieg und Niedergang Der Römischen Welt*, edited
by Wolfgang Haase, vol. II.25.1, 648–793. Berlin/New York: Walter de Gruyter, 1982.

____. "σταυρός, σταυρόω." In *EDNT*, edited by Horst Balz and Gerhard Schneider, vol. 3,
267–71. Grand Rapids: Eerdmans, 1993.

Kundert, Lukas. *Die Opferung/Bindung Isaaks*. 2 vols. WMANT 78 & 79. Neukirchen-
Vluyn: Neukirchener Verlag, 1998.

Lahey, Lawrence. "Jewish Biblical Interpretation and Genuine Jewish-Christian Debate in the
Dialogue of Timothy and Aquila." *JJS* 51 (Autumn 2000): 281–96.

Lampe, G. W. H., ed. *Patristic Greek Lexicon*. Oxford: Clarendon Press, 1961–1968.

Lane, William L. *Hebrews*. 2 vols. WBC 47 a&b. Dallas: Word Books; Nashville: Thomas
Nelson, 1991.

____. *The Gospel According to Mark*. NICNT. Grand Rapids: Eerdmans, 1974.

Langmuir, Gavin I. "Historiographic Crucifixion." In *Les Juifs au Regard de L'Histoire*,
edited by Gilbert Dahan, 109–27. Paris: Picard, 1985.

Laporte, Jean. *De Iosepho*. Les oeuvres de Philon d'Alexandrie 21. Paris: Éditions du Cerf,
1964.

Lawlor, Hugh Jackson, and John Ernest Leonard Oulton. *Eusebius Bishop of Caesarea: The
Ecclesiastical History and the Martyrs of Palestine*. 2 vols. London: SPCK, 1927–1928.

Levenson, Jon D. *The Death and Resurrection of the Beloved Son: The Transformation of
Child Sacrifice in Judaism and Christianity*. New Haven: Yale University Press, 1993.

Lewis, Charlton T. and Charles Short. *A Latin Dictionary*. Oxford: Clarendon Press, 1896.

Liddell, Henry George and Robert Scott. *A Greek-English Lexicon*. Revised by Henry Stuart
Jones and Roderick McKenzie. 9th ed. Oxford: Clarendon Press, 1996.

Lieu, Judith M. "Reading in Canon and Community: Deuteronomy 21.22–23, A Test Case for
Dialogue." In *The Bible in Human Society*, edited by M. Daniel Carroll, David J. A.
Clines, and Philip R. Davies, JSOTSup 200, 317–34. Sheffield: Sheffield Academic Press,
1995.

Lightfoot, J. B. *The Epistle of St. Paul to the Galatians*. Reprint. Grand Rapids: Zondervan,
1957.

Lipsius, J. *De Cruce libri tres*. Amsterdam, 1670.

Lockshin, Martin I. *Rabbi Samuel ben Meir's Commentary on Genesis: an Annotated Translation*. Jewish Studies 5. Lewiston, NY: Edwin Mellen, 1989.

Lust, J., E. Eynikel, and K. Hauspie. *A Greek-English Lexicon of the Septuagint*. 2 vols.
Stuttgart: Deutsche Bibelgesellschaft, 1992/1996.

Macuch, Rudolf. *Grammatik des samaritanischen Hebräisch*. Studia Samaritana 1. Berlin:
Walter de Gruyter, 1969.

Maier, Johann. *Jesus von Nazareth in der talmudischen Überlieferung*. ErFor 82. Darmstadt:
Wissenschaftliche Buchgesellschaft, 1978.

Mann, C. S. *Mark*. AB 27. Garden City, N.Y.: Doubleday, 1986.

Marcus, David. "'Lifting up the Head': On the Trail of a Word Play in Genesis 40."
Prooftexts 10 (1990): 17–27.

Margoliouth, J. P. *Supplement to the Thesaurus Syriacus of R. Payne Smith, S.T.P.* Oxford: Clarendon Press, 1927.

Martyn, J. Louis. *Galatians*. AB 33a. New York: Doubleday, 1997.

Mason, Steve. *Life of Josephus: Translation and Commentary*. Leiden: Brill, 2001.

McCarter, P. Kyle. *I Samuel*. AB 8. Garden City: Doubleday, 1980.

_____. *II Samuel*. AB 9. Garden City, New York: Doubleday, 1984.

Meier, John P. "Jesus in Josephus: a modest proposal." *CBQ* 52 (1990): 76–103.

Mendelsohn, S. *The Criminal Jurisprudence of the Ancient Hebrews: Compiled from the Talmud and other Rabbinical Writings, and Compared with Roman and English Penal Jurisprudence*. 2nd ed. New York: Hermon Press, 1968.

Milgrom, Jacob. *Numbers*. JPS Torah Commentary. Philadelphia: Jewish Publication Society, 1990.

Millar, Fergus. "The Background to the Maccabean Revolution: Reflections on Martin Hengel's 'Judaism and Hellenism'." *JJS* 29 (1978): 1–21.

Moatti-Fine, Jacqueline. *La Bible Alexandrie: Jésus (Josué)*. Paris: Les Éditions du Cerf, 1996.

Møller-Christensen, Vilhelm. "Skeletal Remains from Giv'at ha-Mivtar." *IEJ* 26 (1976): 35–8.

Moore, Carey A. *Esther*. AB 7b. Garden City, New York: Doubleday, 1971.

Moore, Carey A., ed. *Studies in the Book of Esther*. LBS. New York: Ktav, 1982.

Mørkholm, Otto. *Antiochus IV of Syria*. Classica et mediaevalia – Dissertationes 8. Copenhagen: Gyldendalske Boghandel, 1966.

Morland, Kjell Arne. *The Rhetoric of Curse in Galatians: Paul Confronts Another Gospel*. Atlanta: Scholars Press, 1995.

Moscati, Sabatino, Anton Spitaler, Edward Ullendorff, and Wolfram Von Soden. *An Introduction to the Comparative Grammar of the Semitic Languages: Phonology and Morphology*. Edited by Sabatino Moscati. PLO, n.s. 6. Wiesbaden: Otto Harrassowitz, 1964.

Myers, Jacob M. *Ezra, Nehemiah*. AB 14. New York: Doubleday, 1965.

Nairne, A. *The Epistle to the Hebrews*. CGTC. Cambridge: Cambridge University Press, 1922.

Naveh, J. "The Ossuary Inscriptions from Giv'at ha-Mivtar." *IEJ* 20 (1970): 33–7.

Neale, D. "Was Jesus a *Mesith*? Public Response to Jesus and His Ministry." *TynBul* 44 (1993): 89–101.

Neusner, Jacob. *A History of the Jews in Babylonia*. 5 vols. SPB. Leiden: E. J. Brill, 1965–1970.

_____. *The Rabbinic Traditions about the Pharisees before 70*. 3 vols. Leiden: E. J. Brill, 1971.

Newman, Hillel I. "The Death of Jesus in the *Toledot Yeshu* Literature." *JTS* n.s. 50 (1999): 59–79.

Neyrey, Jerome H. "Despising the Shame of the Cross: Honor and Shame in the Johannine Passion Narratives." *Semeia* 68 (1996): 113–37.

_____. *Honor and Shame in the Gospel of Matthew*. Louisville: Westminster John Knox Press, 1998.

Nickelsburg, George W. E., Jr. "An Antiochan Date for the Testament of Moses." In *Studies on the Testament of Moses*, edited by George W. E. Nickelsburg, Jr., SBLSBS 4, 33–7. Cambridge, Mass.: Society of Biblical Literature, 1973.

Nock, Arthur Darby. "Thackeray's Lexicon to Josephus." *HTR* 25 (1932): 361–2.

Nöldeke, Theodor. *Neue Beiträge zur semitischen Sprachwissenschaft*. Strassburg: Karl J. Trübner, 1910.

Nolland, John. *The Gospel of Matthew: A Commentary on the Greek Text.* NIGTC. Grand Rapids: Eerdmans; Bletchley: Paternoster, 2005.

____. *Luke.* 3 vols. WBC 35. Dallas: Word, 1989–1993.

Noth, Martin. *Numbers: A Commentary.* Translated by James D. Martin. OTL. London: SCM Press, 1968. Originally published as *Das vierte Buch Mose, Numeri.* Göttingen: Vandenhoeck & Ruprecht, 1966.

O'Collins, Gerald G. "Crucifixion." In *ABD,* edited by David Noel Freedman, vol. 1, 1207–10. New York: Doubleday, 1992.

Olson, Dennis T. *Deuteronomy and the Death of Moses.* OBT. Minneapolis: Fortress Press, 1994.

Otto, I. C. Th. *Corpus Apologetarum christianorum saeculi secundi.* 9 vols. Ienae: Hermann Dufft, 1857–1879.

Palumbo, Arthur E. "A New Interpretation of the Nahum Commentary." *Folia Orientalia* 29 (1992–1993): 153–62.

Payne Smith, J. (Mrs. Margoliouth), ed. *A Compendious Syriac Dictionary.* Oxford: Clarendon Press, 1903, 1967.

Payne Smith, R., ed. *Thesaurus Syriacus.* 2 vols. Oxford: Clarendon Press, 1879/1901.

Phillips, Anthony. *Ancient Israel's Criminal Law: A New Approach to the Decalogue.* Oxford: Basil Blackwell, 1970.

Pines, Shlomo. *An Arabic Version of the Testimonium Flavianum and its Implications.* Jerusalem: Israel Academy of Sciences and Humanities, 1971.

Pobee, John S. *Persecution and Martyrdom in the Theology of Paul.* JSNTSup 6. Sheffield: JSOT Press, 1985.

Polzin, Robert. "*HWQY^c* and Covenantal Institutions in Early Israel." *HTR* 62 (1969): 227–40.

Prigent, Pierre. *Les Testimonia dans le Christianisme primitif. L'Épître de Barnabé (I–XVI) et ses sources.* Ebib. Paris: J. Gabalda, 1961.

Prostmeier, Ferdinand R. *Der Barnabasbrief.* Kommentar zu den Apostolischen Vätern 8. Göttingen: Vandenhoeck & Ruprecht, 1999.

Provan, Iain W. *Lamentations.* New Century Bible Commentary. Grand Rapids: Eerdmans, 1991.

Puech, Émile. "Die Kreuzigung und die altjüdische Tradition." *Welt und Umwelt der Bibel* 9 (1998): 73–75.

Qimron, Elisha. *The Hebrew of the Dead Sea Scrolls.* HSS 29. Atlanta: Scholars Press, 1986.

Rabin, C. "Alexander Jannaeus and the Pharisees." *JJS* 7 (1956): 3–11.

Rabinowitz, Isaac. "The Meaning of the Key ('Demetrius')-Passage of the Qumran Nahum-Pesher." *JAOS* 98 (1978): 394–9.

Rehkopf, Friedrich. *Septuaginta-Vokabular.* Göttingen: Vandenhoeck & Ruprecht, 1989.

Renkema, Johan. *Lamentations.* Translated by Brian Doyle. Historical Commentary on the Old Testament. Leuven: Peeters, 1998.

Reyburn, William D. *A Handbook on Lamentations.* UBS Handbook Series. New York: United Bible Societies, 1992.

Rosenberg, Roy A. "Jesus, Isaac, and the 'Suffering Servant'." *JBL* 84 (1965): 381–88.

Rosenblatt, Samuel. "The Crucifixion of Jesus from the Standpoint of Pharisaic Law." *JBL* 75 (1956): 315–21.

Rowley, H. H. "4QpNahum and the Teacher of Righteousness." *JBL* 75 (1956): 188–93.

Royse, James R. *The Spurious Texts of Philo of Alexandria: A Study of Textual Transmission and Corruption with Indexes to the Major Collections of Greek Fragments.* ALGHJ 22. Leiden: Brill, 1991.

Runia, David T. "Philo's *De aeternitate mundi*: The Problem of its Interpretation." *VC* 35 (1981): 105–51.

Salvesen, Alison. *Symmachus in the Pentateuch*. JSS Monograph 15. Manchester: University of Manchester, 1991.

Sarna, Nahum M. *Genesis*. JPS Torah Commentary. Philadelphia: Jewish Publication Society, 1989.

Schaaf, Carolo. *Lexicon Syriacum Concordantiale*. 2nd ed. Leiden: Typis Joh. Mulleri, Joh. fil; Apud Cornelium Boutesteyn & Samuelem Luchtmans, 1717.

Schalit, Abraham. "Alcimus." In *EncJud*, vol. 2, 549. Jerusalem: Keter, 1971.

Schiffman, Lawrence H. "Pharisees and Sadducees in *Pesher Nahum*." In *Minhah le-Nahum*, edited by Marc Brettler and Michael Fishbane, JSOTSup 154, 272–90. Sheffield: JSOT Press, 1993.

Schneider, J. "σταυρός, σταυρόω, ἀνασταυρόω." In *TDNT*, edited by Gerhard Kittel and Gerhard Friedrich, translated by Geoffrey Bromiley, vol. 7, 572–84. Grand Rapids: Eerdmans, 1971.

Schoeps, Hans Joachim. "The Sacrifice of Isaac in Paul's Theology." *JBL* 65 (1946): 385–92.

Schonfield, Hugh J. *According to the Hebrews*. London: Duckworth, 1937.

Schreckenberg, Heinz. *Die christlichen Adversus-Judaeos-Texte und ihr literarisches und historisches Umfeld (1.–11.Jh.)*. Europäische Hochschulschriften xxiii.172. Frankfurt: Peter Lang, 1999.

Schulthess, Fridericus, ed. *Lexicon Syropalaestinum*. Berlin: George Reimer, 1903.

Schürer, Emil. *The History of the Jewish People in the Age of Jesus Christ (175 B.C.–A.D. 135)*. Edited by Geza Vermes, Fergus Millar, Martin Goodman, Pamela Vermes, and Matthew Black. Revised English ed. 3 vols. Edinburgh: T. & T. Clark, 1973–1987.

Schwartz, Daniel R. "'The Contemners of Judges and Men' (11Q Temple 64:12)." In *Studies in the Jewish Background of Christianity*, WUNT 60, 81–8. Tübingen: J. C. B. Mohr (Paul Siebeck), 1992. Originally published in *Leshonenu* 47 (1982–83), 18–24.

Schwemer, Anna Maria. *Studien zu den frühjüdischen Prophetenlegenden Vitae Prophetarum: Einleitung, Übersetzung und Kommentar*. 2 vols. TSAJ 49–50. Tübingen: J. C. B. Mohr [Paul Siebeck], 1995–1996.

Seeley, David. *The Noble Death: Graeco-Roman Martyrology and Paul's Concept of Salvation*. JSNTSup 28. Sheffield: JSOT Press, 1990.

Segal, M. H. *A Grammar of Mishnaic Hebrew*. Oxford: Clarendon Press, 1927.

Seland, Torrey. *Establishment Violence in Philo and Luke: A Study of Non-Conformity to the Torah and Jewish Vigilante Reactions*. Biblical Interpretation Series 15. Leiden: E. J. Brill, 1995.

Senior, Donald. *The Passion of Jesus in the Gospel of John*. Collegeville, Minn.: Michael Glazier, 1991.

____. *The Passion of Jesus in the Gospel of Matthew*. Collegeville, Minn.: Michael Glazier, 1985.

Shaw, Brent D. "Tyrants, Bandits and Kings: Personal Power in Josephus." *JJS* 44 (1993): 176–204.

Simon, Marcel. *Verus Israel: A study of the relations between Christians and Jews in the Roman Empire (135–425)*. Oxford: Oxford University Press, 1986.

Skarsaune, Oskar. *The Proof from Prophecy: A Study in Justin Martyr's Proof-Text Tradition: Text-Type, Provenance, Theological Profile*. NovTSup 56. Leiden: E. J. Brill, 1987.

Skinner, John. *A Critical and Exegetical Commentary on Genesis*. 2nd ed. ICC. Edinburgh: T. & T. Clark, 1930.

Smith, Henry Preserved. *A Critical and Exegetical Commentary on the Books of Samuel*. ICC. Edinburgh: T. & T. Clark, 1899.

Smith, Morton. *Jesus the Magician.* London: Victor Gollancz, 1978.

Smith, William Robertson. *Lectures on the Religions of the Semites.* 3rd ed. London: A. & C. Black, 1927.

Smolar, Leivy, Moses Aberbach, and Pinkhos Churgin. *Studies in Targum Jonathan to the Prophets and Targum Jonathan to the Prophets.* Library of Biblical Studies. New York: KTAV, 1983.

Sokoloff, Michael. *A Dictionary of Jewish Palestinian Aramaic of the Byzantine Period.* Dictionaries of Talmud, Midrash and Targum 2. Ramat-Gan, Israel: Bar Ilan University Press, 1990.

Speiser, E. A. "Census and Ritual Expiation in Mari and Israel." *BASOR* 149 (February 1958): 17–25.

_____. *Genesis.* AB 1. Garden City, NY: Doubleday, 1964.

Sperber, Daniel. *A Dictionary of Greek and Latin Legal Terms in Rabbinic Literature.* Dictionaries of Talmud, Midrash and Targum 1. Ramat-Gan: Bar-Ilan University Press, 1984.

Stanton, Graham N. "Jesus of Nazareth: A Magician and a False Prophet Who Deceived God's People?" In *Jesus of Nazareth: Lord and Christ: essays on the Historical Jesus and New Testament Christology*, edited by Joel B. Green and Max Turner, 164–80. Grand Rapids: Eerdmans, 1994.

Stauffer, Ethelbert. *Jerusalem und Rom im Zeitalter Jesu Christi.* Bern: Francke, 1957.

Stemberger, Günter. *Introduction to the Talmud and Midrash.* Translated by Markus Bockmuehl. 2nd ed. Edinburgh: T & T Clark, 1996. Originally published as *Einleitung in Talmud und Midrasch.* 2nd ed. München: C. H. Beck, 1992.

Strack, Hermann L. *Jesus die Häretiker und die Christen nach den ältesten jüdischen Angaben.* Schriften des Institutum Judaicum in Berlin 37. Leipzig: J. C. Hinrichs, 1910.

Strathmann, Hermann. "μάρτυς, etc." In *TDNT*, edited by Gerhard Kittel, translated by Geoffrey W. Bromiley, vol. 4, 474–514. Grand Rapids: Eerdmans, 1967.

Strugnell, John. "Notes en marge du volume V des «Discoveries in the Judaean Desert of Jordan»." *RevQ* 7 (April 1970): 163–276.

Swetnam, James. *Jesus and Isaac: A Study of the Epistle to the Hebrews in the Light of the Aqedah.* AnBib 94. Rome: Biblical Institute Press, 1981.

Tabory, Joseph. "The Crucifixion of the Paschal Lamb." *JQR* 86 (1996): 395–406.

Tantlevskij, Igor R. "The Reflection of the Political Situation in Judaea in 88 B.C.E. in the Qumran Commentary on Nahum (4QpNah, Columns 1–4)." *St. Petersburg Journal of Oriental Studies* 6 (1994): 221–31.

Taylor, Miriam S. *Anti-Judaism and Early Christian Identity: A Critique of the Scholarly Consensus.* SPB 46. Leiden: E. J. Brill, 1995.

Thornton, T. C. G. "The Crucifixion of Haman and the Scandal of the Cross." *JTS* n.s., 37 (1986): 419–26.

Twelftree, Graham H. *Jesus the Exorcist: A Contribution to the Study of the Historical Jesus.* WUNT II/54. Tübingen: J. C. B. Mohr [Paul Siebeck], 1993.

Tzaferis, V. "Jewish Tombs at and near Givʿat ha-Mivtar, Jerusalem." *IEJ* 20 (1970): 18–32.

Van Henten, Jan Willem. *The Maccabean Martyrs as Saviours of the Jewish People: a Study of 2 and 4 Maccabees.* Supplements to the Journal for the Study of Judaism 57. Leiden: Brill, 1997.

Van Henten, Jan Willem and Friedrich Avemarie. *Martyrdom and Noble Death: Selected texts from Graeco-Roman, Jewish and Christian Antiquity.* London/New York: Routledge, 2002.

Veltri, Giuseppe. *Magie und Halakha: Ansätze zu einem empirischen Wissenschaftsbegriff im spätantiken und frühmittelalterlichen Judentum.* TSAJ 62. Tübingen: J.C.B. Mohr [Paul Siebeck], 1997.

Vermes, Geza. "Jewish Literature and New Testament Exegesis: Reflections on Methodology." *JJS* 33 (1982): 361–76.

_____. "New Light on the Sacrifice of Isaac from 4Q225." *JJS* 47 (1996): 140–6.

_____. "Redemption and Genesis XXII: The Binding of Isaac and the Sacrifice of Jesus." In *Scripture and Tradition in Judaism: Haggadic Studies*, SPB 4, 193–227. Leiden: E. J. Brill, 1961.

Vine, W. E. *An Expository Dictionary of New Testament Words.* 4 vols. London: Oliphants, 1939.

von Rad, Gerhard. *Das erste Buch Mose: Genesis.* 10th ed. ATD 2/4. Göttingen: Vandenhoeck & Ruprecht, 1976.

Walbank, F. W. *A Historical Commentary on Polybius.* 2 vols. Oxford: Clarendon Press, 1957/1967.

Weitzman, M. P. *The Syriac Version of the Old Testament: An Introduction.* University of Cambridge Oriental Publications 56. Cambridge: Cambridge University Press, 1999.

Weitzmann, Kurt. "Zur Frage des Einflusses jüdischer Bilderquellen auf die Illustrationen des Alten Testamentes (mit 10 Tafelabbildungen)." In *Mullus*, edited by Alfred Stuiber and Alfred Hermann, Jahrbuch für Antike und Christentum, Ergänzungsband 1, 401–15. Münster: Aschendorffsche Verlagsbuchhandlung, 1964.

Weitzmann, Kurt, and Herbert L. Kessler. *The Cotton Genesis: British Library Codex Cotton Otho B. VI. The Illustrations in the Manuscripts of the Septuagint.* Princeton: Princeton University Press, 1986.

Wellhausen, Julius. *Der Text der Bücher Samuelis.* Göttingen: Vandenhoeck & Ruprecht, 1871.

Westermann, Claus. *Genesis 37–50: A Commentary.* Translated by John J. Scullion. Minneapolis: Augsburg, 1986. Originally published as *Genesis.* Neukirchen-Vluyn: Neukirchener Verlag, 1982.

Wevers, John William. *Notes on the Greek Text of Deuteronomy.* SBLSCS 39. Atlanta: Scholars Press, 1995.

_____. *Notes on the Greek Text of Genesis.* SBLSCS 35. Atlanta: Scholars Press, 1993.

_____. *Notes on the Greek Text of Numbers.* SBLSCS 46. Atlanta: Scholars Press, 1998.

_____. *Text History of the Greek Numbers.* Göttingen: Vandenhoeck & Ruprecht, 1982.

Whealey, Alice. *Josephus on Jesus: The Testimonium Flavianum Controversy from Late Antiquity to Modern Times.* Studies in Biblical Literature 36. New York: Peter Lang, 2003.

Wieder, N. "Notes on the New Documents from the Fourth Cave of Qumran." *JJS* 7 (1956): 71–6.

_____. "Rejoinder." *JJS* 8 (1957): 119–21.

Wilcox, Max. *The Semitisms of Acts.* Oxford: Clarendon Press, 1965.

_____. "'Upon the Tree' – Deut 21:22–23 in the New Testament." *JBL* 96 (1977): 85–99.

Williams, A. Lukyn. *Adversus Judaeos: A Bird's-Eye View of Christian Apologiae until the Renaissance.* Cambridge: Cambridge University Press, 1935.

Williams, Sam K. *Jesus' Death as a Saving Event: the Background and Origin of a Concept.* HDR 2. Missoula: Scholars Press, 1975.

Williamson, H. G. M. *Ezra, Nehemiah.* WBC 16. Waco: Word Books, 1985.

Windisch, Hans. *Die Apostolischen Väter III: Der Barnabasbrief.* HNT. Tübingen: J. C. B. Mohr [Paul Siebeck], 1920.

Winter, Paul. *On the Trial of Jesus*. Edited by T. A. Burkill and Geza Vermes. 2nd rev. ed. SJ 1. Berlin: Walter de Gruyter, 1974.

Wood, J. Edwin. "Isaac Typology in the New Testament." *NTS* 14 (1968): 583–9.

Yadin, Y. "Epigraphy and Crucifixion." *IEJ* 23 (1973): 18–22.

____. "Pesher Nahum (4Q pNahum) Reconsidered." *IEJ* 21 (1971): 1–12.

Zeitlin, Solomon. "The Assumption of Moses and the Revolt of Bar Kokba." *JQR* 38 (1947): 1–45.

____. "The Crucifixion of Jesus Re-examined." *JQR* n.s., 31 (April 1941): 327–69.

____. "The Dead Sea Scrolls: A Travesty on Scholarship." *JQR* 47 (1956–57): 1–36.

____. "The Phrase יתלה אנשים חיים." *JJS* 8 (1957): 117–8.

Zias, Joe, and James H. Charlesworth. "CRUCIFIXION: Archaeology, Jesus, and the Dead Sea Scrolls." In *Jesus and the Dead Sea Scrolls*, edited by James H. Charlesworth, 273–89. New York: Doubleday, 1992.

Zias, Joseph, and Eliezer Sekeles. "The Crucified Man from Givʿat ha-Mivtar: A Reappraisal." *IEJ* 35 (1985): 22–7.

Zimmermann, Johannes. *Messianische Texte aus Qumran: Königliche, priesterliche und prophetische Messiasvorstellungen in den Schriftfunden von Qumran*. WUNT II.104. Tübingen: Mohr Siebeck, 1998.

Citation Index

Old Testament

New Testament

13:29	9, 243	*Hebrews*	
14:19	35	4:15	253
19:13–14	183	6:6	9, 235, 252
26:11	233	7:26–27	253
		7:26	253
Romans		11:17–19	257
2:14f.	242	11:17	257
7:22	243	11:37	259
8:7	243	12:2	252
8:32	257	13:13	252
1 Corinthians		*James*	
1:23	259	2:21–23	257
1:24	259		
2:4	259	*1 Peter*	
5:7	258	1:19	253
9:9	243	2:22	253
9:21	243	2:24	9, 243
		3:18	253
2 Corinthians			
5:21	253	*1 John*	
11:25	35	3:5	253
Galatians		*Revelation*	
3:10	242–243, 247	1:5	254
3:13–14	237	2:13	254
3:13	4, 9, 120, 234, 237, 240,	3:14	254
	241–243, 245, 246, 247,	5:6ff.	258
	249, 251	6:1	258
3:14	122, 242, 247	6:9	254
3:21	243	6:16	258
4:5	242	7	258
		8:1	258
Philippians		11:9–10	244
2:8	252	12:1	258
		12:11	254
Colossians		13:8	258
2:14–15	235, 236	14–17	258
2:14	9	17:6	254
		21–22	258
1 Timothy			
1:13	233		

Old Testament Apocrypha and Pseudepigrapha

Additions to Esther		*1 Esdras*	
C22 (=14:11)	111, 252	5:69	120
E18 (=16:18)	21, 163–164, 165–166	6:22–23	171

Dead Sea Scrolls

Philo

Josephus

Rabbinic Literature

Targumim

Ancient Near Eastern Texts & Pictures

Classical Authors

Patristic Literature (in alphabetical order)

Other Ancient Documents

Author Index

Subject Index

HV 8569 .C465 2008
Ancient Jewish and Christian
perceptions of crucifixion
179381